TO THE WOMEN IN OUR LIVES, WITH LOVE

Dianne and Julia Hales
Beth, Elissa, and Lynn Yudofsky

Contents

Section I: Evaluation and Basic Principles

Section II: Organic Mental Disorders

Contributors

Richard Abrams, M.D.
> *Professor and Vice Chairman, Department of Psychiatry and Behavioral Sciences, UHS/The Chicago Medical School, North Chicago, Illinois*

John L. Black, M.D.
> *Instructor in Psychiatry, Mayo Medical School, Consultant in Adult Psychiatry, Mayo Clinic, Rochester, Minnesota*

Jean Lud Cadet, M.D.
> *Staff Fellow, Neuropsychiatry Branch, National Institute of Mental Health, St. Elizabeths Hospital, Washington, DC*

Steven L. Dubovsky, M.D.
> *Associate Professor of Psychiatry and Medicine, Associate Dean for Faculty Affairs, University of Colorado School of Medicine, Denver, Colorado*

Irl Extein, M.D.
> *Medical Director, Fair Oaks Hospital at Boca/Delray, Delray Beach, Florida*

David V. Forrest, M.D.
> *Associate Professor of Clinical Psychiatry, Consultation-Liaison Psychiatrist in Neurology, Faculty, Columbia Psychoanalytic Center, Columbia University College of Physicians and Surgeons, New York, New York*

Alfred W. Forrester, M.D.
> *Senior Clinical Fellow, Departments of Psychiatry and Behavioral Science and Neuroscience, The Johns Hopkins University School of Medicine, Baltimore, Maryland*

Richard J. Frances, M.D.
> *Professor of Clinical Psychiatry and Vice-Chairman, Department of Psychiatry, Director, Psychiatry Residency Training, New Jersey College of Medicine and Dentistry, Newark, New Jersey*

John E. Franklin, Jr., M.D.
> *Instructor in Psychiatry, The New York Hospital-Cornell Medical Center, White Plains, New York*

Michael D. Franzen, Ph.D.
> *Director of Neuropsychology, Assistant Professor of Behavioral Medicine and Psychiatry, West Virginia University School of Medicine, Morgantown, West Virginia*

Frederick C. Goggans, M.D.
> *Director of Neuropsychiatry, Psychiatric Institute of Ft. Worth, Ft. Worth, Texas*

Mark S. Gold, M.D.
> *Director of Research, Fair Oaks Hospital at Boca/Delray, Delray Beach, Florida, and Fair Oaks Hospital, Summit, New Jersey*

Lawrence S. Gross, M.D.
> *Medical Director, Adult Psychiatric Outpatient Clinic, Los Angeles County/ University of Southern California Medical Center, Assistant Professor of Clinical Psychiatry and the Behavioral Sciences, University of Southern California School of Medicine, Los Angeles, California*

Robert E. Hales, M.D., M.B.A.
> *Associate Professor of Psychiatry, Uniformed Services University of the Health Sciences, F. Edward Hébert School of Medicine, Director, Psychiatry Residency Training, Walter Reed Army Medical Center, Washington, DC*

Helen Hanesian, Ed.D.
> *Assistant Professor of Clincal Psychology (in Psychiatry), Columbia University College of Physicians and Surgeons, Columbia-Presbyterian Medical Center, New York, New York*

Reed J. Kaplan, M.D.
> *Clinical Assistant Professor of Psychiatry and Behavioral Sciences, Medical Director, Inpatient Psychiatric Unit, Stanford University School of Medicine, Stanford, California*

John H. King, M.D.
> *Assistant Professor of Behavioral Medicine and Psychiatry, West Virginia School of Medicine, Morgantown, West Virginia*

David J. Kupfer, M.D.
> *Professor and Chairman, Department of Psychiatry, University of Pittsburgh School of Medicine, Pittsburgh, Pennsylvania*

James B. Lohr, M.D.
> *Neuropsychiatry Branch, National Institute of Mental Health, St. Elizabeths Hospital, Washington, DC*

Mark R. Lovell, Ph.D.
: *Director of Neuropsychology, Department of Psychiatry, Allegheny-Singer Research Institute and Allegheny General Hospital, Pittsburgh, Pennsylvania*

Martha B. Martin, M.D.
: *Assistant Professor of Psychiatry, Georgetown University School of Medicine, Washington, DC*

Maurice J. Martin, M.D.
: *Professor of Psychiatry, Mayo Medical School, Senior Consultant in Adult Psychiatry, Mayo Clinic, Rochester, Minnesota*

John M. Morihisa, M.D.
: *Professor and Chairman, Department of Psychiatry, Georgetown University School of Medicine, and Psychiatry Service, VA Medical Center, Washington, DC*

Cynthia M. Owen, M.A.
: *Psychiatry Service, VA Medical Center, Washington, DC*

Samuel Perry, M.D.
: *Associate Professor of Clinical Psychiatry, Cornell University Medical College, New York, New York*

Richard Pleak, M.D.
: *Research Fellow in Child Psychiatry, Columbia-Presbyterian Medical Center, New York, New York*

William A. Rafuls, M.D.
: *Assistant Director, Neuropsychiatric Evaluation Unit, Fair Oaks Hospital at Boca/Delray, Delray Beach, Florida*

Charles F. Reynolds III, M.D.
: *Associate Professor of Psychiatry and Neurology, Director, Sleep Evaluation Center, Western Psychiatric Institute and Clinic, University of Pittsburgh School of Medicine, Pittsburgh, Pennsylvania*

Robert G. Robinson, M.D.
: *Professor of Psychiatry and Neuroscience, Departments of Psychiatry and Behavioral Science and Neuroscience, The Johns Hopkins University School of Medicine, Baltimore, Maryland*

Richard B. Rosse, M.D.
: *Assistant Professor, Department of Psychiatry, Georgetown University School of Medicine, and Chief, Georgetown Teaching Service, Psychiatry Service, VA Medical Center, Washington, DC*

Frederick S. Sierles, M.D.
: *Associate Professor and Director, Undergraduate Training, Department of Psychiatry and Behavioral Sciences, UHS/The Chicago Medical School, North Chicago, Illinois*

Jonathan M. Silver, M.D.
> *Assistant Professor of Clinical Psychiatry, Columbia University College of Physicians and Surgeons, Clinical Research Specialist in Neuropsychiatry, Department of Clinical Investigation, Hoffmann-La Roche, Inc., Nutley, New Jersey*

David Spiegel, M.D.
> *Associate Professor of Psychiatry and Behavioral Sciences, Director, Adult Psychiatric Outpatient Clinic, Stanford University School of Medicine, Stanford, California*

James M. Stevenson, M.D.
> *Professor and Chairman of Behavioral Medicine and Psychiatry, West Virginia University School of Medicine, Morgantown, West Virginia*

G. Alan Stoudemire, M.D.
> *Assistant Professor of Psychiatry, Director, Medical Psychiatry Unit, Emory University School of Medicine, Atlanta, Georgia*

Carl Rollyn Sullivan, M.D.
> *Assistant Professor of Behavioral Medicine and Psychiatry, West Virginia University School of Medicine, Morgantown, West Virginia*

Michael Alan Taylor, M.D.
> *Professor and Chairman, Department of Psychiatry and Behavioral Sciences, UHS/The Chicago Medical School, North Chicago, Illinois*

Troy L. Thompson II, M.D.
> *Associate Professor of Psychiatry and Medicine, Director, Division of Consultation-Liaison Psychiatry, University of Colorado School of Medicine, Denver, Colorado*

Robert M. Wettstein, M.D.
> *Assistant Professor of Psychiatry, Law and Psychiatry Program, Department of Psychiatry, University of Pittsburgh School of Medicine, Western Psychiatric Institute and Clinic, Pittsburgh, Pennsylvania*

Daniel T. Williams, M.D.
> *Associate Clinical Professor of Psychiatry, Director, Pediatric Neuropsychiatry Service, Columbia Presbyterian Medical Center, New York, New York*

Michael G. Wise, M.D.
> *Associate Professor of Psychiatry, Uniformed Services University of the Health Sciences, F. Edward Hébert School of Medicine, Director, Psychiatry Residency Training, Wilford Hall USAF Medical Center, Lackland Air Force Base, Texas*

Stuart C. Yudofsky, M.D.
> *Associate Professor of Clinical Psychiatry, Columbia University College of Physicians and Surgeons, Director, Department of Psychiatry, Allegheny General Hospital, Pittsburgh, Pennsylvania*

THE CONCEPTUALIZATION OF THIS BOOK began in the fall of 1983 when we began work on Volume 4 of *Psychiatry Update: The American Psychiatric Association Annual Review*. When one of us (REH) with Allen J. Frances, M.D. had reviewed previous volumes of the *Annual Review Series* and were projecting possible sections for future volumes, neuropsychiatry emerged as an important but neglected area. Volume 4 set sales records for the *Annual Review* Series and received excellent reviews in the professional journals, especially the section on neuropsychiatry, of which the other of us (SCY) was Section Editor. However, because of space limitations, many critical areas of neuropsychiatry remained uncovered in the 1985 *Annual Review*.

A second impetus for organizing a textbook of neuropsychiatry came from our clinical experience and training of psychiatric residents in the general hospital setting. We were both struck by the increasing numbers of patients with symptoms with overlap between psychiatry and neurology. We, as well as the residents, increasingly felt the need for scientific data and the benefit of expert clinical guidance in assessing and establishing treatment plans for these patients. In this process we referred frequently to scientific journals and to the previously published and excellent neuropsychiatry-related volumes. Included among these works are Lishman's classic book, *Organic Psychiatry: The Psychological Consequences of Cerebral Disorder*; Pincus and Tucker's excellent *Behavioral Neurology*, which is an outstanding volume for teaching and a landmark in the field; and Cummings' *Clinical Neuropsychiatry*, which is both practical and scholarly.

Notwithstanding these valuable contributions and several other volumes by both psychiatrists and neurologists that also emphasize the interface between neurology and psychiatry, we became convinced that the data base, complexity, and relevance of the field have expanded to the point that a new format, utilizing many individual investigators and clinicians with specialized knowledge of critical areas of neuropsychiatry, would have value and usefulness.

We have endeavored to assemble a comprehensive text that is also clinically relevant and practical to use by residents, psychiatrists, neurologists, neuropsychologists, and other professionals who work in a variety of clinical settings. Although the text was specifically designed to be of use to professionals who work in the general hospital setting, clinicians and health personnel in many other settings—in private practice, in private and state psychiatric hospitals, in community mental health centers, in drug and rehabilitation programs, and in alcohol treatment centers—may also find the information in this text relevant to treatment of their patients.

Chapters have been structured in an attempt to address each topic comprehensively. Clearly, there is some overlap among similar topics discussed in different chapters from varying perspectives. For instance, one may read about the neurochemical basis of depression in the chapter on neurotransmitters and neuroreceptors, learn how depression may mimic dementia in the chapter entitled "Dementia," review the many etiologies of the depression of organic affective syndrome in the chapter on "Selected Organic Mental Disorders," explore the scientific substantiation that the most disabling aspect of stroke is often significant depression following the event in the chapter entitled "Neuropsychiatric Aspects of Cerebrovascular Disease," and learn psychopharmacologic and psychosocial treatment strategies in each of the chapters of similar name. Although we have worked extensively to eliminate redundancy from this book, we have allowed a certain amount of overlap to enable the reader to explore a specific area of neuropsychiatry in depth without having to be continuously and distractingly referred to other chapters of the *Textbook*.

This book would not have been possible without the help and support of many individuals. First, we thank the chapter authors who have labored so diligently to produce what we consider to be contributions that are unique and of high quality. We have endeavored to select chapter authors who are not only recognized leaders in their fields but who are also good writers. In every instance the chapter authors exceeded our requests and expectations. Nonetheless, many chapters were edited and rewritten several times to enhance clarity of exposition, to emphasize the clinical relevance to practitioners who treat patients with neuropsychiatric disorders, and to minimize overlap. The chapter authors were all cooperative and demonstrated good humor, restraint, and good sportmanship in the compulsive and even sometimes painful process of editing and revising. Our chapter authors were encouraged to present research findings that are up-to-date and well documented, and we commend them for demonstrating the clinical applicability of all research findings presented.

We also express our deep appreciation to our mentor for this project, Shervert H. Frazier, M.D., who, as one of the leaders of American Psychiatry, has provided sound advice and counsel in suggesting topics and contributors for this volume. As a former Chairman of the Editorial Advisory Board of the American Psychiatric Press, Inc. and as Director of The National Institute of Mental Health, Sherv has guided us and has always been available to advise us when problems arose. His gracious and scholarly Introduction does honor to all who worked on this project. We thank our administrative assistant for this volume, Ms. Sandy Landfried, who organized all the administrative aspects related to its publication. Her meticulous attention to detail and her continued good humor throughout this complex process were exceptional. The Managing Editor of the American Psychiatric Press, Mr. Timothy Clancy, deserves special praise for his coordination of all the editorial activities necessary to have the volume published in an accurate and timely fashion. Ms. Karen E. Sardinas-Wyssling, who copyedited the manuscript, has done an expert and thorough job in enhancing the quality and consistency of the text. This book would not have been possible without the firm and unwavering support of Mr. Ronald E. McMillen, the General Manager of the American Psychiatric Press. Ron was supportive of the concept of this book since its inception and has shepherded it through its publication. Mrs. Evelyn Stone deserves special recognition as a leading advocate of our work and, in particular, for her support of this textbook. She has helped numerous psychiatrists throughout the years with their publication efforts, and she can add us to the long list of her many devotees. We also thank Mrs. Kathy Woznicki, Mrs. Lorraine Smith, Ms. Olga Petruska, and the outstanding typing pool at Allegheny General Hospital for generously accommodating the enumerable revisions in the final provision of a clear and accurate manuscript.

Finally, we thank our wives, Dianne Hales and Beth Yudofsky, M.D., for their encouragement, advice, and editorial assistance concerning many aspects of this book. In addition, since our work was accomplished on weekends, evenings, and holidays, they also deserve special credit for assuming increased familial responsibilities to permit us to spend so much of our free time on this project. We hope that our efforts and those of the chapter authors and other contributors will be translated into a textbook that is useful to the reader in providing excellent care for the many patients who are afflicted with neuropsychiatric illnesses.

Robert E. Hales, M.D.
Stuart C. Yudofsky, M.D.

Introduction

IT IS WIDELY RECOGNIZED that a large part of what we now regard as psychiatry stems from the ideas and works of 19th century neurologists who devoted their attention to disorders of thought and mood (Cummings 1986). Works such as *Mental Pathology and Therapeutics*, by Griesinger (1845), discounted historical antecedents almost entirely in order to counter the ancient conceptualization of insanity as resulting from demonic possession or more modest departures from religious principles. Griesinger also diminished psychological perspectives of personality and focused on a model that viewed mental illness almost exclusively in terms of organic alterations of the brain. This perspective is often termed the organicistic perspective (Mora 1980). As Griesinger's book became the standard textbook in medical schools, the organicistic trend became increasingly popular and culminated in the so-called theory of degeneration, which conceptualized mental diseases as stages of deteriorating pathological processes that progressed from neurosis to psychosis to mental deficiency (Mora 1980).

In the first six decades of this century, the convergence of psychoanalysis (which places large emphasis on the role of life experience and the unconscious representations of such experience in the understanding and treatment of emotional illness) with the emerging discipline of social psychiatry (which places emphasis on environmental, economic, cultural, and political interfaces of psychiatric illness) resulted in the fields of neurology and psychiatry moving apart. Between 1930 and 1960, it became common to attribute disorders of thinking, social behavior, and mood to the province of psychiatry, whereas disorders involving sensory and motor dysfunction were deemed the clinical responsibility of neurology.

Nevertheless, even in the decades in which psychiatry and neurology seemed to be the greatest distance apart, there were crucial grey zones that blurred the boundaries of these two disciplines. Included among these grey areas were disorders of language, memory, attention, concentration, arousal, and perception. For example, the expressive aphasia associated with the lesion in Broca's area of the cortex most likely would be assigned to the realm of neurology, while a patient with word salad associated with the language disorder of schizophrenia would most often be referred for treatment to a psychiatrist. It has not always been clear, however, as to which discipline should assume clinical responsibility for the assessment and treatment of auditory hallucinations in a patient with temporal lobe epilepsy, or whether a psychiatrist or neurologist should manage a drug-induced organic mental disorder in which a patient has both confusion and cerebellar disturbance.

With the recent and broad acceptance of the important role of biologic intervention in the treatment of many psychiatric illnesses, and with new electrodiagnostic and neurobiologic assessments that suggest the prominent role of brain structure and dysfunction in major psychiatric illnesses such as schizophrenia and bipolar disorders (Mackinnon and Yudofsky 1986), the fields of neurology and psychiatry are again moving together.

Despite the major advances in biologic assessment and treatment, and despite the important grey zones between neurologic and psychiatric symptomatologies, those disease entities comprising symptomatologies traditionally treated both by neurology and psychiatry provide the strongest link between the two specialties and manifest the need for and the reality of neuropsychiatry. A prototypic example is advanced Parkinson's disease wherein motor changes (bradykinesia) and mood changes (major depression) are both likely to be derivative, in part, of a disordered catecholamine system. This and other diseases that encompass both sets of symptomatologies are common and highly disabling, but the care of these patients is often unsatisfactory because of confused interdisciplinary responsibility.

In documenting the reengagement and ultimate inseparability of psychiatry and neurology, the *American Psychiatric Press Textbook of Neuropsychiatry* argues persuasively for the need for neuropsychiatric conceptualizations of disease. Dr. Hales is a graduate of West Point, an authority in military psychiatry, the current Training Director in Psychiatry at Walter Reed Army Medical Center, and the chairperson of the American Psychiatric Association's Scientific Program Committee. For over a decade, Dr. Yudofsky directed the Neuropsychiatric and Diagnostic Treatment Service of Columbia Presbyterian Medical Center, a program which he organized, while simultaneously conducting pioneering research in the psychopharmacology of aggressive disorders related to brain injury. The editors, both psychiatrists, drew upon their broad clinical experience, their extensive organizational skills, and an outstanding group of contributors to craft a cohesive, relevant, and usable book that addresses topics ranging from an overview of neurotransmitters and neuroreceptors to the legal aspects of neuropsychiatry.

This textbook defines disease entities that should be subsumed under the rubric of neuropsychiatry, documents the public health impact of these conditions, and reviews clinical factors relevant to their assessment and treatment. Epilepsy and epileptic seizures, headache and facial pain, sleep disorders, substance-induced organic mental disorders, and neuroendocrine disorders all are defined as common and disabling neuropsychiatric conditions, and elegant and comprehensive reviews of each constitute chapters in this book.

The public health impact of various neuropsychiatric conditions is shown to be extensive. Drs. Frances and Franklin, for example, provide data

which corroborate that alcoholism is the leading public health problem in the United States (directly affecting more than 14 million people) and that alcohol-related syndromes—including intoxication, alcohol withdrawal syndromes, Wernicke's syndrome, Korsakoff's syndrome, and other alcohol dementias—are common and challenging to treat. Dr. Thompson documents that approximately 2 to 5 percent of individuals over 65 years of age have significant dementia; this figure increases to 15 to 20 percent for people over 80. In their chapter on cerebrovascular disease, Drs. Robinson and Forrester note that thromboembolic stroke, estimated to affect between 300,000 and 400,000 patients annually, constitutes the third leading cause of morbidity and mortality in this country. Drs. Silver, Yudofsky, and Hales, writing on traumatic brain injury, report that over 500,000 people per year suffer from severe traumatic injury to the brain, and that a far larger number of people endure the chronic sequelae of such injuries. The authors estimate that total economic costs resulting from traumatic brain injury are exceeded only by those associated with cancer. It is noted, as well, that the psychosocial disruptions of stroke and traumatic brain injury may be far more devastating to patients than are the sensory or motor dysfunctions.

Chapters on clinical assessment and treatment—Dr. Forrest's review of psychosocial treatment in neuropsychiatry, Dr. Dobovsky's paper on neuropsychopharmacology, and Drs. Franzen and Sullivan's focus on cognitive rehabilitation of patients afflicted with neuropsychiatric dysfunction—are similarly valuable parts of this volume.

As Dr. Yudofsky has noted previously (Yudofsky 1985), much of what we know about the so-called "normal" derives from our study of the abnormal; that through the painful and disabling lesions studied and treated by psychiatrists and neurologists, we are discovering ourselves. In this discovery, he wrote, "we ultimately will not only free ourselves of illnesses but also free ourselves of limitations—ranging from anxiety to aging—that have been accepted for millennia as the human condition."

Asserting in a recent editorial in the *Archives of Neurology* that "it is time again to challenge our neuroscientific understanding with the task of explaining mental disorders as a product of brain structure and function interacting with personal and social experience," the authors concluded that "after a century of separation, psychiatry and neurology are coming together again. Neuropsychiatry is the bridge" (Caine and Joydt 1986). I concur with the sentiments and substance of this editorial and submit that the outstanding accomplishment of the *American Psychiatric Press Textbook of Neuropsychiatry* will serve to buttress the foundation and reinforce the suspension of that bridge.

Shervert H. Frazier, M.D.
Director, National Institute of Mental Health

☐ REFERENCES

Caine ED, Joydt RJ: Neuropsychiatry . . . Again. Arch Neurol 43:325–327, 1986

Cummings JL: Introduction to clinical neuropsychiatry, in Clinical Neuropsychiatry. New York, Grune & Stratton, 1986, pp 1–5

Griesinger W: Mental Pathology and Therapeutics [Facsimile of 1887 edition]. Translated by Robertson CL, Rutherford J. New York, Macmillan, 1965

Mackinnon RA, Yudofsky SC: Biological testing in psychiatry, in The Psychiatric Evaluation in Clinical Practice. Philadelphia, J.B. Lippincott Co, 1986

Mora G: Historical and theoretical trends in psychiatry, in Comprehensive Textbook of Psychiatry/III. Edited by Kaplan HI, Freedman AM, Sadock BJ. Baltimore, Williams & Wilkins Co, 1980, pp 4–98

Yudofsky SC: The paradox of Broca, in Psychiatry Update: American Psychiatric Association Annual Review, Vol. 4. Edited by Hales RE, Frances AJ. Washington, DC, American Psychiatric Press, 1985, p 255

Section I

Evaluation and Basic Principles

Chapter 1

The Neuropsychiatric Evaluation

Michael Alan Taylor, M.D.
Frederick S. Sierles, M.D.
Richard Abrams, M.D.

THE NEUROPSYCHIATRIC EVALUATION should be integral to every complete patient evaluation. Many hospitalized medical and surgical patients suffer from significant cognitive impairment interfering with management of their systemic illness, and 15 to 20 percent of acute psychiatric patients suffer from coarse or behavioral neurologic disorder (i.e., "organic" mental disorder) (Taylor et al. 1985). The modern psychiatrist is expected to be expert in diagnosing and caring for such patients. The knowledge and skill required for this purpose are fundamental to the practice of modern psychiatry.

The neuropsychiatric evaluation conducted by a psychiatrist may best be compared with examinations performed by other specialists (e.g., the cardiologist's evaluation of the heart). It is more elaborate and skilled than that of the nonpsychiatric clinician, but it remains a part of the complete patient evaluation in which context it must be performed. It should be structured: questions and testing of cognitive functions should proceed logically,

while remaining responsive to the patient's needs and behaviors. Passive, nondirective, open-ended questioning permits the patient to control the interview and is rarely useful. The sequence of questions can vary and "lead-ins" to questions must be individualized, but a basic outline of topic areas and a standard tactical approach for each symptom area should characterize the examination.

The traditional, "routine" evaluation of neurologic functions focuses almost exclusively on subcortical structures, with only cursory attention paid to cortical associational areas and their projections (areas primarily associated with behavior). This narrow focus derives partly from prior unreliability of clinical testing procedures and the consequent difficulty in localizing lesions that result in defects of higher cortical functions. Testing of these higher cortical functions, however, can be reliable, valid, and sensitive, often identifying a lesion before it is noted on computed tomography (CT) scan or electroencephalogram (EEG) (Folstein et al. 1975; Golden et al. 1978; Matarazzo 1972; Matarazzo et al. 1976; Tsai and Tsuang 1979). Whether clinicians use standard assessment instruments or develop their own neuropsychiatric examination, a knowledge of modern neuropsychological concepts is integral for any meaningful understanding of a patient's disorder.

The importance of the neuropsychiatric/behavioral neurologic evaluation extends beyond the identification and localization of coarse brain disease; many patients with the classic "functional" psychiatric syndromes exhibit cognitive deficits that may be localized to specific brain regions (Silverstein 1983; Taylor and Abrams 1984). For example, catatonia may result from frontal lobe dysfunction (Abrams et al. 1979), and Capgras' syndrome from nondominant parietal lobe dysfunction (Alexander et al. 1979; Hayman and Abrams 1977).

☐ DOMINANT AND NONDOMINANT HEMISPHERES

The "dominant hemisphere" is the cerebral hemisphere that subserves language. In approximately 97 percent of people, it is in the left hemisphere, with the remainder exhibiting right hemisphere or mixed dominance. Hemispheric dominance and hand preference are closely related, but not synonymous. Of the 90 percent of right-handed (dextral) people, 99 percent have left hemisphere dominance for language. Of the 10 percent of left-handed (sinistral) people, about two-thirds have language subserved by the left hemisphere, with the remainder exhibiting "mixed" dominance or language functioning in the right hemisphere (Geschwind 1974, 1974a, 1974b; Levy 1974).

The two hemispheres process information differently and have different functional specializations. The dominant hemisphere processes information in a sequential, analytic, linear fashion and is particularly efficient at processing language and other symbolic information. The nondominant hemisphere processes information in a gestaltic, holistic, parallel fashion and is particularly efficient at processing visuospatial information (Levy 1974; Seamon 1974). Anatomical and biochemical asymmetries underlie these functional differences (Geschwind 1974a, 1974b).

The determination of a patient's preferred hand for writing provides a useful approximation of language dominance. To confirm that the patient's

hand preference for writing is biologically rather than socially determined, the patient should also demonstrate how he or she pours liquids, holds a knife to cut food, holds scissors, throws a ball, and holds a thread when threading a needle. Most individuals who write with their right hand will also use their right hand for these purposes. Left-handers often give a mixed response.

Interhemispheric Connections

The corpus callosum and other deep hemispheric structures transfer and integrate information between hemispheres. Although sensory and motor long tracts do not pass through these interhemispheric structures, interhemispheric messages do pass from one cortical region to another. "Disconnections" of these information bridges can result in several syndromes. One theory of schizophrenia proposes a callosal transfer deficit as a major etiologic factor (Wade and Taylor 1984).

☐ THE NEUROPSYCHIATRIC EVALUATION

The comprehensive neuropsychiatric evaluation includes an assessment of systemic and neurologic functions, an examination for "soft" neurologic signs, a detailed mental status and cognitive assessment, plus ancillary clinical (e.g., the "Mini-mental State," the Aphasia Screening Test) and laboratory tests (e.g., neuropsychological assessment, electrophysiologic studies, brain imaging, spinal fluid studies, cerebral angiography, skull X ray, blood chemistries, urinalysis, VDRL, electrocardiogram [EKG], chest X ray, endocrine and nutritional studies). Space limitations preclude a discussion of some of the above areas.

The Mental Status Examination

A change in behavior is usually the earliest sign of brain dysfunction. Inefficiency at work, inattentiveness, lassitude, moodiness, or slight circumstantiality in speech may occur in the early stages of dementia. Although CT scan and EEG are usually still within normal limits at this early stage of illness, a thorough behavioral history and mental status examination may reveal psychopathological and cognitive stigmata of coarse brain disease even in the absence of more traditional neurologic indicators (Fitzhugh-Bell 1978; Peterson 1978).

Techniques for Testing of Cognitive Functions

A valid cognitive examination must be thorough and systematic, including assessments of (1) motor behavior, (2) language, (3) memory and the temporal lobe functions, (4) frontal lobe functions, (5) parietal lobe functions, (6) occipital lobe functions, and (7) "soft" neurologic signs. The various examination findings can then be intercorrelated (e.g., if motor testing reveals Gegenhalten and expressive aphasia, the combination suggests frontal lobe dysfunction; see Tables 1 and 2).

Most examination tasks focus on specific higher cortical functions and associational cortical regions and systems. Nevertheless, functional intactness

of the entire system (afferent and efferent) is generally required for the correct performance of a given task. No single error is pathognomonic (Golden et al. 1978; Heilman and Valenstein 1979; Matarazzo et al. 1976). Findings should be reported objectively; all errors should be recorded. An examiner's statement, "Well, the patient got that wrong only because of fatigue, so it's not a real error," is an interpretation, not an observation. If an incorrect or unduly slow response is given, the patient should usually be asked to repeat the task. Unclear instructions, lack of fluency in the examiner's language, and an uncooperative or poorly motivated patient are sources of false positive responses.

Motor Functions. In the traditional mental status examination, the examiner notes the patient's level of motor activity, gait, presence of choreo-athetoid movements, tremors, intrusiveness, agitation, and

TABLE 1. CORTICAL MAPPING OF NORMAL FUNCTION

	Frontal	Dominant Temporo-parietal	Dominant Parietal	Non-dominant Parietal	Non-dominant Temporo-parietal	Occipital	Corpus Callosum
Motor Behavior	• Motor persistence • Initiation and stopping • Rapid sequential movement • Resistance to stimulus binding • Learned complex motor behavior	• Writing	• Ideokinetic (ideomotor) praxis • Kinesthetic praxis	• Constructional praxis • Dressing praxis • Kinesthetic praxis			• Tying shoelaces with eyes closed • Ideokinetic praxis in hand ipsilateral to dominant hemisphere
Language	• Verbal fluency • Spontaneous prosody and gesturing* • Ability to repeat with prosodic affective variation*	• Comprehension of spoken language • Reading • Relevance and word usage • Naming • Writing • Letter gnosis • Number gnosis	• Symbolic categorization • Reading • Naming		• Auditory comprehension of affective components of prosody • Visual comprehension of affective components of prosody	• Writing • Reading	
Memory	• Short-term memory store	• Rehearsed consolidated memory (30 sec to 30 min)			• Rehearsed consolidated memory (30 sec to 30 min) • Musical memory	• Visual memory	
Other	• Concentration • Global orientation • Judgment • Problem solving • Abstracting ability • Right spatial recognition		• Finger gnosis • Calculation • Right-left orientation • East-west orientation • Stereoagnosis • Graphesthesia	• Stereoagnosis • Graphesthesis • Recognition of familiar faces and other things		• Visual pattern recognition (visual gnosis)	• Stereoagnosis • Graphesthesis

*Nondominant frontal lobe.

TABLE 2. CORTICAL MAPPING OF BRAIN DYSFUNCTIONS

	Frontal	Dominant Temporo-parietal	Dominant Parietal	Non-dominant Parietal	Non-dominant Temporo-parietal	Occipital	Corpus Callosum
Motor Abnormalities	• Motor impersistence • Inertia • Impaired rapid sequential movements • Stimulus-bound behavior (e.g., echopraxia, gegenhalten)	• Dysgraphia	• Ideokinetic (ideomotor) dyspraxia • Kinesthetic dyspraxia	• Constructional dyspraxia • Dressing dyspraxia • Kinesthetic dyspraxia			• Inability to tie shoes with eyes closed • Ideokinetic dyspraxia in hand ipsilateral to dominant hemisphere • Constructional dyspraxia in hand contralateral to dominant hemisphere • Alexia without agraphia
Language Abnormalities	• Broca's aphasia • Transcortical aphasia • Motor aprosodia* • Verbigeration	• Wernicke's aphasia • Pure word deafness • Driveling, word approximations, neologisms, stock phrases, phonemic paraphasias, private use of words • Dysgraphia • Dyslexia • Dysnomia • Letter agnosia • Number agnosia • Sensory aprosodia	• Dyslexia • Dysnomia				
Memory Abnormalities	• Impaired short-term memory store	• Impairment of rehearsed consolidated memory			• Impaired musical memory	• Impaired visual memory	
Other Abnormalities	• Impaired concentration • Global disorientation • Impaired judgment • Impaired problem solving • Impaired abstraction • Right spatial neglect		• Finger agnosia • Dyscalulea • Right-left disorientation • East-west disorientation • Dysstereognosis • Dysgraphesthesis • Impaired symbolic categorization	• Dysstereognosis • Dysgraphesthesis • Anosognosia • Prosopagnosia • Paragnosia • Reduplicative paramnesia • Left spatial neglect			• Dysstereognosis of hand ipsilateral to dominant hemisphere • Dysgraphesthesis of hand ipsilateral to dominant hemisphere

*Nondominant frontal lobe.

inertia. The behavioral neurologic examination requires further testing of motor regulation.

The ability to start and stop motor actions is a frontal lobe function. Loss of this ability, termed *perseveration*, results in unnecessary repetition or maintenance of an action. It can occur spontaneously. It may be elicited by asking the patient to copy a design or shape that lends itself to unnecessary repetition, or to perform a three-stage command such as, "Take this piece of paper in your right hand, fold it in half, and return it to me." A common perseveration is the patient continuing to fold the paper in fourths or eighths (Luria 1973).

Difficulty initiating motor tasks is related to motor perseveration. Some patients will be virtually immobile, or will be hesitant, or will move extremely slowly. The combination of difficulty initiating motor tasks and difficulty stopping them once started is termed *motor inertia* (Luria 1973). Because of dysfunctions such as perseveration, frontal lobe abnormalities often produce false positive findings when testing of other brain regions (e.g., perseverating a previous response when requested to perform a new task) (Heilman and Valenstein 1979).

Motor persistence, the ability to maintain an action, is tested by asking the patient to perform at least four tasks, such as, (1) "hold out your arms," (2) "make a fist with both of your hands," (3) stick out your tongue," and (4) "close your eyes tightly." Inability to persist at each task for about 20 seconds may be due to frontal lobe dysfunction (i.e., motor impersistence), or to motor weakness (Ben-Yishay et al. 1968; Heilman and Valenstein 1979). To distinguish between the two, muscle strength is tested conventionally.

The ability to control one's motor actions despite distracting stimuli is principally a frontal lobe function (Heilman and Valenstein 1979; Luria 1973). Abnormalities of stimulus-resistant motor regulation (i.e., *stimulus-bound* behavior) include *echopraxia* and *Gegenhalten*, each a feature of catatonia. The *catatonic* patient may also exhibit other signs of motor dysregulation: (1) stupor with mutism, (2) automatic obedience, (3) catalepsy, (4) stereotypies, (5) mannerisms, (6) posturing, and (7) mitgehen. Catatonic behaviors are often seen in patients with frontal lobe dysfunction (Abrams et al. 1979; Heilman and Valenstein 1979; Luria 1973). Further descriptions of catatonia and its assessment are available elsewhere (Taylor 1981).

The examiner should also test *rapid sequential fine movement* performance by asking patients to pronate their hands on a flat surface and tap their fingers rapidly and in sequence. Patients without upper limb pathology should be able to do this easily; if not, it is likely that there is a contralateral frontal lobe dysfunction (Heilman and Valenstein 1979; Luria 1973). If, as the examiner tests one hand for sequential finger movements, and the fingers of the other hand wiggle or tap, the patient has *adventitious motor overflow* (choreiform movements are another example). This sign sometimes localizes to the frontal lobe and is considered a neurologic "soft sign" (Paulson and Gottlieb 1968; Quitkin et al. 1976).

Ideokinetic (ideomotor) praxis (Critchley 1953; Geschwind 1965; 1974b; Heilman and Valenstein 1979; Luria 1973) is the ability to perform an action from memory on request without props or cues. Primary motor and sensory function must be intact and patients must understand the task. To exclude interhemispheric dysconnection as the cause, the nonpreferred hand is tested first. For the same reason, patients should not be allowed to cue themselves by restating the instruction. Patients are asked to demonstrate the use of simple objects (e.g., key, hammer) with each hand. Common errors include awkwardness, miming only with proximal movements (movements of the shoulder and arm) while distal movements (hand and wrist) are stiff or absent, use of the hand *as* the object itself instead of as the bearer of the object (e.g., extending the index finger as if it were the key), or having to perform the task by first verbalizing it (verbal overflow). In patients with interhemispheric dysconnection, ideokinetic praxis may be normal in the hand contralateral to the dominant hemisphere, and impaired in the other. Patients with dominant parietal lobe dysfunction will usually exhibit ideokinetic dyspraxia with both hands.

Kinesthetic praxis is tested by having the patient mimic hand, finger, or other limb positions demonstrated by the examiner. Inability to reproduce these positions reflects dysfunction in the contralateral parietal lobe (Critchley 1953; Geschwind 1965, 1974b; Heilman and Valenstein 1979; Luria 1973).

Constructional ability is tested by having the patient copy the outline of a shape (e.g., a square, a triangle, a Greek cross) (Heilman and Valenstein 1979; Wheeler and Reitan 1962). Only the outline of the drawing is copied, as the accurate copying of details within the object's boundaries may require verbal reasoning (dominant hemisphere) as well as nondominant parietal lobe functioning (Gainotti et al. 1977). Abnormal performance includes a markedly distorted drawing and inability to complete the drawing without lifting pen from paper. The patient who does poorly should repeat the drawing with the nonpreferred hand. If the preferred-hand drawing is worse than that of the nonpreferred hand, the dysfunction is likely the result of interhemispheric dysconnection or dysfunction in dominant hemisphere structures (LeDoux et al. 1978). If drawings with both hands are inaccurate, the dysfunction is probably in the nondominant parietal region (Heilman and Valenstein 1979).

Dressing praxis is the ability to dress and undress oneself. When patients make errors such as putting on clothes inside out or putting their feet in their shirtsleeves, they likely have nondominant parietal dysfunction (Heilman and Valenstein 1979).

Language Functions. Assessment of language (e.g., spontaneous speech, naming, reading, writing) is an extension of the thought processes and content section of the mental status. *Speech* localizes primarily to the parasylvian areas in the frontal, temporal, and parietal lobes in the dominant hemisphere for words and word usage, and in the nondominant hemisphere for the "affectivity" of speech (prosody) (Benson 1979; Geschwind 1965, 1974b; Heilman and Valenstein 1979; Ross 1981).

Fluency of speech is a function of Broca's area, the associated deep frontal cortex, and the supplementary motor cortex. Speech fluency includes the extent, smoothness, and continuity of the patient's utterances. Abnormalities of speech fluency include Broca's aphasia, transcortical motor aphasia, and mixed aphasias (Benson 1979; Geschwind 1974b; Heilman and Valenstein 1979).

Broca's (motor) aphasia results from pathology in the posterior inferior region of the dominant frontal lobe (Broca's area). Although they may have some comprehension and thinking deficits, these patients usually understand speech. Typically, however, they are unable to speak fluently and struggle to "get the words out." Their speech is often dysarthric, utterances labored or mispronounced (e.g., "Messodist Epistopal" for "Methodist Episcopal"). Speech is telegraphic. Because of the extent of brain tissue damage associated with many diseases causing Broca's aphasia, problems not directly related to speech often accompany it (Benson 1979; Geschwind 1974b). These include: (1) ideokinetic dyspraxia of the ipsilateral hand; (2) buccolingual dyspraxia (the patient may have trouble whistling, puffing out the cheeks, or blowing out an imagined match); (3) weakness or paralysis of the contralateral extremity; and (4) dysgraphia of the ipsilateral (and sometimes the contralateral) hand. *Transcortical motor aphasia* results from frontal lobe damage deep to Broca's area and is characterized by a paucity of speech and labored speech. However, speech is not telegraphic. Comprehension and reasoning may also be affected.

Lesions in or near Wernicke's area result in fluent, jargon-filled speech (driveling speech); paraphasic utterances; loss of word complexity; phonemic errors; and impaired comprehension of speech. Syntax appears intact but the content is often meaningless: hence, *Wernicke's (receptive or posterior) aphasia*. Writing is usually aphasic. Poor auditory comprehension is almost always present and non sequiturs frequently occur. Posterior aphasics often have difficulty naming objects (*dysnomia* or *anomia*). This is tested by asking the patient to name a series of common objects (e.g., a pen, a picture frame, a light switch) and then asking the patient to point to items that the examiner names (e.g., "Point to your sleeve," "Show me a shoe"). Dysnomia can result from dominant temporal or parietal lesions.

Faber et al. (1983) demonstrated that patients with schizophrenia and formal thought disorder, and neurologic patients with posterior aphasia, exhibited elements of aphasic speech with equal frequency. Both groups had fluent speech and speech with reduced content or meaning (fewer nouns and more pronouns). The schizophrenic patients, however, could use multisyllabic words (e.g., military industrial complex), whereas the posterior aphasics could not. The schizophrenic patients also tended to exhibit auditory comprehension deficits.

In addition to speech, reading and writing are also associated with the dominant temporoparietal region (Benson 1979; Critchley 1953; Geschwind 1974b; Heilman and Valenstein 1979; Luria 1973; Seamon 1974). To test *reading*, the patient is asked to read several words and sentences. *Writing* is tested by asking the patient to write one or several words from memory and to write a sentence. The patient should be instructed to write in script as the most sensitive test of dysgraphia. The examiner also evaluates what is written for letter construction, syntax, and word usage.

Recent studies of regional blood flow during spontaneous speech have revealed changes in the parasylvian regions of the nondominant hemisphere, suggesting these regions subserve the affective components of language (i.e., *prosody* and *emotional gesturing*) (Benson 1979; Heilman and Valenstein 1979; Ross 1981; Seamon 1974). Patients with normal dominant hemispheric functioning and lesions in the nondominant hemisphere manifest normal spontaneity, clarity, and comprehension of speech. They have, however, impairments of vocal range, modulation, and melody; of gesturing with speech; or of comprehension of the emotional tone of the speech of others. These abnormalities are analogous to aphasic disturbances from dominant hemisphere dysfunction. For example, in an anterior (e.g., frontal) prosodic disturbance, there is impaired spontaneous emotionality and gesturing with speech; in posterior (e.g., temporal) prosodic disturbance, there is impaired comprehension of the prosody and gesturing of others. Assessment of language-related functions of the nondominant hemisphere includes the following four aspects.

1. Observing vocal range, modulation, and melody; the spontaneity of gestures; and the ability to convey feeling.

2. Assessing the ability to repeat a sentence with the same affective quality as the examiner. The examiner makes statements using a happy, sad, tearful, angry, disinterested, or surprised voice, and the patient is asked to repeat these statements in the same manner.

3. Testing the ability to comprehend (rather than mimic) the emotions of others. The examiner stands behind the patient and presents sentences, devoid of emotionally laden words, but with varying affective tones. The patient must then identify whether the sentence was spoken with an angry, sad, happy, disinterested, surprised, or tearful tone. This is comparable to the assessment of the comprehension of speech.

4. Determining the ability to comprehend emotional gesturing. The examiner faces the patient and mimes a facial expression to convey one of the above moods. The patient is then asked to describe the mood conveyed. If the patient cannot do this, choices are given and the patient is asked to choose which one is correct. Dysprosodia differs from emotional blunting in that moods are experienced normally, but cannot be properly expressed, and the patient is troubled by this. Additionally, emotional blunting is associated with other affective deficits, whereas dysprosodia is often a solitary affective dysfunction.

Memory and the Temporal Lobes. Adequate memory assessment is rarely performed during mental status examinations. This is unfortunate, as there are numerous tests of memory function. Memory assessment should include an evaluation of span of immediate retention, learning, and retrieval of recently learned and long-stored information. Specific verbal and visual memory testing should be done (Barbizet 1970; Heilman and Valenstein 1979; Luria 1973).

Questioning patients about their past, and the sequence of events and details of their recent illness, provides an impression of their memory function (Barbizet 1970). Standardized assessment of memory should also be done. *Rote memory* can be tested by asking the patient to recite information learned in early childhood (e.g., alphabet, number series, simple multiplication tables, days of the week and months of the year, childhood rhymes and prayers, the Pledge of Allegiance). Any error or

inability to start or complete these verbal automatisms suggests significant impairment. *Immediate recall* can be tested by asking the patient to repeat series of random numbers (digit span) presented 1 second apart, starting with a sequence of three digits and increasing the length by one digit each time (to a total of seven digits, if the preceding sequence is correctly reproduced). A normal person can repeat six to eight digits forward and four to five backward. Inability to repeat at least five digits forward and three digits backward indicates substantial impairment.

Short-term retention can be tested by a paired-associate task in which the examiner reads aloud a list of word pairs—usually 10 word pairs consisting of 6 easy pairs (e.g., baby-cries) and 4 hard pairs (e.g., cabbage-pen). After a 5-second pause, the examiner then reads aloud, in random order, 1 word from each pair and the patient tries to recall each co-word. The patient is given three trials to learn the 10 word pairs. An attentive and alert adult can recall 7 or 8 pairs on the third trial. If 7 or more pairs are reproduced correctly within three trials, the examiner returns in 5 minutes to test for the number of half-pairs correctly recalled in response to the first word of each pair. Inability to recall at least 3 easy pairs and 2 hard pairs indicates substantial impairment of recall.

Short-term retention and recall can also be assessed by having the patient listen to a standardized 21-unit story paragraph (Figure 1), which the patient is asked to recall immediately (recall of fewer than one-third of the story elements indicates significant dysfunction) (Lezak 1983). Story recall can then be used to test short-term retention by reading it a second time, and asking the patient to try to recall it after 20 minutes (recall of one-third or less of the story elements indicates severe dysfunction).

Visual memory can be tested by displaying a series of geometric designs (Figure 2), each for 5 seconds. The patient immediately tries to reproduce each design. The presence of rotations, reversals, missed important elements, or loss of

---

December 6./ Last week/ a river/ overflowed/ in a small town/ ten miles/ from Albany./ Water covered the streets/ and entered the houses./ Fourteen persons/ were drowned/ and 600 persons/ caught cold/ because of the dampness/ and cold weather./ In saving/ a boy/ who was caught/ under a bridge,/ a man/ cut his hands.

Figure 1. Story Recall Test

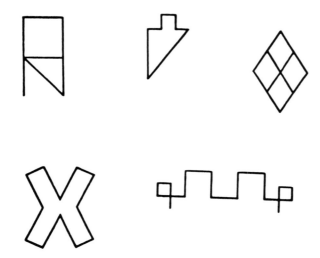

Figure 2.   Visual Memory for Designs

configuration suggests dysfunction (Benton et al. 1983; Lezak 1983).

Language and memory assessment, in part, tests temporal lobe function. Temporal lobe dysfunction is also expressed as psychomotor symptoms. Their presence should suggest a temporal lobe lesion, although discharges elsewhere in the brain can also produce psychomotor phenomena.

Patients with temporal lobe epilepsy or with stroke, head injury, viral disease (particularly herpes), vascular malformations, and degenerative disease involving the temporal lobes can all present with delusions, hallucinations (particularly auditory and panoramic visual), and mood disturbances. Thus, even in the absence of a classic epileptic picture and course, temporal lobe disease should be considered in the differential diagnosis of psychosis (Benson and Blumer 1982; Davidson and Bagley 1969; Heilman and Valenstein 1979; Koella and Trimble 1982; Taylor 1981).

Disturbances in language and memory often occur in patients with temporal lobe dysfunction. Most illnesses with bilateral temporal lobe involvement typically lead to dementia. When the dysfunction is in the dominant temporal lobe, euphoria, auditory hallucinations, formal thought disorder, and primary delusional ideas are frequently observed. These will be associated with impaired learning and retention of verbal material and deficits in verbal and reading comprehension. When the dysfunction is in the nondominant temporal lobe, dysphoria, depression, irritability, and inappropriate emotional expression (aprosodia) may

occur in association with cognitive deficits of decreased recognition and recall of visual and environmental sounds, amusia (loss of ability to repeat musical sounds), poor visual memory, decreased auditory discrimination and comprehension of tonal patterns, and decreased ability to learn and recognize nonsense figures and geometric shapes (Cummings 1982; Heilman and Valenstein 1979).

Frontal Lobe Functions.   The frontal lobes comprise 25 percent of adult brain weight. The portion anterior to the motor areas has executive function over other cortical areas. Many consider this the association cortex for the limbic system, and dysfunction here may adversely affect performance on tests of other cortical areas. The clinician must be cautious in localizing lesions in the presence of frontal lobe dysfunction (Heilman and Valenstein 1979; Luria 1973).

Motor behavior and expressive language are regulated by frontal lobe systems. Other frontal lobe functions include concentration and attention, which is reliably tested by asking the patient to subtract 7s serially from 100 (Folstein et al. 1975; Spear and Green 1966). Reasoning and thinking abilities should also be assessed as part of the evaluation of frontal lobe, as well as other dominant hemisphere functioning.

Some items from the comprehension subtest of the Wechsler Adult Intelligence Scale (WAIS) (Lezak 1983, pp. 259–262; Matarazzo 1972) can be used to assess *comprehension*:

1. Why do we wash clothes?
2. Why does a train have an engine?
3. Why should we keep away from bad company?
4. Why should people pay taxes?
5. Why are child labor laws needed?
6. Why are people who are born deaf usually unable to talk?
7. Why does land in the city cost more than land in the country?
8. Why does the state require people to get a license in order to be married?

Encouragement may be needed to obtain the patient's best performance, but the examiner should terminate the test after three consecutive failures. When each response is scored as 0 = poor, 1 = fair, or 2 = full comprehension, a score of 8 or less suggests significant impairment.

The similarities subtest of the WAIS is a good test of *verbal concept formation* (Lezak 1983; Matarazzo 1972). The examiner should introduce each item by saying, "In what way are *A* and *B* alike"?

For item 1 (orange . . . banana), if the patient replies "they are both fruit," the examiner proceeds with item 2. If the subject's response to item 1 is inadequate, the examiner should state, "They are alike in that they are both fruit," and then proceed with item 2, (coat . . . dress), offering no further help on this or on succeeding items (e.g., table . . . chair; egg . . . seed). After three consecutive failures, the test should be terminated. Each item may be scored 0, 1, or 2, with a score of 10 or less suggesting serious dysfunction.

The verbal and pictorial absurdities sections of the Stanford-Binet Intelligence Scale provide a test of reasoning (Lezak 1983, pp. 494–495). The patient is asked to listen to a statement and then tell the examiner what is "foolish" about the statement. Two examples are:

1. A man had the flu twice. The first time it killed him, but the second time he got well quickly.

2. When there is a collision, the last car of the train is usually damaged most. So they decided that it will be best if the last car is always taken off before the train starts.

Visual reasoning is similarly tested by showing the patient several pictures (Figure 3), each of which is "foolish" in some way. Verbal and visual reasoning can be scored in a fashion similar to tests of comprehension, with 0 = poor, 1 = fair, and 2 = a good response. In a five-item reasoning test, a score less than 5 suggests significant impairment.

Parietal Lobe Functions. Touch, pain, and temperature are represented in the primary cortex in

Figure 3. Picture Absurdities

the posterior central gyrus of the parietal lobe opposite to the side of the body being tested. Proprioception, stereognosis, and graphesthesia are represented in secondary cortex in the contralateral parietal lobe, just caudal to the posterior central gyrus. Much of each parietal lobe is tertiary cortex. The nondominant parietal lobe coordinates motor, sensory, and spatial perception. Its functions include the recognition of faces, the awareness of one's body in space, and the ability to copy the outline of simple objects. The dominant parietal lobe coordinates visual and language functions, including reading and writing. Two other parietal lobe functions, kinesthetic praxis and ideokinetic (ideomotor) praxis, have also been discussed. Others include finger gnosis, calculation, right-left orientation, symbolic categorization, graphesthesia, and stereognosis (Critchley 1953; Heilman and Valenstein 1979; Luria 1973; Neilsen 1938).

The examiner tests *finger gnosis* by pointing, without touching, to each of the patient's fingers (interlocked, as if in prayer), and then asking the patient to name them. *Calculation*, or ability to do simple math, is assessed by asking the patient to perform, on paper, several calculations that require "carrying" one or two digits. *Right-left orientation* is tested with several tasks that require the patient to tell left from right while crossing his or her body midline (e.g., "Touch your left hand to your right ear"; "Touch your right hand to your left elbow"). *Symbolic categorization* is tested by asking the patient to identify family relationships (e.g., "What would be the relationship to you of your brother's father"). Symbolic categorization requires that the patient make a "mental diagram" in order to respond correctly.

Just as in the assessment of kinesthetic praxis, the evaluation of *graphesthesia* and *stereognosis* tests the parietal lobe contralateral to the hand being tested, and interhemisphere connections (Critchley 1953; Heilman and Valenstein 1979; Luria 1973). Graphesthesia is tested by tracing letters, one at a time, on the patient's palms while the patient's eyes are closed. The patient is required to name each letter. Stereognosis is tested by placing objects (e.g., key, coins, button, paper clip), one at a time, in the patient's palms while the patient's eyes are closed. Impairment of these tasks is due to dysfunction of the contralateral parietal lobe, or of the interhemispheric connections such as the corpus callosum, if errors are primarily lateralized to the nonpreferred hand.

Additional nondominant parietal lobe functions include the ability "to recognize" people and objects. Abnormalities include nonrecognition of (1) obvious serious medical disability (anosognosia), (2) the left side of one's body or of objects in the left visual field (left spatial nonrecognition), and (3) familiar people and faces (prosopagnosia). *Prosopagnosia* (Critchley 1953; Luria 1973; Meadows 1974) is suggested when the patient accuses one or more familiar people, usually a family member, of being an impostor (i.e., *Capgras' syndrome*) (Alexander et al. 1979; Hayman and Abrams 1977). Some recent evidence suggests prosopagnosia extends to the nonrecognition of other nonfacial visual phenomena and that lesions are often bilateral. *Reduplicative paramnesia* is a related alternative explanation of Capgras' syndrome (Critchley 1953; Luria 1973; Weinstein and Kahn 1955); here a patient insists that a duplicate of a person or place exists elsewhere.

Some patients with intact left-right orientation ignore the left side of their body or objects in their left visual field. Another nondominant parietal lobe dysfunction (Critchley 1953; Heilman and Valenstein 1979; Luria 1973; Weinstein and Kahn 1955), *left spatial nonrecognition*, manifests itself as not shaving the left half of the face, bumping into objects on the left, or reading only the right side of printed materials. *East-west orientation* is also a "spatial" orientation function of the nondominant parietal lobe. The examiner assesses this by drawing two crossed arrows representing the directions on an imaginary map and asking the patient to identify north, south, east, and west (Critchley 1953; Luria 1973; Weinstein and Kahn 1955).

Occasionally, a hospitalized patient with normal global orientation (who chose correctly from a series of choices about present location) cannot state spontaneously where he or she is. When asked to do so, the patient will make a series of wild guesses (e.g., "At the MacDonald's"; "At the railway station"; "In a high-rise building"). This wild guessing is called paragnosia, and is associated with lesions in the nondominant parietal lobe (Critchley 1953; Luria 1973).

Parietal lobe dysfunction may produce significant psychopathology (e.g., delusional ideas, experiences of alienation), leading to misdiagnoses and inappropriate psychiatric treatment (Critchley 1953; Heilman and Valenstein 1979; Luria 1973). Dominant parietal lobe lesions often produce language disorders, dyscalculia, dyspraxias, difficulties in spatially related abstraction, and contralateral sensory deficits (graphasthesia, astereoagnosis) and motor deficits (hypotonia, posturing, paucity of movement). Gerstmann's syndrome (dysgraphia, dyscalculia, right-left disorientation, finger agnosia) is the best known dominant parietal syndrome (Neilsen 1938). Although its validity has been questioned by some authors, it has been reported (Birkett 1967) in 19 percent of chronic psychiatric patients and is believed the result of a lesion in the angular gyrus.

Nondominant parietal lobe lesions may produce denial of illness, left-sided spatial neglect, constructional difficulties, dressing dyspraxia, contralateral sensory and motor deficits, Capgras' syndrome, and the first-rank symptom of experience of alienation (body parts or thoughts not belonging to one). These patients may have trouble orienting themselves in their environment. They complain that things look "confused" or "jumbled"; they cannot find their way along previously familiar routes, and can no longer drive a car because they lose track of the other vehicles around them. They may report that their body is somehow different; that an arm or leg feels heavy, or larger than usual; or that they are unsure of the location of an arm or leg.

Occipital Lobe Functions. Except for primary occipital cortical functions (visual fields or color vision), it is difficult to test separately for right and left occipital lobe functioning. One such test requires the patient to identify a visual pattern in the presence of a distracting background (Luria 1973).

"Soft" Neurologic Signs. "Soft" neurologic signs are clinical features that indicate brain dysfunction but that cannot be precisely localized or lateralized. When present, these signs are well correlated with psychiatric illnesses and other behavior disorders (Ben-Yishay et al. 1968; Cox and Ludwig 1979; Nasrallah et al. 1983).

The examiner tests the *palmar-mental reflex* by repeatedly scratching the base of the patient's thumb. A positive response occurs when the lower lip and jaw move slightly downward, and does not extinguish with repeated stimulation. The examiner elicits the *grasp reflex* by pressing his or her fingers into the palm of one or both of the patient's hands. A positive response occurs when the patient's hand grasps the examiner's fingers. The *snout (rooting) reflex* is tested by stroking the corner of the patient's mouth. Pursing of the lips and movement of the lips or head toward the stroking is a positive response. *Adventitious motor overflow* was described above in the section on motor functions.

Double simultaneous stimulation discrimination is tested with the patient's eyes closed. The examiner simultaneously brushes a finger against one of the patient's cheeks and another finger against one of the patient's hands, asking the patient where he or she has been touched. Patients with impaired double simultaneous discrimination usually do not perceive the touch on the hands. Occasionally, only stimuli on one side of the body are extinguished, suggesting contralateral dysfunction. Some patients with large parietal lobe lesions (usually on the right) locate the stimuli outside their body parts.

The Neurologic History

The neurologic history and examination is part of a complete neuropsychiatric evaluation, and generally precedes the cognitive and behavioral examinations. Frequent manifestations of nervous system dysfunction include: headache; pain in the extremities or spine; memory and thinking disorders; loss of interest, drive, and energy; clumsiness or weakness of the extremities; tremors and involuntary movements; change in speech; difficulty in swallowing; vertigo and loss of balance; tinnitus and loss of hearing; blurring or dimness of vision; diplopia; sensory loss or distortions (paresthesias); difficulty urinating; and signs and symptoms of convulsive disorder (Cummings 1982; Fitzhugh-Bell 1978; Peterson 1978).

Important Historical Antecedents of Coarse Brain (Neurologic) Disease. Head trauma is the most common historical antecedent of brain syndromes. A closed head injury of sufficient magnitude to result in subsequent behavioral changes will likely be associated with a skull fracture, unconsciousness of 30 minutes or longer, anterograde amnesia of several hours or longer, focal neurologic signs (even if transient), or blood in the spinal fluid. "Bumps on the head," even when suturing is required, do not correlate highly with most brain syndromes (Luria 1969; Sisler 1978). Mild to moderate trauma is, however, a typical antecedent of the postconcussion syndrome (Rowe and Carlson 1980). A documented history of epilepsy is also commonly associated with behavioral syndromes (Benson and Blumer 1982; Davidson and Bagley

1969; Koella and Trimble 1982), as is a history of major systemic disease (Hall 1980).

Physical Signs of Coarse Brain Disease. Physical findings consistent with coarse neurologic disease include focal neurologic abnormalities (e.g., abnormal cranial nerve signs, paralysis, pathological reflexes) and clear signs of a systemic illness known to produce behavioral change (Hall 1980; Peterson 1978). Soft neurologic signs have been reported in 40 to 70 percent of "functional" psychotics and are not useful in discriminating neurologic from psychiatric conditions (Cox and Ludwig 1979; Nasrallah et al. 1983; Quitkin et al. 1976).

Laboratory Studies

The value of laboratory studies in distinguishing neurologic from psychiatric disorders has been diluted by recent findings that some schizophrenics and patients with affective disorder exhibit substantial abnormalities on a variety of such measures. Nevertheless, there are specific differences in laboratory findings between psychiatric patients and those with coarse brain disease.

Numerous computer-enhanced tomographic studies (Weinberger et al. 1982) have reported that, compared to normal controls, schizophrenics have enlarged lateral ventricles, reduced cortical thickness, decreased gray matter density, greater or reversed cerebral asymmetry, and reduced cerebellar mass. Several investigators report similar findings in patients with affective disorder (Nasrallah et al. 1982) and in psychiatrically ill children (Reiss et al. 1983). Although theoretically interesting, these findings are primarily based on group mean comparisons, and few individual subjects have CT scan images that would be clinically reported as abnormal. Therefore, a scan characterized as clinically abnormal (e.g., circumscribed lesion, significant cortical atrophy) remains consistent with the diagnosis of neurologic coarse brain disease (Cummings 1982; Peterson 1978).

Similarly, 40 to 50 percent of schizophrenics have clinically abnormal resting EEGs (Abrams and Taylor 1979). However, a characteristic schizophrenic EEG pattern has not been demonstrated. EEG studies in affective disorder (Abrams and Taylor 1979) and other psychiatric conditions (Kiloh et al. 1974) have also failed to identify specific abnormalities. A resting EEG with a specific clinical abnormality (e.g., spike and slow wave complexes,

paroxysmal bursts of slow waves, circumscribed abnormalities) is inconsistent with a "functional" psychiatric diagnosis, and indicates the patient may have coarse brain disease. Evoked response studies can also be helpful in determining the presence of demyelinating disease (Green and Walcoff 1982).

Neuropsychological test abnormalities have been widely reported in affective disorder patients and schizophrenics, with the general findings that most schizophrenics exhibit bilateral impairment and that a smaller proportion of patients with affective disorder exhibit bilateral anterior impairment and general nondominant hemisphere dysfunction (Silverstein 1983; Taylor and Abrams 1984). A circumscribed neuropsychological deficit is inconsistent with the major functional psychoses and suggests coarse brain disease (Fitzhugh-Bell 1978; Heilman and Valenstein 1979).

Any cerebrospinal fluid abnormality, a blood test result associated with dementia (e.g., low serum B12, low serum T3), or other laboratory finding consistent with a systemic illness known to produce behavioral change (e.g., X-ray evidence of pneumonia, EKG evidence of a recent myocardial infarct) strongly suggests a diagnosis of coarse brain disease (Peterson 1978). In some samples of psychotic patients (Hall 1980), nearly 40 percent had systemic illness that appeared to be the most likely cause of the behavioral syndrome. Investigative techniques such as brain electrical area mapping (Morihisa et al. 1983) and cerebral blood flow studies (Mathew et al. 1982; Uytdenhoef et al. 1983) show promise as discriminating measures of different behavioral syndromes. Many more patients, however, will have to be studied by these techniques before consistent and clear-cut differences emerge.

Ancillary Clinical Tests

The Reitan-Indiana Aphasia Screening Test (Wheeler and Reitan 1962), the Minimental State Examination of Folstein, Folstein, and McHugh (Folstein et al. 1975; Tsai and Tsuang 1979), the Luria-Nebraska Neuropsychological Battery (Golden et al. 1978), and the Halstead-Reitan Neuropsychological Battery (Klove 1974; Matarazzo et al. 1976) are the most commonly used neuropsychological tests for identification and localization of coarse brain disease and the assessment of cognitive dysfunction. The Reitan-Indiana Aphasia Screening Test and the Minimental State Examination are easily administered, brief (5 to 20 minutes), noninvasive tests designed to identify, localize, and lateralize brain dysfunction. Wheeler and Reitan (1962) have demonstrated the concurrent validity of the Reitan-Indiana Aphasia Screening Test in terms of its capacity to lateralize lesions in neurologic patients. Folstein et al. (1975) compared the results of the Minimental State Examination with clinical diagnoses and WAIS scores and demonstrated its capacity to distinguish diffuse from focal cortical dysfunction and from normal cortical function. Tsai and Tsuang (1979) confirmed this in a CT scan study.

The Luria-Nebraska Neuropsychological Battery was inspired by the work of Alexander Luria (1973). Standardization of testing was begun by Christensen (1975), and a formal scoring system was developed by Golden et al. (1978). The battery consists of tests of a wide variety of cognitive functions. The concurrent validity of the Luria battery is good. Golden et al. (1978) compared 50 hospitalized control patients with 50 matched neurological patients with a clinical diagnosis of coarse brain disease and were able to separate the groups "with 100 percent accuracy."

The Halstead-Reitan Neuropsychological Battery is Reitan's modification of Halstead's test for the investigation of behavior in brain-damaged and normal persons. It is longer than the Luria battery, but is preferred by more psychologists. It contains 10 subtests, including the Minnesota Multiphasic Personality Inventory (a self-report inventory), the WAIS, and the Reitan-Indiana Aphasia Screening Test. In addition to identifying and localizing brain dysfunction, it provides data for vocational rehabilitation and other rehabilitation programs (Klove 1974; Matarazzo 1972; Matarazzo et al. 1976; Wheeler and Reitan 1962). Matarazzo et al. (1976) demonstrated high test-retest reliability for this battery. The validity of the battery is also high.

☐ REFERENCES

Abrams R, Taylor MA: Differential EEG patterns in affective disorder and schizophrenia. Arch Gen Psychiatry 36:1355–1358, 1979

Abrams R, Taylor MA, Stolrow KAC: Catatonia and mania: patterns of cerebral dysfunction. Biol Psychiatry 14:111–117, 1979

Alexander MP, Struss DT, Benson DF: Capgras syndrome: a reduplicative phenomena. Neurology 29:334–339, 1979

Barbizet J: Human Memory and Its Pathology. Translated by Jardine DK. San Francisco, WH Freeman and Co, 1970

Benson DF: Aphasia, Alexia and Agraphia. Edinburgh, Churchill Livingstone, 1979

Benson DF, Blumer D: Psychiatric manifestations of epilepsy, in Psychiatric Aspects of Neurologic Disease, Vol. 2. Edited by Benson DF, Blumer D. New York, Grune & Stratton, 1982, pp 25–47

Benton AL, des Hamsher K, Varney NR, et al: Contributions to Neuropsychological Assessment: A Clinical Manual. New York, Oxford University Press, 1983, pp 23–29

Ben-Yishay Y, Diller L, Gerstman L, et al: The relationship between impersistence, intellectual function and outcome of rehabilitation in patients with left hemiplegia. Neurology 18:852–861, 1968

Birkett DP: Gerstmann's syndrome. Br J Psychiatry 113:801, 1967

Christensen A-L: Luria's Neuropsychological Investigation. New York, Spectrum Publications, 1975

Cox SM, Ludwig AM: Neurological soft signs and psychopathology, I: findings in schizophrenia. J Nerv Ment Dis 167:161–165, 1979

Critchley M: The Parietal Lobes. New York, Hafner Press, 1953

Cummings JL: Cortical dementias, in Psychiatric Aspects of Neurologic Disease, Vol. 2. Edited by Benson DF, Blumer D. New York, Grune & Stratton, 1982, pp 93–121

Davidson K, Bagley CR: Schizophrenia-like psychoses associated with organic disorders of the central nervous system: a review of the literature, in Current Problems in Neuropsychiatry (Br J Psychiatry Special Publication No. 4), 1969, pp 113–184

Faber R, Abrams R, Taylor MA, et al: Formal thought disorder and aphasia: comparison of schizophrenic patients with formal thought disorder and neurologically impaired patients with aphasia. Am J Psychiatry 140:1348–1351, 1983

Fitzhugh-Bell KB: Neuropsychological evaluation in the management of brain disorders. Psychiatr Clin North Am 1:37–50, 1978

Folstein MF, Folstein SW, McHugh PR: "Mini-Mental State": a practical method of grading the cognitive state of patients for the clinician. J Psychiatr Res 12:189–198, 1975

Gainotti G, Miceli G, Caltagirone C: Constructional apraxia in left brain-damaged patients: a planning disorder? Cortex 13:109–118, 1977

Geschwind N: Disconnection syndromes in animals and man (in two parts). Brain 88:237–294, 585–644, 1965

Geschwind N: The anatomical basis of hemisphere differentiation, in Hemisphere Function in the Human Brain. Edited by Dimond SJ, Beaumont JG. New York, Halsted Press, 1974a, pp 7–24

Geschwind N: Selected Papers on Language and the Brain. Boston, Reidel, 1974b

Golden C, Hammeke T, Purisch A: Diagnostic validity of a standardized neuropsychological battery from Luria's neuropsychological tests. J Consult Clin Psychol 48:1258–1265, 1978

Green JB, Walcoff MR: Evoked potentials in multiple sclerosis. Arch Neurol 39:696–697, 1982

Hall RCW (ed): Psychiatric Presentations of Medical Illness: Somatopsychic Disorders. New York, SP Medical & Scientific Books, 1980

Hayman M, Abrams R: Capgras' syndrome and cerebral dysfunction. Br J Psychiatry 130:68–71, 1977

Heilman KM, Valenstein E (eds): Clinical Neuropsychology. New York, Oxford University Press, 1979

Kiloh LG, McComas AJ, Osselton JW: Clinical Electroencephalography, 2nd ed. London, Butterworths, 1974, pp 168–200

Klove H: Validation studies in adult neuropsychology, in Clinical Neuropsychology: Current Status and Applications. Edited by Reitan R, Davidson L. Washington, DC, VH Winston & Sons, 1974, pp 211–235

Koella WP, Trimble MR (eds): Temporal Lobe Epilepsy, Mania, and Schizophrenia and the Limbic System, in Advances in Biological Psychiatry, Vol 8. Basel, S. Karger, 1982

LeDoux JE, Wilson DH, Gazzaniga MS: Block design performance following callosal sectioning: observations on functional recovery. Arch Neurol 35:506–508, 1978

Levy J: Psychological implications of bilateral asymmetry, in Hemisphere Function in the Human Brain. Edited by Diamond S, Beaumont JG. New York, Halsted Press, 1974, pp 121–183

Lezak MD: Neuropsychological Assessment, 3rd ed. New York, Oxford University Press, 1983, pp 414–474

Luria AR: Frontal lobe syndromes, in Handbook of Clinical Neurology, Vol 2. Edited by Vinken PJ, Bruyn GW. New York, Elsevier-North Holland, 1969, pp 725–775

Luria AR: The Working Brain: An Introduction to Neuropsychology. Translated by Hough B. New York, Basic Books, 1973

Matarazzo J: Wechsler's Measurement and Appraisal of Adult Intelligence. New York, Oxford University Press, 1972

Matarazzo JD, Matarazzo RG, Wiens AM, et al: Retest reliability of the Halstead Impairment Index in normals, schizophrenics and two samples of organic patients. J Clin Psychol 32:338–354, 1976

Mathew RJ, Duncan GC, Weinman ML, et al: Regional cerebral blood flow in schizophrenia. Arch Gen Psychiatry 39:1121–1124, 1982

Meadows J: The anatomical basis of prosopagnosia. J Neurol Neurosurg Psychiatry 37:489–501, 1974

Morihisa JM, Duffy FH, Wyatt RJ: Brain electrical activity mapping (BEAM) in schizophrenic patients. Arch Gen Psychiatry 40:719–728, 1983

Nasrallah HA, McCalley-Whitters M, Jacoby CG: Cerebral ventricular enlargement in young manic males: a controlled CT study. J Affective Disord 4:15–19, 1982

Nasrallah HA, Tippin J, McCalley-Whitters M: Neuropsychological soft signs in manic patients: a comparison with schizophrenics and control groups. J Affective Disord 5:45–50, 1983

Neilsen J: Gerstmann's syndrome: finger agnosia, agraphia, comparison of right and left and acalculia. Archives of Neurology and Psychiatry 39:536–560, 1938

Paulson G, Gottlieb G: Development reflexes: the reappearance of foetal and neonatal reflexes in aged patients. Brain 91:37–52, 1968

Peterson GC: Organic brain syndrome, differential diagnosis and investigative procedures in adults. Psychiatr Clin North Am, 1:21–36, 1978

Quitkin F, Rifkin A, Klein DF: Neurologic soft signs in schizophrenia and character disorders, organicity in schizophrenia with premorbid asociality and emotionally unstable character disorders. Arch Gen Psychiatry 33:845–853, 1976

Reiss D, Feinstein C, Weinberger DR, et al: Ventricular enlargement in child psychiatric patients: a controlled study with planimetric measurements. Am J Psychiatry 140:453–456, 1983

Ross ED: The aprosodias: functional anatomic organization of the affective components of language in the right hemisphere. Arch Neurol 38:561–569, 1981

Rowe MJ, Carlson C: Brain stem auditory evoked potentials in post-concussional dizziness. Arch Neurol 37:679–683, 1980

Seamon JG: Coding and retrieval processes and the hemispheres of the brain, in Hemisphere Function in the Human Brain. Edited by Dimond SJ, Beaumont JG. New York, Halsted Press, 1974, pp 184–203

Silverstein M: Neuropsychological dysfunction in the major psychoses, in Laterality and Psychopathology. Edited by Flor-Henry F, Gruzelier J. New York, Elsevier-North Holland, 1983, pp 143–162

Sisler GC: Psychiatric disorder associated with head injury. Psychiatr Clin North Am 1:137–152, 1978

Spear FG, Green R: Inability to concentrate. Br J Psychiatry 112:913–915, 1966

Taylor MA: The Neuropsychiatric Mental Status Examination. New York, SP Medical & Scientific Books, 1981

Taylor MA, Abrams R: Cognitive impairment in schizophrenia. Am J Psychiatry 141:196–201, 1984

Taylor MA, Sierles FS, Abrams R: General Hospital Psychiatry. New York, Free Press, 1985

Tsai L, Tsuang MT: The "Mini-Mental State" and computerized tomography. Am J Psychiatry 136:436–439, 1979

Uytdenhoef P, Portelange P, Jacquy J, et al: Regional cerebral blood flow and lateralized hemispheric dysfunction in depression. Br J Psychiatry 143:128–132, 1983

Wade J, Taylor MA: Interhemispheric transfer in schizophrenia. Biol Psychiatry 19:107–111, 1984

Weinberger DR, DeLisi LE, Perman GP, et al: Computed tomography in schizophreniform disorder and other acute psychiatric disorders. Arch Gen Psychiatry 39:778–783, 1982

Weinstein EA, Kahn RL: Denial of Illness: Symbolic and Physiological Aspects. Springfield, Ill, Charles C Thomas, 1955

Wheeler L, Reitan RM: Presence and laterality of brain damage predicted from responses to a short aphasia screening test. Percept Mot Skills 15:783–799, 1962

Chapter 2

Brain Imaging and Laboratory Testing in Neuropsychiatry

Richard B. Rosse, M.D.
Cynthia M. Owen, M.A.
John M. Morihisa, M.D.

THE BRAIN IMAGING and other diagnostic tests used in psychiatry today encompass a wide range of procedures, some of which are outlined in Tables 1 to 4. Some of these procedures are used routinely by psychiatrists in screening psychiatric patients for organic brain dysfunction or other medical illnesses, as well as in the pretreatment and follow-up evaluation of some psychotropic medication therapies. The laboratory is also routinely used by psychiatrists to help detect drug and alcohol abuse, intoxication, and overdose. Furthermore, the laboratory is routinely used to detect certain environmental toxins that can result in behavioral changes, such as that seen in manganese, lead, and mercury poisoning.

Tables 3 and 4 list procedures that are primarily used as investigational tools in the search for neurophysiologic markers of psychiatric illness. Some of these tests have recently received a great deal of attention in the psychiatric literature. Biologic markers have a number of potential clinical applications, including increasing or decreasing the probability of a patient having a certain psychiatric diagnosis, aiding in choice of treatment, and predicting treatment response. Biologic markers might also be useful in delineating subgroups in certain psychiatric disorders, as well as in revealing possible biologic overlap among some currently established diagnostic categories (Greden 1981; Sternberg 1984). Possible problems with these markers include a lack of sensitivity, specificity, reliability, and possible contamination from artifactual influences such as the effects of medications or other illnesses.

Although many markers have been studied, none of the markers discussed in this chapter seem

17

Table 1. ELECTROPHYSIOLOGICAL AND BRAIN IMAGING TECHNIQUES IN CLINICAL USE

- Clinical electroencephalogram
- Polysomnography
- Evoked potentials
- Computed tomography
- Magnetic resonance imaging

Table 2. SOME COMMON USES OF THE CLINICAL LABORATORY IN PSYCHIATRY

- Complete blood count with differential; biochemical and endocrine profile
- Screening tests for syphillis (e.g., VDRL) as well as tests for other infectious agents if suspected (e.g., hepatitis screen)
- Urinalysis
- Toxicology for detection of drug abuse, overdose, or environmental intoxications (e.g., mercury, manganese, lead)
- Laboratory evaluation of dementia (including B_{12}, folate levels)
- Pretreatment lithium and electroconvulsive therapy evaluation
- Lithium, antidepressant, and anticonvulsant blood levels
- Follow-up lab evaluation for certain psychotropic and anticonvulsant medications

Table 3. SOME ELECTROPHYSIOLOGICAL AND BRAIN IMAGING TECHNIQUES USED IN NEUROPSYCHIATRIC RESEARCH

- Computerized topographic mapping of electrophysiologic data
- Polysomnography
- Computed tomography (CT)
- Regional cerebral blood flow (rCBF)
- Positron emission tomography (PET)
- Single photon emission computed tomography (SPECT)
- Magnetic resonance imaging (MRI)
- Electrodermal activity
- Magnetoelectroencephalography (MEG)

Table 4. SOME USES OF THE LABORATORY IN NEUROPSYCHIATRIC RESEARCH

- Medication evaluation
  Neuroleptic levels; platelet MAO activity in patients taking MAOIs
- Neuroendocrine markers
  DST, TRHST, GH, and PRL challenge tests
- Peripheral tissue markers
  platelet MAO; 5HT uptake; ^{3}H-imipramine binding; alpha$_2$-adrenergic receptor activity
  lymphocyte beta-adrenergic receptor activity; dopamine receptor binding; lymphocyte response to mitogen stimulation
  fibroblast muscarinic receptor
  red blood cell red blood cell/lithium ratios
- Peripheral and spinal fluid markers
- Melatonin
- Provocative tests for anxiety disorders (e.g., lactate infusion test)

Note. MAO = monoamine oxidase; MAOI = monoamine oxidase inhibitors; DST = dexamethasone suppression test; TRHST = thyrotropin-releasing hormone stimulation test; GH = growth hormone; PRL = prolactin.

to have the diagnostic accuracy that would make them powerful enough for routine clinical use, and none should replace good clinical sense. However, these markers continue to be powerful research tools that should help in our continuing efforts to understand the neurobiology of psychiatric disorders. Someday, biologic markers may provide an independent system for diagnostic classification.

☐ ROUTINE PSYCHIATRIC DIAGNOSTIC TESTS

Hall et al. (1982) have outlined the need for careful medical evaluation of psychiatric patients. They have shown that significantly large numbers of psychiatric patients suffer from coexisting medical illnesses, many of which either cause or exacerbate their psychiatric symptoms. Medical disorders that may present psychiatric symptomatology include viral infections of the central nervous system (e.g., encephalitis), endocrine disorders (e.g., hypothyroidism), intracranial tumors and vascular malfor-

mations, certain nutritional disorders (e.g., thiamine deficiency), certain inborn errors of metabolism (e.g., Wilson's disease), and environmental intoxication (e.g., manganese madness). DeLisi (1984) reviewed some of the medical disorders that must be differentiated from psychiatric disorders, and outlined the laboratory tests utilized for this purpose. Recommended tests that might be used in an initial psychiatric evaluation include a complete blood count with differential; a biochemical profile, including electrolytes, glucose, hepatic and renal functions, calcium and phosphate levels; thyroid function testing; a screening test for syphilis, B12 and folate levels; and a urinalysis. Blood levels for any measurable medications the patient is taking should also be obtained. A chest X ray, electrocardiogram (EKG), and electroencephalogram (EEG) are also common evaluation procedures. A sleep-deprived EEG is probably more sensitive than a routine EEG. Depending on the patient's history or presenting circumstances, there may be additional tests, such as toxicology or drug screens. Blood and urine tests for a wide variety of potential drugs of abuse are available. A number of different test methodologies with different capabilities for the detection of various substances exist (Gold and Dackis 1986). Sramek et al. (1985) has published a preliminary report on the augmentation of phencyclidine (PCP) blood and urine testing with hair analysis for PCP. Additionally, tests to detect THC in saliva are being developed and tested.

The EEG is particularly important in the differential diagnosis of organic versus functional syndromes. Psychiatrists and neurologists have long used this procedure in the evaluation of patients with possible organic brain disorders, such as delirium, dementia, central nervous system infections and metabolic abnormalities, intracranial masses, head trauma, and epilepsy. Clinical EEG procedures, as well as experimental EEG tests, will be discussed more fully in following sections.

Finally, Weinberger (1984) has argued for the more frequent use of computed tomography (CT) in routine psychiatric evaluation. While some psychiatrists might feel more comfortable with a CT scan being ordered by a neurology consultant, Weinberger contends that such consultations can prove unrewarding; as few neurologists are trained to appreciate that psychiatric symptoms can alone be harbingers of central nervous system pathology. He proposes the following indications for ordering CT scans of psychiatric patients: (1) confusion and/or dementia of unknown cause, (2) first episode of a psychosis of unknown etiology, (3) movement disorder of unknown etiology, (4) anorexia nervosa, (5) prolonged catatonia, and (6) first episode of major affective disorder or personality change after age 50.

☐ CLINICAL MONITORING OF PSYCHOTROPIC DRUG TREATMENT

Tricyclic Antidepressants

The Task Force on the Use of Laboratory Tests in Psychiatry (1985) of the American Psychiatric As-

sociation has concluded "that plasma level measurements of imipramine, desmethylimipramine (desipramine), and nortriptyline are unequivocally useful in certain situations" (p. 155).

Such situations seem to include (1) when patients have a poor response to a "typical" antidepressant dose; (2) when patients will need as low a potentially effective dose of the medication as possible (e.g., because of age, side effects, or medical illness); (3) when patients need to obtain a potentially therapeutic dose of an antidepressant as quickly as possible because of severe illness (e.g., suicidal or without adequate oral nutritional intake); and (4) when patients have questionable compliance.

The Task Force reported on findings (e.g., Glassman et al. 1977; Reisby et al. 1977) that suggested a therapeutic blood level of imipramine is attained when the combined plasma level of imipramine and its metabolite desmethylimipramine exceeds 200 ng/ml. The potential therapeutic effects of very high blood levels (greater than 750 ng/ml) have not been determined. For nortriptyline, the Task Force reported evidence (e.g., Asberg et al. 1971) supporting the concept of a "therapeutic window" for blood levels of this antidepressant. Levels less than 50 ng/dl and those greater than 150 ng/dl have been reported to be less clinically effective than those levels within the 50 to 150 ng/dl range. Finally, for desipramine, the Task Force reported on findings (e.g., Nelson et al. 1982) that suggested that blood levels above 125 ng/ml are probably more effective than lower levels. The utility of blood level determinations for other antidepressants is still under investigation. It should be noted, however, that some investigators (Simpson et al. 1983) are not in complete consensus with some of the literature supporting clear-cut therapeutic antidepressant drug levels for any of the antidepressants. In any case, it would seem reasonable that anyone using these drug levels should closely assess the patient's clinical progress and allow sound clinical judgment to be the final arbiter for necessary treatment decisions.

Lithium

The utility of monitoring serum lithium levels in bipolar patients is well accepted. Serum lithium levels can be determined by either atomic absorption spectrophotometry or by emission flame photometry (Coombs et al. 1975). Emission flame photometry is more sensitive and has a lower limit of detection than atomic absorption spectrophotometry. However, this difference is not considered to be clinically relevant in the determination of currently accepted therapeutic serum lithium levels, and in most cases either technique can be used without preference (Cooper 1980).

Amdisen (1980) described a range for successfully treated long-term patients as being between 0.3 and 1.2 mmol/L (meq/L). Therapeutic ranges for the management of acute mania have been proposed to range from a lower level of 0.8 to 1.0 meq/L to an upper level of 1.4 to 1.5 meq/L (Jefferson et al. 1986). However, Amdisen (1980) characterized a range from about 1.2 to 1.5 mmol/L as a "warning range"; when a patient is in this range, the clinician should be vigilant for early signs of possible lithium toxicity. Toxic reactions to lithium have been reported to be more likely when the serum lithium level is above 1.5 meq/L. However, toxic effects have been described in patients whose serum lithium levels were below the 1.2 to 1.5 meq/L range (Reisberg and Gershon 1979).

Maintenance therapy is generally prescribed at a lower serum lithium level than that recommended for acute mania. Prien and Caffey (1976) and Waters et al. (1982) reported that serum lithium levels of 0.8 meq/L or greater best protected against illness relapse. However, others have reported similar rates of relapse for patients with lower serum lithium levels (e.g., less than 0.5 meq/L) as compared to patients with higher levels (e.g., greater than 0.7 meq/L) (Jerram and McDonald 1978). Hullin (1980) reported increased relapse rates when serum lithium levels fell below 0.4 meq/L. How low one can go with the serum lithium level in some patients and still achieve effective prophylaxis is an area of continuing research. Interestingly, there has even been an anecdotal report that claimed effective treatment for a patient maintained on a plasma lithium level as low as 0.13 meq/L (Yassa et al. 1984).

The currently accepted time to draw the serum lithium level is 12 hours after the last lithium dose (Amdisen 1980). Values obtained in this manner can be compared with serum levels that are reported in the literature. Generally, when lithium is first initiated in a patient, blood samples are drawn more often until a stable lithium level is achieved. Stable lithium levels are usually obtained in about 4 to 5 days after the last dosage adjustment (Jef-

ferson et al. 1986). Blood levels should also be drawn if the patient demonstrates any sign of emerging toxicity.

Lithium treatment has been identified as having potentially significant effects on the thyroid, kidney, heart, white blood count (WBC), and developing fetus (Baldessarini and Lipinski 1975). Therefore, some laboratory evaluation of these systems is considered important in the pretreatment and maintenance phases of therapy. Recommended pretreatment laboratory evaluation generally includes a WBC, serum electrolytes, blood urea nitrogen (BUN), creatinine, thyroid function tests (e.g., TSH, T4, T3), urinalysis, and possibly a 24-hour urine test for creatinine clearance. The integrity of renal function is specifically important as lithium is excreted through the kidney and impaired function can lead to toxicity. Other pretreatment tests include an EKG, as well as a pregnancy test for potentially childbearing women. Follow-up tests during treatment usually include thyroid function tests (e.g., TSH), BUN, creatinine, and periodic EKGs.

☐ ELECTROPHYSIOLOGICAL EVALUATION

Clinical EEG

The development of the EEG by Hans Berger reported in 1929 heralded one of the earliest attempts to search for evidence of disordered brain function in psychiatric patients. The conventional EEG measures the brain's electrical activity from electrodes placed in standardized positions on the scalp. The changing electrical potential of neurons below each electrode location forms the basis of EEG recordings, with the largest contribution presumably originating from neurons in the uppermost cortical cell layers. Clinical reading of the EEG involves visual evaluation of the waveform's amplitude and frequency, as well as detection of paroxysmal events such as spikes or isolated bursts of activity. EEG frequencies have been divided into the following spectral bands: delta activity (<4 Hz), theta activity (4 to <8 Hz), alpha activity (8 to 13 Hz), and beta activity (>13 Hz). Alpha activity is present in the normal adult record when the eyes are closed and is most prevalent over the occipital lobes (Figure 1,

p. 25). When the normal adult is stimulated or if the eyes are open, alpha activity essentially disappears from the record, and faster frequencies (beta activity) predominate. Theta and delta waves are generally only apparent during sleep. Deviations from normal EEG patterns generally indicate underlying brain pathology. For example, the abnormal appearance of delta activity in the awake tracing could reflect a specific structural abnormality (if localized), or could represent a diffuse dysfunction (if generalized). Additionally, the appearance of the EEG varies at different stages of the life cycle (e.g., infancy, early childhood, old age). Therefore, the patient's age must be considered in any clinical EEG evaluation.

In addition to serving as a tool for differentiating organic from functional brain disorders, the EEG has been used in the search for neurophysiologic markers of psychiatric illness. Although most studies concur that the prevalence of EEG abnormalities is greater in psychotic patients than in normal individuals, no diagnostic patterns of abnormality have been identified (Small 1983). Abrams and Taylor (1979) found that schizophrenic patients had twice as many EEG abnormalities as patients with affective disorder. Furthermore, abnormalities in the schizophrenic patients tended to be over the temporal lobes, whereas the abnormalities in affective patients were more frequent over the parietal-occipital regions. Shagass et al. (1983) reported that the EEG records of schizophrenic patients had lower amplitude variability, greater frequency variability, greater wave symmetry, and less reactivity to eye opening than nonpatient controls. Stevens et al. (1979) studied schizophrenic patients using telemetered EEG. In nearly half the patients studied, EEG abnormalities were associated with abnormal behaviors (e.g., hallucinations and psychomotor blocking). However, these findings represent research investigations, and their clinical relevance will require further clarification.

In summary, the current utility of the clinical EEG in psychiatry is limited to screening for organic brain dysfunction. The elucidation of electrophysiologic markers of psychiatric illness is the goal of ongoing research efforts. This includes work utilizing computerized topographic EEG mapping and magnetoencephalography (MEG). MEG measures the minute magnetic fields generated by the electrical activity of neurons and permits the three-dimensional investigation of brain electrical activity (Lopes da Silva and Van Rotterdam 1982).

Polysomnography

Polysomnography involves the recording of EEG activity during sleep (polysomnography can include the measurement of multiple other parameters of potential interest, such as muscle activity, eye movements, and EKG and respiratory activity). Sleep consists of two electrophysiologic phases, one characterized by the presence of rapid eye movements (REM) and one not accompanied by rapid eye movements (non-REM). Non-REM sleep is subdivided into stages 1 through 4, with stage 1 representing light sleep and each successive stage representing progressively deeper sleep. Stage 4, also known as "slow wave" or "deep" sleep, is characterized by a predominance of delta activity. In REM sleep, which normally occurs in cycles throughout the night, the slow delta waves of stage 4 sleep are replaced by low voltage, fast frequency activity that closely resembles the waking alert EEG.

Sleep recordings have revealed a number of potentially important markers of psychiatric illness. Abnormalities in the REM sleep of affective patients have been a relatively consistent finding. These abnormalities include the reduction of REM latency, an increase in the overall amount of REM, and a reversal of the normal REM distribution such that more REM occurs early in the night (Foster et al. 1976; Kupfer et al. 1978). While normal aging is associated with decreased REM latency, depressed patients appear to show even shorter REM latencies with increasing age (Ulrich et al. 1980). The reduction of REM latency induced by cholinergic stimulation (e.g., after administration of intravenous arecoline, a cholinergic agonist) has been reported to be more robust in depressed patients than in healthy controls (Sitaram et al. 1982). Some investigators hypothesize that this finding suggests a cholinergic supersensitivity in depression (Jones et al. 1985; Sitaram et al. 1982). Patients with obsessive-compulsive disorder, subaffective dysthymia, and anorexia nervosa may also show reduced REM latencies (Insel et al. 1982). Sleep studies of EEG activity in schizophrenia have included reports of decreases in the amount of stage 4 sleep (Gillin et al. 1985; Guazzelli et al. 1985; Hiatt et al. 1985).

Evoked Potentials

Evoked potential (EP) testing involves the measurement of EEG response to simple sensory stimulation. The evoking stimulus can be visual, auditory, or somatosensory, resulting in visual evoked potentials (VEPs), auditory evoked potentials (AEPs), or somatosensory evoked potentials (SEPs). Collecting EP data involves the presentation of a series of discrete stimuli, followed by computerized averaging of the EEG activity that follows each stimulus. The computer averages out electrical activity not related to the stimulus (background EEG activity) and produces a characteristic waveform (the EP). The waveform consists of negative and positive peaks spread along a time axis. EP studies typically examine the amplitude and latency of these peaks, as well as overall waveform variability. Early peaks (e.g., in the first 50 msec poststimulus) are thought to represent anatomically specific events related to the relay of sensory information to the cortex, and are sometimes used in the evaluation of certain neurologic diseases (e.g., multiple sclerosis). Some components occurring after 50 to 80 msec poststimulus are hypothesized to reflect cortical events associated with cognitive or psychological processing. Abnormalities of early, middle, and late EP components have been reported in psychiatric disorders (Buchsbaum 1977; Roth 1977; Shagass 1977). For instance, Shagass (1983) found reductions in the amplitude of late EP components in psychiatric patients, a finding that reportedly distinguishes psychotic from nonpsychotic patients. Also reported is an increase in measures of waveshape variability in psychotic patients. Additionally, Cooper et al. (1985) reported a lack of normal lateralization of cortical SEP in 10 out of 21 schizophrenic patients.

Harding et al. (1985) reported that the VEP is a more specific indicator of Alzheimer's disease than the EEG or CT scan. In this study, patients with primary senile dementia showed a slowing of the major positive component (P2) of the VEP to flash stimulation, yet showed no slowing in the major positive component (P100) of the VEP to pattern-reversal stimulation. This is an unusual pattern of results that has not been reported in any other disorder to date. For this reason, Harding and colleagues suggested that it may be a specific marker for this disease. St. Clair et al. (1985) reported that the P3 component of the AEP was significantly longer and of lower amplitude in patients with Alzheimer's disease than in patients with Korsakoff's syndrome or normal controls.

There is another general type of EP, referred to as slow potentials or event-related slow potentials (ERSPs). These can be negative or positive waves, of gradual onset and relatively long duration, that typically precede an expected event. One specific ERSP is the contingent negative variation (CNV), a slowly increasing negative wave that develops prior to an expected sensory stimulus. Psychiatric studies of the CNV have generally used an alerting click (S_1) followed by a train of light flashes (S_2) that must be terminated (e.g., via pressing a button) by the patient. The CNV develops after presentation of the alerting click (between S_1 and S_2). CNV amplitude has generally been found to be lower in both medicated and unmedicated patients with psychosis (Timsit-Berthier 1973). While CNV amplitude reportedly increases during efficacious drug treatment in schizophrenia, it has been reported to remain significantly lower than normal, and has been suggested as a possible trait marker of schizophrenia (Rizzo et al. 1983).

It is hoped that recently developed techniques for analyzing EP data (e.g., computerized topographic mapping) will enhance the utility of evoked potentials in psychiatric patients. Computerized mapping of EP data is discussed in a later section of this chapter on computerized topographic mapping of electrophysiologic data.

Electrodermal Activity

Electrodermal activity (EDA) is gauged in various ways, including measurements such as the skin conductance response (SCR) to stimulation and the tonic skin conductance level (SCL). The resistance of the skin varies inversely with sweat gland activity. Since sweat gland activity seems to be largely controlled by the sympathetic nervous system, changes in EDA are thought to reflect changes in sympathetic arousal. Faster habituation of the skin conductance orienting response (SCOR) has been reported in schizophrenic patients compared to normal controls (Levinson et al. 1984). In depression, although reports are somewhat inconsistent, findings have included reduced EDA in depressed patients when compared to normals (Iacano et al. 1984).

☐ BRAIN IMAGING TECHNIQUES

CT

CT was introduced in the 1970s and has revolutionized radiologic diagnosis in many areas of medicine. In CT scanning of the brain, thousands of X-ray readings are computer processed to yield cross-sectional images. Consecutive cross-sections can be used to generate a three-dimensional image of the brain. In addition to its use in the workup of patients with suspected organic brain dysfunction, CT has been used to identify a number of structural abnormalities in the brains of psychiatric patients (Johnstone et al. 1976; Weinberger et al. 1979).

A number of investigators have reported a significantly higher frequency of reversed cerebral asymmetry in schizophrenic patients compared to patients without schizophrenia (Luchins et al. 1979; Tsai et al. 1983). Nasrallah et al. (1985) have suggested the possible existence of a subset of schizophrenic patients defined by cerebellar atrophy and third ventricle enlargement. Pearlson et al. (1984a, 1984b) have reported abnormally high ventricle-to-brain ratios (VBRs) in chronic schizophrenic and bipolar patients. Furthermore, persistent unemployment and "negative" symptoms (e.g., apathy, poor hygiene, emotional flattening, and asociality) were strongly associated with ventricular enlargement in both these patient groups. Ventricular enlargement in chronic schizophrenia has also been reported to correlate with poor response to neuroleptic treatment (Weinberger et al. 1980). Taken together, these findings have been suggested by some investigators to form a basis for defining meaningful subgroups of schizophrenic patients. In their review of CT scanning and schizophrenia, Dennert and Andreasen (1983) concluded that there is evidence supporting a subgroup of schizophrenia with CT abnormalities. However, the authors pointed out that while these findings may help us understand the pathogenesis of schizophrenia, their current diagnostic value requires further clarification.

Regional Cerebral Blood Flow

Patterns of regional cerebral blood flow (rCBF) in psychiatric disorders are of interest because blood flow in the brain is thought to reflect the metabolic and therefore functional activity of the brain. This research technique now usually involves the inhalation of Xenon-133 gas, although it has alternatively involved the intracarotid injection of a metabolically inert, radioactive isotope. Xenon-133 is a low-energy gamma ray emitter that is metabolically inactive in the brain and exchanges rapidly between blood and tissue. After inhalation (or in-

jection), the arrival of Xenon-133 to brain tissues and its gradual elimination are proportional to regional blood flow. External gamma ray detectors (up to 16 per hemisphere on current equipment) monitor the changes in radioactivity as blood flow eliminates Xenon-133 from the brain, and these desaturation data are used to generate a two-dimensional map of cerebral blood flow.

Ingvar and Franzen (1974) applied the Xenon-133 intracarotid technique to study resting rCBF in chronic schizophrenic patients. The schizophrenic patients demonstrated less blood flow in frontal as compared to posterior brain regions ("hypofrontality"), whereas an alcoholic control group showed greater blood flow in frontal as compared to posterior regions ("hyperfrontality"). In the resting state, Gur et al. (1983) and Gur (1984) found that unmedicated schizophrenics showed higher left hemisphere blood flows, whereas normal controls showed symmetrical hemispheric blood flow. Furthermore, schizophrenic patients demonstrated increased flow in the left hemisphere while engaged in a spatial cognitive task, in contrast to normal controls, who showed increased flow in the right hemisphere. This abnormality was more pronounced in unmedicated patients, and neuroleptics were found to increase right hemisphere blood flow. Gur interpreted these results as indicative of left hemisphere overactivation in schizophrenia. Weinberger et al. (1986) have also used a standardized cognitive task to study "activated" rCBF (as opposed to resting rCBF) in schizophrenia. They reported that schizophrenic subjects do not show increased blood flow to the dorsolateral prefrontal cortex during the Wisconsin Card Sort Test, a task that increases blood flow to this region in normal controls (Figure 2, p. 25). They suggested that their data extend the body of evidence supporting frontal lobe dysfunction in schizophrenia.

Positron Emission Tomography

Positron emission tomography (PET) is an exciting new method of brain imaging whose application to psychiatric research has just begun. In PET, positron-emitting elements (e.g., F-18, C-14, C-11) are incorporated into organic compounds (e.g., deoxyglucose), which are then introduced into the body by injection or inhalation. When these compounds enter the brain, emitted gamma rays are picked up by detectors positioned around the patient's head.

These signals are analyzed by a computer and arranged into cross-sectional images showing relative regional concentrations of the labeled compound/element. Consecutive slice images are developed to yield a three-dimensional image. Use of various PET tracer molecules allows for the visualization of different aspects of brain function, including specific brain receptors, blood flow, and glucose utilization. Techniques for visualizing glucose metabolism, using a fluorine-18-labeled analogue of 2-deoxyglucose (FDG), have been the most frequently used in psychiatric PET studies (Buchsbaum 1984). Studies imaging specific brain receptors, such as dopamine receptors, have been reported (Baron et al. 1985; Wagner et al. 1983).

PET studies of patients with schizophrenia and affective disorder have demonstrated abnormalities of the anteroposterior gradient of glucose utilization (Buchsbaum 1984; Buchsbaum et al. 1984; Phelps et al. 1984). Wolkin et al. (1985) reported lower absolute rates of frontal lobe glucose metabolism in chronic schizophrenic patients. It is interesting that these findings are consistent with the "hypofrontality" reports from rCBF studies of schizophrenia. However, some investigators studying schizophrenic patients have not found "hypofrontality" on the PET scans of these patients (Kling et al. 1986). Studies have varied in regards to whether the study subjects are deprived of sensory input during the scanning procedure. It is thought that variations in sensory input during the PET scan might have an important effect on study results (Mazziotta et al. 1982). Baxter et al. (1985) reported that whole brain metabolic rates for patients with bipolar depression increased going from depression to a euthymic or manic state. Studies using PET to measure cerebral blood flow, blood volume, and oxygen metabolism have suggested that patients with panic disorder, whose panic symptoms can be brought on by a sodium lactate infusion, have an "abnormal hemispheric asymmetry" of blood flow, blood volume, and oxygen metabolism. Attention has focused on a region of the parahippocampal gyrus, and the abnormalities in this area are reported to be less in the left hemisphere than in the right hemisphere of these patients (Reiman et al. 1984, 1986). These patients are also reported as having higher whole brain blood flow compared to normal controls. In patients with Alzheimer's disease, PET scan studies have reported finding markedly decreased cerebral glucose metabolism (de Leon et al. 1983).

Single Photon Emission Computed Tomography

Single photon emission computed tomography (SPECT) is a computerized tomographic approach that uses longer acting radiopharmaceuticals that allow rotating gamma camera(s) to image the entire brain in axial, coronal, or oblique sections. Current SPECT image resolution, however, is not as sharp as that obtained with PET. Like PET, SPECT is capable of visualizing subcortical structures (Buchsbaum 1984).

Using Iodine-123-labeled 3-quinuclidinyl-4-iodobenzilate (123 I-QNB) as a SPECT tracer, Holman et al. (1985) imaged brain muscarinic acetylcholine binding in a patient with Alzheimer's disease. They also imaged brain blood perfusion using 123 I-N-isopropyl-p-iodoamphetamine (123 I-IMP), which reflects the brain's blood flow distribution. They found a profound decrease in the perfusion of posterior-temporal and parietal cortex and decreased 123 I-QNB binding in the patient as compared to a normal age-matched control. Other potentially useful gamma ray emitting radiopharmaceuticals are being developed for use in SPECT studies of psychiatric disease.

Computerized Topographic Mapping of Electrophysiological Data

The sheer amount of data generated in multielectrode EEG recordings is enormous, and this factor has often limited the utility of EEG data. Recent developments in computer technology and mathematical algorithms for data analysis have made possible computer-assisted systems that summarize EEG data in the form of colored topographic maps. To make individual maps, the EEG signal from a specified time period is subjected to a computerized spectral analysis, and a value for each electrode that represents the amount of voltage in a given frequency band (e.g., delta, theta, alpha, or beta) is obtained. Colors are assigned to different voltage ranges, thereby defining a color map of EEG activity in the specified spectral band.

Topographic data from a specific population of individuals can be summarized as a group map, and the group maps from different populations (e.g., patients versus normal controls) can be statistically compared. To compare electrophysiologic data from different groups, multivariate analysis techniques may be applied to the numerical indices used to generate the topographic maps.

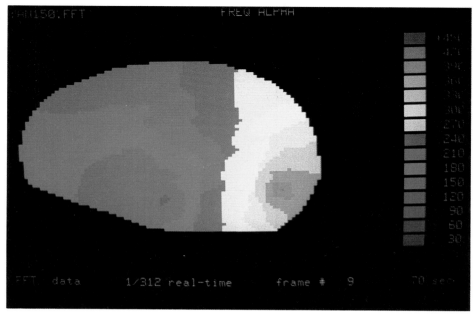

Figure 1. A computerized topographic electroencephalogram map that shows the normal distribution of alpha activity in the left hemisphere of a control subject in the alert resting condition with eyes closed. The region of greatest alpha activity is depicted in red and lies over the occipital region of the brain. (*Source*: Dr. Richard Coppola, National Institute of Mental Health, Bethesda, Md.)

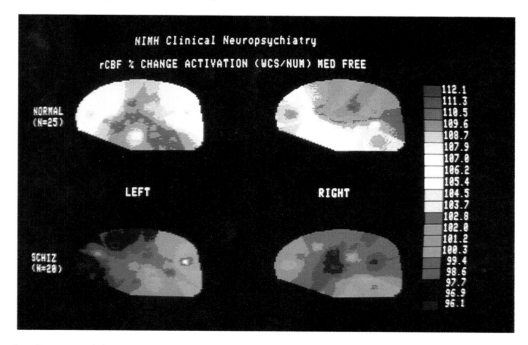

Figure 2. A color map of the regional distribution of cerebral blood flow percent change in a group of control subjects compared to a group of schizophrenic patients comparing two cognitive activation paradigms: a number matching task and the Wisconsin Card Sort (WCS) test. Note the control group increases blood flow to the frontal cortex during the WCS while the schizophrenic patients fail to do so. The numbers task controls for general variables having to do with measuring regional cerebral blood flow during any cognitive activation task. The WSC selectively places a cognitive demand on the dorsolateral prefrontal cortex. The color red denotes the greatest amount of cerebral blood flow. (*Source*: Dr. Daniel R. Weinberger, National Institute of Mental Health, Washington, DC.)

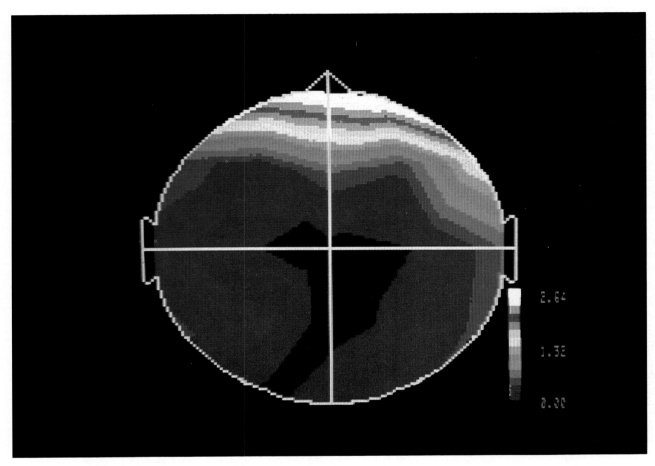

Figure 3. A computerized topographic map defining regional electrophysiological differences between schizophrenic patients with and without computed tomography scan evidence of frontal atrophy. The electrophysiological data were generated by a visual evoked potential. These data suggest that it may be possible to relate electrophysiological differences in schizophrenia to definable morphologic abnormalities of the brain. (*Source*: Dr. John M. Morihisa, Georgetown University School of Medicine and VA Medical Center, Washington, DC.)

There are several topographic mapping systems in use today. These systems differ in the particular electrode montage used, the graphic layout of the maps produced, and the statistical analyses they can apply to data. The Brain Electrical Activity Mapping (BEAM) system, developed by Duffy et al. (1979), places scalp electrodes according to the international 10-20 system and displays the data values in a graphic outline of the entire head viewed from above. In contrast, a system developed by Coppola et al. (1982) uses more electrodes and produces separate maps for the right and left hemispheres, each using a graphic outline of the head in profile.

Employing the BEAM system, Morihisa et al. (1983) found increased delta activity over the entire cortical surface in medicated and drug-free schizophrenic patients compared to normal controls. These findings add further evidence of brain abnormalities in schizophrenia. Recent work from the same laboratory replicated findings of increased delta in schizophrenia but emphasized the importance of on-line electrooculogram monitoring of eye-movement artifact to avoid contamination of delta activity findings that can result in inaccurate topographic localizations of delta (Morihisa 1987a).

EPs can also be topographically visualized using these computerized systems. Morihisa and McAnulty (1985) found regional differences in EP data when comparing schizophrenic patients with frontal lobe atrophy (as evidenced from CT scans) to schizophrenic patients without evidence of frontal atrophy. These differences peaked over the frontal lobes and involved late components of both the AEP and the VEP (Figure 3). This was a preliminary study with a small sample size. However, the results indicate the potential utility of combining structural (e.g., CT scans) and functional (e.g., topographic EEG) imaging techniques. In addition, this research combining structural and functional approaches focuses attention on the frontal lobes in schizophrenia as a possible site of pathophysiologic dysfunction (Morihisa 1986).

Although these EP findings from Morihisa and McAnulty (1985) are consistent with reports of decreased frontal blood flow (Ingvar and Franzen 1974) and decreased frontal glucose utilization (Wolkin et al. 1985) in schizophrenia, the literature in this area is far from consistent. Morihisa (1987a) has suggested that the combined use of different imaging techniques might help to clarify current questions regarding the validity and specificity of the hypothesized frontal lobe dysfunction in schizophrenia.

Magnetic Resonance Imaging

Magnetic resonance imaging (MRI) has also been known as nuclear magnetic resonance (NMR) imaging. The technique currently offers us the ability to visualize brain structure and, at some time in the future, possibly certain brain functions. In MRI, a magnetic field is applied to the brain. The nuclei of exposed hydrogen atoms (protons) are aligned by this magnetic field. The aligned protons are then influenced by brief pulses of radio frequencies. After a pulse, the nuclei relax back to their previously aligned positions and, in so doing, emit energy. This energy is detected and used to construct an image of the brain (Figure 4). The advantages of

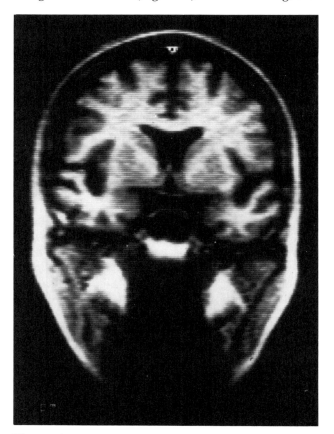

Figure 4. A magnetic resonance image of the human brain. The technique of magnetic resonance imaging (nuclear magnetic resonance) can now provide us with structural information and, in the future, may provide clinically useful functional information as well. (*Source*: Dr. Daniel R. Weinberger, National Institute of Mental Health, Washington, DC.)

MRI over CT include its superior ability to differentiate gray matter from white matter and to display pathology seen in demyelinating disease. CT, however, is superior in imaging bone and small calcifications. Also, MRI does not expose the patient to ionizing radiation, but currently usually requires longer periods of patient cooperation and tolerance for some discomfort (lying in a small, enclosed tunnel during the imaging procedure). Because of some of MRI's ability to better detect and visualize some CNS lesions when compared to CT, MRI might usefully supplement or replace CT in certain clinical situations..

Studies using MRI in the investigations of psychiatric disorders are underway. Andreasen et al. (1986) reported decreased frontal lobe size, as well as smaller cerebrums and craniums in schizophrenic patients. The full potential of different scanning modes requires further study.

Besson et al. (1985) studied spin lattice relaxation time (T1) in dementia patients. In Alzheimer's disease and multi-infarct dementia, they found a significant increase in T1 as compared to normal controls. They also reported that the severity of dementia (as determined by mental status questionnaire) correlated positively with increases in T1. Rangel-Guerra et al. (1983) reported higher T1 values in the temporal brain regions of bipolar patients (pre-lithium) compared to those found in normal controls. After 10 days of lithium treatment, the T1 values were reported to become similar to controls.

MRI has the potential for providing functional imaging, in addition to the currently available anatomic imaging. Current MRI machines image the hydrogen nucleus. Machines of the future, with stronger magnetic fields and other technical improvements, should allow for the imaging of other nuclei. High on the list of possible candidates for visualization is phosphorous (31 P), which could allow for direct imaging of brain cellular metabolism.

☐ EXPERIMENTAL METHODS FOR MONITORING PSYCHOTROPIC DRUG TREATMENT

Antipsychotics

Various methods for the measurement of antipsychotic blood levels are available. Levels have been determined in plasma, serum, and red blood cells (RBCs). Measurement methodologies include gas-liquid chromatography (GLC), high-pressure liquid chromatography (HPLC), gas chromatography-mass spectrometry (GC-MS), fluorimetry, radioimmunoassay, and the radioreceptor assay (RRA) (Creese and Snyder 1977). These methodologies vary in whether they detect solely the parent compound, or the parent compound and a few metabolites, or the activity of the parent compound and its active metabolites (the latter is achieved by RRA). Using these different methodologies, no consistent "therapeutic levels" for any of the antipsychotics have been reported (Tang 1985).

Using RRA, Tang et al. (1984) found no significant differences in plasma chlorpromazine and haloperidol levels in responders and nonresponders. Others have reported similar findings measuring serum levels for various neuroleptics using RRA (Lindenmayer et al. 1984). However, also employing RRA, Brown et al. (1982) reported a significantly higher relapse rate in those patients with low serum neuroleptic levels. Krska et al. (1986) utilized RRA and found correlations between the dose of antipsychotic and the serum level, and these authors went on to suggest that the RRA might be of some use in the assessment of patient compliance or in the evaluation of those patients taking medication but achieving low serum levels. Curry (1985) developed an algorithm that can be used as an aid in the interpretation of blood levels of different neuroleptics obtained by different assay methods. However, at this time, even in the best cases, these levels are only an adjunctive aid to the physician's careful clinical monitoring of the patient for therapeutic response and side effects. Validation of the meaningfulness of antipsychotic blood levels awaits further study.

Monoamine Oxidase Inhibitors

Some studies have suggested that maximal therapeutic effects of the monoamine oxidase inhibitor (MAOI) phenelzine is achieved with amounts of blood platelet monoamine oxidase (MAO) inhibition approximately equal to or greater than 80 percent (Georgotas et al. 1981; Liebowitz et al. 1984; Robinson et al. 1978). Different techniques have been utilized to measure blood MAO activity, including those involving the use of radioisotopes, as well as various chromatographic procedures (Gupta and Steiner 1985). MAO activity can be measured in both isolated washed platelets and platelet rich plasma (Gupta and Steiner 1985). The commercial availability of these techniques for measuring MAO inhibition in patients on MAOI medications is somewhat limited at this time. The clinical usefulness of measuring blood platelet MAO inhibition for patients taking MAOIs will require further elaboration.

Lithium

Other proposed methods for monitoring lithium therapy besides plasma or serum lithium levels have included RBC/plasma lithium ratios (Yassa et al. 1984) and salivary lithium levels (Neu et al. 1975; Ravenscroft et al. 1978). Yassa et al. (1984) presented a single case report of a bipolar patient who was maintained on a very low plasma lithium level but who had a high RBC/plasma lithium ratio. Higher RBC/plasma lithium ratios have been associated with bipolar patients who are lithium responders (Flemenbaum et al. 1978; Mendels et al. 1976) but results have not been consistent (Frazer et al. 1977). The use of salivary lithium levels to monitor lithium treatment seems to require each patient having their saliva/plasma lithium ratio determined so that their individual salivary lithium level will be meaningful (Sims 1980). However, the potential clinical value of any of these methods as alternatives or adjuncts to monitoring serum lithium levels awaits further clarification.

☐ NEUROENDOCRINE MARKERS

A number of neuroendocrine markers are currently being studied. The interest in these markers seems based on the following hypothesis. Psychiatric disease is thought to involve cortical and limbic system dysfunction. Cortical and limbic systems seem to affect secretion of hypothalamic factors and pituitary hormones. It would then follow that measurable hypothalamic-pituitary-target endocrine gland abnormalities might reflect, albeit indirectly, limbic system and/or cortical dysfunction involved in psychiatric illness.

Given this hypothesis, a plethora of different neuroendocrine tests have been studied as potential markers of psychiatric disease. Each test evaluates a particular point on hypothalamic-pituitary-target endocrine gland axes where a measurable hormonal dysregulation might be found. These

neuroendocrine tests have involved baseline measures of endocrine function in psychiatric patients, as well as "challenge" tests. These challenge tests involve the measurement of hormonal response to certain factors. Response patterns in normal and psychiatric populations are compared.

Basal Hormonal Measurement

Gross abnormalities of thyroid, parathyroid, and adrenal gland function are associated with various psychiatric syndromes currently classified as organic mental disorders (Martin 1983). Barring these gross abnormalities reflecting frank medical disease, investigators have searched for potentially more subtle abnormalities associated with functional psychiatric illness.

A frequently reported endocrine abnormality in affective disorder is the hypersecretion of cortisol (Carroll et al. 1976; Cookson et al. 1985). Weiler et al. (1986) found that a 4:00 P.M. baseline cortisol level above 15 μg/dl predicted nonsuppression on the dexamethasone suppression test (DST) with 90.4 percent accuracy. The DST is discussed in a later section.

Thyroid function test abnormalities in hospitalized psychiatric patients have also been noted (Spratt et al. 1982). Cohen and Swigar (1979) found that 9 percent of 480 newly admitted psychiatric patients had an elevated estimated free thyroxine (EFT4), whereas 9 percent had low levels of EFT4. The EFT4 level in some patients in both groups later became spontaneously normal. Preliminary work from Tollefson et al. (1985) suggests that measurement of thyroid function during an acute depressive episode may help predict treatment outcome. In this study, initially high (but still within normal limits) levels of thyroid-stimulating hormone (TSH) and a low free/bound ratio of T4 activity was associated with patients who eventually had a recurrence of their depression. Patients with bipolar affective illness who demonstrate elevated TSH levels have been reported to be at higher risk of a rapid cycling bipolar disorder and for tricyclic-induced rapid mood cycling (Cowdry et al. 1983).

The basal secretion of growth hormone (GH) has been reported to be higher in depression. Mendlewicz et al. (1985) reported GH secretion over a 24-hour period to be higher in affectively ill patients compared to normal controls. Puig-Antich et al. (1984) reported that sleep GH levels in children fully recovered from a major depressive episode were higher than in children who had never been depressed.

Basal level studies of another anterior pituitary hormone, prolactin (PRL), have suggested that plasma PRL concentration in drug-free, chronic schizophrenic patients varies inversely with ratings of their psychopathology, particularly in patients with normal ventricular size as determined by CT. None of these PRL levels were in an established abnormal range (Kleinman et al. 1982).

Dexamethasone Suppression Test

Extensive research has been reported describing DST results in depressed patients. Some of these studies vary in their technical aspects. The clinical usefulness of the DST remains an area of controversy.

In a commonly described version of the test, the patient receives 1 mg of dexamethasone orally at 11 P.M. Some investigators have studied the use of 0.5 mg of dexamethasone; others have used 2 mg of dexamethasone. Blood is drawn over the next 24 hours, generally at 8 A.M. and at 4 and 11 P.M. Most investigators have considered the test abnormal if the postdexamethasone serum cortisol equals or exceeds 5 μg/100 ml at any sample point ("nonsuppression"), although ranges in the literature have varied (Arana et al. 1985; Carroll 1984).

The sensitivity of the DST in depression has been estimated at about 45 percent, but may be higher with increasingly severe depressive disorders. Indeed, some have suggested that this rate may approach 75 percent in psychotic affective disorders (Arana et al. 1985). The DST's specificity varies, depending on whether depressed patients are compared to healthy control subjects or to patients with other psychiatric disorders. DST specificity for differentiating depressives from healthy control subjects has been estimated by some to be over 90 percent. However, nonsuppressors have been found in a significant number of other psychiatric disorders besides depression (Arana et al. 1985). This lack of specificity for other psychiatric diagnoses would seem to limit the usefulness of the DST as an aid in differential diagnosis.

A large number of factors may influence the DST, including withdrawal from alcohol or drugs, weight loss, age, physiological stress, diabetes mellitus, and medications such as steroids, barbiturates, and carbamazepine. These potential artifactual influences have been extensively outlined elsewhere (Arana et al. 1985; Carroll 1984; Shapiro et al. 1983). Low postingestion dexamethasone levels due to individual differences in the metabolism of dexamethasone can be responsible for abnormal DST results (Arana et al. 1984).

Some investigators have suggested that the DST may prove useful in predicting relapse. Nemeroff and Evans (1984) provided preliminary evidence that depressed patients whose DST results "normalize" after treatment have a lower rate of relapse. Godwin et al. (1984) have also demonstrated that manic patients whose DSTs are initially abnormal and fail to normalize with clinical recovery may be more likely to relapse. However, more study is needed to determine whether DST normalization may help predict eventual clinical response (Arana et al. 1985).

Thyrotropin-Releasing Hormone Stimulation Test

Thyrotropin-releasing hormone (TRH) is a tripeptide hormone naturally found in the hypothalamus. Release of TRH from the hypothalamus causes secretion of TSH from the anterior pituitary gland. TSH then acts on the thyroid gland to stimulate the release of thyroid hormone. The thyrotropin-releasing hormone stimulation test (TRHST) was initially developed by endocrinologists to evaluate the hypothalamic-pituitary-thyroid axis. Interest in the TRHST as a potential diagnostic aid in psychiatry was stimulated by experimental trials of TRH in the treatment of depression. These trials revealed that depressed patients showed less TSH release after TRH infusion than did normal controls (Prange et al. 1972).

In a commonly described version of the test, 500 μg of TRH is given intravenously over a 1-minute period to the patient at bed rest after an overnight fast, generally at 9 A.M. Samples for TSH are taken at baseline and 30, 60, 90, and 180 minutes after TRH administration (Garbutt et al. 1983; Loosen and Prange 1982). A delta TSH is then determined by subtracting the baseline TSH from the peak TSH after TRH stimulation. In major depression, a blunted TSH response to TRH has been observed about 25 percent of the time (blunted response generally defined as a delta TSH less than or equal to 5 to 7 IU/ml) (Loosen and Prange 1982). Factors that can adversely affect the delta TSH include thyroid disease, other endocrine disease, hepatic or renal failure, advanced age, weight loss, alcohol intoxication or withdrawal, steroid treatment, diphenylhydantoin, tegretol, estrogens, or lithium (Prange et al. 1972). Recent cocaine use may also cause abnormal TRH test results (Dackis et al. 1985).

Using a delta TSH of ≤7 IU/ml as a definition of a blunted TSH response suggestive of a major depressive disorder in euthyroid patients, Extein et al. (1981a) studied a group of patients with major and "nonmajor" depression (i.e., dysthymic disorder, adjustment reaction, or personality disorder). In this population of patients, they found a sensitivity for the TRHST of 56 percent and a specificity of 93 percent. These same investigators (Extein et al. 1981b) have suggested that the DST and TRHST can be complementary, with each test identifying a significant portion of patients with major depression not identified by the other test.

Some investigators feel that a positive TRH test is related to severity of the depression. McGrath et al. (1984) have found significantly more blunted tests in depressed inpatients than in controls, but they did not find more blunting in depressed outpatients than in controls. Linkowski et al. (1984) found that female patients with past histories of violent suicide attempts had significantly more blunted tests, and felt that a blunted TRH test might help predict suicide risk. However, they found no relationship between TSH response to TRH and severity of depression.

Krog-Meyer et al. (1984) and Targum (1984) have reported that the TSH response increases in some patients after clinical recovery from depression. They found that during the months following the TRHST, the clinical course of patients was closely related to changes in their TSH response; those with an increased response remained in remission, whereas those with an unchanged response had a higher frequency of relapse. Others have also suggested that patients with persistent TRH test abnormality may relapse more frequently despite the prophylactic use of antidepressant medication (Kirkegaard et al. 1975). Finally, Targum et al. (1984) suggested that treatment-resistant depressed patients with an augmented TSH response (>30 μM/ml), with otherwise normal thyroid indices, might benefit from adjunctive thyroid hormone added to their antidepressant regime.

GH and PRL Challenge Tests

GH responses to challenge by dopamine (DA), apomorphine (a dopaminergic agonist), dextroamphetamine, clonidine (an adrenergic agonist), and insulin-induced hypoglycemia have been studied in various psychiatric disorders (Sternberg 1984). Blunted responses have been associated with depressive disorders, and an augmented response of GH to apomorphine has been reported in schizophrenia.

Whalley et al. (1984) reported that GH responses to apomorphine were greater in psychotic patients with Schnederian first-rank symptoms than in those without first-rank symptoms and in normal controls. In this study, apomorphine suppression of plasma PRL was greater in schizophrenic patients than in normal controls. Meltzer et al. (1984b) also found that the apomorphine-induced GH response was significantly correlated with psychosis ratings as well as with negative symptom scale scores. They further reported that the apomorphine-induced PRL suppression was greater in affectively disordered patients than in schizophrenic patients or in normal controls. Moreover, the apomorphine-induced PRL suppression was significantly correlated with various measures of depression in patients with both schizophrenia and major affective disorder. Finally, Judd et al. (1982) reported that depressed patients had lower basal PRL levels and a blunted PRL response to intramuscular methadone.

☐ PERIPHERAL TISSUE MARKERS

Direct measurement of CNS neurotransmitter receptors and enzyme systems is only possible through brain biopsy or in postmortem tissue. At present, in psychiatry, brain biopsy entails too great a risk to the patient to be a useful procedure. However, these same neurotransmitter receptor and enzyme systems can be found in tissues other than brain tissue. Human platelets contain MAO, alpha-2-adrenergic receptors, serotonin reuptake sites, 3-H-imipramine binding sites, and adenylate and guanylate cyclase enzymes. Human lymphocytes contain beta-adrenergic receptors, adenylate and guanylate cyclase enzymes, and DA receptors. Human fibroblasts contain cholinergic receptors. Human RBCs also contain some potential biologic markers, including a mechanism for lithium transport across the cell membrane and the enzyme catechol-O-methyl transferase (COMT) (Stahl 1985). The clinical significance of these peripheral tissue markers remains to be delineated and will require extensive further investigation.

Platelet Markers

The results concerning MAO activity in the blood platelets of psychiatric patients are inconsistent. Tachiki et al. (1984) noted that many workers have reported evidence of a decrease in activity of MAO in the blood of chronic and acute schizophrenics as compared with controls; however, other investigators have been unable to demonstrate any differences between schizophrenic and control subjects. Furthermore, DeLisi et al. (1981) and Meltzer et al. (1982) have reported a significant neuroleptic effect on MAO. Platelet alpha-2-adrenergic receptors have been investigated in patients with major depressive disorder with no clear abnormalities yet identified. Doyle et al. (1985) reported decreased alpha-2-adrenergic receptor binding in depressed elderly patients as identified by 3-H-clonidine. Decreased platelet serotonin uptake has been associated with unipolar and bipolar depressed patients, with no decrease seen in normal controls and schizophrenic patients (Meltzer et al. 1984a; Stahl 1985). Platelet 3-H-imipramine binding sites, which seem related to the platelet serotonin reuptake sites (Paul et al. 1981), are reported to be decreased in patients with major depressive disorder (Stahl 1985). Preliminary work from Mooney et al. (1985) has demonstrated increased platelet adenylate cyclase responses in patients showing an antidepressant response to alprazolam compared to alprazolam nonresponders.

Lymphocyte Markers

Brain neurotransmitter receptor and enzyme systems have also been studied in human lymphocytes. Mann et al. (1985) found that drug-free patients with endogenous depression had lower isoproterenol beta-adrenergic stimulated cyclic adenosine monophosphate (AMP) levels in intact lymphocytes than did normal controls. Some investigators have found elevated plasma norepinephrine in patients with major depression and melancholia, and have speculated that the reports of decreased beta-adrenergic receptor level and function in depressed patients may be related to higher levels of circulating catecholamines (Roy et al. 1985). Other lymphocyte studies include those of Bondy et al. (1985), who found increased binding of the DA antagonist 3-H-spiperone to lymphocyte DA receptors in schizophrenic patients.

Depressed patients have also been reported as having an impairment in lymphocyte response to mitogen stimulation, a measure of cell-mediated immunity (Kronfol et al. 1986a). It has been hypothesized that this decreased lymphocyte function is related to the excessive cortisol secretion that has been observed in many depressed patients. However, Kronfol et al. (1986a) found similarly decreased lymphocyte functioning in depressed patients with both normal and elevated 24-hour urinary free cortisol (UFC) excretion. Kronfol et al. (1986b) have also reported finding significantly higher blood neutrophil and leukocyte counts in untreated manic patients as compared to untreated schizophrenic patients.

Skin Fibroblast Markers

Skin fibroblasts are easily accessible by skin biopsy and can be cultured with relative ease. These fibroblasts contain enzyme and receptor systems that seem similar to those found in neurons. Nadi et al. (1984) demonstrated increased muscarinic cholinergic binding sites in the skin fibroblasts of patients with affective disorders. Others, however, have been unable to confirm these initial findings (Kelsoe et al. 1985; Lenox et al. 1985).

RBC Markers

Individual variations in RBC lithium transport have been proposed as being responsible for differences among psychiatric patients in their RBC/plasma lithium ratios. Pandy et al. (1984) reported that patients with bipolar illness had significantly lower measures of lithium transport than normal controls. On the other hand, Werstiuk et al. (1984) were unable to find significant differences in measures of lithium influx and efflux between bipolar patients and healthy controls.

Richelson et al. (1986) did not find measures of RBC lithium transport or the RBC/plasma lithium ratio to be useful markers of affective illness. Garver et al. (1984) examined the utility of an in vitro RBC/lithium ratio assay as a possible marker for subgroups of lithium-responsive psychotic patients. Finally, regarding another potential RBC marker, the measurement of RBC COMT activity does not currently appear to be a reliable marker of affective illness (Egeland et al. 1984) or schizophrenia (Baron et al. 1984).

☐ PERIPHERAL AND SPINAL FLUID MARKERS

These fluids include plasma, serum, urine, and cerebrospinal fluid (CSF). Potential fluid markers for psychiatric disease that have been investigated include neurotransmitter substances and their metabolites, as well as enzymes involved in their metabolism, such as dopamine beta-hydroxylase (DBH). These studies, however, have yielded mixed results (Jimerson and Berrettini 1985; Van Kammen and Antelman 1984). Some interesting findings have included the reports of reduced CSF 5-hydroxyindole acetic acid (5-HIAA) and homovanillic acid (HVA) in patients with melancholia (Asberg et al. 1984) and the reported association between reduced CSF 5-HIAA and suicidal behavior (Asberg et al. 1976). High urinary corticosteroids have also been associated with depression and suicidal behavior (Bunney et al. 1969). In a study of another potential fluid marker, Wood et al. (1986) reported lower plasma levels of the immunoglobulin IgM in depressed patients compared to normal controls.

Decreased levels of urinary 3-methoxy-4-hydroxyphenylglycol (MHPG), the major metabolite of norepinephrine (NE), have been reported in depression (Schildkraut et al. 1978), although results here have also been inconsistent. Some have reported an association between low MHPG in urine and a good clinical response to noradrenergic antidepressants such as imipramine (Maas et al. 1982). However, subsequent reports suggest that low MHPG levels predict response to imipramine only in a subgroup of affective patients, perhaps in bipolar but not in unipolar patients (Maas et al. 1984). There have also been conflicting reports regarding low urinary MHPG in schizophrenia (Meltzer et al. 1984a).

☐ MELATONIN

Brown et al. (1985) demonstrated a blunted nighttime rise in serum melatonin secretion in depressed patients. Lewy et al. (1985) showed that exposure to light reduced plasma melatonin levels in depressed and manic patients twice as much as in normal controls. They also reported similar findings in euthymic bipolar patients, suggesting that supersensitivity to light might be a trait marker for bipolar affective disorder. The diagnostic specificity of these findings is unknown at this time.

☐ PROVOCATIVE TESTS FOR ANXIETY DISORDERS

Probably the best known and most intensively studied provocative test for anxiety disorders is the lactate infusion test. It has been suggested that intravenous lactate infusions can precipitate panic attack in patients with histories of panic attack, but not as commonly in normal controls. The standard procedure involves the intravenous infusion of 10 ml of .5 molar racemic sodium lactate per kilogram body weight over a 20-minute period (Liebowitz et al. 1985; Pitts and McClure 1967). An abnormal response consists of an attack typical of a spontaneous panic attack. Studies suggest that approximately 70 to 90 percent of patients with panic disorder and 0 to 30 percent of control subjects experience anxiety states meeting the criteria for panic attack (Rainey and Nesse 1985). Compared to normal controls, patients with panic disorder show lower preinfusion blood pCO_2 and bicarbonate levels, as well as higher heart rates and diastolic blood pressures (Liebowitz et al. 1985).

Other provocative tests of anxiety states include isoproterenol, beta-carboline, yohimbine, caffeine, CO_2, and hyperventilation challenge tests (Rainey and Nesse 1985). The specificity of any of these challenge tests as well as their clinical utility awaits further clarification.

☐ NEURO-OPHTHALMOLOGIC MARKERS

Evaluation of Abnormal Eye Movements

Eye-tracking dysfunctions (ETDs) consist of a larger than expected number of jerky movements of the eyes during the visual tracking of a moving object. ETDs have been evaluated using a wide range of tracking tasks and recording techniques (Lipton et al. 1983).

As reviewed by Holzman et al. (1984), ETDs have been reported in up to 50 to 80 percent of schizophrenic patients, about 40 percent of manic-depressive patients, and about 8 percent of the normal population. ETDs are also found in many organic brain disorders. A greater frequency of ETDs has been found in the parents of schizophrenic patients than in the parents of manic-depressive patients or in the general population (Holzman et al. 1984). Holzman has therefore suggested that

ETDs represent familial markers of vulnerability to schizophrenia. ETDs have also been associated with lithium use (Levy et al. 1985).

CONCLUSION

The demonstration of certain brain imaging and laboratory test abnormalities in patients with behavioral disturbances has returned psychiatry to its original foundations in the neurosciences (Morihisa 1987b). The psychiatrist should be knowledgeable about the brain imaging techniques, electrophysiological procedures, and laboratory tests employed in the evaluation of organic mental disorders and screening of underlying medical illnesses in psychiatric patients. Psychiatrists should also be knowledgeable about the pretreatment and follow-up laboratory evaluation for certain psychotropic medications, the pretreatment laboratory evaluation of electroconvulsive therapy (ECT), as well as the laboratory screening tests for drug abuse and environmental intoxications.

The current state of neurophysiologic markers of psychiatric disease is in evolutionary flux, and some of the ideas presented in this chapter will no doubt have to be modified as new data are reported. No markers have been clearly accepted at this time for routine clinical use in the evaluation of psychiatric disorders. Further research into these markers should, at some point in the future, bring some of these techniques into the realm of diagnostic procedures for practicing clinicians. Biologic marker study should also help us in our continuing effort to understand the neurobiology of psychiatric disease. This research might support the creation of new diagnostic categories around certain markers or combinations of markers. Additionally, future advances in the fields of genetics and molecular biology should allow for the identification of specific areas of the genome responsible for psychiatric illness. This has already been done for Huntington's disease (Gusella et al. 1983, 1984). These genetic markers will perhaps be the ultimate trait markers of psychiatric disease.

As with all diagnostic tests in medicine, physicians should treat patients and not laboratory test results. Neuropsychiatrists should be wary not to overinterpret brain imaging and laboratory data out of clinical context. None of these diagnostic tests have absolute sensitivity or specificity. However, it should be remembered that our current clinical diagnostic schema can be fallible. The biologic markers and diagnostic tests discussed in this chapter, as well as others perhaps not mentioned or yet to be defined, are likely to have a growing role as aids in the diagnostic and prognostic assessment of psychiatric patients.

REFERENCES

Abrams R, Taylor MA: Differential EEG patterns in affective disorder and schizophrenia. Arch Gen Psychiatry 36:1355–1358, 1979

Amdisen A: Monitoring lithium dose levels: clinical aspects of serum lithium estimation, in Handbook of Lithium Therapy. Edited by Johnson FN. Lancaster, England, MTP Press, 1980

Andreasen N, Nasrallah HA, Dunn V: Structural abnormalities in the frontal system in schizophrenia. Arch Gen Psychiatry 43:136–144, 1986

Arana GW, Baldessarini RJ, Ornsteen M: The dexamethasone suppression test for diagnosis and prognosis in psychiatry: commentary and review. Arch Gen Psychiatry 42:1193–1204, 1985

Arana GW, Workman RJ, Baldessarini RJ: Association between low plasma levels of cortisol in psychiatric patients given dexamethasone. Am J Psychiatry 141:1619–1620, 1984

Asberg M, Bertilsson L, Martensson, et al: CSF monoamine metabolites in melancholia. Acta Psychiatr Scand 69:201–219, 1984

Asberg M, Cronholm B, Sjoqvist F, et al: Relationship between plasma level and therapeutic effect of nortriptyline. Br Med J 3:331–334, 1971

Asberg M, Traskman C, Thoren P: 5-HIAA in the cerebrospinal fluid: a biochemical suicide predictor. Arch Gen Psychiatry 33:1193–1197, 1976

Baldessarini RJ, Lipinski JF: Lithium salts: 1970–1975. Ann Intern Med 83:527–533, 1975

Baron JC, Comar D, Zaritian E, et al: Dopaminergic receptor sites in human brain: positron emission tomography. Neurology 35:16–24, 1985

Baron M, Gruen R, Levitt M, et al: Erythrocyte catechol O-methyltransferase activity in schizophrenia: analysis of family data. Am J Psychiatry 141:29–32, 1984

Baxter CR, Phelps ME, Mazziotta JC, et al: Cerebral metabolic rates for glucose in mood disorders: studies with positron emission tomography and fluorodeoxyglucose F18. Arch Gen Psychiatry 42:441–447, 1985

Besson J, Corrigan F, Foreman E, et al: NMR imaging in dementia. Br J Psychiatry 146:31–35, 1985

Bondy B, Ackenheil M, Elbers R, et al: Binding of 3H-spiperone to human lymphocytes: a biological marker in schizophrenia. Psychiatry Res 15:41–48, 1985

Brown R, Kocsis JH, Caroff S: Differences in noctural melatonin secretion between melancholic depressed patients and control subjects. Am J Psychiatry 142:811–816, 1985

Brown WA, Laughren T, Chisholm E, et al: Low serum neuroleptic levels predict relapse in schizophrenic patients. Arch Gen Psychiatry 30:998–1000, 1982

Buchsbaum MS: Middle evoked potentials. Schizophr Bull 3:93–104, 1977

Buchsbaum MS: Positron emission tomography (PET) in psychiatry, in Brain Imaging in Psychiatry. Edited by Morihisa JM. Washington, DC, American Psychiatric Press, 1984

Buchsbaum MS, DeLisi LE, Holcomb HH, et al: Anterioposterior gradients in cerebral glucose use in schizophrenia and affective disorders. Arch Gen Psychiatry 41:1159–1166, 1984

Bunney WE, Fawcett JA, Davis JM, et al: Further evaluation of urinary 17-hydroxycorticosteroids in suicidal patients. Arch Gen Psychiatry 21:138–150, 1969

Carroll BJ: Dexamethasone suppression test, in Handbook of Psychiatric Diagnostic Procedures, Vol 1. Edited by Hall RCW, Beresford TP. New York, Spectrum Publications, 1984

Carroll BJ, Curtis GC, Davies BM, et al: Urinary cortisol excretion in depression. Psychol Med 6:43–50, 1976

Cohen KL, Swigar ME: Thyroid function screening in psychiatric patients. JAMA 242:254–257, 1979

Coombs HI, Coombs RRH, Mee UG: Methods of serum lithium estimation, in Lithium Research and Therapy. Edited by Johnson FN. New York, Academic Press, 1975

Cookson JC, Silverstone T, Williams S, et al: Plasma cortisol levels in mania: associated clinical ratings and changes during treatment with haloperidol. Br J Psychiatry 146:498–502, 1985

Cooper JE, Andrews H, Barber C: Stable abnormalities in the lateralization of early cortical somatosensory evoked potentials in schizophrenic patients. Br J Psychiatry 146:585–593, 1985

Cooper TB: Monitoring lithium dose levels: estimation of lithium in blood, in Handbook of Lithium Therapy. Edited by Johnson FN. Lancaster, England, MTP Press, 1980

Coppola R, Buchsbaum MS, Rigal F: Computer generation of surface distribution maps of measures of brain activity. Comput Biol Med 12:191–199, 1982

Cowdry RW, Wehr TA, Zis AP, et al: Thyroid abnormalities associated with rapid-cycling bipolar illness. Arch Gen Psychiatry 40:414–420, 1983

Creese I, Snyder SH: A simple and sensitive radioreceptor assay for antischizophrenic drugs in blood. Nature 270:180–182, 1977

Curry SH: Commentary: the strategy and value of neuroleptic drug monitoring. J Clin Psychopharmacol 5:263–271, 1985

Dackis CA, Estroff TW, Sweeney DR, et al: Specificity of the TRH test for major depression in patients with serious cocaine abuse. Am J Psychiatry 142:1097–1099, 1985

de Leon MJ, Ferris SH, George AE, et al: Positron emission tomographic studies of aging and Alzheimer's disease. AJNR 4:568–571, 1983

DeLisi LE: Use of the clinical laboratory, in Biomedical Psychiatric Therapeutics. Edited by Sullivan JL, Sullivan PD. Boston, Butterworths, 1984

DeLisi LE, Wise CD, Bridge TP, et al: A probable neuroleptic effect on platelet monoamine oxidase in chronic schizophrenic patients. Psychiatry Res 4:95–107, 1981

Dennert JW, Andreasen NC: CT scanning and schizophrenia: a review. Psychiatr Dev 1:105–122, 1983

Doyle MC, George AJ, Ravindran AV, et al: Platelet alpha-2-adrenoreceptor binding in elderly depressed patients. Am J Psychiatry 142:1489–1490, 1985

Duffy FH, Burchfiel JL, Lombroso CT: Brain electrical activity mapping (BEAM): a method for extending the clinical utility of EEG and evoked potential data. Ann Neurol 5:309–332, 1979

Egeland JA, Kidd JR, Frazer A, et al: Amish study, V: lithium-sodium countertransport and catechol-O-methyltransferase in pedigrees of bipolar probands. Am J Psychiatry 141:1049–1054, 1984

Extein I, Pottash ALC, Gold MS: Thyrotropin-releasing hormone test in the diagnosis of unipolar depressives. Psychiatry Res 5:311–316, 1981a

Extein I, Pottash ALC, Gold MS: Relationship of thyrotropin-releasing hormone test and dexamethasone suppression test abnormalities in unipolar depression. Psychiatry Res 4:49–51, 1981b

Flemenbaum A, Weddige R, Miller J: Lithium erythrocyte/plasma ratio as a predictor of response. Am J Psychiatry 135:336–338, 1978

Foster FG, Kupfer DJ, Coble P, et al: Rapid eye movement sleep density: an objective indicator in severe medical-depressive syndromes. Arch Gen Psychiatry 33:1119–1123, 1976

Frazer A, Gottlieb J, Mendels J: Lithium ratio and clinical response in manic depressive illness. Lancet 1:41–42, 1977

Garbutt JC, Loosen PT, Tipermans A, et al: The TRH test in patients with borderline personality disorder. Psychiatry Res 9:107–113, 1983

Garver DL, Hirschowitz J, Fleishman R, et al: Lithium response and psychoses: a double-blind, placebo-controlled study. Psychiatry Res 12:57–68, 1984

Georgotas A, Mann J, Friedman E: Platelet monoamine oxidase inhibition as a potential indicator of favorable response to MAOI's in geriatric depressions. Biol Psychiatry 16:997–1001, 1981

Gillin IC, Reynolds CF, Shipley JE: Sleep studies in selected adult neuropsychiatric disorders, in Psychiatry Update: American Psychiatric Association Annual Review, Vol 4. Edited by Hales RE, Frances AJ. Washington, DC, American Psychiatric Press, 1985

Glassman AH, Perel JM, Shostak M, et al: Clinical implications of imipramine plasma levels of depressive illness. Arch Gen Psychiatry 34:197–204, 1977

Godwin LD, Greenberg LB, Skukla S: Predictive value of the dexamethasone suppression test in mania. Am J Psychiatry 141:1610–1612, 1984

Gold MS, Dackis CA: Role of laboratory in the evaluation of suspected drug abuse. J Clin Psychiatry 47(Suppl):17–23, 1986

Greden JF: The dexamethasone suppression test: an established biological marker of melancholia, in Biological Markers in Psychiatry and Neurology. Edited by Usdin E, Hanin I. New York, Pergamon Press, 1981

Guazzelli M, Maggini C, Landino G, et al: Similarity of non-REM abnormalities in schizophrenia and depression. Arch Gen Pshciatry 42:834–835, 1985

Gupta RN, Steiner M: Liquid chromatographic determination of inhibition of monoamine oxidase activity in platelet-rich plasma of depressed patients treated with phenelzine. Clin Chim Acta 152:63–69, 1985

Gur RE: Regional cerebral blood flow in psychiatry: the resting and activated brains of schizophrenic patients, in Brain Imaging in Psychiatry. Edited by Morihisa JM. Washington, DC, American Psychiatric Press, 1984

Gur RE, Skolnick BE, Gur RC: Brain function in psychiatric disorders, I: regional cerebral blood flow in medicated schizophrenia. Arch Gen Psychiatry 40:1250–1254, 1983

Gusella JF, Wexler NS, Conneally PM, et al: A polymorphic DNA marker genetically linked to Huntington's disease. Nature 306:234–238, 1983

Gusella JF, Tanzi RE, Anderson MA, et al: DNA markers for nervous system diseases. Science 225:1320–1326, 1984

Hall RC, Beresford TP, Gardner ER: The medical care of psychiatric patients. Hosp Community Psychiatry 33:25–34, 1982

Harding GFA, Wright CE, Orwin A: Primary presenile dementia: the use of the visual evoked potential as a diagnostic indicator. Br J Psychiatry 147:532–539, 1985

Hiatt JF, Floyd TL, Katz PH, et al: Further evidence of abnormal non-rapid eye movement sleep in schizophrenia. Arch Gen Psychiatry 42:797–802, 1985

Holman BL, Gibson RE, Hill TC, et al: Muscarinic acetylcholine receptors in Alzheimer's disease: in vivo imaging with iodine 123-labeled 3-quinuclidinyl-4-iodobenzilate and emission tomography. JAMA 254:3063–3066, 1985

Holzman PS, Solomon CM, Levin S, et al: Pursuit eye movement dysfunction in schizophrenia: family evidence for specificity. Arch Gen Psychiatry 41:136–139, 1984

Hullin RP: Minimum serum lithium levels for effective prophylaxis, in Handbook of Lithium Therapy. Edited by Johnson FN. Baltimore, University Park Press, 1980

Iacono W, Lykken O, Peloquin L, et al: Electrodermal activity in euthymic unipolar and bipolar affective disorders. Arch Gen Psychiatry 40:557–565, 1984

Ingvar DH, Franzen G: Distribution of cerebral activity in chronic schizophrenia. Lancet 2:1484–1486, 1974

Insel TR, Gillin JL, Moore A, et al: The sleep of patients with obsessive-compulsive disorder. Arch Gen Psychiatry 39:1372–1377, 1982

Jefferson JW, Greist JH, Ackerman DL, et al: Lithium encyclopedia for clinical practice, 2nd ed. Washington, DC, American Psychiatric Press, 1986

Jerram TC, McDonald R: Plasma lithium control with particular reference to minimum effective levels, in Lithium in Medical Practice. Edited by Johnson FN, Johnson S. Lancaster, England, MTP Press, 1978

Jimerson DC, Berrettini W: Cerebrospinal fluid amine metabolite studies in depression: research update, in Pathochemical Markers in Major Psychoses. Edited by Beckmann H, Riederer P. New York, Springer-Verlag, 1985

Johnstone EC, Crow TJ, Frith CD, et al: Cerebral ventricular size and cognitive impairment in chronic schizophrenia. Lancet 2:924–926, 1976

Jones D, Kelwala S, Bell J, et al: Cholinergic REM sleep induction response correlation with endogenous major depression. Psychiatry Res 14:99–110, 1985

Judd LL, Risch SC, Parker DC, et al: Blunted prolactin response: a neuroendocrine abnormality manifested by depressed patients. Arch Gen Psychiatry 39:1413–1416, 1982

Kelsoe JR, Gillin JC, Janowsky DS, et al: Failure to confirm muscarinic receptors on skin fibroblasts. N Engl J Med 312:861–862, 1985

Kirkegaard C, Norlem N, Birk-Lauridsen U, et al: Protirelin stimulation test and thyroid function during treatment of depression. Arch Gen Psychiatry 32:115–118, 1975

Kleinman JE, Weinberger DR, Rogol AD, et al: Plasma prolactin concentration and psychopathology in chronic schizophrenia. Arch Gen Psychiatry 39:655–657, 1982

Kling, AS, Metter EJ, Riege WH, et al: Comparison of PET measurement of local brain glucose metabolism and CAT measurement of brain atrophy in chronic schizophrenia and depression. AM J Psychiatry 143:175–180, 1986

Krog-Meyer I, Kirkegaard C, Kijine B, et al: Prediction of relapse with the TRH test and prophylactic amitriptyline in 39 patients with endogenous depression. Am J Psychiatry 141:945–948, 1984

Kronfol Z, House JD, Silva J, et al: Depression, urinary free cortisol excretion and lymphocyte function. Br J Psychiatry 148:70–73, 1986a

Kronfol Z, Turner R, House JD, et al: Elevated blood neutrophil concentration in mania. J Clin Psychiatry 47:63–65, 1986b

Krska J, Sampath G, Shah A, et al: Radio receptor assay of serum neuroleptic levels in psychiatric patients. Br J Psychiatry 148:187–193, 1986

Kupfer DJ, Foster FG, Loble P, et al: The application of EEG sleep for the differential diagnosis of affective disorders. Am J Psychiatry 135:69–74, 1978

Lenox RH, Hitzemann RJ, Richelson E, et al: Failure to confirm muscarinic receptors on skin fibroblasts. N Engl J Med 312:861, 1985

Levinson DF, Edelberg R, Bridger WH: The orienting response in schizophrenia: proposed resolution of a controversy. Biol Psychiatry 19:489–507, 1984

Levy DL, Dorus E, Shaughnessy R, et al: Pharmacologic evidence for specificity of pursuit dysfunction in schizophrenia. Arch Gen Psychiatry 42:335–341, 1985

Lewy AJ, Nurnberger JI, Wehr TA, et al: Supersensitivity to light: possible trait marker for manic-depressive illness. Am J Psychiatry 142:725–727, 1985

Liebowitz MR, Gorman JM, Fyer AJ, et al: Lactate provocation of panic attacks, II: biochemical and psychological findings. Arch Gen Psychiatry 42:709–719, 1985

Liebowitz MR, Quitkin FM, Stewart JW, et al: Phenelzine versus imipramine in atypical depression: a preliminary report. Arch Gen Psychiatry 41:669–677, 1984

Lindenmayer JP, Smith D, Katz I: Radioreceptor assay of neuroleptics in refractory chronic schizophrenic patients. J Clin Psychiatry 45:117–119, 1984

Linkowski P, Van Wettere JP, Kerkhofs M, et al: Violent suicidal behavior and the thyrotropin-releasing hormone test: a clinical outcome study. Neuropsychobiology 12:19–22, 1984

Lipton RB, Levy DL, Holzman PS, et al: Eye movement dysfunction in psychiatric patients: a review. Schizophr Bull 9:13–32, 1983

Loosen PT, Prange AJ: The serum thyrotropin response to thyrotropin releasing hormone in psychotic patients: a review. Am J Psychiatry 139:405–416, 1982

Lopes da Silva FH, Van Rotterdam A: Biophysical aspects of EEG and MEG generation, in Electroencephalography: Basic Principles, Clinical Applications, and Related Fields. Edited by Niedermeyer E, Lopes da Silva FH. Baltimore, Urban and Schwarzenberg, 1982

Luchins DJ, Weinberger DR, Wyatt RJ: Schizophrenia: evidence of a subgroup with reversed cerebral asymmetry. Arch Gen Psychiatry 36:1309–1311, 1979

Maas JW, Kocsis JE, Bowden CL, et al: Pretreatment neurotransmitter metabolities and response to imipramine or amitriptyline treatment. Psychol Med 12:37–43, 1982

Maas JW, Koslow SH, Katz MM, et al: Pretreatment neurotransmitter metabolite levels and response to tricyclic antidepressant drug response. Am J Psychiatry 141:1159–1171, 1984

Mann JJ, Brown RP, Halper JP, et al: Reduced sensitivity of lymphocyte beta-adrenergic receptors in patients with endogenous depression and psychomotor agitation. N Engl J Med 313:715–720, 1985

Martin MJ: A brief review of organic diseases masquerading as functional illness. Hosp Community Psychiatry 34:328–332, 1983

Mazziotta JC, Phelps ME, Carson RE, et al: Tomographic mapping of human cerebral metabolism: sensory deprivation. Ann Neurol 12:435–444, 1982

McGrath RJ, Quitkin FM, Stewart JW, et al: A comparative study of the pituitary TSH response to thyrotropin in outpatient depressives. Psychiatry Res 12:185–193, 1984

Meltzer HY, Duncavage MB, Jackman H, et al: Effect of neuroleptic drugs on platelet monoamine oxidase in psychiatric patients. Am J Psychiatry 139:1242–1248, 1982

Meltzer HY, Arora RC, Metz J: Biological studies of schizoaffective disorders. Schizophr Bull 10:49–70, 1984a

Meltzer HY, Kalakowska T, Fang US, et al: Growth hormone and prolactin response to apomorphine in schizophrenia and the major affective disorders. Arch Gen Psychiatry 41:512–519, 1984b

Mendels J, Frazer A, Baron J, et al: Intra-erythrocyte lithium ion concentration and long-term maintenance treatment. Lancet 1:966, 1976

Mendlewicz J, Linkowski P, Kerhofs M, et al: Diurnal hypersecretion of growth hormone in depression. J Clin Endocrinol Metab 60:505–512, 1985

Mooney JJ, Schatzberg AF, Cole JO: Enhanced signal transduction by adenylate cyclase in platelet membranes of patients showing antidepressant responses to alprazolam: preliminary data. J Psychiatr Res 19:65–75, 1985

Morihisa JM, Duffy FH, Wyatt RJ: Brain electrical activity mapping (BEAM) in schizophrenic patients. Arch Gen Psychiatry 40:719–728, 1983

Morihisa JM, McAnulty GB: Structure and function: brain electrical activity mapping and computed tomography in schizophrenia. Biol Psychiatry 20:3–19, 1985

Morihisa JM: Electrophysiological evidence implicating frontal lobe dysfunction in schizophrenia. Psychopharmacol Bull 22:885–889, 1986

Morihisa JM: Computerized EEG and evoked potential mapping, in Brain Imaging for Psychiatrists. Edited by Andreasen NC. Washington, DC, American Psychiatric Press, 1987a

Morihisa JM: Functional brain imaging techniques, in Psychiatry Update: The American Psychiatric Association Annual Review, Vol. 6. Edited by Hales RE, Frances AJ. Washington, DC, American Psychiatric Press, 1987b

Nadi NS, Nurnberger JI, Gershon ES: Muscarinic cholinergic receptors on skin fibroblasts in familial affective disorder. N Engl J Med 26:225–230, 1984

Nasrallah HA, Jacoby CG, Chapmans J, et al: Third ventricular enlargement on CT scan in schizophrenia: association with cerebellar atrophy. Biol Psychiatry 20:443–450, 1985

Nelson JC, Jatlow P, Quinlan DM, et al: Desipramine plasma concentration and antidepressant response. Arch Gen Psychiatry 39:1419–1422, 1982

Nemeroff CB, Evans DL: Correlation between the dexamethasone suppression test in depressed patients and clinical response. Am J Psychiatry 141:247–249, 1984

Neu C, Dimascio A, Williams D: Saliva lithium levels: clinical applications. Am J Psychiatry 132:66–68, 1975

Pandy GN, Dorus E, Casper RC, et al: Lithium transport in red cells of patients with affective disorders. Prog Neuropsychopharmacol Biol Psychiatry 8:547–555, 1984

Paul SM, Rehavi M, Rice KC, et al: Does high affinity [^{3}H]imipramine binding label serotonin reuptake sites in brain and platelet? Life Sci 28:2753–2760, 1981

Pearlson GD, Garbacz DJ, Breakey WR, et al: Lateral ventricular enlargement associated with persistent unemployment and negative symptoms in both schizophrenia and bipolar disorder. Psychiatry Res 12:1–9, 1984a

Pearlson GD, Garbacz DJ, Tompkins RH, et al: Clinical correlates of lateral ventricular enlargement in bipolar affective disorder. Am J Psychiatry 141:253–256, 1984b

Phelps ME, Mazziotta JC, Baxter L, et al: Positron emission tomographic study of affective disorders: problems and strategies. Ann Neurol 15:s149–s156, 1984

Pitts FN, McClure JM: Lactate metabolism in anxiety neuroses. N Engl J Med 277:1328–1336, 1967

Prange AJ, Wilson IC, Lara PP, et al: Effects of thyrotropin-releasing hormone in depression. Lancet 2:999–1002, 1972

Prien RF, Caffey EM: Relationship between dosage and response to lithium prophylaxis in recurrent depression. Am J Psychiatry 133:567–570, 1976

Puig-Antich J, Goetz R, Davies M, et al: Growth hormone secretion in prepubertal children with major depression, IV: sleep-related plasma concentrations in a drug-free, fully recovered clinical state. Arch Gen Psychiatry 41:479–483, 1984

Rainey JM, Nesse RM: Psychobiology of anxiety and anxiety disorders. Psychiatr Clin North Am 8:133–144, 1985

Rangel-Guerra R, Perez-Payan H, Minkoff L, et al: Nuclear magnetic resonance in bipolar affective disorders. AJNR 4:229–231, 1983

Ravenscroff P, Vozeh S, Weinstein M, et al: Saliva lithium concentrations in the management of lithium therapy. Arch Gen Psychiatry 35:1123–1127, 1978

Reiman EM, Raichle ME, Butler FK, et al: A focal brain abnormality in panic disorder, a severe form of anxiety. Nature 310: 683–685, 1984

Reiman EM, Raichle ME, Robins E, et al: The application of positron emission tomography to the study of panic disorder. Am J Psychiatry 143:469–477, 1986

Reisberg B, Gershon S: Side effects associated with lithium therapy. Arch Gen Psychiatry 36:879–887, 1979

Reisby N, Gram LF, Bech P, et al: Imipramine: clinical effects and pharmacokinetic variability. Psychopharmacology 54:263–272, 1977

Richelson E, Synder K, Carlson J, et al: Lithium ion transport by erythrocytes of randomly selected blood donors and manic-depressive patients: lack of association with affective illness. Am J Psychiatry 143:457–462, 1986

Rizzo PA, Albani GF, Spadaro M, et al: Brain slow potentials (CNV), prolactin, and schizophrenia. Biol Psychiatry 18:175–183, 1983

Robinson DS, Nies A, Ravaris C, et al: Clinical pharmacology of phenelzine. Arch Gen Psychiatry 35:629–635, 1978

Roth WT: Late event related potentials and psychopathology. Schizophr Bull 3:105–120, 1977

Roy A, Pickar D, Linnoila M, et al: Plasma norepinephrine level in affective disorder: relationship to melancholia. Arch Gen Psychiatry 42:1181–1185, 1985

Schildkraut JJ, Orsulak PJ, Schatzberg AF, et al: Toward a biochemical classification of depressive disorders. Arch Gen Psychiatry 35:1427–1433, 1987

Shagass C: Early evoked potentials. Schizophr Bull 3:80–92, 1977

Shagass C: Evoked potentials in adult psychiatry, in EEG and Evoked Potentials in Psychiatry and Behavioral Neurology. Edited by Hughes JR, Wilson WP. Boston, Butterworths, 1983

Shagass C, Roemer RA, Straumanis JJ: Relationships between psychiatric diagnosis and some quantitative EEG variables. Arch Gen Psychiatry 39:1423–1435, 1983

Shapiro MF, Lehman AF, Greenfield S: Biases in the laboratory diagnosis of depression in medical practice. Arch Intern Med 143:2085–2088, 1983

Simpson GM, Pi EH, White K: Plasma drug levels and clinical response to antidepressants. J Clin Psychiatry 44(Suppl):27–34, 1983

Sims A: Monitoring lithium dose levels: estimation of lithium in saliva, in Handbook of Lithium Therapy. Edited by Johnson FN. Lancaster, England, MTP Press, 1980

Sitaram N, Nurnberger JI, Gershon ES, et al: Cholinergic regulation of mood and REM sleep: potential model and marker of vulnerability of affective disorder. Am J Psychiatry 139:571–576, 1982

Small JG: EEG in schizophrenia, in EEG and Evoked Potentials in Psychiatry and Behavioral Neurology. Edited by Hughes JR, Wilson WP. Boston, Butterworths, 1983

Spratt DT, Pont A, Miller MB, et al: Hyperthyroxinemia in patients with acute psychiatric disorders. Am J Med 73:41–48, 1982

Sramek JJ, Baumgartner WA, Tallos JA, et al: Hair analysis for detection of phencyclidine in newly admitted psychiatric patients. Am J Psychiatry 142:950–953, 1985

Stahl SM: Peripheral models for the study of neurotransmitter receptors in man. Psychopharmacol Bull 21:663–671, 1985

St. Clair DM, Blackwood DHR, Christie JE: P3 and other long latency auditory evoked potentials in presenile dementia Alzheimer type and alcoholic Korsakoff syndrome. Br. J Psychiatry 147:702–706, 1985

Sternberg DE: Biologic tests in psychiatry. Psychiatr Clin North Am 7:639–650, 1984

Stevens JR, Bigelow L, Denroy D, et al: Telemetered EEG-EOG during psychotic behaviors of schizophrenia. Arch Gen Psychiatry 36:251–262, 1979

Tachiki KH, Kurtz N, Kling AS, et al: Blood monoamine oxidases and CT scans in subgroups of chronic schizophrenics. J Psychiatr Res 18:233–243, 1984

Tang SW: Prediction of treatment response in schizophrenia: clinical use of neuroleptic blood levels. Can J Psychiatry 30:249–250, 1985

Tang SW, Glaister J, Davidson L, et al: Total and free plasma neuroleptic levels in schizophrenic patients. Psychiatry Res 13:285–293, 1984

Targum SD: Persistent neuroendocrine dysregulation in major depressive disorder: a marker for early relapse. Biol Psychiatry 14:305–318, 1984

Targum SD, Greenberg RD, Harmon RL, et al: Thyroid hormone and the TRH stimulation test in refractory depression. J Clin Psychiatry 45:345–346, 1984

Task Force on the Use of Laboratory Tests in Psychiatry: Tricyclic antidepressants—blood level measurements and clinical outcome: an APA Task Force Report. Am J Psychiatry 142:155–162, 1985

Timsit-Berthier M: CNV, slow potentials and motor potential studies in normal subjects and psychiatric patients, in Human Neurophysiology, Psychology, Psychiatry: Average Evoked Responses and Their Conditioning in Normal Subjects and Psychiatric Patients. Edited by Fessard A, Lelord G. Paris, Inserm, 1973

Tollefson G, Valentine R, Hoffman N, et al: Thyroxine binding and TSH in recurrent depressive episodes. J Clin Psychiatry 46:267–272, 1985

Tsai LY, Nasrallah HA, Jacoby CG: Hemispheric asymmetries on computed tomographic scans in schizophrenia and mania: a controlled study and a critical review. Arch Gen Psychiatry 40:1286–1289, 1983

Ulrich RF, Shaw DH, Kupfer DJ: Effects of aging on EEG sleep in depression. Sleep 3:31–40, 1980

Van Kammen DP, Antelman S: Minireview: impaired noradrenergic transmission in schizophrenics. Life Sci 34:1403–1413, 1984

Wagner HN, Burns HD, Dannals RF, et al: Imaging dopamine receptors in the human brain by positron tomography. Science 221:1264–1266, 1983

Waters B, Lapierre Y, Gagnon A, et al: Determination of the optimal concentration of lithium in the prophylaxis of manic-depressive disorder. Biol Psychiatry 17:1323–1329, 1982

Weiler MA, Jobe TH, Nasr SJ, et al: 4 p.m. baseline cortisol level as a predictor of DST results in depression. J Clin Psychiatry 47:60–62, 1986

Weinberger DR: Brain disease and psychiatric illness: when should a psychiatrist order a CAT scan? Am J Psychiatry 141:1521–1527, 1984

Weinberger DR, Berman KF, Zec RF: Physiological dysfunction of dorsolateral prefrontal cortex in schizophrenia, I: regional cerebral blood flow (rCBF) evidence. Arch Gen Psychiatry 43:114–124, 1986

Weinberger DR, Bigelow LB, Kleinman JF, et al: Cerebral ventricular enlargement in chronic schizophrenia: an association with poor response to treatment. Arch Gen Psychiatry 37:22–23, 1980

Weinberger DR, Torrey EF, Neophytides AN, et al: Structural abnormalities in the cerebral cortex of chronic schizophrenic patients. Arch Gen Psychiatry 36:935–939, 1979

Werstiuk ES, Rathbone MP, Grof P: Erythrocyte lithium efflux in bipolar patients and control subjects: the question of reproducibility. Psychiatry Res 13:175–185, 1984

Whalley LJ, Christie JE, Brown S, et al: Schneider's first-rank symptoms of schizophrenia: an association with increased growth hormone response to apomorphine. Arch Gen Psychiatry 41:1040–1043, 1984

Wolkin A, Kaegar J, Brodie J, et al: Persistence of cerebral metabolic abnormalities in chronic schizophrenia as detemined by positron emission tomography. Am J Psychiatry 142:564–571, 1985

Wood K, Harwood J, Cooper A: Plasma immunoglobulins in depressed and lithium treated patients. Br J Psychiatry 148:581–582, 1986

Yassa R, Nair V, Kraus DJ: A possible indication for red cell lithium determinations: case report. Can J Psychiatry 29:44–45, 1984

Neuropsychological Assessment

Michael D. Franzen, PH.D.
Mark R. Lovell, PH.D.

OVER THE LAST 30 YEARS, clinical neuropsychology has come to play an increasingly important role in the application of neurobehavioral theory to clinical problems. As with most phenomena, neuropsychological assessment has undergone many changes during the course of its history. These changes can be seen as occurring both in the context of influences from inside the field as well as from external influences (Costa 1983). This chapter will trace some of the developments that have occurred, relating them: (1) to the external influences of demands from other professionals; (2) to the internal influences of psychometric theory and psychological assessment; and (3) most importantly, to the internal influence of changes in neuropsychological theory. The current state of neuropsychological assessment will be surveyed. Implications for the utility of neuropsychological assessment with neuropsychiatric populations will be discussed.

☐ HISTORICAL DEVELOPMENTS

Neuropsychological assessment procedures were first developed in response to a need by medical practitioners for diagnostic and localization information in brain-damaged individuals. The earliest form of neuropsychological assessment was actually performed by physicians rather than by psychologists, having its origin with the European neurologists Wernicke, Broca, and Dax in the mid 1800s (Golden 1981). The profession of clinical neuropsychology is a much more recent development.

Influence of Localization Theory

The prevailing spirit of neurologic investigation at that time was the theory of localization. Localization theory posited that individual behaviors could be strictly associated to a specific neurologic substrate and that injury to particular areas of the brain resulted in specific behavioral sequelae. The subjects of assessment were those individuals who were unfortunate enough to receive an acquired form of brain impairment such as a cerebral vascular accident or trauma to the head. The method of assessment in these early days was to uncover the behavioral deficit caused by the damage. Later, at autopsy, the behavioral deficit or deficits could be correlated with the location of the lesion. This form of assessment merely required that a deficit be demonstrated; thus only a dichotomous form of information-impaired or nonimpaired was needed. Generally, the performance of a subject on behavioral tasks was compared against informal, internal expectations or norms that the clinician had acquired through clinical experience. Because the information requested from an adherent of localization theory was qualitative (whether or not there was brain damage and the most likely site of the damage), there was no apparent need to quantify the results.

The Influence of Equipotentiality Theory

The next major neuropsychological theory to gain currency was equipotentiality, which directly opposed localization theory. The name most often associated with equipotentiality theory is that of Karl Lashley (1947), although the earlier work of Flourens (1824) helped set the stage. Lashley (1947) held that each area of the brain performed a given function, but that all areas of the brain had equal potential to perform every task for which the brain was ultimately responsible. He found that the region of the brain ablated had a weaker relation to the type and amount of deficit manifested than did the amount of brain mass destroyed. The major problem with generalizing these results to the human brain was and still is the anatomic differences between the rat brain and human brain. The rat brain lacks the development of the neocortex seen in humans and in other "higher" mammals. Also, structurally, the human brain appears more differentiated than the rat brain.

Despite these problems in transferring knowledge gained through research with rats to the human brain, the work of Lashley had an enormous influence on neuropsychological theory. His work also had a large, albeit indirect, influence on neuropsychological assessment as practiced at that time.

Because it was assumed that brain tissue was equipotential, it was further assumed that all brain injuries had similar clinical presentations. This notion was contained in the unitary construct or organicity so popular during the early and middle 1900s (Goldstein 1948). It was felt that a single test for organicity could diagnose most instances of brain damage regardless of the site, etiology, or extent of the impairment. Once again, dichotomous information was requested. However, now the information requested was whether the patient was "organic" or "functional." This development in neuropsychological assessment did not occur under the solitary influence of Lashley's theory. Another influence was the rise of optimism regarding the efficacy of treatment for the functionally impaired patient coupled with pessimism regarding the effectiveness of any treatment for patients with neurologic disorders.

The Need for Discrimination Between Functional and Organic Disorders

Functional and organic patients (or in current nomenclature, psychiatric and neurologic patients) can have very similar clinical presentations. Early neuropsychiatrists needed a method that would allow them to distinguish psychiatric patients, for whom the new weapons of humane treatment and psychological therapies could constitute treatment modalities, from organic patients, for whom these treatments would be relatively ineffective. Also at this time, psychologists were being attracted away from their academic laboratories and into clinical settings. The war effort of the U.S. government during World War II played no small role in this transformation; a significant number of psychologists with training in experimental psychology were pressed into service to assist medical professionals in assessing injuries obtained on the battlefield. Consistent with their academic and research backgrounds, these psychologists began to introduce psychometric testing into clinical settings. Until this time, assessment of a patient consisted of informal interviews and bedside procedures. The psychologists brought the rigor of experimental measurement and psychometric theory to the problem of measuring the kind and degree of mental activity present in the patient who had suffered damage to the central nervous system.

Transformation of Laboratory Tasks into Clinical Tools

In this environment, laboratory tasks were transformed into instruments that could meet the needs of the assessor. For example, tasks of visual-motor integration were used as components in the Bender-Gestalt Test, a common test of "organicity" at that time. Sometimes, a procedure would end up with an entirely different purpose than for which it was originally designed. This was the case with the Rorschach Ink Blot Test. The Rorschach was originally designed as a method of assessing the visual-perceptual integrity of a subject and was thus intended as a method of indicating the presence of organic impairment. However, it was not long before the inkblot technique was put to a much different use as a projective psychological test. More often, a laboratory task was adapted to serve a purpose in the clinical setting that was similar to the purpose it served in the research setting. Another example of the trend for laboratory tasks to be incorporated into clinical procedures was the development and use of the Wechsler Memory Scale. This test was originally designed as a global test of brain dysfunction but has since been utilized more specifically as a measure of memory.

The Wechsler Memory Scale. Following his success with the development of the Bellevue-Wechsler Intelligence Scale—later known after revision as the Wechsler Adult Intelligence Scale-Revised (WAIS-R)—David Wechsler (1945) attempted to meld laboratory procedures with clinical methods. Wechsler extracted tasks that were widely used in laboratory evaluations of memory. He standardized these procedures and provided normative information against which the performance of a single subject could be judged. He scaled the scores such that the mean performance was equal to 100 and 1 standard deviation was equal to 15, making the score similar to the scores provided by the Wechsler-Bellevue Intelligence Scale. Wechsler's thinking was that if the memory quotient (MQ) score was more than 1 standard deviation lower than the intelligence quotient (IQ), this would constitute evidence of organic impairment. He reasoned that a person of average intelligence should also possess average memory. A relatively poorer memory scale score would therefore indicate that something had happened to impair memory. Using similar logic, the proponents of the Bender-Gestalt Test pro-

posed that impaired performance in copying geometric designs indicated the presence of organic impairment.

Both of these notions rely on an implication of equipotentiality theory, which posits that physical damage to the brain results in nonspecific behavioral impairment. The developers of the Wechsler Memory Scale were seemingly asserting that all brain damage would, in fact, impair memory. The users of the Bender-Gestalt Test were depending upon brain damage always to impair some part of the complex task of accurately perceiving and reproducing geometric designs. As might be expected, the use of these tests results in a high rate of false negatives, especially in the case of focal brain damage, which might have highly specific effects not tapped by the particular tasks. However, these tests enjoyed popularity for a long period of time and, unfortunately, are still employed as measures of "organicity." These tests could be administered and interpreted by the general clinical psychologist, and they provided the type of information that was typically requested—the binary decision of "organic" versus "functional" impairment.

Although no other single function tests were to enjoy as much popularity as the Wechsler Memory Scale and the Bender-Gestalt Test, there has since been the development of a plethora of screening instruments based on the same concept of the nonspecific effects of brain damage. Although these instruments continued to remain popular in clinical settings, research conducted in experimental neuropsychological settings began to reflect a return to aspects of localization theory in the mid-1900s. At approximately the same time, medical neurologists and neurosurgeons were developing methods of treating structural impairments, especially tumors and cardiovascular accidents. Although their success rates were far from the surgical successes of the present day, they did raise the need for noninvasive techniques to help localize the site of damage. Once again, it was a movement from the laboratory into the clinical setting that provided the impetus for new assessment methods.

The Rise of the Battery Approach

The next era of clinical neuropsychological assessment was ushered in by an experimental neuropsychologist. Ward Halstead (1947) was dissatisfied with the concept of intelligence as measured by the WAIS and the Wechsler Intelligence Scale for Children (WISC). He felt that there were aspects of intelligence that were not tapped by the tests. He called his notion "biological" intelligence and hypothesized that since intelligence was subserved in the brain, we could study its biological substrate by finding tests that were sensitive to brain damage. In his basement laboratory at the University of Chicago, and with the help of the department of neurosurgery at the University of Chicago School of Medicine, Halstead reviewed nearly 3,000 tests in an effort to find those that were most sensitive to brain damage. The eventual collection of 10 tests (plus the WAIS and Minnesota Multiphasic Personality Inventory) were to make up the first standardized neuropsychological battery. Halstead was interested in these tests as useful tools in studying the brain. It was his doctorate student Ralph Reitan, however, who adapted these tests for clinical purposes in his work, first at the Indiana University School of Medicine and later at the University of Washington and the University of Arizona.

The subtests of the Halstead-Reitan Neuropsychological Battery are homogeneous. That is to say, each item in a given test is intended to tap the same skill. It is by isolating the task demands into specific skill requirements and then devising a test for each specific skill that Halstead could accurately assess brain function. Naturally, not all possible skills are represented. Only those tests found to discriminate impaired subjects from nonimpaired subjects were retained in the test battery.

Advantages of the Battery Approach. There were several advantages to using a battery of tests in this way. First, by sampling different areas of brain function, the rate of diagnostic false negatives could be decreased to less than that that occurs with the use of single screening devices like the Bender-Gestalt Test. Second, the evaluation of multiple skills allowed for a differentiation of strengths and weaknesses, or of impaired and intact skills. This also allowed a nondichotomous conception of organicity. The use of numerical scores also allows a description of the relative degree of impairment, as compared to the impaired–nonimpaired dichotomy. Lastly, the uses of a standardized battery approach facilitated the comparison of research results across laboratories.

Since the development of the Halstead-Reitan, we have witnessed the development of other battery approaches, the most commonly used one being the Luria-Nebraska Neuropsychological Battery (LNNB). The LNNB was developed under the influence of Aleksandr Luria's theories of brain organization. Luria posited that all observable behavior was the result of cooperation among multiple brain areas. These areas are organized into functional units. Inability to perform a certain behavior, therefore, could not be related to a lesion in one specific location. Localization, instead, relied on what Luria called qualification of the symptom. This process involved subtle changes in the task demands of what appeared to be similar behaviors. For example, a subject might be asked to read, write from dictation, write from visual stimuli, and repeat the same word to qualify what aspect of the behavior of producing the word was impaired. For this reason, the subtests of the LNNB are not homogeneous in the same way as are the subtests of the Halstead-Reitan.

☐ CLINICAL ISSUES IN THE SELECTION AND USE OF NEUROPSYCHOLOGICAL TESTS

As highlighted through the previous discussion, the field of clinical neuropsychology has made tremendous strides over the last several decades. These developments have parallel advances in the medical specialties of psychiatry, neurology, and neurosurgery. At present, a careful neuropsychological evaluation has a great deal to add to the assessment and treatment of brain-injured individuals.

With the development of sophisticated neurodiagnostic techniques such as computed tomography, positron emission tomography, and magnetic resonance imaging, physicians have become increasingly adept at identifying and localizing brain injury. However, these traditional medical procedures, although extremely useful in guiding medical and surgical treatment, do not provide specific information as to the *behavioral* impact of the insult to the brain-injured individual. Modern neuropsychological assessment procedures have developed to fill this gap, and are designed to provide complementary rather than redundant information (Boll 1978).

In general, a thorough neuropsychological evaluation should be structured to provide the following information: (1) to establish the existence of cognitive and behavioral deficits following some form of insult to the brain (i.e., trauma or disease); (2) to provide information on the likely localization of the injury or disease process; (3) to establish the severity or magnitude of the deficits caused by insult to the brain; (4) to establish the remaining strengths and weaknesses of the afflicted individual; (5) to estimate the brain-impaired individual's ability to function within his or her environment (i.e., at work and at home); (6) and to suggest rehabilitation strategies to help the brain-impaired person recover optimally.

Determining the Presence of Organic Impairment

The question of whether deficits exist following brain insult transcends diagnosis of the afflicted individual as "organic," "functional," or "normal" (although this information is often yielded through a careful evaluation of the patient's level of neuropsychological functioning) and seeks to provide information on the behavioral significance of the brain lesion or disease process for the impaired person. This is important because actual response to damage in a particular area of the brain varies from individual to individual due to individual differences in brain organization, educational level, age at time of injury, and a host of other factors. This makes determination of level of functioning based on data obtained via traditional neurologic diagnostic techniques a risky business. However, neuropsychological assessment, with its reliance on the measurement of behavioral skills, is uniquely suited for this activity.

Localization of Impairment

Although modern neurologic procedures often enable accurate evaluations of lesion site, localization of some forms of brain impairment via these techniques is problematic. This is particularly true following mild closed head trauma, metabolic disturbances, or the early stages of progressive neurologic disorders. Neuropsychological assessment is often able to provide hypotheses as to the area of the brain responsible for dysfunction through a careful analysis of test results.

Determination of Severity of Injury

Given that standardized neuropsychological assessment enables comparison of test results with

other populations, statements can be made with regard to severity of deficits based on rigorously obtained objective criteria. This facilitates accurate determination of the level of cognitive dysfunction in a given individual.

Determination of Neuropsychological Strengths and Weaknesses

In all but the most pervasive brain injuries, certain functional abilities are "spared" while some abilities are lost. A thorough neuropsychological evaluation can provide valuable data on remaining abilities and is a prerequisite to making predictions on future adjustment in various environments in which the patient is likely to be placed. The identification of strengths allows suggestions to be made regarding capitalization on these strength areas to compensate for deficits.

Assessment of Ability to Return to Pre-injury Activities

This stage of the assessment process is an extremely important one. Without a careful translation of neuropsychological assessment data into predictions of likely adjustment "in the real world," the brain-impaired individual may be placed in an occupational or other environment in which he or she cannot perform adequately or where there is potential danger to the self or to others. For example, years of heavy alcohol abuse often result in impairment in visual-spatial functioning that may go unnoticed by the patient's family or employer. If an individual with this form of neuropsychological dysfunction is allowed to operate mechanized equipment such as in a factory environment, the individual is likely to make serious errors in judgment that would result in injury.

Rehabilitation Planning

Although the field of cognitive rehabilitation (see Chapter 24) is still in its infancy, and debate still exists as to the extent that brain-damaged individuals can be rehabilitated following serious injury or disease, recent information suggests that rehabilitation of the brain-damaged patient may serve to enhance adjustment to the disability as well as to build new skill areas (Goldstein and Ruthven 1983; Miller 1984). Neuropsychological assessment is essential to rehabilitation planning because it allows a determination of impairment by identifying those areas that need rehabilitation. Additionally, by determining areas of strength, skills on which to build compensatory mechanisms are identified. Finally, assessment can help document progress during the rehabilitation process.

☐ USES OF NEUROPSYCHOLOGICAL TESTING IN NEUROPSYCHIATRIC SETTINGS

Neuropsychological assessment has a variety of practical applications in neuropsychiatric settings, and can provide the physician with very important information with regard to the diagnosis and subsequent treatment of brain-impaired individuals. Accordingly, in the next section of this chapter, we will focus on some of the most useful applications of neuropsychological testing.

Differentiation of Psychiatric Patients from Organic Patients

As mentioned earlier, a major impetus for the development of neuropsychological tests was the need for instruments to help determine whether an individual's symptoms were more likely to have a psychiatric rather than an organic etiology. At the present time, this question remains an important one. Psychiatric patients often present with symptomatology that is suggestive of organic impairment in the absence of corroborative neurodiagnostic evidence. A diagnostic question that is often asked, but is difficult to answer, concerns the differentiation of patients with degenerative neurologic disease (dementia) from patients who suffer from depressive illness (pseudodementia). As is well known, severely depressed individuals often present with symptoms quite similar to those displayed by patients with dementing illness. (Wells 1979, 1982). A careful review of neuropsychological test results combined with consideration of other neurodiagnostic and historical information can often help to resolve this question. For example, although the memory deficits that frequently occur in Alzheimer's patients and in depressed patients seem similar when assessed informally, there are often subtle differences that can be teased out by neuropsychological testing. Impaired short-term memory with relatively nonimpaired long-term

memory is more characteristic of demented than depressed patients. Conversely, depressed patients usually display more uniform memory problems. Psychomotor retardation is also usually associated with pseudodementia but not with organic disease (Wells 1979).

Cerebral Vascular Disorders

Cerebral vascular disorders are often accompanied by changes in cognitive functioning, with disturbances of language being particularly common when the language-dominant (usually left) hemisphere is affected. This is due to the high incidence of cerebral vascular accidents that involve the middle cerebral artery, the artery that nourishes the perisylvian areas of the brain, which are integrally involved in the comprehension and production of speech (Boll 1978; Golden et al. 1983). Neuropsychological assessment procedures can be particularly useful in charting recovery from stroke. Cognitive deficits can be documented during specific phases of recovery, and rehabilitation can be structured in accordance with the patient's current level of functioning. The results of neuropsychological testing can be extremely important in choosing appropriate referral sources, such as speech and physical therapy. Neuropsychological testing can be particularly helpful in documenting cognitive decline in individuals who suffer from cerebral arteriosclerosis.

Neuropsychological Sequelae of Chronic Medical Disorders

Many chronic medical disorders have neurologic and psychiatric sequelae. Conditions such as diabetes mellitus and multiple sclerosis, as well as a host of other congenital or acquired conditions, can cause neuropsychological dysfunction. For example, Turner's syndrome is often accompanied by impairment of visual perception and deficits in attentional processes (McGlone 1985). Determination of the type and severity of neuropsychological deficit is extremely important because early identification of neuropsychological deficits associated with this and other disorders can result in remedial efforts. This can minimize the seriousness of these deficits and promote optimal educational, occupational, and social adjustment.

Determination of Cognitive Deficits Following Head Trauma

Many patients who sustain traumatic injury to the brain manifest neuropsychological difficulties. Deficits such as reduced attention span, impaired ability to process information, and memory problems have been documented even after minor head trauma (Barth et al. 1983). One situation frequently encountered in neuropsychiatric settings is the "frontal lobe syndrome," which often accompanies a blow to the anterior region of the skull (Damasio 1985). In addition to the psychiatric disturbance that often occurs in frontal lobe patients (see Chapter 10), damage to this area of the brain often leads to highly specific cognitive deficits such as lack of judgment, deficits in abstract thinking, concentration problems, and perseveration (Stuss and Benson 1984; Taylor 1981). Neuropsychological testing is often useful in documenting these deficits and in helping to design strategies to help remediate the deficits. The results of neuropsychological testing can also be important in helping the family to adjust to the patient's difficulties (Henry et al., in press; Rosenthal 1984).

Assessment of Recovery Following Surgery

One of the most useful applications of neuropsychological testing is the documentation of cognitive functioning before and after surgical intervention. If neuropsychological assessment is carried out prior to surgery, recovery can be objectively charted at various intervals following the surgical procedure. Serial neuropsychological testing assessment following surgery can establish residual deficits and strengths as well as help to determine the permanency of the disability. This information, in turn, is valuable to the physician in assisting with discharge planning, and can also provide useful information to the family and employer in assuring optimal readjustment to the home or work environment.

Assessment of Learning Disabilities in Children

Until quite recently, children labeled as "learning disabled" were treated more or less as a homogeneous group. Indeed, as late as the 1970s, children who suffered from different types of learning disabilities often received the same form of remedial treatment (Rourke 1985). As our knowledge has grown over the last several decades, this approach to the treatment of the learning disabled child has given way to more sophisticated evaluation strategies. It is now well established that learning disabled children vary in clinical presentation, with some children displaying deficits in the processing of verbal information and some displaying more visually based difficulties (Joschko and Rourke 1985). The proper diagnosis of learning disabilities through neuropsychological testing is extremely important because it promotes the development of remediation programs that are specifically tailored to utilize the relative cognitive strengths of the learning disabled child. Improper diagnosis of neuropsychological functioning can lead to the placement of the child in an inappropriate educational or social environment, which in turn can lead to behavioral and psychiatric disturbances (as is the case when a learning disabled child is placed in a classroom with mentally retarded individuals).

Neuropsychological Functioning and Epilepsy

Psychiatric disturbances have long been associated with epilepsy (Bear and Fedio 1977; Pond and Bidwell 1960; Tizard 1962), although the strength of this relationship has been questioned (Scott 1978; Standage and Fenton 1975). Over the last 30 years, deficits in neuropsychological functioning have also been linked with epileptic conditions, with the type of deficit being influenced by such factors as diagnosis (Fedio and Mirsky 1969; Glowinski 1973; O'Leary et al. 1983) and age at onset of first symptoms (Chelune and Edwards 1981; O'Leary et al. 1981). Neuropsychological testing can help pinpoint individual strengths and weaknesses. Test results can be utilized for educational planning. Neuropsychological testing can also be useful in the discrimination of suspected seizure disorders from psychiatric disorders (Golden et al. 1983). Neuropsychological testing is especially useful when the existence of absence seizures has been suggested because a thorough neuropsychological evaluation allows for a careful assessment of the child's performance under structured conditions.

Vitamin Deficiencies

Patients with severe, chronic malnutrition sometimes present with cognitive dysfunction. Deficiencies in B complex vitamins are most often associated with brain impairment (Lishman 1978). Wernicke's encephalopathy is a condition in which cognitive changes are particularly evident. This condition is most often accompanied by severe disturbance in short-term memory, as in Korsakoff's encephalopathy. Neuropsychological testing can be utilized in several ways. First, a complete neuropsychological evaluation can be helpful in the differentiation of Korsakoff patients from individuals who suffer from degenerative diseases (Golden et al. 1983). It is important to note that the severe memory problems that accompany Korsakoff's encephalopathy often exist in the absence of any measurable intellectual deterioration (Boll 1978). This highlights the danger of utilizing tests of intelligence as indicators of neuropsychological functioning. Second, serial neuropsychological testing can provide information regarding the recovery of cognitive abilities after a period of abstinence from alcohol and thus allow for a more precise prediction of the permanency of the impairment and allow for more effective discharge planning.

☐ CURRENT APPROACHES TO NEUROPSYCHOLOGICAL ASSESSMENT

Lezak (1983) described three major approaches to neuropsychological assessment. However, she herself has stated that two of these approaches, the clinical intuitive approach and the standardized approach, exist only as platonic ideals. Most current practitioners use what she termed "the flexible approach," which falls on a continuum between the other two assessment strategies.

The Clinical Intuitive Approach

The clinical intuitive approach eschews the use of standardized procedures or scoring systems and has much in common with the behavioral neurology tradition of Eastern Europe. The decision regarding which skill areas to assess is made with reference to the present problem and history. Examinations are usually performed at bedside, and procedures may be idiosyncratic to the particular examiner. Scoring is dichotomous (impaired versus nonimpaired) and is conducted by comparison to a set of internal expectations or norms. If a disorder of speech is suspected, assessment is concentrated

to reveal deficits in this area, often to the exclusion of evaluation in other areas of neuropsychological functioning.

Although this approach to assessment has the advantage of flexibility and often requires a minimum of time to complete, the clinical approach relies on subjective interpretation of test data rather than an objective comparison of performance to statistically determined standards or norms. In addition, use of the clinical approach may result in less apparent but significant deficits not being recognized because the assessment procedure has been overly focused on only one problem area. A third disadvantage of the clinical approach is that it may encourage a focus on pinpointing impairment without providing an assessment of relative strengths.

The Standardized Approach

The quantitative or standardized approach to neuropsychological assessment provides an empirically derived criterion for comparing performance to that of nonimpaired individuals. Numerical cutoff scores that allow objective assessment of degree of severity of impairment are provided. However, the standardized approach requires more time than the intuitive approach.

On the other hand, the advantages offered by a standardized battery of tests are several. This approach allows individuals to be studied in a uniform fashion, making possible comparisons among patients with various deficits. When the same set of tests is given uniformly, it allows for psychometric evaluations of the relationships among the component tests. When these relationships are known, it is possible to identify relative strengths and weaknesses in the brain-injured patient. Conversely, when tests that are normed on different samples are given to the same individual, differences across tests might reflect differences in the tested individual or differences in the two samples on which the test was normed. A standardized battery obviates this problem.

The use of a battery approach also allows for pattern analysis of test scores. It is a risky if not foolish endeavor to attempt to localize or diagnose brain impairment simply on the basis of a single identified deficit. However, a combination of two types of deficits combined with evidence of spared abilities in a third skill area often adds valuable information and facilitates proper diagnosis and treatment. For example, the presence of short-term memory problems, word finding difficulties, and the need for verbal cueing, combined with an intact ability to interpret proprioceptive information and intact reading skills may suggest the possibility of Alzheimer's disease in a given individual.

Lastly, the use of a standardized battery also facilitates the application of multivariate statistical techniques to the study of neuropsychological phenomena. Although it is theoretically possible to use multivariate statistics with individual tests, the number of research subjects required would necessitate either extremely long data collection periods or collection of data across more than one site.

The Flexible Approach

The third method of neuropsychological assessment, the flexible approach, is the strategy that most practitioners actually use. There is great variability among the proponents of this approach, with applications ranging from practitioners who start with a fixed battery and then use additional, smaller tests to more specifically address problematic areas, to practitioners who employ a different set of small, individual tests for each client. For example, users of the Halstead-Reitan Neuropsychological Battery often will include one or more allied procedures. At its best, this approach may be said to combine the best features of the standardized approach with the adaptability of the clinical intuitive approach. At its worst, the flexible approach may be no better than either the standardized or intuitive approach.

☐ A SURVEY OF SELECTED NEUROPSYCHOLOGICAL ASSESSMENT INSTRUMENTS

Neuropsychological assessment procedures can consist of a number of smaller individual tests or of larger test battery approaches. There are more than 100 tests that either were designed for the purpose of neuropsychological assessment or have subsequently been used toward that end. In this section, we will review some of the more commonly used instruments as determined by a survey of clinical practice (Hartlage et al. 1981). At present, the two most popular battery approaches to neu-

ropsychological assessment are the Halstead-Reitan Neuropsychological Battery and the Luria-Nebraska Neuropsychological Battery.

The Benton Visual Retention Test

The Benton Visual Retention Test (BVRT) is a short test of visual perception, memory, and construction. As such, there are several types of neuropsychological impairment that might cause deficient performance on this instrument. The BVRT has been used in some settings as a screening device, although it is more properly used as a measure of the integrity of visual constructive processes. There are three sets of 10 cards that are equivalent forms of the test. There are also four different types of administration, depending on the question at issue.

Each of the cards contains an abstract geometrical design. With administration A, the patient is shown the card for 10 seconds, after which the patient is asked to reproduce the design from memory. With administration B, the patient is allowed only 5 seconds to examine the card. With administration C, the patient copies the design while the card is still in view. With administration D, there is a 15-second delay between the examination and reproduction of the design. Norms are available for each of the administrations.

The Bender-Gestalt Visual Motor Test

The Bender-Gestalt has a long history. It was originally devised as a measure of visual-perceptive skills. Lauretta Bender based her instrument on the theories of the Gestalt school of experimental psychology. However, she intended her instrument to be a measure of organicity, to provide an estimate of intellectual level, and to provide a projective measure of psychodynamics. It is best used as a measure of visual construction skills. The Bender-Gestalt consists of a set of cards with geometric designs. The subject is shown the cards and then asked to reproduce them. The Bender-Gestalt is fairly accurate in identifying individuals with visual perceptive or visual constructive impairments. However, it is prone to misidentify schizophrenic individuals as being organically impaired. The Cantor Background Interference Procedure has been found to increase the diagnostic validity of the Bender-Gestalt in neuropsychiatric settings.

The Wechsler Memory Scale

The Wechsler Memory Scale is a collection of six subtests that measure different aspects of memory. However, all but five of the subtests deal with verbally presented material, so it cannot be said to provide a balanced assessment of memory. Similarly, there is no measurement of intermediate memory, of incidental memory, or of memory with interference. However, the Wechsler Memory Scale does measure some aspects of long-term memory and of memory for a list of words, pairs of words, a short story, and serial digits. It is best used as a screening device only for memory problems, which can then be followed up by a more detailed assessment of memory processes.

The Wechsler Adult Intelligence Scale—Revised and Wechsler Intelligence Scale for Children— Revised

The WAIS-R and WISC-R are similar in structure. They differ in content and in normative referents. Both are composed of subtests that are divided into Performance and Verbal scales. The subscales reflect what David Wechsler considered to be the components of intelligence. The raw scores of the subscales are transformed into scaled scores with a mean of 10 and a standard deviation of 3 points. These subscale scores are then summed into Verbal and Performance scores and then transformed into IQ. The IQs derived from the Wechsler tests are deviations from the estimated population average. The average is assigned a score of 100 and the value of 1 standard deviation is 15 points. Currently, controversy exists concerning the use of the WAIS-R and WISC-R to diagnose acquired brain impairment on the basis of either the Verbal-Performance split or the scatter of scores among subscales. However, the information derived from the use of these instruments can be useful in describing the current level of standard intelligence in subjects.

The Halstead-Reitan Neuropsychological Battery

The Halstead-Reitan Neuropsychological Test Battery for Adults consists of 13 tests and is designed to be employed with persons 15 years of age or older. This battery was originally developed by Ward Halstead in 1949 and has since been modified by Reitan (1955), a student of Halstead's.

For the *Tactual Performance* test, the patient is blindfolded and instructed to place blocks of various shapes in a form board. This test assesses tactile recognition, motor speed, and the ability to form a visual "map." Time, Memory, and Localization scores are derived. The *Category* test requires the patient to choose a number between 1 and 4 that reminds the patient of designs that are projected on an opaque screen via a slide projector. The test is comprised of 208 such designs. The Category test is a measure of new learning and of mental efficiency. The *Speech Sounds Perception* test is made up of 60 groups of four "nonsense syllables" that are played on a tape recorder. The patient is instructed to match and identify the correct sound on a response sheet. This test provides a measure of auditory-verbal perception. The *Rhythm* test requires the patient to determine whether 30 pairs of rhythmic beats are the same or are different from each other. This test is a measure of attention/concentration and of nonverbal auditory discrimination. The *Finger Tapping* test measures the ability of the patient to depress a lever with his or her index finger as rapidly as possible. A score for each hand is recorded and is used as a basis of comparing motor speed for both sides of the body.

From scores obtained on these individual tests, an Impairment index can be calculated to yield a general indication of level of brain dysfunction. A number of allied procedures such as a sensory-perceptual examination, the Wechsler Memory Scale, and the WAIS-R are often employed in conjunction with the standard procedures. Downward extension of the Halstead-Reitan Neuropsychological Battery is available for children aged 5 to 8 and another procedure has been standardized for use with children aged 9 to 14. The test data are organized in terms of four "methods of inference" devised by Reitan (1967) to facilitate organization of diverse test results.

Methods of Inference. Analysis of level of performance is no doubt the most widely used method of inference employed by psychologists in the interpretation of psychological tests. It involves an assessment of how an individual performs on the test measure. This assessment is made by comparing test performance to that of a normative population. Analysis of level of performance data does not, in and of itself, provide an adequate assessment of brain impairment, but is a starting point in the evaluation process.

As the name implies, evaluation of patterns of scores on different tests and subtests involves going beyond analysis of level of performance data to consider specific relationships between obtained test scores. For example, impaired expressive speech capacity in the presence of intact receptive speech skills is interpreted as reflecting a different process than is impairment in both skill areas. This approach to neuropsychological assessment has the advantage of highlighting specific areas of preserved functioning as well as areas that have been affected by injury to the brain.

Evaluation of specific behavioral deficits or pathognomonic signs represents an assessment of performance on test items that, when failed, almost always indicate brain impairment. Inability to copy or to draw a simple object is an example of a test item that is almost never missed by individuals without brain injuries. Similarly, visual field defects are also quite rare in individuals whose neuropsychological functioning is intact.

Finally, evaluation of differences in motor and sensory functioning of both sides of the body is the fourth method of inference recommended by Reitan (1967). This level of analysis relies on evaluation of test performance on tasks that require intact abilities in the area of tactile and motor functioning and are often useful in lateralization of a brain lesion to one side of the body.

The Halstead-Reitan Neuropsychological Battery represents a popular and useful approach to neuropsychological assessment. However, there are several drawbacks to the use of this test battery. First of all, the battery requires up to 2 full days to administer and hence is difficult to use in general medical settings where the patient must remain under the constant attention of medical professionals. The equipment required to complete this examination is also quite bulky and is not easily adapted for inpatient testing. Another criticism of the Halstead-Reitan is that the individual tasks that make up the battery do not yield test scores that are directly comparable to each other. Lastly, although provisional norms exist for the evaluation of test performance with regard to the age of the patient, this battery does not allow adjustment for the educational level.

The Luria-Nebraska Neuropsychological Battery

The LNNB (Golden et al. 1982) consists of 14 scales that provide information on motor, tactile, auditory (rhythm), visual, memory, and intellectual functioning as well as assessment of receptive and ex-

pressive language abilities. The inclusion of writing, reading, and arithmetic scales allows for the assessment of educationally related skills.

The *Motor* scale assesses a variety of abilities, including motor speed, coordination, oral motor movement, the ability to respond motorically to verbal and nonverbal instructions, and visual constructive functioning. The *Rhythm* scale evaluates perception and discrimination of rhythm and pitch and also provides a measure of attentional processes. The patient is required to perform such tasks as to identify rhythmic patterns played on a tape recorder as being the same or different, to count a series of beeps, to identify pitch relationships between tones, and to generate rhythmic patterns from verbal description. The *Tactile* scale provides an evaluation of a variety of tactile and kinesthetic skills. The patient is blindfolded throughout the administration of the entire scale. Scale items include tasks that require discrimination of sharp and dull sensations on the hand, the localization of touch on various parts of the body, the identification of verbal and nonverbal symbols traced on the wrist (graphesthesia), and the tactile identification of objects placed in the hand (stereognosis). The *Visual* scale is designed to provide measures of both visual and spatial processes. This scale is composed of tasks that assess the patient's capacity to recognize common objects, to identify objects in a line drawing that are overlapping, to integrate various forms within a larger "gestalt," to identify times from clock faces, to count three-dimensional piles of blocks, and mentally to rotate geometric objects in space.

The *Receptive Speech* scale assesses the patient's ability to understand spoken language. Scale items include simple collections of phonemes, words, and sentences that the patient is required to repeat and reproduce in written form, items that require the patient to follow instructions, tasks that involve the comprehension of logical relationships, and inverted grammatical structure. The *Expressive Speech* scale evaluates the patient's oral expressive speech ability. This includes the repetition of phonemes, words, and sentences, naming from pictures, naming from verbal description, narration of a story from a picture, the "unscrambling" of a number of words to form a sentence, and the construction of a sentence using three words that are given to the patient. The *Writing* scale evaluates basic writing skills and involves the copying of letters from cards, writing one's name, writing from dictation, and writing on a specified topic in 60 seconds. The *Reading* scale requires the patient to read individual letters, syllables, words, sentences, and a short story. The *Arithmetic* scale involves number identification, simple algebraic operations, number comparison, and serial subtraction tasks. The *Memory* scale is composed of a variety of verbal and nonverbal memory tasks. These tasks include the memorization of a list of seven words in five trials, the memorization of both verbal and nonverbal material under conditions of interference from extraneous stimuli, the memorization of rhythmic pattern, the memorization of a series of hand gestures, and a paired associate learning task in which the patient is required to associate a word with a particular picture. Form II of the Luria-Nebraska also includes an *Intermediate Memory* scale that is composed of items taken from the other clinical scales. This scale is administered immediately following the other clinical scales and is better considered as a test of delayed memory with interference rather than a test of intermediate memory. Finally, the *Intellectual* scale provides a measure of the patient's intellectual level and includes items similar to those included in standard tests of intellectual functioning, such as the WAIS-R.

In addition to the basic scale scores listed above, the LNNB also provides localization scores, and factor scores that allow more exact identification of deficit areas. The LNNB also yields information on strength areas. This test battery has the advantage of requiring only 2 to 4 hours to administer. The LNNB provides cutoffs for identifying brain impairment, adjusted for both the patient's age and educational background. This allows for a more sensitive appraisal of impairment, relatively free of these extraneous factors. Finally, LNNB raw scores are converted to scale scores (T-scores), which allow for direct comparison between scales.

Levels of Interpretation. Similar to the "methods of inference" developed by Reitan (1967), Golden et al. (1980) have suggested a multilevel approach to interpretation of the LNNB.

The strategy of analysis of the original 14 scales of the test allows a relatively quick assessment of the likelihood of brain impairment, employing empirically derived "hit rates." This strategy also represents the first step in the overall interpretive scheme.

Analysis of localization scales provides useful information concerning localization of brain impairment in the cerebral hemispheres and involves

evaluation of scores on clusters of test items that were found empirically to be indicative of brain dysfunction in the frontal, temporal, and parietal-occipital regions of the brain. Scores are provided on these scales for both left and right hemispheres.

Assessment of factor scales involves the evaluation of 30 scale scores developed through separate factor analyses that further divide the original 14 scales into more basic skill areas (McKay and Golden 1981). Analysis of the factor scales of the LNNB facilitates pattern analysis of skills.

Item analysis involves the reanalysis of interpretative information gleaned from the other methods of evaluation in light of performance on the individual test items. This level of analysis involves an evaluation of strengths and weaknesses at the most basic skill level and is often instrumental in helping to determine rehabilitation strategies that will exploit the individual's preserved abilities.

Finally, qualitative analysis of performance focuses on how the test item was performed rather than on whether the items were performed correctly and can provide valuable information that is often overlooked when concentrating on quantitative information. Evaluation of how a given task is performed often yields important cues as to how an individual has compensated (or has not compensated) for an injury. For example, knowing that an impaired person can complete a nonverbal sequential task only by using verbal cues to guide performance might be particularly important in helping that individual adjust to his or her home or work environment.

It must be emphasized that a thorough neuropsychological evaluation should not only involve analysis of data from the five methods described above but should also rely on supportive historical data on premorbid level of functioning in a variety of areas. Because most individuals who sustain injury to the brain have not been evaluated neuropsychologically prior to their injury, the neuropsychologist must frequently rely on less precise data to ascertain the severity of behavioral compromise. Investigation into the highest level of educational achievement and into the level of functioning at work are likely to provide the best estimates of premorbid functioning.

□ REFERENCES

Barth JT, Macciocchi SN, Giordani B, et al: Neuropsychological sequelae of minor head injury. Neurosurgery 13:529–533, 1983

Bear DM, Fedio P: Quantitative analysis of interictal behavior in temporal lobe epilepsy. Arch Neurol 34:454–467, 1977

Boll TJ: Diagnosing brain impairment, in Clinical Diagnosis of Mental Disorders. Edited by Wolman B. New York, Plenum, 1978

Chelune GJ, Edwards P: Early brain lesions: ontogenetic-environmental considerations. J Consult Clin Psychol 49:777–790, 1981

Costa L: Clinical neuropsychology: a discipline in evolution. Journal of Clinical Neuropsychology 5:1–11, 1983

Damasio AR: The frontal lobes, in Clinical Neuropsychology, 2nd ed. Edited by Heilman KM, Valenstein E. New York, Oxford University Press, 1985

Fedio P, Mirsky AF: Selective intellectual deficits in children with temporal lobe or centrencephalic epilepsy. Neuropsychologia 7:287–300, 1969

Flourens P: Recherches Experimentales sur les proprietes et les fonctions du systeme nerveux dans les animaux vertebres. Paris, Crevot, 1824

Glowinski H: Cognitive deficits in temporal lobe epilepsy. J Nerv Ment Dis 171:624–629, 1973

Golden CJ: Diagnosis and Rehabilitation in Clinical Neuropsychology, 2nd ed. Springfield, Ill, Charles C Thomas, 1981

Golden CJ, Ariel RN, McKay SE, et al: The Luria-Nebraska Neuropsychological Battery: theoretical orientation and comment. J Consult Clin Psychol 50:291–300, 1982

Golden CJ, Hammeke T, Purisch A: The Luria-Nebraska Neuropsychological Battery: Manual, rev ed. Los Angeles, Western Psychological Services, 1980

Golden CJ, Moses JA, Coffman JA, et al: Clinical Neuropsychology: Interface with Neurologic and Psychiatric Disorders. New York, Grune and Stratton, 1983

Goldstein G, Ruthven L: Rehabilitation of the Brain Damaged Adult. New York, Plenum, 1983

Goldstein K: Language and Language Disturbances. New York, Grune and Stratton, 1948

Halstead WC: Brain and Intelligence: A Quantitative Study of the Frontal Lobes. Chicago, University of Chicago Press, 1947

Hartlage LC, Chelune G, Tucker D: Survey of professional issues in the practice of clinical neuropsychology. Presented at the Annual Meeting of the American Psychological Association, Los Angeles, 1981

Henry PW, Knippa J, Golden CJ: A systems model for therapy with brain injured adults and their families. Family Systems in Medicine (in press)

Joschko M, Rourke BF: Neuropsychological subtypes of learning disabled children who exhibit the ACID pattern on the WISC, in Neuropsychology of Learning Disabilities. Edited by Rourke BP. New York, Guilford, 1985

Lashley KS: Brain Mechanisms and Intelligence. Chicago, University of Chicago Press, 1947

Lezak MD: An individualized approach to neuropsychological assessment, in Clinical Neuropsychology: A Multidisciplinary Approach. Edited by Logue PE, Schear JM. Springfield Ill, Charles C Thomas, 1983

Lishman WA: Organic Psychiatry: The Psychological Consequences of Cerebral Disorder. Oxford, Blackwell Scientific, 1978

McGlone J: Can spatial deficits in Turner's syndrome be explained by focal CNS dysfunction or atypical speech lateralization? J Clin Exp Neuropsychol 7:375–394, 1985

McKay SE, Golden CJ: The assessment of specific neuropsychological skills using scales derived from factor analysis of the Luria-Nebraska Neuropsychological Battery. Int J Neurosci 14:189–194, 1981

Miller E: Recovery and Management of Neuropsychological Impairments. New York, Wiley, 1984

O'Leary DS, Lovell MR, Sackellares JC, et al: Effects of age at onset of partial and generalized seizures on neuropsychological performance in children. J Nerv Ment Dis 22:197–204, 1983

O'Leary DS, Seidenberg M, Berent S, et al: Effects of age at onset of tonic clonic seizures in neuropsychological performance in children. Epilepsia 22:197–204, 1981

Pond DA, Bidwell BH: A survey of epilepsy in fourteen general practices, II: social and psychological aspects. Epilepsia 1:282–289, 1960

Reitan RM: Investigation of the validity of Halstead's measure of biological intelligence. Archives of Neurology and Psychiatry 77:134–139, 1955

Reitan RM: Psychological assessment of deficits associated with brain lesions in subjects with normal and subnormal intelligence, in Brain Damage and Mental Retardation: A Psychological Evaluation. Edited by Khanna JL. Springfield, Ill, Charles C Thomas, 1967

Rosenthal M: Strategies for intervention with families of brain impaired patients, in Behavioral Assessment and Rehabilitation of the Traumatically Brain-Injured. Edited by Edelstein BA, Couture ET. New York, Plenum, 1984

Rourke BP: Overview of learning disability subtypes, in Neuropsychology of Learning Disabilities. Edited by Rourke BP. New York, Guilford, 1985

Scott DF: Psychiatric aspects of epilepsy. Br J Psychiatry 132:417–430, 1978

Standage KF, Fenton GW: Psychiatric symptom profiles of patients with epilepsy: a controlled investigation. Psychol Med 5:152–160, 1975

Stuss DT, Benson DF: Neuropsychological studies of the frontal lobes. Psychol Bull 95:3–28, 1984

Taylor MA: The Neuropsychiatric Mental Status Examination. Jamaica, NY, Spectrum, 1981

Tizard B: The personality of epileptics: a discussion of the evidence. Psychol Bull 59:196–210, 1962

Wechsler D: The Wechsler Memory Scale. New York, Psychological Corporation, 1945

Wells CE: Pseudodementia. Am J Psychiatry 136:895–900, 1979

Wells CE: Pseudodementia and the recognition of organicity, in Psychiatric Aspects of Neurologic Disease. Edited by Benson DF, Blumer D. New York, Grune and Stratton, 1982

Chapter 4

An Overview of Neurotransmitters and Neuroreceptors

Martha B. Martin, M.D.
Cynthia M. Owen, M.A.
John M. Morihisa, M.D.

THE FORTUITOUS DISCOVERY of effective psychotropic medications began in the 1950s. Chlorpromazine was originally developed as an antihistamine and was found to be particularly effective in calming agitated, psychotic patients. Efforts to find increasingly effective antitubercular drugs led to the discovery of monoamine oxidase (MAO) inhibitors. Although not effective against tuberculosis, these agents were found to be useful in treating depression. The chance discovery of these and other psychotropic drugs prompted investigations concerned with delineating their mechanisms of action. The results of such studies have generally supported the notion that psychotropic drugs exert their effects by altering specific chemical processes involved in neuronal communication. Accordingly, basic research efforts in psychopharmacology have zealously pursued the identification of neurotrans-

mitter substances, the characterization of neuroreceptors, and the mapping of neuronal systems ("neurochemical pathways"), that utilize a given neurotransmitter. The observed association between psychotropic drug effects and alterations in neurotransmitter processes has also had profound effects on clinical research in psychiatry. Over the past three decades, a number of hypotheses that propose various aspects of disordered neurotransmission as etiologic factors in psychiatric illness have been formulated. Investigations of such hypotheses influence the current therapeutic regimes applied to psychiatric patients and contribute to the ongoing refinement of psychotropic medications.

Rapid advances in the areas of neurotransmitter and neuroreceptor research contribute to the theoretical foundations on which psychiatrists must base their clinical use of psychotropic medications. Therefore, the purpose of this chapter is to provide the clinician with an overview of recent research in these areas. Our purpose is to highlight classic neurochemical hypotheses of psychiatric illness as well as current research directions, thus providing the groundwork from which readers can pursue further examination of this important aspect of psychiatry. We will first review general aspects of neurotransmitters and neuroreceptors, focusing on the anatomy and physiology of the synapse, general principles of neurotransmission, and the research strategies used in investigations in this field. Then we will consider the theories of disordered neurotransmission associated with each of the major psychiatric illnesses. We will begin with an overview of schizophrenia, focusing on a critical review of the potential role of dopamine in this disorder. We will then look at the affective disorders, with particular attention to a discussion of the monoamine hypothesis, examining the proposed etiologic roles of norepinephrine and serotonin in these disorders. The evidence regarding involvement of various neurotransmitters and receptors in the anxiety disorders will be reviewed next, looking specifically at panic attacks and generalized anxiety disorder. Finally, we will conclude with cognitive disorders, focusing on the putative role of derangements in the cholinergic system in the Alzheimer's type of dementia.

☐ GENERAL

Fundamentals of Neurotransmission

The functional building block of the central nervous system (CNS) is the synaptic unit. The synaptic unit consists of two neurons (the *pre*synaptic and the *post*synaptic neurons) and the specialized area of functional contact between the two neurons, known as the synapse. The term *synapse* derives from the Greek word *synapto*, meaning "to clasp," and was coined by Sir Charles Sherrington in 1897 to describe the junctional areas between neurons that he observed with the light microscope.

Each neuron of the synaptic unit consists of three compartments: the *cell body*, the fine tubular extensions from the cell body called *dendrites*, and a single tubular projection known as the *axon*. The synaptic unit and the three structural components of neurons are shown in Figure 1. The cell body of the neuron contains the nucleus and ribosomes, that is, the cellular apparatus needed for synthesizing protein materials. The structural and metabolic materials needed by the neuron are thus manufactured in the cell body and transported, as necessary, to the dendrites and axon. The functional role of the axon is to carry electrical impulses away from the cell body toward the synaptic junction between the pre- and postsynaptic neurons. The length of the axon depends on the type and location of the neuron, and it *may* branch at the end to make synaptic contact with more than one neuron. The axon terminates closely opposed to the postsynaptic neuron in a swelling called the nerve terminal or *terminal bouton* (see Figure 1). Many axons terminate adjacent to a dendrite of the postsynaptic neuron, and such synapses are termed *axodendritic*. Dendrites, therefore, function as the primary receptive structures of neuronal communication. It should be noted, however, that axons can also form synaptic connections with other axons (axoaxonic synapses) as well as with the cell bodies of other neurons (axosomatic synapses).

Communication between the two neurons of a synaptic unit involves a combination of bioelectrical and chemical processes. The bioelectrical processes depend partly on properties of the neuron's cell membrane. This membrane shows selective permeability to various ions and contains energy-dependent ion pumps that transport ions across the membrane against their concentration gradients. As a result of these properties, there is a voltage difference maintained across the membrane of an inactive or "resting" neuron. This voltage difference is approximately -70 millivolts (inside of neuron is negative with respect to outside) and is called the resting potential. Incoming stimuli from other neurons can locally influence the membrane's permeability to ions so as to decrease the resting voltage difference. If such a depolarization reaches a threshold level, an action potential is generated. An action potential is a self-limiting event in which the rapid influx of sodium ions temporarily reverses the polarity of the membrane. In the action potential, a series of depolarizations moves along the membrane and down the axon toward the synapse. Propagation of the action potential down the axon can reach extraordinary velocities when the axon is encased in an insulating covering called a myelin sheath. When an action potential reaches the axon's terminal bouton, it causes the release of a chemical messenger, the neurotrans-

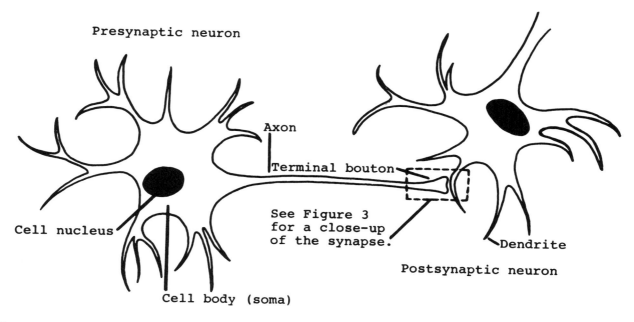

Figure 1. Synaptic connection between two neurons. Neurotransmitter precursors are commonly synthesized in the cell body of the presynaptic neuron and transported down the axon to the terminal bouton where they are produced and stored in vesicles. An action potential traveling down the axon causes release of the neurotransmitter into the narrow space between the two neurons, the synaptic cleft. Many axons terminate adjacent to dendrites of the postsynaptic neuron, as shown here. This is known as an axodendritic synapse. Some axons terminate on the postsynaptic cell body (axosomatic synapses), and others terminate on other axons (axoaxonic synapses).

mitter, into the synaptic cleft. The neurotransmitter diffuses across the cleft and binds to specialized receptor sites on the postsynaptic membrane (see Figure 2). The receptor "translates" the information encoded in the neurotransmitter molecule and initiates a physiologic response in the postsynaptic neuron.

To summarize, neurotransmission depends on electrochemical events and chemical messengers. Information is transmitted across the presynaptic neuron as a series of electrochemical events known as action potentials. The transfer of information between neurons, that is, from pre- to postsynaptic neuron, depends on chemical messengers known as neurotransmitters.

Neurotransmitters

In 1921, Otto Loewi performed a classic experiment in which he electrically stimulated the vagus nerve of a frog's heart and found that this stimulation could arrest the beat of a second heart that was being transfused with ventricular fluid from the first. This experiment offered the first evidence of chemically mediated neurotransmission. Loewi named this inhibitory chemical released from the vagus nerve *vagusstoff*, a substance later identified as acetylcholine.

To be designated as a neurotransmitter, a substance must satisfy a number of criteria (see Table 1). Investigations utilizing these criteria for putative transmitters in the brain represent a difficult task. Nevertheless, many putative neurotransmitters have been identified in the brain thus far, and it is possible that these represent only a small percentage of the actual number of neurotransmitters used in the brain. Table 2 lists a number of putative neurotransmitters. As shown in Table 2, the putative neurotransmitters fall into one of three general categories: (1) amino acids, (2) biogenic amines, and (3) neuropeptides.

Neurons are generally thought to synthesize and use only one neurotransmitter, although Coyle (1985a) pointed out that exceptions to this principle are currently emerging. Neurons that utilize the same neurotransmitter are grouped together in the brain, forming neurochemical systems that are thought to serve distinct functions. An example of

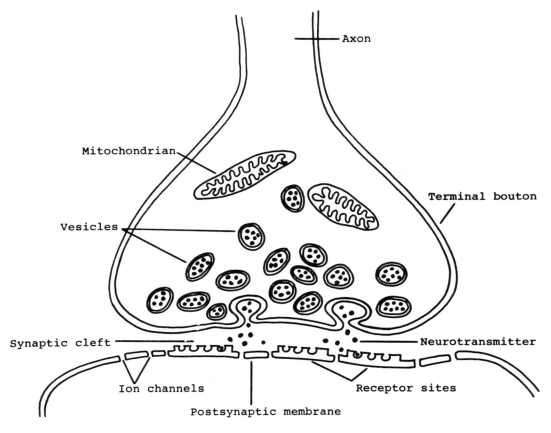

Figure 2. Close-up of a synapse. Molecules of neurotransmitter are enclosed in vesicles in the terminal bouton of the axon. Two vesicles are shown fused to the presynaptic membrane, releasing neurotransmitter into the synaptic cleft. The neurotransmitter initiates activity in the postsynaptic neuron by binding to receptor sites in the postsynaptic membrane. See Figure 3 for a schematic close-up of the receptor site.

TABLE 1. NEUROTRANSMITTER CRITERIA

1. Substance must be concentrated in the presynaptic nerve terminal.
2. Substance must be released when a depolarizing stimulus is applied to the neuron.
3. Neuron must have the necessary enzyme systems for synthesizing the putative neurotransmitter.
4. Effects on the postsynaptic receptor should be the same whether the putative neurotransmitter is released from the presynaptic neuron or applied exogenously.
5. Known antagonists of the postsynaptic receptor should block the effects caused by exogenous application of the putative neurotransmitter, as well as the effects caused by presynaptic release of the putative neurotransmitter.
6. There must be mechanism for inactivating the putative neurotransmitter after its release from the presynaptic nerve terminal (e.g., a catabolic enzyme system or an active reuptake mechanism).

---

such a neurochemical system is the nigrostriatal tract, which has cell bodies in the substantia nigra and innervates areas of the basal ganglia. These neurons utilize dopamine as their neurotransmitter and seem to function as a distinct system for coordinating fine motor control. Localizing neurochemical pathways in the brain depends on histochemical methods for detecting neurotransmitters or their metabolic enzymes—these methods include the use of fluorescence techniques, neurotoxins, and specific antibodies—as well as on autoradiographic techniques for visualizing neuroreceptors. Determining the functional roles of these pathways is an even more difficult and elusive task that relies heavily on inferences drawn from lesioning and pharmacologic studies in animals.

Neurotransmitters are generally synthesized in the cell body of the neuron, packaged in vesicles,

---

TABLE 2.   PUTATIVE CNS NEUROTRANSMITTERS

I. *Amino Acids*
  A. Excitatory
    1. Glutamic acid
    2. Aspartic acid
  B. Inhibitory
    1. Gamma-aminobutyric acid
II. *Biogenic Amines*
  A. Catecholamines
    1. Dopamine
    2. Norepinephrine
    3. Epinephrine
  B. Acetylcholine
  C. Histamine
  D. Indoleamines
    1. Serotonin
III. *Neuropeptides*
  A. Beta-endorphin
  B. Cholecystokinin
  C. Somatostatin
  D. Substance-P
  E. Vasopressin
  F. Neurotensin

---

and transported down the axon for storage in the nerve terminal. In some cases, one or more synthetic steps may occur within the vesicle or within the nerve terminal. Many neurons have reuptake mechanisms for transporting the neurotransmitter back into the presynaptic terminal after release. (In the case of cholinergic neurons, the reuptake mechanism transports choline, the precursor of acetylcholine, back into the nerve terminal.) This recycling capability allows the neuron to function during periods of sustained firing without continual de novo synthesis of neurotransmitter.

Receptors

As noted above, receptors on the postsynaptic membrane bind the neurotransmitter released from the presynaptic neuron, translate the neurotransmitter's message, and affect an appropriate physiologic response in the postsynaptic neuron. Although the scope of this chapter does not permit a detailed discussion of these specialized membrane structures, a few general principles merit discussion. Receptors are generally supramolecular, proteinaceous structures with two functional components: the *recognition site* and the *transducer site*. The recognition site is located on the external surface of the neuronal membrane. Its specific configuration allows for high affinity binding of its associated neurotransmitter. Exogenous agonists

and antagonists of the receptor will compete with the neurotransmitter for occupation of the recognition site. By definition, receptor agonists will mimic the effects of the endogenous ligand (the neurotransmitter), and receptor antagonists will block binding of the neurotransmitter, thus preventing its effect. Neurotransmitter occupation of the recognition site activates the transducer site of the receptor, which, in turn, initiates the physiologic response. Molecular components of the transducer are thought to be located within the neuronal membrane and on its inner surface. There appear to be two general types of transducers. One directly regulates the size of ion pores in the membrane, thus affecting membrane permeability and the electrochemical excitability of the neuron. The other type seems to initiate enzymatic changes in the neuron via activation of a so-called "second messenger" such as a cyclic nucleotide. The receptor and its components are depicted in Figure 3.

Pharmacologic studies have revealed more than one type of receptor for some neurotransmitters. For example, two types of dopamine receptors, D_1 and D_2, have been identified. D_1 receptors appear to activate adenylate cyclase activity. D_2 receptors are labeled by tritiated butyrophenones and seem to inhibit adenylate cyclase. In sum, there appear to be multiple receptors for certain neurotransmitters, and their different natures are characterized by different ligand affinities and/or different pharmacological effects.

Action of Psychotropic Drugs

Psychotropic drugs can exert their effects by augmenting or by diminishing the action of a given neurotransmitter at the synapse via one of several mechanisms of action: (1) by affecting the *enzymes* that are involved in the synthesis or breakdown of the neurotransmitter, (2) by affecting *storage* or *reuptake* of the neurotransmitter, or (3) by affecting the *receptor site* to enhance or to diminish the action of the neurotransmitter.

Overview of Research Methods

The remainder of this chapter will examine some of the evidence for disordered chemical neurotransmission in various psychiatric disorders. Some of the research methods used in gathering this evidence are introduced below to familiarize the reader with their various strengths and weaknesses.

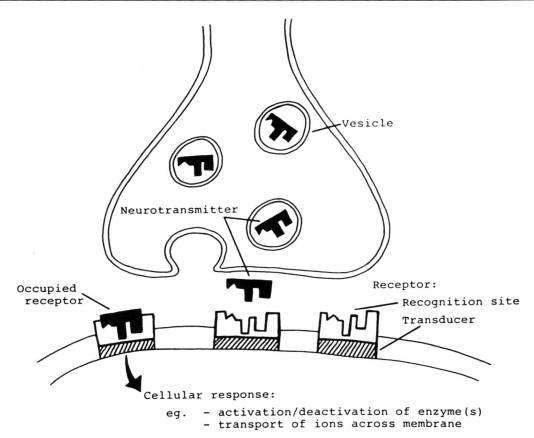

Figure 3. Receptor sites. The receptor site has two components: a recognition site and a transducer. The recognition site exhibits high specificity for binding the associated neurotransmitter. Occupation of the recognition site, as shown here on the far left receptor, acti- vates the transducer, which in turn produces the cellular response. This response may involve the activation or deactivation of enzyme(s), and/or the transport of ions across the cell membrane.

Highly specific and sensitive assay procedures have been developed for measuring tissue and fluid levels of many putative neurotransmitters, their metabolites, and their metabolic enzymes. There- fore, one common approach to studying neuro- transmitter activity in psychiatric patients involves measuring their concentration (or that of their me- tabolites and metabolic enzymes) in plasma, urine, cerebrospinal fluid (CSF), or postmortem brain tis- sue. When evaluating the results of such studies, it is important to consider the sensitivity and spec- ificity of the assay technique employed. However, even when the assay technique is sound, there are inherent weaknesses in this approach. Levels of neurotransmitters (or their enzymes) measured in plasma, urine, or CSF can provide only an indirect reflection of levels in the brain. Since many CNS neurotransmitters are also found in the periphery, urine and plasma concentrations are potentially confounded by peripheral contributions to the as- say pool. In contrast, CSF assays should theoreti- cally provide a more accurate index of brain levels. CSF samples, however, reflect an average of whole CNS concentrations (brain *and* spinal cord) and thus provide no information regarding localization of an observed abnormality. In fact, a highly localized abnormality in neurotransmitter levels may not be detectable by any of these indirect measurements. Direct measurement of neurotransmitter levels in postmortem brain tissue can potentially detect lo- calized abnormalities. However, postmortem stud- ies must address a different potential problem, specifically, the possibility that changes in brain levels occur at death. Overall, despite the current availability of accurate assay techniques, this re- search strategy has inherent methodological limi- tations that must be considered in the interpretation of this data.

Studies that measure levels of neurotransmit- ters and their enzymes are concerned with evaluating presynaptic processes (e.g., metabolic turnover of the neurotransmitter). Postsynaptic processes involving receptor functions can also be assessed. There are two basic approaches to assessing receptor function in psychiatric patients: in vivo measurements and in vitro measurements.

In vivo studies test the response capacity of a particular receptor system known to show a characteristic response to a specific agonist or antagonist. The induced response is then compared between experimental and control groups. An example of such a "pharmacologic challenge" test is the clonidine-induced decrease in plasma levels of 3-methoxy-4-hydroxyphenylglycol (MHPG). Clonidine is a specific agonist of alpha-2 adrenergic receptors, and stimulation of these receptors inhibits the release of norepinephrine (NE) in the brain, thereby reducing plasma levels of NE's major metabolite, MHPG. Thus, in this challenge test, the MHPG response to clonidine can potentially reveal differences in the functioning of alpha-2 adrenergic receptors between patient groups and control groups. The response in pharmacologic challenge studies is the end result of a cascade of physiologic events. Herein lies a major disadvantage of this research strategy: It is difficult to localize the abnormality and to determine how this may relate to the complexities of physiology and behavior.

In vitro studies of receptor function have become possible with the development of radioactive ("labeled") ligands, which show specific, high affinity binding to certain receptors. Radioligand binding studies usually involve incubating a tissue slice or homogenate with a labeled receptor agonist or antagonist. The labeled ligand-receptor complexes are then separated from the unbound ligand (e.g., by filtration, precipitation, or centrifugation) and quantified. By analyzing multiple samples in which sample size is held constant while the amount of added ligand is increased, a saturation curve can be generated. This saturation data can be used to estimate the absolute number of receptor sites in the sample as well as the binding affinity of these sites for the ligand. In studies of psychiatric patients, various tissues are utilized for receptor assays. The most direct approach is to apply these assays to postmortem brain tissue. As with all postmortem studies, there is the possibility that changes may have occurred in the tissue following death. Platelets, lymphocytes, red blood cells, and skin fibroblasts have been found to contain receptors for certain CNS neurotransmitters. These tissues are thus used to assay neurotransmitter receptors

in the living subject. However, the degree to which such peripheral models reflect the functioning of brain receptors is unknown.

Finally, when evaluating the literature on chemical neurotransmission in psychopathology, one should bear in mind that neurotransmitter systems are dynamic. Therefore, studies of these dynamic systems should control for possible confounding factors, such as circadian rhythms, the medication status of the patient, and the clinical state of the patient.

☐ SCHIZOPHRENIA

The Dopamine Hypothesis

The classical dopamine hypothesis proposes that the symptoms of schizophrenia result from a functional overactivity of dopamine in the CNS. Several lines of indirect pharmacological evidence converged to inspire this hypothesis. One contributing line of evidence came from studies of amphetamine. Chronic abuse or ingestion of a large amount of amphetamine can produce an acute psychotic state similar to paranoid schizophrenia (Angrist and Gershon 1970; Connell 1958). Furthermore, amphetamine has been reported to exacerbate existing symptoms in schizophrenic patients (Janowksy and Davis 1976). On a neurochemical level, amphetamine potentiates the synaptic levels of both dopamine and norepinephrine (NE) by increasing their presynaptic release and inhibiting their reuptake from the synaptic cleft. Owing largely to other lines of pharmacological evidence, early attention focused on dopamine rather than NE.

Additional evidence contributing to early statements of the dopamine hypothesis came from studies of antipsychotic medications. For example, Hornykiewicz (1963) observed that antipsychotic medications can cause a neurologic syndrome similar to Parkinson's disease. Since idiopathic Parkinson's disease is linked to a loss of dopaminergic neurons in the substantia nigra and a resultant depletion of dopamine in the striatum, this observation suggested that antipsychotic medications may exert their effects through a mechanism that diminishes dopamine activity. Carlsson and Lindqvist (1963) were the first to suggest that neuroleptics may diminish dopaminergic activity by blocking postsynaptic dopamine receptors. They proposed that a feedback mechanism would communicate this receptor blockade to the presynaptic neurons, which, in turn, would increase their firing rate and release of dopamine. In support of their hypothesis, Carlsson and Lindqvist found that neuroleptic administration produced an increase in dopamine metabolites in the mouse brain. Since antipsychotic drugs have diverse biochemical effects, establishing this type of correlation is necessary for relating the therapeutic effects of these drugs to a specific pharmacologic effect.

To investigate the hypothesis that antipsychotic medications block postsynaptic dopamine receptors, a method was needed to assess dopamine receptor function. In 1972, Kebabian et al. reported that exposure to dopamine increases adenylate cyclase activity, thereby stimulating the accumulation of cyclic adenosine monophosphate (cAMP) in homogenates of rat corpus striatum. Since this effect appears somehow linked to stimulation of the dopamine receptor, measurements of dopamine-induced cAMP accumulation can be used as an indirect index of dopamine receptor activity. Studies that applied this method found that neuroleptics inhibit dopamine-induced cAMP accumulation (Clement-Cormier et al. 1974; Miller et al. 1974). These findings thus supported the notion that antipsychotic medications exert their therapeutic effects through blockade of postsynaptic dopamine receptors. One important exception to these findings was noted, however. The butyrophenones (e.g., haloperidol) were found to be less potent than phenothiazines in preventing dopamine-stimulated cAMP accumulation. Since butyrophenones are generally more potent than phenothiazines in terms of antipsychotic properties, there appeared to be a discrepancy between the in vivo and in vitro effects of the butyrophenones. This apparent discrepancy has been addressed by subsequent studies using another method of assessing dopamine receptors. These radioligand binding studies will be discussed in a later section.

Efforts to localize the dopaminergic hyperactivity proposed by the dopamine hypothesis must naturally consider the distribution of dopamine in the brain. Of the dopamine tracts that have been identified in the brain, there appear to be four of potential clinical significance in schizophrenia (see Figure 4). The *mesolimbic tract* originates in the midbrain ventral tegmental area and innervates various limbic structures. The *mesocortical tract* also originates in the ventral tegmental area and projects to areas of the frontal cortex. The mesolimbic and mesocortical tracts have been associated with emo-

tional and intellectual functions. The *nigrostriatal tract* has its cell bodies in the substantia nigra and projects to the basal ganglia. This tract is part of the extrapyramidal motor system and is thus involved in movement. The fourth tract of significance is the *tuberoinfundibular tract* (also termed the *tuberohypophyseal tract*), which originates in the hypothalamus and projects to the pituitary. This system is functionally involved in regulating some of the pituitary's endocrine functions. The proposed involvement of these four dopaminergic systems in schizophrenia is as follows. Many of the symptoms of schizophrenia, such as delusions, hallucinations, and disordered cognition, are thought to involve derangements in the mesolimbic and mesocortical dopaminergic systems. The extrapyramidal side effects of antipsychotic medications are thought to reflect the effects of these drugs on the nigrostriatal system. Additionally, certain motoric symptomatology (e.g., catatonia) may be related to abnormalities of the nigrostriatal system. Finally, the endocrinologic side effects of antipsychotic medications (e.g., the elevation of plasma prolactin levels) appear to be mediated by their effects on the tuberoinfundibular dopamine system.

With these anatomic considerations in mind, some investigators have searched for direct evidence of enhanced dopamine activity in postmortem brain tissue from schizophrenic patients. In this type of study, dopamine-rich areas of the brain are assayed to determine concentrations of dopamine, its metabolites, or its metabolic enzymes. Several studies have reported increased dopamine concentrations in the brains of schizophrenic patients compared to nonpsychiatric controls. In a series of some 50 schizophrenic patients, Bird et al. (1979b) observed increased dopamine concentrations in limbic forebrain areas, including the nucleus accumbens and olfactory tubercle. In an extension of this study, these findings were confirmed and extended to include elevations of dopamine in the caudate nucleus as well (MacKay et al. 1982). Furthermore, based on a small subset of patients who were medication-free for at least 1 month prior to death, MacKay and associates suggested that previous neuroleptic medication did not cause the observed dopamine elevations. In contrast to the above, Kleinman et al. (1982) did not find increased dopamine concentrations in the nucleus accumbens of schizophrenic patients. Given that some studies have found increased dopamine concentrations in the brains of schizophrenic pa-

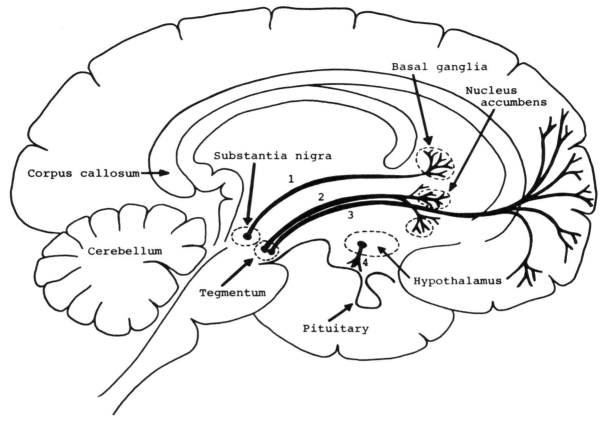

Figure 4. The four major dopamine tracts: (1) nigro-striatal tract—also known as the extrapyramidal pathway, begins in the substantia nigra and ends in the caudate nucleus and putamen of the basal ganglia; (2) mesolimbic tract—originates in the midbrain tegmentum and innervates the nucleus accumbens and adjacent limbic struc-

tures; (3) mesocortical tract—originates in the midbrain tegmentum and innervates anterior cortical areas; and (4) tuberohypophyseal tract—projects from the arcuate and periventricular nuclei of the hypothalamus to the intermediate lobe of the pituitary and to the portal blood system surrounding the anterior pituitary.

tients, one might state on a simplistic level that such studies support the dopamine hypothesis. However, increased dopamine concentrations do not necessarily reflect an increase in the *functional* activity of dopamine. To support a presynaptic mechanism of functional overactivity, this evidence of elevated dopamine levels should be associated with evidence of increased dopamine turnover (indicating increased synaptic usage of dopamine). Increased dopamine turnover could be inferred if levels of dopamine metabolites were found to be elevated in postmortem brain tissue. Unfortunately, postmortem assays of the two major dopamine metabolites, homovanillic acid (HVA) and 3,4-dihydroxyphenylacetic acid (DOPAC), have not shown such elevations (Owen et al. 1978). Therefore, the reports of elevated brain dopamine in schizophrenia are difficult to interpret. Several

studies have assayed the enzyme dopamine beta-hydroxylase (DBH) in postmortem brain tissue from schizophrenic patients. One group, in fact, reported decreased levels of brain DBH in schizophrenic patients (Wise and Stein 1973). However, this finding has not been confirmed in subsequent studies (Cross et al. 1978; Wyatt et al. 1975). To summarize, postmortem studies have not yielded conclusive evidence supporting a presynaptic excess of dopamine in schizophrenia. The reader should be reminded, however, that such studies pose tremendous methodologic problems, including potential contamination from residual neuroleptic effects and postmortem tissue deterioration.

Dopamine metabolites and metabolic enzymes have also been measured in the CSF and peripheral tissues of schizophrenic patients. Studies that measured HVA concentrations in the CSF of schizophrenic patients have consistently failed to demonstrate an elevation in dopamine turnover (Berger et al. 1980; Bowers 1973; Post et al. 1975). However, based on trends observed within groups of schizophrenic patients, some investigators have suggested that CSF HVA levels may delineate certain subgroups of schizophrenia. For example, patients with more Schneiderian first-rank symptoms seem to show lower CSF HVA levels (Bowers 1973; Post et al. 1975), and one study reported higher CSF HVA levels in patients with paranoid schizophrenia (Rimon et al. 1971). These subgroup observations are at best preliminary, and current evidence finds no universal abnormalities in CSF HVA, a finding consistent with the postmortem data mentioned above (Owen et al. 1978). The activity of MAO has also been investigated in schizophrenic patients, with most studies using platelets as a peripheral model. Within the CNS, MAO is responsible for the intracellular deamination of the monoamine neurotransmitters. In theory then, a decrease in CNS MAO activity could lead to a buildup of dopamine in the brain. Given this, considerable excitement was generated by early reports of decreased MAO activity in the platelets of schizophrenic patients (Berger et al. 1978; Murphy and Wyatt 1972). However, subsequent studies revealed that this observation was not specific to schizophrenia, with similar deficiencies also found in manic-depressive patients (Wyatt et al. 1979) and in alcoholic patients (Major and Murphy 1978). Moreover, antipsychotic medications have now been shown to decrease MAO activity (DeLisi et al. 1981a; Meltzer et al. 1982). Many positive reports of reduced MAO activity in schizophrenia have come from studies of medicated and/or chronic patients with a long history of neuroleptic treatment (reviewed by DeLisi et al. 1981b). The neuroleptic effect on MAO activity may have been a confounding factor in many of these studies. In summary, CSF and peripheral assays have not proven any more successful than postmortem studies in terms of revealing clear evidence for a presynaptic abnormality of dopaminergic activity in schizophrenia.

The lack of evidence for a presynaptic dopaminergic abnormality in schizophrenia is not sufficient to discount the dopamine hypothesis. The functional overactivity of dopaminergic systems proposed by this hypothesis could also be due to a postsynaptic abnormality such as a supersensitivity of postsynaptic dopamine receptors. With the development of specific radioligand binding techniques (in the early to mid-1970s), direct quantification of receptor activity became possible, and investigators began using these techniques to probe dopamine receptor function in schizophrenia. The reader will recall that indirect studies of the postsynaptic dopamine receptor produced discrepant findings regarding the actions of butyrophenones as compared to phenothiazines. Whereas phenothiazines were found to inhibit dopamine-stimulated cAMP accumulation in direct proportion to their clinical potency, butyrophenones did not exhibit the same correlation between in vitro and in vivo effects. This discrepancy suggested that butyrophenones might act on a different neurotransmitter system or on a dopamine receptor that is "different" from the one blocked by phenothiazines. Creese et al. (1976) used radioligand binding techniques to resolve this issue. The investigators labeled striatal dopamine receptors with either tritiated haloperidol or tritiated dopamine and measured the ability of various neuroleptics to compete with these labeled compounds for dopamine receptors. They found that the clinical potencies of all neuroleptics tested correlated with their ability to displace tritiated haloperidol. Competition for the sites labeled by tritiated dopamine correlated less well with clinical potencies. These results thus distinguished two subtypes of dopamine receptors, one selectively labeled by tritiated dopamine and one selectively labeled by tritiated haloperidol. Moreover, these results linked the clinical potencies of antipsychotic medications to their affinity for the receptor subtype labeled by tritiated haloperidol.

Subsequent studies have confirmed and expanded on the above findings (reviewed by Creese 1985). The two subtypes of dopamine receptors mentioned above are now referred to as D_1 and D_2 receptors. The D_1 receptors are associated with stimulation of adenylate cyclase. The D_2 receptors are selectively labeled by tritiated butyrophenones and are possibly associated with the reduction of adenylate cyclase activity. The clinical potencies of antipsychotic medications correlate very closely with their affinity for the D_2 receptor. The therapeutic effects of antipsychotic medications appear to be linked to their affinity to D_2 receptors. The functional role of the D_1 receptor remains to be characterized. Since it was the D_1 receptor activity that was being assessed by studies of dopamine-stimulated cAMP accumulation, it is not surprising that these studies revealed apparent discrepancies between the in vitro and in vivo effects of certain neuroleptics.

Since the D_2 dopamine receptor appears to mediate the therapeutic effects of antipsychotic medications, this receptor has been quantitatively investigated in postmortem studies of brain tissue from schizophrenic patients. Assuming that this receptor is the site of dopaminergic dysfunction in schizophrenia, the dopamine hypothesis would predict that D_2 receptors are increased in number or affinity in schizophrenic patients. Early studies by Lee and Seeman (1978, 1980) did, in fact, report increased tritiated haloperidol (D_2) binding in the caudate and putamen of schizophrenic patients. Owen et al. (1978) reported an increase in D_2 receptor number in the caudate, putamen, and nucleus accumbens of schizophrenic patients. Interestingly, there was also an apparent decrease in the affinity of the D_2 receptor for labeled haloperidol. Since most of the patients had been on neuroleptic medication prior to death, the authors hypothesized that this decreased affinity may be due to competitive inhibition by residual neuroleptic in the receptor preparations. Similar results were reported by MacKay et al. (1982). That is, increased numbers of D_2 receptors were observed in the caudate and nucleus accumbens, and the D_2 receptors also exhibited a decreased affinity for tritiated butyrophenone. These investigators subjected some of their membrane preparations to an unusually rigorous washing procedure in an attempt to remove any residual neuroleptic from the receptors. After this washing, the binding affinity of the D_2 receptors for labeled ligand increased, suggesting that the decreased affinity observed in both of these studies was potentially due to neuroleptic contamination.

A key issue remaining to be resolved is whether the observed increase in D_2 receptor number might also be an artifact of prior neuroleptic treatment. In animals, long-term neuroleptic treatment produces increases in brain dopamine receptors (Clow et al. 1980; Owen et al. 1980). In the study by Owen et al. (1980), the increase in D_2 receptors was apparent in their small subset of patients who had been neuroleptic-free for at least 1 year prior to death. However, MacKay et al. (1982) observed an increase in D_2 density only in those patients who had received medication up until the time of death. In the few patients studied who were neuroleptic-free for at least 1 month prior to death, the increase was not observed. To summarize, increased D_2 re-

ceptor density has been reported in dopamine-rich areas of the brain in schizophrenic patients. It is not clear at this time whether this increase is a valid marker for schizophrenia or merely an effect of prior neuroleptic treatment. Future studies must carefully address this issue by attempting to control for potential medication effects. This will be a difficult task in postmortem studies because most schizophrenic patients at autopsy will have been treated, usually for significant periods, with antipsychotic medications. A possible solution to this problem may involve the application of recently developed techniques (e.g., positron emission tomography) for imaging dopamine receptors in the living brain.

To conclude this discussion of the dopamine hypothesis, we have seen that this neurochemical model of schizophrenia originated from and continues to draw support from multiple lines of indirect pharmacologic evidence. The strongest of these appears to be the apparent link between the clinical effects of antipsychotic drugs and their relative ability to block the D_2 dopamine receptor. There is little clear evidence to support a presynaptic dopaminergic abnormality in schizophrenia. That is, despite several reports of increased concentrations of dopamine in the brains of schizophrenic patients, there is no conclusive evidence for increased dopamine turnover or abnormal dopamine metabolism. The reports of increased D_2 receptors in autopsied brains of schizophrenic patients are tantalizing in terms of delineating a possible postsynaptic dopaminergic abnormality. However, the clinical relevance of this finding awaits clarification.

One weakness in the dopamine hypothesis is the wide discrepancy between the time course for neuroleptic blockade of dopamine receptors and that required for amelioration of schizophrenic symptoms. Receptor blockade is essentially complete within hours of intramuscular injection, whereas symptomatic improvement may require weeks or months. This implies the involvement of long-term, adaptive changes. Such adaptive changes might include changes in receptor number or sensitivity, as well as homeostatic adjustments in the interaction between dopaminergic systems and other neurotransmitter systems. Future research in this area will probably focus on delineating these adaptive changes within the dopaminergic systems and their dynamic consequences for other neurotransmitter systems.

Possible Involvement of Other Neurotransmitter Systems

It would be somewhat naive to assume that a solitary neurochemical defect (e.g., an abnormality in the D_2 receptor) could be responsible for the protean and complex behavioral manifestations of schizophrenia. However, even if there were such an initial biochemical abnormality (that predisposes an individual toward schizophrenia), one cannot ignore the entire cascade of biochemical changes, possibly encompassing many neurotransmitter systems, that would derive from the initial defect. As we emphasized above, neurotransmitter systems are dynamic and interactive. Therefore, in recent years, there has been an increasing interest in examining other neurotransmitter systems for possible involvement in schizophrenia.

Norepinephrine. Some of the early pharmacologic evidence that suggested a role for excess dopaminergic activity in schizophrenia could also have been interpreted as indirect evidence implicating excess NE activity in schizophrenia. For example, the ability of amphetamine to produce a psychotic state similar to paranoid schizophrenia could have been attributed to amphetamine's potentiation of noradrenergic activity, rather than to its similar potentiation of dopamine activity. Similarly, early clinical studies of reserpine generally attributed the antipsychotic properties of this drug to its depletion of brain dopamine stores. However, reserpine depletes brain NE stores in a similar fashion.

A reinterpretation of the early pharmacologic data was perhaps inspired when Yorkston et al. (1974) reported therapeutic effects of propranolol (a beta-adrenergic receptor blocker) in a group of chronic schizophrenic patients. Although the antipsychotic efficacy of propranolol has not been confirmed (Bigelow et al. 1979), CSF and postmortem studies have observed NE abnormalities in schizophrenic patients. Lake et al. (1980) reported elevated NE concentrations in the lumbar CSF of unmedicated schizophrenic patients, a finding that appeared more robust in paranoid patients. An initial postmortem study, which examined 4 paranoid schizophrenic patients, found elevated NE concentrations in many areas of the limbic forebrain, including the nucleus accumbens, mammillary bodies, bed nucleus of the stria terminalis, and the ventral septum (Farley et al. 1978). In a larger postmortem study, which employed both normal

and psychiatric controls, Kleinman et al. (1982) found increased NE levels in the nucleus accumbens and hypothalamus of paranoid schizophrenics. In contrast to paranoid schizophrenics, undifferentiated schizophrenic patients exhibited NE elevations only in the hypothalamus. Furthermore, levels of MHPG, a major NE metabolite, were elevated in the nucleus accumbens of paranoid schizophrenic patients in this study. Based on these postmortem studies and on the CSF study by Lake et al. (1980), there appears to be a potential connection between elevated NE levels and paranoid schizophrenia. It should be noted that two postmortem studies did not find increased NE concentrations in the limbic forebrain of schizophrenic patients (Bird et al. 1979a; Crow et al. 1978). However, these studies did not analyze diagnostic subgroups and thus may have missed potential positive findings in those patients with paranoid schizophrenia.

Additional indirect support for an NE excess in schizophrenia derives from clinical trials of clonidine. For example, Freedman et al. (1982) reported that clonidine showed an antipsychotic efficacy similar to that of trifluoperazine (Stelazine). To date, there have not been many studies of noradrenergic receptor function in schizophrenic patients. Kafka and van Kammen (1983) reported that alpha-adrenergic receptors were decreased on the platelets of schizophrenic patients, a finding that could be interpreted as a down-regulation of these receptors in response to excessive NE levels. However, since neuroleptics have alpha-adrenergic blocking properties, this observation could merely reflect an effect of neuroleptic treatment. In summary, the CSF and postmortem studies provide the most convincing evidence for possible NE excess in schizophrenia. The potential link between excess NE and paranoid symptomatology merits further investigation.

Serotonin. Historically, serotonin had been investigated in schizophrenic patients based on the following rationale. Lysergic acid diethylamide (LSD) is a psychotomimetic that interacts with the serotonin system to produce psychotic symptomatology (e.g., hallucinations) in normal individuals. Increased serotonergic activity has been proposed as a possible mechanism for producing the psychotic symptoms of schizophrenia (Green and Grahame-Smith 1976). Other lines of investigation suggest that schizophrenia may involve an imbalance between serotonergic (hypoactive) and dopaminergic (hyperactive) activity in the brain. The hypothesis that such a serotonin-dopamine balance exists is derived from animal studies that found that potentiation of brain serotonin could attenuate dopamine-induced motor activity, whereas antagonizing brain serotonin could increase these dopamine-induced behaviors (Gershon and Baldessarini 1980). Thus both increases and decreases in serotonergic activity have been proposed as possible contributing factors in schizophrenia. The available evidence is just as divergent as these hypotheses. A postmortem study by Joseph et al. (1979) found no differences between schizophrenic and control brains in levels of serotonin, tryptophan (a precursor to serotonin), and 5-hydroxyindole acetic acid (5-HIAA) (a serotonin metabolite). In contrast, Korpi et al. (1986) found elevations of serotonin and 5-HIAA in the putamen and globus pallidus of schizophrenic patients. In another postmortem study, Owen et al. (1981) found no differences in serotonin receptor binding between schizophrenic and control brains. CSF studies have not found abnormalities in the levels of 5-HIAA in schizophrenic patients (Berger et al. 1980; Post et al. 1975). Finally, Rotman et al. (1982) reported that the active reuptake of serotonin is decreased on platelets from schizophrenic patients. However, as we point out in our discussion of affective disorders later in this chapter, this effect is not specific to schizophrenia. In summary, if there is, in fact, a serotonergic derangement in schizophrenia, it is not possible to delineate its nature from the currently available evidence.

Gamma-Aminobutyric Acid. As will be discussed later in this chapter, gamma-aminobutyric acid (GABA) is thought to be the major inhibitory neurotransmitter in the CNS, with a major role in modulating the activity of other neurotransmitter systems. With this functional role in mind, Robert (1972) proposed that a deficiency of GABAergic activity might underlie the proposed dopaminergic hyperactivity in schizophrenia. Unfortunately, there is little evidence to corroborate this hypothesis. Postmortem studies have not found abnormalities in the activity of glutamic acid decarboxylase (GAD) (the synthetic enzyme for GABA) or in GABA receptor binding in schizophrenic brains (Bennett et al. 1979; McGreer and McGreer 1979). One postmortem study, however, did report decreased GABA concentrations in the nucleus accumbens and thalamus of brains from schizophrenic patients (Perry

et al. 1979). Clinical trials of GABAergic agents (reviewed by Garbutt and van Kammen [1983]) have not generally supported the notion of diminished GABAergic activity in schizophrenia. In summary, there is little evidence available at this time to support the hypothesis of diminished GABAergic activity in schizophrenia.

Endorphins. Endorphin is the class name given to endogenous neuropeptides that act as agonists of specific opiate receptors in the brain. Nearly a half-dozen such peptides were isolated shortly after three research groups (Pert and Snyder 1973; Simon et al. 1973; Terenius 1973) discovered specific opiate receptors in the human brain. These endogenous "opioid peptides" include the two pentapeptides, leu- and met-enkephalin, as well as larger peptides such as beta-endorphin and dynorphin. The distribution of endorphins and opiate receptors in the brain shows highest densities in the limbic structures, basal ganglia, hypothalamus, medial thalamus, and midbrain periaqueductal gray (Simantov et al. 1976). Given their close proximity to the dopaminergic systems implicated in schizophrenia, it is not surprising that opioid systems have received significant attention in recent neurochemical investigations of schizophrenia.

Early studies of the behavioral effects produced by injecting beta-endorphin into the CNS led to two divergent hypotheses concerning the possible role of endorphins in schizophrenia. Bloom et al. (1976) observed prolonged muscular rigidity and immobility in rats after beta-endorphin injections and suggested that this resembled the catatonia sometimes seen in schizophrenic patients. Based on this inferential evidence, these investigators proposed an "excess opioid" hypothesis of schizophrenia. On the other hand, Jacquet and Marks (1976) felt that the motoric effects of beta-endorphin resembled Parkinsonian symptoms. On the basis of this interpretation, these authors suggested that opioid peptides may be "endogenous neuroleptics" and schizophrenia may thus involve a deficit in opioid activity.

A number of clinical trials have examined both the excess and the deficit opioid hypotheses of schizophrenia. The excess hypothesis has been tested by administering opiate receptor antagonists to schizophrenic patients, whereas the deficit hypothesis has been tested by administration of opiate agonists. Of the two hypotheses, the former has been more extensively investigated. Berger and

Barchas (1983) reviewed five clinical trials that administered beta-endorphin to schizophrenic patients and concluded that there is no convincing evidence supporting a therapeutic role for this peptide in schizophrenia treatment. A number of studies have administered naloxone (an opiate receptor antagonist) to schizophrenic patients. The first of these, a single-blind study by Gunne et al. (1977), reported a dramatic decrease in the auditory hallucinations of 4 out of 6 patients for several hours after injection. Subsequent studies have produced both positive findings (Davis et al. 1977; Watson et al. 1978) and negative findings (Janowsky et al. 1977; Volavka et al. 1977). The results of a large double-blind investigation (Pickar et al. 1982) suggest that administering naloxone in conjunction with a neuroleptic may have synergistic effects on schizophrenic symptomatology. This notion is consistent with basic pharmacologic studies that suggest important functional links between dopaminergic and opioid systems (Enjalbert et al. 1979; Pert 1978; Volavka et al. 1979). In summary, clinical studies provide no overwhelming support for a clear-cut excess or deficiency of endorphin activity in schizophrenia. Basic pharmacologic studies as well as the clinical study of Pickar et al. (1982) suggest that endorphins may interact with dopaminergic systems.

At present, there have not been many assay studies of endorphin activity carried out in schizophrenic patients. In a postmortem study, Kleinman et al. (1983) found decreased met-enkephalin concentrations in the caudate nucleus of paranoid schizophrenic patients. Using radioreceptor techniques, Naber et al. (1981) found decreased opioid activity in the CSF of schizophrenic males compared to normal males. Clearly, more assay studies of endorphin levels and opiate receptor activity are needed before any conclusions can be drawn. Given the potential interaction between endorphins and neuroleptics, it is crucial that future assay studies control for possible neuroleptic effects.

Other Neuropeptides. Histochemical studies have recently suggested that neurons may contain a neuropeptide transmitter in addition to a "classic" neurotransmitter (Lundberg and Hokfelt 1983). This finding has led to the speculation that these "colocalized" neuropeptides might have a modulatory influence on the neuron's classic neurotransmitter. Two neuropeptides, neurotensin (NT) and cholecystokinin (CCK), are of possible interest in schizo-

phrenia because they have been found to coexist with dopamine in certain dopaminergic neurons (Hokfelt et al. 1984; Snyder 1980). Studies of these neuropeptides in schizophrenic patients are in their infancy and await more extensive investigation.

Conclusion. To summarize, other neurotransmitter systems, in addition to dopaminergic systems, have been investigated for potential involvement in schizophrenia. Although much of this literature currently defies integration into a comprehensive neurochemical model of schizophrenia, it is clear that dopamine is only part of the total picture. What appears more likely is that dopamine has an important role in a complex system of neurotransmitter interactions that ultimately produce the manifestations of schizophrenia.

☐ AFFECTIVE DISORDERS

The Monoamine Hypothesis of Affective Disorders

In the 1950s and early 1960s, several lines of evidence suggested a link between affective disorders and disturbances in central monoamine transmission. Iproniazid, an agent that increases brain monoamine levels by inhibiting the deaminating enzyme MAO, was found to have mood-elevating effects in patients with tuberculosis (Loomer et al. 1957). Reserpine, which depletes brain monoamines by interfering with intracellular storage, was found to produce severe depression in some patients who were receiving the drug for treatment of hypertension (Achor et al. 1955; Muller et al. 1955). Finally, MAO inhibitors and tricyclic drugs were found to be efficacious antidepressant medications (Cole 1964; Klerman and Cole 1965; Kuhn 1958; Pare and Sandler 1959). Both of these drug classes were found to increase functional levels of brain NE. The MAO inhibitors accomplish this by preventing intracellular deamination of NE (Kopin 1964), whereas the tricyclics increase synaptic concentrations of NE by inhibiting neuronal reuptake (Glowinski and Axelrod 1964; Hertting et al. 1961). Based on this pharmacologic evidence, the classic catecholamine hypothesis of affective disorders was proposed (Bunney and Davis 1965; Schildkraut 1965). This hypothesis states that depression is related to a deficiency of NE at functionally important noradrenergic synapses in the brain.

The same evidence used to formulate the catecholamine hypothesis can also be used to substantiate an indoleamine hypothesis of affective disorders. That is, the effects produced on brain serotonin (5-HT) by reserpine, MAO inhibitors, and tricyclic antidepressants (TCAs) are similar to those produced on brain NE by these agents. The potential importance of 5-HT in affective disorders was, in fact, acknowledged in early reviews of evidence supporting the catecholamine hypothesis of depression. Referring to the roles of NE and 5-HT, Bunney and Davis (1965) wrote, "It is premature to argue that one and not the other is important in human depression, since both are implicated by indirect evidence. . . . It may also be found that the interaction between serotonin and norepinephrine may be important" (p. 492). Research efforts over the past 20 years have, in fact, supported the involvement of both noradrenergic and serotonergic systems in affective disorders. Current literature, therefore, tends to address a "monoamine hypothesis" of affective disorders, which proposes that clinical depression results from functional deficiencies in NE and/or 5-HT. The remainder of this section will present a summation of the evidence related to this hypothesis, as well as data implicating the involvement of other neurotransmitters in affective disorders.

Monoamine Metabolism in Affective Disorders

The monoamine hypothesis of affective disorders has stimulated numerous investigations of monoamine metabolism in depressed patients. Assessment of monoamine turnover has generally involved the measurement of metabolite concentrations in peripheral fluids (e.g., urine, CSF) or in postmortem samples of brain tissue. In the case of NE, the major metabolite is MHPG. For 5-HT, the major metabolite is 5-HIAA. The metabolic pathways for NE and 5-HT are diagramed in Figures 5 and 6, respectively. The evidence regarding levels of these metabolites in depressed patients is summarized below.

MHPG. In theory, CSF concentrations of MHPG should provide the best peripheral index of central NE turnover. However, current evidence suggests that MHPG diffuses readily from plasma to CSF (Kopin et al. 1983). Therefore, CSF levels of MHPG may reflect more peripheral contamination than was initially thought. This could be important in light

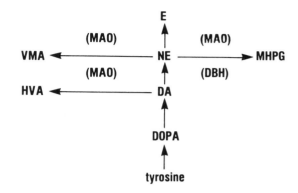

Products:
DA = dopamine, NE = norepinephrine, E = epinephrine
MHPG = 3-methoxy-4-hydroxy-phenylglycol
HVA = homovanillic acid
VMA = 3-methoxy-4-hydroxy-mandelic acid

Enzymes:
DBH = dopamine-beta-hydroxylase
MAO = monoamine oxidase

Figure 5. Catecholamine metabolism.

of data suggesting a hyperactive sympathetic nervous system in depressive disorders (Koslow et al. 1983). Given these considerations, it is not surprising that CSF studies of MHPG levels in depressed patients have produced inconsistent results. There have been reports of reduced (Post et al. 1973), normal (Oreland et al. 1981), and elevated (Koslow et al. 1983) CSF MHPG levels in depressed patients.

In the first study of urinary levels of MHPG in affective disorders, Maas et al. (1968) reported a reduction of MHPG excretion in a heterogeneous group of depressed patients compared to a healthy control group. However, other investigations have not found significant differences in the urinary excretion of MHPG in depressed patients compared to healthy controls (Beckman and Goodwin 1980; Hollister 1981; Koslow et al. 1983).

On closer examination, discrepancies in the urinary MHPG literature may be related in part to the heterogeneity of affective disorders. Several studies that examine urinary MHPG levels within subgroups of depressed patients have reported lower MHPG levels in bipolar patients as compared to unipolar patients (Beckman and Goodwin 1980; Edwards et al. 1980; Schildkraut 1978). Schatzberg et al. (1982) found decreased urinary excretion of

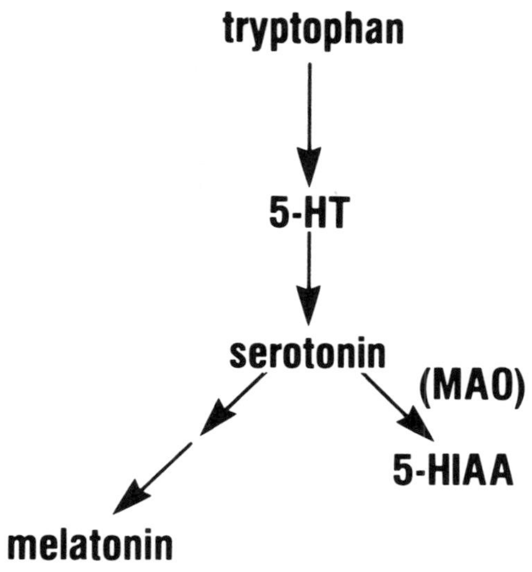

Products:
5-HT = 5-hydroxytryptophan
5-HIAA = 5-hydroxyindoleacetic acid

Enzymes:
MAO = monoamine oxidase

Figure 6. Serotonin metabolism.

MHPG in bipolar patients compared to normal controls. In this study, no statistically significant difference was found in the MHPG levels of unipolar patients compared with normal controls. However, based on the distribution of MHPG levels found in these unipolar patients, the authors suggested the existence of three biochemical subtypes of unipolar depression, characterized by low, normal, and high pretreatment levels of MHPG. By applying "metaanalytic techniques," Davis and Bresnahan (1987) combined the data from several studies that measured 24-hour urinary excretion of MHPG in depressed patients. The results of this "metaanalysis" state that bipolar patients excrete significantly less MHPG than unipolar patients (although not significantly less than healthy controls), and unipolar patients excrete higher levels of MHPG than normal controls.

In summary, studies of urinary excretion of MHPG have produced inconsistent results, particularly within the group of studies that did not examine subgroups of depressed patients for possible differences. There is some evidence suggesting that urinary MHPG levels may delineate biochemical subgroups of affectively disordered patients. A possible distinction between unipolar and bipolar patients based on this measure remains an open question that is under active investigation. The data which suggest that MHPG levels may distinguish between unipolar and bipolar depressed patients has contributed to a reevaluation of Maas' (1975) "two-disease" model of depression. This model proposes the existence of two biochemically and pharmacologically distinct subgroups of depression, one characterized by low pretreatment levels of urinary MHPG and good treatment response to imipramine, and the other characterized by normal or high levels of urinary MHPG and good treatment response to amitriptyline. Since imipramine (in vivo) is thought to affect primarily NE uptake, whereas amitriptyline affects primarily 5-HT uptake, Maas further suggested that the former subgroup has a noradrenergic disorder, and the latter subgroup has a serotonergic disorder. Some studies have investigated the hypothesized power of MHPG levels to predict response to antidepressant medication. Although some have supported the hypothesis (Beckman and Goodwin 1975; Cobbin et al. 1979; Hollister et al. 1980; Rosenbaum et al. 1980), recent studies have failed to confirm these findings (Coppen et al. 1979; Janicak et al. 1985; Sacchetti et al. 1976).

Given the recent reports suggesting that unipolar and bipolar subgroups can be distinguished by urinary MHPG levels (discussed above), it may prove enlightening to examine the predictive power of MHPG levels in bipolar and unipolar patients separately. This approach was employed by Maas et al. (1984) in a National Institute of Mental Health collaborative study. In this investigation, low values of urinary MHPG were associated with response to imipramine in bipolar, but not unipolar, patients. For methodological reasons, the question of whether higher values of MHPG predict response to amitriptyline in bipolar patients versus unipolar patients could not be addressed in this study. To summarize, the evidence to date does not justify the use of pretreatment urinary MHPG levels as a predictive clinical tool. However, new findings suggest that continued research in this area is potentially worthwhile.

5-HIAA. Although a number of studies have reported decreased levels of CSF 5-HIAA in depressed patients (Ashcroft et al. 1966; Coppen et al. 1972; Dencker et al. 1966; Mendels et al. 1972; van Praag et al. 1973), there have also been numerous studies that found no significant differences between depressed patients and controls (Berger et al. 1980; Bowers 1944; Goodwin et al. 1973; Koslow et al. 1983; Papeschi and McClure 1971; Vestergaard et al. 1978).

Evidence has been reported supporting an association between low CSF 5-HIAA and suicidal behavior in depressed patients. Asberg et al. (1976) found a bimodal distribution of CSF 5-HIAA levels in depressed patients, and reported that patients with low levels of 5-HIAA attempted suicide more often than patients with higher levels of this metabolite. The authors suggested that low levels of CSF 5-HIAA may therefore be a biochemical predictor of suicidal acts. Traskman-Bendz et al. (1984) also reported a bimodal distribution of CSF 5-HIAA in depressed patients. In this study, suicidal depressed patients had low 5-HIAA levels, whereas nonsuicidal depressed patients had 5-HIAA values more similar to those of controls. Given this possible association between low CSF 5-HIAA and suicidal behavior, it is also interesting to note that several research groups have reported reductions in brain 5-HIAA (Korpi et al. 1986) and brain 5-HT (Lloyd et al. 1974; Korpi et al. 1986) in postmortem studies of suicide victims.

Although there is a growing body of evidence regarding this link between suicidal acts and low CSF 5-HIAA, it is becoming apparent that low levels of this metabolite may not be specific for suicidal people suffering from affective disorders. Ninan et al. (1984) found low CSF 5-HIAA levels in suicidal schizophrenic patients, and Brown et al. (1982) presented evidence relating low CSF 5-HIAA to aggressive behavior or impulsivity in general.

Receptor Studies

As described above, the acute effects of antidepressant medications (MAO inhibitors and TCAs) enhance monoamine transmission in the brain, and thus support the monoamine hypothesis of depression. However, the acute effects of these medications occur very shortly after the administration of a single dose (Iversen and MacKay 1979), whereas the clinical effects may not become apparent for several weeks. Furthermore, there are a number of "atypical" antidepressants (e.g., iprindole), which are clinically effective yet have little or no effect on monoamine uptake and/or metabolism. As a result

of these observations, recent investigations concerned with delineating the therapeutic mechanisms of antidepressants have focused on the chronic effects of antidepressant treatment. The emphasis is on delineating adaptive changes in the monoaminergic systems, such as compensatory changes in receptor function.

Beta Adrenergic Receptors.

The most consistent changes observed following chronic administration of antidepressants involve the beta adrenergic receptors. Vetulani and Sulser (1975) were the first to report that chronic administration of various antidepressants (including the atypical TCA, iprindole) reduces the activity of NE-stimulated adenylate cyclase in rat brain slices. This response is mediated, at least partially, by beta adrenergic receptors (Blumberg et al. 1976). As reviewed by Charney et al. (1981), this observation has been consistently replicated. Furthermore, virtually all types of antidepressant treatments, including MAO inhibitors (Vetulani et al. 1976), atypical antidepressants (Mishra et al. 1980), and electroconvulsive therapy (ECT) (Gillespie et al. 1979) have been found to reduce NE- or isoproterenol-stimulated production of cAMP.

Banerjee et al. (1977) reported a decrease in the number of beta adrenergic receptors in homogenates of rat brain following chronic administration of either TCAs or the atypical antidepressant, iprindole. Numerous studies have replicated and expanded these findings (refer to Charney et al. [1981] for a detailed review). This decrease in the number of beta adrenergic receptors has been found not only in association with chronic pharmacologic treatment, but also following ECT (Bergstrom and Kellar 1979) and rapid eye movement (REM) sleep deprivation (Mogilnicka et al. 1980).

Animal studies have thus provided consistent evidence that beta adrenergic receptors are "downregulated" (desensitized and/or decreased in number) by chronic administration of virtually all effective antidepressants. In depressed patients, this avenue of investigation must reply on peripheral models of central receptor function. As with all peripheral models, the degree to which central receptor function can be inferred is unknown, and effects of peripheral transmitters further complicate the picture. Three human studies have reported reduced isoproterenol-stimulated adenylate cyclase production in the lymphocytes of unmedicated patients with affective illness (Extein et al. 1979; Mann et al. 1985; Pandey et al. 1979). Investigations of possible changes in these receptors following long-term antidepressant treatment remain to be done.

With antidepressants that increase synaptic levels of NE (e.g., TCAs and MAO inhibitors), down-regulation of the beta adrenergic receptors may be a compensatory response of the receptors to chronic increases in NE levels. However, since all antidepressants do not significantly affect NE metabolism (e.g., the atypical antidepressant, iprindole), there must be other mechanisms by which this down-regulation is produced. For example, certain atypical antidepressants may exert direct effects on the beta adrenergic receptors. It is also possible that certain antidepressant treatments may affect the regulation of NE release. NE release is partially regulated by presynaptic alpha-2 adrenergic receptors, such that an increase in synaptic concentrations of NE will normally result in a feedback inhibition of NE release via stimulation of these alpha-2 receptors. Pharmacologic blockade or desensitization of these alpha-2 receptors would, therefore, increase synaptic levels of NE and could thus contribute to compensatory changes in beta adrenergic receptors. This mechanism may, in fact, underlie the clinical efficacy of the atypical antidepressant, mianserin. Whereas mianserin appears to have little effect on NE reuptake, it has been found to stimulate NE release, presumably through its ability to act as an alpha-2 receptor antagonist (Fludder and Leonard 1978, 1979).

Finally, it is interesting to note that functional interactions between the noradrenergic and serotonergic systems might be involved in mediating the down-regulation of beta adrenergic receptors by antidepressants. For example, when the serotonergic system is destroyed by chemical lesioning techniques, chronic antidepressant treatment fails to reduce the density of beta adrenergic receptors (Janowsky et al. 1982). Delineating possible interactions between the noradrenergic and serotonergic systems is an intriguing research approach, one that could possibly lead to an integrated understanding of the involvement of these monoamines in affective illness.

Alpha-2 Adrenergic Receptors. In rat brain, Spyrakic and Fibiger (1980) found that chronic administration of desipramine reduced the alpha-2 receptor's inhibition of NE release. If chronic antidepressant treatment does, in fact, down-regulate the presynaptic alpha-2 receptor, it has been theo-

rized that these receptors might be supersensitive in unmedicated depressed patients. Studies that have examined this issue, however, are equivocal. Siever et al. (1984) reported a decreased MHPG response to clonidine in unmedicated depressed patients, a result suggesting a subsensitivity of the presynaptic alpha-2 receptors. In contrast, Charney et al. (1982) found no difference in this same response between unmedicated depressed patients and healthy controls. Price et al. (in press) examined the MHPG response to yohimbine (an alpha-2 antagonist) and found this response to be unaffected in unmedicated depressed patients. The question of whether presynaptic alpha-2 receptors are abnormal in depression thus remains open.

Studies regarding postsynaptic alpha-2 adrenergic receptors in depressed patients are more consistent. Since growth hormone (GH) release appears to be mediated by postsynaptic alpha-2 receptors (Terry and Martin 1981), several studies have compared clonidine-stimulated release of GH in depressed patients and healthy controls. These studies reported a blunting of the GH response to clonidine in unmedicated depressed patients, thus suggesting a subsensitivity of postsynaptic alpha-2 receptors in depression (Charney et al. 1982; Mattussek et al. 1980; Siever et al. 1982).

Serotonin Receptors. There are at least two types of 5-HT receptors: the 5-HT$_1$ receptors, which are labeled by tritiated 5-HT, and the 5-HT$_2$ receptors, which are labeled by tritiated spiroperidol (Peroutka and Snyder 1979). Chronic, but not acute, treatment with various antidepressants (including TCAs, MAO inhibitors, and iprindole) has been found to reduce the number of 5-HT receptor sites in the frontal cortex of rats (Peroutka and Snyder 1980). The decrease observed in this study was dramatic (about 40 percent) and was more pronounced for 5-HT$_2$ receptors than for 5-HT$_1$ receptors. This decrease in 5-HT$_2$ receptor density after chronic antidepressant treatment has also been reported by other investigators (Blackshear et al. 1980; Kellar et al. 1981).

Although these binding studies suggest a down-regulation of 5-HT$_2$ receptors with antidepressant treatment, the literature is not as congruent as that which supports a down-regulation of beta adrenergic receptors. For example, Kellar et al. (1981) reported that the administration of ECT actually increase the density of 5-HT$_2$ receptors in rat brain. Furthermore, studies that have examined the physiologic responses of these receptors suggest that their sensitivity is enhanced by long-term antidepressant treatment (Anderson 1983; Charney et al. 1981). Finally, Stanley and Mann (1983) reported that 5-HT$_2$ receptors are increased in the frontal cortex of suicide victims.

Tritiated Imipramine Receptors. High affinity binding sites for ^{3}H-labeled imipramine have been found in rat brain (Raisman et al. 1979), human brain (Rehavi et al. 1980), and human platelets (Paul et al. 1980). These binding sites are thought to be associated with the reuptake mechanism for 5-HT on neurons and platelets (Langer et al. 1980; Paul et al. 1981b). Although the pharmacologic significance of these receptors has yet to be established, Paul et al. (1984) suggested that they may be associated with the inhibition of 5-HT uptake caused by tricyclic antidepressants.

Several research groups have reported that tritiated imipramine binding sites are decreased on the platelets of depressed patients compared to healthy controls (Arsarch et al. 1980; Briley et al. 1980; Paul et al. 1981c). Furthermore, a normalization in the number of platelet ^{3}H-imipramine binding sites appears to follow successful ECT or tricyclic antidepressant treatment (Suranyi-Cadotte et al. 1983). In addition, Stanley et al. (1982) reported a decreased density of tritiated imipramine binding sites in the frontal cortex of suicide victims.

If these tritiated imipramine binding sites are, in fact, associated with the neuronal mechanism for 5-HT uptake, these findings may be related to the decreased 5-HT uptake in the platelets of depressed patients observed by Kaplan and Mann (1982). However, there cannot be an accurate interpretation of this literature until the functional role of the tritiated imipramine binding sites is more clearly defined.

Involvement of Other Neurotransmitters in Affective Disorders

The catecholamine and idoleamine hypotheses have emphasized the involvement of norepinephrine and serotonin in affective illness. The possible involvement of other neurotransmitters, particularly dopamine and acetylcholine, has also been investigated, although not as extensively.

Several lines of evidence suggest that the functional activity of dopamine systems may be reduced in affective illness. Chronic treatment with

TCAs, MAO inhibitors, as well as ECT has been found to decrease the sensitivity of presynaptic dopamine receptors (Antelman et al. 1981; Serra et al. 1979). Since these presynaptic receptors inhibit dopamine release, a decrease in their sensitivity would theoretically increase dopamine release. In light of these observations, it is interesting that Jimerson and Post (1984) reported successful clinical trials in depressed patients with the dopamine agonists, piribedil and bromocriptine. Halaris et al. (1975) reported that a variety of antidepressants block dopamine uptake in synaptosomes from rat brain, and, based primarily on this indirect evidence, Halaris (1982) inferred the involvement of dopamine in affective illness. As additional evidence, Halaris (1982) pointed to the case of the antidepressant, bupropion. This agent inhibits dopamine uptake, whereas it appears to have little effect on NE or 5-HT. Studies of dopamine metabolism in depressed patients have not produced consistent results. Kasa et al. (1982) reported a decrease in CSF levels of the major metabolite, HVA, in depressed patients. Other investigators report a decrease in CSF HVA, but only in subgroups of depressed patients (Davis and Bresnahan 1987; Koslow et al. 1983). Berger et al. (1980) found no difference between depressed patients and normal controls when baseline CSF HVA was examined; however, after the administration of probenecid (an organic acid that inhibits transport of metabolites from the CSF), accumulation of CSF HVA was decreased in depressed patients.

The possible involvement of acetylcholine in affective illness has been even less investigated than dopamine. Janowsky et al. (1972) proposed a cholinergic-adrenergic hypothesis of mania and depression. According to this hypothesis, a given affective state represents a balance between central cholinergic and adrenergic activity, with depression resulting from a predominance of cholinergic activity and mania resulting from a predominance of adrenergic activity. The authors supported this hypothesis with indirect evidence, including preliminary evidence that cholinomimetic agents can produce depression, whereas anticholinergic agents may have antidepressant effects. More recent evidence supporting this hypothesis came from Davis et al. (1978), who reported transient antimanic effects from administration of an acetylcholine agonist. Also, Sitaram et al. (1980) reported that depressed patients show faster REM induction by arecoline (a cholinergic agonist) than do healthy controls, an observation that may suggest a supersensitivity of the cholinergic system in affective illness. Using a different cholinomimetic agent, RS 86, Berger et al. (1985) also observed faster REM induction in depressed patients compared to healthy controls.

Summary

The catecholamine and indoleamine hypotheses were originally formulated on the basis of indirect pharmacologic evidence that suggested that these neurotransmitters may be involved in the pathophysiology of affective illness. Over the past three decades, extensive research concerned with monoamine metabolism and monoamine receptor function has revealed numerous abnormalities of the noradrenergic and serotonergic systems in depressed patients. However, absolute consistency in the literature regarding the nature of these abnormalities is rare. The heterogeneity of affective illness may greatly contribute to the lack of consensus of the literature, and current research efforts are emphasizing the importance of investigating various subgroups of depressed patients. Given the time lag between treatment initiation and the therapeutic effect of antidepressant medications, current research efforts are also emphasizing the delineation of gradual, adaptive changes in the monoamine systems associated with chronic antidepressant treatment. These studies generally focus on adrenergic and serotonergic receptors. The most consistent finding revealed by such studies is the down-regulation of beta adrenergic receptors associated with virtually all types of antidepressant treatments. It is important to bear in mind that such findings derive largely from animal studies. Although some receptor studies have been conducted in postmortem samples of brain tissue, the majority of human receptor studies must rely on peripheral models of CNS receptors or on endocrine challenge tests. Therefore, the available receptor data should be interpreted cautiously. That is, extrapolation from animal to human brain is problematic, and in human studies, the degree to which peripheral receptors reflect central receptor function is unknown.

Overall, the monoamine hypothesis continues to stand as a useful model for stimulating research that will hopefully resolve current inconsistencies in the literature and expand our knowledge of how monoamines contribute to the pathophysiology underlying affective illness. Recent evidence has

suggested a functional link between the NE and 5-HT systems involved in mediating the effects of antidepressant treatment, and delineating this interaction is an area of current interest. Finally, the monoamine hypothesis does not rule out possible contributions from other neurotransmitter systems in affective disorders, and these contributions are under investigation.

☐ ANXIETY DISORDERS

Generalized Anxiety Disorder

The development of the benzodiazepines in the 1960s heralded a new era in the treatment of anxiety disorders. In addition to their sedative, anticonvulsant, and muscle relaxant properties, the benzodiazepines were found to alleviate anxiety effectively. The antianxiety effects of benzodiazepines are observed at dosage levels that are typically insufficient to cause sedation. To reflect this specific effect on anxiety, the benzodiazepines have come to be known as "anxiolytics," as opposed to "sedatives" or "tranquilizers." There is widespread agreement that benzodiazepines are the most effective agents available for treating generalized anxiety disorder (GAD). Therefore, research efforts aimed toward elucidating the neurochemistry of GAD have focused on delineating the mechanisms of action of the benzodiazepines. In 1977, research groups found high-affinity, stereospecific binding sites for benzodiazepines in the rat brain (e.g., Squires and Braestrup 1977). In vitro binding studies in human brain tissue also revealed specific binding sites for benzodiazepines (Braestrup et al. 1977). These sites were irregularly distributed in the brain, with highest densities occurring in the cerebral cortex, hippocampus, and cerebellar cortex. Most importantly, the relative binding affinities of various benzodiazepines for these sites were found to correlate with their recommended daily dosages as anxiolytic medication. This observation provides indirect evidence suggesting that these receptors mediate the anxiolytic effects of benzodiazepines.

The discovery of a specific receptor site for benzodiazepines in the human brain raises the question of whether there is an endogenous ligand that normally interacts with this site. Such a ligand could be the brain's natural anxiolytic chemical. Alternately, it is equally possible that the proposed ligand could be "anxiogenic," in which case benzodiazepines would be termed antagonists of this receptor. Braestrup et al. (1980) isolated a compound from urine that was initially thought to be an endogenous anxiogenic compound. This compound, beta-carboline carboxylate ethyl ester (beta-CCE), shows high affinity binding to the benzodiazepine receptor site, blocks some pharmacologic effects of the benzodiazepines (Tenen and Hirsch 1980), and produces acute "anxiety" reactions in rhesus monkeys (Ninan et al. 1982). Unfortunately, beta-CCE was found to be a by-product of the chemical extraction procedure rather than an endogenous chemical (Braestrup and Nielsen 1980). Nicatinamide and certain purines (e.g., inosine, hypoxanthine) have also been suggested as possible endogenous ligands of the benzodiazepine receptor (for review see Skolnick and Paul [1982]). Guidotti et al. (1983) isolated a polypeptide from brain extracts that competitively inhibits diazepam binding (hence named DBI, diazepam-binding inhibitor). In animal behavioral paradigms, DBI appears to have anxiogenic effects. However, the question of whether this peptide has a natural physiologic function remains to be answered. The search for endogenous ligands that interact with the benzodiazepine receptor site continues to be a lively area in anxiety research.

Another avenue of benzodiazepine research has focused on determining which neurotransmitter system(s) might be involved in mediating the pharmacologic effects of these drugs. A large body of evidence points to a relationship between benzodiazepine binding and the neurotransmitter, GABA. This relationship appears to involve a functional linkage between the receptors for each, such that benzodiazepine binding enhances GABAergic transmission (MacDonald and Barker 1978; Polc et al. 1974). Before discussing this benzodiazepine-GABA interaction, a brief overview of the GABAergic system is necessary.

On the basis of numerous studies, GABA is generally thought to be the major inhibitory neurotransmitter in the brain. GABA neurons appear to be widely distributed throughout the human brain and typically possess short axons. This pattern of diffuse distribution and short-axon innervation suggests that GABA neurons generally serve a localized, perhaps modulatory, function. There appear to be two subtypes of GABA receptors, designated $GABA_A$ and $GABA_B$, which are identified by selective radioligands and seem to mediate

different functions (Bowery 1983). $GABA_A$ receptors are located postsynaptically and are associated with chloride ionophores (membrane components that regulate the opening and closing of chloride ion channels). When the $GABA_A$ receptor is activated, the chloride ionophore is modified such that membrane permeability to chloride ions is increased, resulting in chloride influx and hyperpolarization of the cell (Enna and Gallagher 1983).

A subpopulation of $GABA_A$ receptor sites appears to be associated with benzodiazepine receptors (Unnerstall et al. 1981). Although a discussion of the supporting literature is beyond the scope of this chapter, extensive biochemical studies have led to the formulation of a molecular model of the benzodiazepine-GABA interaction. This model proposes a supramolecular receptor complex, consisting of a functionally coupled benzodiazepine recognition site, GABA receptor, and chloride ionophore (Costa et al. 1978; Paul et al. 1981a; Skolnick and Paul 1982). When benzodiazepine binds to this complex, the affinity of the $GABA_A$ receptor is increased (Costa et al. 1978), resulting in enhanced GABAergic transmission. It appears that benzodiazepine binding effects this change on the GABA receptor by an allosteric modification that may involve the removal of a membrane protein that normally masks the GABA receptor (Baraldi et al. 1979; Costa et al. 1978; Massotti et al. 1981).

Animal studies show that GABA antagonists can block the anxiolytic effects of benzodiazepines (Stein et al. 1975), and thus support the involvement of this benzodiazepine-GABA receptor complex in anxiolysis. It is also possible that other neurotransmitter systems are involved in the anxiolytic effects of benzodiazepines. As mentioned above, GABA neurons are generally short-axon "interneurons" that may function as modulators of other neurotransmitter systems. The benzodiazepine-GABA receptor complex may thus mediate some anxiolytic effects through modulation of other neurotransmitter systems. Recently, some investigators have employed the beta-CCE model of "induced anxiety" (mentioned above) as a tool for examining the possible contributions of noradrenergic and serotonergic systems to anxiety (Crawley et al. 1985; Insel et al. 1984). Crawley et al. (1985) found that pretreatment with diazepam (a benzodiazepine), clonidine (an alpha-2 adrenergic agonist), cyproheptadine (a serotonin receptor antagonist), propranolol (a beta-adrenergic antagonist), and THIP (a GABA agonist) could selectively attenuate or alleviate certain aspects of the induced "anxiety syndrome." These results suggest the involvement of several neurotransmitter systems in the anxiety syndrome. Further research using this model to tease apart the relative contributions of these neurotransmitter systems appears warranted, especially in light of a recent study by Dorow et al. (1983) that suggests that the beta-CCE model is a valid analogue of human anxiety. In this study, a similar beta-carboline ester was reported to produce severe anxiety reactions in normal volunteers.

In summary, the ability of benzodiazepines to enhance GABAergic transmission is implicated in the clinical efficacy of these drugs. Other neurotransmitter systems may also be involved (perhaps secondarily to abnormal GABAergic regulation) in the myriad complex of behavioral and autonomic symptoms that characterize GAD.

Panic Attacks

Panic attacks occur in panic disorder and in frequent association with agoraphobia. These acute, often spontaneous reactions are characterized by intense feelings of apprehension, nervousness, terror, and mental confusion, accompanied by somatic and autonomic symptoms that include rapid pulse, palpitations, chest discomfort, dyspnea, dizziness, sweating, trembling, and nausea. The symptoms themselves suggest acute, massive activation of beta-adrenergic receptors, and support for such a mechanism is derived from studies of isoproterenol infusions. Isoproterenol (a beta-adrenergic agonist) has been reported to induce panic attacks in patients with panic disorder but not in healthy controls (Pohl et al. 1985). Furthermore, two studies have reported that isoproterenol-induced attacks can be ameliorated with injections of propranolol, a beta-adrenergic antagonist (Easton and Sherman 1976; Frolich et al. 1969).

Based on studies of brain noradrenergic function in the stump-tailed monkey, Redmond and colleagues (Huang et al. 1976; Redmond and Huang 1979; Redmond et al. 1976a, 1976b) proposed that acute anxiety reactions are related to increased activity in brain noradrenergic systems. In brief, electrical stimulation of the locus coeruleus (a major noradrenergic nucleus) induces a behavioral syndrome in monkeys similar to that produced by natural fear-inducing situations. These same behaviors were also increased by administration of yohim-

bine and piperoxane, alpha-2 adrenergic antagonists that increase NE release in the brain. Finally, bilateral lesions of the locus coeruleus decreased the occurrence of these behaviors, both in social situations and in fear-inducing situations. Reviewing the evidence for this noradrenergic hypothesis of acute anxiety states, Redmond and Huang (1979) suggested that drugs that reduce NE turnover (e.g., clonidine) might be useful in treating panic attacks in humans, whereas drugs that increase NE turnover (e.g., yohimbine) may produce anxiety states in humans. As summarized below, these predictions have been upheld by several human studies.

Charney et al. (1983) reported that yohimbine induced symptoms of panic attacks in healthy volunteers. In a subsequent study, the anxiogenic effects of yohimbine were found to be greater in patients with panic disorder and agoraphobia than in healthy controls (Charney et al. 1984). Furthermore, patients in this study who had a high frequency of panic attacks showed an enhanced MHPG response to yohimbine (yohimbine increases plasma MHPG levels by increasing NE turnover). The authors suggested that this enhanced MHPG response to yohimbine could reflect impaired presynaptic regulation of NE release, possibly due to down-regulated alpha-2 adrenergic autoreceptors.

In several clinical studies, clonidine has shown potential for decreasing the frequency and symptoms of panic attacks (Hoehn-Saric et al. 1981; Ko et al. 1983; Liebowitz et al. 1981). In the study by Ko et al. (1983), plasma MHPG levels were observed to rise following a panic attack, and this increase correlated with severity of the symptoms. Clonidine treatment suppressed the MHPG increase associated with panic symptoms. These results suggest an association between the therapeutic effect of clonidine and its effect on noradrenergic activity.

As noted throughout this chapter, clues regarding the neurochemistry of psychiatric disorders are often derived from examining the mechanism of action of clinically therapeutic drugs. In the case of panic attacks, useful medications include TCAs and MAO inhibitors (Sheehan et al. 1980; Tyrer et al. 1973; Zitrin et al. 1980, 1983). The benzodiazepines have not proven particularly effective in the treatment of panic attacks, suggesting that different neurochemical substrates underlie panic disorder and generalized anxiety disorder. The TCAs and MAO inhibitors have major effects on both noradrenergic and serotonergic systems. In light of other evidence implicating the noradrenergic system, it has been proposed that it is the ability of TCAs and MAO inhibitors to decrease locus coeruleus firing, NE turnover, and beta-adrenergic receptor function that underlies their efficacy in ameliorating panic attacks (Redmond 1979). The search for evidence that links the antipanic efficacy of these drugs to their effects on brain NE is the subject of ongoing investigations. Charney and Heninger (1985b) reported that imipramine reduced plasma MHPG levels in patients being treated for panic attacks, and imipramine did not affect yohimbine-induced increases in MHPG. The authors concluded that the therapeutic effect of imipramine is thus due to its effect on NE turnover, but does not appear to involve alterations of alpha-2 autoreceptor function.

In contrast to other benzodiazepines, alprazolam (Xanax) appears to reduce the occurrence and symptoms of panic attacks (Charney and Heninger 1985a; Chouinard et al. 1982). Charney and Heninger (1985a) reported that alprazolam treatment reduces plasma MHPG levels in panic disorder patients and also reduces yohimbine-induced increases in anxiety and MHPG levels. They speculated that alprazolam may suppress both NE turnover and yohimbine effects via stimulation of putative benzodiazepine-GABA receptors located on NE neurons of the locus coeruleus.

The available evidence thus implicates noradrenergic hyperactivity in panic attacks. Where this dysregulation occurs in the noradrenergic system has yet to be determined. By some unknown mechanism, infusions of sodium lactate have been repeatedly reported to induce "panic attacks" in panic disorder patients but not in healthy controls (Liebowitz et al. 1984, 1985; Pitts and McClure 1967; Pohl et al. 1985). Future studies using this model may add to our knowledge concerning neurochemical aspects of panic attacks.

□ ALZHEIMER'S DISEASE

Alzheimer's Disease

Alzheimer's disease involves a progressive, often rapid deterioration of cognitive functions and affects both the presenile (less than 65 years) and senile age groups. A clinical diagnosis of Alzheimer's disease can be advanced after carefully ruling out all other possible causes for a patient's dementia. Confirmation of the diagnosis, however, relies on microscopic examination of the patient's brain (usually done at autopsy, although occasionally done with a biopsy). The specific neuropathologic findings that distinguish Alzheimer's disease are neurofibrillary tangles (twisted, cross-linked filaments accumulated inside swollen neurons), neuritic plaques (spherical deposits of amyloid, surrounded by misshapen neurons), and granulovacuolar degeneration in the hippocampus. When evaluating the research literature on Alzheimer's disease, one must bear in mind whether or not the data were collected from patients with a pathologically confirmed diagnosis.

In 1977, Drachman reported that blocking central acetylcholine receptors of the muscarinic type could produce symptoms of memory loss in young adults. This led to the notion that dementias such as Alzheimer's disease might result from a physiologic process involving central cholinergic systems. Central cholinergic systems consist of neurons that make, store, and release acetylcholine as their neurotransmitter. Acetylcholine synthesis and catabolism are diagrammed in Figure 7. Choline is actively taken up by cholinergic neurons and is converted to acetylcholine when choline acetyltransferase transfers an acetyl group from acetyl CoA to the choline molecule. After presynaptic release of acetylcholine, the neurotransmitter is hydrolyzed to its original components by acetylcholinesterase. A number of studies that examined the brains of Alzheimer's patients have revealed abnormalities in these processes of acetylcholine metabolism. For example, Terry and Davies (1980) reported profound decreases (60 to 90 percent, depending on area of the brain examined) in choline acetyltransferase in the brains of Alzheimer's patients, as well as significant decreases in acetylcholinesterase activity. Using biopsied cortical samples, Sims et al. (1983) found reduced choline uptake in Alzheimer's patients. Furthermore, in biopsied brain samples from Alzheimer's patients, the in vitro synthesis of acetylcholine appears to be impaired (Francis et al. 1985; Sims et al. 1983). Francis et al. (1985) reported that this reduction in synthesis correlated with severity of cognitive impairment. Since this particular study examined "young" Alzheimer's patients, the authors suggested that such cholinergic deficits are an early, perhaps primary, factor in Alzheimer's disease. The available evidence thus tends to sup-

CAT = choline acetyl transferase
ACE = acetylcholinesterase

Figure 7. Choline metabolism. CAT = choline acetyltransferase; ACE = acetylcholinesterase.

port a possible presynaptic derangement of cholinergic systems in Alzheimer's disease.

In the brain, acetylcholine is concentrated in the basal ganglia and in the basal forebrain cholinergic complex (BFCC). The BFCC is a complex neuronal system thought to play a critical role in memory processes (Drachman 1977). The cell bodies of the BFCC are located in the globus pallidus and the nucleus basalis of Meynert, as well as in septal areas and the diagonal band of Broca. The axons of these cell bodies project to areas of the frontal cortex, hippocampus, and temporal cortex (refer to Coyle [1985b] for review of BFCC anatomy). Cell loss in areas of the BFCC (e.g., in the nucleus basalis of Meynert) has been reported in the brains of Alzheimer's patients, and this evidence lends additional support to the hypothesis of cholinergic involvement in Alzheimer's disease (Coyle et al. 1983; Whitehouse et al. 1982).

Other neurotransmitter systems have also been investigated for possible involvement in Alzheimer's disease. Gottfries et al. (1969) reported reductions in CSF levels of HVA, the major metabolite of dopamine, in patients with a clinical diagnosis of Alzheimer's disease. However, this finding was not confirmed in a subsequent study that examined the CSF from patients with biopsy-confirmed Alzheimer's disease (Bowen et al. 1981). Postmortem levels of 5-HT have been reported to be decreased in the brains of some Alzheimer's patients (Bowen et al. 1983). Cross et al. (1984) reported reductions in the number of 5-HT recep-

tors as well. Neither of these abnormalities, however, appears to correlate with cognitive impairment (Francis et al. 1985) and may thus represent secondary events in Alzheimer's disease. Substantial cell loss in the locus coeruleus, a major site of noradrenergic cell bodies, has been observed in the brains of some Alzheimer's patients (Bondareff et al. 1982). Although this finding may implicate noradrenergic systems in Alzheimer's disease, it was not consistently found in all patients. Somatostatin, a neuropeptide and putative neurotransmitter, has been measured in the autopsied brains of pathologically confirmed Alzheimer's patients and found to be reduced (by about 50 percent) in areas of the cortex and hippocampus. Whether this reduction is related to cell loss in these areas remains open to question. Davies (1983) cautions that this reduction may only reflect illness-related stress because induced stress in animals may cause depletion of somatostatin stores.

In summary, the most consistent neurochemical data pertaining to Alzheimer's disease are the observed reductions in choline acetyltransferase activity and the impaired ability of brain tissue from Alzheimer's patients to synthesize acetylcholine. Coupled with reports of cholinergic cell loss in Alzheimer's patients, this evidence suggests a primary defect in CNS cholinergic systems. There is some evidence for the possible involvement of other neurotransmitter systems in this disorder. Such involvement may, however, be secondary to cholinergic derangements. The cause of the cholinergic derangements in Alzheimer's disease remains elusive. Although there appears to be some genetic predisposition toward Alzheimer's disease, a latent viral etiology has also been proposed.

☐ CONCLUSION

Many of the most effective pharmacologic interventions in psychiatry have been discovered by chance. Over the last two decades, we have begun to delineate the neurochemical mechanisms by which these drugs effect the brain. This indirect pharmacologic evidence has led to the formulation of several major biochemical hypotheses of psychiatric illness, such as the dopamine hypothesis of schizophrenia and the monoamine hypothesis of affective disorders. Although more recent metabolic and receptor binding studies have supported some aspects of these hypotheses, they have also served to expand these theories to encompass complex dynamic relationships between neurotransmitter systems as well as adaptive interactions between neurotransmitters and their receptors.

This field of investigation has the formidable goal of linking neurochemical events with human behavior. Within the heart of this challenge lives the tantalizing hope of delineating fundamental neuroscience principles that can provide the basis for more efficacious therapeutic interventions in psychiatry.

☐ REFERENCES

Achor TWP, Hanson NO, Gifford RW Jr: Hypertension treated with rauwolfia serpentina (whole root) and with reserpine. JAMA 159:841–845, 1955
Anderson JL: Serotonin receptor changes after chronic antidepressant treatments: ligand binding, electrophysiological, and behavioral studies. Life Sci 32:1791–1801, 1983
Angrist B, Gershon S: The phenomenology of experimentally induced amphetamine psychosis: preliminary observations. Biol Psychiatry 2:95–107, 1970
Antelman S, Chiodo LA: Dopamine autoreceptor subsensitivity: a mechanism common to the treatment of depression and the induction of amphetamine psychosis. Biol Psychiatry 16:717–727, 1981
Arsarch KB, Shih JC, Kulcsar A: Decreased ^{3}H-imipramine binding in depressed males and females. Communications in Psychopharmacology 4:425–432, 1980
Asberg M, Traskman L. Thoren P: 5-HIAA in the cerebrospinal fluid: a biochemical suicide predictor? Arch Gen Psychiatry 33:1193–1197, 1976

Ashcroft GW, Crawford TB, Eccleston D, et al: 5-Hydroxyindole compounds in the cerebrospinal fluid of patients with psychiatric or neurological diseases. Lancet 2:1049–1052, 1966
Banerjee SP, Kung LS, Riggi SJ, et al: Development of beta-adrenergic receptor subsensitivity by antidepressants. Nature 268:455–456, 1977
Baraldi M, Guidotti A, Schwarz J, et al: GABA receptors in clonal cell lines: a model for study of benzodiazepine action at molecular level. Science 205:821–823, 1979
Beckman H, Goodwin F: Antidepressant response to tricyclics and urinary MHPG in unipolar patients: clinical response to imipramine or amitriptyline. Arch Gen Psychiatry 32:17–21, 1975
Beckman H, Goodwin FK: Urinary MHPG in subgroups of depressed patients and normal controls. Neuropsychobiology 6:91–100, 1980
Bennett JP, Enna SJ, Bylund DB, et al: Neurotransmitter receptors in frontal cortex of schizophrenics. Arch Gen Psychiatry 36:927–934, 1979
Berger M, Holchli D, Zulley J, et al: Cholinomimetic drug RS 86, REM sleep, and depression. Lancet 1:1385–1386, 1985
Berger PA, Barchas JD: Pharmacological studies of beta-endorphin in psychopathology. Psychiatr Clin North Am 6:377–391, 1983
Berger PA, Faull KF, Kilkowski J, et al: CSF monoamine metabolites in depression and schizophrenia. Am J Psychiatry 137:174–180, 1980
Berger PA, Ginsburg RA, Barchas JD, et al: Platelet monoamine oxidase in chronic schizophrenic patients. Am J Psychiatry 135:95–99, 1978
Bergstrom DA, Kellar KJ: Effect of electroconvulsive shock on monoaminergic receptor binding sites in rat brain. Nature 278:464–466, 1979
Bigelow LB, Zalcman S, Kleinman JE, et al: Propranolol treatment of chronic schizophrenia: clinical response, catecholamine metabolism and lymphocyte B-receptor, in Catecholamine Basic and Clinical Frontiers. Edited by Usdin E, Kopin I, Barchas J. New York, Pergamon Press, 1979
Bird ED, Spokes EG, Iversen LL: Brain norepinephrine and dopamine in schizophrenia. Science 204:93–94, 1979a
Bird ED, Spokes EG, Iversen LL: Increased dopamine concentration in limbic areas of brain from patients dying with schizophrenia. Brain 102:347–360, 1979b
Blackshear MA, Steranka R, Sanders-Bush E: Serotonin receptor subtypes after chronic treatment with tricyclic antidepressant drugs. Neuroscience Abstracts 6:860, 1980
Bloom F, Segal D, Ling N, et al: Endorphins: profound behavioral effects in rats suggest new etiological factors in mental illness. Science 194:630–632, 1976
Blumberg JB, Vetulani J, Stawarz RJ, et al: The noradrenergic cyclic AMP generating system in the limbic forebrain: pharmacological characterization in vitro and possible role of limbic noradrenergic mechanisms in the mode of action of antipsychotics. Eur J Pharmacol 37:357–366, 1976

Bondareff W, Mountjoy CQ, Roth M: Loss of neurons of origin of the adrenergic projection to cerebral cortex (nucleus locus ceruleus) in senile dementia. Neurology 32:164–168, 1982

Bourne HR, Bunney WE, Colburn RW, et al: Noradrenaline, 5-hydroxytryptamine and 5-hydroxyindoleacetic acid in the hindbrains of suicidal patients. Lancet 2:805–808, 1968

Bowen DM, Allen SJ, Benton JS, et al: Biochemical assessment of serotoninergic and cholinergic dysfunction and cerebral atrophy in Alzheimer's disease. J Neurochem 41:266–272, 1983

Bowen DM, Sims N, Benton JS, et al: Treatment of Alzheimer's disease: a cautionary note. N Engl J Med 305:1016, 1981

Bowers MB: Lumbar CSF 5-hydroxyindoleacetic acid and homovanillic acid in affective syndromes. J Nerv Ment Dis 158:325–330, 1944

Bowers MD: 5-HIAA and HVA following probenecid in acute psychotic patients treated with phenothiazine. Psychopharmacologia 28:309–318, 1973

Bowery NG: Classification of GABA receptors, in The GABA Receptors. Edited by Enna SJ. Clifton, NJ, Humana Press, 1983

Braestrup C, Nielsen M: Searching for endogenous benzodiazepine receptor ligands. Trends in Pharmacological Science 2:424–427, 1980

Braestrup C, Albrechtsen R, Squires RF: High densities of benzodiazepine receptors in human cortical areas. Nature 269:702–704, 1977

Breastrup C, Nielsen M, Olsen CF: Urinary and brain beta-carboline-3-carboxylates as potent inhibitors of brain benzodiazepine receptors. Proc Natl Acad Sci USA 77:2288–2292, 1980

Briley MS, Langer SZ, Raisman R, et al: Tritiated imipramine binding sites are decreased in platelets of untreated depressed patients. Science 209:303–305, 1980

Brown GL, Ebert MH, Goyer PF, et al: Aggression, suicide and serotonin: relationships to CSF amine metabolites. Am J Psychiatry 139:741–746, 1982

Bunney WE, Davis JM: Norepinephrine in depressive reactions. Arch Gen Psychiatry 13:483–494, 1965

Carlsson A, Linqvist M: Effect of chlorpromazine or haloperidol on formation of 3-methoxytyramine and normetanephrine in mouse brain. Acta Pharmacol Toxicol (Copenh) 20:140–144, 1963

Charney DS, Heninger GR: Noradrenergic function and the mechanism of action of antianxiety treatment, I: the effect of long-term alprazolam treatment. Arch Gen Psychiatry 42:458–467, 1985a

Charney DS, Heninger GR: Noradrenergic function and the mechanism of action of antianxiety treatment, II: the effect of long-term imipramine treatment. Arch Gen Psychiatry 42:473–481, 1985b

Charney DS, Heninger GR, Breier A: Noradrenergic function in panic anxiety: effects of yohimbine in healthy subjects and patients with agoraphobia and panic disorder. Arch Gen Psychiatry 41:751–763, 1984

Charney DS, Heninger GR, Redmond DE: Yohimbine-induced anxiety and increased noradrenergic function in humans: effects of diazepam and clonidine. Life Sci 33:19–29, 1983

Charney DS, Heninger GR, Sternberg DE, et al: Adrenergic receptor sensitivity in depression: effects of clonidine in depressed patients and healthy subjects. Arch Gen Psychiatry 39:290–294, 1982

Charney DS, Menkes DB, Heninger GR: Receptor sensitivity and the mechanism of action of antidepressant treatment: implications for the etiology and therapy of depression. Arch Gen Psychiatry 38:1160–1180, 1981

Chouinard G, Annable L, Fontaine R, et al: Alprazolam in the treatment of generalized anxiety and panic disorders: a double-blind placebo-controlled study. Psychopharmacology 77:229–233, 1982

Clement-Cormier YC, Kebabian JW, Petzold GL, et al: Dopamine-sensitive adenylate cyclase in mammalian brain: a possible site of action of antipsychotic drugs. Proc Natl Acad Sci USA 71:1113–1117, 1974

Clow A, Theodorou A, Jenner P, et al: Changes in rat striatal dopamine turnover and receptor activity during one year's neuroleptic administration. Eur J Pharmacol 63:135–144, 1980

Cobbin DM, Requin-Blow B, Williams LR: Urinary MHPG levels and tricyclic antidepressant drug selection. Arch Gen Psychiatry 36:1111–1116, 1979

Cole JO: Therapeutic efficacy of antidepressive drugs. JAMA 190:448–462, 1964

Connell PH: Amphetamine Psychosis. London, Oxford University Press, 1958

Coppen A, Prange AJ, Whybrow PC, et al: Abnormalities of indoleamines in affective disorders. Arch Gen Psychiatry 26:474–478, 1972

Coppen A, Ramo Rao VA, Ruthven CRJ, et al: Urinary 4-hydroxy-3-methoxyphenyl-glycol is not a predictor for clinical response to amitriptyline in depressive illness. Psychopharmacology 64:95–97, 1979

Costa E, Guidotti A, Toffano G: Molecular mechanisms mediating the action of diazepam on GABA receptors. Br J Psychiatry 133:239–248, 1978

Coyle JT: Introduction to the pharmacology of the synapse, in Psychiatry Update: American Psychiatric Association Annual Review, Vol 4. Edited by Hales RE, Frances AJ. Washington, DC, American Psychiatric Press, 1985a

Coyle JT: The cholinergic systems in psychiatry, in Psychiatry Update: American Psychiatric Association Anual Review, Vol 4. Edited by Hales RE, Frances AJ. Washington, DC, American Psychiatric Press, 1985b

Coyle JT, Price DL, DeLong MR: Alzheimer's disease: a disorder of cholinergic innervation. Science 219:1184–1190, 1983

Crawley JN, Ninan PT, Pickar D, et al: Neuropharmacological antagonism of the beta-carboline-induced "anxiety" response in rhesus monkeys. J Neurosci 5:477–485, 1985

Creese I: Dopamine and antipsychotic medications, in Psychiatry Update: American Psychiatric Association Annual Review, Vol 4. Edited by Hales RE, Frances AJ. Washington, DC, American Psychiatric Press, 1985

Creese I, Burt DR, Snyder SH: Dopamine receptor binding predicts clinical and pharmacological potencies of antischizophrenic drugs. Science 192:481–483, 1976

Cross AJ, Crow TJ, Johnson JA, et al: Studies on neurotransmitter receptor systems in neocortex hippocampus in senile dementia of the Alzheimer type. J Neurol Sci 64:109–117, 1984

Cross AJ, Crow TJ, Killpack WS, et al: The activities of brain dopamine beta-hydroxylase and catechol-o-methyl transferase in schizophrenics and controls. Psychopharmacology (Berlin) 59:117–121, 1978

Crow TJ, Owen F, Cross AJ, et al: Brain biochemistry in schizophrenia. Lancet 1:36–37, 1978

Davies P: The neurochemistry of Alzheimer's disease and senile dementia. Med Res Rev 3:221–236, 1983

Davis GC, Bunney WE, DeFraites EG, et al: Intravenous naloxone administration in schizophrenia and affective illness. Science 197:74–77, 1977

Davis JM, Bresnahan D: Psychopharmacology in clinical psychiatry, in Psychiatry Update: American Psychiatric Association Annual Review, Vol 6. Washington, DC, American Psychiatric Press, 1987

Davis KL, Berger PA, Hollister LE, et al: Physostigmine in mania. Arch Gen Psychiatry 35:119–122, 1978

DeLisi LE, Wise CD, Bridge TP, et al: A probable neuroleptic effect on platelet monoamine oxidase in chronic schizophrenic patients. Psychiatry Res 4:95–107, 1981a

DeLisi LE, Wise CD, Bridge TP, et al: Monoamine oxidase and schizophrenia, in Biological Markers for Mental Illness. New York, Pergamon Press, 1981b

Dencker SJ, Malm U, Ross BE, et al: Acid monoamine metabolites of cerebrospinal fluid in mental depression and mania. J Neurochem 13:1545–1548, 1966

Dorow R, Horowski R, Paschelke G, et al: Severe anxiety induced by FG 7142, a beta-carboline ligand for benzodiazepine receptors. Lancet 1:98–99, 1983

Drachman DA: Memory function in man: does the cholinergic system have a specific role? Neurology 27:783–790, 1977

Easton JD, Sherman DG: Somatic anxiety attacks and propranolol. Arch Neurol 33:689–691, 1976

Edwards DJ, Spiker DG, Neil JF, et al: MHPG excretion in depression. Psychiatry Res 2:295–305, 1980

Enjalbert A, Ruby M, Fiore L, et al: Effect of morphine on the dopamine inhibition of pituitary release in vitro. Eur J Pharmacol 53:211–212, 1979

Enna SJ, Gallagher JP: Biochemical and electrophysiological characteristics of mammalian GABA receptors. Int Rev Neurobiol 24:181–212, 1983

Extein I, Tallman J, Smith CC, et al: Changes in lymphocyte beta-adrenergic receptors in depression and mania. Psychiatry Res 1:191–197, 1979

Farley IJ, Price KS, McCullough E, et al: Norepinephrine in chronic paranoid schizophrenia: above normal levels in limbic forebrain. 200:456–458, 1978

Fludder JM, Leonard BE: Interaction between mianserin and clonidine in the rat in vivo. Communications in Psychopharmacology 2:487–490, 1978

Fludder JM, Leonard BE: Chronic effects of mianserin on noradrenergic metabolism in the rat brain: evidence for a pre-synaptic alpha-adrenolytic action in vivo. Psychopharmacology 64:329–332, 1979

Francis PT, Palmer AM, Sims NR, et al: Neurochemical studies of early-onset Alzheimer's disease. N Engl J Med 313:7–11, 1985

Freedman R, Kirch D, Bell J, et al: Clonidine treatment of schizophrenia: double-blind comparison to placebo and neuroleptic drugs. Acta Psychiatr Scand 65:35–45, 1982

Frolich ED, Tarazi RC, Dustan HP: Hyperdynamic beta-adrenergic circulatory state. Arch Intern Med 123:1–7, 1969

Garbutt JC, van Kammen DP: The interaction between GABA and dopamine: implications for schizophrenia. Schizophr Bull 9:336–353, 1983

Gershon SC, Baldessarini RJ: Motor effects of serotonin in the central nervous system. Life Sci 27:1435–1451, 1980

Gillespie DD, Manier DH, Sulser F: Electroconvulsive treatment: rapid subsensitivity of the norepinephrine receptor-coupled adenylate cyclase system in brain linked to down regulation of beta-adrenergic receptors. Communications in Psychopharmacology 3:191–194, 1979

Glowinski J, Axelrod J: Inhibition of uptake of tritiated noradrenalin in the intact rat brain by imipramine and structurally related compounds. Nature 204:1318–1319, 1964

Goodwin FK, Post RM, Dunner DL, et al: Cerebrospinal fluid amine metabolities in affective illness: the probenecid technique. Am J Psychiatry 130:73–79, 1973

Gottfries CG, Gottfries I, Roos BE: HVA and 5-HIAA in the CSF of patients with senile dementia, presenile dementia and parkinsonism. J Neurochem 16:1341–1345, 1969

Green RA, Grahame-Smith DE: Effects of drugs on the processes regulating the functional activity of brain 5-hydroxytryptamine. Nature 260:487–491, 1976

Guidotti A, Forchetti CM, Corda MG, et al: Isolation, characterization and purification to homogeneity of an endogenous polypeptide with agonistic action on benzodiazepine receptors. Proc Natl Acad Sci USA 80:3531–3535, 1983

Gunne LM, Lindstrom L, Terenius L: Naloxone-induced reversal of schizophrenic hallucinations. J Neural Transm 40:13–19, 1977

Halaris AE: Evidence in support of a role of dopamine in affective illness. Psychopharmacol Bull 18:31–34, 1982

Halaris AE, Belendiuck KT, Freedman DX: Antidepressant drugs affect dopamine uptake. Biochem Pharmacol 24:1896–1898, 1975

Hertting G, Axelrod J, Whitby LG: Effect of drugs on the uptake metabolism of H^3-norepinephrine. J Pharmacol Exp Ther 134:146–153, 1961

Hoehn-Saric R, Merchant AF, Keyser ML, et al: Effects of clonidine on anxiety disorders. Arch Gen Psychiatry 28:1278–1282, 1981

Hokfelt T, Everitt B, Foster G, et al: Occurrence and distribution of neurons with multiple synaptic messengers and some functional aspects. Clin Neuropharmacol 7(Suppl 1):6–7, 1984

Hollister LE: Excretion of 3-methoxy-4-hydroxyphenylglycol in depressed and geriatric patients and normal persons. International Pharmacopsychiatry 16:138–143, 1981

Hollister LE, Davis KL, Berger PA: Subtypes of depression based on excretion of MHPG and response to nortriptyline. Arch Gen Psychiatry 37:1107–1110, 1980

Hornykiewicz O: Die topische Localisation und das Verhalten von Noradrenalin und Dopamin (3-hydroxytyramin) in der Substantia Nigra des Normalen und Parkinson kranken Menschen (The specific areas and action of noradrenalin and dopamine 3-hydroxytyramine in the substantia nigra on normal and parkinsonian population). Wien Klin Wochenschr 75:309–312, 1963

Huang YH, Redmond DE, Synder DR, et al: Loss of fear following bilateral lesions on the locus coeruleus in the monkey. Neuroscience Abstracts 2:573, 1976

Insel TR, Ninan PT, Aloi J, et al: A benzodiazepine receptor-mediated model of anxiety: studies in nonhuman primates and clinical implications. Arch Gen Psychiatry 41:741–750, 1984

Iversen LL, MacKay AVP: Pharmacodynamics of antidepressants and antimanic drugs, in Psychopharmacology of Affective Disorders. Edited by Paykel ES, Coppen A. New York, Oxford University Press, 1979, pp 60–90

Jacquet Y, Marks N: The C-fragment of beta-lipotropin: an endogenous neuroleptic or antipsychotogen? Science 194:632–635, 1976

Janicak PG, Davis JM, Chan C, et al: Urinary MHPG does not predict response to treatment in unipolar depressed patients. Paper presented at the Annual Meeting of the American Psychiatric Association, Dallas, May 1985

Janowsky AJ, Okada F, Applegate C, et al: Role of serotonergic input in the regulation of the beta-adrenoceptor coupled adenylate cyclase system in brain. Science 218:900–901, 1982

Janowsky DS, Davis JM: Methylphenidate, dextroamphetamine, levoamphetamine effects on schizophrenic symptoms. Arch Gen Psychiatry 33:304–308, 1976

Janowsky DS, Khaled El-Yousef M, Davis JM, et al: A cholinergic adrenergic hypothesis of mania and depression. Lancet 2:632–635, 1972

Janowsky DS, Segal DS, Bloom F, et al: Lack of effect of naloxone on schizophrenic symptoms. Am J Psychiatry 134:926–927, 1977

Jimerson DC, Post RM: Psychomotor stimulants and dopamine agonists in depression, in The Neurobiology of Mood Disorders. Edited by Post RM, Ballenger JC. Baltimore, Williams & Wilkins, 1984, pp 619–628

Joseph MH, Baker HF, Crow TJ, et al: Brain tryptophan metabolism in schizophrenia: a postmortem study of metabolites on the serotonin and kynureine pathways in schizophrenic and control subjects. Psychopharmacology 62:279–285, 1979

Kafka MS, van Kammen DP: Alpha-adrenergic receptor function in schizophrenia. Arch Gen Psychiatry 40:264–270, 1983

Kaplan RD, Mann JJ: Altered platelet serotonin uptake kinetics in schizophrenia and melancholia. Life Sci 31:583–588, 1982

Kasa K, Otsuki S, Yamamoto M, et al: Cerebrospinal fluid aminobutyric acid and homovanillic acid in depressive disorders. Biol Psychiatry 17:877–883, 1982

Kebabian JW, Petzold GL, Greengard P: Dopamine sensitive adenylate cyclase in caudate nucleus of rat brain and its similarity to the "dopamine receptor." Proc Natl Acad Sci USA 79:2145–2149, 1972

Kellar KJ, Cascio CS, Butler JA, et al: Differential effects of electroconvulsive shock and antidepressant drugs on serotonin-2 receptors in rat brain. Eur J Pharmacol 69:515–518, 1981

Kleinman JE, Iadarola M, Govoni S, et al: Postmortem measurements of neuropeptides in human brain. Prog Neuropsychopharmacol Biol Psychiatry 19:375–377, 1983

Kleinman JE, Karoum F. Rosenblatt JE, et al: Postmortem neurochemical studies in chronic schizophrenia, in Biological Markers in Psychiatry and Neurology. Edited by Usdin E, Handin I. New York, Pergamon Press, 1982

Klerman GL, Cole JO: Clinical pharmacology of imipramine and related antidepressant compounds. Pharmacol Rev 17:101–141, 1965

Ko GN, Elsworth JD, Roth RH, et al: Panic-induced elevation of plasma MHPG levels in phobic-anxious patients. Arch Gen Psychiatry 40:425–430, 1983

Kopin IJ: Storage and metabolism in catecholamines, the role of monoamine oxidase. Pharmacol Rev 16:179–191, 1964

Kopin IJ, Gordon EK, Jimerson DC, et al: Relation between plasma and cerebrospinal fluid levels of 3-methoxy-4-hydroxyphenylglycol. Science 219:73–75, 1983

Korpi ER, Kleinman JE, Goodman SI: Serotonin and 5-HIAA in brains of suicide victims: comparison in chronic schizophrenic patients with suicide as cause of death. Arch Gen Psychiatry 43:594–600, 1986

Koslow SH, Maas JW, Bowden CL, et al: CSF and urinary biogenic amines and metabolites in depression and mania. Arch Gen Psychiatry 40:999–1010, 1983

Kuhn R: The treatment of depressive states with G22355 (imipramine hydrochloride). Am J Psychiatry 115:459–464, 1958

Lake CR, Steinberg P, van Kammen D, et al: Schizophrenia: elevated cerebrospinal fluid norepinephrine. Science 207:331–333, 1980

Langer SZ, Moret C, Raisman R, et al: High affinity [^{3}H] binding in rat hypothalamus: association with uptake of serotonin but not of norepinephrine. Science 210:1133–1135, 1980

Lee T, Seeman P: Binding of 3-H neuroleptics and 3-H apomorphine in schizophrenic brains. Nature 274:897–900, 1978

Lee T, Seeman P: Elevation of brain neuroleptic/dopamine receptors in schizophrenia. Am J Psychiatry 137:191–197, 1980

Liebowitz MR, Fyer AJ, Gorman JM, et al: Lactate provocation of panic attacks, I: clinical and behavioral findings. Arch Gen Psychiatry 41:764–770, 1984

Liebowitz MR, Fyer AJ, McGrath P, et al: Clonidine treatment of panic disorder. Psychopharmacol Bull 17:122–124, 1981

Liebowitz MR, Gorman JM, Fyer AJ, et al: Lactate provocation of panic attacks, II: biochemical and physiological findings. Arch Gen Psychiatry 42:709–719, 1985

Lloyd KF, Farley IJ, Deck JHN, et al: Serotonin and 5-hydroxyindoleacetic acid in discrete areas of the brain stem of suicide victims and control patients. Adv Biochem Psychopharmacol 11:387–397, 1974

Loomer HP, Saunders JC, Kline NS: Clinical and pharmacodynamic evaluation of iproniazid as psychic energizer. Psychiatry Research Reports 8:129–141, 1957

Lundberg JM, Hokfelt T: Coexistence of peptides and neurotransmitters. Trends in Neuroscience 6:325–333, 1983

Maas JW; Biogenic amines and depression: biochemical and pharmacological separation of two types of depression. Arch Gen Psychiatry 32:1357–1361, 1975

Maas JW, Fawcett JA, Dekirmenjian H: 3-Methoxy-4-hydroxyphenylglycol (MHPG) excretion in depressive states. Arch Gen Psychiatry 19:129–134, 1968

Maas JW, Koslow SH, Katz MM, et al: Pretreatment neurotransmitter metabolite levels and response to tricyclic antidepressant drugs. Am J Psychiatry 141:1159–1171, 1984

MacDonald R, Barker J: Benzodiazepines specifically modulate GABA-mediated postsynaptic inhibition in cultured mammalian neurons. Nature 271:563–564, 1978

MacKay AVP, Iversen LL, Rossor M, et al: Increased brain dopamine and dopamine receptors in schizophrenia. Arch Gen Psychiatry 39:991–997, 1982

Mair RG, McEntee WJ: Korsakoff's psychosis: noradrenergic systems and cognitive impairment. Behav Brain Res 9:1–32, 1983

Major LF, Murphy DL: Platelet and plasma amine oxidase activity in alcoholic individuals. Br J Psychiatry 132:548–554, 1978

Mann JJ, Brown RP, Halper JP, et al: Reduced sensitivity of lymphocyte beta-adrenergic receptors in patients with endogenous depression and psychomotor agitation. N Engl J Med 313:715–720, 1985

Massotti M, Guidotti A, Costa E: Characterization of benzodiazepine and gamma-aminobutyric recognition sites and their endogenous modulators. J Neurosci 1:409–418, 1981

Mattussek N, Ackenheil M, Hippius H, et al: Effect of clonidine on growth hormone release in psychiatric patients and controls. Psychiatry Res 2:25–36, 1980

McEntee WJ, Mair RG: Memory impairment in Korsakoff's psychosis: a correlation with brain noradrenergic activity. Science 202:905–907, 1978

McGreer EG, McGreer PL: GABA-containing neurons in schizophrenia, Huntington's chorea, and normal aging, in GABA-Neurotransmitters. Edited by Korsgaard-Larsen P, Scheel-Kriiger H, Kofod H. New York, Academic Press, 1979

Meltzer HY, Duncavage MB, Jackman H, et al: Effect of neuroleptic drugs on platelet monoamine oxidase in psychiatric patients. Am J Psychiatry 139:1242–1248, 1982

Mendels J, Frazier A, Fitzgerald RG, et al: Biogenic amine metabolites in cerebrospinal fluid of depressed and manic patients. Science 175:1380–1382, 1972

Miller RJ, Horn AS, Iversen LL: The action of neuroleptic drugs on dopamine-stimulated adenosine 3'5'-monophosphate production in rat neostriatum and limbic forebrain. Mol Pharmacol 10:759–766, 1974

Mishra R, Janowsky A, Sulser F: Action of mianserin and Zimeldine on the norepinephrine receptor coupled adenylate cyclase system in brain: subsensitivity without reduction in beta-adrenergic receptor binding. Neuropharmacology 19:983–987, 1980

Mogilnicka E, Arbilla S, Depoortere H, et al: Rapid-eye-movement sleep deprivation decreased the density of ^{3}H-dihydroalprenolol and ^{3}H-imipramine binding sites in the rat cerebral cortex. Eur J Pharmacol 65:289–292, 1980

Muller JC, Pryor WW, Gibbons JE, et al: Depression and anxiety occurring during rauwolfia therapy. JAMA 159:836–839, 1955

Murphy D, Wyatt RJ: Reduced MAO activity in blood platelets from schizophrenia patients. Nature 238:225–226, 1972

Naber D, Pickar D, Post RM, et al: Endogenous opioid activity and beta-endorphin immunoreactivity in CSF of psychiatric patients and normal volunteers. Am J Psychiatry 138:1457–1462, 1981

Ninan PT, van Kammen DP, Scheinin M, et al: CSF 5-hydroxyindoleacetic acid levels in suicidal schizophrenic patients. Am J Psychiatry 141:566–569, 1984

Ninan P, Insel TR, Cohen RM, et al: A benzodiazepine receptor mediated model of anxiety. Science 218:1332–1334, 1982

O'Donnell VM, Pitts WM, Fann WE: Noradrenergic and cholinergic agents in Korsakoff's syndrome. Clin Neuropharmacol 9:65–70, 1986

Oreland L, Wiberg A, Asberg M, et al: Platelet MAO activity and monoamine metabolites in cerebrospinal fluid in depressed and suicidal patients and in healthy controls. Psychiatry Res 4:21–29, 1981

Owen F, Cross AJ, Crow TJ, et al: Increased dopamine-receptor sensitivity in schizophrenia. Lancet 2:223–226, 1978

Owen F, Cross AJ, Crow TJ, et al: Neurotransmitter receptors in the brain in schizophrenia. Acta Psychiatr Scand 63:20–27, 1981

Owen F, Cross AJ, Waddington JL, et al: Dopamine-mediated behavior 3-H spiperone binding to striatal membranes in rats after nine months of haloperidol administration. Life Sci 26:55–59, 1980

Pandey GN, Dysken MW, Garver DL, et al: Beta-adrenergic receptor function in affective illness. Am J Psychiatry 136:675–678, 1979

Papeschi R, McClure DJ: Homovanillic and 5-hydroxyindoleacetic acid in cerebrospinal fluid of depressed patients. Arch Gen Psychiatry 25:354–358, 1971

Pare CMB, Sandler M: Clinical and biochemical study of a trial of iproniazid in the treatment of depression. J Neurol Neurosurg Psychiatry 22:247, 1959

Pare CMB, Young DPH, Price KS, et al: 5-Hydroxytryptamine, noradrenaline, and dopamine in brainstem, hypothalamus and caudate nucleus of controls and of patients committing suicide by coal-gas poisoning. Lancet 2:133–135, 1969

Paul SM, Rehavi M, Skolnick P, et al: Demonstration of specific high affinity binding sites for [^{3}H]imipramine on human platelets. Life Sci 26:953–959, 1980

Paul SM, Marangos PJ, Skolnick P: The benzodiazepine-GABA-chloride ionophore receptor complex: common site of minor tranquilizer action. Biol Psychiatry 16:213–229, 1981a

Paul SM, Rehavi M, Rice KC, et al: Does high affinity [3H]imipramine binding label serotonin reuptake sites in brain and platelet? Life Sci 28:2753–2760, 1981b

Paul SM, Rehavi M, Skolnick P, et al: Depressed patients have decreased binding of tritiated imipramine to platelet serotonin "transporter." Arch Gen Psychiatry 38:1315–1317, 1981c

Paul SM, Rehavi M, Skolnick P, et al: High affinity binding of antidepressants to biogenic amine transport sites in human brain and platelet, in Studies in Depression in Neurobiology of Mood Disorders, Vol 1. Edited by Post RM, Ballenger JC. Baltimore, Williams & Wilkins, 1984

Peroutka SJ, Snyder SH: Multiple serotonin receptors: differential binding of [3H]5-hydroxytryptamine, [3H]lysergic acid diethylamide and [3H]spiroperidol. Mol Pharmacol 16:687–699, 1979

Peroutka SJ, Snyder SH: Long-term antidepressant treatment decreases spiroperidol-labeled serotonin receptor binding. Science 210:88–90, 1980

Perry TL, Buchanan J, Kish SJ, et al: Gamma-aminobutyric acid deficiency in brain of schizophrenic patients. Lancet 1:237–239, 1979

Pert A: The effects of opiates on nigrostriatal dopaminergic activity, in Characteristics and Functions of Opioids. Edited by van Ree JM, Terenius L. Amsterdam, Elsevier/North Holland, 1978

Pert C, Snyder S: Opiate receptor: demonstration in nervous tissue. Science 179:1011–1014, 1973

Pickar D, Vartanian F, Bunney WE, et al: Short-term naloxone administration in schizophrenics and manic patients. Arch Gen Psychiatry 39:313–319, 1982

Pitts FN, McClure JN: Lactate metabolism in anxiety neurosis. N Engl J Med 277:1328–1336, 1967

Pohl R, Rainey J, Ortiz A, et al: Isoproterenol-induced anxiety states. Psychopharmacol Bull 21:424–427, 1985

Polc P, Mohler H, Haefely W: The effect of diazepam on spinal cord activities: possible sites and mechanism of action. Archives of Pharmacology 284:319–337, 1974

Post RM, Fink E, Carpenter WT, et al: Cerebrospinal fluid amine metabolites in acute schizophrenia. Arch Gen Psychiatry 32:1063–1069, 1975

Post RM, Gordon EK, Goodwin FK, et al: Central norepinephrine metabolism in affective illness: MHPG in the cerebrospinal fluid. Science 179:1002–1003, 1973

Price LH, Charney DS, Heninger GR, et al: Alpha-2 adrenergic receptor function in depression: the cortical response to yohimbine. Arch Gen Psychiatry (in press)

Raisman R, Briley M, Langer SZ: Specific tricyclic antidepressant binding sites in rat brain. Nature 281:148–150, 1979

Redmond DE: New and old evidence for the involvement of a brain norepinephrine system in anxiety, in Phenomenology and Treatment of Anxiety. Edited by Fann WE, Karacan I, Pokorny A, et al. New York, Spectrum Books, 1979, pp 152–203

Redmond DE, Huang YH: New evidence for a locus coeruleus-norepinephrine connection with anxiety. Life Sci 25:2149–2162, 1979

Redmond DE, Huang YH, Snyder DR, et al: Behavioral changes following lesions of the locus coeruleus in Macaca arctoides. Neuroscience Abstracts 1:472, 1976a

Redmond DE, Huang YH, Snyder DR, et al: Behavioral effects of stimulation of locus coeruleus in the stumptail monkey (Macaca arctoides). Brain Res 116:502–520, 1976b

Rehavi M, Paul SM, Skolnick P, et al: Demonstration of specific high affinity binding sites for [3H]imipramine in human brain. Life Sci 26:2273–2279, 1980

Rimon R, Roos BE, Rakkolainen V, et al: The content of 5-HIAA and HVA in the CSF of patients with acute schizophrenia. J Psychosom Res 15:375–378, 1971

Robert E: A hypothesis suggesting that there is a defect in the GABA system in schizophrenia. Neuroscience Research Progress Bulletin 10:468–481, 1972

Rosenbaum AH, Schatzberg AF, Maruta T, et al: MHPG as a predictor of antidepressant response to imipramine and maprotiline. Am J Psychiatry 137:1090–1092, 1980

Rotman A, Zemishlany Z, Munitz H, et al: The active uptake of serotonin by platelets of schizophrenic patients and their families: possibility of a genetic marker. Psychopharmacology 77:171–174, 1982

Sacchetti E, Smeraldi E, Cagnasso M, et al: MHPG, amitriptyline, and affective disorder: a longitudinal study. International Pharmacopsychiatry 11:157–162, 1976

Schatzberg AF, Orsulak PJ, Rosenbaum AH, et al: Toward a biochemical classification of depressive disorders, IV: heterogeneity of unipolar disorders. Am J Psychiatry 139:471–475, 1982

Schildkraut JJ: The catecholamine hypothesis of affective disorders: a review of supporting evidence. Am J Psychiatry 122:509–522, 1965

Schildkraut JJ: Current status of the catecholamine hypothesis of affective disorders, in Psychopharmacology: A Generation of Progress. Edited by Lipton MA, DiMascio A, Killam KF. New York, Raven Press, 1978, pp 1223–1234

Serra G, Argiolas A, Klimek V, et al: Chronic treatment with anti-depressants prevents the inhibitory effect of small doses of apomorphine on dopamine synthesis and motor activity. Life Sci 25:415–424, 1979

Sheehan DV, Ballenger J, Jacobsen G: Treatment of endogenous anxiety with phobic, hysterical, and hypochondriacal symptoms. Arch Gen Psychiatry 37:51–59, 1980

Siever LJ, Uhde TW, Jimerson DC, et al: Differential inhibitory noradrenergic responses to clonidine in 25 depressed patients and 25 normal control subjects. Am J Psychiatry 141:733–741, 1984

Siever LJ, Uhde TW, Silberman EK, et al: The growth hormone response to clonidine as a probe of noradrenergic receptor responsiveness in affective disorder patients and controls. Psychiatry Res 6:171–183, 1982

Simantov R, Kuhar MJ, Pasternak GW, et al: The regional distribution of morphine-like factor enkephalin in monkey brain. Brain Res 106:189–197, 1976

Simon EJ, Hiller JM, Edelman I: Stereospecific binding of one potent narcotic analgesic (3-H) etorphine to rat-brain homogenate. Proc Natl Acad Sci USA 70:1947–1949, 1973

Sims NR, Boen DM, Neary D, et al: Metabolic processes in Alzheimer's disease: adenine nucleotide content and production of $^{14}CO_2$ from [U-14C]glucose in vitro in human neocortex. J Neurochem 41:339–1324, 1983

Sitaram N, Nurnberger JI, Gershon ES: Faster cholinergic REM sleep induction in euthymic patients with primary affective illness. Science 208:200–202, 1980

Skolnick P, Paul SM: Benzodiazepine receptors in the central nervous system. International Review of Neurobiology 23:103–140, 1982

Snyder SH: Brain peptides as neurotransmitters. Science 209:976–983, 1980

Spyrakic C, Fibiger HC: Functional evidence for subsensitivity of noradrenergic alpha-receptors after chronic desipramine treatment. Life Sci 27:1863–1867, 1980

Squires RF, Braestrup C: Benzodiazepine receptors in rat brain. Nature 266:732–734, 1977

Stanley M, Mann J: Increased serotonin$_2$ binding sites in frontal cortex of suicide victims. Lancet 1:214–216, 1983

Stanley M, Virgilio J, Gershon S: Tritiated imipramine binding sites are decreased in the frontal cortex of suicides. Science 216:1337–1339, 1982

Stein L, Wise CD, Belluzzi JD: Effects of benzodiazepines on central serotonergic mechanisms. Adv Biochem Psychopharmacol 14:29–44, 1975

Suranyi-Cadotte BE, Wood PL, Nair NPV, et al: Normalization of platelet [^{3}H]imipramine binding in depressed patients. Eur J Pharmacol 85:351–357, 1983

Tenen SS, Hirsch JD: Beta-carboline-3-carboxylic acid ethyl ester antagonizes diazepam activity. Nature 288:609–610, 1980

Terenius L: Stereospecific interaction between narcotic analgesics and a synaptic plasma membrane fraction of rat cerebral cortex. Acta Pharmacol Toxicol (Copenh) 32:317–320, 1973

Terry LC, Martin JB: Evidence for alpha-adrenergic regulation of episodic growth hormone and prolactin secretion in the undisturbed male rat. Endocrinology 108:1869–1873, 1981

Terry RD, Davies P: Dementia of the Alzheimer type. Annu Rev Neurosci 3:77–95, 1980

Traskman-Bendz L, Asberg M, Betilsson L, et al: CSF monoamine metabolites of depressed patients during illness and after recovery. Acta Psychiatr Scand 69:333–342, 1984

Tyrer P, Candy J, Kelly DA: A study of the clinical effects of phenelzine and placebo in the treatment of phobic anxiety. Psychopharmacologia 32:237–254, 1973

Unnerstall J, Kuhar M, Niehoff DL, et al: Benzodiazepine receptors are coupled to a subpopulation of gamma-aminobutyric acid (GABA) receptors: evdence from a quantitative autoradiographic study. J Pharmacol Exp Ther 218:797–804, 1981

van Praag HM, Korf J, Schut D: Cerebral monoamines and depression: an investigation with the probenecid technique. Arch Gen Psychiatry 28:827–831, 1973

Vestergaard P, Sorensen T, Hoppe E, et al: Biogenic amine metabolites in cerebrospinal fluid of patients with affective disorders. Acta Psychiatr Scand 58:88–96, 1978

Vetulani J, Sulser F: Action of various antidepressant treatments reduce reactivity of noradrenergic cyclic AMP-generating system in limbic forebrain. Nature 257:495–496, 1975

Vetulani J, Stawarz RJ, Sulser F: Adaptive mechanisms of the noradrenergic cyclic AMP generating system in the limbic forebrain of the rat: adaptation to persistent changes in the availability of norepinephrine (NE). J Neurochem 37:661–666, 1976

Volavka J, Davis LG, Ehrlich YH: Endorphins, dopamine, and schizophrenia. Schizophr Bull 5:227–239, 1979

Volavka J, Mallya A, Baig S, et al: Naloxone in chronic schizophrenia. Science 196:1227–1228, 1977

Watson SJ, Berger PA, Akil H, et al: Effects of naloxone on schizophrenia: reduction in hallucinations in a subpopulation of subjects. Science 201:73–76, 1978

Whitehouse PJ, Price DL, Stuble RG: Alzheimer's disease and senile dementia: loss of neurons in the basal forebrain. Science 215:1237–1239, 1982

Wise CD, Stein L: DBH deficits in the brains of schizophrenia patients. Science 181:344–347, 1973

Wyatt RJ, Schwartz MD, Erdelyi E, et al: Dopamine-beta-hydroxylase activity in brains of chronic schizophrenic patients. Science 187:368–369, 1975

Yorkston NJ, Zaki SA, Malik MKU, et al: Propranolol in the control of schizophrenia symptoms. Br Med J 14:633–635, 1974

Zitrin CM, Klein DF, Woerner MG, et al: Treatment of agoraphobia with group exposure in vivo and imipramine. Arch Gen Psychiatry 37:63–72, 1980

Zitrin CM, Klein DF, Woerner MG, et al: Treatment of phobias: comparison of imipramine hydrochloride and placebo. Arch Gen Psychiatry 40:125–138, 1983

Section
II

Organic Mental Disorders

Chapter 5

Delirium

Michael G. Wise, M.D.

DELIRIUM MAY WELL BE the most common psychiatric syndrome found in a general medical hospital. Its mortality and morbidity may surpass all other psychiatric diagnoses. Only dementia, when followed for several years, has a higher mortality rate (Roth 1955; Varsamis et al. 1972). In addition, demented or other brain-damaged patients have a lower threshold for developing a delirium and do so with greater frequency (Epstein and Simon 1967; Hodkinson 1973). Although commonly seen by consultation psychiatrists and other physicians, delirium remains an ignored, underresearched phenomenon. Lipowski (1978) stated, "Organic brain syndromes are the most neglected areas of psychiatry in this country. Little is known about their epidemiology, their classification is inadequate, and their terminology is a prime example of semantic bedlam" (p. 309).

Figure 1 presents a conceptual overview of delirium. Note the wide variety of different physiologic insults that can produce the symptom cluster of the delirium syndrome. This multifactorial etiology accounts both for the high incidence of the syndrome and for the evolution of so many "equivalent" diagnostic terms. Delirium can manifest clinically as a hypoactive state (decreased arousal), hyperactive state (increased arousal), or as a mixed state with fluctuations between hypoactive and hyperactive forms. Accurate diagnosis, of course, precedes treatment. However, if the clinician cannot find a specific reason or reasons for a delirium, there are nonspecific treatments that can decrease symptoms, decrease morbidity, and may decrease mortality. The prognosis for delirium, without proper diagnosis and treatment, is bleak.

☐ DEFINITION

Defining delirium is not an easy task because many terms have been used to describe this clinical syndrome (Table 1). These terms are sometimes used synonymously and, at other times, are used as though they describe different clinical syndromes. For example, Peura and Johnson (1985), who described the use of intravenous cimetidine in gastroduodenal mucosal lesions, stated that one patient had delirium, one patient had hallucinations, and a third patient had mental confusion. Do these three patients have different disorders or do they all have a delirium? A computerized literature search for recent articles using the subject headings "delirium," "encephalopathy" (a term often used by internists and neurologists), and "confusion" revealed

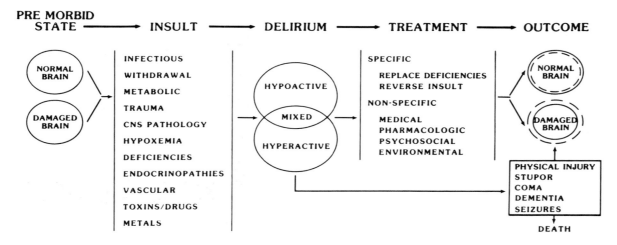

Figure 1. Conceptual overview of delirium.

TABLE 1. TERMS USED/MISUSED TO DENOTE DELIRIUM

acute brain failure	infective-exhaustive
acute brain syndrome	psychosis
acute brain syndrome	ICU psychosis
with psychosis	metabolic encephalopathy
acute confusional state	oneiric state
acute organic psychosis	organic brain syndrome
acute organic reaction	reversible cerebral
acute organic syndrome	dysfunction
acute reversible psychosis	reversible cognitive
acute secondary	dysfunction
psychosis	reversible dementia
cerebral insufficiency	reversible toxic psychosis
confusional state	toxic confusion state
dysergastic reaction	toxic encephalopathy
exogenous psychosis	

the following. Of the many references catalogued under each subject, none was catalogued as common to all three headings, and fewer than 0.5 percent were common to any combination of two of these subject headings. It would appear that confusion describes both the syndrome and its literature.

The diagnostic criteria for delirium found in DSM-III-R (1987) is outlined in Table 2. Both DSM-III (1980) and DSM-III-R criteria evolved from a committee effort but underrepresent the wide array of neuropsychiatric abnormalities found in the delirious patient. The section of this chapter on clinical features attempts to amplify and expand these criteria. DSM-III-R does unify a broad spectrum of clinical states under the diagnostic umbrella of delirium (i.e., hypoactive, hyperactive, and mixed deliriums). This approach is not accepted by many of

TABLE 2. DSM-III-R DIAGNOSTIC CRITERIA FOR DELIRIUM

A. Reduced ability to maintain attention to external stimuli (e.g., questions must be repeated because attention wanders) and to appropriately shift attention to new external stimuli (e.g., perseverates answer to a previous question).

B. Disorganized thinking, as indicated by rambling, irrelevant or incoherent speech.

C. At least two of the following:
   (1) reduced level of consciousness, e.g., difficulty keeping awake during examination
   (2) perceptual disturbances: misinterpretations, illusions or hallucinations
   (3) disturbance of sleep-wake cycle with insomnia or daytime sleepiness
   (4) increased or decreased psychomotor activity
   (5) disorientation to time, place, or person
   (6) memory impairment, e.g., inability to learn new material, such as the names of several unrelated objects after five minutes, or to remember past events, such as history of current episode of illness

D. Clinical features develop over a short period of time (usually hours to days) and tend to fluctuate over the course of a day.

E. Either (1) or (2):
   (1) evidence from the history, physical examination, or laboratory tests of a specific organic factor (or factors) judged to be etiologically related to the disturbance
   (2) in the absence of such evidence, an etiologic organic factor can be presumed if the disturbance cannot be accounted for by any nonorganic mental disorder, e.g., Manic Episode accounting for agitation and sleep disturbance

our medical colleges, particularly neurologists. Adams and Victor (1981), for example, feel that the diagnosis of delirium should be reserved for a subgroup of confused patients with agitation, autonomic instability, and hallucinations. Delirium tremens (DTs) is the conceptual model they used. Patients who become acutely confused, incoherent, and disoriented, but without autonomic instability and hallucinations, would be said to have "acute confusional states," not delirium. These classification disparities are rooted in the history and evolution of the concept of delirium and have been discussed by Lipowski (1980b) and Berrios (1981).

Pending further research, the unified approach of DSM-III-R, which labels both hyperactive and hypoactive forms as delirium, seems appropriate. This concept is supported by Engel and Romano (1959), who hypothesized that delirium represents a metabolic derangement. Several other aspects of the syndrome must be incorporated into a definition. Delirium usually has a sudden onset and a brief duration, and is reversible. Therefore, delirium is herein defined as a transient, essentially reversible dysfunction in cerebral metabolism that has an acute or subacute onset and is manifest clinically by a wide array of neuropsychiatric abnormalities.

☐ EPIDEMIOLOGY

A discussion of the epidemiology of delirium implies the existence of a reasonable body of scientific study into the factors that influence its frequency and distribution. However, systematic research on the epidemiology of delirium is, for the most part, lacking. Therefore, conclusions drawn are tentative.

Incidence

The incidence of delirium varies depending on the type of insult and the predisposition of the individual involved. On general medical or surgical hospital services, Lipowski (1980a) has estimated that 5 to 10 percent of patients display symptoms of delirium. Engel (1967) estimated a rate of 10 to 15 percent on acute medical and surgical wards.

Six groups of patients reportedly have a higher risk of developing a delirium: (1) elderly patients, (2) children, (3) postcardiotomy patients, (4) burn patients, (5) patients with preexisting brain dam-

age, and (6) patients with drug addiction. Advancing age increases the risk, with age 60 or over usually cited as the highest risk group (Lipowski 1980a). If children are excluded, the incidence of delirium increases with the age of the patient population studied. Sir Martin Roth (1955), while studying the natural history of mental disorders in older people, reported acute confusional states among psychiatric patients in 7.5 percent of patients age 60 to 69, 9 percent in patients age 70 to 79, and 12 percent in patients over age 80. Bedford (1959) reported that 80 percent of the 5,000 patients aged 65 years or more admitted to the Oxford Geriatric Unit during an 8-year period had confusional states.

There are very few studies of delirium in children, but there is general consensus, based on anecdotal information, that delirium occurs frequently in this population: "In the milder forms, the child or adolescent may be thought to be exhibiting provocative behavior or acting-out behavior; if the underlying delirium is undetected, the patient may gradually become more delirious to the point of injuring himself or interfering with his medical treatment" (Prugh 1980, p. 189). This statement applies equally to delirious adults. Children have a negligible incidence of postcardiotomy delirium. Kornfeld et al.'s (1965) sample of 119 unselected open heart patients included 20 children who had surgical procedures for repair of congenital lesions. No child developed delirium whereas 30 percent of the adults operated on for congenital repairs experienced delirium.

Postcardiotomy delirium has been the focus of more neuropsychiatric research than any other aspect of delirium. Dubin et al. (1979) wrote a thorough review of postcardiotomy delirium in which they reported that the incidence across studies varied from 13 to 67 percent. A number of factors in addition to increased age and preexisting brain damage may increase the incidence of postcardiotomy delirium. These include time on bypass (Heller et al. 1970; Kornfeld et al. 1974), severity of postoperative illness (Kornfeld et al. 1974), serum levels of anticholinergic drugs (Tune et al. 1981), increased levels of central nervous system (CNS)-adenylate kinase and subclinical brain injury (Aberg et al. 1982, 1984), decreased cardiac output (Blachly and Kloster 1966), complexity of the surgical procedure (Dubin et al. 1979), complement activation (Chenoweth et al. 1981), and nutritional status as measured by albumin levels. Preoperative psychiatric interviews may reduce postoperative psychosis by 50 percent (Kornfeld et al. 1974; Layne and Yudofsky 1971).

According to Andreasen et al. (1972), about 30 percent of adult burn patients have symptoms of delirium and the "frequency increases with both the age of the patient and the severity of the burn" (p. 68). Blank and Perry (1984) described an 18 percent incidence of delirium in burn patients. Antoon et al. (1972) reported a 14 percent incidence of burn encephalopathy in children, but they defined burn encephalopathy as "Neurologic disturbances ranging from hallucination, personality changes, and delirium to seizures and coma" (p. 609), so the actual incidence of delirium in this study was much lower.

The presence of preexisting brain damage, whether preoperative CNS neurologic abnormalities (Branthwaite 1972; Kornfeld et al. 1974; Layne and Yudofsky 1971) or dementia (Epstein 1967; Hodkinson 1973), lowers the patient's threshold for developing a delirium. Withdrawal from drug addiction, particularly withdrawal from alcohol, is without question a risk factor for developing delirium.

Prevalence

The prevalence of delirium is largely unknown. Anthony et al. (1982) used the "Mini-Mental State" examination and tested consecutively admitted patients to a general medical ward of the Johns Hopkins Hospital. They found a point prevalence for delirium of 24 percent and also found that 34 percent of patients had some cognitive impairment on the day of admission.

Predisposing Factors

Although one assumes that anyone can develop delirium, some patients have a greater risk. Research indicates that as the severity of a physiologic stress increases, so does the probability of developing a delirium. This is particularly true in burn patients (Andreasen 1974) and in postoperative and postcardiotomy deliriums (Dubin et al. 1979).

Additional factors, such as sleep deprivation and perceptual (sensory) deprivation, are felt to facilitate the development of a delirium. Lipowski (1980a), after a thorough review of the literature on the relationship of sleep to delirium stated, "the results of experimental and clinical studies converge to support a relationship between sleep dis-

turbance and delirium. The precise nature of this relationship remains unclear" (p. 133). Without question, sleep-wake abnormalities are an integral part of the symptomatology found in delirium. How critical sleep deprivation is to the development of the delirium remains an unanswered question. Both sensory deprivation and sensory overload are felt to be facilitating factors in delirium (Lipowski 1980a). The crucial issue may not be the quantity of stimuli but rather the quality. It is known, for example, that the electroencephalogram (EEG) of a subject exposed to monotonous stimuli shows more slowing than the EEG of a sensory-deprived subject (Zubek and Welch 1963). Patients in an intensive care unit (ICU) do not lack stimulation; rather, they lack the kinds of stimuli that orient them to time and environment.

The predisposition associated with personality and psychological variables has been investigated as well. In their review of the postoperative literature, Dubin et al. (1979) indicated that no specific personality profile correlated with delirium. Lipowski (1980a) agreed, reporting that "it may be stated that so far not a single psychological variable has been conclusively shown to predispose one to delirium" (p. 115).

☐ CLINICAL FEATURES OF DELIRIUM

Prodrome

The patient will often manifest symptoms such as restlessness, anxiety, irritability, or sleep disruption prior to the onset of a delirium. Review of the

---

TABLE 3.   CLINICAL FEATURES OF DELIRIUM

Prodrome - Restlessness, anxiety, sleep disturbance, irritability
Rapidly Fluctuating Course, Reversible
Attention Decreased (easily distractable)
Altered Arousal and Psychomotor Abnormality
Sleep-Wake Disturbance
Impaired Memory (can't register new information)
Thinking and Speech Disorganized
Disorientation - time, place, person (very rare)
Perceptions Altered - misperceptions, illusions, delusions (poorly formed), hallucinations
Emotional Lability
Dysgraphia/Constructional Apraxia/Dysomic Aphasia
Motor Abnormalities - tremor, asterixis, myoclonus, reflex and tone changes

delirious patient's medical chart, particularly the nursing notes, will often reveal these prodomal features.

Fluctuating Course

The clinical features of delirium are protean (Table 3) and, to complicate the picture further, will vary rapidly over time. This variability and fluctuation of clinical findings are not only characteristic of delirium but can lead to diagnostic difficulties. Thus the surgery team that sees Mr. Jones on early morning rounds may find him friendly, alert, and noncomplaining, but the psychiatric consultant later that day may find Mr. Jones grossly confused, paranoid, agitated, uncooperative, and visually hallucinating. Convincing the surgeons that Mr. Jones has a severe delirium that requires immediate evaluation and treatment can be a difficult and often frustrating task. The appearance of lucid intervals in the clinical course of a patient is an important observation and is diagnostic of a delirium.

Wells and Duncan's (1980) statement that the symptom complex of delirium is manifest by "marked variability from patient to patient and from time to time in the same patient" (p. 46) is certainly true. There is a subgroup of patients who manifest what has been called "reversible dementia" (Task Force sponsored by the National Institute on Aging 1980). These patients lack the dramatic fluctuations that are so typical of delirium and, as a result, are often misdiagnosed as dementia.

Attentional Deficits

The delirious patient has difficulty sustaining attention. The patient is easily distracted by incidental activities in the environment. If one were interviewing a delirious patient in the hospital and a housekeeping person walked by, the patient would most likely attend to the distraction. When the patient then looked back, the patient may say, "Did you ask me a question?" The patient's inability to sustain attention undoubtedly plays a key role in memory and orientation difficulties.

Arousal Disturbance and Psychomotor Abnormalities

The activating system of the brain stem in delirium may be hypoactive, in which case the patient would appear apathetic, somnolent, and quietly con-

fused. In other patients, the brain stem's activating system may be hyperactive, in which case the patient is agitated and hypervigilant, exhibiting psychomotor hyperactivity. Some patients have a mixed picture, with swings back and forth between hypoactive and hyperactive states. According to Lipowski (1980a), the latter group of delirious patients is "very common" (p. 53). The patient with a retarded (hypoactive) type delirium is less apt to be diagnosed as delirious and is often labeled as depressed or uncooperative. The diagnosis of clinical depression in an apathetic, quietly confused patient can lead to inappropriate treatment (e.g., antidepressants). This misdiagnosis increases morbidity and mortality from failure to diagnose and treat underlying causes for the delirium, and adds the anticholinergic burden from antidepressants to the already malfunctioning brain.

Sleep-Wake Disturbance

Sleep-wake disturbance is not only symptomatic of a delirium, but exacerbates the confusion via sleep deprivation. The normal sleep-wake cycle of the delirious patient is often reversed. The patient may be somnolent during the day and active during the night when the nursing staff is sparse. Restoration of the normal diurnal sleep cycle is an important part of treatment.

Impaired Memory

The ability of a delirious patient to register events into memory is severely impaired. Whether because of attentional deficits, perceptual disturbances, or malfunction of the hippocampus, the patient will fail tests of immediate and recent memory. Following recovery from a delirium, some patients will be amnestic for the entire episode; others will have islands of memory for events during the episode. Whether these islands of memory correspond to the previously described "lucid intervals" is unknown.

Disorganized Thinking and Speech

The delirious patient's thought patterns are disorganized and reasoning is defective. Ask a presumptively delirious patient to explain the following story: "I have a friend by the name of Frank Jones whose feet are so large he has to put on his pants by pulling them over his head. Can Mr. Jones do that?" Typical responses, often with a smile and a laugh, are, "Sure, as long as he does one pant leg at a time" or "I guess so, if he takes off his shoes." The delirious patient does not understand the problem at hand and is unable to reason normally. Using DSM-III-R terminology, the patient's consciousness is clouded. In addition, as the severity of the delirium increases, spontaneous speech becomes "incoherent, rambling, and shifts from topic to topic" (Cummings 1985, p. 68).

Disorientation

The patient with a delirium, except for lucid intervals, is usually disoriented to time, often disoriented to place, but very rarely, if ever, disoriented to person. It is not unusual for a delirious patient to feel he or she is in a familiar place (e.g., "a room in the attic of my house") while also nodding agreement that he or she is being monitored in a surgical intensive care unit. The extent of the patient's disorientation will fluctuate with the severity of the delirium.

Altered Perceptions

The delirious patient will often experience misperceptions that involve illusions, delusions, and hallucinations. Virtually all patients with a delirium will have misperceptions. The patient will often weave these misperceptions into a loosely knit delusional, often paranoid system. The patient may, for example, overhear the nurses say, "We're going to move him out" (i.e., move to another room). The patient may then hear another patient moaning and have the illusion that the sound of a falling bedpan is a gunshot. The patient may then put these events together and suspect that he is about to be transferred to a torture chamber and be killed.

Visual hallucinations are common and can involve simple visual distortions or complex scenes. During a delirium, visual hallucinations occur more frequently than auditory hallucinations. Tactile hallucinations are the least frequent. In this author's experience, many of the so-called auditory and tactile hallucinations are, in fact, illusions. For example, intravenous tubing brushing the skin may be perceived as a snake crawling on the arm.

Emotional Lability

Emotional disturbances are common in delirious patients. The intensity of the patient's emotional response to mental confusion may fluctuate relatively rapidly and may also change in character with the passage of time (i.e., from fear with associated hyperarousal to apathy with hypoarousal). Thus, the delirious patient is often described as emotionally labile.

The emotional responses seen in delirious patients include anxiety, panic, fear, anger, rage, sadness, apathy, and—rarely except in self-induced delirium—euphoria. Medical care givers may identify the emotional or behavioral disturbance of the critically ill patient without recognizing the underlying confusional state. Lipowski (1967, 1980a) notes that the determinates of the individual's response to delirium are personality structure, the nature of the underlying illness, the contents of thoughts and hallucinations, and the characteristics of the environment.

Dysgraphia/Constructional Apraxia/Dysnomic Aphasia

There are a number of neuropsychiatric signs that are found in delirium. Testing for these signs at the bedside not only strengthens the clinician's suspicion but, when added to the chart, assists other physicians to acknowledge the presence of a confusional state. Draw a large circle on an unlined blank sheet of paper and ask the patient to draw a clock face with the hands showing 10 minutes before 11 o'clock (Figure 2). This, and other constructional tasks, are very sensitive indicators for the degree of confusion present. Ask the patient to name objects (testing for dysnomia) and to write a sentence (testing for dysgraphia). Dysgraphia is one of the most sensitive indicators of a delirium. In Chedru and Geschwind's study (1972), 33 of 34 acutely confused patients had impaired writing. Writing shows motor impairment (from tremor to illegible scribble), spatial impairment (letter malalignment and line disorientation), misspelling, and linguistic errors.

Motor Abnormalities

Delirious patients may not have motor system abnormalities, although many patients manifest tremor, myoclonus, asterixis, or reflex and muscle tone changes. The tremor associated with delirium, particularly toxic-metabolic, is absent at rest but apparent during movement. Myoclonus and asterixis (so-called liver flap) occur in many toxic and metabolic conditions. Symmetric reflex and muscle tone changes can also occur.

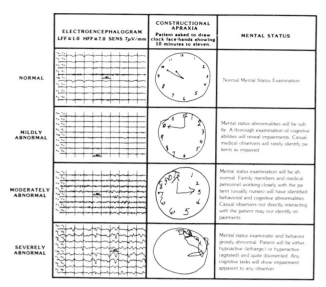

Figure 2. Comparison of electroencephalogram, constructional apraxia, and mental status.

☐ PATHOPHYSIOLOGY AND EEG ABNORMALITIES

Although delirium is a common clinical entity, remarkably little of its pathophysiology has been studied. Significant information has been provided by early EEG investigators. From 1944 to 1947, Engel, Romano, and others (Engel et al. 1947; Romano and Engel 1944) wrote a series of classic papers correlating the severity of delirium (i.e., cognitive dysfunction) with EEG findings (Figure 2). Their clinical research established that: (1) a correlation existed between the electrical abnormality and disturbance of consciousness, which they termed "the primary psychological symptom of delirium;" (2) EEG changes were reversible to the extent that the clinical delirium was reversible; (3) the character of the EEG change appeared to be independent of the specific underlying disease process; (4) the character of the EEG changes was determined by the intensity, duration, and reversibility of the noxious factors as modified by the essential premorbid integrity of the CNS; and (5) clinical interventions (e.g., administration of oxygen in congestive heart failure and pulmonary insufficiency) improved (normalized) the EEG and improved the mental status.

Engel and Romano's (1959) classic paper, entitled "Delirium, a Syndrome of Cerebral Insufficiency," proposed that the basic etiology of all delirium was a derangement in functional metab-olism that was manifest at the clinical level by characteristic disturbances in cognitive functions and at the physiologic level by characteristic slowing of the EEG. Pro and Wells (1977) reported that EEG changes virtually always accompany delirium. The EEG changes found in delirium are *not* always slowing and the pattern can be low voltage fast activity, as in delirium tremens (Kennard et al. 1945). Low voltage fast activity is usually found in hyperactive, agitated patients with heightened arousal (Pro and Wells 1977). EEG slowing is found in lethargic, anergic, abulic patients. The EEG slowing illustrated in Figure 2 is typical for deliriums caused by toxic-metabolic etiologies.

An individual's EEG can have significant slowing but still be read as normal if, for example, a patient's normal background activity is 12 cycles/sec and during a metabolic encephalopathy the background slows to 8 cycles/sec. Significant slowing has occurred, although the reported rate, 8 cycles/sec, still falls within the "normal" range and the EEG could be read as normal. Documentation of the encephalopathy might only occur if the patient has a previous EEG on record or if a second EEG is obtained once the patient is again cognitively normal. EEG abnormalities can also occur before, and also linger after, the clinical manifestations of a delirium (Andreasen et al. 1977).

Since the Engel and Romano's (1959) hypothesis that delirium represents a metabolic derangement, little additional research information has been forthcoming. When Lipowski (1980a) reviewed the studies on cerebral metabolism, cerebral blood flow, and delirium, he stated, "Studies of rCBF [regional cerebral blood flow] in delirium have only begun." This is still an accurate assessment. Two recent textbooks, *Cerebral Blood Flow and Metabolism Measurement* (Hartmann and Hayer 1985, p. 167) and *Positron Emission Tomography* (Reivich and Abass 1985) contain information on psychiatric disorders, but neither sheds any further light on the pathophysiology of delirium.

☐ DIFFERENTIAL DIAGNOSIS FOR DELIRIUM

The differential diagnosis of delirium is so extensive that there may be a clinical tendency to avoid the search for etiologies. It is also important to realize that confusional states, particularly in the elderly, may have multiple causes. For example, an elderly delirious patient may be found to have a low hematocrit, multiorgan system disease (e.g., pulmonary insufficiency, cardiac failure, or preexisting brain damage) and be taking multiple medications. Each potential contributor to the delirium needs to be pursued and reversed independently.

Nonspecific terms such as *ICU psychosis* may be used as an explanation, when, in fact, these nonspecific terms simply mask our lack of knowledge. The task for the clinician is to organize the wide array of potential causes of delirium into a usable diagnostic system. The following is an attempt to present a systematic approach to the differential diagnosis of delirium.

Emergent Items (WHHHHIMP)

A two-tiered differential diagnostic system is very helpful when consulting on a delirious patient. The first level of this diagnostic system is demonstrated in Table 4, and is represented by the mnemonic WHHHHIMP. WHHHHIMP diagnoses must be made early in the course of a delirium because failure to do so may result in irreversible damage to the patient. The mnemonic can help the clinician recall these critical items. Table 4 also contains many of the clinical questions that must be asked to determine the diagnosis.

W—Wernicke's encephalopathy/Withdrawal: A patient with Wernicke's encephalopathy will have a triad of findings that consists of confusion, ataxia, and ophthalmoplegia (usually lateral gaze paralysis). If Wernicke's encephalopathy is not promptly treated with parenteral thiamine, the patient will be left with a permanent Korsakoff's psychosis, in DSM-III called organic amnestic syndrome. A precise history of alcohol intake is critical for the diagnosis of alcohol withdrawal and/or DTs. Other findings that increase the suspicion of alcohol withdrawal/DTs are a history of alcohol-related arrests, alcoholic blackouts, medical complications associated with alcohol abuse, liver function abnormalities, and elevated red cell mean corpuscular volume (MCV). Hyperreflexia and sympathetic discharge (e.g. tachycardia, tremor, sweating, hyperarousal) at the time of examination should lead the clinician to suspect a hyperadrenergic withdrawal state.

H—(4 *Hs*) Hypoxemia/Hypertensive encephalopathy/Hypoglycemia/Hypoperfusion: Checking the arterial blood gases and checking the current and past vital signs should quickly establish whether hypoxemia or hypertensive encephalopathy is present. The patient with hypoglycemic-induced

TABLE 4. DIFFERENTIAL DIAGNOSIS FOR DELIRIUM: EMERGENT ITEMS (WHHHHIMP)

Diagnoses	Clinical Questions
Wernicke's Encephalopathy/ Withdrawal	Ataxia? ophthalmoplegia? alcohol/drug history, ↑ MCV ↑ sympathetic activity? (e.g., ↑ pulse, ↑ BP, sweating), hyperreflexia?
Hypertensive Encephalopathy	↑ ↑ BP, papilledema?
Hypoglycemia	History of insulin-dependent diabetes mellitus? ↓ glucose?
Hypoperfusion of CNS	↓ BP, ↓ cardiac output? (e.g., myocardial infarct, arrhythmia, cardiac failure), ↓ hemocrit
Hypoxemia	Arterial blood gases (↓ pO₂), history of pulmonary disease?
Intracranial Bleed	History of unconsciousness? focal neurologic signs?
Meningitis/Encephalitis	Meningeal signs, ↑ white blood count, ↑ temp?; viral prodrome?
Poisons/Medications	Should toxic screen be ordered? signs of toxicity? (e.g., pupillary abnormality, nystagmus, ataxia); is the patient on a drug that may cause delirium?

delirium almost always has a history of insulin-dependent diabetes mellitus. Hypoglycemic delirium is also a hyperadrenergic delirium. There are a number of clinical phenomena that can singularly, or additively, decrease brain perfusion. These are "relative" hypotension (relative to usual perfusion pressures), decreased cardiac output from a myocardial infarction, cardiac failure or arrhythmias, and anemia.

I—Intracranial bleeding: Has the patient had a subarachnoid bleed or any other type of CNS hemorrhage? If the patient had a brief period of unconsciousness, with or without headache, and is now delirious, or if the patient had or now has focal neurologic signs, an intracranial bleed must be suspected. Immediate neurologic/neurosurgical evaluation is necessary.

M—Meningitis/Encephalitis: These are typically acute febrile illnesses (check vital signs for fever) and usually have either nonspecific localizing neurologic signs (e.g., meningismus with stiff neck) or more focal neurologic signs.

P—Poisons/Medications: When a delirious patient is encountered in the emergency room, the clinician must consider a toxic organic reaction and order a toxic screen. Other considerations such as pesticide or solvent poisoning are less likely but should be considered. In hospital and emergency room patients, a common cause of delirium is prescribed medications (Table 5). The importance of taking a thorough medication history cannot be overemphasized. For hospitalized patients who become delirious, the examiner must thoroughly review the patient's medication records. The doctor's order sheets can be misleading because drugs may have been ordered but not given. Correlation of behavior with medication administration or discontinuation can be very helpful in sorting through a difficult case.

Critical Items (I WATCH DEATH)

Space limitations in this text preclude a complete discussion of each category contained within the I WATCH DEATH mnemonic. Table 6 lists many of the insults that can cause delirium. Because the list is lengthy, it may be helpful for the clinician to carry a card containing the entire differential diagnosis of delirium.

The use of the mnemonic I WATCH DEATH may sound melodramatic. This is not the case. The appearance of a delirium, which is equivalent to acute brain failure, should marshal the same medical forces as failure of any other vital organ. The morbidity and mortality that result from an untreated or undertreated delirium are substantial and should not be ignored.

☐ COURSE (PROGNOSIS)

The clinical course of a delirious patient is variable. The possibilities are: (1) full recovery, (2) progression

---

TABLE 5. DRUGS CAUSING DELIRIUM (REVERSIBLE DEMENTIA)

Antibiotics
acyclovir (antiviral)
amphotericin B (antifungal)
cephalexin (Keflin)
chloroquine (antimalarial)
Anticholinergic
antihistamines
chlorpheniramine (Ornade, Teldrin)
antiparkinson drugs
benztropine (Cogentin)
biperiden (Akineton)
antispasmodics
atropine/homatropine
belladonna alkaloids
diphenhydramine (Benadryl)
phenothiazines (especially thioridizine)
promethazine (Phenergan)
scopolamine
tricyclic antidepressants (especially amitriptyline)
trihexyphenidyl (Artane, Pipanol, Tremin)

Anticonvulsant
phenobarbital
phenytoin (Dilantin)
sodium valproate (Depakene)
Antiinflammatory
adrenocorticotropic hormone
corticosteroids
ibuprofen (Motrin, Advil)
indomethacin (Indocin)
naproxen (Naprosyn)
phenylbutazone (Butazolidin, Azolid)
Antineoplastic
5-fluorouracil
Antiparkinson
amantadine (Symmetrel)
carbidopa (Sinemet)
levodopa (Larodopa)
Antituberculous
isoniazid
rifamipicin
Analgesics
opiates
salicylates
synthetic narcotics

Cardiac
beta-blockers
propranolol (Inderal)
clonidine (Catapres)
digitalis (Digoxin, Lanox)
disopyramide (Norpace)
lidocaine (Xylocaine)
mexilitene
methyldopa (Aldomet)
quinidine (Quinidine, Quiaglute, Duraquine)
procainamide (Pronestyl)
Drug Withdrawal
alcohol
barbiturates
benzodiazepines
Sedative-Hypnotics
barbiturates (Miltown, Equanil)
benzodiazepines
glutethemide (Doriden)
Sympathomimetics
amphetamines
phenylephrine
phenylpropanolamine

Miscellaneous
aminophylline
bromides
chlorpropamide (Diabinese)
cimetidine (Tagamet)
disulfiram (Antabuse)
lithium
metrizamide (Amipaque)
metronidazole (Flagyl)
podphylline by absorption
propylthiouracil
quinacrine
theophylline
timolol ophthalmic
Over-the-Counter
Compoz
Excedrin-PM
Sleep-Eze
Sominex

**TABLE 6.   CAUSES OF DELIRIUM
(I WATCH DEATH)**

Infectious	Encephalitis, meningitis, syphilis
Withdrawal	Alcohol, barbiturates, sedatives-hypnotics
Acute Metabolic	Acidosis, alkalosis, electrolyte disturbance, hepatic failure, renal failure
Trauma	Heat stroke, postoperative, severe burns
CNS Pathology	Abscesses, hemorrhage, normal pressure hydrocephalus, seizures, stroke, tumors, vasculitis
Hypoxia	Anemia, carbon monoxide poisoning, hypotension, pulmonary/cardiac failure
Deficiencies	B12, hypovitaminosis, niacin, thiamine
Endocrinopathies	Hyper(hypo)adrenalcorticism, hyper(hypo)glycemia
Acute Vascular	Hypertensive encephalopathy, shock
Toxins/Drugs	Medications, pesticides, solvents (see Table 5)
Heavy Metals	Lead, manganese, mercury

to stupor and/or coma, (3) seizures, (4) chronic brain syndromes, (5) death, or (6) 1 through 4 above with associated morbidity (e.g., fracture or subdural hematomas from falls). The majority of patients who experience delirium probably have a full recovery, although the actual probability of this outcome is unknown. Some patients will progress to stupor and/or coma and either recover, with or without chronic brain damage, or become chronically vegetative, or die. Seizures can accompany delirium, but are more likely to occur with drug withdrawal, particularly alcohol, and burn encephalopathy (Antoon et al. 1972). Lastly, a number of patients will not completely recover and will have residual brain injury. The chronic brain syndrome may be global or focal (e.g., amnestic syndrome, organic personality disorder).

Morbidity

There are no direct studies of morbidity in delirium. Research indicates hospitalization is prolonged (Kay et al. 1956). In one study, 38.9 percent of acute brain syndromes became chronic brain syndromes (Titchener et al. 1956). In another study,

15 percent of postcardiotomy delirious patients had persistent neurologic signs at discharge (Tufo et al. 1970).

Any clinician who performs hospital consultations has seen patients, as Moore (1977) described, who "became agitated, struck a nurse, and pulled out his nasogastric tube" (p. 1431). Delirious patients pull out intravenous lines, nasogastric tubes, arterial lines, nasopharyngeal tubes, and intra-aortic balloon pumps.

Mortality

Most psychiatrists, and physicians in general, underestimate the mortality associated with delirium. Three months following diagnosis, the mortality rate for delirium is 14 times greater (Weddington 1982) than the mortality rate for affective disorders. A patient diagnosed with delirium during a hospital admission has a 5.5 times greater hospital mortality rate than a patient diagnosed with dementia (Rabins and Folstein 1982). Furthermore, the elderly patient who develops a delirium in the hospital has a 22 percent (Rabins and Folstein 1982) to 76 percent (Flint and Richards 1956) chance of dying during that hospitalization. Patients who survive hospitalization have a very high death rate during the months immediately following discharge. Patients with a diagnosis of delirium followed for several months show a mortality rate equal to dementia patients followed for several years (Roth 1955; Varsamis et al. 1972).

☐ MAKING THE DIAGNOSIS OF DELIRIUM

Regardless of the suspected diagnosis, the neuropsychiatric evaluation of a patient follows a particular generic process. A specific diagnosis, such as delirium, follows from an appreciation of the clinical features of the syndrome (Table 3) and a thorough evaluation of the patient's mental and physical status (Table 7). In addition to the usual mental status examination, the examiner should, at a minimum, test for praxis (see Figures 2 and 3 for tests of spatial abilities and motor fluency), writing ability, and the ability to name objects. Folstein et al.'s (1975) Mini-Mental State examination (Appendix 1) provides a good screening tool for organicity and

TABLE 7. NEUROPSYCHIATRIC EVALUATION OF THE PATIENT

Mental Status
    Interview (Assess: Level of consciousness, psychomotor activity, appearance, affect, mood, intellect, thought processes)
    Performance tests (memory, concentration, reasoning, motor and constructional apraxia, dysgraphia, dysnomia)

Physical Status
    Brief neurologic exam (reflexes, limb strength, Babinski's, cranial nerves, meningeal signs, gait)
    Review past and present vital signs (pulse, temperature, BP, respiration rate)
    Review chart (labs, abnormal behavior noted and if so when it began, medical diagnoses, VDRL, or FTA − ABS + ?)
    Review medication records (correlate abnormal behavior with starting or stopping medications)

Laboratory Exam—Basic
    Blood chemistries (electrolytes, glucose, Ca^{++} albumin, blood urea nitrogen, NH_4^+, liver functions)
    Blood count (hematocrit, white count and differential, MCV, sedimentation rate)
    Drug levels (need toxic screen? medication blood levels?)
    Arterial blood gases
    Urinalysis
    Electrocardiogram
    Chest X ray

Laboratory—Based on Clinical Judgment
    Electroencephalogram (seizures? focal lesion? confirm delirium)
    Computed tomography (normal pressure hydrocephalus, stroke, space occupying lesion)
    Additional blood chemistries (heavy metals, thiamine and folate levels, thyroid battery, LE prep, ANA, urinary porphobilinogen)
    Lumbar puncture (if indication of infection or intracranial bleed)

is also used to follow the patient's clinical course serially. Should a delirium be present, every effort must be made to identify the specific etiology (etiologies).

The laboratory evaluation of a delirious patient can be conceptualized as having two levels. The basic laboratory battery will be ordered in virtually every patient with a diagnosis of delirium. Other tests are available to the clinician. When information concerning the patient's mental and physical status is combined with the basic laboratory battery, the specific etiology (etiologies) is often apparent. If not, the clinician should review the case and consider ordering further diagnostic studies.

☐ TREATMENT

After thoroughly evaluating the patient, the consulting psychiatrist is likely to be faced with one of the following situations: (1) a specific etiology or several etiologies have been identified and the patient's inappropriate behavior endangers medical care and requires treatment; or (2) no specific etiology has been identified and the patient's inappropriate behavior endangers medical care and requires treatment. When faced with managing a patient in one of these situations, it is helpful to divide the treatment of delirium into specific etiologies and nonspecific treatments.

Treatments—Etiologies Known

Many causes of delirium have specific treatments; therefore, the clinician must systematically attempt to establish a diagnosis. The goal of diagnosis is to discover reversible causes for delirium. For example, a delirious patient found to have a blood pressure of 260/150 and papilledema must immediately receive antihypertensive medications. The alcoholic patient having withdrawal symptoms must receive appropriate pharmacologic intervention with drugs such as thiamine and oxazepam. Without an organized approach to diagnosis, one might attempt to treat the agitation and hallucinations of the patient having DTs with chlorpromazine. This would increase the likelihood of withdrawal seizures.

Treatments—Etiologies Unknown

There are a number of treatments that will help the patient medically and psychologically through the ordeal of a delirium. These treatments are particularly applicable for the patient who is delirious and the exact etiology is unknown. These interventions are classified as medical, pharmacologic, psychosocial, and environmental.

Medical. In addition to ordering the laboratory tests essential to identify the cause of a delirium, one of the important roles of the neuropsychiatrist is to raise the level of awareness of the medical and nursing staff concerning the morbidity and mortality associated with a delirium. The patient should be placed in a room near the nursing station. Obtaining frequent vital signs is essential. Increased observation of the patient ensures closer monitoring for medical deterioration as well as for frequent

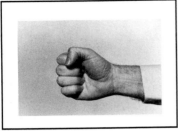 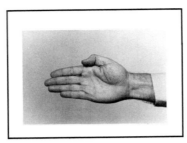 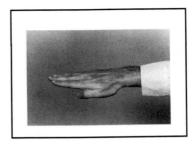

1. LURIA HAND SEQUENCE: Examiner demonstrates movements A→B→C, A→B→C, A→B→C and then asks the patient to copy the sequence.

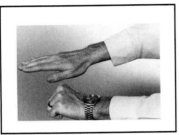 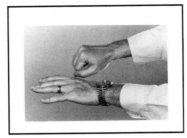 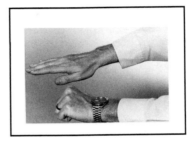

2. RAPID ALTERNATING MOVEMENTS: Examiner demonstrates movements A→B→A→B→A→B (rapidly) and then asks the patient to copy the sequence.

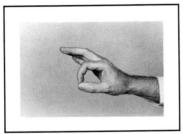 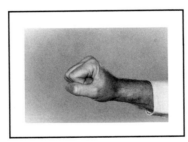 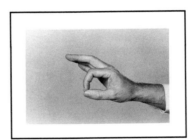

3. RING-FIST SEQUENCE: Examiner demonstrates movements A→B→A→B→A→B and then asks the patient to copy the sequence.

Figure 3.   Tests of motor fluency (praxis).

checks for dangerous behavior such as trying to crawl over bed rails or pulling out intravenous or central venous lines. Fluid input and output must be monitored and good oxygenation ensured. All nonessential medications should be discontinued.

Remember that the brain is a very sensitive forecaster of medical perils ahead. When an etiology for the confusional state has not been identified, daily laboratory examinations (e.g., blood count, blood chemistries, urinalysis) and physical examinations are essential.

Pharmacologic.   There is no consensus in the literature on the pharmacologic treatment of delirium when the etiology is unknown. To this author's

knowledge, there have been no double-blind trials using drug(s) to treat delirium. Therefore, one must rely on clinical experience, known properties of drugs (particularly side effects), and anecdotal reports of various treatments. The scenario for pharmacologic intervention often involves consultation on an agitated, combative, hallucinating, paranoid, medically ill patient whose behavior is a threat to continuing medical treatment.

A drug used to control agitated psychotic behavior in an ICU should result in calming and quieting any agitation, cessation of hallucinations and paranoid ideation, and sedation without further obtunding consciousness. A drug should not suppress respiratory drive, cause hypotension, or be deliriogenic (e.g., anticholinergic). The drug should be available in a parenteral form. Review of the literature and clinical experience indicates that haloperidol comes closest to meeting these criteria and is the drug of first choice when treating a delirium with an unknown etiology (Lipowski 1980b). Haloperidol is a potent antipsychotic with virtually no anticholinergic or hypotensive properties, and it can be given parenterally. In fact, intravenous haloperidol has been used in high doses for many years in seriously ill patients without harmful side effects (Sos and Cassem 1980; Tesar et al. 1985). (*Note*: Haloperidol is not approved by the FDA for intravenous use.) Although extrapyramidal side effects are more likely with the higher potency antipsychotic drugs, the actual occurrence rate in medically ill patients, particularly using intravenous administration, is strikingly low.

Other antipsychotic medications that have been found useful are thiothixene (Navane) and droperidol (Inapsine). Droperidol is used by anesthesiologists as a preanesthetic agent and by other physicians for the control of nausea and vomiting. It is, like haloperidol, a butyrophenone and has comparable antipsychotic potency. Droperidol is approved for intravenous use but has the disadvantage of having a higher potential than haloperidol for causing hypotension. Antipsychotic medications that are less potent (i.e., require a higher milligram dose for equal effect) are more likely to cause hypotension and to have more anticholinergic side effects.

Regardless of the route of administration, the usual initial dosage of haloperidol in the agitated younger patient is 2 mg for mild agitation, 5 mg for moderate agitation, and 10 mg for severe agitation. The initial dosage for the elderly patient is 0.5 mg for mild agitation, 1 mg for moderate agitation, and 2 mg for severe agitation. The dose is repeated every 30 minutes until the patient is sedated and/or calm.* After the confusion has cleared,

---

*Neuroleptic prescribing practices remain controversial. Issues of rapid neuroleptization, speculation regarding the presence of a therapeutic window, and ultimate dosage levels continue to be debated. The clinical issue, however, must be the individual patient's situation and response to medications. Delirium is defined by its variability; thus one consultation assessment will evoke management and medical recommendations that are time-limited in efficacy. Only constant follow-up of the delirious patient will suffice, regardless of what eventually prevails about the pharmacology of specific neuroleptics.

continue the medications for 3 to 5 days. Abrupt discontinuation of medication immediately following improvement may, within 24 hours, be followed by recurrence of the delirium. A more rational approach is to taper the medication over a 3- to 5-day period, administering the largest dosage of the medication before bedtime to help normalize the sleep-wake cycle.

The use of benzodiazepines in delirium has its proponents. Benzodiazepines are the drugs of choice in DTs. However, the sedation that accompanies benzodiazepines may further impair the delirious patient's sensorium. In addition, some patients may be further disinhibited when given benzodiazepines. Therefore, with the exceptions of drug withdrawal states, benzodiazepines are not recommended as a sole agent in the treatment of the confused patient. Benzodiazepines have been used with success as adjuncts to high potency neuroleptics like haloperidol (Adams 1984). Small doses of intravenous lorazepam, particularly in patients who have not responded to high doses of haloperidol alone, have been found useful.

Psychosocial. The psychological support of a patient both during and after a delirium is important. For the paranoid, agitated patient, having a calm family member remain with the patient is reassuring and can stop mishaps (e.g., pulling out arterial lines, falling out of bed). In lieu of a family member, close supervision by reassuring nursing staff is crucial.

After the delirium has resolved, helping the patient understand the bizarre experience can be therapeutic (MacKenzie and Popkin 1980). An explanation to the family about delirium can reduce anxiety and calm fears. Many patients, if they remember the delirious period, will be reluctant to discuss their experiences. Patients may be encouraged to talk if the physician makes statements such as, "Many patients get confused after ———— (e.g., surgery). Some patients experience frightening visions, some hear strange conversations or noises, and others believe that people they trust are trying to harm them. These experiences, if you had any of them, might cause you to worry." Simple explanation is usually all that is required to reduce this type of morbidity.

Environmental. Environmental interventions are sometimes helpful but should not be considered as the primary treatment. Both nurses and family members can frequently reorient the patient to date and surroundings. Placing a clock, calendar, and familiar objects in the room may be helpful. Adequate light in the room during the night will usually decrease frightening illusions. Despite recommendations to the contrary, a private room for the delirious patient is appropriate only if adequate supervision can be assured. A room with a window may be helpful to orient the patient to normal diurnal cues (Wilson 1972). If the patient normally wears eyeglasses or a hearing aid, improving the quality of sensory input by returning these devices may help the patient better understand the surroundings.

A common error occurring on medical and surgical wards is to place delirious patients in the same room. This makes reorientation of these patients impossible and often leads to confirmation, based on conversations with a paranoid roommate, that strange things are indeed happening in the hospital.

☐ FUTURE DIRECTIONS

The need for future research regarding delirium is clear, given its high morbidity and mortality. Basic questions need to be answered. Is delirium the final common pathway in brain dysfunction? Are there predisposing physiologic, personality, emotional, genetic, and environmental factors in the development of a delirium? The resurgence of interest in the field of neuropsychiatry may provide the impetus needed to perform this crucial research.

☐ REFERENCES

Aberg T, Ronquist G, Tyden H, et al: Release of adenylate kinase into cerebrospinal fluid during open-heart surgery and its relation to postoperative intellectual function. Lancet 1:1139–1141, 1982

Aberg T, Ronquist G, Tyden H, et al: Adverse effects on the brain in cardiac operations as assessed by biochemical, psychometric, and radiologic methods. J Thorac Cardiovasc Surg 87:99–105, 1984

Adams F: Neuropsychiatric evaluation and treatment of delirium in the critically ill cancer patient. The Cancer Bulletin 36:156–160, 1984

Adams RD, Victor M: Principle of Neurology. New York, McGraw-Hill, 1981

American Psychiatric Association: Diagnostic and Statistical Manual of Mental Disorders, 3rd ed. Washington, DC, American Psychiatric Association, 1980

American Psychiatric Association: Diagnostic and Statistical Manual of Mental Disorders, 3rd ed, revised. Washington, DC, American Psychiatric Association, 1987

Andreasen NJC: Neuropsychiatric complications in burn patients. Int J Psychiatry Med 5:161–171, 1974

Andreasen NJC, Noyes R, Hartford C, et al: Management of emotional reactions in seriously burned adults. N Engl J Med 286:65–69, 1972

Andreasen NJC, Hartford CE, Knott JR, et al: EEG changes associated with burn delirium. Diseases of the Nervous System 38:27–31, 1977

Anthony JC, LeResche L, Niaz U, et al: Limits of the "mini-mental state" as a screening test for dementia and delirium among hospital patients. Psychol Med 12:397–408, 1982

Antoon AY, Volpe JJ, Crawford JD: Burn encephalopathy in children. Pediatrics 50:609–616, 1972

Bedford PD: General medical aspects of confusional states in elderly people. Br Med J 2:185–188, 1959

Berrios GE: Delirium and confusion in the 19th century: a conceptual history. Br J Psychiatry 139:439–449, 1981

Blachly PH, Kloster FE: Relation of cardiac output to postcardiotomy delirium. J Thorac Cardiovasc Surg 52:423–427, 1966

Blank K, Perry S: Relationship of psychological processes during delirium to outcome. Am J Psychiatry 141:843–847, 1984

Branthwaite MA: Neurological damage related to open-heart surgery: a clinical survey. Thorax 27:748–753, 1972

Chedru F, Geschwind N: Writing disturbances in acute confusional states. Neuropsychologia 10:343–353, 1972

Chenoweth DE, Cooper SW, Hugli TE, et al: Complement activation during cardiopulmonary bypass. N Engl J Med 304:497–502, 1981

Cummings J, Benson DF, LoVerme S: Reversible dementia. JAMA 243:2434–2439, 1980

Cummings JL: Acute confusional states, in Clinical Neuropsychiatry. Edited by Cummings JL. New York, Grune & Stratton, 1985, pp 68–74

Dubin WR, Field NL, Gastfriend DR: Postcardiotomy delirium: a critical review. J Thorac Cardiovasc Surg 77:586–594, 1979

Engel GL: Delirium, in Comprehensive Textbook of Psychiatry. Edited by Friedman AM, Kaplan HS. Baltimore, Williams & Wilkins Co, 1967

Engel GL, Romano J: Delirium, a syndrome of cerebral insufficiency. J Chronic Dis 9:260–277, 1959

Engel GL, Romano J, Ferris EB: Effect of quinacrine (atabrine) on the central nervous system. Archives of Neurology and Psychiatry 58:337–350, 1947

Epstein LJ, Simon A: Organic brain syndrome in the elderly. Geriatrics 22:145–150, 1967

Flint FJ, Richards SM: Organic basis of confusional states in the elderly. Br Med J 2:1537–1539, 1956

Folstein MF, Folstein SE, McHugh PR: "Mini-mental state": a practical method for grading the cognitive state of patients for the clinician. J Psychiatr Res 12:189–198, 1975

Hartmann A, Hayer S: Cerebral Blood Flow and Metabolism Measurement. New York, Springer-Verlag, 1985

Heller SS, Frank KA, Malm JR, et al: Psychiatric complications of open-heart surgery. N Engl J Med 283:1015–1020, 1970

Hodkinson HM: Mental impairment in the elderly. J R Coll Physicians Lond 7:305–317, 1973

Kay DWK, Norris V, Post F: Prognosis in psychiatric disorders of the elderly. J Ment Sci 102:129–140, 1956

Kennard MA, Bueding E, Wortis WB: Some biochemical and electroencephalographic changes in delirium tremens. Quarterly Journal of Studies on Alcohol 6:4–14, 1945

Kornfeld DS, Heller SS, Frank KA, et al: Personality and psychological factors in postcardiotomy delirium. Arch Gen Psychiatry 31:249–253, 1974

Kornfeld DS, Zimberg S, Malm JR: Psychiatric complications of open-heart surgery. N Engl J Med 273:287–292, 1965

Layne OL, Yudofsky SC: Postoperative psychosis in cardiotomy patients: the role of organic and psychiatric factors. N Engl J Med 284:518–520, 1971

Lipowski ZJ: Delirium, clouding of consciousness and confusion. J Nerv Ment Dis 145:227–255, 1967

Lipowski ZJ: Organic brain syndromes: a reformulation. Compr Psychiatry 19:309–322, 1978

Lipowski ZJ: Delirium: Acute Brain Failure in Man. Springfield, Ill, Charles C Thomas, 1980a

Lipowski ZJ: Delirium updated. Compr Psychiatry 21:190–196, 1980b

MacKenzie TB, Popkin MK: Stress response syndrome occurring after delirium. Am J Psychiatry 137:1433–1435, 1980

Moore DP: Rapid treatment of delirium in critically ill patients. Am J Psychiatry 134:1431–1432, 1977

Peura DA, Johnson LF: Cimetidine for prevention and treatment of gastroduodenal mucosal lesions in patients in an intensive care unit. Ann Intern Med 103:173–177, 1985

Pro JD, Wells CE: The use of the electroencephalogram in the diagnosis of delirium. Diseases of the Nervous System 38:804–808, 1977

Prugh DG, Wagonfeld S, Metcalf D, et al: A clinical study of delirium in children and adolescents. Psychosom Med 42 (Suppl):177–197, 1980

Rabins PV, Folstein MF: Delirium and dementia: diagnostic criteria and fatality rates. Br J Psychiatry 140:149–153, 1982

Reivich M, Abass A: Positron Emission Tomography. New York, Alan R Liss, 1985

Romano J, Engel GL: Delirium, I: electroencephalographic data. Archives of Neurology and Psychiatry 51:356–377, 1944

Roth M: The natural history of mental disorder in old age. Journal of Mental Science 101:281–301, 1955

Sos J, Cassem NH: Managing postoperative agitation. Drug Therapy 10(3):103–106, 1980

Task Force Sponsored by the National Institute on Aging: Senility reconsidered. JAMA 244:259–263, 1980

Tesar GE, Murray GB, Cassem NH: Use of high-dose intravenous haloperidol in the treatment of agitated cardiac patients. J Clin Psychopharmacol 5:344–347, 1985

Titchener JL, Swerling I, Gottschalk L, et al: Psychosis in surgical patients. Surg Gynecol Obstet 102:59–65, 1956

Tufo HM, Ostfeld AM, Shekelle R: Central nervous system dysfunction following open-heart surgery. JAMA 212:1333–1340, 1970

Tune LE, Damlouh NF, Holland A, et al: Association of postoperative delirium with raised serum levels of anticholinergic drugs. Lancet 2:651–653, 1981

Varsamis J, Zuchowski T, Maini KK: Survival rates and causes of death in geriatric psychiatric patients: a six-year follow-up study. Canadian Psychiatric Association Journal 17:17–21, 1972

Weddington WW: The mortality of delirium: an underappreciated problem? Psychosomatics 23:1232–1235, 1982

Wells CE, Duncan GW: Neurology for Psychiatrists. Philadelphia, FA Davis Co, 1980

Wilson LM: Intensive care delirium. Arch Intern Med 130:225–226, 1972

Zubek JP, Welch G: Electroencephalographic changes after prolonged sensory and perceptual deprivation. Science 139:1209–1210, 1963

APPENDIX 1. MINI-MENTAL STATE EXAMINATION AND INSTRUCTIONS

Patient _____

Examiner _____

Date _____

MINI-MENTAL STATE EXAMINATION

Maximum score	Score	
		Orientation
5	( )	What is the (year) (season) (date) (day) (month)?
5	( )	Where are we: (state) (county) (town) (hospital) (floor).
		Registration
3	( )	Name 3 objects: 1 second to say each. Then ask the patient all 3 after you have said them. Give 1 point for each correct answer. Then repeat them until he learns all 3. Count trials and record.

Trials_____

Attention and Calculation

5 ( ) Serial 7's. 1 point for each correct. Stop after 5 answers. Alternatively spell "world" backwards.

Recall

3 ( ) Ask for the 3 objects repeated above. Give 1 point for each correct.

Language

9 ( ) Name a pencil, and watch (2 points)
Repeat the following "No ifs ands or buts." (1 point)
Follow a 3-stage command:
"Take a paper in your right hand, fold it in half, and put it on the floor" (3 points)
Read and obey the following:

Close your eyes (1 point)

Write a sentence (1 point)
Copy design (1 point)
Total score
ASSESS level of consciousness along a continuum

Alert   Drowsy   Stupor   Coma

INSTRUCTIONS FOR ADMINISTRATION OF
MINI-MENTAL STATE EXAMINATION

Orientation

1. Ask for the date. Then ask specifically for parts omitted, e.g., "Can you also tell me what season it is?" One point for each correct.
2. Ask in turn "Can you tell me the name of this hospital?" (town, county, etc.). One point for each correct.

Registration

Ask the patient if you may test his memory. Then say the names of 3 unrelated objects, clearly and slowly, about one second for each. After you have said all 3, ask him to repeat them. This first repetition determines his score (0–3) but keep saying them until he can repeat all 3, up to 6 trials. If he does not eventually learn all 3, recall cannot be meaningfully tested.

Attention and Calculation

Ask the patient to begin with 100 and count backwards by 7. Stop after 5 subtractions (93, 86, 79, 72, 65). Score the total number of correct answers.

If the patient cannot or will not perform this task, ask him to spell the word "world" backwards. The score is the number of letters in correct order. E.g., dlrow = 5, dlorw = 3.

Recall

Ask the patient if he can recall the 3 words you previously asked him to remember. Score 0–3.

Language

Naming: Show the patient a wrist watch and ask him what it is. Repeat for pencil. Score 0–2.
Repetition: Ask the patient to repeat the sentence after you. Allow only one trial. Score 0 or 1.
3-Stage command: Give the patient a piece of plain blank paper and repeat the command. Score 1 point for each part correctly executed.
Reading: On a blank piece of paper print the sentence "Close your eyes", in letters large enough for the patient to see clearly. Ask him to read it and do what it says. Score 1 point only if he actually closes his eyes.
Writing: Give the patient a blank piece of paper and ask him to write a sentence for you. Do not dictate a sentence, it is to be written spontaneously. It must contain a subject and verb and be sensible. Correct grammar and punctuation are not necessary.
Copying: On a clean piece of paper, draw intersecting pentagons, each side about 1 in., and ask him to copy it exactly as it is. All 10 angles must be present and 2 must intersect to score 1 point. Tremor and rotation are ignored.
Estimate the patient's level of sensorium along a continuum, from alert on the left to coma on the right.

Reproduced with permission from Folstein MF, Folstein SE, McHugh PR: Mini-mental state: a practical method for grading the cognitive state of patients for the clinician. J Psychiatr Res 12:189–198, 1975 (Copyright © 1975 Pergamon Press, Ltd.)

Chapter 6

Dementia

Troy L. Thompson II, M.D.

WHAT IS NOW TERMED DEMENTIA and is a subcategory of the organic mental disorders (American Psychiatric Association 1980) has been known by many names in recent years, including senility and chronic organic brain syndrome. These changes in nomenclature reflect the advances in knowledge about these conditions in recent years. Senility used to be viewed as a normal part of aging, and forgetfulness and intellectual decline would often be attributed to arteriosclerosis. This ageism probably caused many treatable dementias to be overlooked (Butler 1975). For example, the word *chronic* in *chronic organic brain syndrome* sometimes led physicians to believe that they were dealing with an untreatable condition; therefore, a thorough workup and vigorous treatment efforts were not done. After a thorough workup of 80 patients diagnosed as having chronic organic brain syndrome, 77 were given a more specific diagnosis (Seltzer and Sherwin 1978). Most of these patients were recategorized to primary degenerative dementia, alcoholic dementia, or Korsakoff's syndrome; however, 15 percent of these patients were diagnosed as having functional psychiatric disorders and not an organic brain syndrome.

☐ DEFINITION

Dementia is a disorder of decline in multiple cognitive functions from the individual's previous intellectual level (McHugh and Folstein 1985). The cardinal feature of dementia is cognitive and intellectual impoverishment and lack of mental alertness in thinking, leading to inappropriate reasoning and behavior. The term *dementia* is derived from the Latin meaning "out of one's mind" (Wells 1985). In the past, the word *dementia* was used to describe processes that would be categorized quite differently today, such as *dementia praecox*, which today would be termed *schizophrenia*.

☐ CLINICAL FEATURES

Today, the term *dementia* should be used only if a patient fits a specific set of criteria (Table 1). It is important to differentiate dementia from delirium, amnestic syndrome, organic delusional syndrome, organic hallucinosis, organic affective syndrome, organic personality syndrome, and intoxication or withdrawal states (American Psychiatric Associa-

TABLE 1. DSM-III-R DIAGNOSTIC CRITERIA FOR DEMENTIA

A. Demonstrable evidence of impairment in short- and long-term memory. Impairment of short-term memory (inability to learn new information) may be indicated by inability to remember three objects after five minutes. Long-term memory impairment (inability to remember information that was known in the past) may be indicated by inability to remember past personal information (e.g., what happened yesterday, birthplace, occupation) or facts of common knowledge (e.g., past Presidents, well-known dates).

B. At least one of the following:
   (1) impairment in abstract thinking, as indicated by inability to find similarities and differences between related words, difficulty in defining words and concepts, and other similar tasks
   (2) impaired judgment, as indicated by inability to make reasonable plans to deal with interpersonal, family, and job-related problems and issues
   (3) other disturbances of higher cortical function, such as aphasia (disorder of language), apraxia (inability to carry out motor activities despite intact comprehension and motor function), agnosia (failure to recognize or identify objects despite intact sensory function), and "constructional difficulty" (e.g., inability to copy three-dimensional figures, assemble blocks, or arrange sticks in specific designs)
   (4) personality change, i.e., alteration or accentuation of premorbid traits

C. The disturbance in A and B significantly interferes with work or usual social activities or relationships with others.

D. Not occurring exclusively during the course of Delirium.

E. Either (1) or (2):
   (1) there is evidence from the history, physical examination, or laboratory tests of a specific organic factor (or factors) judged to be etiologically related to the disturbance
   (2) in the absence of such evidence, an etiologic organic factor can be presumed if the disturbance cannot be accounted for by any nonorganic mental disorder, e.g., Major Depression accounting for cognitive impairment

Note. Copyright © 1987 American Psychiatric Association. Reproduced with permission.

tion 1987). However, it is also important to remember that these conditions may occur together. Dementias may be further categorized as arising in the senium and presenium and into primary degenerative dementia (of senile or presenile onset) and multi-infarct dementias. Within each of these categories, the patient may also be classified as to whether there is associated delirium, delusions, or depression or whether the dementia is uncomplicated by these symptoms. Presenile (those under age 65) dementia, for which no other etiology was determined premortem, used to be called Alzheimer's disease; the senile form was called senile dementia. However, no difference in symptoms or pathology exists in these two forms; therefore, that disorder is now called Alzheimer's disease regardless of the patient's age (Schneck 1982).

As with other physiologic functions, mental capacities slow to some degree with normal aging, and occasional forgetting is normal for individuals of all ages. "Benign senescent forgetfulness" is more common with aging and is characterized by occasionally being unable to remember some relatively unimportant aspect of an experience but at other times being able to recall it and the overall experience is remembered (Kral 1978). With dementia, the facts continue to be forgotten or confused. The nondemented elderly may need a little longer to remember or learn something, or may have to take a somewhat circuitous route to do so. For example, they may not be able to remember a person's name but can describe what they want to discuss with the person or when that person was last seen. However, memory deficits do not significantly interfere with the nondemented persons' abilities to manage and enjoy their business or personal relationships.

Alzheimer's disease and other forms of dementia have received a great deal of media attention in recent years. It is not uncommon for elderly patients to become frightened that they are developing Alzheimer's in response to normal forgetting or benign senescent forgetfulness. Individuals who have been "worriers," hypochondriacal, anxious, obsessive, and perfectionistic seem to develop these concerns more frequently. A tip off is if they are able to give a detailed history of their memory lapses.

Depression, especially in the elderly, may mimic dementia. Because depression is usually treatable, it is critical that it be considered in anyone suspected of dementia. In fact, depression in the elderly so often has a dementia-like picture that it has sometimes been termed *pseudodementia* (Solomon 1985; Wells 1979) (Table 2). This term has been criticized, but it does serve as a reminder to consider a covert depression as etiologic of cognitive impairment.

In the early stage of dementia, it is common for a patient to come to a physician complaining

TABLE 2. SOME DIFFERENTIAL DIAGNOSTIC COMPARISONS OF DEMENTIA AND PSEUDODEMENTIA

Dementia of Organic Disease	Pseudodementia of Psychiatric Disease
Age is nonspecific, usually adult	Elderly—60 years or older
Onset vague: months, years	Onset more precise: days, weeks
Course: slow; worse at night	Course: rapid and uneven; no nocturnal change
Past history of systemic illness or of drug or alcohol abuse	Past history of depression or mania; or somatic manifestations of depression
Often unaware of cognitive defect; unconcerned or denies problem	Often complains of memory loss; distressed and emphasizes problem
Organic signs of neurologic disease, such as dysphasia, dyspraxia, agnosia, incontinence	Psychological symptoms of sadness, self-accusation, preoccupation, anxiety, delusions, or somatic symptoms of depression
Greater impairment of cognitive features, such as recent memory and orientation for time and date	Greater impairment of personality features, such as confidence, drive, interests, and attention
Mental status examination shows spotty responses, with some features much poorer than others; consistent on repeated exams	Mental status examination shows variability of impairment of different modalities on repeated exams
Behavior and affect consistent with degree of cognitive defect	Behavior and affect incongruent with degree of cognitive impairment
Cooperative but frustrated by struggle to perform well; relies on notes to remember	Poorly cooperative, with little effort to remember or do well
Responses to queries approximate, confabulated, or perseverated	Responses to queries often "I don't know"; apathetic
Emphasizes trivial accomplishments	Emphasizes failures
Responses to funny or sad situations normal or exaggerated; mood is shallow or labile	Little or no response to funny or sad circumstances; depression of mood
Neurologic studies (e.g., CT and EEG) usually abnormal	Neurologic studies usually normal

Note. The differences listed above are not mutually exclusive, and there is considerable overlap between the two categories; moreover, depression may be an early reaction to dementia. From Solomon (1985); Copyright © 1985 Williams & Wilkins Co.; reproduced with permission.

of being anxious or depressed and having many classic signs and symptoms of these disorders; up to 40 percent of Alzheimer's patients have significant symptoms of anxiety or depression (McHugh and Folstein 1985). Anxiety and depression are less frightening and more treatable disorders than most dementias, so the patient hopes this "self-diagnosis" is correct. An especially useful differential diagnostic point is to talk with the patient's nurses and review the nursing notes, or talk with family members for outpatients, to note any diurnal fluctuation of symptoms. Patients with dementia usually worsen during the evening ("sundowner" syndrome) and at night, whereas anxious or depressed patients usually do not have such an affective fluctuation. If the physician prescribes an antidepressant, anxiolytic, or sedative-hypnotic to sundowning patients, their underlying dementia may become worse. If this is recognized and a dementia workup follows, the patient may indirectly have been done a favor by such a failed clinical trial. If worsened dementia symptoms are not recognized as such, and the patient remains on those medications, a potentially treatable dementia may progress or a delirium may develop, especially if other factors also become present, such as overmedication, an infection, dehydration, or a psychosocial stress (such as a move or disrupted important relationship) (Lipowski 1983; McHugh and Folstein 1985). (Also see the chapter on delirium.)

A previous history or family history of depression makes that diagnosis more likely. Depression also may coexist in about one-fourth of cognitively impaired patients, but the rate and severity of depression tends to decrease as the severity of the dementia increases (Reifler et al. 1982). A profound depression is uncommon for patients during any stage of dementia. The dexamethasone suppression test (DST) may not be useful in differentiating advanced Alzheimer's from pseudodementia, because the DST may be abnormal in Alzheimer's patients who are not depressed (Raskind et al. 1982). However, the DST may be valuable in detecting depression in mildly demented patients (McAllister et al. 1982).

☐ EPIDEMIOLOGY

Approximately 2 to 5 percent of individuals over 65 years of age have a significant dementia; this figure increases to 15 to 20 percent for those over 80, with at least half of those having Alzheimer's disease (McHugh and Folstein 1985; Terry and Katzman 1983; Thompson 1982). An additional 5 to 15 percent of people over 65, and probably at least two to three times that percentage for those over 80, have mild to moderate symptoms of dementia (Kral 1978; Mortimer 1980). Just under 2 million individuals are currently in nursing homes in the United States; almost 60 percent of those patients have dementia (Schneck et al. 1982). Those patients are often not able to care for themselves in even rudimentary ways, cannot be compliant with medical treatments, and may not report symptoms of a significant medical disorder, such as a myocardial infarction. There is a marked decrease (6 to 8 or more years) in the life expectancy of demented patients compared to nondemented age-matched individuals (Kay et al. 1964; Schneck et al. 1982). Following the onset of Alzheimer's disease, the usual length of life is 2 to 20 years. For these reasons, in addition to the deterioration in the brain itself, Alzheimer's disease is thought to be the fourth leading cause of death in this country (Katzman 1976).

The significance of the prevalence of Alzheimer's is magnified by the great increase in the number of elderly individuals in our society. The number of elderly individuals has increased several hundredfold in recent decades. At the turn of the century, only a small percentage of individuals lived into their 70s and 80s. Today, almost 13 percent of our population is over 65 years of age, and this will increase to 15 to 20 percent over the next few decades. Alzheimer's has been reported to occur more frequently in elderly women than men, but this is probably due to the longer life expectancy of women, resulting in a much larger number of women living long enough to develop the disorder.

Since the elderly have the highest percentage of virtually all types of medical and surgical disorders and carry many psychiatric disorders with them into old age, the percentage of the health care dollar that is spent on the elderly will be several times greater than their percentage of the population. The current annual cost of dementia alone to our society is 12 billion dollars.

At least 50 percent of elderly patients who develop dementia are suffering from Alzheimer's disease or some other disorder for which there is currently no cure. However, it is important to do a thorough workup in each case because about one-fourth of demented patients have a disorder underlying their dementia that can be specifically treated. About 10 percent of demented patients have an underlying disorder that may be cured if properly treated. Other diagnoses often causing dementia and their approximate frequencies include: alcoholic dementia (Korsakoff's syndrome), 10 percent; multi-infarct dementia, 9 percent; normal pressure hydrocephalus, 6 percent; pseudodementia (depression or other treatable psychiatric disorders), 6 percent; intracranial masses, 5 percent; and Huntington's disease, drug toxicity, and posttraumatic dementia, 2 to 3 percent each (Wells 1979, 1985).

☐ COURSE

Dementia tends to have an insidious onset and to progress slowly, especially if caused by Alzheimer's disease. Of course, if the dementia is caused by some other type of acute or chronic medical disorder, the dementia will tend to worsen, improve, or stabilize in relation to the underlying disorder. The usual course of dementia may be divided into early, middle, and late phases (Wells 1985).

Early Phase

The patient, family, and friends rarely identify the earliest signs and symptoms of an incipient dementing process as such. A number of other psychiatric symptoms are more prominent than memory loss, including anxiety, a vague feeling of "disease," insomnia, feeling frustrated or aggravated, and often multiple somatic symptoms. A dementia workup should be conducted on patients who have these types of persistent symptoms. This is especially true if the patient worsens rather than improves after a benzodiazepine, sedative-hypnotic, or antidepressant has been prescribed for anxiety, insomnia, or depression.

In the early stage of dementia, a previously hard-driving individual may uncharacteristically decide to retire or give up a valued hobby. Some personality traits may become amplified. The individual's usual psychological defenses may be fortified to conceal or compensate for the developing mental deficits; therefore, the person may become a "caricature" of himself or herself. The type A individual may become more driven, intolerant, and hostile. The more relaxed individual may become a "sweet little old lady or man" and begin to "kill everyone with kindness." The former will more often be labeled as pathologic and the latter missed. It is more difficult to consider that someone who brings you cookies and compliments is doing so because they are developing a mental disorder than to consider mental illness in someone who disagrees with and is hostile toward you.

In early dementia, patients tend to deny memory loss and are often able to conceal it. Calendars and address and appointment books may allow them to compensate (Stoudemire and Thompson 1981). If a memory deficit is detected, the patient usually attributes it to just having lost interest in the area being questioned. Replies such as "I was never interested in politics" to general questions like "Who is the President?" should alert the physician. Other common examples are "I was never good at arithmetic" or "I don't watch the news anymore." Anyone, even a functionally illiterate individual, should know who is the President and be able to make change from a dollar unless dementia or mental retardation is present.

Middle Phase

The middle phase is characterized by the progression of symptoms to a degree where they can no longer be concealed from family and friends. It is evident to anyone who interacts to a significant degree with the patient that cognition is impaired. Memory for recent events usually becomes impaired before memories in the distant past, although, as dementia progresses, even remote memories may become quite distorted or lost. At this stage, the patient clearly begins to demonstrate deficits on the cognitive questions of a standard mental status examination. This would include naming the presidents in reverse order, subtracting serial 7s or 3s, other arithmetical tasks, proverbs, abstractions, or similarities.

As the patient progresses through the middle phase, errors of judgment become more common. Disorientation may develop. At times, the patient may become lost or totally confused. The patient may become overwhelmed and tremendously anxious at such times and develop a "catastrophic reaction," which may include fight or flight response patterns (McHugh and Folstein 1985). In conversation, the patient will often wander aimlessly and endlessly, demonstrating circumstantiality and tangentiality. The patient may also perseverate; that

is, go over the same material repeatedly, sometimes without realizing it or without the ability to stop if it is pointed out.

Late Phase

During the late phases of dementia, patients lose their personality and, in a sense, their identity. Patients may not recognize their closest family members and friends and not even realize when their own name is being referred to and when their part in recent or remote events is being discussed. Patients may become totally unable to find their way around, even at home. Patients may become paranoid of others, but often their memory is so poor that they cannot sustain a paranoid delusional system, because they cannot remember its components.

Patients may progress to being unable to carry on even the most simple conversation and may not be able to recognize and utilize properly even the most basic household items, such as a spoon, toothbrush, or toilet paper. Patients may lose their appetite or forget that they are hungry and be unable to prepare food or feed themselves. Severe weight loss may result; without regular nursing care, many of these patients die of malnutrition or frank starvation. Patients may forget how to use the toilet or simply no longer care; therefore, soiling, incontinence, and urinating or defecating in inappropriate places are common. Some of these patients will lie in one position in their bed almost all day, literally causing an impression of their bodily form in the mattress, and thereby are very vulnerable to decubitus ulcers. Others may wander aimlessly and be at great risk for leaving their home or a nursing facility. Such patients have stepped in front of cars, or wandered into winter nights to their deaths, not realizing the danger.

☐ DIAGNOSIS

Although the diagnosis of dementia is based on the criteria in Table 1, the diagnosis "dementia" does not in any way specify the underlying cause. Wells (1984) suggested an algorithmic approach involving three questions in diagnosing dementia. First, do the patient's symptoms and signs result from functional or organic brain disease? If they are functional, proceed to treat that disorder. Second, do the patient's symptoms and signs result from focal or diffuse cerebral disease? If they appear to be focal, a neurologist or neurosurgeon should be consulted. Third, are the patient's symptoms and signs resulting from delirium or dementia? In either case, a thorough workup for possibly reversible or treatable underlying causes should proceed (Table 3).

Concerning tests for syphilis, the FTA is recommended instead of, or at least in addition to, the VDRL because the serum VDRL may be negative in older individuals with tertiary syphilis. If the FTA is positive, a spinal tap should be done so serology can be performed on the cerebrospinal fluid to diagnose tertiary CNS syphilis (O'Daniel et al. 1981). If a demented patient has a completely normal computed tomography (CT) or magnetic resonance imaging (MRI) scan of the head, the physician should look more carefully for toxic, metabolic, and other etiologies, including functional psychiatric conditions. An electroencephalogram (EEG) and lumbar puncture are usually done only if there is a specific clinical indication for them. Psychological testing may also be useful, especially in detecting functional psychiatric disorders that

---

TABLE 3. DIAGNOSTIC WORKUP FOR DEMENTIA

A. Physical exam, including thorough neurologic exam
B. Vital signs
C. Review of medications and drug levels
D. Blood and urine screens for alcohol, drugs, and heavy metals[a]
E. *Physiologic workup*
  Electrolytes
  Liver, renal function tests
  SMA-12 (broad screening of blood chemistries), or equivalent
  Urinalysis
  Complete blood cell count with differential cell type count
  Thyroid function tests
  FTA, VDRL
  Serum B12, folate levels
  Urine corticosteroids[a]
  Sedimentation rate, lupus erythematosus cell test, antinuclear antibody[a]
  Arterial blood gases[a]
    HTLV-III screen[a]
F. Chest X ray, electrocardiogram
G. *Neurologic workup*
  CT or MRI scan of head
  Lumbar puncture[a]
  EEG[a]
H. Neuropsychologic testing[b]

Note. Modified from Stoudemire and Thompson (1981).
[a]If indicated.
[b]May be useful in differentiating dementia from other psychiatric syndromes if this cannot be done clinically.

---

may have been overlooked or concealed or denied by the patient during routine interviewing. The evaluation in Table 3 may appear expensive; however, if even a small percentage of patients are found to have a treatable disorder, the human savings may be considerable, as well as the economic savings of avoiding long-term institutionalization. Also, disruption of neuronal functioning may occur that leads to symptoms of dementia before the neuron is permanently damaged or killed. Therefore, early diagnosis and treatment may decrease the ultimate degree of dementia.

A sodium amobarbital interview may be useful in distinguishing an organic from a functional psychiatric disorder. Patients who have dementia or delirium will tend to become more sedated due to the barbiturate; however, patients with a psychosocial disorder often become more talkative and discuss psychological conflicts that they otherwise would deny or repress.

If the above tests and any additional tests indicated by the history or physical exam are essentially nonrevealing, the patient (regardless of age) should be followed closely and some or all of these tests repeated periodically. It is erroneous to assume that it is normal for someone to develop significant memory or other cognitive deficits just because they are elderly. If nothing definitive appears on the tests, the patient probably has Alzheimer's disease, which remains a diagnosis of exclusion without brain biopsy or postmortem pathologic examination.

☐ CAUSES AND PATHOPHYSIOLOGY

The differential diagnosis of dementia is long and complex. In fact, one must consider almost every diagnosis in textbooks of medicine and neurology before assuming the disorder is a primary degenerative dementia. In addition, one must remember that several etiologic problems may coexist. Specific treatments are not available for some causes, including Alzheimer's, Pick's, Huntington's, and Creutzfeldt-Jacob diseases. However, dementia may be secondary to other conditions, some of which are treatable or at least their progression may be slowed (Table 4).

Dementia is a disease of the brain, not of the mind, and is not a "functional" disorder. The syndrome results when cortical or subcortical, including limbic, regions of the central nervous system

TABLE 4. CLASSIFICATION OF CAUSES OF MOST COMMON SECONDARY DEMENTIAS**

Medications
Psychoactives—sedative-hypnotics, minor tranquilizers, major tranquilizers, cyclic antidepressants, lithium carbonate
Antihypertensives—methyldopa (especially combined with haloperidol), clonidine (especially combined with fluphenazine), propranolol (or other beta-blockers)
Anticonvulsants—phenytoin, barbiturates
Anticholinergics—atropine and related compounds, antispasmodics
Other—L-dopa, narcotics, steroids, digitalis, quinidine, diuretics, oral hypoglycemics, antiinflammatory agents, disulfiram, bromides, cimetidine

Chemical intoxications
Heavy metals—arsenic, lead, mercury
Exogenous or industrial agents—alcohol–chronic (see Chapter 8), carbon monoxide, carbon disulfide, organophosphates, toluene, trichloroethylene
Anesthesia

Metabolic or electrolyte disturbances
Hepatic encephalopathy
Uremic encephalopathy (including dialysis dementia)
Hypercalcemia
Hyponatremia
Volume depletion

Endocrinopathies
Hypo- and hyperthyroidism
Parathyroid disease
Addison's disease
Cushing's disease and exogenous steroids
Hypoglycemia
Panhypopituitarism

Other systemic disorders
Cardiac—arrhythmias, congestive heart failure, endocarditis
Pulmonary failure—hypoxia, hypercapnia, COPD
Parkinson's disease

Hepatolenticular degeneration (Wilson's disease)
Severe anemia
Polycythemia vera
Stroke
Sarcoidosis
Collagen vascular disease: lupus
Carcinoma: remote effect, usually lung
Generalized infections: tuberculosis
Fecal impaction

Intracranial disorders
Trauma
Subdural hematoma
Cerebral anoxia or hypoxia
Postconcussive syndrome
Cerebrovascular accident
Multi-infarct dementia
Tumors—meningioma, glioma, metastatic carcinoma
Hydrocephalus—communicating (normal pressure) or noncommunicating
Multiple sclerosis
Seizures

Cerebral infections
Acquired immune deficiency syndrome (AIDS)
Meningitis (e.g., tubercular, fungal)
Brain abscess
Neurosyphilis

Nutritional deficiencies
Wernicke-Korsakoff syndrome (thiamine)
Anemias (B12, folate)
Pellagra (niacin)

Environmental
Sensory deprivation or impairments—visual or hearing problems
Overstimulation or change—hospitalization, nursing home placement

Psychiatric
Depression (pseudodementia)
Chronic schizophrenia
Repeated electroconvulsive therapy

Note. Adapted from Stoudemire and Thompson (1981) and from Wells (1985). Copyright © 1985 Williams & Wilkins Co.; reproduced in revised form with permission.

(CNS) are not functioning properly. Emotional stresses and conflicts may make a person with a clinical or previously subclinical dementia more symptomatic, but nonorganic factors, by definition, are not the underlying cause of the syndrome.

Alzheimer's Disease

This disorder used to be considered rare and received little attention. However, in recent years, it has been appreciated that it probably accounts for more than one-half of all cases of dementia and is the fourth leading cause of death in the Western world (Katzman 1976; Reisberg 1983a). The pathophysiology of Alzheimer's disease characteristically includes several features on microscopic examination: neurofibrillary tangles, senile plaques, and granulovacuolar degenerations (Cummings and Benson 1983; Reisberg 1983a; Schneck 1982) (Figures 1 and 2). In Alzheimer's patients, senile plaques tend to be extensively spread through the cerebral cortex and sometimes coalesce together into large

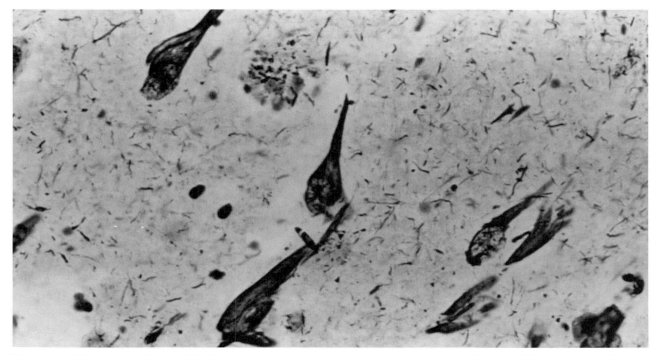

Figure 1. Flame-shaped neurofibrillary tangles from the hippocampus of a 61-year-old male with Alzheimer's disease. Bodian stain. Original magnification, 140×.

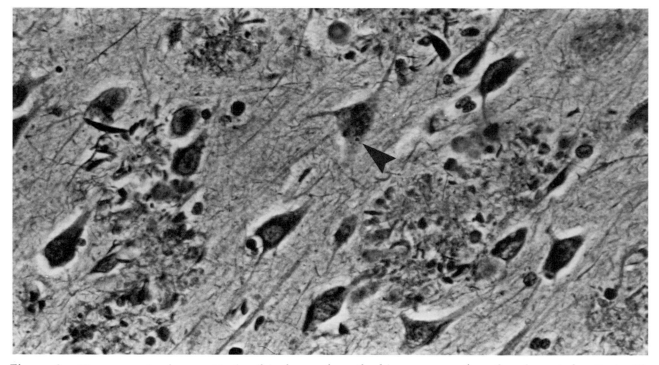

Figure 2. Numerous circular neuritic (senile) plaques from the hippocampus of another demented patient with Alzheimer's disease. Note granulovacuolar degeneration (arrowhead); these cytoplasmic granules lie within a clear space. Modified Bodian stain. Original magnification, 100×.

dense plaques. The severity of the dementia can be directly correlated with the prevalence of senile plaques in the cerebral cortex, as well as with the number of neurofibrillary tangles (Farmer et al. 1976). In Alzheimer's disease, neurofibrillary tangles are spread throughout the cerebral cortex, whereas they are usually located only in the hippocampal regions in normal elderly individuals. Senile plaques and neurofibrillary tangles also appear in subcortical areas (e.g., thalamus, hypothalamus, mamillary bodies) of Alzheimer patients' brains. Granulovacuolar degeneration usually occurs only in the hippocampal region (in pyramidal cells in the normal elderly) but are diffusely spread throughout the cortex in Alzheimer's patients. Cortical cell death is an important manifestation of Alzheimer's disease; more than one-half of the cells in the frontal and temporal cortical regions may die in Alzheimer's patients.

Alzheimer's cannot be diagnosed by gross examination of the brain. Although the Alzheimer's brain may have diffuse cortical atrophy with consequent widening of the cortical sulci and dilation of the cerebral ventricles, so may the brain of patients with other dementing illnesses and some normal elderly individuals (Figure 3).

Although an exact connection has not yet been determined, it is interesting to note that dementia and identical brain changes as in Alzheimer's tend to occur in Down's syndrome patients who live into middle age. Relatives of Alzheimer's patients also appear to be at increased risk for Down's syndrome. If these observations are valid, they may indicate some as yet unknown genetic factor linking these disorders. Alzheimer's-like brain changes also occur in some postencephalitic patients and "punch-drunk" boxers with "dementia pugilistica" (McHugh and Folstein 1985).

A number of exciting discoveries have occurred in recent years regarding biochemical abnormalities in the brains of Alzheimer's patients. However, what may become evident as more is learned is

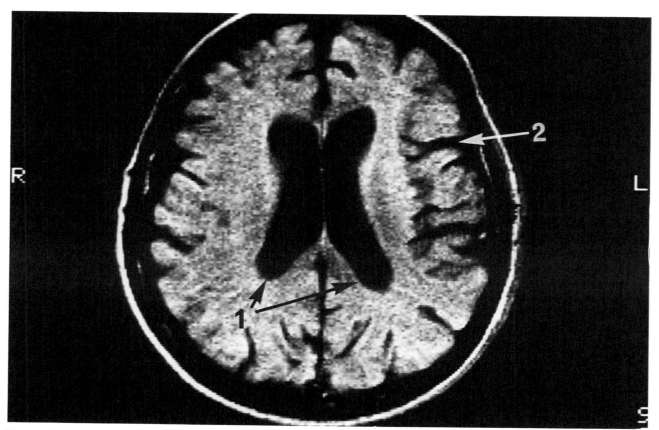

Figure 3. MRI scan brain section showing diffuse cortical atrophy and ventricular enlargement. 1. (arrows) enlarged ventricles bilaterally. 2. (arrow) example of enlarged sulcus.

that Alzheimer's disease is actually a syndrome, a final common pathway, that may result from a number of biochemical, traumatic, or other factors that significantly disrupt the functioning or cause the death of certain types or pathways of cortical neurons.

Deficits in the presynaptic cholinergic system are an early change in Alzheimer's patients (Francis et al. 1985). A common defect in Alzheimer's brains tends to be in the enzyme choline acetyltransferase, which is necessary for the production of a critical neurotransmitter, acetylcholine. A strong correlation has been found between decreased choline acetyltransferase activity and formation of senile plaques, as well as decreased mental acuity scores (Perry et al. 1978). The enzyme that breaks down acetylcholine, acetylcholinesterase, also typically is decreased in some Alzheimer's patients. These biochemical changes have been observed in cortical neurons as well as in subcortical, including limbic, structures in some cases (Whitehouse et al. 1982). The latter is important because some subcortical structures, such as the nucleus basalis of Maynert, appear to play a major role in the cholinergic innervation of cortical structures (Wells 1985). About 70 percent of brain acetylcholine neurons originate in the nucleus basalis (McHugh and Folstein 1985), and a great deal of nucleus basalis cell loss occurs in Alzheimer's patients (Coyle et al. 1983). Noradrenergic dysfunction (associated with problems in memory, arousal, and attention) may also appear in some Alzheimer's patients (Kubanis and Zornetzer 1981), as may degeneration of somatostatinergic and corticotropin-releasing factor containing neurons (Bissette et al. 1985).

Since problems in acetylcholine metabolism may play a major role in many Alzheimer's patients, attempts have been made to increase the amount of acetylcholine available to neurons. Acetylcholine is produced from choline, of which a common source in food is lecithin. Therefore, patients have been fed large doses of lecithin in hopes of increasing the choline available to cholinergic neurons; however, this has proven to be of little value (Reisberg et al. 1981). Another approach that has been tried is the administration of physostigmine, a centrally acting cholinesterase inhibitor. Cholinesterase breaks down acetylcholine; therefore, at least theoretically, an anticholinesterase, which would inhibit the enzyme breaking down acetylcholine, might increase the amount of acetylcholine available to

neurons. Some transient improvement may occur in Alzheimer's patients given physostigmine orally, intravenously, or intrathecally, and more research is indicated; however, no long-term or practical therapeutic approach of this type yet has been devised. Also, physostigmine may cause many side effects, including anergia, anxiety, depression, nausea, vomiting, and ventricular arrhythmias (Dysken and Janowsky 1985; Mohs et al. 1985). Oral tetrahydroaminoacridine (THA), a centrally active anticholinesterase, has been found to be at least temporarily useful in long-term palliative treatment of Alzheimer's patients (Summers et al. 1986). Further research also should probably be conducted in treating some forms of dementia with compounds such as adrenocorticotropic hormone (ACTH), vasopressin, and piracetam (Reisberg et al. 1981). Intravenous naloxone also merits further study, because it has shown temporary positive effects in some Alzheimer's patients (Reisberg et al. 1983).

Genetic or at least some inherited factors appear to be important in some cases of Alzheimer's, but most Alzheimer's patients appear to have no family history of the disorder. Overall, family members of Alzheimer's patients appear to have a three to four times increased risk of developing the disorder (Heston et al. 1981). That is, the risk of developing Alzheimer's appears to be between 10 and 30 percent if a first degree relative (parent, sibling, or child) has the disorder (Schneck 1982). That risk may be even greater if the Alzheimer's patient has associated symptoms of aphasia or agraphia. Among the latter group of patients, Alzheimer's may be transmitted as an autosomal dominant (Breitner and Folstein 1984). Relatives of Alzheimer's patients with aphasia or agraphia appear to have a 50 percent probability of developing the disorder by age 90, whereas relatives of Alzheimer's patients who do not have aphasia or agraphia symptoms have less than a 10 percent risk of developing Alzheimer's. However, the actual incidence may be lower than an autosomal dominant type of transmission would suggest because many individuals do not live long enough to develop the disorder.

Some investigators have wondered if increased dietary aluminum or a decreased capacity of some patients to metabolize aluminum might lead to Alzheimer's. In fact, the level of aluminum in the brain tends to increase with age, even in individuals who have no evidence of Alzheimer's (McHugh and Folstein 1985), but there does not appear to be an increased incidence of Alzheimer's in communities that have relatively higher aluminum levels in their drinking water or in individuals using aluminum cookware. However, injecting high levels of aluminum into the brains of some laboratory animals may cause structures similar to neurofibrillary tangles to appear, although other anatomical changes associated with Alzheimer's do not typically develop. "Aluminum phobia" has sometimes resulted from this hypothesis, resulting in families throwing away their aluminum cookware and utensils. The amount of aluminum that is acquired from cooking or eating with aluminum is negligible, and there appears to be no justification for such actions.

An autoimmune disorder or an unknown virus also has been suggested as a possible cause of Alzheimer's. Senile plaques have an amyloid core, but it is not clear if this is derived from serum immunoglobulin. Since Creutzfeldt-Jacob disease has been demonstrated to be due to a viral agent, it has been natural to look closely at Alzheimer's patients in this regard. However, no viral inclusion particles or other evidence of viral disease have been found in Alzheimer's patients with increased frequency when compared with normals. However, some laboratory animals have developed plaques that are similar to the senile plaques of Alzheimer's disease when certain strains of scrapie virus were inoculated into their brains.

A more recent hypothesis regarding Alzheimer's disease might be termed the head trauma theory. Some investigators suspect that Alzheimer's develops more commonly in individuals who have suffered a severe head injury, usually closed head trauma like a concussion that causes at least temporary loss of consciousness, within a decade or so before the onset of symptoms. If this observation is borne out, the question would still remain as to whether the trauma per se initiates the typical degenerative changes or if the trauma might make the brain more susceptible to other pathogenic processes.

Pick's Disease

This disorder is much rarer than but quite similar to Alzheimer's disease in several ways. Like Alzheimer's, Pick's disease is classified as a primary degenerative dementia. It is characterized by reactive gliosis, especially in frontal and temporal cortical areas, and intraneuronal inclusions called Pick bodies. The Pick bodies are dense and have a granulovacuolar profile, containing neurofilamentous and neurotubular structures.

CT or MRI scans of the head tend to show involvement of the frontal and temporal cortical areas initially in Pick's, as opposed to Alzheimer's, which has more diffuse involvement. As a result, Pick's patients often present as "frontal lobe" patients with dramatic behavioral changes of dysinhibition and social inappropriateness, in contrast to Alzheimer's patients who initially have memory problems. Later, as both disorders progress, it is difficult, if not impossible, to distinguish Pick's from Alzheimer's.

Huntington's Disease (or Chorea) and Other Subcortical Disorders

Huntington's usually becomes manifest in the 30s and 40s. The patient may survive 15 to 20 years after onset. Huntington's is inherited as a sex-linked dominant. The choreiform movements, which usually begin first, and the psychiatric symptoms are progressive. The psychiatric symptoms usually resemble a recurrent schizophrenic-type psychosis, which may account for the high incidence of suicide, or a frank dementia. It is impossible to differentiate the symptoms or course of this dementia from that of Alzheimer's in most cases, although some feel that apathy or lack of inertia occur more commonly early in the course of Huntington's (Wells 1985). Some do not develop the chorea movements. It is probably wiser to think of this condition as Huntington's disease, rather than chorea, so those who develop only the psychiatric symptoms will not be as likely to be overlooked.

Other subcortical disorders (e.g., Parkinson's, Wilson's disease, supranuclear palsy) may also produce dementia. A number of features may be helpful in differentiating them from cortical dementias (Table 5). Patients with subcortical dementias do not develop aphasia, jargon paraphrasia, agnosia, or apraxia (Huber and Paulson 1985; McHugh and Folstein 1985). Wilson's disease (hepatolenticular degeneration) is a rare cause of dementia that especially should be considered in patients who also have symptoms of basal ganglia or cerebellar dysfunction.

TABLE 5. DIFFERENTIAL DIAGNOSIS OF CORTICAL VERSUS SUBCORTICAL DEMENTIA

Clinical Features	Cortical Dementia[a]	Subcortical Dementia[b]
Appearance	Alert, healthy (often appear younger than stated age)	Abnormal (infirm, disheveled, strange)
Activity	Normal	Abnormal (slow)
Stance	Erect	Abnormal (stooped, hyperextended, twisted)
Gait	Normal (pacing is common)	Abnormal (dancing, ataxic, festinating)
Movements	Normal	Abnormal (tremor, chorea, dystonia)
Verbal output	Normal	Abnormal (dysarthric, hypophonic mute)
Language	Abnormal (anomia, paraphasia)	Normal
Cognition	Abnormal (unable to manipulate knowledge)	Dilapidated (less than normal)
Memory	Abnormal (disorder of learning)	Forgetful (disorder of retrieval)
Visual spatial	Abnormal (constructional disturbance)	Sloppy (due to movement problem)
Emotional state	Abnormal (unaware, unconcerned)	Abnormal (apathetic, lacking drive)

Note. From Beck et al. (1982); reproduced with permission.
[a]Alzheimer's disease, Pick's disease.
[b]Huntington's disease, Wilson's disease, progressive supranuclear palsy, Parkinson's disease.

Multi-Infarct Dementia

Multiple emboli may arise outside the brain and migrate to occlude cerebral vessels, producing multi-infarct dementia (MID) (Hachinski et al. 1974) (Table 6). Pseudobulbar palsy with weakness of the mouth, tongue, and swallowing muscles may result from bilateral damage to cortical and subcortical (bulbar) structures. Slurring of words, difficulty swallowing, choking, and general psychomotor slowing may result (McHugh and Folstein 1985). Pseudobulbar patients may also have affective lability and inappropriate expression of emotions. Despite this, MID patients tend to have more preservation of their premorbid personality than Alzheimer's patients.

Within the last 10 to 20 years, it has been discovered that arteriosclerosis is not the most common cause of dementia. Prior to that time, carotid endarterectomies were sometimes performed to relieve mild to moderate carotid blockage when Alzheimer's disease or some other dementing illness, and not decreased cerebral perfusion and hypoxia, was causing the patient's dementia. However, MID may be the primary etiology in about 10 percent of dementias. Because many of the medical disorders that cause or increase the risk for embolization can be managed, it is especially important that these conditions be evaluated. For example, uncontrolled hypertension, diabetes, atrial fibrillation, and hypercoagulable states may greatly increase the risk for and incidence of embolization. It is critical that severe hypertension be controlled in MIA patients, but reducing the blood pressure dramatically in a

patient who has had long-standing hypertension, paradoxically, may lead to further cerebral infarction. In such patients, a gradual reduction of blood pressure and accepting a higher than optimal blood pressure may be the prudent clinical course to avoid possible compromised perfusion through arteriosclerotic carotid and cerebral vessels.

MID often has an earlier age of onset than Alzheimer's, and tends to occur more often in men, especially in those with the above or other cardiovascular risk factors, including positive family history; high serum cholesterol, serum triglyceride, and lipoprotein profiles associated with arteriosclerosis; cigarette smoking; and obesity. The CT or MRI scan will sometimes identify numerous areas of infarction throughout the brain, although small lacunar infarcts may be too small to be picked up.

TABLE 6. DSM-III-R DIAGNOSTIC CRITERIA FOR MULTI-INFARCT DEMENTIA

A. Dementia (see Table 1).
B. Stepwise deteriorating course with "patchy" distribution of deficits (i.e., affecting some functions, but not others) early in the course.
C. Focal neurologic signs and symptoms (e.g., exaggeration of deep tendon reflexes, extensor plantar response, pseudobulbar palsy, gait abnormalities, weakness of an extremity, etc.).
D. Evidence, from the history, physical examination, or laboratory tests of significant cerebrovascular disease that is judged to be etiologically related to the disturbance.

Note. Copyright © 1987 American Psychiatric Association. Reproduced with premission.

The EEG will usually demonstrate slow wave activity, indicating decreased functioning, in the multiple areas of damage.

Creutzfeldt-Jakob Disease

Creutzfeldt-Jakob is a fatal disease that may present with a wide variety of vague "neurotic-appearing" symptoms or as dementia. This disorder usually begins in the 40s or 50s and is rapidly progressive, with patients often becoming severely demented and dying within a year. Possibly the most interesting aspect of the disorder is that it has been demonstrated to be infectious; that is, a transmissible agent, in some ways similar to a "slow" (long incubation period) virus, has been transmitted from one laboratory animal to another and produced the disease.

Normal Pressure Hydrocephalus

Normal pressure, or occult, hydrocephalus should be suspected in patients with progressive dementia who also develop ataxia and urinary incontinence. Their gait may appear similar to the astasia-abasia of hysterics. The symptoms appear to be due to impaired flow of cerebrospinal fluid over the cortex to the arachnoid villi, where it is reabsorbed. A CNS infection, subarachnoid hemorrhage, or idiopathic factors may lead to the onset of the disorder. The CT or MRI scan will demonstrate enlarged cerebral ventricles without significant cortical atrophy. Neurosurgical shunting procedures may prevent the dementia, if performed early in the disease.

Brain Tumors

A CT or MRI scan of the head is indicated to rule out brain tumors, as well as other anatomically distorting disorders, in demented patients. Dementia, in the absence of other neurologic signs or symptoms, may be due to tumors in the frontal or anterior temporal lobes or to extracerebral tumors, such as subdural hematomas or meningiomas. The latter disorders are nonmalignant and proper treatment may lead to curing an associated dementia.

Other Systemic Disorders

A number of other systemic disorders (Table 4) may also cause dementia, and several will be discussed briefly; however, more detailed discussions may be found in standard internal medicine or subspecialty medical texts or other psychiatric sources (Benson 1982; Cummings and Benson 1983; Glen and Whalley 1979; Mayeux and Rosen 1983; McHugh and Folstein 1985; Thompson et al. 1985; Wells 1985). Cerebral dysfunction may be caused by a number of metabolic and endocrine disorders. Apathetic hyperthyroidism is thought to produce dementia in the elderly more often than hypothyroidism. Therefore, thyroid function studies should be performed as part of the evaluation of any patient suspected of having dementia. Thyroid hormone replacement may correct the dementia of hypothyroidism, but brain damage may become permanent after a variable period of time if that diagnosis is overlooked. Idiopathic hypoparathyroidism, which usually responds very well to treatment, may also cause dementia. Hypopituitarism, hypoadrenalism (Addison's disease), and hyperadrenalism (Cushing's disease) usually cause depression or other primarily affective symptoms rather than dementia, although such disorders should be considered in the differential diagnosis.

Chronic liver failure may also cause dementia due to hepatic encephalopathy. Chronic renal failure may produce dementia as one of the symptoms of uremic encephalopathy. Patients treated with hemodialysis over several years may develop "dialysis dementia"; speech abnormalities (e.g., stuttering, dysarthria) are usually the initial indication that this syndrome is developing, and myoclonic jerks and seizures may follow. Dialysis dementia may be due to aluminum toxicity from the dialysate fluid or from the frequent use of antacids; stopping the aluminum intake may lead to symptom reversal.

Cardiac arrhythmias or chronic pulmonary disease may also produce dementia through persistent hypoxia. A collagen-vascular disorder may cause cerebral vessels to become inflamed and, thereby, produce dementia. If signs of a collagen disease, such as an elevated sedimentation rate and proteinuria or casts in the urine, are present, even if a specific collagen-vascular disease cannot be diagnosed, a therapeutic trial of steroids is indicated. Steroid therapy may also improve dementia due to sarcoidosis; this disorder may cause dementia alone but usually is associated with other symptoms of meningeal disease.

Nutritional deficiency states may also produce dementia. The classic triad (three Ds) of pellagra due to nicotinic acid deficiency consists of dementia, dermatitis, and diarrhea. Vitamin B12 (cyano-cobalamin) deficiency usually, but not always, produces blood dyscrasias and other nervous system dysfunctions, such as peripheral neuropathy and dorsal or lateral column spinal cord disorders, prior to the onset of symptoms of dementia. The above symptoms, associated with B12 deficiency, may also develop due to folic acid deficiency; therefore, serum B12 and folate levels should routinely be part of a dementia workup.

Cryptococcal meningitis and neurosyphilis are infections that should be considered in cases of slowly progressive dementia. Other classic symptoms of meningitis, such as stiff neck, headache, fever, increased intracranial pressure, and fluctuating consciousness, will virtually always be present in association with meningitis. Acquired immune deficiency syndrome (AIDS) also may produce symptoms of dementia and delirium.

A large number of drugs, heavy metals, and other chemical and industrial compounds also may produce dementia. These topics are discussed in Chapter 9. However, it should be remembered that many elderly individuals use a number of over-the-counter medications (Guttmann 1977) and alcohol (Atkinson 1984); therefore, an especially thorough history is indicated in those areas.

☐ GENERAL TREATMENT APPROACHES

A number of treatment approaches have been discussed in conjunction with specific disorders in previous sections. This section will be a general discussion of the management of demented patients. First, the physician should assure that it is primarily an organic, not a functional, process that is causing the symptoms. If in doubt, the physician should consider a clinical trial to treat a possible underlying or associated functional disorder.

Many patients with dementia will have Alzheimer's disease or some other "untreatable" disorder. However, it is critical that the physician realize that although a specific treatment, or cure, is not yet available for some causes of dementia, that does not imply that the symptoms with which those patients suffer are not treatable. The patient's level of general functioning and the severity of symptoms may be significantly improved by proper management.

The demented patient's symptoms may be managed in several ways. First, the physician should assure that the patient's general health is as good as possible. A healthy environment and life-style, including a good diet, adequate sleep, and as much exercise as is possible to maintain fitness, are important. Perceptual and sensory problems, such as vision and hearing, should also be evaluated and corrected (e.g., eyeglasses, cataract surgery, hearing aids) as fully as possible (Stoudemire and Thompson 1981). Also, any concurrent medical disorders should be managed as well as is possible. The patient and family should also be instructed to see the physician as soon as possible if any new symptoms appear. What might be a minor illness (e.g., a cold, the flu, or a urinary tract infection) for someone else, may cause symptoms of dementia or delirium in the usually subclinical or mildly demented patient. The environment should also be organized in a structured and consistent manner so that changes, which may exceed the patient's mental capacities, are minimized. Hospitalizations or moves to a nursing home or any unfamiliar environment may be very distressing and may cause confusion or other dementia symptoms.

Regular orientation and use of orienting aids may also be very helpful. The same individual should interact with each patient as often as possible and have at least brief chats whenever possible. These conversations might focus on discussions of the date, day of week, time of day, season, news, or other events as indicated. Confused or frightened patients should also be placed in rooms as close as possible to the nursing station or other centers of activity (Thompson 1982). Familiar, reassuring, and orienting objects in the patient's room may include personal clothing, family photos and other mementos, a night-light, clock, calendar, television, radio, and current newspapers and magazines.

Many symptoms associated with dementia can be effectively managed through judicious use of medications. However, demented patients are often noncompliant because they may not remember to take medications properly or may be apathetic about doing so. Therefore, someone should oversee medication administration, including the use of memory aid pill counters, in demented patients (Stoudemire and Thompson 1983).

A secondary or coexistent depression may be improved by use of an antidepressant. The dosage of the antidepressant should usually be much smaller and increased more slowly than usual (Thompson et al. 1983). Also, anticholinergic and sedating side effects of some antidepressants, especially amitriptyline and doxepin but many others to a lesser degree, may worsen dementia or produce delirium. The antidepressants with the fewest anticholinergic and sedative side effects, such as desipramine (Norpramin) or trazodone (Desyrel), should generally be used initially in demented patients. However, trazodone has been reported to cause sexual problems, including anorgasmia in women and priapism requiring surgical intervention resulting in permanent impotence in men; therefore, it is not the antidepressant of first choice for demented patients with sexual activity or interest.

The demented patient often becomes most symptomatic in the evening or at night. "Sundowner" syndrome often develops, as its name implies, around sundown because the sensory stimulation that is needed by the demented patient to maintain orientation decreases as night falls. Sensory input also tends to decrease at that time of day because visitors may leave, and the general amount of activity tends to decrease as others settle in for the night. A heavy evening meal may also shunt blood into the splanchnic vascular bed and be sedating to the patient.

If given 1 or 2 hours before sundown, a small dose of neuroleptic may be helpful in decreasing or aborting the anxiety, agitation, confusion, and possibly psychotic symptoms, including illusions, delusions, and hallucinations, that might otherwise develop in sundowning patients. As little as 0.5 mg of haloperidol may be useful, but the dosage may be gradually escalated upward until the optimal dosage (i.e., maximal decrease in symptoms for minimal side effects) is found. If extrapyramidal or other side effects develop to haloperidol, other neuroleptics should be tried. Since they are relatively less sedating than other neuroleptics, haloperidol or one of the other higher potency neuroleptics especially are indicated for demented patients who tend to be lethargic or withdrawn.

If the patient is extremely agitated or anxious, one of the less potent but more sedating neuroleptics, such as thioridazine or chlorpromazine, may provide more symptomatic relief for the equivalent dosage required. The greater risk of anticholinergic side effects or alpha-adrenergic blockade leading to orthostatic hypotension with these agents is usually not a major clinical problem if the dosage is gradually titrated upward and the patient regularly monitored for their development. As little as 10 to

25 mg of thioridazine or chlorpromazine 1 or 2 hours before the usual onset of symptoms may be very effective in decreasing agitation and aborting sundowner syndrome.

Another therapeutic point that is often not recognized is that sunset occurs at different times of the day as the seasons change. Some institutions routinely give evening medications at about 9 P.M. That is too late virtually throughout the year to treat sundowner syndrome optimally. During the summer months, when sundown is usually 8 to 9 P.M., the neuroleptic will be most effective if given between 6 and 7 P.M. During the winter months, when darkness may occur between 5 and 6 P.M., the neuroleptic should be given mid-afternoon. To wait until 8 or 9 P.M. during the winter, 3 or 4 hours after sunset, to give the neuroleptic will almost always lead to a much larger dose being required to control the symptoms, which may be rapidly escalating or full-blown by that time.

If agitation or other symptoms persist throughout the day, a neuroleptic may need to be administered in divided doses; for may patients, however, a single early evening dosage is adequate. A nap or two during the day may do more to improve the demented patient's mental functioning than anything else, and should be encouraged in patients whose mental functioning tends to deteriorate progressively as the day goes on.

The role of ergot alkaloids (Hydergine) to treat dementia has been controversial. The Food and Drug Administration approved dose of 1 mg tid may be homeopathic for some patients; in Europe, dosages equivalent to 6 to 9 mg daily often are more effective. A new, more bioavailable form, Hydergine-LC, has recently become available in the United States. Patient selection is also critical in achieving good results; that is, the ergot alkaloids have never been claimed to be effective for severely demented individuals. However, ergot alkaloids have been demonstrated to significantly improve a number of functional areas, including attention and concentration, in nursing home patients (vanLoveren-Huyben et al. 1984). Therefore, a clinical trial of at least several months is recommended for mild to moderately demented patients. Physicians who are skeptical might consider utilizing a structured mental status exam or other relatively objective measure, such as psychological testing or the Mini-Mental State (Folstein et al. 1975), to assess change.

The more severely demented patient who is paranoid, wanders endlessly, has insomnia, and exhibits persistent psychotic symptoms usually can be managed by higher dosages of neuroleptics. The use of benzodiazepines or sedative-hypnotics for such symptoms may be problematic. Longer half-life benzodiazepines, such as flurazepam (Dalmane), may accumulate and worsen depression or dementia, especially due to pharmacokinetic changes associated with aging that often double or triple their time of elimination (Thompson et al. 1983). If a trial of a benzodiazepine is desired for anxiety control, one of the shorter half-life agents is recommended; lorazepam (Ativan), oxazepam (Serax), and alprazolam (Xanax) are good initial choices.

Antihistamines should generally not be used as a sedative-hypnotic; other agents are as effective, and antihistamines may cause further dementia or delirium due to their anticholinergic effects. Chloral hydrate should be avoided as a sedative-hypnotic for patients concurrently taking acidic drugs, including warfarin, diphenylhydantoin, and many other frequently used medications. A metabolite of chloral hydrate displaces acidic drugs from their protein binding sites and, therefore, may significantly disrupt their steady state metabolism.

If a trial of a benzodiazepine sedative-hypnotic seems indicated, temazepam (Restoril) is the drug of choice. Its half-life of about 8 to 10 hours parallels the desired length of sleep. Also, because it bypasses the oxidative hepatic enzyme system, as do lorazepam and oxazepam, its half-life remains basically constant with aging, in the presence of most hepatic disorders, and in combination with other medications. An even shorter half-life agent, triazolam (Halcion), may cause mental confusion or other side effects, partly due to its rapid absorption, especially in neurologically impaired patients. Also, triazolam's half-life of 3 to 4 hours may not maintain sleep through the second half of the night, which tends to be the most restless portion for elderly or demented individuals.

Counseling or psychotherapy may be helpful for mildly and some moderately demented patients and may be directed toward learning coping methods to minimize their deficits. Education regarding memory aids and reminders may be especially useful. These patients may also learn and be supported to avoid activities that may be beyond their mental capacities, and grief work may be helpful for their loss of previously enjoyed cognitively based activities.

Therapeutic planning should involve an assessment of the patient's environment and social support systems; most important among these is often the family (Mace and Rabins 1981). Can the family safely care for the patient at home? What types of support does the family need to do so without "burning out"? Can brief nursing home or other institutional stays (called respite programs) be periodically arranged for the patient to provide the caretakers a much needed vacation? Arranging for a nurse or housekeeper to come to the patient's home may be even less disruptive to the patient. These types of measures may also be cost effective in the long run by delaying or preventing the need for long-term institutionalization.

The physician also should realize that a great deal may be learned from the family or other caretakers about what works best for a particular patient. Therefore, the caretakers should be actively involved in every step of treatment assessment and planning (Reisberg 1983b). This will also bolster their morale and sense of being a valued part of the caretaking team. The physician may need to counsel some families that the patient needs to be placed in a nursing home for the patient's own safety. This may lead to guilt in some families because they may believe that a "good family" should personally care for its own members regardless. In such situations, the physician may provide education and support that the most caring act at times is to assure that round-the-clock trained personnel will be involved with the patient. Institutional placement may also free up the family so that when they do visit, they may have more energy and may be able to spend more "quality" time with the patient.

The judgment of many Alzheimer's or otherwise demented patients is impaired, and their families may understandably be frightened and eager to try any possible "cure." Therefore, these patients and their families may be relatively easy "marks" for con artists or misguided and unscientific individuals selling folk, dietary, or health food remedies, wanting to replace all of their dental fillings, or other unproven schemes to treat their disorder. The physician should be alert to question patients and their families regularly about such approaches, which may be quite expensive and may falsely elevate hopes.

☐ SUMMARY

In recent years, much has been learned about the syndrome of dementia. It has been recognized as a serious and frequent clinical disorder; it is the fourth leading cause of death in the Western world. Alzheimer's disease accounts for more than one-half of dementias, especially in the elderly. However, signs and symptoms of dementia may be caused by a broad spectrum of medical, neurologic, and psychiatric disorders. Therefore, a thorough evaluation is indicated for every suspected case of dementia; about 25 percent of those may be due to a specifically treatable condition and 10 percent may be curable. Even for those cases of dementia where there is not a specific treatment, good medical and psychiatric management may significantly improve the quality of life for these patients and their families, plus sometimes slow the progression of the dementia and delay or prevent the need for long-term care. The challenging and critical nature of the physician's role in coordinating integrated care for demented patients and their families is at least as great as for any other group of medical disorders.

☐ REFERENCES

American Psychiatric Association: Diagnostic and Statistical Manual of Mental Disorders, 3rd ed, revised. Washington, DC, American Psychiatric Association, 1987

Atkinson RM (ed): Alcohol and Drug Abuse in Old Age. Washington, DC, American Psychiatric Press, 1984

Beck JC, Benson DF, Scheibel AB, et al: Dementia in the elderly: the silent epidemic. Ann Intern Med 97:231–241, 1982

Benson DF: The treatable dementias, in Psychiatric Aspects of Neurologic Disease, Vol 2. Edited by Benson DF, Blumer D. New York, Grune & Stratton, 1982

Bissette G, Reynolds GP, Kilts CD, et al: Corticotropin-releasing factor-like immunoreactivity in senile dementia of the Alzheimer type. JAMA 234:3067–3069, 1985

Breitner JCS, Folstein MF: Familial Alzheimer dementia: a prevalent disorder with specific clinical features. Psychol Med 14:63–80, 1984

Butler RN: Why Survive? Being Old in America. New York, Harper & Row, 1975

Coyle JT, Price DL, DeLong MR: Alzheimer's disease: a disorder of cortical cholinergic innervation. Science 219:1184–1190, 1983

Cummings JL, Benson DF: Dementia: A Clinical Approach. Woburn, MA, Butterworth, 1983

Dysken MW, Janowsky DS: Dose-related physostigmine-induced ventricular arrhythmia: case report. J Clin Psychiatry 46:446–447, 1985

Farmer PM, Peck A, Terry RD: Correlations among neuritic plaques, neurofibrillary tangles and the severity of senile dementia. (abstract) J Neuropathol Exp Neurol 35:367, 1976

Folstein MF, Folstein SE, McHugh PR: "Mini-mental state": a practical method for grading the cognitive state of patients for the clinician. J Psychiatr Res 12:189–198, 1975

Francis PT, Palmer AM, Sims NR, et al: Neurochemical studies of early-onset Alzheimer's disease: possible influence on treatment. N Engl J Med 313:7–11, 1985

Glen AIM, Whalley LJ: Alzheimer's Disease: Early Recognition of Potentially Reversible Deficits. New York, Churchill Livingstone, 1979

Guttmann D: Patterns of legal drug use by older Americans. Addict Dis 3:337–356, 1977

Hachinski VC, Lassen NA, Marshall J: Multi-infarct dementia: a cause of mental deterioration in the elderly. Lancet 2:207–210, 1974

Heston LL, Mastri AR, Anderson E, et al: Dementia of the Alzheimer type: clinical genetics, natural history, and associated conditions. Arch Gen Psychiatry 38:1085–1090, 1981

Huber SJ, Paulson GW: The concept of subcortical dementia. Am J Psychiatry 142:1312–1317, 1985

Katzman R: The prevalence and malignancy of Alzheimer disease: a major killer. Arch Neurol 33:217–218, 1976

Kay DWK, Beamish P, Roth M: Old age mental disorders in Newcastle upon Tyne. Br J Psychiatry 110:146–148, 1964

Kral VA: Benign senescent forgetfulness, in Aging, Vol 7. Edited by Katzman R, Terry RD, Bick KL. New York, Raven Press, 1978

Kubanis P, Zornetzer SF: Age-related behavioral and neurobiological changes: a review with an emphasis on memory. Behav Neural Biol 31:115–172, 1981

Lipowski ZJ: Transient cognitive disorders (delirium, acute confusional states) in the elderly. Am J Psychiatry 140:1426–1436, 1983

Mace NI, Rabins PV: The 36 Hour Day: A Family Guide to Caring for Patients with Alzheimer's Disease, Related Dementing Illnesses, and Memory Loss in Later Life. Baltimore, Johns Hopkins University Press, 1981

Mayeux R, Rosen W (eds): The Dementias: Advances in Neurology, Vol. 38. New York, Raven Press, 1983

McAllister TW, Ferrell RB, Price TRP, et al: The dexamethasone suppression test in two patients with severe depressive pseudodementia. Am J Psychiatry 139:479–481, 1982

McHugh PR, Folstein MF: Organic mental disorders, in Psychiatry, Vol 1. Edited by Cavenar JO, Jr. Philadelphia, JB Lippincott Co, 1985, pp 1–21

Mohs RC, Davis BM, Johns CA, et al: Oral physostigmine treatment of patients with Alzheimer's disease. Am J Psychiatry 142:28–33, 1985

Mortimer JA: Epidemiologic aspects of Alzheimer's disease, in Advances in Neurogerontology, Vol. 1, The Aging Nervous System. Edited by Maletta GJ, Pirozzolo FJ. New York, Praeger, 1980

O'Daniel R, Lippmann S, Piyush P: Depressive pseudodementia. Psychiatric Annals 11:10–15, 1981

Perry EK, Tomlinson BE, Blessed G, et al: Correlation of cholinergic abnormalities with senile plaques and mental test scores. Br Med J 2:1457–1459, 1978

Raskind M, Peskind E, Rivard MF, et al: Dexamethasone suppression test and cortisol circadian rhythm in primary degenerative dementia. Am J Psychiatry 139:1468–1471, 1982

Reifler BV, Larson E, Hanley R: Coexistence of cognitive impairment and depression in geriatric outpatients. Am J Psychiatry 139:623–626, 1982

Reisberg B (ed): Alzheimer's Disease. New York, Free Press, 1983a

Reisberg B: A Guide to Alzheimer's Disease for Families, Spouses, and Friends. New York, Free Press, 1983b

Reisberg B, Ferris SH, Gershon S: An overview of pharmacologic treatment of cognitive decline in the aged. Am J Psychiatry 138:593–600, 1981

Reisberg B, Ferris SH, Anand R, et al: Effects of naloxone in senile dementia: a double-blind trial. (letter) N Engl J Med 308:721–722, 1983

Schneck MK, Reisberg B, Ferris SH: An overvew of current concepts of Alzheimer's disease. Am J Psychiatry 139:165–173, 1982

Schneck SA: Aging of the nervous system and dementia, in Clinical Internal Medicine in the Aged. Edited by Schrier RW. Philadelphia, WB Saunders, 1982

Seltzer B, Sherwin I: "Organic brain syndromes": an empirical study and critical review. Am J Psychiatry 135:13–21, 1978

Solomon S: Application of neurology to psychiatry, in Comprehensive Textbook of Psychiatry (4th ed). Edited by Kaplan HI, Sadock BJ. Baltimore, Williams & Wilkins, 1985, p 151

Stoudemire A, Thompson TL II: Recognizing and treating dementia. Geriatrics 136:112–120, 1981

Stoudemire A, Thompson TL II: Medication noncompliance: systematic approaches to evaluation and intervention. Gen Hosp Psychiatry 5:233–239, 1983

Summers WK, Majovski LV, Marsh GM, et al: Oral tetrahydroaminoacridine in long-term treatment of senile dementia, Alzheimer type. N Engl J Med 315:1241–1245, 1986

Terry RD, Katzman R: Senile dementia of the Alzheimer's type. Ann Neurol 14:497–506, 1983

Thompson TL II: Psychosocial and psychiatric problems of the aged, in Clinical Internal Medicine in the Aged. Edited by Schrier RW. Philadelphia, WB Saunders, 1982

Thompson TL II, Moran MG, Nies AS: Psychotropic drug use in the elderly. N Engl J Med 308:134–138, 194–199, 1983

Thompson TL II, Scully JH, Thompson WL: The "difficult" medical patient, and the importance of consultation-liaison psychiatry, in Understanding Human Behavior in Health and Illness (3rd ed). Edited by Simons RC. Baltimore, Williams & Wilkins, 1985

vanLoveren-Huyben CMS, Engelaar HFWJ, Hermans MBM, et al: Double-blind clinical and psychologic study of ergoloid mesylates (Hydergine) in subjects with senile mental deterioration. J Am Geriatr Soc 32:584–588, 1984

Wells CE: Pseudodementia. Am J Psychiatry 136:895–900, 1979

Wells CE: Diagnosis of dementia: a reassessment. Psychosomatics 25:183–190, 1984

Wells CE: Organ syndromes: dementia, in Comprehensive Textbook of Psychiatry (4th ed). Edited by Kaplan HI, Sadock BJ. Baltimore, Williams & Wilkins, 1985

Whitehouse PJ, Price DL, Struble RG, et al: Alzheimer's disease and senile dementia: loss of neurons in the basal forebrain. Science 215:1237–1239, 1982

Chapter 7

Selected Organic Mental Disorders

G. Alan Stoudemire, M.D.

☐ HISTORICAL PERSPECTIVE

One may trace identifiable roots of the DSM-III (American Psychiatric Association 1980) schema for the diagnosis of mental disorders to Kraeplin and Bleuler. Kraepelin used the term *organic dementias* for psychoses due to primary central nervous system (CNS) diseases (such as neurosyphilis) (Lipowski 1981). In 1916, Bleuler described the "organic psychosyndrome," which was characterized by a constellation of behavioral symptoms due to chronic diffuse cortical damage (Lipowski 1981). Bleuler's organic psychosyndrome consisted primarily of global impairments in memory, perception, attention, orientation judgment, and emotional and impulse control as well as personality changes. Bleuler emphasized, however, that cognitive functions were not always uniformly impaired and that focal brain lesions could, at times, cause more affective than cognitive abnormalities (Lipowski 1981).

The concept of focal abnormalities causing specific syndromes was further delineated by Bleuler's son Manfred (Bleuler 1951). The essential feature of a focal organic psychosyndrome was that even though the patient might exhibit evidence of disruption in emotional, drive, and impulse control, the overall cognitive dysfunctioning could remain relatively intact (Lipowski 1984). These focal disruptions were in contrast to the global disruptions in cerebral functioning typical of dementia.

The first edition of the Diagnostic and Statistical Manual of Mental Disorders (American Psychiatric Association 1952) essentially overlooked the concept of the focal organic psychosyndrome and essentially applied the conceptual description of the organic psychosyndrome, which required global disruptions in memory, attention, concentration, personality, affect, impulse control, and intellect. The nomenclature, therefore, did not allow for focal abnormalities that could potentially leave cognitive functioning relatively unimpaired (Lipowski 1981).

DSM-II (American Psychiatric Association 1968) did little to clarify the focal organic brain syndrome as diagnostic possibility (Lipowski 1981). DSM-II retained the concept of a "basic" organic brain syndrome resulting from diffuse cerebral impairment whose component features were marked by global impairments in orientation, memory, intellectual functioning, judgment, and affect. The fundamental difficulty in this scheme was the failure to describe syndromes in which brain and behavior abnormalities were relatively focal rather than global. These conceptual difficulties led to the revisions in DSM-III which recognized the possibility of focal brain dysfunction due to specific causes.

In DSM-III-R (American Psychiatric Association 1987), the "essential" feature of the general category organic mental disorders is the presence of psychological or behavioral abnormalities that are associated with transient or permanent dysfunction of the brain. As such, the diagnostic criteria for an organic mental disorder should include: (1) recognizing on clinical assessment the presence of signs and symptoms of one of the organic brain syndromes (see below) and (2) demonstrating on the basis of history, physical examination, or laboratory tests, the presence of a specific etiologic factor relating to the altered mental status.

DSM-III-R categorizes the organic mental syndromes into the following broad categories: delirium, dementia, amnestic syndrome, organic delusional syndrome, organic hallucinosis, organic mood syndrome, organic anxiety syndrome, organic personality syndrome, and organic brain syndrome NOS (residual category). Delirium and dementia have been discussed in previous chapters. In this chapter, we will selectively discuss the amnestic syndrome, organic mood syndrome (manic and depressed), organic delusional syndrome, organic hallucinosis, organic personality syndrome (including aggressive type), and the organic anxiety syndrome.

SELECTED ORGANIC BRAIN SYNDROMES

The fundamental feature of dementia and delirium is that these disorders are characterized by global (rather than circumscribed) disruptions in cognitive functioning as part of the symptom complex. In contrast, the organic brain syndromes discussed in this section (amnestic, affective, delusional, hallucinosis, mood, anxiety) are marked by relatively focal abnormalities in behavioral and psychological functioning. The cardinal inclusion criteria for these specific syndromes include "demonstrating, by means of the history, physical examination, or laboratory tests, the presence of a specific organic fac-

tor (or factors) judged to be etiologically related to the abnormal mental state" (American Psychiatric Association 1987). Cardinal exclusion criteria for the diagnosis of these particular syndromes are that there is no clouding or fluctuation in the level of consciousness (as in delirium) and there is no significant global loss of intellectual abilities (as in dementia). Hence, for the diagnosis of these disorders, delirium and dementia must be excluded. Mild cognitive deficits, however, may be present in any of these particular syndromes but they should not be pervasive; even in the organic amnestic syndrome, cognitive/memory deficits are relatively focal rather than global. Each of these syndromes will now be individually considered.

AMNESTIC SYNDROME

DSM-III-R Criteria and Clinical Features

The essential feature of the amnestic syndrome is an impairment in short-term and long-term memory occurring in a normal state of consciousness. Patients should not be delirious, nor should they have dementia. To appreciate the relatively focal aspect of this syndrome, a brief discussion of memory functioning relative to clinical diagnosis will be considered.

Memory

Memory may be divided into three aspects: (1) immediate recall, (2) the ability to learn new information (short-term memory), and (3) the ability to retrieve previously stored information (long-term memory) (Benson 1978). Immediate recall (or immediate retention) is the ability to reproduce with accuracy information that has just recently been received. Information is essentially not stored in this step. The basic test for immediate recall is the digit span or some similar test. The norm in clinical psychiatry for the test is usually seven digits (plus or minus two). Disturbances in immediate recall are usually indicative of an inability to maintain attention and are thus most commonly found in delirium. Immediate recall is usually normal in the amnestic syndrome.

The components of memory functioning disturbed in the amnestic syndrome are the ability to learn new information (the DSM-III-R corollary term being *short-term memory*) and long-term memory.

The phase of learning new information is an active memory storage process. Psychologists may refer to the basic process of learning new information as consisting of selection and registration. The ability to learn new information (or short-term memory) is usually tested at the bedside by asking the patient to remember three unrelated objects for 5 to 10 minutes. Other tests such as the paired associate learning task (adapted from the Wechsler Memory Scale) may also be used (Taylor et al. 1985).

Short-term memory is usually most severely affected in the amnestic syndrome. This short-term memory deficit, which essentially represents an inability to register or learn new information, is also referred to as anterograde amnesia. It describes the inability to form new memories (i.e., to learn new information), from the time of the illness onset. Since orientation is aided by the ability to store information regarding time, date, location, and circumstance, most patients with this form of memory impairment may, at times, appear disoriented and confused but without fluctuating disturbances in their level of consciousness typical of delirium.

The ability to retrieve information, or long-term or remote memory, is also impaired in the amnestic syndrome. Testing this memory function is aided by the examiner knowing, or being able to confirm, certain historical aspects of the patient's life. Other tests may involve sequential recall of the names of presidents, historical events within the patient's life span, and specific dates in the patient's life (e.g., birthdays, wedding dates, years of graduation). A similar manifestation of long-term memory impairment is referred to as retrograde amnesia, that is, impairment in recall of memories established prior to illness onset. It tends to be somewhat less affected than short-term memory functioning in the amnestic syndrome.

The tendency to confabulate is often associated with the amnestic syndrome. Confabulation is characterized by responses that are not only grossly inaccurate, but are often bizarre and fantastic. The responses may be so farfetched or unrealistic as to sound "psychotic." Confabulation has traditionally been considered to be essentially a secondary phenomenon to the memory deficits, as patients were felt to be attempting to "fill in the gaps." This conceptualization is probably simplistic. The degree of confabulation is not necessarily correlated with the degree of memory disorder, and correlation tends to vary more with the loss of ability to monitor responses and to be self-corrective (Mercer et al.

1977). Bifrontal lobe disease tends to be a more reliable anatomical correlate of confabulation rather than temporal lobe dysfunction (Benson 1978; Stuss et al. 1978).

Etiology

The primary disorders that should be considered in the differential diagnosis in patients presenting with memory disturbances are delirium and dementia. In delirium, the memory disturbance is accompanied by a disturbed level of consciousness and usually fluctuates with time. Pervasive signs of cerebral dysfunction are usually present. Immediate memory, due to difficulties with attention and concentration (as evidenced by problems with digit span), may be present; this is in contrast to amnestic syndrome, where the digit span should be essentially normal. In dementia, evidence of global intellectual deterioration should be present (Wells 1985a).

One disorder that bears close resemblance to the amnestic syndrome is transient global amnesia (TGA). TGA usually occurs in middle-aged or elderly individuals and is manifested by the sudden loss of memory for recent events and inability to recall new information with secondary confusion. The level of consciousness is normal and personal identity remains intact (Shuping et al. 1980). Patients tend to be aware of their deficits and may ask repeated questions about their circumstances. The episodes may last from minutes to hours, with attacks sometimes being episodic events. The "spells" usually remit within 24 hours. Most experts consider the episodes to be due to episodic transient vascular insufficiency of the mesial temporal lobe, but other disorders, such as tumors, diazepam overdosage, digitalis-induced cardiac arrhythmias, cerebral embolism, migraine, polycythemia vera, and myxomatous mitral valvular disease, have also been reported. The majority of patients with TGA also have associated risk factors for cerebrovascular stroke (Shuping et al. 1980). Most common angiographic findings tend to be occlusion or stenosis of the posterior cerebral artery (Mathew and Meyer 1974). The occurrence of TGA usually necessitates a neurologic and cardiovascular search for underlying causes for cerebral insufficiency or emboli.

Amnestic syndrome should also be differentiated from the dementia associated with chronic alcoholism. The dementia associated with alcoholism, as the term *dementia* implies, is associated with global intellectual deterioration rather than relatively focal memory deficits. The amnestic syndrome, however, may be superimposed on patients with alcoholic dementias in various stages of development (Cutting 1978).

The most common syndrome associated with the amnestic syndrome is the Wernicke-Korsakoff syndrome, but the two syndromes should not be considered synonymous. The Wernicke-Korsakoff syndrome is attributed to thiamine deficiency, primarily occurring in chronic alcoholics, although any individual subjected to thiamine depletion due to dietary reasons or malabsorption (i.e., comatose patients or patients with disseminated infections and malignancies, eating disorders, or undergoing hemodialysis) may develop the syndrome (McEvoy 1981). The Wernicke's component of the syndrome presents as an acute encephalopathy and consists of ophthalmoplegia (often a sixth nerve palsy), peripheral neuropathy, ataxia, nystagmus, and delirium. The Wernicke's encephalopathic component of the syndrome occurs in 50 to 90 percent of cases (Adams 1983; Cutting 1978; Victor et al. 1971). Mood changes ranging from euphoria to apathy may herald onset of the syndrome as well as delusional symptoms and (rarely) auditory hallucinations. The acute neurologic component of the syndrome responds to thiamine repletion. The ocular changes respond most promptly. Improvement in mentation and gait disturbances may take days to weeks to resolve, however, and the recovery may be limited. The residual of the Wernicke-Korsakoff syndrome may be a persistent amnestic syndrome. The prognosis in the Korsakoff's type of amnestic syndrome is variable. Victor et al.'s (1971) series of 104 patients followed over 5 years revealed that 20 percent recovered completely, 28 percent were significantly improved, and 25 percent were slightly improved. The remainder were either not improved or were considered to worsen; most required some degree of chronic custodial care.

The most common neuroanatomical abnormality associated with the amnestic syndrome associated with thiamine deficiency invokes bilateral sclerosis of the mammillary bodies, probably due to hemorrhage (Benson 1978). Significant degenerative changes have also been observed in the dorsal medial nucleus of the thalamus (Victor 1969; Victor et al. 1971), which serves as a "relay" point between memory centers and the frontal cortex.

Thiamine deficiency is not the only etiologic cause of the amnestic syndrome. The syndrome may occur from any disease process affecting the diencephalic and medial temporal structures (mammillary bodies, fornix, hippocampal complex). The amnesia caused by trauma, cerebrovascular events, surgery, and possibly herpes encephalitis appears to involve the medial temporal region—particularly the hippocampal area—rather than mammillary bodies in the diencephalic areas. The fornix, if injured, may also cause amnestic difficulties (Benson 1978). Although most amnestic syndromes are associated with bilateral damage to these brain structures, amnestic syndromes have been described with unilateral brain insults, particularly left-sided temporal lobe and thalamic structures (Benson et al. 1974).

In psychogenic types of amnesia, the memory loss is usually related to personal information, including information regarding the individual's identity. Short-term memory is intact, in striking contrast to the deficits in this area found in organic amnestic states.

Memory deficits after head trauma may be both anterograde (inability to learn new information) and retrograde. Most patients recover the ability to learn new information but may have "lacunae" of permanent memory loss during the period of posttraumatic amnesia. The retrograde memory deficits initially may extend backward for long periods of time (years), but memories tend to return gradually as the period of time affected by retrograde amnestia "shrinks."

Electroconvulsive therapy (ECT) may cause an amnestic syndrome, but memory deficits associated with the treatments usually resolve within 6 months. There is little scientific evidence of permanent memory impairment with properly performed ECT, although retrograde amnesia gaps for periods of time preceding, during, and after treatments may persist. The technique of unilateral nondominant lobe electrode placement markedly reduces the transient memory impairments associated with ECT.

Other miscellaneous reported causes of the amnestic syndrome include heavy metal poisoning (arsenic, lead), carbon monoxide poisoning, and cerebral anoxia (Lipowski 1980b). Temporal lobectomy for intractable complex partial seizures may result in memory deficits, but is usually of major significance only when surgery is bilateral.

Treatment

Direct treatment for amnestic syndrome is possible primarily in cases due to thiamine deficiency but may also be possible in some cases of vascular insufficiency or by early removal from exposure to toxic substances. Most cases, however, will require cognitive and behavioral rehabilitation to facilitate recovery and adaptation to residual deficits. For example, "cognitive retraining" for patients and counseling for their family members are especially valuable. Specialized rehabilitation programs have been developed for such patients, particularly those with a history of head trauma (Kwentus et al. 1985; Lezak 1978). Treatment of head-injured patients is discussed elsewhere in this volume (Chapter 10). (See also the section on treatment of organic personality syndrome, this chapter.)

☐ ORGANIC MOOD SYNDROME

DSM-III-R Criteria and Clinical Features

The essential feature of an organic mood syndrome is a mood disturbance with characteristics of major depression or mania caused by a specific organic factor. The presence of delirium or dementia excludes the diagnosis. Mild cognitive impairment may be present. Any or all of the symptoms of major depression and mania may be seen as part of the syndrome, including secondary delusions and hallucinations (American Psychiatric Association 1987).

Etiology

A seemingly endless litany of diseases and medications have been associated with causing depression. Whitlock and Evans (1978) listed approximately 200 drugs associated with depression. Hall (1980) listed 25 medical illnesses that may induce depression, 23 medical conditions associated with "reactive" depression, 20 causes of dementia that produce secondary "depressive responses," and 75 other medical conditions that could present with depression. There are, however, a number of serious problems with interpreting these catalog-style lists. First, one must carefully state what is meant by "depression." Rarely are the diagnoses in case reports from which such lists are compiled based

on rigorous, systematic structured diagnostic interviews. Secondly, a drug or disease causing certain symptoms associated with depression does not constitute a formal diagnosis of depression. For example, many drugs and physical illnesses may be accompanied by symptoms similar to the somatic symptoms of major depression—such as fatigue, lassitude, lethargy, weakness, headache, abdominal pain, insomnia, anxiety, and difficulty concentrating. Thus, depression may be mimicked rather than induced. For example, over half of patients entering a general hospital have been found to complain of fatigue (Adams 1983) as do 60 to 80 percent of depressed patients (Mathew et al. 1981; Wittenborn and Buhler 1979). The complaint of insomnia is another example. Complaints of insomnia have been found in 30 to 35 percent of the general population (Kales et al. 1982) but are also typical in clinical depression as well, occurring in 60 to 70 percent of patients (Wittenborn and Buhler 1979).

Attributing a medication or disease as the cause of depression should therefore be approached with some degree of caution and skepticism, and case reports and lists of such should be approached and evaluated critically. Demonstrating a causal link between a drug or illness as inducing a major depressive disorder would ideally be approached in a prospective controlled manner; unfortunately, this is rarely possible. We are aware of only one such study that used the methodology of the randomized controlled prospective clinical trial in this manner—Stoudemire et al. (1984) examined the possible depressive effects of propranolol—and the results of the study were essentially negative. A recent epidemiologic case-control study of hypertensive patients revealed, however, that the prevalence of tricyclic antidepressant use was higher in patients being treated with beta-blockers than with other antihypertensives (Avorn et al. 1986).

Despite these caveats, a number of illicit drugs, medications and illnesses have nevertheless been associated with depression. Antihypertensives, primarily reserpine, are the most frequently mentioned medications associated with depression. Of patients treated with reserpine, 20 percent will develop symptoms of depression, and 5 percent will develop true clinical depressive disorders (Wells 1985b). Due to reserpine's relatively clear association with depression, this medication is contraindicated in patients with a history of depression.

With respect to other antihypertensives, Paykel et al. (1982) noted in an exhaustive review of the literature that only with alpha-methyldopa did there appear to be a definite link to depression. The authors called for the same precautions in its use in depressed patients. The evidence for a primary depressive effect of clonidine, beta-adrenergic blockers (primarily propranolol), and guanethidine remains relatively weak (Paykel et al. 1982). In the case of beta-blockers, if the question of depression is a clinical issue, clinicians may select beta-blockers that are less lipophilic than propranolol, such as atenolol, which are less likely to penetrate the blood-brain barrier and cause CNS symptoms (Stoudemire et al. 1984).

A study by Okada (1985) has implicated diuretic agents as "causing" depression. This report suffered from the same problems as did other such reports in this area, further mitigated by the relatively high prevalence of depression in the general medical population. Medications and drugs most commonly mentioned as associated with depression are listed in Table 1 (Dietch and Zetin 1983; Whitlock and Evans 1978).

Steroids, primarily cortisone and prednisone, and treatment with adrenocorticotropic hormone (ACTH) have been strongly associated with depression (Ling et al. 1981). In a review of case reports (up to 1981) of corticosteroid reactions, 40 percent reported depressive symptoms (Ling et al. 1981). Although depression is common, the more typical reaction is induction of anxiety and affective instability with both depressive and manic features. Hypomanic, manic, and euphoric reactions often precede or are intermixed with depressive mood swings. Steroid dosage may be correlated, at times, to the risk of developing depression and other psychiatric disturbances, but neither dosage nor duration of treatment seems to correlate directly to the risk of depression.

Depressive reactions may remit with tapering or discontinuation of the steroid, but some cases may require antidepressant or even ECT to remit. Lithium has been used with positive results prophylactically in the prevention of manic behavior following corticotropin treatment for multiple sclerosis (Falk et al. 1979).

A variety of medical illnesses, as noted earlier, have presented with depression or depressive symptoms as the chief complaints. The most frequently mentioned illnesses in this regard include occult carcinomas (pancreatic) and lymphomas, viral illnesses (hepatitis, mononucleosis, influenza), and endocrinopathies (Cushing's syndrome, adrenal insufficiency, hypoglycemia, hyper- and hypocalcemia, hypo- and hyperthyroidism). As many as one-third of patients who have suffered cerebrovascular stroke will experience depression in the 6- to 12-month-period after the acute event. The depressive episode may be due to direct structural and biochemical effects (rather than "reactive" psychological adjustments) because patients tend to respond to nortriptyline (Lipsey et al. 1984). Depression, often of melancholic and psychotic proportions, occurs in one-third to one-half of patients with Parkinson's disease (Mayeux 1981; Wells 1985b).

Endocrinopathies, particularly Cushing's syndrome and hypothyroidism, are the classic illnesses that present as organic mood syndromes. As many as 40 to 86 percent of patients with Cushing's syndrome have significant depression (Cohen 1980; Dietch and Zetin 1983; Ettigi and Brown 1978; Jeffcoate et al. 1979). A family history of depression, suicide, early bereavement, or separation was found in half of the cases of Cushing's-related depression in one series of patients (Cohen 1980). Severity of depression does not appear to be consistently related to circulating levels of serum cor-

TABLE 1. MAJOR REPORTED CAUSES OF ORGANIC MOOD SYNDROME (DEPRESSED)

- Medications
  - Antihypertensives (reserpine, methyldopa, propranolol)
  - Psychostimulants (amphetamine and cocaine in the post-withdrawal phase)
  - Barbiturates
  - Guanethidine
  - Indomethacin
  - Levodopa
  - Corticosteroids
- Medical Illnesses
  - Carcinomas (pancreatic)
  - Lymphomas
  - Viral illnesses (hepatitis, mononucleosis, influenza)
  - Endocrinopathies (Cushing's syndrome, Addison's disease, hypoglycemia, hyper- and hypocalcemia, hyper- and hypothyroidism)
  - Cerebrovascular disease (stroke)
  - Parkinson's disease
  - Pernicious anemia (B12 deficiency)
  - Carcinoid syndrome
  - Collagen-vascular disease (systemic lupus erythematosus)

tisol, although low ACTH levels may be associated with milder rather than pronounced depressed mood (Starkman et al. 1981). Depression tends to remit with appropriate medical-surgical treatment (Kelly et al. 1983).

Hypothyroidism is also classically associated with depression, as is adrenal insufficiency (or Addison's disease). In contrast, hyperthyroidism usually presents psychiatrically primarily with symptoms of agitation and anxiety. Hyperthyroidism in the elderly may present as an organic mood syndrome resembling agitated depression or melancholia (Brenner 1978). The condition of "apathetic hyperthyroidism" has been described as presenting with apathy, lethargy, depression, and high output cardiac failure. The syndrome improves markedly with correction of the underlying endocrine disturbance. Other diseases associated with organic mood syndrome include pernicious anemia (B12 deficiency), carcinoid syndrome, and collagen vascular disease (including systemic lupus erythematosus).

Mania may also present as an organic mood syndrome caused by drugs, medications, or illnesses. The major etiologic possibilities are found in Table 2 (Krauthammer and Klerman 1978; Stasiek and Zetin 1985). Disorders felt more likely to primarily be characterized as delirium with manic features have been deleted from Table 2, as have esoteric etiologies that may be found in the original reviews noted above. To the etiologic possibilities are added manic syndromes after thyroid supplementation for hypothyroidism (Josephson and MacKenzie 1980), baclofen withdrawal (Arnold et

al. 1980), and cimetidine (Hubain et al. 1982). The usual cautions, however, in interpreting case reports that were discussed in considering possible causes of depressive organic mood syndrome should be applied.

Treatment

Treatment of depressed organic mood syndrome requires correction of the underlying physiologic abnormality or removal from the offending medication. Depressed mood may nevertheless persist after these efforts, and some patients will also need concurrent antidepressant treatment or ECT (Hales and Hershey 1984; Ling et al. 1981).

The treatment of manic organic mood syndrome lies in correctly identifying and removing the offending agent or underlying disease that is causing the disorder. Phenothiazines are most commonly reported for suppressing acute psychotic symptoms and may usually be tapered once the underlying etiologic process is effectively treated. In some cases, the manic syndrome may be persistent. In a number of reports with a variety of etiologies, these patients, primarily those with manic syndromes induced by antidepressants and steroids, responded to treatment with lithium carbonate (Falk et al. 1979; Krauthammer and Klerman 1978; Ling et al. 1981).

☐ ORGANIC DELUSIONAL SYNDROME

DSM-III-R Criteria and Clinical Features

Organic delusional syndrome is characterized by the presence of delusions due to a specific organic factor. As in amnestic and organic mood syndromes, the symptoms should occur in a clear state of consciousness. The patient should not have a dementia or delirium. Mild cognitive deficits may be present, and hallucinations may occur, but neither should be a predominant feature of the patient's clinical presentation. Many associated symptoms may occur such as rambling speech, incoherency, disheveled dress, hyperactivity, apathy, ritualistic behavior, dysphoria, and personality changes (American Psychiatric Association 1987). As might be surmised, based on symptoms alone, the syndrome may initially be difficult to distin-

---

TABLE 2. REPORTED CAUSES OF ORGANIC MOOD SYNDROME (MANIC)

Medications
  Levodopa
  Decongestants (containing phenylephrine)
  Sympathomimetics/bronchodilators (containing theophylline and/or ephedrine/isophedrine)
  Corticosteroids/ACTH
  Antidepressants
  Monoamine oxidase inhibitors
Metabolic abnormalities
  Hyperthyroidism
Seizure/neurologic disorders
  Temporal lobe seizures
  Multiple sclerosis
  Right hemispheric damage
Neoplasms

guish from paranoid schizophrenia. The clinical history, however, will usually aid in the diagnostic discrimination. Evidence should be available from the history, physical examination, or laboratory tests to point toward a specific factor causing the organic delusional symptoms.

Etiology

A wide range of disorders has been reported to cause delusions based on organic factors (Cummings 1985). If one selects out cases where delirium and/or dementia would have most likely been the principal diagnosis according to DSM-III-R criteria, however, the possibilities become more restricted. Cummings (1985) published an exhaustive review of the reported causes of "organic delusions," but included in this group patients with dementia and delirium. In reviewing the possible causes of organic delusional syndrome, it is important to eliminate cases where the principal diagnosis would have most appropriately been delirium or dementia. A modification of Cummings' summary is listed in Table 3, with deletion of cases that were judged most likely due to delirium or dementia.

Drugs and medications are the most common causes of organic delusional syndrome, particularly hallucinogens, amphetamines, cannabis, and steroids. The delusions associated with amphetamines are most commonly paranoid and persecutory in nature. Visual and auditory hallucinations may occur along with irritability, hostility, and aggression. Ideas of reference, hypervigilance, and agitation usually are present to some degree. The paranoid delusions may persist for days or weeks. Treatment usually involves the use of neuroleptics. Postamphetamine depression frequently follows the syndrome and may require specific pharmacologic antidepressant treatment.

Steroids also are frequently implicated as causing psychotic episodes. The phenomenological nature of "steroid psychosis" is quite variable. The presence of depression, mania, and varying degrees of affective instability have been previously mentioned. Some patients had been described as having "toxic psychosis" with paranoia, hallucinations, agitation, confusion, stupor, and catatonia—perhaps better characterized as delirium (Ling et al. 1981). The majority of cases in a series of 14 cases studied in depth had some evidence of delirium on clinical grounds (Hall et al. 1979). Hall and associates also found that steroid-related psychoses tended to occur with doses of prednisone

TABLE 3. MAJOR ETIOLOGIC FACTORS IN ORGANIC DELUSIONAL SYNDROME

Endocrinopathies
  Adrenal insufficiency
  Cushing's disease
  Hypothyroidism
  Hyperthyroidism
  Hypo- and hypercalcemia
  Panhypopituitarism
Deficiency states
  B12
  Folate
  Niacin
Connective tissue disease
  Systemic lupus erythematosus
  Temporal arteritis
Drug/medications
  Antiparkinson agents
  Antituberculosis agents
  Antimalarials, anticonvulsants
  Antidepressants
  Antihypertensives
  Hallucinogens
Miscellaneous
  Porphyria
  Huntington's chorea
  Amphetamines
  Corticosteroids
  Pentazocine
  Bromide
  Heavy metal toxicity
CNS disorders
  Multiple sclerosis
  Parkinson's disease
  Idiopathic basal ganglia calcification
  Spinocerebellar degeneration
  Temporal lobe epilepsy
  Neoplasms
  Cerebrovascular disease

(or its equivalent) in excess of 40 mg/day similar to findings of the Boston Collaborative Drug Surveillance Program (1972). The majority of cases reported responded to treatment with phenothiazines (chlorpromazine and thioridazine) with a mean dose of 200 mg/day.

Areas of Controversy

One significant disorder that has been associated with delusions presumably of an organic nature is the interictal schizophrenia-like psychoses of temporal lobe epilepsy (Bear et al. 1985; Stoudemire et al. 1983). Interictal schizophrenia-like behavior may develop in patients with temporal lobe epilepsy often after years (overall 12 to 14) of suffering from a primary seizure disorder. In contrast to schizophrenia, most of these patients show a relative lack of premorbid schizoid personality traits, have the capacity to retain close interpersonal relationships, do not tend to deteriorate, and lack a strong family history for schizophrenia. The degree of psychotic symptoms may vary at times inversely with degree of seizure control, thus leading to speculation regarding "antagonism" between seizure activity and the frequency of psychotic symptoms. Some authorities feel that schizophrenia-like symptoms are more commonly associated with left-sided temporal lobe lesions, but this is not a consistent finding. Treatment has varied between raising (or lowering) anticonvulsant levels, adding haloperidol and/or carbamazepine to the treatment regimen, ECT, and temporal lobectomy of seizure foci. Improvements have occurred with all these therapeutic maneuvers, but responses are variable and not predictable.

A number of other intriguing delusional syndromes have been described that may at times be characterized as organic delusional syndromes vis-à-vis DSM-III. These include the Capgras' syndrome, Fregoli syndrome, intermetamorphosis syndrome, de Clerambault syndrome, and Othello syndrome (delusional jealousy). These syndromes, which have been occasionally reported to be induced by organic factors, have been reviewed by Cummings (1985). Illicit drugs and medications reported as a cause of organic delusional syndrome include L-dopa, indomethacin, marijuana, and cocaine (Lipowski 1980b).

Treatment

Treatment of organic delusional syndrome is based on identifying the offending agent or treating the underlying condition causing the patient's brain syndrome. Neuroleptic medications are most often used for short-term symptomatic control until the primary etiology can be treated (Cummings 1985).

☐ ORGANIC HALLUCINOSIS

DSM-III-R Criteria and Clinical Features

Organic hallucinosis is an organic brain syndrome characterized by persistent or recurrent hallucinations that occur in a clear state of consciousness and in the absence of other associated findings indicative of either delirium or dementia. Delusions are not a prominent part of the syndrome; if de-

lusions predominate in the clinical presentation, the patient is more appropriately diagnosed as having an organic delusional disorder (with associated hallucinations) if their sensorium is relatively clear and an organic process is suspected. Delusions may be auditory, visual, tactile, or olfactory in nature in organic hallucinosis.

Etiology

Alcohol-related hallucinosis is the most common cause of this syndrome. Kraepelin used the term *hallucinatory insanity of drunkards* to describe the syndrome. Bonkoeffer used the term *clear minded delirium*. Bleuler coined the term *alcoholic hallucinosis* but mistakenly regarded it as a form of alcohol-induced schizophrenia (Surawicz 1980; Victor and Hope 1958).

The hallucinations may develop abruptly. The hallucinations may occur while the individual is drinking or after a period of abstinence of hours, days, or even weeks (Surawicz 1980). Hallucinations are auditory, and may be persecutory and paranoid in nature. Fleeting visual hallucinations may also occur. The syndrome is distinct from alcohol withdrawal delirium (delirium tremens), although alcohol hallucinosis may begin prior to the withdrawal delirium and persist during and after the course of the withdrawal period. Cognitive functioning is usually intact unless the patient has an underlying alcohol-related dementia or amnestic syndrome. Most patients recover within a week, although in as many as 10 percent of the cases the symptoms may persist for weeks or months (Wells 1985). If superimposed on a physiologic withdrawal syndrome, the disorder should be treated with medications such as benzodiazepines, thiamine replacement, and the usual supportive measures. In persistent cases, neuroleptics may help suppress the symptoms.

The other prominent drugs associated with hallucinations are the hallucinogens, primarily LSD. Recurrences of previous hallucinogen-induced experiences may occur and involve both auditory and visual phenomena (flashbacks). More pervasive schizophrenia-like symptoms may develop after heavy repetitive hallucinogen use (Wells 1985). There are no reliable systematic data as to the treatment of these hallucinatory experiences, although neuroleptics are reported to be of variable benefit (Wells 1985).

Seizure foci may cause isolated, yet persistent hallucinatory phenomena. The nature of hallucinatory phenomenon will largely depend on the seizure foci. Limbic region and temporal lobe structures are often involved in auditory, tactile, and olfactory phenomena. Various tumors, structural lesions, and infections involving these areas may also present with hallucinations. Medications that have been reported to cause relatively isolated hallucinatory episodes include L-dopa, bromocriptine, amantadine, ephedrine, pentazocine, propranolol, and methylphenidate (Lipowski 1980b).

The other major cause for organic hallucinatory phenomenon relates to occipital lobe and visual pathway disease. Visual hallucinations may arise as a result of practically any injury or disease, from the cortical to the peripheral ends of the visual pathway (White 1980). Visual hallucinations related to primary eye disease are usually unformed (e.g., flashes of light, zigzag lines) whereas disorders of deeper structures (cerebral peduncles, cerebral hemispheres, optic chiasm, occipital lobes) tend to cause formed hallucinations (White 1980). Complex visual hallucinations are relatively common events in the partially blind following cataract extraction (Weisman and Hackett 1958) or following bandaging of the eyes after corneal grafting.

Cogan (1973) divided visual hallucinations into "irritable" and "release" types. Release hallucinations tend to occur as a result of sensory deprivation, lesions of eye, optic nerve, optic chiasm, optic tract, and occipital lobe. Release hallucinations have also been described in patients with posterior cerebral artery occlusion (Brust and Behrens 1977). Complex formed visual hallucinations also may occur due to primary eye disease such as macula degeneration and choroideremia (White 1980).

The elderly may be at somewhat greater risk for the release type of visual and auditory hallucinations due to progressive sensory degeneration as a form of insiduous sensory deprivation. This partially explains why such phenomena are more frequent at night when sensory input is the least, and emphasizes the importance of correcting potentially treatable ophthalmic and otologic problems when they exist, and of maximized orientation efforts (particularly at night) for the hospitalized elderly.

Treatment

As with the other organic syndromes, treatment is dependent on identifying the etiology of the syndrome. As noted earlier, neuroleptic agents have

been reported to be of some benefit for alcoholic-related hallucinosis, but no controlled treatment trials of these or other medications have been published for this condition (Surawicz 1980). Efforts to correct sensory impairments in the elderly, or to provide special orientation efforts, may help diminish hallucinations due to relative sensory deprivation.

☐ ORGANIC PERSONALITY SYNDROME

DSM-III-R Criteria and Clinical Features

The predominant feature of the organic personality syndrome is a marked change in personality due to an organic factor. Dementia is excluded because pervasive intellectual deterioration should not be present. Cognitive functioning should be largely intact in organic personality syndrome and pathologic changes are primarily confined to personality and behavior. The nature of the clinical syndrome in any given case is determined by the location and extent of the cerebral injury or type of disease process.

Etiology

Practically any injury or disease process that affects cerebral structures and brain functioning can cause an organic personality syndrome. The most common causes tend to be head trauma, neoplasms, temporal lobe seizure disorders, and vascular disease. Multiple sclerosis and collagen vascular diseases such as systemic lupus erythematosus may cause an organic personality syndrome as well. Endocrinopathies such as hypothyroidism, adrenocortical disease, and practically any toxic-metabolic insult to the brain (such as heavy metal poisoning) that primarily affects personality and leaves cognitive functioning, intellectual capabilities, and level of awareness intact may cause this syndrome. Subcortical dementias such as Huntington's chorea may also primarily affect personality in the early stages. This section will focus on direct injuries to cerebrum from vascular accidents, head trauma, and temporal lobe seizure disorders in the differential diagnosis.

The frontal and temporal lobes are most frequently associated with organic personality syndromes. Two organic personality syndromes—

pseudopsychopathic (characterized by emotional lability, impulsivity, socially inappropriate behavior, and hostility) and pseudodepressive syndrome (characterized by apathy, indifference, and social disconnectedness)—have been described. The syndromes are usually referred to as frontal lobe syndromes and are marked by indifference for the consequences of behavior and an inability to perceive appropriately the effects of such behavior on others (Blumer and Benson, 1975). Although frontal lobe tumors and cerebrovascular accidents involving the anterior cerebral arteries may at times cause an organic personality syndrome, the most common cause is head trauma—primarily from motor vehicle accidents. As memory deficits such as anterograde and retrograde amnesia recede after head trauma, the residual may be the organic personality syndrome.

Treatment

Regardless of etiology, organic personality syndromes cause major problems for the families of such patients. Lezak (1978) divided the problematic aspects of the "characterologically" altered brain-injured patient into five broad aspects: (1) self-centered behavior that shows limited capability for self-awareness, self-criticism, or empathy; (2) impaired self-control resulting in restlessness, impulsivity, and impatience; (3) "stimulus-bound" behavior manifested by dependency, difficulty in planning and organizing, and lack of motivation; (4) emotional instability resulting in apathy, silliness, irritability, and either hypo- or hypersexuality; and (5) an inability to profit from experience. Lezak (1978) also outlined practical steps in which these patients' behaviors can be best managed by families. Readers are referred to this article for an excellent discussion of the subject.

With respect to pharmacologic treatment, some cases of organic personality syndrome will respond to carbamazepine (McAllister 1985), but most cases are treated with neuroleptics for agitated, disruptive, paranoid behavior. The neuropsychiatric aspects of head injury are also discussed in Chapter 10.

Areas of Controversy

The other major cause of the organic personality syndrome is seizures, usually complex partial seizures of temporal lobe origin (Trimble 1983). (Interictal schizophrenia-like psychoses have previously been considered under organic delusional syndromes.) Although the concept has been, and remains, controversial, a number of clinicians and investigators have described the clustering of a number of peculiar personality traits associated with temporal lobe epilepsy (Bear and Fedio 1977). The basic components of the "temporal lobe personality" consist of changes in personality, including some hypersexuality but more commonly hyposexuality. Emotional "viscosity" or "stickiness" has been described that is marked by slow, pedantic, overly inclusive, detailed conversation that usually does not provide the listener with an opportunity to disengage from the interaction. The patient often appears oblivious to the usual social and interpersonal cues that signal the desire for interpersonal distancing. Hyperreligiosity may be seen as well as intellectual preoccupation with philosophical matters involving fate and destiny. A "deepening of emotionality" is usually described, which may be characterized by moodiness, easy frustration, anger, and hostile violent outbursts. Hypergraphia has also been observed, which consists of compulsive writing and drawing with many of the same tendencies apparent in their conversation, such as verbosity, circumstantiality, and overinclusiveness (Waxman and Geschwind 1975). Other traits that have been associated with this personality syndrome include paranoid tendencies, humorlessness, and hypermoralism (Bear et al. 1982, 1985).

Most of the studies prior to 1977 involving personality characteristics of temporal lobe epilepsy involved the Minnesota Multiphasic Personality Inventory. However, in 1977, a landmark paper that continues to stir controversy appeared when Bear and Fedio published their findings based on their own 18-item rating scale devised to measure specifically the behavioral abnormalities postulated to be associated with temporal lobe epilepsy. The scale was administered to two groups of patients with right and left temporal lobe epilepsy, and to two control groups, one healthy and the other a group of patients with neuromuscular disorders. The results of the study separated out the patients with temporal lobe epilepsy and noted lateralization differences between the right and left temporal lobe patients. The paper stirred significant criticism, the most prominent being a lack of control patients with seizure disorders of nontemporal lobe origin. Mungas (1982), in a similar study, tested Bear and Fedio's findings by using two control groups: nonepileptic neurobehavioral disorder patients and nonepileptic psychiatric patients. This study failed to replicate the discriminating ability of the Bear and Fedio inventory to delineate specific symptom profiles associated with temporal lobe epilepsy.

Other studies (Hermann and Reil 1981; Nielsen and Kristensen 1981), however, tended to support specific personality traits for temporal lobe epilepsy. Subsequently, Bear et al. (1982), using controls of nonepileptic patients and nontemporal lobe epileptic patients, largely repeated his previous findings (Bear and Fedio 1977). While the matter remains controversial and the symptom complex described above is not totally applicable to *all* patients with temporal lobe epilepsy, the trend of clinical opinion generally favors such an association at least in some patients with temporal lobe seizure disorders.

Organic Personality Syndrome—Explosive Type (Explosive Disorder, Episodic Dyscontrol Syndrome)

The explosive subtype of organic personality syndrome in DSM-III-R is characterized by recurrent outbursts of aggression or rage that are grossly out of proportion to any precipitating psychosocial stressors (American Psychiatric Association 1987; Yudofsky 1985). The pathophysiology usually appears to relate to a history of some type of specific organic factor or brain damage such as attention deficit disorder, head trauma, complex partial seizures, cerebral tumors, and encephalitis (Elliott 1984). Irritable seizure foci in the limbic regions are the most common lesions; episodic rage reactions have also occurred in lesions involving the thalamus, midbrain, pons, and possibly midline cerebellar nuclei (Elliott 1984). Alcohol is the most common pharmacologic trigger for the syndrome.

Treatment. Pharmacologic approaches to controlling the syndrome have included carbamazepine and phenytoin to dampen irritable epileptic foci, but these medications may help control symptoms even in the absence of detectable seizure foci. Amphetamines and psychostimulants such as methylphenidate have been reported to help control explosive behavior in adults with residual features of attention deficit disorder (Wood et al. 1976). Elliott (1977, 1984) reported the usefulness of propranolol (in doses up to 320 mg/day) in controlling behavior in patients with a history of acute brain insults and in adults with residual attention deficit

disorder, head injury, stroke, and brain tumor. Propranolol may be used in conjunction with anticonvulsants in seizure disorders associated with the syndrome. Metoprolol, a selective beta-1 adrenoreceptor blocker, has been reported in two patients to suppress symptoms of the disorder, which had failed to respond to propranolol and carbamazepine (Mattes 1985). Medications with disinhibiting effects such as benzodiazepines may worsen the disorder.

☐ ORGANIC ANXIETY SYNDROME

DSM-III-R Criteria and Clinical Features

Organic conditions such as hyperthyroidism and pheochromocytoma may present as an organic anxiety syndrome (American Psychiatric Association 1987; MacKenzie and Popkin 1983). The essential feature is recurrent or persistent anxiety and/or panic due to a specific organic factor. The diagnosis is not made in the presence of significant cognitive dysfunction or delirium or dementia, although mild cognitive impairments may be present. No primary mood disturbance, hallucinations, or delusions should be present. The presence of the following associated symptoms may be associated with an organic anxiety syndrome: diaphoresis, tachycardia, palpitations, systolic hypertension, dyspnea, chest pain, choking, dizziness, vertigo, tremor, hot/cold flashes, faintness, diarrhea, irritability, fatigue, and urinary frequency. Evidence should be present from the history, physical examination, or laboratory tests of a specific organic factor judged to be etiologically related to the disorder.

Etiology

Potential etiologies of the disorder include endocrinopathies (e.g., hyperthyroidism, fasting hypoglycemia, hypercortisolism). Substance-related agents include caffeine, psychostimulants/amphetamine, sympathomimetics, and withdrawal from CNS depressants. Pheochromocytomas, tumors in the vicinity of the third ventricle, and seizure foci in the diencephalon may also be rare possibilities as well as temporal lobe epilepsy.

Treatment

Since the concept of organic anxiety syndrome is relatively new, no controlled treatment trials using this diagnosis have been published. The case report literature, however, emphasizes identifying the specific etiologic factor involved in each instance. Benzodiazepines may be beneficial in controlling anxiety symptoms until underlying disorders have remitted or been effectively treated, but are generally not necessary for longer-term treatment.

☐ CONCLUSION

The present DSM-III-R classification of organic brain syndromes, as with other psychiatric disorders, is primarily based on symptom clusters that are operationally defined as representing certain diagnostic entities. The availability of more precise diagnostic techniques, such as positron emission tomography, not only will aid in more precise diagnosis of altered cerebral functioning, but may permit standardization of "biologic markers" to be used as part of the diagnostic criteria.

Any diagnostic classification of organic mental disorders, however, is based on currently available knowledge and on our understanding of the etiologies, clinical manifestations, prognostic factors, and underlying biologic mechanisms. As our knowledge and diagnostic techniques increase, the nomenclature will further evolve toward greater diagnostic precision. As Lipowski (1984) has eloquently stated: "the present classification reflects no more than our limited knowledge and working hypotheses, and will have to be revised in the future in the light of new data which will inevitably accrue as the hypotheses are tested" (p. 203).

☐ REFERENCES

Adams RD: Anxiety, depression, asthenia, and personality disorders, in Harrison's Principles of Internal Medicine (10th ed). Edited by Petersdorf RG, Adams RD, Braunwald E, et al. New York, McGraw-Hill, 1983, pp 68–75

American Psychiatric Association: Diagnostic and Statistical Manual of Mental Disorders. Washington, DC, American Psychiatric Association, 1952

American Psychiatric Association: Diagnostic and Statistical Manual of Mental Disorders, 2nd ed. Washington, DC, American Psychiatric Association, 1968

American Psychiatric Association: Diagnostic and Statistical Manual of Mental Disorders, 3rd ed. Washington, DC, American Psychiatric Association, 1980

American Psychiatric Association: Diagnostic and Statistical Manual of Mental Disorders, 3rd ed, revised. Washington, DC, American Psychiatric Association, 1987

Arnold ES, Rudd SM, Kirshner H: Manic psychosis following rapid withdrawal from baclofen. Am J Psychiatry 137:1466–1477, 1980

Avorn J, Everitt DE, Weiss S: Increased antidepressant use in patients prescribed beta-blockers. JAMA 255:357–360, 1986

Bear DM, Fedio P: Quantitative analysis of interictal behavior in temporal lobe epilepsy. Arch Neurol 34:454–467, 1977

Bear DM, Levin K, Blumer D, et al: Interictal behaviour in hospitalized temporal lobe epileptics: relationship to idiopathic psychiatric syndromes. J Neurol Neurosurg Psychiatry 45:481–488, 1982

Bear D, Freeman R, Schiff D, et al: Interictal behavioral changes in patients with temporal lobe epilepsy, in Annual Review, Vol 4. Edited by Hales RE, Frances AJ. Washington, DC, American Psychiatric Association, 1985, pp 197–199

Benson DF: Amnesia. South Med J 71:1221–1227, 1978

Benson DF, Marsden DC, Meadows JC: The amnestic syndrome of posterior cerebral artery occlusion. Acta Neurol Scand 50:133–145, 1974

Bleuler M: Psychiatry of cerebral disease. Br Med J 2:1233–1238, 1951

Blumer D, Benson DF: Personality changes with frontal and temporal lobe lesions, in Psychiatric Aspects of Neurologic Disease. Edited by Benson DF, Blumer D. New York, Grune & Stratton, 1975, pp 151–170

Boston Collaborative Drug Surveillance Program. Acute reverse reaction to prednisone in relation to dosage. Clin Pharmacol Ther 13:694–697, 1972

Brenner I: Apathetic hyperthyroidism. J Clin Psychiatry 39:479–480, 1978

Brust JCM, Behrens MM: "Release hallucinations" as the major symptom of posterior cerebral artery occlusion: a report of 2 cases. Ann Neurol 2:432–436, 1977

Cogan DG: Visual hallucinations as release phenomena. Albrecht von Graefes. Arch Klin Ophthalmol 188:139–150, 1973

Cohen SI: Cushing's syndrome: a psychiatric study of 29 patients. Br J Psychiatry 136:120–124, 1980

Cummings JL: Organic delusions: phenomenology, anatomical correlations, and review. Br J Psychiatry 146:184–197, 1985

Cutting J: The relationship between Korsakov's syndrome and "Alcoholic dementia." Br J Psychiatry 132:240–251, 1978

Dietch JT, Zetin M: Diagnosis of organic depressive disorders. Psychosomatics 24:971–979, 1983

Elliott FA: Propranolol for the control of belligerent behavior following acute brain damage. Ann Neurol 1:489–491, 1977

Elliott FA: The episodic dyscontrol syndrome and aggression. Neurol Clin 2:113–125, 1984

Ettigi PG, Brown GM: Brain disorders associated with endocrine dysfunction. Psychiatr Clin North Am 1:117–135, 1978

Falk WE, Mahnke MW, Poskanzer DC: Lithium prophylaxis of corticotropin-induced psychosis. JAMA 241:1011–1012, 1979

Hales RE, Hershey SC: Psychopharmacologic issues in the diagnosis and treatment of organic mental disorders. Psychiatr Clin North Am 7:817–829, 1984

Hall RCW: Depression, in Psychiatric Presentations of Medical Illness: Somatopsychic Disorders. Edited by Hall RCW. New York, SP Medical and Scientific Books, 1980, pp 37–64

Hall RCW, Popkin MK, Stickney SK, et al: Presentation of the steroid psychoses. J Nerv Ment Dis 167:229–236, 1979

Hermann BP, Reil P: Interictal personality and behavioural traits in temporal lobe and generalized epilepsy. Cortex 17:125–128, 1981

Hubain PP, Sobolski J, Mendlewicz J: Cimetidine-induced mania. Neuropsychobiology 8:223–224, 1982

Jeffcoate WJ, Silverstone JT, Edwards CRW, et al: Psychiatric manifestations of Cushing's syndrome: response to lowering plasma cortisol. Q J Med 48:465–472, 1979

Josephson AM, MacKenzie TB: Thyroid-induced mania in hypothyroid patients. Br J Psychiatry 137:222–228, 1980

Kales A, Kales JD, Soldatos CR: Insomnia and other sleep disorders. Med Clin North Am 66:971–991, 1982

Kelly WF, Checkley SA, Bender DA, et al: Cushing's syndrome and depression: a prospective study of 26 patients. Br J Psychiatry 142:16–19, 1983

Krauthammer C, Klerman GL: Secondary mania: manic syndromes associated with antecedent physical illness on drugs. Arch Gen Psychiatry 35:1333–1339, 1978

Kwentus JA, Hart RP, Peck ET, et al: Psychiatric complications of closed-head trauma. Psychosomatics 26:8–17, 1985

Lezak MD: Living with the characterologically altered brain injured patient. J Clin Psychiatry 39:592–598, 1978

Ling MHM, Perry PJ, Tsuang MT: Side effects of corticosteroid therapy: psychiatric aspects. Arch Gen Psychiatry 38:471–477, 1981

Lipowski ZJ: A new look at organic brain syndromes. Am J Psychiatry 137:674–677, 1980a

Lipowski ZJ: Organic mental disorders: introduction and review of syndromes, in Comprehensive Textbook of Psychiatry, Vol. 2 (3rd ed). Edited by Kaplan HI, Freedman AM, Sadock BJ. Baltimore, Williams & Wilkins, 1980b, pp 1359–1392

Lipowski ZJ: Organic mental disorders: their history and classification with special reference to DSM-III. Aging 15:37–45, 1981

Lipowski ZJ: Organic brain syndromes: new classification, concepts, and prospects. Can J Psychiatry 29:198–204, 1984

Lipsey JR, Robinson RG, Pearlson GD, et al: Nortriptyline treatment of post-stroke depression: a double blind study. Lancet 1:297–300, 1984

MacKenzie, TB, Popkin MK: Organic anxiety syndrome. Am J Psychiatry 140:342–344, 1983

Mathew RJ, Meyer JS: Pathogenesis and natural history of transient global amnesia. Stroke 5:303–311, 1974

Mathew RJ, Weinman ML, Mirabi M: Physical symptoms of depression. Br J Psychiatry 139:293–296, 1981

Mattes JA: Metoprolol for intermittent explosive disorder. Am J Psychiatry 142:1108–1109, 1985

Mayeux R, Stern Y, Rosen J, et al: Depression, intellectual impairment and Parkinson's disease. Neurology 31:645–650, 1981

McAllister TW: Carbamazepine in mixed frontal lobe and psychiatric disorders. J Clin Psychiatry 46:393–394, 1985

McEvoy JP: Organic brain sydromes. Ann Intern Med 95:212–220, 1981

Mercer B, Wepner W, Gardner H, et al: A study of confabulation. Arch Neurol 34:429–433, 1977

Mungas D: Interictal behavior abnormality in temporal lobe epilepsy. Arch Gen Psychiatry 39:108–111, 1982

Nielsen H, Kristensen O: Personality correlates of sphenoidal EEG foci in temporal lobe epilepsy. Acta Neurol Scand 64:298–300, 1981

Okada F: Depression after treatment with thiazide diuretics for hypertension. Am J Psychiatry 142:1101–1102, 1985

Paykel ES, Fleminger R, Watson JP: Psychiatric side effects of antihypertensive drugs other than reserpine. J Clin Psychopharmacol 2:14–39, 1982

Shuping JR, Rollinson RD, Toole JF: Transient global amnesia. Ann Neurol 7:281–285, 1980

Starkman MN, Schteingart DE, Schork MA: Depressed mood and other psychiatric manifestations of Cushing's syndrome: relationship to hormone levels. Psychosom Med 43:3–18, 1981

Stasiek C, Zetin M: Organic manic disorders. Psychosomatics 26:394–402, 1985

Stoudemire A, Brown JT, Harris RT, et al: Propranolol and depression: a reevaluation based on a pilot clinical trial. Psychiatric Medicine 2:211–218, 1984

Stoudemire A, Nelson A, Houpt JL: Interictal schizophrenia-like psychoses in temporal lobe epilepsy. Psychosomatics 24:331–339, 1983

Stuss DT, Alexander MP, Lieberman A, et al: An extraordinary form of confabulation. Neurology 28:1166–1172, 1978

Surawicz FG: Alcoholic hallucinosis: a missed diagnosis: differential diagnosis and management. Can J Psychiatry 25:57–63, 1980

Taylor MA, Sierles F, Abrams R: The neuropsychiatric evaluation, in Annual Review, Vol 4. Edited by Hales RE, Frances AJ. Washington, DC, American Psychiatric Association, 1985, pp 109–141

Trimble MR: Personality disturbances in epilepsy. Neurology 33:1332–1334, 1983

Victor M: The amnestic syndrome and its anatomical basis. Can Med Assoc J 100:1115–1125, 1969

Victor M: Hope JM: The phenomenon of auditory hallucinations in chronic alcoholism. J Nerv Ment Dis 126:451–481, 1958

Victor M, Adams RD, Collins GH: The Wernicke-Korsakoff syndrome. Contemporary Neurology Series, Vol 7. Philadelphia, FA Davis Co., 1971, pp 15–32

Waxman SG, Geschwind N: The interictal behavior syndrome of temporal lobe epilepsy. Arch Gen Psychiatry 32:1580–1586, 1975

Weisman AD, Hackett TP: Psychosis after eye surgery. N Engl J Med 258:1284–1289, 1958

Wells CE: Organic syndromes: amnestic syndrome, in

Comprehensive Textbook of Psychiatry, Vol. 1 (4th ed). Edited by Kaplan HI, Sadock BJ. Baltimore, Williams & Wilkins, 1985a, pp 870–872

Wells CE: Other organic brain syndromes, in Comprehensive Textbook of Psychiatry, Vol. 1 (4th ed). Edited by Kaplan HI, Sadock BJ. Baltimore, Williams & Wilkins, 1985b, pp 873–882

White NJ: Complex visual hallucinations in partial blindness due to eye disease. Br J Psychiatry 136:284–286, 1980

Whitlock FA, Evans LEF: Drugs and depression. Drugs 15:53–71, 1978

Wittenborn JR, Buhler R: Somatic discomforts among depressed women. Arch Gen Psychiatry 36:465–471, 1979

Wood DR, Reimer F, Wender P, et al: Diagnosis and treatment of minimal brain dysfunction in adults. Arch Gen Psychiatry 33:1453–1460, 1976

Yudofsky SC, Silver JM: Psychiatric aspects of brain injury: trauma, stroke, and tumor, in Psychiatry Update: The American Psychiatric Association Annual Review, Vol. 4. Edited by Hales RE, Frances AJ. Washington, DC, American Psychiatric Press, 1985, pp 147–148

Chapter 8

Alcohol-Induced Organic Mental Disorders

Richard J. Frances, M.D.
John E. Franklin, Jr., M.D.

ALCOHOLISM IS ONE OF THE LEADING public health problems in the United States, directly affecting 14 million people (West et al. 1984). Robins et al. (1984) found that substance abuse disorders rank first among 15 DSM-III (American Psychiatric Association 1980) diagnoses, and lifetime prevalence of alcohol abuse or dependence is 13.6 percent. The cost to society of alcoholism is estimated to be 116.7 billion dollars annually (Niven 1984). Mass media campaigns have increased public awareness of the problem. Medical schools and residency programs are becoming increasingly aware of the importance of educating future health care providers about alcoholism. Attention has focused on early identification and prevention in high-risk populations, the search for biologic markers, and improvement of legal control and public education. Family history of alcoholism increases the risk of developing alcoholism four- or fivefold in both sexes (Goodwin 1985). Alcoholism is frequently seen in combination with other chemical abuse.

Pathologic neuropsychologic findings in alcoholism are prevalent (Table 1). Problems range from transient organic brain syndromes during intoxication to permanent dementia and memory difficulty. Psychiatric and neuropsychologic assessment is important in treatment selection and implementation. Effective recognition and treatment of signs and symptoms of alcoholism require knowledge of its major neuropathologic findings.

☐ ALCOHOL INTOXICATION

Alcohol intoxication is a common, time-limited, organic condition, precipitated by varying amounts of alcohol use. Stages of intoxication can range from mild inebriation to anesthesia, coma, respiratory depression, and, rarely, death. Pathologic ramifications include acute organic brain syndrome, seizures, pathologic or idiosyncratic intoxication, and blackouts. Alcohol is a central nervous system de-

141

TABLE 1.   PATHOLOGIC NEUROPSYCHIATRIC SIGNS AND SYMPTOMS

Syndrome	Key Signs and Symptoms	Key Neuropsychiatric Signs and Symptoms	Time of Onset of Syndrome	Treatment (Medication)
Alcohol intoxication	Disinhibition, sedation at high doses	Acute organic brain syndrome	Rapid, depends on tolerance of individual	Time, protective environment
Alcohol idiosyncratic intoxication	Marked aggressive or assaultive behavior	Absence of focal neurologic signs and symptoms	Erratic occurrence	None
Alcohol withdrawal	Tremulousness, irritability, nausea, vomiting, insomnia, malaise, autonomic hyperactivity	Transient sensory disturbances possible	Several hours; peak symptoms 24–48 hours after last drink or relative drop-in level	See Table 3
Alcohol seizures	Grand mal seizures can occur in bursts of 2–6 seizures; rarely status epilepticus	Loss of consciousness, tonic-clonic movements, urinary incontinence, post ictal confusion; look for focal signs	7–38 hours after cessation of alcohol	Diazepam, phenytoin; maintenance phenytoin if underlying seizure disorder is present; prevent by chlordiazepoxide detox
Alcohol withdrawal delirium	Confusion, disorientation, fluctuating consciousness, preceptual disturbances, autonomic hyperactivity	Marked variations in levels of consciousness and disorientation; may be fatal	Gradual onset 2–3 days after cessation of alcohol; peak intensity at 4–5 days	Chlordiazepoxide detox; haloperidol 2–5 mg po bid for psychotic symptomology may be added if necessary
Alcohol hallucinosis	Vivid auditory hallucination with affect appropriate to content (often threatening)	Clear sensorium	Usually within 48 hours or less of last drink; may last several weeks	Haloperidol 2–5 mg po bid for psychotic symptoms
Wernicke's	Oculomotor disturbances, cerebellar ataxia	Mental confusion	Abrupt onset; ataxia may precede mental confusion	Thiamine 100 mg iv with $MgSO_4$ 1–2 ml in 50% solution should be given prior to glucose loading
Korsakoff's	Alcohol stigmata may be present	Retrograde and anterograde amnesia; confabulation early; intellectual functioning generally spared	Several days following occurrence of Wernicke's	No effective treatment; institutionalization often needed
Alcohol dementia	Absence of other causes for dementia	Nonprogressing dementia if alcohol free	Associated with greater than 10-year history of drinking	None

pressant that, in low amounts, disinhibits higher cortical activity, producing clinical excitement (Adams and Victor 1981). A direct depressant action on cortical neurons produces sedation at higher blood levels. Phenomenologic presentations of intoxication depend not only on absolute blood levels but also on the rate of rise of blood alcohol level, duration of consumption, and the tolerance of the individual involved.

In nonhabituated persons, blood levels of 30 mg per 100 ml can lead to mild euphoria and 50 mg per 100 ml can cause mild coordination problems. Ataxia is present at 100 mg per 100 ml. Confusion and decreased consciousness can occur at

200 mg per 100 ml. Blood levels of 400 mg per 100 ml may produce anesthesia, coma, and death (Adams and Victor 1981). The legal definition of an intoxicated driver is 100 mg per 100 ml in most states. Due to tolerance, chronic drinkers consume larger quantities and reach proportionally higher blood levels without obvious signs of drunkenness. When alcohol levels are raised very slowly by gradual consumption or reduced absorption, few symptoms may appear, even in nonhabituated individuals. An increased degree of neuronal adaptation to alcohol has been proposed as an explanation, but the neurochemical basis is not clearly delineated (Adams and Victor 1981).

Inebriation can produce exhilaration, excitement, and gregariousness, often described by alcoholics as a "glow." Other manifestations are impaired motor performance with poor muscular control, slurred speech, and ataxia. Thinking is slowed, with impaired concentration, reasoning, attention, judgment, and ability to form word associations (Lishman 1978). Fairly consistent psychophysiologic symptoms occur with intoxication, an increase in heart rate, nystagmus, electromyographic (EMG) and electroencephalographic (EEG) changes, and slowed reaction times (Cohen et al. 1983). Severe intoxication may contribute to emotional lability, personality changes, and loss of control. The consequences of these states may result in driving while intoxicated, physical assault, and increased suicidal or homicidal behavior (Frances and Franklin in press). Individual and cultural variations of tolerance may influence the manifestation of intoxication. For example, an "alcohol flush" reaction due to an inborn variation of alcohol dehydrogenase enzyme, which causes increased acetaldehyde, may contribute to a lower rate of alcoholism in Orientals (Schwittes et al. 1982).

Treatment of Intoxication

Intoxication is a time-limited condition. General management principles include decreasing threatening external stimuli, interrupting alcohol ingestion, and, when necessary, protecting individuals from damaging themselves and others. There is no effective method of hastening ethanol removal, except in potentially fatal cases, where hemodialysis has been attempted. In patients with alcoholism, prevention of severe intoxication requires total abstinence due to a tendency toward loss of control. In the nonalcoholic population, teaching more sen-

sible patterns of alcohol use, especially among young people, may prevent unfortunate and sometimes disastrous consequences.

Blackouts

Alcohol blackouts are transient episodes of amnesia that accompany varying degrees of intoxication. These phenomena are characterized by relatively dense retrograde amnesia for events and behavior during periods of intoxication, even though the state of consciousness is not grossly abnormal as observed by others. Behavior during these episodes may be relatively benign or grossly abnormal. A blackout is a symptom indicative of impaired functioning in the DSM-III-R (American Psychiatric Association 1987) criteria for alcohol dependence. Blackouts can occur in isolated episodes of drinking in persons who never become alcoholic as well as at any time in the course of the disease of alcoholism (Adams and Victor 1981). In general, blackouts occur relatively late in the course of the illness and are directly correlated with severity and duration (Goodwin et al. 1969). The sharpness of the rise and fall of the blood alcohol level has been proposed as an associated factor, although the etiologic mechanism of this phenomenon is not clear or well studied (Lishman 1978).

Explanations of pathogenesis have ranged from psychological repression to organic etiologies such as deep seizures and problems in capacity for laying down long-term memory during these episodes (Ballenger and Post 1984; Lishman 1978). There is evidence that some memories may be recovered when prompted by others, but classically, there is a complete amnesia for the period during intoxication.

☐ ALCOHOL IDIOSYNCRATIC INTOXICATION

Alcohol idiosyncratic intoxication (DSM-III-R), or pathologic intoxication, has been a controversial concept that is associated with blind unfocused assaultive and destructive behavior with intoxication. DSM-III-R defines alcohol idiosyncratic intoxication as a marked aggressive or assaultive behavioral change, with drinking, that is not typical of the person when sober. In susceptible individuals, this reaction occurs with small amounts of alcohol ingestion, insufficient to induce intoxication in most people. Differentiation of idiosyncratic intoxication from severe intoxication, frank epileptic phenomena, delirium tremens (DTs), compromised brain function from trauma, or hysterical phenomena may be difficult. There may be certain individuals with a genetic vulnerability and possible subclinical epileptic focus, but these phenomena have not been well studied and cases are anecdotal. Workup includes an EEG and a computed tomography (CT) scan if focal neurologic signs or symptoms are present.

☐ ALCOHOL WITHDRAWAL SYMPTOMS

Alcohol withdrawal symptoms can occur after cessation of alcohol in chronic abusers or secondary to a relative drop in blood levels. Therefore, clear-cut withdrawal symptoms may be present during a period of continuous alcohol consumption. Alcohol withdrawal proper (DSM-III-R) may precede or accompany more pathologic withdrawal phenomena such as DTs, seizures (rumfits), and alcohol hallucinosis. A pattern of pathologic use of alcohol, which can include withdrawal or tolerance symptoms, has been defined in DSM-III-R as alcohol dependence. Increased duration of drinking and binge patterns of alcohol ingestion are clearly tied to an increase in withdrawal phenomena. By far, the most common and earliest symptoms are tremulousness, combined with general irritability, nausea, and vomiting occurring several hours after the last drink, frequently the next morning. These individuals may use a drink to "calm the nerves." Peak symptoms occur 24 to 48 hours after the last drink and, in uncomplicated cases, subside in 5 to 7 days, even without treatment, although mild irritability and insomnia may last 10 days or longer. It is helpful to educate patients about the time course of withdrawal because a rapid return to drinking may be precipitated by these residual withdrawal symptoms.

The generalized tremor is coarse, fast frequency (5 to 7 cycles/sec), can worsen with motor activity or emotional stress, and is most likely observed when the hands or the tongue is extended. Often patients complain only of feeling shaky inside. In addition, patients manifest malaise and autonomic hyperactivity, tachycardia, increased blood pressure, sweating, and orthostatic hypotension. Careful attention should be given to vital signs in a suspected alcoholic. Individuals may complain of disturbed sleep with nightmares, transitory illusions, or hallucinations. Recently, extrapyramidal symptoms also have been associated with alcohol withdrawal (Shen 1984). The usual occurrence of withdrawal symptoms is after several weeks of continuous drinking although symptoms can occur in susceptible highly dependent individuals after an intensive brief binge of days' duration.

Several studies have tried to explain withdrawal. Due to the observed autonomic hyperactivity during withdrawal mediated by the sympathetic nervous system, neurochemical studies have focused on the noradrenergic system. Increased cerebrospinal fluid (CSF) norepinephrine has been associated with intensity of withdrawal symptoms (Fujimato et al. 1983). Alcohol by-products, including acetaldehyde, may have an inhibitory effect on the adrenergic receptors. Increased cyclic adenosine monophosphate (AMP) in neurons with long-term alcohol exposure may increase norepinephrine receptor sensitivity and increase norepinephrine turnover (Hawley et al. 1981). Ethanol has also been reported to induce changes in postsynaptic dopamine receptors; monoamine oxidase (MAO), which is low in platelets of alcoholics, is increased during withdrawal (Alexopoulos et al. 1981; Black et al. 1980).

Ballenger and Post (1984) have proposed a "kindling model," first demonstrated in rat studies, where repeated mild withdrawal from alcohol increases presumed subcortical nerve spiking serving as a kindling focus for limbic, hypothalamic, and thalamic areas, increasing severity of withdrawal. Early studies reported a decrease in rapid eye movement (REM) sleep during alcohol use and REM rebound during abstinence (Greenberg and Pearlman 1967). Besson and Glen (1985) reported an increase in brain water content during withdrawal and a decrease during intoxication in nuclear magnetic resonance (NMR) studies of the brain. Berglund and Risberg (1981) reported a decrease in regional cerebral blood flow in the first 2 days of withdrawal. This is associated with a decrease in clear sensorium and correlates positively with duration of drinking.

Alcohol Withdrawal Seizures

Seizures are associated with cessation of long-term use of alcohol. Ninety percent of these occur 7 to

38 hours after last use, with the peak incidence somewhat greater than 24 hours (Adams and Victor 1981; Holloway et al. 1984; Sellers and Kalant 1976). Half of these occur in bursts of two to six grand mal seizures. Less than 3 percent develop status epilepticus, which can be a life-threatening condition unless interrupted (Adams and Victor 1981). Focal seizures suggest a focal lesion, which may be the result of trauma or idiopathic epilepsy. Seizures can be precipitated during a short bout of drinking by lowering seizure threshold. These alcohol-precipitated seizures usually occur after the period of acute intoxication (Adams and Victor 1981). EEG findings in nonepileptic individuals can be abnormal during withdrawal, with occurrences of brief periods of dysrhythmia that usually result in a normal EEG with clearance. In a study of nonaddicted adults, Zilm et al. (1981) reported that evoked potentials are sensitive to tolerance and withdrawal. Two studies of alcoholic seizures reported 50 percent had abnormal CT scans (Feissner et al. 1981; Tarter et al. 1983). Feissner et al. (1981) found that 39 percent had generalized cerebral atrophy and 15 percent had focal structural lesions. Positive focal neurologic signs were found in 30 percent of those with a focal deficit on CT scan versus 6 percent of those without a focal deficit. A careful neurologic exam may predict those who may need a CT scan.

Hypomagnesemia, respiratory alkalosis, hypoglycemia, and increased intracellular sodium have been associated with alcohol seizures, and the seizures may be the result of hyperexcitability of the neuron systems caused by these conditions (Victor and Wolfe 1973). Serum magnesium should be tested in alcoholic patients who develop seizures.

These seizures have an important prognostic value in predicting a complicated withdrawal period. Approximately one-third of patients with generalized seizures secondary to alcohol withdrawal go on to develop alcoholic withdrawal DTs (Adams and Victor 1981). Tarter et al. (1983) reported that alcoholics who experience withdrawal seizures do not suffer decreased intellectual or neuropathologic performances on tests and that seizures are not a marker for severity of alcoholism.

Alcohol Withdrawal Delirium (DTs)

Alcohol's association with DTs was first described in the 18th century, but it was not until 1955 that Isbell (1955) related it specifically to sudden withdrawal from alcohol. DTs are distinguished from uncomplicated withdrawal symptoms by a characteristic delirium. Confusion, disorientation, fluctuating or clouded consciousness, and perceptual disturbances may all be present. The syndrome includes delusions, vivid hallucinations, agitation, insomnia, mild fever, and marked autonomic arousal that can appear suddenly, but more usually gradually, 2 to 3 days after cessation of drinking, with peak intensity on the fourth or fifth day. Terror, agitation, and primarily visual hallucinations of insects, small animals, or other perceptual distortions are classic, although a wide variation in presentation can occur.

The clinical picture can vary from quiet confusion, agitation, and peculiar behavior lasting several weeks to marked abnormal behavior, vivid terrifying delusions, and hallucinations. Hallucinations may be auditory and of a persecutory nature or they may be kinesthetic, such as a tactile sensation of crawling insects. The level of consciousness may fluctuate widely. Approximately half of cases present in an atypical manner (Victor and Adams 1953). In most cases, the DTs are benign and short lived. Less commonly, the delirious state may be characterized by several relapses separated by lucid intervals. The majority of cases subside after 3 days of full-blown DTs, although DTs may last as long as 4 to 5 weeks. When cases are complicated by medical conditions, it has been reported that up to 20 percent of cases may end fatally (Victor 1966). Recent reports, however, have found overall fatality may be less than 1 percent (Gessner 1979). Deaths in DTs may be related to infections, fat emboli, or cardiac arrhythmias associated with hyperkalemia, hyperpyrexia, poor hydration, and hypertension.

DTs generally occur in alcoholics with 5 to 15 years of heavy drinking who decrease their blood alcohol levels and who have a major physical illness, such as infection, trauma, liver disease, or metabolic disorders. Only 1 to 10 percent of alcoholics hospitalized for detoxification develop DTs (Holloway et al. 1984). There is some evidence that the severity of DTs is related to the severity of the acute drinking bout before admission, the amount of insomnia, and gastrointestinal disturbance. Other associated factors that have been discussed are hypocalcemia, hypophosphatemia, and hypokalemia. Although hypomagnesemia has been associated with seizures, it is probably not an associated agent in DTs (Kramp and Hemmingsen 1984; Tønnesen 1982).

Alcohol Hallucinosis

Alcohol hallucinosis is described in DSM-III-R as a vivid auditory hallucination, occurring shortly after the cessation or reduction of heavy ingestion of alcohol. Differential diagnoses include DTs, withdrawal syndrome, paranoid psychosis, and borderline transient psychotic episodes. In contrast to delirium, the hallucinations usually occur in a clear sensorium. A paucity of autonomic symptoms also differentiates the syndrome from withdrawal syndrome. The hallucinations may range from sounds such as clicks, roaring, humming, ringing bells, or chanting to frank voices of friends or enemies, which often are threatening or maligning (Lishman 1978). A single derogatory remark may proceed to a relentless persistence of auditory accusations by several voices and auditory commands. Patients usually respond appropriately with fear, anxiety, and agitation. These symptoms may resemble paranoid schizophrenia (Surawicz 1980). However, the diagnosis is usually made on the basis of heavy alcohol use, lack of formal thought disorder, and lack of schizophrenia or mania in past or family history.

The onset is classically after cessation of drinking, but onset during drinking bouts has been reported. In the great majority of cases, the symptoms recede in a few hours to days, with patients fully realizing that the voices were imaginary. A small percentage of patients may proceed to develop a quiet chronic paranoid delusional state or frank schizophrenia (Sellers and Kalant 1976). A period of 6 months has been reported as a cutoff point beyond which remission is not expected (Lishman 1978).

Treatment of the Withdrawal Syndrome

Treatment and prevention of complications from the cessation of alcohol use in an alcohol-dependent individual depends on recognition of patterns of alcohol abuse and a careful evaluation of the stage of the illness, complicating medical problems, and flexibility in the use of treating medications. Alcohol-related medical disorders are often not detected as such and are evident in approximately 23 percent of general hospital admissions (Beresford 1979). These can include gastritis, ulcers, pancreatitis, liver disease, cardiomyopathy, anemia, neu-

rologic complications, sexual dysfunction, and cancer. Withdrawal symptoms are most dangerous when accompanied by medical illness such as pneumonia, liver failure, and subdural hematomas. A high suspicion is needed to treat target symptoms in individuals undergoing withdrawal. Denial is a major defense mechanism in alcoholism, and the magnitude of an individual's drinking may not be evident until withdrawal phenomena appear.

Inpatient Versus Outpatient Treatment.   The choice of setting for treatment of withdrawal symptoms depends on the severity of symptoms, medical complications, the use of other substances, patient cooperation, ability to follow instructions, social support systems, and past history. Patients with organic brain syndrome, low intelligence, Wernicke's encephalopathy, dehydration, history of trauma, neurologic symptoms, medical complications, psychopathology that may require psychotropic medications, DTs, alcoholic seizures, or alcoholic hallucinosis are probably best treated in an inpatient setting. Supervision, observation, and proper medical backup is often required. A past history of withdrawal seizures, DTs, or poor compliance also warrants withdrawal in an inpatient setting. Concomitant use of other substances (e.g., barbiturates and benzodiazepines) may complicate alcohol withdrawal. Concomitant opiate addiction may require cautious use of more than one agent for detoxification.

General Management of Inpatient Treatment.   If inpatient treatment is deemed necessary for withdrawal, an atmosphere that avoids overstimulation and that is well structured is preferable. A closed unit with good lighting, minimal noise, frequent orientation, and a nonthreatening approach is recommended. A good medical history and physical and neurologic examinations are required. Standard laboratory tests are listed in Table 2. An EEG, head CT scan, and gastrointestinal (GI) series are frequent ancillary tests. An EEG may rule out metabolic or focal seizure focus. A CT scan helps rule out structural deficits and masses. GI series are helpful to rule out peptic ulcers or esophageal varices. Vital signs should be routinely taken every 8 hours, and the patient should be observed closely.

Patients with alcoholism are often nutritionally deficient. Deficiencies in thiamine, B12, and folic acid level are commonly found. For patients who

TABLE 2. MEDICAL WORK-UP FOR ALCOHOL WITHDRAWAL

Medical History and Complete Physical Examination

Routine Laboratory Tests
  Complete blood count with differential
  Serum electrolytes
  Liver function tests (including bilirubin)
  Blood urea nitrogen
  Creatinine
  Fasting blood sugar
  Prothrombin time
  Cholesterol
  Triglycerides
  Calcium
  Magnesium
  Albumin with total protein
  Hepatitis B surface antigen
  B12 folic acid levels
  Stool Guiac
  Urinalysis
  Urine drug and alcohol screen
  Chest X ray, electrocardiogram

Ancillary Tests
  Electroencephalogram
  Head computed tomography
  Gastrointestinal series

are not severely debilitated, daily oral thiamine 100 mg, along with 1 mg of folic acid and one multivitamin plus adequate nutrition is sufficient to prevent Wernicke-Korsakoff's and to replenish vitamin stores if given throughout the hospitalization. In patients suspected of very poor nutrition, thiamine 100 to 200 mg im or iv should be administered immediately followed by 100-mg po doses daily. Thiamine should be given prior to any situation where glucose loading is required, as glucose infusion can further exhaust stores of thiamine. Recently, some have suggested that beverage companies fortify alcoholic beverages with thiamine to prevent thiamine deficiencies. However, high levels of thiamine (7.5 mg per liter) would be necessary to overcome malabsorption, and thiamine would be detectable in taste (Meilgaard 1985). Attention to the total protein, albumin, and prothrombin time may determine if hyperalimentation or vitamin K (5 to 10 mg parenterally) should be given. Hyperalimentation is rarely needed for alcoholic malnutrition.

Magnesium sulfate 1 g (2 mg in 50 percent solution) im q 6 hours for 2 days should be given to any individual with a past history of alcohol withdrawal seizures. In mild to moderate withdrawal, dehydration is not usually a problem that requires parenteral iv fluids, and overhydration may occur. In severe cases where autonomic hyperarousal, sweating, and fever cause considerable dehydration, careful rehydration and attention to electrolyte replacement should be done with medical supervision.

Inpatient Nonpharmacologic Treatment. In mild uncomplicated cases of withdrawal, nonpharmacologic withdrawal can be attempted. Many alcoholics have had the experience of stopping alcohol rather suddenly and tolerating withdrawal symptoms without complication. Femino and Lewis (1982) described withdrawing patients nonpharmacologically in a secure hospital setting over 2 to 7 days, observing for any complications. They suggested this approach may help provide the alcoholic with the experience of nonpharmacologic control. In our experience, convenience and legal issues have limited the use of this technique.

Pharmacologic Treatment. The rationale for pharmacologic treatment of withdrawal symptoms is to relieve discomfort secondary to autonomic symptoms and to prevent complications such as seizures and DTs. An ideal medication is currently unavailable, although numerous medications have been tried. An ideal medication for withdrawal would produce adequate sedation, abort autonomic hyperarousal, be easy to administer, provide a good therapeutic safety index, be without primary liver metabolism, and be nonaddicting. Numerous medications have been reported to be effective for uncomplicated withdrawal symptoms, such as alcohol, paraldehyde, chloral hydrate, antihistamines, barbiturates, chlormethiazole, major tranquilizers, phenytoin, propranolol, piracetam, and benzodiazepines.

Cross-tolerance with alcohol and sedation have been the main rationale for these medications. On these parameters, several medications have been found to be efficacious when properly used. No clearly demonstrated superiority is derived from any one. Recommendations have been made on the basis of safety, ease, and comfort of administration and clinical experience. Moskowitz et al. (1983) reviewed 81 therapeutic trials in 2,313 randomized patients and found only four deaths. These studies generally lacked either clear endpoints, proper handling of drop-outs, or adequate details of side effects. No definite conclusions other than the efficacy of benzodiazepines could be ascertained.

General principles of pharmacologic detoxification providing the maximum degree of safety include the adequate sedation of the patient and gradual withdrawal of blood levels of a medication cross-tolerant with alcohol. Alcohol itself is often used by alcoholics as a weaning device. Clinically, its disadvantages include short half-life, gastric irritation, excessive sedation, and the confusing of the abstinence message to the patient. Antihistamines have been used in mild withdrawal and provide sedation but no cross-tolerance or prevention against DTs or seizures. Chlormethiazole has similar effects but is not available in the United States and has not been well studied. Propranolol (Inderal) and clonidine (Catapres) have been used to prevent the hyperadrenergic manifestations and tremor. Propranolol can decrease anxiety, tremor, mild hypertension, tachycardia, and subjective symptoms. The relationship of a central versus peripheral mechanism is unclear. In severe withdrawal, propranolol up to 160 mg a day may decrease tremor but provides no protection from seizures or DTs (Sellers and Kalant 1976). Major tranquilizers do produce sedation but are not cross-tolerant with alcohol; they have the disadvantage of causing hypotension and lowering seizure threshold. Successful use of high potency antipsychotics in controlling the agitated psychotic symptoms associated with delirium has been reported (Holloway et al. 1984). This may be due to their general sedating effects. Chloral hydrate is not cross-tolerant. It has a relatively short half-life of 6 to 8 hours, can only be given orally or rectally, and im use is limited secondary to possible nerve damage, risks of sterile abscess, fat embolization, and poor rectal absorption. It leads the patient to have a strong, unpleasant breath odor when given orally. It may be hepatotoxic, and its elimination is slow in severe hepatic disease (Sellers and Kalant 1976).

Barbiturates and benzodiazepines are both cross-tolerant. The major advantage of cross-tolerance is the prevention of seizure activity during withdrawal. Barbiturates have had a decreased popularity in recent years, secondary to high incidence of respiratory depression and a low therapeutic safety index compared to benzodiazepines. In the presence of severe liver disease, oversedation is a danger with the use of barbiturates due to their decreased liver metabolism. Longer-acting barbiturates such as phenobarbital are preferable over short-acting medications and can be used with equivalent doses to benzodiazepines. Barbital, a long-acting barbiturate, is used widely in Denmark and reportedly is not metabolized by the liver (Hemmingsen et al. 1979).

Benzodiazepines are clearly the medication of choice for withdrawal symptoms because of a relatively high therapeutic safety index, oral and iv administration, anticonvulsant properties, and good prevention of DTs. Disadvantages include poor im absorption (except for lorazepam), primary liver metabolism, high cost, and abuse potential. There are no clear advantages to any one benzodiazepine, although special circumstances may favor one over another. Short-acting benzodiazepines, such as triazolam (Halcion), should generally be avoided. Rapidly fluctuating blood levels may promote withdrawal seizures. In patients with severe liver disease and in the elderly, intermediate-acting benzodiazepines such as lorazepam (Ativan) or oxazepam (Serax) can be used. Oxazepam has the added advantage of renal versus liver excretion. Intermediate-acting benzodiazepines must be given at short intervals and must be carefully tapered. Lorazepam 1 to 4 mg orally q 6 to 8 hours and oxazepam 15 to 60 mg q 8 hours are standard doses. Diazepam (Valium) and chlordiazepoxide (Librium), longer-acting benzodiazepines, are comparable in length of action, with half-lives of 24 to 36 hours. The onset of action is slow, thus rapid loading doses are often needed. Chlordiazepoxide and diazepam have the advantage of smooth induction and gradual decline in blood levels so that there are fewer symptoms on discontinuation of low dosages. Chlordiazepoxide may be preferable due to its greater sedation. In severe withdrawal cases with a history of seizures, and in cases of cross-addiction with other depressant drugs, diazepam is used because of its greater anticonvulsant effect. Equivalent doses of diazepam and chlordiazepoxide are 10 to 25 mg.

Outpatient Management. For the majority of people with mild withdrawal symptoms, an outpatient medical detoxification is possible. Close follow-up, including daily visits, is essential to assure adequate sedation and observation for complications. This method has the advantages of leaving the patients in their own work and social settings, and of fostering a positive therapeutic alliance with the treating outpatient therapist.

In uncomplicated outpatient withdrawal, chlor-

TABLE 3. STANDARD TREATMENT REGIMEN FOR ALCOHOL WITHDRAWAL

Outpatient
- Chlordiazepoxide 25–50 mg po, qid on first day: 20% decrease in dose over a 5-day period
- Daily visits to assess symptoms

Inpatient
- Chlordiazepoxide 25–100 mg po qid on first day; 20% decrease in dose over 5–7 days
- Chlordiazepoxide 25–50 mg po qid prn for agitation, tremors, or change in vital signs
- Thiamine 100 mg po qid
- Folic acid 1 mg po qid
- Multivitamin one per day
- Magnesium sulfate 1 g im q 6 hours × 2 days (if status post withdrawal seizures)

---

diazepoxide 25 to 50 mg po qid should be prescribed on the first day, with a 20 percent decrease in dose over a 5-day period and with daily visits to assess symptoms (Table 3). The advantage of inpatient detoxification is the security of being able to assess subjective and objective symptomatology rapidly and to adjust the dose properly.

Inpatient Detoxification

For inpatient withdrawal, generally 100 to 400 mg of chlordiazepoxide is given the first day in quarterly divided dosages (Table 3). This generally provides adequate sedation and control of autonomic symptoms, although chlordiazepoxide may not take away all subjective discomforts of withdrawal. Skilled staff should be available to assess adequacy of dosage and give prn doses if objective signs are present. Countertransference problems may lead staff to over- or undermedicate withdrawal symptoms secondary to fears of promoting addiction or anger at the patient. Our standard inpatient detoxification is chlordiazepoxide 25 to 100 mg po qid with 25 to 50 mg q 2 hours prn for agitation, tremulousness, or change of vital signs. If some sedation is not achieved 1 hour after the first dose, chlordiazepoxide 25 mg can be prescribed hourly until the patient is sedated. Sellers and Kalant (1976) suggested higher levels of chlordiazepoxide may be necessary in cigarette smokers. The total 24-hour dose on the first day should be tapered over 5 to 7 days in equally divided dosages per day. Holloway et al. (1984) suggested that if 600 mg is used over a 24-hour period, the entire situation should be reevaluated. A patient may have mild chronic

withdrawal symptoms that may last for several weeks. Kolin and Linet (1981) found equal efficacy comparing alprazolam (Xanax) and diazepam in subchronic withdrawal symptoms (5 to 21 days after last drink).

Ballenger and Post (1984) reviewed several studies on the efficacy of carbamazepine (Tegretol) in withdrawal from alcohol. Open trials and one double blind comparison study of carbamazepine showed good efficacy and good anticonvulsant protection. They postulated that a subcortical epileptic discharge builds in a kindling fashion during repeated withdrawal. Carbamazepine has good antikindling properties. Interestingly, phenytoin (Dilantin) is an anticonvulsant, but is not antikindling and has not been found useful for withdrawal.

Treatment of Status Epilepticus

Patients with known idiopathic or traumatic epilepsy may require the additional anticonvulsant properties of phenytoin but it is not indicated in uncomplicated withdrawal or seizures. Status epilepticus is a major neurologic emergency. Diazepam 10 mg iv usually aborts status epilepticus. However, phenytoin loading 1000 mg iv slowly over 20 minutes (50 ml per minute in glucose-free solution) may be necessary. Patients with abnormal EEGs repeated 2 to 3 weeks after withdrawal may require maintenance phenytoin 100 mg po tid with follow-up blood levels.

Treatment of Alcohol Hallucinosis

Patients with alcohol hallucinosis should receive the same basic appropriate withdrawal treatment. For those patients with hallucinosis and extreme agitation, a potent antipsychotic such as haloperidol (Haldol) 2 to 5 mg po bid successfully decreases symptoms. Medication should not be continued indefinitely and reassessment should take place shortly after cessation of symptoms.

☐ WERNICKE-KORSAKOFF SYNDROME

Wernicke-Korsakoff's is a spectrum neurologic disorder associated with thiamine deficiency. It is most often associated with alcoholism, but it can occur in any condition that causes thiamine deficiency such as malabsorption syndrome, severe anorexia,

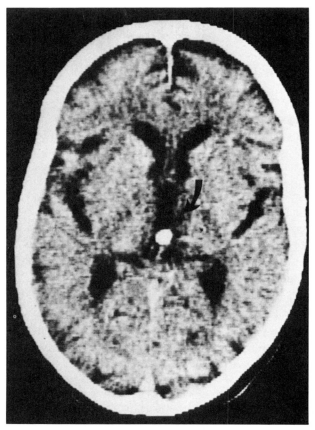 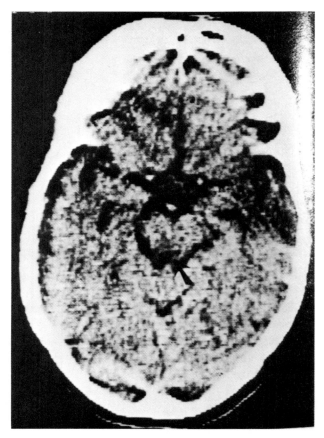

Figure 1. Computed tomographic scan of a patient with Wernicke's encephalopathy, made one day after admission. *Left:* Scan shows poor definition of the walls of the third ventricle and an adjacent hypodense area (curved arrow). *Right:* Scan shows a poorly defined hy-podense area around the aqueduct, near the quadri-geminal plate (arrow). These changes, typically arranged around the midline of the brain, strongly suggest Wernicke's encephalopathy. Reproduced from Mensing et al. (1984), reprinted with permission.

upper GI obstruction, prolonged intravenous feeding, thyrotoxicosis, and hemodialysis. The first case was described by Wernicke in 1881; it is estimated that the syndrome constitutes 3 percent of all alcohol-related disorders (Nakada and Knight 1984). Wernicke-Korsakoff's is a spectrum disease where Wernicke's encephalopathy can evolve into a Korsakoff permanent memory disorder.

Wernicke's Encephalopathy

Classically, Wernicke's encephalopathy has an abrupt onset with oculomotor disturbances, cerebellar ataxia, and mental confusion. The oculomotor disturbances range from various types of nystagmus to complete gaze palsy. The ataxia is truncal and these conditions may precede the mental confusion by days. A general confusional state with disorientation, inattention, and slow response may proceed to frank stupor and coma in 10 to 80 percent of cases (Nakada and Knight 1984). Wernicke's encephalopathy should be suspected in any unexplained case of coma. It has a 17 percent mortality rate and should be considered a medical emergency. If a patient does not respond quickly (within 48 to 72 hours) to treatment, the development of Korsakoff's psychosis is likely.

Alcohol Amnestic Disorder (Korsakoff's)

Korsakoff's psychosis is classically a chronic condition, with both retrograde and anterograde amnesia. The period of retrograde amnesia may cover up to a few years before the onset of the illness. Confabulation may be typical in the early stages but it is not always present. Numerous studies have outlined some of the neuropathologic aspects of the syndrome. Selzer and Benson (1974) confirmed the classic Korsakoff memory problem in which recent, well-known public events were poorly remembered compared to remote events. Albert et al. (1979) also reported a positive study for retrograde amnesia in Korsakoff's and suggested that it was not related to the difficulty of the fact to be remembered. Zola-Morgan and Oberg (1980) suggested the need to study Korsakoff patients in more naturalistic settings to get a better view of their functional memory difficulties. Sensory, motivational, and visual-spatial difficulties have also been found in Korsakoff's, but intellectual functioning is generally spared.

Korsakoff patients may have faulty memory retrieval due to increased reactive inhibition, they can encode semantically, and some association mechanisms can help them remember (Mattis et al. 1981). Butters (1985) reviewed studies that indicated that the patients present with an inability to acquire new information because of interference from previously learned material (perseveration of response).

Structural and neurochemical findings have also characterized the Wernicke-Korsakoff syndrome. Punctate lesions in the periventricular, periaquaductal regions of the brain stem and diencephalon have been found on brain autopsy (McEntee and Mair 1980). Periventricular lesions of the thalamus, hypothalamus, mammillary bodies, the reticular activating system, periaquaductal areas of the midbrain, and the floor of the fourth ventricle have been found, and may relate to the memory problems and various stages of consciousness. CT scans of Wernicke patients have correlated with postmortem findings (Figures 1–3). Edema has been found in the mammillary bodies around the third ventricle and the aquaductal floor of the fourth ventricle (Mensing et al. 1984).

Weingartner et al. (1983) suggested that the memory pathology in Korsakoff's may be based on a disruption of the functional anatomic linkages between the reward-reinforcement and memory systems. The patients may have access to semantic memory, unlike Alzheimer's patients, so psychobiologic mechanisms have been proposed. Decreases in CSF levels of norepinephrine, dopamine, and serotonin have been found, with the greatest decrease in norepinephrine levels. Negative studies have also been reported (McEntee and Mair 1978). The hypothesis is that norepinephrine sys-

tems are selectively damaged in Korsakoff's psychosis, producing memory deficits but not global dementia. Others have reported deficits in the acetylcholine system, suggesting a milder form of damage to the basalis of Meynert compared to what is found in Alzheimer's (Butters 1985). Butters (1985) characterized this as a basal forebrain rather than a diencephalon amnesia. At this time, Korsakoff's disease cannot be attributed to damage of any one structure.

Abnormalities in the metabolism of thiamine have been postulated as a contributory factor in the development of severe thiamine deficiency. Transketolase activity in the muscle fibroblasts of Wernicke-Korsakoff patients have been found to be decreased but the expression of the syndrome may

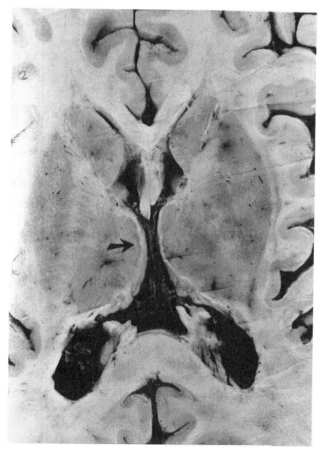

Figure 2. Postmortem slide of brain tissue from a patient with Wernicke's encephalopathy, showing smooth walls of the third ventricle, with an adjacent small discolored zone (arrow). Reproduced from Mensing et al. (1984), reprinted with permission.

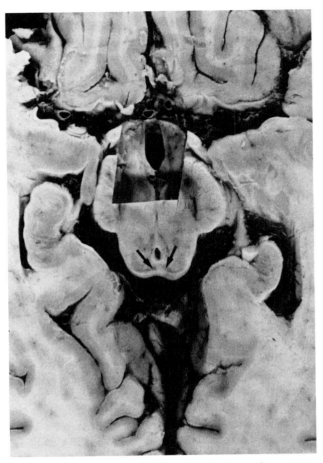

Figure 3. Postmortem slide of brain tissue from a patient with Wernicke's encephalopathy, showing discolored zone near the quadrigeminal plate (arrows). Reproduced from Mensing et al. (1984), reprinted with permission.

not become evident unless there is a thiamine-deficient diet (Blass and Gibson 1977). A report of monozygotic twins, both having a decrease in erythrocyte transketolase activity, with one developing Wernicke-Korsakoff secondary to alcoholism, suggested a possible genetic basis, although this is currently speculative (Leigh et al. 1981).

Treatment of Wernicke's Encephalopathy

Wernicke's encephalopathy is a life-threatening condition; treatment should be considered a medical emergency. Treatment consists of parenteral thiamine 100 mg with titration of thiamine upward until ophthalmoplegia has resolved. Resistance to thiamine replacement may result from hypomag-

nesemia because magnesium is a co-factor for thiamine transketolase. Magnesium sulfate 1 to 2 ml im in 50 percent solution should be administered. Thiamine should be given prior to any glucose loading. Ophthalmoplegia usually responds fairly quickly but truncal ataxia may persist.

Treatment of Korsakoff's Psychosis

Korsakoff's can be a devastating illness that often requires institutionalization. Korsakoff's and alcoholic dementia may occur in combination and may be difficult to separate clinically. Clonidine, an alpha-norepinephrine agonist, has been reported (0.3 mg bid) to improve recent memory and recall, perhaps as a result of hypothesized damage to the ascending norepinephrine-containing neurons in the brain stem and diencephalon (McEntee et al. 1981). Propranolol, up to 20 mg per kilogram per day, has been used for rage attacks in Korsakoff's psychosis (Yudofsky et al. 1984). This points to a chronic catacholamine supersensitivity. Unfortunately, none of these pharmacologic approaches is terribly effective.

Neuropsychological Changes with Alcohol Abuse

Alcohol's neurotoxicity is the result of years of alcohol abuse and occurs independently of thiamine deficiency. Impaired abstracting ability, problem solving, tactile and spatial performance, visual perception, olfactory acuity, visual learning, and memory have all been reported in alcoholics (Parsons 1977; Drejer et al. 1985). Basic intellectual functioning is generally spared, but a small number of patients do manifest general cognitive deficits and have a dementia-like picture. Determining what processes are impaired, when in the course of the drinking history problems become evident, and permanent versus temporary deficits becomes important in establishing prognosis, appropriateness of treatment, and discharge plans.

Duration and quantity of drinking, sensitivity of tests, patterns of drinking, and length of abstinence are factors that affect neuropsychological studies. Selection of patients may be fundamental in determining results in neuropsychological testing. Age, length of drinking, history of poor nutrition, and other drug abuse will vary outcome. Increased age is an important variable in poor neuropsychological performance, and it may not correlate with abstinence. Alcohol has greater effects in older individuals because their brains are more sensitive to the toxic effects of alcohol and because they are more likely to have had longer drinking histories. Social drinking in the elderly may produce decreases in cognitive functioning, but the hypothesis that alcohol leads to premature aging has not been supported by the data (Ryan 1982). Porjesz and Begleiter (1982) found very different evoked potentials between elderly individuals and alcoholics. In studies of young alcoholic men versus nonalcoholic controls, there was no difference in psychological findings (Grant et al. 1974). There is a significant difference between middle-aged alcoholics and elderly nonalcoholics. Reversibility of cognitive deficits also argues against the premature aging hypothesis.

Patterns of drinking may effect neuropsychological findings. Alcoholics with more than 10 years of heavy drinking show greater cognitive deficits. Binge drinking may be more neurotoxic. Social drinkers show greater decrease in cognitive performance when larger amounts are consumed at one time rather than spread out over time (Parker and Nobel 1977).

Various studies have stressed the importance of the length of sobriety on neuropsychological testing. Page and Schwaub (1977) studied 51 recovering alcoholics and found no further improvement of their specific intellectual functions after 3 weeks. At 7 weeks, Yohman et al. (1985) still found verbal memory, abstracting ability, problem solving, perceptual motor skills, and learning deficits, which cleared at 13 months of abstinence. Large-scale studies of sober alcoholics over longer periods of time (e.g., 3 years) are needed to characterize permanent deficits. The general wisdom is that most neuropsychological findings will clear in the majority of alcoholics after several weeks. In others, a more permanent although limited deficit may be evident.

In short-term (21 to 28 days) rehabilitation programs, educational efforts may be hampered by cognitive deficits. There is evidence that cognitive impairment may be predictive of poor treatment outcome (Caster 1977). Kupke and O'Brien (1985) found neuropsychological test scores predictive of completion of inpatient program, outpatient attendance, future drinking episodes, work behavior, and behavior while in the program. Recidivism is higher with patients with greater neuropsychological deficit (Abbott and Gregson 1981). Donovan

et al. (1984) found no prediction of success of abstinence at 6 months, but found decreased employment with poor neuropsychological scores. Focusing efforts at behavioral change or insight in treatment programs may be hampered by cognitive deficits. Programs need to take these problems into account in designing treatment. Patients are more fragile and less open to treatment when cognitive problems are most likely to affect judgment, learning, and attention.

Two hypotheses have been raised to explain these neuropsychological findings. One states that deficits are the consequence of prolonged drinking. Another states that cognitive deficits in individuals predispose one to develop alcoholism. A prospective longitudinal study of sons of alcoholics at high risk for developing alcoholism revealed relatively poorer vocabulary and worse performance on categorizing ability, organization, and planning compared to controls (Stejer et al. 1985). Minimal brain dysfunction symptoms have been associated with primary alcoholism and poor neuropsychological testing. A history of these symptoms in childhood may be associated with later impairment in neuropsychological testing (De Obaldia and Parsons 1984). Tarter and Alterman (1984) suggested that minimal brain dysfunction may predispose one toward alcoholism. In the families of alcoholics, abstracting and problem-solving deficits have been found. This suggests that learning and memory problems may antedate alcoholism, and that alcoholism plus neuropsychological deficits may have additive effects in susceptible individuals.

Begleiter et al. (1983) described a characteristic P300 wave attenuation on the evoked potential found in alcoholics and sons of alcoholics that may provide a trait marker for alcoholism. The P300 wave is thought to be characteristic of the decreased reaction to novel experience related to a hippocampal deficit. Prospective studies are needed to see if evoked potential would discriminate those at highest risk.

There are some similarities between neuropsychological findings in long-term alcoholics and Korsakoff patients, although there are also important differences. Both have impairments with visual perception and problem solving, which are both association cortex tasks. Ryback (1971) suggested that there is a continuum of decrease in function from abstinent individuals to moderate to chronic drinkers and Korsakoff patients. However, recent evidence has not supported the notion that

Korsakoff's is at the extreme end of the spectrum of alcohol dementia (Butters 1985). Compared to Korsakoff's, long-term alcoholics have less learning impairment, dissimilar memory impairment processes, and less verbal memory impairment.

ALCOHOL DEMENTIA

Alcohol dementia is dementia presumably caused by long-term alcohol use. Because it may be difficult to separate effects from subacute Wernicke-Korsakoff, trauma, and hepatic encephalopathy, careful exclusion criteria may decrease the reported incidence of this entity. Cala and Mastaglia (1981) reviewed the literature on CT scans in chronic alcoholics. There is positive evidence for cortical shrinkage but no direct correlation between CT atrophy and neuropsychologcal deficits, except in the frontal lobe areas. This accompanies findings in Alzheimer's where cortical atrophy does not necessarily predict level of dementia. Reversal of cortical atrophy can follow a prolonged period of abstinence, suggesting that neuronal fallout is not the only factor responsible for alcohol brain atrophy. Advances in the use of positron emission tomography (PET) scans now provide a potential for further study of alcohol's effect on the brain.

OTHER NEUROLOGIC COMPLICATIONS

Alcoholic polyneuropathy is characterized by stocking-glove paresthesia with decreased reflexes and autonomic nerve dysfunctions such as impotence, orthostatic hypotension, and bowel or bladder difficulties (Nakada and Knight 1984). It is a degenerative nerve process that may be partially improved by vitamin B supplementation. Alcohol cerebellar degeneration is a slowly evolving condition encountered along with long-standing history of excessive alcohol use. It affects the cerebellar cortex and produces truncal ataxia and gait disturbance. The exact course is unknown but typical symptoms, alcoholic history, and supporting CT findings may make the diagnosis. Central pontine myelinolysis, Marchiafava-Bignami disease, and nutritional amblyopia are rare neurologic conditions associated with chronic alcoholism. Pontine dysfunction evident in central pontine myelinolysis is of unknown etiology and often causes death.

Marchiafava-Bignami disease is a rare demyelinating disease of the corpus callosum, whose etiology is totally unknown. A nutritional amblyopia is associated with alcohol and tobacco use and is treated with B complex vitamins. Alcoholism is also associated with an increased risk of stroke, possibly due to hyperlipidemia, hypertension, or blood flow abnormalities.

SUMMARY

Alcohol can have acute and chronic effects that can lead to neuropsychiatric impairment, making diagnosis difficult. Intoxication, withdrawal, and temporary and lasting brain effects require careful history taking, mental status evaluation, selective laboratory testing, and treatment planning. Frequently these problems become complicated by interactions of alcohol-related organic brain syndromes with psychiatric, medical, and neurologic conditions. Further research is needed to establish the specific pathogenesis of these neuropsychiatric problems. New approaches such as PET scanning and tools for study of neurotransmitters and receptor sites may help us to understand these effects better. Ultimately, prevention and early diagnosis are the best ways to minimize the devastating consequences of alcohol abuse and dependence.

REFERENCES

Abbott W, Gregson RAM: Cognitive dysfunction in the prediction of relapse in alcoholics. J Stud Alcohol 42:230–245, 1981

Adams RD, Victor M: Principles of Neurology. New York, McGraw-Hill, 1981

Albert MS, Butters N, Levin J: Temporal gradients in the retrograde amnesia of patients with alcoholic Korsakoff's disease. Arch Neurol 36:211–216, 1979

Alexopoulos GS, Lieberman KW, Frances R, et al: Platelet MAO during the alcohol withdrawal syndrome. Am J Psychiatry 138:1254–1255, 1981

American Psychiatric Association: Diagnostic and Statistical Manual of Mental Disorders, 3rd ed. Washington, DC, American Psychiatric Association, 1980

American Psychiatric Association: Diagnostic and Statistical Manual of Mental Disorders, 3rd ed, revised. Washington, DC, American Psychiatric Association, 1987

Ballenger JC, Post RM: Carbamazepine in alcohol withdrawal syndromes and schizophrenic psychosis. Psychopharmacol Bull 20:72–84, 1984

Begleiter H, Porjesz B, Chou CL, et al: P_3 and stimulus incentive value. Psychophysiology 1:95–101, 1983

Beresford, TP: Alcoholism consultation and general hospital psychiatry. Gen Hosp Psychiatry 1:293–300, 1979

Berglund M, Risberg J: Regional cerebral blood flow during withdrawal. Arch Gen Psychiatry 38:351–355, 1981

Besson JA, Glen AI: Brain water in alcoholics (letter). Lancet 2:50, 1985

Black RF, Hoffman RL, Tabakoff B: Receptor-mediated dopaminergic function after ethanol withdrawal. Alcoholism 4:294–297, 1980

Blass JP, Gibson GE: Abnormality of a thiamine requiring enzyme in patients with Wernicke-Korsakoff syndrome. N Engl J Med 297:7–70, 1977

Butters N: Alcoholic Korsakoff's syndrome: some unresolved issues concerning etiology: neuropathology and cognitive deficits. Journal of Clinical and Experimental Neuropsychology 7:181–210, 1985

Cala LA, Mastaglia FL: Computerized tomography in chronic alcoholics. Alcoholism (NY) 5:283–294, 1981

Caster DU: The treatment of the recidivist alcoholic. Alcoholism (NY) 1:87–90, 1977

Cohen MJ, Schandler SL, Naliboff BD: Psychophysiological measures from intoxicated and detoxified alcoholics. J Stud Alcohol 44:271–282, 1983

De Obaldia R, Parsons OA: Relationship of neuropsychological performance to primary alcoholism and self-reported symptoms of childhood minimal brain dysfunction. J Stud Alcohol 45:386–392, 1984

Donovan DM, Kivlahan DR, Walker RD: Clinical limitations of neuropsychological testing in predicting treatment outcome among alcoholics. Alcoholism (NY) 8:470–475, 1984

Drejer K, Theilgaard A, Teasdale TW, et al: Prospective study of young men at high risk for alcoholism: neuropsychological assessment. Alcoholism 6:498–502, 1985

Feissner J, Linfus E, Blessing C, et al: CAT scanning in ETOH withdrawal syndromes: value of the neurological exam. Ann Intern Med 94:519–522, 1981

Femino J, Lewis DC: Clinical Pharmacology and Therapeutics of the Alcohol Withdrawal Syndrome. Report 0372. Rockville, MD, National Institute on Alcohol Abuse and Alcoholism, 1982

Frances RJ, Franklin JE: Alcoholism and suicidality. Ann NY Acad Sci (in press)

Fujimato A, Nagaao T, Ebara T, et al: Cerebrospinal fluid monoamine metabolite during alcohol withdrawal syndrome and recovered state. Biol Psychiatry 18:1141–1152, 1983

Gessner PK: Drug withdrawal therapy of the alcohol withdrawal syndrome, in Biochemistry and Pharmacology of Ethanol, Vol. 2. Edited by Majchowicz E, Moble E. New York, Plenum Press, 1979, pp 375–435

Goodwin DW: Alcoholism and genetics. Arch Gen Psychiatry 42:171–174, 1985

Goodwin DW, Crane JB, Guze SB: Alcoholic blackouts: a review and clinical study of 100 alcoholics. Am J Psychiatry 126:174–177, 1969

Grant I, Adams K, Reed R: Normal neuropsychological abilities of alcoholic men in their late thirties. Am J Psychiatry 136:1263–1269, 1974

Greenberg P, Pearlman C: Delirium tremens and dreaming. Am J Psychiatry 124:133–142, 1967

Hawley BJ, Major LF, Schulman EA, et al: CSF levels of norepinephrine during alcohol withdrawal. Arch Neurol 38:289–292, 1981

Hemmingsen R, Kramp P, Rafaelsen OJ: DT's and related clinical states: Etiology, pathophysiology and treatment. Acta Psychiatr Scand 59:337–369, 1979

Holloway HC, Hales RE, Wantanabe HK: Recognition and treatment of acute alcohol withdrawal syndrome. Psychiatr Clin North Am 7:729–743, 1984

Isbell H, Fraser HF, Wikler A, et al: An experimental study of the etiology of "rum fits" and delirium tremens. Q J Stud Alcohol 16:1–13, 1955

Kolin IS, Linet OT: Double blind comparison of alprazolam and diazepam for subchronic withdrawal from alcohol. J Clin Psychiatry 42:169–173, 1981

Kramp P, Hemmingsen R: Delirium tremens and related clinical states: changes in calcium and inorganic phosphate concentrations in plasma and cerebrospinal fluid. Acta Psychiatr Scand 69:250–258, 1984

Kupke T, O'Brien W: Neuropsychological impairment and behavioral limitation exhibited within an alcoholic treatment program. Journal of Clinical and Experimental Neuropsychology 7:292–304, 1985

Leigh D, McBurney A, McIlwain H: Wernicke-Korsakoff syndrome in monozygotic twins: a biochemical peculiarity. Br J Psychiatry 139:156–159, 1981

Lishman WA: Cerebral disorder in alcoholism: syndromes of impairment. Brain 104:1–20, 1981

Lishman WA: Organic Psychiatry. Philadelphia, JB Lippincott Co, 1978

Mattis S, Kovner R, Gartner J, et al: Deficits in retrieval of category exemplors in alcoholic Korsakoff patients. Neuropsychologia 19:357–363, 1981

McEntee WJ, Mair RG: Memory impairment in Korsakoff's psychosis: a correlation with brain norepinephrine activity. Science 202:905–907, 1978

McEntee WJ, Mair RG: Memory enhancement in Korsakoff's psychosis by clonidine: further evidence for a norepinephrine deficit. Ann Neurol 79:466–470, 1980

McEntee WJ, Mair RG, Langlas PJ: Clonidine in Korsakoff disease: pathophysiologic and therapeutic implications. Prog Clin Biol Res 71:211–223, 1981

Meilgaard: Wernicke's encephalopathy (letter). N Engl J Med 313:637–638, 1985

Mensing JW, Hoogland PH, Slooff JL: Computed tomography in the diagnosis of Wernicke's encephalopathy: a radiological-neuropathological corelation. Ann Neurol 16:363–365, 1984

Moskowitz G, Chalmers TC, Sacks HS, et al: Deficiencies of clinical trials of alcohol withdrawal. Alcoholism (NY) 7:42–46, 1983

Nakada T, Knight RT: Alcohol and the central nervous system. Med Clin North Am 68:121–131, 1984

Niven RG: Alcoholism: a problem in perspective. JAMA 252:1912–1914, 1984

Page RD, Schaub LH: Intellectual functioning in alcoholics during six months abstinence. J Stud Alcohol 38:1240–1246, 1977

Parker ES, Noble E: Alcohol consumption and cognitive functioning in social drinkers. J Stud Alcohol 38:1224–1232, 1977

Parsons O: Neuropsychological deficits in chronic alcoholics: facts and fantasies. Alcoholism (NY) 1:51–56, 1977

Porjesz B, Begleiter H: Evoked brain potential deficits in alcoholism and aging. Alcoholism (NY) 6:53–63, 1982

Robins LN, Helzer JE, Weissman MM, et al: Lifetime prevalence of specific psychiatric disorders in three sites. Arch Gen Psychiatry 41:949–958, 1984

Ryan C: Alcoholism and premature aging: a neuropsychological perspective. Alcoholism (NY) 6:22–30, 1982

Ryback R: The continuum and specificity of the effects of alcohol on memory. Q J Stud Alcohol 32:995–1016, 1971

Schwittes SY, Johnson RC, McClean GE, et al: Alcohol use and the flushing response in different rural and ethnic groups. J Stud Alcohol 43:1254–1262, 1982

Sellers EM, Kalant H: Alcohol intoxication and withdrawal. N Engl J Med 294:757–762, 1976

Selzer B, Benson DF: The temporal pattern of retrograde amnesia in Korsakoff's disease. Neurology 24:527–530, 1974

Shen WW: Extrapyramidal symptoms associated with alcohol withdrawal. Biol Psychiatry 19:1037–1043, 1984

Surawicz FG: Alcoholic hallucinosis: a missed diagnosis: differential diagnoses and management. Can J Psychiatry 1:57–63, 1980

Tarter RE, Alterman AL: Neuropsychological deficits in alcoholics: etiological considerations. J Stud Alcohol 45:1–9, 1984

Tarter RE, Goldstein G, Alterman A, et al: Alcoholic seizures: intellectual and neuropsychological sequelae. J Nerv Ment Dis 171:123–125, 1983

Tønnesen E: Delirium tremens and hypokalemia (letter). Lancet 2:97, 1982

Victor M: Treatment of alcohol intoxication and the withdrawal syndrome: a critical analysis of the use of drugs and other forms of therapy. Psychosom Med 28:636–650, 1966

Victor M, Adams RD: The effect of alcohol on the nervous system. Res Publ Assoc Res Nerv Ment Dis 32:526–573, 1953

Victor M, Wolfe SM: Causation and treatment of the alcohol withdrawal syndrome, in Alcoholism: Progress in Research and Treatment. Edited by Bourne PG, Fox R. New York, Academic Press, 1973, pp 137–166

Weingartner H, Groifman J, Boutelle W, et al: Forms of memory failure. Science 221:380–383, 1983

West LJ, Maxwell DS, Noble EP, et al: Alcoholism. Ann Intern Med 100:405–416, 1984

Yohman RY, Parsons OA, Leber WR: Lack of recovery in male alcoholics neuropsychological performance one year after treatment. Alcoholism (NY) 9:114–117, 1985

Yudofsky SC, Stevens L, Silver J, et al: Propranolol in the treatment of rage and violent behavior associated with Korsakoff's Psychosis. Am J Psychiatry 141:114–115, 1984

Zilm DH, Kaplan HC, Capell H: Electroencephalographic tolerance and abstinence phenomena during repeated alcohol ingestion by non-alcoholics. Science 212:1175–1177, 1981

Zola-Morgan SM, Oberg RG: Recall of life experience in an alcoholic Korsakoff patient: a naturalistic approach. Neuropsychologia 18:549–557, 1980

Chapter

9

Substance-Induced Organic Mental Disorders

Samuel Perry, M.D.

THE DIAGNOSIS OF A SUBSTANCE-INDUCED organic mental disorder, according to DSM-III-R (American Psychiatric Association 1987), is made whenever a patient has a psychological or behavioral sign or symptom that is caused by the direct effect on the nervous system of any substance. The overall incidence of this disorder is not known, but a perusal through the *Physician's Desk Reference* (1986) should help convince any clinician that most medications cross the blood-brain barrier and, at least in some patients, cause alterations in alertness, thinking, perception, memory, mood, coordination, impulse control, personality, or behavior. There are thousands of case reports describing both common and rare neuropsychiatric symptoms induced by medication as well as several recent attempts to summarize the accumulated data (Hall et al. 1980; Johnson 1981; Lipowski 1980; Perl et al. 1980; Shader 1972).

In addition to not knowing how often substance-induced organic mental disorders occur, we

also do not know how often this diagnosis is missed. We do know from many large studies that organic mental disorders in general are frequently not recognized or are misinterpreted (Bunce et al. 1982; Hall et al. 1978, 1981; Hoffman 1982; Koranyi 1979; Leeman 1975; Perry and Cella 1985). Based partly on these and other studies and partly on clinical experience, the presumption is that substance-induced neuropsychiatric phenomena are especially prone to be overlooked or misdiagnosed. Several factors contribute to this failure:

1. The mental changes may occur insidiously and may not be apparent when the medication is first administered; therefore, neither the patient nor the clinician may consider that the new symptoms are possibly due to a drug that has been taken regularly for weeks, months, or even years (e.g., reserpine, oral contraceptives, isoniazid).

2. The mental changes caused by prescribed

157

medication occur in the presence of someone who is already physically or emotionally ill; therefore, the changes may mistakenly be attributed to the underlying illness and not to its pharmacologic treatment (e.g., fatigue and depression in a patient receiving digitalis for cardiac failure; emotional withdrawal and visual misperceptions in a patient receiving methysergide for migraine headaches; conduct disturbance in a child with cancer receiving antineoplastic agents (Weiss et al. 1974); restlessness and agitation in a psychotic patient receiving neuroleptics).

3. The prescribed drugs often affect mood, personality, or behavior without noticeably affecting alertness, cognition, or sensorimotor function; therefore, to the patient, the mental changes may be egosyntonic and, to the clinician, the changes may not be discernible either on neurologic examination or on the mental status examination of higher integrative functions (e.g., the mood changes induced by corticosteroids; personality changes induced by sulindac; aggressive behavioral changes induced by bromocriptine, which may even persist for 6 weeks after the drug is discontinued).

4. The occurrence of drug-induced mental changes as well as their expression is influenced by the patient's situation, psychodynamics, personality, and style; therefore, emotional symptoms may be erroneously viewed as only "functional" in origin while the organic component is neglected (e.g., excitability in a histrionic patient with asthma who is administered xanthine bronchodilators; irritability in an elderly patient with parkinsonism administered levodopa; nightmares in an actor prescribed propranolol for stage fright).

5. Many adverse reactions to medication are idiosyncratic and "typically atypical"; therefore, they cannot be easily categorized and may be unfamiliar to the clinician (e.g., persecutory hallucinations with vincristine; suspiciousness with cimetidine; grandiose delusions after withdrawal from baclofen).

6. Adverse mental changes may occur with small, single doses of a given drug; therefore, the diagnosis is missed by the clinician who considers the possibility only in the presence of higher, sustained doses (bizarre behavior af-

ter a single injection of procaine penicillin G; suspiciousness after a single 1-g dose of chloroquine).

7. Many patients misrepresent, minimize, deny, or frankly lie about how they are taking drugs, both those that are prescribed and those that are illicit; therefore, the clinician may be misled and not suspect a toxic reaction (e.g., benzodiazepines, nicotine, caffeine, alcohol, and all "street" drugs).

8. For countertransferential reasons, the clinician may unconsciously be reluctant to acknowledge the iatrogenic effect of a medication personally prescribed.

To address this problem of misdiagnosis, the usual approach has been to provide a description of mental changes associated with various drugs, then to supplement this discussion with a list of commonly prescribed medications and their possible adverse neuropsychiatric effects (Abramowicz 1981; Guggenheim and Erman 1985; Hall et al. 1980; Lipowski 1980; Perl et al. 1980; Shader 1972; Zavodnick 1984). Although a valuable reference source, such a summary tends to be encyclopedic, cannot easily be remembered, and, most importantly, may fail to distinguish between those mental changes that are frequent, immediate, egodystonic, and easily diagnosed from those that are rare, delayed, egosyntonic, subtle, and easily missed. For example, a clinician may readily realize a patient's complaint of "yellow-tinted vision" is due to digitalis yet fail to consider that the same patient's increasing belligerence may also be due to this drug. Moreover, any summary or list may be misleading in that it cannot adequately convey the possibility of an atypical idiosyncratic response or the interplay between the drug-induced mental changes and the patient's unique situation and psychodynamics.

This chapter, therefore, takes a different approach; rather than presenting a long list of drugs with condensed descriptions for each, this chapter selects those substances that are representative of the diagnostic difficulties that most commonly challenge psychiatrists. Special emphasis is given to commonly abused substances because, as noted above, patients often misrepresent their self-administration of these drugs. A knowledge of the neuropsychiatric presentation thereby becomes the clinician's best method of making the appropriate diagnosis. Emphasis is also given to psychotropic medication because the mental changes induced by these drugs can so easily be confused with the underlying emotional disturbance for which the psychotropics are being prescribed.

In addition to being selective, this chapter departs from the standard approach by introducing each of the discussed categories of drugs with a case vignette. The intention is not only to make the various drug-induced mental changes more memorable and to illustrate how situation, personality, and psychodynamics may influence the clinical presentation, but also to indicate some of the difficulties in either diagnosis or management of these disorders. In alphabetical order, the overlapping categories of drugs discussed are: (1) anticholinergics and antidepressants; (2) antihypertensives; (3) depressants; (4) hallucinogens; (5) inhalants; (6) lithium; (7) marijuana; (8) neuroleptics; (9) opioids; (10) steroids; and (11) stimulants. The diagnostic indicators of organic mental disorders induced by these substances are listed in Table 1.

☐ ANTICHOLINERGICS AND ANTIDEPRESSANTS

Mr. A, a 72-year-old retired carpenter, developed a severe agitated depression following the death of his wife in a car accident in which he was the driver. The surgeon who had treated Mr. A's wife prescribed amitriptyline 25 mg tid. After 2 days, Mr. A became lightheaded on standing, groggy, forgetful, and felt "weird." He interpreted these symptoms as a worsening of his depression and, on his own, increased the amitriptyline to 150 mg/day. He immediately felt more confused, restless, and despondent. When he awoke alone in the night, he envisioned his wife standing at the foot of his bed. Now convinced that he was losing his mind, Mr. A stumbled to the bathroom and, in an impulsive suicide attempt, ingested the remaining amitriptyline, 800 mg total.

The next morning Mr. A's daughter fortuitously discovered him slumped on the floor in a stupor. He was rushed by ambulance to the emergency room (ER) where physical examination disclosed a delirious elderly man with dilated and unreactive pupils, dry skin, heart rate 140, temperature 39°C, absent bowel sounds, and distended bladder. With a test dose of physostigmine 1.0 mg slowly injected intravenously over 1 minute, Mr. A became more alert and his pupils responsive to light. An intravenous drip of physostigmine 2 mg/hour was administered, then gradually discontinued during the next 7 hours in the intensive care unit where Mr. A had been transferred for monitoring.

The next day, with no signs of cardiac complications or aspiration pneumonia, Mr. A was admitted to the psychiatric service. For the next 3 days his sensorium continued to clear off all medication; however, the irrational guilt over "causing" his wife's death was compounded by the shame about the overdose. He became even more suicidally despondent. Nine electroconvulsive therapies (ECT) were administered, leading to a complete and uncomplicated recovery from his depression.

This case illustrates both the mild and severe mental changes associated with tricyclic antidepressants (TCAs), and how these changes can be misinterpreted by the depressed patient—postural hypotension; decrement in short-term memory; sedation; estrangement; and agitation—followed, at higher doses, by an anticholinergic delirium—misperceptions; impulsivity; impaired judgment; dry, warm skin; dilated, fixed pupils; fever; tachycardia; diminished peristalsis; atonic bladder; and improvement after an intravenous test dose of physostigmine (Preskorn and Irwin 1982).

Similar atropinic-like effects may occur with mydriadic eyedrops; antiemetics; many over-the-counter hypnotics; drugs administered prior to surgery or ECT to reduce respiratory tract secretions; and antiparkinsonian medication such as benztropine (Cogentin), biperiden (Akineton), diphenhydramine (Benadryl), and trihexyphenidyl (Artane) (Greenblatt and Shader 1973). When such drugs are inadvertently administered in toxic doses to reduce extrapyramidal symptoms associated with neuroleptics, the resulting dysphoria, agitation, and confusional state may be attributed to the underlying psychotic process and erroneously lead to an increase of the neuroleptic rather than to a reduction of the antiparkinsonian agent (Tune et al. 1982). The availability without a prescription of diphenhydramine and similar drugs may help explain the increasing abuse of anticholinergics by adolescents who enjoy the substance's euphoriant effect. As a result of cumulative "pill popping" during a long night of partying, these teenagers present in the ER with either a psychotic delirium or a life-threatening stupor similar to Mr. A's.

As described in this case, when the anticholinergic poisoning is severe and requires more than gastric lavage and observation, physostigmine (Antilirium), a short-acting cholinesterase inhibitor, should be used, especially in the presence of a significant cardiac arrhythmia. The usual required dose is 1 to 4 mg iv or im every 2 hours; however, since anticholinergic agents act over an

TABLE 1.   DIAGNOSTIC INDICATORS OF COMMON SUBSTANCE-INDUCED ORGANIC MENTAL DISORDERS

Drug Category	Name[a]	Diagnostic Signs/Symptoms	Comments
Anticholinergics			
	Benztropine (Cogentin) Biperiden (Akineton) Diphenhydramine (Benadryl) Trihexyphenidyl (Artane)	Subtle: Postural hypotension Tachycardia Diminished memory Sedation; agitation Estrangement Dysphoria Impulsivity Poor judgment Severe: Illusions; hallucinations Dry, warm skin; fever Dilated, fixed pupils Atonic bladder Decreased peristalsis	Diagnosis often missed when used in conjunction with neuroleptics for psychotic disorder Overdose treated with gastric lavage and parenteral physostigmine
Antidepressants Heterocyclics		Anticholinergic activity:	All antidepressants may elicit schizophrenic-like, hypomanic, or manic episode, and long half-life requires 24-hour monitoring after overdose
	Amitriptyline (Elavil)	+ + +	
	Protriptyline (Vivactil)	+ + +	
	Doxepin (Sinequan)	+ +	
	Trimpramine (Surmontil)	+ +	
	Nortriptyline (Aventyl)	+ +	
	Imipramine (Tofranil)	+ +	
	Desipramine (Norpramin)	+	Rapid induction causes seizures
	Maprotiline (Ludiomil)	+	
	Amoxapine (Asendin)	+	Extrapyramidal symptoms, tardive dyskinesia
	Trazodone (Desyrel)	0	Possible priapism
Monamine oxidase inhibitors			
	Phenelzine (Nardil) Isocarboxazid (Marplan) Tranylcypromine (Parnate)	Insomnia, agitation Weight gain Impotence; compulsive rituals; delirium	Intravenous phentolamine for hypertensive crisis Meperidine contraindicated
Antihypertensives			
	Reserpine (Serpasil) Methyldopa (Aldomet)	Insidiously developing depression	Guanethidine (Ismelin) does not cross blood-brain barrier Cross-reactions with TCAs and MAOIs with many antihypertensives
	Hydralazine (Apresoline)		Lower risk of depression
	Clonidine (Catapres)		Hypomania with abrupt withdrawal
	Propranolol (Inderal)		Nightmares, agitation, etc. may be confused with underlying mania, schizophrenia, or anxiety disorder

TABLE 1. (Continued)

Drug Category	Name[a]	Diagnostic Signs/Symptoms	Comments
Depressants			
Benzodiazepines	Flurazepam (Dalmane) Diazepam (Valium) Chlordiazepoxide (Librium) Lorazepam (Ativan) Alprazolam (Xanax) Temazepam (Restoril) Oxazepam (Serax) Triazolam (Halcion)	Sedation Paradoxical hyperactivity and affective lability Accentuation of depression (less with alprazolam) Withdrawal syndrome: anxiety, tremor, muscle cramps, dysphoria, insomnia, seizures, hallucinations, delirium Memory loss ("blackouts") at normal doses	Listed in order of longest to shortest half-life Withdrawal syndrome confused with anxiety disorder Accumulation in elderly leads to "sundowning" and subtle delirium
Barbiturates	Phenobarbital Secobarbital (Tuinal) Pentobarbital	Induce mental disorders similar to benzodiazepines	Low therapeutic index for psychiatric disorders
Methaqualone			
Hallucinogens			
Arylcyclohexylamine derivatives	PCP, TCP, "Angel Dust"	Horizontal and vertical nystagmus Ataxia, dysarthria Grimacing Catatonic posturing Numbness, analgesia Salivation, diaphoresis Delirium with rapid fluctuations Self-destructive and violent behavior	Prompt treatment with restraints, calm environment, diazepam Profound depression during withdrawal
Lysergic acid diethylamide	LSD; "Acid"; "Microdot"	Body distortions Depersonalization Paranoia Hallucinations Recurrent misperceptions ("flashbacks")	Reassurance and correction of misperceptions usually sufficient
Mescaline	"Mesc"; "Speed"		
Peyote	"Cactus"		
Ketamine		Frightening misperceptions following anesthesia	More prominent with adults
Inhalants			
Amyl nitrate	"Poppers"; "Snappers"	Hypotension, vasodilation Paranoia, panic, dysphoria	Complications rare
Solvents	Shoe polish, glue, paint, and many others	Smell of solvent on breath Excitement, hallucinations, delusions (acute) Cognitive decline (chronic) Abnormal kidney and liver functions	Sudden deaths attributed to cardiac arrhythmias
Lithium	(Eskalith, Lithobid)	Tremor, nausea, polyuria Diminished concentration, creativity, memory, and sensorimotor function Toxic: ataxia, dysphoria, irritability, restlessness, impulsivity Overdose: delirium, seizures, arrhythmia, stupor	Confused with reactive depression Confused with hypomania Infusion of sodium chloride

TABLE 1. (Continued)

Drug Category	Name[a]	Diagnostic Signs/Symptoms	Comments
Marijuana			
Cannabinoid	"pot"; "weed"; "grass"; "joint"	Euphoria; detachment Increased appetite Depersonalization Preoccupations	Complications rare and influenced by setting and personality Urine screening available
Tetrahydrocannibol	"THC"	Paranoia, panic reactions Conjunctival injection Decreased short-term memory Hallucinations (rare) Amotivational syndrome (chronic)	Adverse reactions usually respond to reassurance
Neuroleptics			
Phenothiazines	Chlorpromazine (Thorazine)	Sedation, depression, mental slowing	Leads to poor compliance; confused with reactive depression
	Thioridazine (Mellaril)	Acute dystonia	Early onset; males > females
	Trifluoperazine (Stelazine) Perphenazine (Trilafon)	Akathesia: restlessness, dysphoria, impulsivity	Confused with underlying psychosis; females > males
	Fluphenazine (Prolixin)	Parkinsonism	Early onset; females > males
Thioxanthenes	Chlorprothixene (Taractan) Piperazine (Navane)	Neuroleptic malignant syndrome: fever, tachycardia, delirium, rigidity	Later onset (unlike acute dystonia)
Butyrophenones	Haloperidol (Haldol)	Tardive dyskinesia	Late onset; females > males
Indolic derivatives Dibenzoxazepine	Molindone (Moban) Loxapine (Loxizane)	"Rabbit syndrome" (facial muscles but not tongue)	Late onset but, unlike tardive dyskinesia, responds to antimuscarinic agents
Opioids			
Opium alkaloids and semisynthetic derivatives	Morphine Diacetylmorphine (Heroin) Hydromorphone (Dilaudid)	Sedation; mental slowing Dysphoria; euphoria	Confused with depressive or physical response to underlying illness
		Overdose: respiratory suppression, coma, pulmonary edema, pupillary constriction	Ventilation; naloxone
	Codeine Oxycodone (Percodan)	Addiction: cigarette burns, subcutaneous abscesses, needle "tracks"	
Synthetic narcotics	Levorphinol (Levo-Dromoran) Propoxyphene (Darvon) Methadone (Dolophine)	Withdrawal: perspiring, dilated pupils, abdominal cramps, piloerection, muscular spasm	Reduced by clonidine
	Meperidine (Demerol)	Myoclonic twitches	Accumulation of normeperidine may lead to seizures and delirium
	Pentazocine (Talwin)	Psychotomimetic	Antagonist properties can precipitate withdrawal syndrome

TABLE 1. (Continued)

Drug Category	Name[a]	Diagnostic Signs/Symptoms	Comments
Steroids			
Corticosteroids	Hydrocortisone Prednisone	Insomnia Affective lability: hypomania, dysphoria; depression Delirium with illusions, hallucinations	Mood changes without cognitive impairment; increased risk with higher dose, prior steroid-induced episode, and family or personal history of affective illness
Adrenocorticotropic hormone	ACTH		
Oral contraceptives		Depression; dysphoria	Mental changes in > 5% women
Stimulants			
Cocaine	"coke"; "line"; "crack"	Chronic abuse: personality change; impaired judgment; impulsivity; aggressivity; suspiciousness; anorexia with weight loss; insomnia; irritability; delusions; inflamed nasal mucosae; hyperreflexia; parkinsonism; auditory, tactile, and olfactory hallucinations	Often subtle and insidious; confused with antisocial personality or paranoid disorders
		Withdrawal: depression	Bromocriptine may reduce psychophysiological withdrawal reactions and drug craving
		Acute toxic reactions: dilation; hypertension; tachycardia; delirium; hyperpyrexia; seizures; cardiovascular collapse	Intravenous diazepam
Amphetamines	Dextroamphetamine (Dexedrine) Methylphenidate (Ritalin)	Psychological symptoms and signs similar to cocaine	Toxicity, addiction, and withdrawal usually less severe than cocaine
Appetite suppressants	Phenmetrazine (Preludin) Diethylpropion (Tenuate)		

[a]Generic name given, with an example of a brand name in parentheses. "Street" or common names given for hallucinogens, inhalants, marijuana, and cocaine.

8- to 12-hour period and TCA toxicity may have a duration of 24 hours or longer, the original dose of physostigmine may need to be repeated several times or, as with Mr. A, an intravenous drip can be administered (Stern 1983). Physostigmine can itself induce confusion, hallucinations, and seizures; this cholinergic toxicity can be distinguished from an anticholinergic effect by the presence of bradycardia, meiosis, increased secretions, abdominal colic with diarrhea, and urinary urgency or incontinence. Atropine 0.5 to 2.0 mg im will promptly reverse these symptoms should they arise as a result of injudicious administration of physostigmine.

Because the elderly or physically ill are more sensitive to the anticholinergic side effects of TCAs, the physician may choose to prescribe a monoamine oxidase inhibitor (MAOI) or one of the newer antidepressants. These agents, however, are also associated with adverse mental changes. The MAOIs commonly produce dose-related sleeplessness, restlessness, and a "racy feeling," and less commonly cause compulsive rituals or even a psychotic delirium. As with *all* antidepressants, the MAOIs may elicit a hypomanic or manic syndrome, especially in those with a personal or family history of bipolar illness. Antidepressants may also elicit a schizophrenic-like syndrome in those with a personal or family history of schizophrenia or with a vulnerability to psychosis, such as patients with either a borderline or schizoid personality disorder, or with an organic mental disorder. Amoxapine (Asendin), a tetracyclic, causes mental changes similar to the tricyclics and has the additional risk of tardive dyskinesia with extended use. Trazodone (Desyrel) and maprotiline (Ludiomil) are chemically unrelated to the TCAs or MAOIs and may have a lower risk of adverse mental changes.

☐ ANTIHYPERTENSIVES

Mrs. K, a 42-year-old housewife, is referred by her internist for psychiatric consultation because she has become increasingly depressed over the past 3 months since her youngest child left for college. The year before when her first child left home, Mrs. K had some mild depressive symptoms—insomnia, fatigue, somatic concerns. When she consulted the internist on that occasion, however, he chose to treat Mrs. K with reassurance and did not believe that antidepressant medication was necessary. At that time the internist also discovered that Mrs. K had essential hypertension (180/125), which he initially treated with methyldopa (Aldomet), adding reserpine (Serpasil) a few months later.

On that regime, Mrs. K's blood pressure has remained stable over the past 6 months, but her depression has become profoundly worse. She wakes up early every morning, staring at the ceiling and wondering what is her purpose in life now that the children are gone. She has lost all interest in her friends, husband, sex, and food, and has lost 15 pounds, which makes her appear 10 years older. She feels tired and worthless. Whenever she irritably flares up at her husband over dinner or with her children over the phone, she is convinced that everyone would be better off without her. She has thought about taking an overdose with all the drugs in her medicine cabinet, and the previous night went into the bathroom and stared at a handful of pills before putting them back. Her husband is completely baffled by Mrs. K's behavior. Although she had a severe postpartum depression long ago, in recent years she has been physically and emotionally healthy in contrast to her mother and sister, both of whom have been repeatedly hospitalized for depression. The husband is also annoyed at his wife and has started to spend less time at home to avoid the outbursts and arguments that often ensue.

Because of the risk of suicide and the current emotional unavailability of the husband, Mrs. K was psychiatrically hospitalized. In conjunction with the internist, her previous antihypertensive medication was discontinued. She was gradually begun on pargyline, with adequate control of her blood pressure as well as a lifting of her mood over the ensuing weeks.

The case of Mrs. K illustrates many features of depression associated with antihypertensive medication, which induces at least a mild depression in 20 percent of patients (Bunney 1978; Pottash et al. 1981). This high incidence is not surprising in that most antihypertensives impede or deplete neurotransmitters. As with Mrs. K, the diagnosis of a drug-induced depression may be missed because the symptoms typically develop several months after starting the drug and may be attributed to psychosocial stressors that contribute to the depression, but are not its sole cause. In addition, Mrs. K's personal and family history of affective illness may bias the clinician toward assuming that the psychiatric symptoms are not drug-induced, but actually these factors predispose an individual to an iatrogenic depression when antihypertensives are administered (Paykel et al. 1982).

The treatment of a mild depression in a patient receiving antihypertensives is to decrease the dosage, to change to a lower risk alternative (diuretics and hydralazine), or to change to an antihypertensive that does not cross the blood-brain barrier, such as guanethidine (Ismelin). If the depression is more severe, as with Mrs. K, the combined treatment of hypertension and depression is more of a problem. One possibility is to administer ECT for the depression and continue the antihypertensive, but this plan runs the risk of recurrent depression in the future as the brain stores of norepinephrine and dopamine again become depleted. Another possibility is to stop the antihypertensive and begin a TCA, which may provide adequate control of the blood pressure as well. However, if TCAs are administered to patients receiving guanethidine, clonidine (Catapres), bethanidine, or debrisoquin, the TCAs may inhibit nerve reuptake of these antihypertensives and the result may be an actual rise in blood pressure. Similarly, when combined with antihypertensive medications, MAOIs may cause a paradoxical rise in blood pressure. For example, since guanethidine initially causes the release of norepinephrine from nerve endings, a patient being maintained on an MAOI may experience a hypertensive reaction. An elevated blood pressure may also result if either hydralazine or methyldopa is administered to a patient receiving an MAOI. The decision reached with Mrs. K is one possible solution; namely, prescribing pargyline, which is both an antihypertensive drug and an antidepressant (Risch et al. 1981).

Depression is not the only neuropsychiatric problem induced by hypertensives; for example, the protracted use of inderal has been associated with insomnia, nightmares, drowsiness, visual hallucinations, and delirium (Petrie et al. 1982). These symptoms may be confused with the underlying disorder when inderal is prescribed for anxiety, panic states, schizophrenia, or mania.

☐ DEPRESSANTS

Mrs. B, a 29-year-old housewife, became increasingly anxious following an uncomplicated appendectomy. On her third postoperative day, psychiatric consultation reveals an attractive woman who articulately indicates that she is relieved the emergency surgery was successful but does not understand why she is so "shaky" (by which she means a coarse, intention tremor). She also complains of muscle cramps in her calves and lightheadedness and weakness on standing. On the basis of Mrs. B's rather histrionic style and the absence of a prior psychiatric history, the psychiatrist concludes that the patient's anxiety and other symptoms are no more than exaggerated emotional and physical reactions to surgery and anesthesia. He reassures Mrs. B and leaves, failing to note her hyperreflexia and myclonic twitches.

The night after the consultation, Mrs. B awakens with a nightmare, is given meperidine 75 mg im (the only "sedating" medication on order), but she fails to calm down. As the night progresses, she begins thrashing and screaming in bed to the point that four-limb restraints are required, which Mrs. B in her delirious state misinterprets as punishment by Gestapo guards. While the surgeons are gathering for early morning rounds, Mrs. B has a generalized seizure, which lasts for 4 minutes until diazepam 10 mg iv is administered. She immediately becomes more calm.

A few minutes later the paged psychiatrist is on the scene and this time takes a more detailed history. He learns that Mrs. B always regarded herself a "hyperemotional" person and was therefore not surprised when she was more anxious than most mothers when her only child began nursery school 9 months ago. At that time Mrs. B mentioned to her gynecologist during a routine examination that she was "a nervous wreck." Although realizing that Mrs. B was inclined to be overdramatic, the gynecologist prescribed 50 capsules of chlordiazepoxide (Librium) 25 mg tid to help her through the stressful life event. Mrs. B found that the medication not only calmed her nerves but also helped her sleep. During the next several weeks, without giving the matter much thought, she gradually began taking

more of the drug at bedtime (two and occasionally three pills) and, in addition, became in the habit of taking "a pill or two" when feeling unsettled by an upsetting daily event, such as a fight with the plumber or a minor injury to her son.

When the prescription ran out, along with the two renewals, Mrs. B called the gynecologist who ordered more of the drug; but after 4 months, when Mrs. B again called for a renewal, he suggested over the phone that Mrs. B now try to solve her problems on her own. Taking this advice, Mrs. B discontinued the medicine—but within 2 or 3 days, she felt "jittery" and unable to sleep. She interpreted these symptoms as an indication that she simply was too anxious a person to manage life's stresses on her own.

Too ashamed to contact her gynecologist again, she asked her son's pediatrician to write a prescription and later asked her husband's internist, both of whom agreed because by all appearances Mrs. B was a highly functional, responsible woman. With even less self-confidence, she began taking the drug in anticipation of stressful events. Although Mrs. B was aware that she now needed the medicine to help her nerves and to "manage," at no time did she suspect that she was physically dependent. It was the life-threatening events that followed her emergency appendectomy that made this fact all too clear.

For treatment, Mrs. B was immediately given chlordiazepoxide 100 mg po, then transferred to a detoxification service. On the basis of history, Mrs. B's total daily dose of chlordiazepoxide was estimated to be 100 to 250 mg per day. This total daily dose was divided by 4 and the amount, 50 mg po, was administered every 6 hours for the first 2 days. If Mrs. B appeared sedated at the time of administration, the dose was halved or eliminated; conversely, if Mrs. B appeared apprehensive or tremulous, the dosage was increased by 50 to 100 percent. By the third day, having been stabilized on 200 mg/day, the total daily dose was decreased by 25 mg every other day while "hard" signs (tremor, myoclonic twitches) were monitored as early indications that the withdrawal was too rapid. During this detoxification, Mrs. B was also educated about drug dependency and taught relaxation techniques as an alternative method for controlling her anxiety. She left the hospital after 19 days. No evidence of substance abuse has been apparent during the 8 years since discharge.

This case illustrates several features regarding the development of benzodiazepine dependency: the occurrence in a relatively well-adjusted individual; the rather casual prescribing patterns of physicians; the development of psychological and physical dependency within a few months of taking two to three times the prescribed dose (Covi et al. 1973); the mistaken belief that withdrawal symptoms are signs of an underlying anxiety disorder; the reinforcement of that belief when an anxiolytic relieves the restlessness, dysphoria, and insomnia associated with withdrawal; and the resulting lack of confidence and self-esteem when the patient is unable to manage without medication.

This case also illustrates many features of an acute withdrawal syndrome common to benzodiazepines, barbiturates, alcohol, and methaqualone: discovery in a situation where a patient does not have usual access to the drug; apprehension; a coarse, rhythmic, nonpatterned tremor most evident during voluntary movement; postural hypotension and associated tachycardia (i.e., heart rate increased by 18 beats/minute recumbent to standing); hyperreflexia; muscle cramps; weakness; myoclonic twitches; insomnia with nightmares; the lack of cross-tolerance with narcotics; and ultimately panic; delirium; hallucinatory misperceptions; and seizures that may progress to a fatal status epilepticus. Withdrawal phenomena not shown by Mrs. B include anorexia, vomiting, hyperpyrexia, and cardiovascular collapse. In general, the severity of the withdrawal syndrome increases if more drug is regularly taken, if the drug's half-life is shorter, and if the duration of abuse has been longer (Winokur et al. 1980).

For Mrs. B, detoxification was conducted using the "cumulative test dose" method, and the same drug of abuse was used for withdrawal. In less reliable patients and in those who have abused a drug with a shorter half-life (e.g., triazolam, amytal), the "pentobarbital test dose" method may be preferable. A sober patient is given 200 mg im pentobarbital 4 to 6 hours after last receiving a depressant. Depending on the extent of sedation 1 hour later, an estimate is made of the total daily dose requirement. Shorter-acting depressants are converted to an equivalent dose of phenobarbital, which has a longer half-life and thereby provides a smoother withdrawal as the total daily dose is decreased by 30 mg/day (Smith and Wesson 1971).

Unlike Mrs. B, whose sensorium remained deceptively clear despite increased doses of her anxiolytic, elderly or physically ill patients may present a somewhat different clinical picture when administered depressants. They may appear more relaxed and sleep more soundly the first few days, but as the drug accumulates—particularly those with longer half-lives, such as flurazepam (Dalmane) or diazepam (Valium)—these patients begin to "sundown" (i.e., become more confused in the evening when external structure and stimuli diminish). The resulting agitation and disorientation may mistakenly lead to an increase in the sedative rather than to its discontinuance. For these reasons, the "routine" prescription of hypnotics in nursing homes and hospitals should be avoided. Except for the treatment of transient situational insomnia, the efficacy of these hypnotics is doubtful (Perry and Wu 1984).

☐ HALLUCINOGENS

Mr. E, a 20-year-old college sophomore, is brought to the ER late at night by the police after he was discovered breaking several furniture store windows then smashing the furniture on display. Before being taken to the precinct for arrest, he requires treatment for the lacerations of his face and arms. Because of Mr. E's imbalance, slurred speech, brief bout of vomiting, and seeming indifference to his bleeding, the police and surgeons presume that Mr. E is drunk with alcohol. This impression is supported by Mr. E's behavior during suturing as he laughs along with the nurses and feels no pain.

After the minor surgical procedure, while the chart note is being completed by the nurse, Mr. E sits rigidly on the edge of the bed and appears to "space out" as he stares at his bandages; then unpredictably and with no apparent provocation, he grimaces wildly, hurls the surgical tray against the wall, and starts to strangle the unsuspecting nurse, who fortunately is rescued by the police waiting outside the ER booth. Now slobbering and screaming wildly, Mr. E is restrained face down on a stretcher, and an emergency psychiatric consultation is obtained. The psychiatrist is informed of the recent events and notes the blood pressure of 180/110, dilated pupils, vertical and horizontal nystagmus, muscular rigidity, excessive perspiration, and absence of fever. She administers diazepam 10 mg iv, then clears the room of all other personnel, turns off the light in the ER booth, and sits with Mr. E (who is still restrained), calmly reassuring him whenever body image distortions or visual hallucinatory flashes are described. An hour later, after a repeat of diazepam injection, Mr. E is sufficiently calm to provide a recent history. At a fraternity party that night he had ingested "two tabs of TCP," the thiophene derivative of phencyclidine (PCP). He had taken PCP ("angel dust") once before but at that time only experienced a strange delirious euphoria.

Mr. E agrees to psychiatric hospitalization. The following day he appears moderately depressed, which is at first attributed to his understandable guilt and shame over the events of the previous night. Considering that Mr. E had no prior psychiatric history, that he was calm and cooperative with the staff, and appeared comforted by his fraternity brothers who came during visiting hours, the treating psychiatrist saw no reason to prescribe extra precautions. That night, Mr. E is found hanging by his belt in his room—a fatal suicide attempt.

This case dramatically illustrates the changes induced by arylcyclohexylamine derivatives. The physical changes include ataxia; dysarthria; slightly elevated blood pressure; vomiting; horizontal and vertical nystagmus; grimacing; catatonic posturing with muscular rigidity; numbness and indifference to pain (as well as decreased proprioceptive and temperature sensations); and increased salivation and diaphoresis (in contrast to anticholinergic drugs). The psychological changes include delirious euphoria; unpredictable fluctuations in mood, perceptions, and behavior; impulsivity; body image distortions; visual hallucinations; hyperactivity; self-destructive and violent behavior; and depression with increased suicidal risk during the immediate recovery period (Showalter and Thornton 1977; Tong et al. 1975).

Treatment of the acute phase includes the provision of adequate restraints and a calm environment (Perry and Gilmore 1981). As compared to other drugs, diazepam has the advantage of reducing both agitation and the risk of convulsions without compounding the muscular rigidity (which may occur with haloperidol) and without lowering the seizure threshhold and increasing the confusion (as may occur with phenothiazines).

LSD ("acid," "microdot"), mescaline ("mesc"), peyote ("cactus"), and ketamine (Winters et al. 1972) can induce similar body distortions, depersonalization, and unusual hallucinatory experiences, but are less likely to cause violent behavior and self-inflicted injury. The treatment for toxic reactions usually requires no more than a calm environment, reassurance, and correction of misperceptions when they occur; but benzodiazepines or even haloperidol can be administered acutely for extreme reactions. "Flashbacks," brief recurrent intrusive hallucinatory experiences, may occur months or even years after ingestion of any hallucinogen. Psychoeducation, and not neuroleptics, is generally sufficient if no other psychotic symptoms are present.

☐ INHALANTS

R is a 12-year-old boy referred for psychological evaluation by his seventh-grade math teacher be-

cause of a decline in his performance as well as an apathetic "dazed" classroom behavior. R's wealthy parents, in the midst of a bitterly contested divorce, have assumed that their son's decline is simply a response to that stress. They agree to make arrangements for psychological testing after the principal insists. The Wechsler Intelligence Scale for Children (WISC) reveals a marked discrepancy between superior verbal and only average performance scores. There is also marked "scatter" on subtests, suggesting an organic impairment. Projective tests show a surprising paucity of responses, most of which are depressive in nature. No evidence of autism or psychotic thinking is present.

R is then referred for neurologic evaluation. A mild fine motor incoordination and dysarthia are noted, and the electroencephalogram (EEG) shows very mild diffuse slowing. Hepatic and renal blood tests are normal. No definitive etiology for the subtle deficits can be found. Psychiatric referral is then recommended to help R cope with his cognitive impairment and the turmoil in his family. Again his parents resist and procrastinate. Only after R absolutely refuses to go to summer camp do the parents arrange for psychotherapy, which now R himself rejects. A full year has passed since the math teacher's initial recommendation. By now R has failed all his seventh-grade courses, is repeating the year in a private school, and is living alternately with his mother and father. He has no friends, no interests, and blankly stares at the television night after night without bothering to switch channels. Finally, his father's new (and young) girlfriend suspects what might be going on; she searches through all of R's personal possessions and ultimately discovers in a stereo speaker several full tubes of airplane glue and bottles of liquid correction fluid as well as plastic sandwich bags.

Because of R's disruptive home situation and his cognitive, social, and academic decline, a 2-month psychiatric hospitalization is eventually prescribed and followed by weekly outpatient psychotherapy. After 3 years of remaining drug-free, R's repeat psychological testing, neurologic examination, liver and kidney function, and EEG are all normal.

This case of R illustrates the value of both direct knowledge and a high index of suspicion for diagnosing drug-induced mental changes. Despite consultation with experts, R's problems were ultimately diagnosed by his father's girlfriend. This case also illustrates how drug-induced changes are "typically atypical." Although experimentation with inhaling solvents or paints usually occurs around R's age, other features are unusual; most often these substances are not inhaled ("huffed") on a regular basis for several months, but rather are temporarily abused then discontinued without evidence of withdrawal. If sustained abuse does occur, the toxic effects on the liver or kidney are usually apparent. However, since chronic abuse of inhalants is more common in lower socioeconomic classes, perhaps subtle cognitive changes are not detected until the somatic effects of chronic toxicity have become apparent.

Patients who present in the ER acutely intoxicated by an inhalant at first appear to be drunk with alcohol; however, the correct diagnosis can be made by the smell of the solvent on their breath as well as possible pigmentation around the nose and mouth of the paint or shoe polish that has been inhaled. In extreme cases, excitement, illusions, hallucinations, and delusions occur. Sudden death, probably caused by cardiac arrhythmias, has been reported, such as when an intoxicated sniffer is unexpectedly discovered and attempts to flee. No specific acute treatment is available; antiarrhythmics, neuroleptics, benzodiazepines, and/or reassurance are administered as necessary during the minutes to hours until the sensorium clears.

The abuse by young adolescents of various solvents (and the variety is endless) should not be confused with the inhalation of amyl nitrate by young adults. The contents of "snappers" or "poppers" (the sound of opening the amyl nitrate capsule) are inhaled just prior to orgasm to prolong the pleasurable sensation. Occasionally a dysphoric, panic, or paranoid reaction will occur as the result of the circulatory vasodilation, but these complications are rare (Cohen 1979; Pearlman and Adams 1970).

☐ LITHIUM

Mr. R, a 38-year-old corporate attorney with bipolar affective illness, is admitted to the psychiatric service because of a delusional manic episode. He has had two other such episodes in the past 5 years, each occurring several months after he discontinued his lithium. As in the past, this episode responds within 1 week to rapid tranquilization followed by a resumption of lithium. At his first outpatient visit 1 week after discharge, Mr. R frankly admits that he will "probably" stop taking his lithium at some point in the future because he finds the side effects intolerable in a business that demands creativity and productivity. He feels that the lithium produces an effect that is "like driving a high-powered car with the left foot resting on the brake." When asked to be more specific, he finds it difficult to do so, describing only a vague sense that his memory and concentration are not "sharp." On mental status examination, Mr. R appears alert, facile, and

has no difficulty remembering three items after 3 minutes, reversing 6-digit numbers, or subtracting serial 7s; yet while performing these and other mental tasks, he berates himself for not being able to perform as well as usual. He has a fine nonintentional tremor, which is noticeable but about which he has no complaint. His lithium level is 0.9 mEq/L. All laboratory tests are normal.

This case of Mr. R illustrates the difficulty in diagnosing the mild neuropsychiatric manifestations induced by lithium. Reports have documented the frequency with which the patients complain of symptoms similar to Mr. R's: diminished concentration, memory, and productivity (Jamison et al. 1979; Lund et al. 1982; Schou 1979). Until more recently, clinicians were not sure if these symptoms were directly due to lithium's pharmacologic effects or were more functional in origin (i.e., that patients "missed" the inflated self-esteem and euphoria accompanying hypomanic or manic episodes). This problem was confounded in patients such as Mr. R who might be inclined to blame the lithium for professional or personal failures that were actually the psychosocial consequences of repeated manic or depressive episodes. However, recent neuropsychological studies have examined memory and sensorimotor tasks in patients on and off lithium, using the patient as his or her own control (Shaw et al. 1986). These studies provide persuasive evidence that lithium does indeed induce subtle cognitive changes at nontoxic, therapeutic lithium levels, and that the complaints of patients about lithium's mental side effects are justified. Other side effects, such as nausea and polyuria, are usually transient; if they persist, slow-release preparations of lithium (Eskalith CR or Lithobid) avoid high plasma peaks and may reduce these symptoms. In the event of an incapacitating tremor, atenolol 25 mg tid or qid may be useful. Complaints of headache or blurred vision may be due to pseudotumor cerebri, a rare complication (Saul et al. 1985).

For patients like Mr. R who repeatedly have difficulty in complying with lithium maintenance, the clinician can consider: (1) prescribing lithium at the lowest possible therapeutic dose; (2) prescribing drug "holidays," while following the patient with frequent appointments to observe the prodromal symptoms of hypomania; or (3) trying carbamazepine (Tegretol) at an initial dose of 400 mg/day and gradually increasing as necessary to a maximum of 1600 mg/day while closely observing for clinical and laboratory signs of toxic reactions in the blood or liver.

The manifestations of lithium toxicity are far easier to diagnosis than the subtle changes associated with lithium maintenance. At blood levels between 1.5 and 2.0 mEq/L, many patients experience dysarthria, ataxia, vomiting, and gross tremor. The forgetfulness, disorientation, restlessness, dysphoria, and irritability may be confused by patients and their families with hypomania; however, the recommended treatment is to stop or decrease rather than increase the lithium. As always, prevention is the best cure; patients should be told to discontinue their lithium during bouts of vomiting or diarrhea and prior to elective surgery. When lithium toxicity is more severe, such as following a suicide attempt, serum levels are usually above 2.0 mEq/L. The associated stupor, seizures, and arrhythmias may be life-threatening. Emergency treatment includes (1) gastric lavage if the patient is conscious; (2) infusion of 1500 to 3000 mEq of sodium chloride over 6 hours; and/or (3) hemodialysis.

☐ MARIJUANA

Mr. D, a 17-year-old high school junior, is brought to the ER because of a severe panic reaction at a party following mid-year exams. After a couple of beers, Mr. D began smoking "reefers of Acapulco Gold," something he had done only once or twice previously at a friend's house but without much effect other than "the munchies" and "the giggles." This time, however, Mr. D started to feel as though he were outside his body looking down on himself. He then grew suspicious that others could see that he was "going crazy." His heart began racing and as he grew lightheaded, Mr. D grew convinced that he was having a heart attack. He was rushed to the ER by his peers.

Psychiatric evaluation discloses no prior psychiatric or drug history; in fact, Mr. D has always been regarded by his friends as reserved and in control. Physical examination reveals conjunctival injection, dry mouth, and mild tachycardia, but otherwise no more than an anxious young man who responds to reassurance.

The case of Mr. D illustrates many typical features of a panic reaction induced by cannabis: the occurrence in a relatively stable individual who is inclined to be in control of his environment and who has had little experience with the drug; the simultaneous ingestion of alcohol (or other drugs);

a confusing environment (a rock concert or a large party with strangers); depersonalization; paranoia; tachycardia with palpitations; conjunctival injection; decreased short-term memory; and response to cessation of the drug, to removal from the scene, and to simple reassurance and correction of misperceptions. Panic reactions are unusual; most individuals report a mild euphoria that is associated with diminished short-term memory, a sensation of decreased time, a preoccupation with external and internal stimuli, increased appetite, and a slight apathetic detachment (Grinspoon 1969). In severe toxic reactions, induced by tetrahydrocannabinol (THC), hallucinations may occur, and a paranoid or depersonalization syndrome may persist (Szymanski 1981). Benzodiazepines (e.g., diazepam 10 mg iv) or even neuroleptics (e.g., haloperidol 5 mg po concentrate or im) may then be necessary; but such occurrences remain very rare considering that marijuana is the most widely used illicit drug in the United States (Willette 1976).

The manifestations of chronic use are more controversial. No doubt chronic smoking can cause a decrease in serum testosterone and an increase in bronchitis and precancerous lung lesions. Whether chronic use can in itself lead to social withdrawal and a "light-up, drop-out" amotivational syndrome has not been absolutely documented. Nevertheless, clinical experience suggests that if heavy chronic use continues, apathy and diminished achievement will persist despite psychotherapy (Brill and Christie 1974; Mellinger et al. 1976). If such use is suspected but denied, the patient's urine can be tested for THC metabolites using an enzyme multiple immunoassay (EMIT). Depending on the potency and amount of marijuana taken, urine samples will remain positive (i.e., greater than 100 ng/ml) for several days (Willette 1976).

☐ NEUROLEPTICS

Mr. H, a 32-year-old file clerk with a 9-year history of schizophrenia, is admitted for his third psychotic break 3 months after discontinuing his maintenance neuroleptic, trifluoperazine (Stelazine) 30 mg/day. He stopped the medicine on his own because he believed that it interfered with his concentration at work and with playing chess, his one source of pride and pleasure. After a week of psychiatric hospitalization on trifluperazine 40 mg/day, he remains agitated and spends his days and nights pacing up and down in his room, presumably preoccupied by a persistent delusional preoccupation that his previous girlfriend has spread rumors that he is a homosexual (although Mr. H has not actually admitted to this belief since admission). On psychiatric interview, he complains only of being "depressed." He connects this despair to having a severe illness, to his menial marginal existence, and to his involuntary tongue movements.

In a attempt to diminish his dysphoria and agitation, the psychiatrist increases the trifluperazine to 50 then 60 mg/day. During the next week, Mr. H appears even more restless and less capable of attending activities or interacting on the ward. After a violent altercation with another patient who insisted that Mr. H "sit still," an emergency dose of chlorpromazine 100 mg im is administered. Mr. H is found in bed 3 hours later delirious, rigid, perspiring profusely, and with a blood pressure of 100/60, a respiratory rate of 40, a heart rate of 130, and temperature of 38°C. Mr. H is closely observed; all neuroleptics are discontinued and amantadine HCl 100 mg is given orally twice a day for 2 weeks, and his delirium gradually clears. A month later, Mr. H is discharged on 100 mg chlorpromazine/day with improved functioning and outpatient compliance over the ensuing years.

This case illustrates many chronic and acute neuropsychiatric complications associated with neuroleptics: subjective mental slowing and sedation leading to noncompliance with maintenance medication; tardive dyskinesia; akathisia with restlessness, dysphoria, and impulsivity erroneously attributed to the underlying chronic illness; and a neuroleptic malignant syndrome consisting of delirium, rigidity, diaphoresis, hyperthermia, labile blood pressure, tachycardia, and tachypnea.

As with Mr. H, the subtle cognitive changes induced by maintenance neuroleptics are often difficult to discern in a patient with an underlying psychotic illness. These changes are also difficult to study systematically because of the inherent dangers of discontinuing maintenance medication to see if side effects improve. For this reason, the best evidence for neuroleptic-induced cognitive obtunding comes from studies of patients with Tourette syndrome who are not psychotic (Shapiro and Shapiro 1980). Here there is compelling evidence that phenothiazines and haloperidol affect alertness, motivation, concentration, attention, and memory. These potential cognitive impairments should be explained to patients who may erroneously attribute these symptoms to the underlying disease or to a superimposed secondary depression. Since these deficits are dose related, low daily dosage and/or drug holidays should be prescribed when at all possible.

Tardive dyskinesia, characterized by the relatively late onset of abnormal, persistent movements of the tongue, lips, face, and sometimes trunk, occurs in about half of all patients maintained on neuroleptic therapy, and about half of these are unresponsive to treatment for this movement disorder. The cause is unknown. Currently most favored is the "dopaminergic imbalance theory," which hypothesizes that continuous neuroleptic treatment leads to a supersensitivity of the inhibitory dopamine receptors on the cholinergic neurons of the corpus striatum; alternative theories, however, have been proposed (Richelson 1985). Empirically, many different treatments of tardive dyskinesia have been tried: choline and choline precursors (deanol, lecithin) to increase acetylcholine levels in the central nervous system (CNS); levodopa and amantadine to decrease the supersensitive dopamine receptors; gamma-vinyl gamma-aminobutyric acid (GABA); diazepam; propranolol; baclophen; and reserpine. None of these has proved widely efficacious; therefore, the best treatment at this writing is to use treatments that may be less likely to cause the disorder (clozapine, thioridazine, molindone) and to treat patients in the shortest possible period of time with the lowest possible doses, especially for those patients most at risk (women over 40 years old). The rare "rabbit syndrome," which involves the oral facial muscles, may be confused with tardive dyskinesia; this late onset extrapyramidal side effect does not involve the tongue, however, and does respond to antimuscarinic agents such as benztropine (Cogentin) 2 mg bid (Todd et al. 1984).

As the case of Mr. H. dramatically reveals, akathisia is commonly confused with the underlying psychotic illness. This side effect is characterized not only by fidgeting, pacing, and "restless legs," but also by dysphoria and decreased impulse control, occasionally leading to homicidal or suicidal behavior. This side effect can easily be misinterpreted as an indication for increased neuroleptic dosage, which only makes the symptoms worse. Unlike parkinsonian side effects, akathisias do not respond as well to antimuscarinic agents, antihistamines, or amantadine; therefore, the choice is either to lower the dose of the neuroleptic or to change to one with a lower affinity for dopamine receptors, such as molindone, thioridazine, or chlorpromazine.

The neuroleptic malignancy syndrome illustrated by Mr. H might initially be confused with an acute dystonic reaction in that both occur after neuroleptic administration and are accompanied by muscular rigidity; however, the two adverse reactions have distinguishing characteristics. Acute dystonia, characterized by abrupt muscle spasms of the eye, tongue, and neck, occurs during the first weeks of treatment, especially in young males; is not accompanied by delirium or abnormal vital signs; and responds rapidly to parenteral administration of benztropine (Cogentin) 2 mg or diphenhydramine (Benadryl) 50 mg. In contrast, the neuroleptic malignant syndrome may occur after more prolonged drug administration; is characterized by markedly abnormal vital signs (increased heart and respiratory rate and temperature, labile blood pressure), leukocytosis, and elevated creatine phosphokinase; and is less immediately responsive to treatment (Caroff 1980; Lazarus 1985). Amantadine 100 mg bid (McCarron et al. 1982), bromocriptine (Ayd 1983), and dantrolene (Coons et al. 1982) have been reported to be helpful in a small number of cases, suggesting that the pathophysiology of this disorder is related to dopamine receptor antagonism.

☐ OPIOIDS

Mrs. G, a 56-year-old secretary with insulin-dependent diabetes, is admitted to the surgical service for chronic osteomyelitis of the right foot. Intravenous antibiotics are begun and, for severe pain, meperidine 75 mg im q 3 hours prn is administered. On the fourth hospital day, psychiatric consultation is requested because she has become increasingly dysphoric and irritable, presumably in anticipation of possible amputation. Psychiatric evaluation reveals a cooperative, but excitable woman sobbing in bed. She feels out of control and in no shape for surgery, and has therefore refused to sign informed consent. Normally a pleasant and outgoing woman, she now just wants "to be left alone to die" and snaps at the psychiatrist when he attempts to offer reassurance. Except for some difficulty concentrating when asked serial 7s, Mrs. G has no evidence of cognitive impairment; however, a diffuse tremor and myoclonic twitches are noted in both thighs.

This case illustrates the subtle adverse neuropsychiatric changes that may be associated with meperidine: dysphoria, irritability, and myclonic twitches. Greater toxicity with accumulation of the metabolite normeperidine may lead to seizures and delirium. Changing to another narcotic at equian-

algesic dosages (e.g., morphine 10 mg im) is usually all that is required for treatment.

The adverse mental changes induced by narcotic analgesics are common, yet are generally less appreciated than problems of addiction or overdosage. Although narcotics are presumed to produce euphoria, most patients do not obtain a blissful "rush" with intramuscular or oral administration; in fact, many patients feel dysphoric and nauseated, but tolerate these side effects to obtain pain relief (Perry 1984). The psychotomimetic and depressogenic effects of opioids are also underappreciated; pentazocine (Talwin), for example, can induce an acute schizophrenic-like picture with nightmares, depersonalization, and visual hallucinations. Continuous narcotic administration can induce apathy, withdrawal, and lethargy that may mistakenly be attributed to a psychological reaction to pain or the underlying physical illness, such as cancer.

The neuropsychiatric manifestations of narcotic overdose are far less subtle and rarely missed: severe respiratory depression to the point of apnea in severe cases; possible pulmonary edema secondary to impairment of capillary permeability; and pupillary constriction (although pupils may be dilated if hypoxia is extreme). If the patient arrives in coma and a history cannot be obtained, skin changes associated with intravenous abuse are helpful diagnostically: cigarette burns from "nodding" while under the influence of narcotics; needle puncture marks over superficial veins; "skin popping" subcutaneous abscesses or scars over the upper arm, abdomen, and thigh; skin "tracks" (i.e., linear, discolored brownish streaks found along the course of subcutaneous veins as a result of unsterile injections and deposits of particulate materials); and "shooting tattoos" (i.e., black spots caused by carbon from a repeatedly flamed needle). These skin changes as well as urine samples are also helpful for the diagnosis of chronic narcotic abuse in the denying or lying patient.

Emergency treatment of narcotic overdose includes: open airways; provision of ventilation; and naloxone (Narcan), a narcotic antagonist, 0.4 to 3.0 mg iv. Response is usually obtained within 30 to 50 seconds. Since naloxone's duration of action (½ to 3 hours) is shorter than the depressant action of narcotics (morphine 3 to 8 hours and methadone 24 to 72 hours), close observation is necessary to determine if repeated administration of the antagonist is necessary.

When a narcotic withdrawal syndrome in a physically dependent individual is precipitated by administration of naloxone, an intense withdrawal syndrome may be evident: nausea, vomiting, diarrhea, deep breathing, restlessness, fever, and insomnia. Except in the elderly or physically ill, even this intense withdrawal is usually not life-threatening and, if necessary, can be rapidly reversed by parenteral administration of a short-acting narcotic at one-fourth the total equivalent daily dosage. The withdrawal symptoms that occur after stopping of narcotics vary greatly with specific agent, dosage, intervals between dosage, duration of use, and the psychological state of the patient. The earliest symptom is anxiety, usually manifested by drug-seeking behavior, which reaches its peak intensity by 36 to 72 hours after the last narcotic administration. During the first 10 hours of withdrawal, the individual experiences perspiring, rapid short respirations, slight rhinorrhea and lacrimation, and dilated reactive pupils. During the second 10 hours, the signs and symptoms include more marked lacrimation and rhinorrhea; increased heart rate; tremor; abdominal pain with nausea, vomiting, and diarrhea; fever; elevated blood pressure; and leukocytosis. The "goose flesh" are due to piloerecta stimulation from which the term *cold turkey* arose. Severe muscular spasms in the legs are less common, although the term *kicking the habit* persists. Despite the subjective complaints of addictive individuals during withdrawal, most symptoms are not intolerable if adequate support is provided. Often missed are the long-term consequences of physical dependence, including irritability, fatigue, and depression, which may last for several months. Also missed are withdrawal syndromes precipitated when a narcotic with agonist-antagonist characteristics (pentazocine) is administered to a physically dependent patient with a chronic painful illness. Withdrawal symptoms, and perhaps opioid craving, may be abated by clonidine 5 μg/kg bid (Gold et al. 1978).

☐ STEROIDS

Psychiatric consultation is requested for Miss A, a 38-year-old district bank manager, who has become increasingly depressed since being hospitalized 1 week ago for acute low back pain with bilateral reflex changes. The referring neurologist suspects that Miss A, "a compulsive hard worker," cannot accept the necessary imposed bed rest; he further suspects her depression may also stem from "personal problems—no husband, no children, that kind of stuff."

During the psychiatric interview, Miss A cries fitfully when discussing any subject, past or present, that is the least bit upsetting. She states, "I just don't know what's come over me" and explains that she has always prided herself for being "level-headed." She reveals no serious emotional problems in the past, but is now afraid she will "flip out" if she does not calm down and get some sleep. She does not complain, however, of much back pain ("just some spasms") and is not hopeless about her physical recovery in that "the same disc slipped" a few years ago and improved with no medication and 2 weeks of bed rest at home. No cognitive impairment is noted.

Chart review discloses that since admission Miss A has received prednisone 75 mg/day to diminish the acute inflammation and possibly to reduce residual scarring. When Miss A is told that she is experiencing a common toxic reaction to steroids, her dysphoria is reduced and her pride restored. Over the next week, the daily dosage of prednisone is decreased to 30 mg, and Miss A's "depression" resolves.

The case of Miss A illustrates several features of steroid-induced mental changes: insomnia, lability of affect, egodystonic alteration in mood, unimpaired cognitive functioning, and a reduction of symptoms at a prednisone dose below 40 mg/day (Whybrown and Hurwitz 1976). Euphoria with increased appetite is also a common effect of steroid administration, and delirium can occur. Depending on the study and the methods used, the frequency of psychiatric symptoms in patients receiving corticosteroids ranges between 5 and 30 percent. In general, the risk increases with dosage, a history of a prior steroid-induced episode, and a personal or family history of affective illness. However, many patients have no apparent neuropsychiatric manifestations even at very high doses (1000 mg prednisone/day); toxic reactions on one occasion then not on another; a history of a serious psychiatric illness yet no exacerbations of psychopathology while on steroids; or, conversely, no psychiatric history and marked steroid-induced mental changes. For these reasons, the research in this area is quite confusing; different methods within different patient populations yield different results. Whatever their incidence, if and when psychotic symptoms do emerge, they respond to dose reduction or, if medically infeasible, to neuroleptics (e.g., haloperidol 5 to 15 mg/day) (Hall et al. 1979). Lithium prophylaxis has been recommended to diminish subsequent reactions (Falk et al. 1979). Another alternative, if medically feasible, is to prescribe salicylates or nonsteroidal antiinflammatory drugs (e.g., phenylbutazone, indomethacin, diflunisal), although the latter also have neuropsychiatric side effects (e.g., dysphoria, disorientation, drowsiness, and hallucinations) (Stimmel 1983).

When steroids are administered to treat a disease that affects the CNS, the diagnosis of drug-induced mental change is more difficult to make. For example, when psychotic symptoms occur in patients receiving prednisone for systemic lupus erythematosus, the tendency is to attribute these mental phenomena to the drug and to reduce the dose. However, available studies indicate that if psychotic symptoms arise in the presence of active CNS disease and if they are accompanied by a delirium with misperceptions, then steroids are more likely to be the solution and not the cause; that is, *increased* steroid dosage may be necessary to treat the etiologic cerebritis with neuroleptics administered temporarily until psychotic symptoms resolve (Perry 1986).

Depressions that are milder and more insidious in their development than Miss A's have been associated with oral contraceptives. The exact incidence is not known because the affective changes are subtle and either do not come to medical attention or are attributed to some other cause; a conservative estimate is that some drug-induced alteration in mood occurs in at least 5 percent of women who use or have used oral contraceptives (Fleming and Seager 1978, Weissman and Klerman 1977).

☐ STIMULANTS

Mr. C, a 40-year-old recently fired corporate manager, is referred for psychiatric consultation by his lawyer 3 weeks before a grand jury investigation in which Mr. C is accused of embezzling company funds. The lawyer wants psychiatric advice because he cannot understand what caused his client to change in just 2 years from a conscientious businessman intensely devoted to his firm and family into an irresponsible, impulse-ridden criminal. The lawyer also does not know why Mr. C, despite obvious emotional distress, has continually put off seeking psychiatric help until the last minute before the trial.

During the psychiatric evaluation, Mr. C appears a thin, restless man who states from the start that he has come only because his lawyer threatened to drop the case if Mr. C did not keep the appoint-

ment. In a coherent but guarded manner, Mr. C adds that he doubts the psychiatrist can be of much help because his former partner will arrange for Mr. C to be convicted by bribing the judge; this ex-partner will then be able to continue more freely the extramarital affair he is currently having with Mr. C's wife. Despite Mr. C's conviction that this partner is "out to get me," the patient can offer little evidence to support this belief other than the fact that Mr. C did take a swing at his partner during a business meeting 4 months ago, one of the several such incidents that prompted Mr. C's dismissal—after which the missing corporate funds were discovered.

Although Mr. C minimizes any emotional difficulties and repeatedly deflects the psychiatric inquiry, he does admit to chronic insomnia and a weight loss of 15 pounds during the past year. No cognitive changes are noted, including adequate memory recall. Physical examination reveals a slightly masked facies; heart rate of 130; blood pressure of 180/100; dilated but reactive pupils; thin, ulcerated nasal mucosa; worn teeth; brisk reflexes; and a mild parkinsonian tremor.

In a concerned but straightforward manner, the psychiatrist informs Mr. C that he reveals many signs of cocaine abuse for which an effective treatment can be provided. Mr. C vehemently denies any such problem, is now convinced the psychiatrist is in collaboration with his ex-partner, and abruptly leaves the office. A month later Mr. C is indicted and ultimately convicted, and he enters a rehabilitation drug program. He thereafter remains drug-free by regularly attending a self-help group (Cocaine Anonymous), but a moderate depression persists for 2 years as he attempts to repair his professional and personal life.

The case of Mr. C illustrates several common features associated with chronic cocaine abuse: personality change; impaired judgment; impulsive, aggressive, and antisocial behavior; hypervigilance and suspiciousness developing into a fixed delusional belief; denial of substance abuse and emotional problems; anorexia with weight loss; insomnia; restlessness; irritability; tachycardia; hypertension; pupillary dilatation; inflamed nasal mucosa from repeated inhalation; worn teeth from bruxism; hyperreflexia; masked facies; and a tremor that, in Mr. C's case, had slight parkinsonian characteristics.

The case also reveals that chronic cocaine abuse can insidiously lead to a picture that closely resembles a paranoid functional disorder. The physical manifestations may be quite subtle or absent, and the delusions can occur in a clear state of consciousness without cognitive impairment. Furthermore, if hallucinations are present, they may be only auditory in nature (Siegel 1978). In a more cooperative patient, however, a careful history may also disclose the occurrence of visual, olfactory, and (especially) tactile hallucinations (i.e., formication, "cocaine bugs"). A similar clinical picture can be seen with chronic abuse of amphetamines (Snyder 1973), methylphenidate, and appetite suppressants such as phenmetrazine (Preludin) and diethylpropion (Tenuate).

Because of the magnificent feelings of confidence and euphoria that occur almost immediately following inhalation, intravenous injection, or smoking ("free-basing") cocaine, the addictive potential of cocaine is extraordinarily great. This euphoria appears to be mediated by the dopamine system; cocaine blocks the synaptic reuptake of dopamine, resulting in increased postsynaptic receptor stimulation (Ross and Renyi 1966). This addictive potential is then reinforced by the "crash" into a dysphoric state when administration of cocaine is discontinued. The depression during withdrawal in chronic cocaine abusers may derive from dopamine depletion (Taylor and Ho 1977). Individuals like Mr. C may therefore have a pharmacologic basis for going to self-destructive extremes in order to obtain cocaine and to avoid any treatment in which access will be denied. Recent reports have indicated that bromocriptine (a dopamine receptor agonist) may be effective in treating both cocaine craving and the symptoms of cocaine withdrawal (Dackis and Gold 1985). Bromocriptine 0.625 to 1.25 mg tid may help stabilize several neurochemical disruptions induced by continuous cocaine administration: hyperprolactinemia, dopamine depletion, and increased dopamine receptor binding.

An acute delirious state may occur in both the naive cocaine experimenter as well as in the chronic user. This delirium is more easily diagnosed than chronic abuse: the obvious confusion and disorientation are accompanied by life-threatening hypertension, hyperpyrexia, systemic acidosis, and potential convulsions and cardiovascular collapse. A fever above 39° C should be vigorously treated with both hypothermic blankets and ice packs to reduce the risk of convulsions. If seizures do occur, intravenous diazepam 5 to 20 mg every 15 to 45 minutes will help prevent status epilepticus. To treat the agitation and frightening visual, tactile, olfactory, and auditory hallucinations, the patient should be removed to a quiet area free of the excessive external stimuli so common in emergency rooms. Neuroleptics (haloperidol 5 to 15 mg oral concentrate q 2 hours prn) may be given if frank psychotic symptoms persist; however, perhaps as a result of dopamine depletion, chronic cocaine abusers may be very sensitive to the extrapyramidal side effects of neuroleptics. These dopamine antagonists may actually increase cocaine craving during the first few weeks of abstinence. Because an untreated, severe hypertensive crisis can lead to a subdural or subarachnoid hemorrhage, propranolol may be necessary if the systolic blood pressure remains above 200 mmHg for an hour or more despite the measures described above.

☐ CONCLUSION

This chapter has illustrated the challenge of diagnosing and treating substance-induced organic mental disorders. The case vignettes remind us that simply memorizing common and severe adverse drug reactions, although helpful, is not sufficient. The drug-induced mental changes are often subtle, idiosyncratic, insidious, egosyntonic, and confounded by the patient's situation, psychodynamics, psychopathology, physical illness, and misrepresentation of what substances have been used or abused. Ironically, the knowledge of how drugs adversely affect thinking, memory, perception, mood, personality, and behavior may prove to be an invaluable tool for understanding and treating neuropsychiatric disorders that are not drug-induced.

☐ REFERENCES

Abramowicz M (ed): Drugs that cause psychiatric symptoms. Med Lett Drugs Ther 23:9, 1981

American Psychiatric Association: Diagnostic and Statistical Manual of Mental Disorders, 3rd ed, revised. Washington, DC, American Psychiatric Association, 1987

Ayd FJ: Bromocriptine therapy for the neuroleptic malignant syndrome. Drug Therapy News 18:33, 1983

Brill NQ, Christie RL: Marijuana use and psycho-social adaptation. Arch Gen Psychiatry 31:713–719, 1974

Bunce DFM II, Jones LR, Badger LW, et al: Medical illness in psychiatric patients: barrier to diagnosis and treatment. South Med J 75:941, 1982

Bunney WE: Psychopharmacology of the switch process in affective illness, in Psychopharmacology: A Generation of Progress. Edited by Lipton MA, DiMascio A, Killam KF. New York, Raven Press, 1978

Caroff S: The neuroleptic malignant syndrome. J Clin Psychiatry 41:79–83, 1980

Cohen S: Inhalants, in Handbook on Drug Abuse. Edited

by Dupont R, Goldstein A, O'Donnell J. Washington, DC, National Institute on Drug Abuse, 1979

Coons DJ, Hillman FJ, Marshall RW: Treatment of neuroleptic malignant syndrome with dantrolene sodium: a case report. Am J Psychiatry 139:944, 1982

Covi L, Lippmann HH, Pattison JH, et al: Length of treatment with anxiolytic sedatives and response to their sudden withdrawal. Acta Psychiatr Scand 49:51–64, 1973

Dackis CA, Gold MS: Bromocriptine as a treatment of cocaine abuse. Lancet 1:1151–1152, 1985

Falk W, Mahnke MW, Poskanzer DC: Lithium prophylaxis of corticotropin-induced psychosis. JAMA 241:1011–1012, 1979

Fleming O, Seager C: Incidence of depressive symptoms in users of oral contraceptives. Br J Psychiatry 132:432–440, 1978

Gold MS, Redmond E Jr, Kleber HD: Clonidine blocks acute opiate withdrawal symptoms. Lancet 2:599–602, 1978

Greenblatt D, Shader R: Anticholinergics. N Engl J Med 288:1215–1219, 1973

Grinspoon L: Marijuana. Sci Am 221:17–25, 1969

Guggenheim FG, Erman MK: Medication-induced psychiatric symptoms and disorders, in Psychiatry. Edited by Michels R. New York, JB Lippincott Co, 1985

Hall RCW, Popkin MW, De Vaul RA, et al: Physical illness presenting as psychiatric disease. Arch Gen Psychiatry 35:1315, 1978

Hall RCW, Popkin MK, Stickney SK, et al: Presentation of the steroid psychoses. J Nerv Ment Dis 167:229, 1979

Hall RCW, Stichney SK, Gardner E: Behavioral toxicity of nonpsychiatric drugs, in Psychiatric Presentations of Medical Illness: Somatopsychic Disorders. Edited by Hall RCW. Jamaica, NY, Spectrum Publications, 1980, pp 337–349

Hall RCW, Gardner ER, Popkin MK, et al: Unrecognized physical illness prompting psychiatric admission: a prospective study. Am J Psychiatry 138:629, 1981

Hoffman RS: Diagnostic errors in the evaluation of behavioral disorders. JAMA 248:964, 1982

Jamison KR, Gerner RH, Goodwin FK: Patient and physician attitudes toward lithium. Arch Gen Psychiatry 36:866–869, 1979

Johnson DAW: Drug-induced psychiatric disorders. Drugs 22:57–69, 1981

Koranyi EK: Morbidity and rate of undiagnosed physical illnesses in a psychiatric population. Arch Gen Psychiatry 36:414, 1979

Lazarus A: Neuroleptic malignant syndrome: detection and management. Psychiatric Annals 15:715–725, 1985

Leeman CP: Diagnostic errors in emergency room medicine: physical illness in patients labeled "psychiatric" and vice versa. Int J Psychiatry Med 6:533, 1975

Lipowski ZJ: Intoxication with medical drugs, in Delirium. Edited by Kugelmass IN. Springfield, Ill, Charles C Thomas, 1980, pp 255–316

Lund Y, Nissen M, Rafaelsen OJ, et al: Long-term lithium treatment and psychological functions. Acta Psychiatr Scand 65:233, 1982

McCarron MM, Boettger ML, Peck JJ: A case of neuro-

leptic malignant syndrome successfully treated with amantadine. J Clin Psychiatry 43:381, 1982

Mellinger GD, Somers RH, Davidson ST, et al: The amotivational syndrome and the college student. Ann NY Acad Sci 282:37–55, 1976

Paykel ES, Fleminger R, Watson JP: Psychiatric side effects of antihypertensive drugs other than reserpine. J Clin Psychopharmacol 2:14, 1982

Pearlman J, Adams G: Amyl nitrite inhalation fad. JAMA 212:160, 1970

Perl M, Hall RCW, Gardner E: Behavioral toxicity of psychiatric drugs, in Psychiatric Presentations of Medical Illness: Somatopsychic Disorders. Edited by Hall RCW. Jamaica, NY, Spectrum Publications, 1980, pp 311–336

Perry S: Classical management of postop pain with narcotics. Infection in Surgery 3:115–124, 1984

Perry S: Psychiatric aspects of SLE, in Systemic Lupus Erythematosus. Edited by Lahita R. New York, John Wiley & Sons, 1986

Perry S, Cella DF: Missed diagnosis of OMS in hospitalized medical patients. Am J Psychiatry 142:525–526, 1985

Perry S, Gilmore, M: The disruptive patient or visitor. JAMA 245:755–757, 1981

Perry S, Wu A: Rationale for the use of hypnotic agents in a general hospital. Ann Intern Med 100:441–446, 1984

Petrie W, Maffucci R, Woosley R, et al: Propranolol and depression. Am J Psychiatry 139:92–93, 1982

Physicians' Desk Reference (PDR) (40th ed). Oradell, NJ, Medical Economics Co, 1986

Pottash A, Black HR, Gold MS: Psychiatric complications of antihypertensive medications. J Nerv Ment Dis 169:430–438, 1981

Preskorn SH, Irwin HA: Toxicity of tricyclic antidepressants: kinetics, mechanism, intervention: a review. J Clin Psychiatry 43:151–156, 1982

Richelson E: Schizophrenia: treatment, in Psychiatry. Edited by Michels R. Philadelphia, JB Lippincott Co, 1985

Risch SC, Groom GP, Janowsky DS: Interfaces of psychopharmacology and cardiology: II. J Clin Psychiatry 42:47–59, 1981

Ross SB, Renyi AL: Uptake of some tritiated sympathomimetic amines by mouse brain cortex in vitro. Acta Pharmacol Toxicol (Copenh) 24:297–309, 1966

Saul RF, Hamburger HA, Selhorst JB: Pseudotumor cerebri secondary to lithium carbonate. JAMA 253:2869, 1985

Schou M: Artistic productivity and lithium prophylaxis in manic-depressive illness. Br J Psychiatry 135:97–103, 1979

Shader RI (ed): Psychiatric Complications of Medical Drugs. New York, Raven Press, 1972

Shapiro AK, Shapiro ES: Tics, Tourette Syndrome and Other Movement Disorders. Bayside, NY, Tourette Syndrome Association, 1980

Shaw ED, Mann JJ, Stokes PE, et al: Effects of lithium carbonate on associative productivity and idiosyncrasy in bipolar outpatients. Am J Psychiatry 143:1166–1169, 1986

Showalter CV, Thornton WF: Clinical pharmacology of phencyclidine toxicity. Am J Psychiatry 134:1234–1238, 1977

Siegel RK: Cocaine hallucinations. Am J Psychiatry 135:309–314, 1978

Smith DE, Wesson DR: Phenobarbital technique for treatment of barbituate dependence. Arch Gen Psychiatry 25:56–60, 1971

Snyder S: Amphetamine psychosis. Am J Psychiatry 130:61–67, 1973

Stern T: Continuous infusion of physostigmine in anticholinergic delirium: case report. J Clin Psychiatry 44:463–464, 1983

Stimmel B: Pain, Analgesia, and Addiction. New York, Raven Press, 1983

Szymanski HV: Prolonged depersonalization after marijuana use. Am J Psychiatry 138:231–233, 1981

Taylor D, Ho BT: Neurochemical effects of cocaine following acute and repeated injection. J Neurosci Res 3:95–101, 1977

Todd R, Lippman S, Manshadi M, et al: Recognition and treatment of rabbit syndrome, uncommon complication of neuroleptic therapies. Am J Psychiatry 140:1519–1520, 1984

Tong TG, Benowitz NL, Becker CE, et al: Phencyclidine poisoning. JAMA 234:512, 1975

Tune LE, Strauss ME, Lew MF, et al: Serum levels of anticholinergic drugs and impaired recent memory in chronic schizophrenic patients. Am J Psychiatry 139:1460, 1982

Weiss HD, Walker MD, Wiernik PH: Neurotoxicity of commonly used antineoplastic agents: I and II. N Engl J Med 291:75–81, 128–133, 1974

Weissman MM, Klermann GL: Sex differences and the epidemiology of depression. Arch Gen Psychiatry 34:98, 1977

Whybrow PC, Hurwitz T: Psychological disturbance associated with endocrine disease and hormone therapy, in Hormones, Behavior and Psychopathology. Edited by Sacher EJ. New York, Raven Press, 1976, pp 125–143

Willette R (ed): Cannabinoid Assays in Humans. NIDA Research Monograph Series No 7. Rockville, MD, National Institute of Drug Abuse, 1976

Winokur A, Rickels K, Greenblatt OJ, et al: Withdrawal reactions from long-term, low dosage administration of diazepam. Arch Gen Psychiatry 37:101–105, 1980

Winters WD, Ferrer-Allado T, Guzman-Flores C: The cataleptic state induced by ketamine: a review of the neuropharmacology of anesthesia. Neuropharmacology 11:303–315, 1972

Zavodnick S: Psychopharmacology, in Psychiatric Emergencies. Edited by Dubin WR, Hanke N, Nickens HW. New York, Churchill Livingstone, 1984

Section
III

Neuropsychiatric
Disorders

Chapter 10

Neuropsychiatric Aspects of Traumatic Brain Injury

Jonathan M. Silver, M.D.

Stuart C. Yudofsky, M.D.

Robert E. Hales, M.D.

EACH YEAR IN THE UNITED STATES over 500,000 people suffer severe traumatic injuries to the brain (Frankowski et al. 1985). A far larger number are afflicted with the chronic sequelae of such injuries. In this population, the psychosocial and psychological deficits are a major source of disability to the victim and of stress to the families. The psychiatrist is often called on by other medical specialists or by families to treat these patients. In this chapter, the role of the psychiatrist in the prevention, diagnosis, and treatment of the cognitive, behavioral, and emotional aspects of central nervous system (CNS) injury will be reviewed.

☐ EPIDEMIOLOGY

It is commonly taught in introductory courses in psychiatry that suicide is the second most common

cause of death in persons under 35 years of age. What is often not stated is that the number one cause of death in this population is automobile accidents. In the United States in 1984, there were 46,200 automobile-related deaths (National Safety Council 1985). These accidents resulted in 1,700,000 disabling injuries. Approximately 70 percent of automobile-related deaths result from head trauma (Poleck 1967). It has been estimated that 500,000 cases of brain injury occur per year (Frankowski et al. 1985). Of these cases 30 to 50 percent are associated with moderate to severe brain injury or are fatal; 5 to 10 percent of the survivors have residual neurologic dysfunction. In an epidemiologic survey conducted in San Diego County in which the incidence and etiology of brain damage were studied, it was found that 44 percent of brain injuries were secondary to motor vehicle accidents, 21 percent from falls, 12 percent from assaults, 10 percent from sports, and 6 percent from firearms (Kraus et al. 1984). The incidence of brain injuries in the United States of 180 per 100,000 population is approximately one and one-half times the incidence of schizophrenia.

The economic cost of brain injury is staggeringly high. Hartunian et al. (1980) compared the economic costs of various illnesses and found that the total economic cost per year for cancer was 23.1 billion dollars; for motor vehicle injuries 14.4 billion dollars; for heart disease 13.7 billion dollars; and for stroke 6.5 billion dollars.

Children are highly vulnerable in accidents as passengers and, as pedestrians, to falls, to impacts from moving objects, (e.g. rocks or baseballs), and to sports injuries (Hendrick et al. 1965). It has been estimated that as many as 5 million children sustain head injuries each year; of this group, 200,000 children are hospitalized (Raphaely et al. 1980). Prolonged hospitalization is required for 15,000 children, with 2 to 5 percent of these remaining severely handicapped. Four thousand children per year die as a result of head trauma.

Statistics form only a piece of the picture of the cost of traumatic brain injury. As psychiatrists, we deal with individuals and families who have suffered such tragic events. The psychological and social disability after head injury can be dramatic. Studies examining the psychosocial functioning and adjustment at 1 month, 2 years, or 7 years after injury have shown that patients have extreme difficulties in a number of areas of functioning, including work, school, leisure, and recreational activities, and suffer from extreme personality changes (Crawford 1983; McLean et al. 1984; Oddy et al. 1985; Weddell et al. 1980).

As opposed to many other common neurologic and psychiatric disorders, many severe injuries are potentially preventable. Thus all practitioners, in their roles as advisors and authority figures, should encourage preventive measures. To focus solely on the accurate diagnosis and state-of-the-art treatment of head injury is short-sighted and incomplete. Prevention of brain injury will be discussed later in this chapter.

□ ETIOLOGY

Brain injury may arise from many etiologies. Almost any portion of the brain, especially the frontal regions, may be injured by direct impact on the skull during automobile, motorcycle, or bicycle accidents. Powerful shearing forces incurred by the brain during deceleration in automobile accidents may severely damage frontal or temporal lobes. Falls may produce acute or chronic subdural hematomas. Gunshot wounds and other penetrating injuries may cause focal damage. Extensive discussions of the pathophysiology, mechanisms, and assessment of severity of head injury can be found elsewhere (Becker and Povlishock 1985; Brooks 1984; Cooper 1982; Levin et al. 1982). Although brain injuries subsequent to serious automobile, occupational, or sports accidents may not result in diagnostic enigmas for the psychiatrist, less severe trauma may first present as relatively subtle behavioral or affective change. Prototypic examples of brain damage in which the patient, while providing a history, may fail to associate with the traumatic event include the alcoholic who is amnestic for a fall that occurred while inebriated; the 10-year-old boy whose head was hit while falling from his bicycle, but who fails to inform his parents; or the wife who was beaten by her husband, but who is either fearful or ashamed to report the injury to her family physician. Such trauma may be associated with confusion, intellectual changes, affective lability, or psychosis; and the patient may first present to the psychiatrist for evaluation and treatment.

Patients with affective illness, with problems of substance abuse, with impulse disorders, and with characterologic disorders (such as antisocial, borderline, and narcissistic personality disorders) are prone to the taking of risks. Representative examples include: the suicidally depressed patient who drives at high speeds under the influence of alcohol; the irritable manic patient who provokes a fight in a bar; and the construction worker with narcissistic personality disorder who takes unnecessary risks and refuses to wear protective gear in order to capture the attention and admiration of co-workers. Sports such as boxing, football, rugby, ice hockey, skydiving, mountain climbing, hang gliding, and professions such as law enforcement, fire fighting, and above-ground construction not only attract risk-takers but also result in a disproportionately high incidence of head trauma. Psychiatrists should be aware that self-destructive behavior may be camouflaged by the violence, contact, and other dangers inherent in such activities.

Guns and war give rise to a significant amount of serious head trauma. In the United States, 50 percent of reported suicides in men and 25 percent of reported suicides in women are from gunshot wounds. Homicides and assaults in the United States involve guns in an exponentially higher number of cases than in countries where handguns are strictly prohibited. In some surveys, gunshot wounds accounted for 20 to 40 percent of cases of head trauma (Frankowski et al. 1985). In a study of World War II veterans, those victims of penetrating head injury who develop subsequent posttraumatic epilepsy have a decreased life expectancy compared to those with penetrating head injury without epilepsy or patients with peripheral nerve injuries (Corkin et al. 1984). The psychiatrist is often reluctant to inquire of the ownership of or access to weapons, especially by the violent, paranoid, or impulsive patient. These patients, as well as others with diagnoses of affective illness, substance abuse disorders, and antisocial personalities, should be encouraged by the psychiatrist to dispose of their weapons prior to a crisis. This may prove to be a life-saving intervention.

☐ CLINICAL FEATURES

The prognosis for recovery in the brain-injured patient has been found to be dependent on several factors. Levin et al. (1982) reviewed this topic extensively. At the time the patient with acute brain injury presents to the hospital, a poorer outcome is seen in patients with impaired bilateral pupillary response, physical underactivity or agitation, or increased age. The duration of posttraumatic amnesia is correlated with subsequent cognitive recovery.

Personality Changes

Prominent behavioral traits such as disorderliness, suspiciousness, argumentativeness, isolativeness, disruptiveness, and anxiousness become more pronounced with brain injury (Fordyce et al. 1983; Oddy et al. 1985; Thomsen 1984). For example, the affective lability of the borderline patient may intensify to the point that previous feelings of sadness and depression become life-threatening suicidal or self-mutilative behaviors. Nonpsychiatric physicians may dismiss these behaviors as "crazy and intolerable"; however, the alert psychiatrist will detect from a careful history and mental status examination that an exacerbation of preexisting

psychopathology has occurred that is not fully explained by social or psychological events. As always, when discrete mental changes cannot be traced to specific stresses, an organic etiology must be suspected and explored.

Because of the vulnerability of the prefrontal and frontal regions of the cortex to injury, specific changes in personality known as the frontal lobe syndrome are not uncommon. In the prototypic patient with frontal lobe syndrome, the cognitive functions of the patient are preserved while personality changes abound. These changes include decreased motivation, impaired social judgment, and labile affect. Patients may display uncharacteristic lewdness, inability to appreciate the effects of their behavior or remarks on others, a loss of social graces (such as eating manners), a lack of attention to personal appearance and hygiene, and boisterousness. In addition, impaired judgment may be prominent and take the form of diminished concern for the future, an increase in risk taking, unrestrained drinking of alcoholic beverages, and indiscriminate selection of food. Patients may appear shallow, indifferent, or apathetic, with a global lack of concern for the consequences of their behavior. This syndrome is labeled organic personality syndrome in DSM-III-R (American Psychiatric Association 1987).

Intellectual Changes

Problems with intellectual functioning may be among the most subtle manifestations of brain injury. Changes may occur in the capacity to concentrate, use language, abstract, calculate, reason, remember, and process information (Barth et al. 1983; Levin et al. 1985; Stuss et al. 1985). Many children who survive severe head trauma and return to school may still have mild behavioral and learning problems (Mahoney et al. 1983). Children who have suffered mild head injuries showed neuropsychological sequelae when carefully tested (Gulbrandsen 1984). These intellectual changes, even if not perceptible to others, influence the social rehabilitation of the head-injured patient (Tyerman and Humphrey 1984). The results of several studies suggest that a long-term sequelae of brain trauma may include Alzheimer's disease (Amaducci et al. 1986; Heyman et al. 1984; Mortimer et al. 1985). Thus DSM-III-R categorization of these intellectual changes may include dementia and amnestic syndrome.

Affective Changes

Preexisting affective illnesses are aggravated by brain injuries. Head trauma, like other stresses, precipitates manic or depressive states in patients with bipolar illness. Others may develop major depressive episodes de novo subsequent to the brain damage (Robinson and Szetela 1981). Mania also has been reported as a sequel to head trauma (Sinanan 1984). These are conditions classified as an organic affective syndrome in DSM-III-R. Patients whose affective illness fails to respond to aggressive psychiatric treatment, and patients who exhibit side effects at relatively low doses of psychotropic medications or other drugs that affect the brain, may have CNS lesions.

Psychotic Changes and Delirium

Posttraumatic psychoses can occur either immediately following brain injury, or after a latency of many months of normal functioning. The psychiatrist is often consulted as the brain-injured patient is emerging from coma. At that time, the patient may be restless, agitated, confused, disoriented, delusional, or hallucinatory. Delirium is a frequent mental change associated with subdural hematomas (Black 1984). Although usually summoned to manage the behavior of the patient, the psychiatrist should be aware that the patient's agitation or psychosis may be secondary to etiologies other than the trauma that initiated the coma. In the acute phase of the injury, delusions (organic delusional syndrome) or hallucinations (organic hallucinosis) have many possible etiologies. The etiologies of psychoses or delusions in patients emerging from coma include fluid and electrolyte imbalance, side effects of medications, environmental factors such as sensory monotony or decreased oxygen levels, infections, disorders of blood, blood viscosity, and intoxication or withdrawal from drugs that were being administered prior to the traumatic event.

Psychosis that occurs after a span of time subsequent to trauma may be more difficult to diagnose and to treat. Such psychoses may be associated with posttraumatic seizures that develop in 5 percent of patients with closed head injuries and 50 percent of those patients with compound skull fractures and wounds of the brain (Adams and Victor 1985). While only 1 percent of posttraumatic seizures occur within moments of the injury, the remainder occur from 1 to 3 months after the injury

(Adams and Victor 1985). Hillbom (1960) surveyed a large number of patients whose head injuries occurred during war. He found that left-sided injuries were more often associated with psychiatric illness, in particular with psychosis. Salazar et al. (1985) studied Vietnam veterans who had suffered penetrating head injuries; 53 percent had posttraumatic epilepsy. In 18 percent, the first seizure was after 5 years; in 7 percent, the first seizure was after 10 years. In addition, 26 percent of those with epilepsy had an organic mental syndrome as defined in DSM-III (American Psychiatric Association 1980). Lishman (1978) reported that patients with schizophrenic-like symptoms subsequent to brain injury may be "indistinguishable" from symptoms of the "naturally occurring" disorder. These symptoms may persist despite improvement in cognitive deficits caused by the trauma (Nasrallah et al. 1981). Reviews of the literature revealed 1 to 15 percent of schizophrenic inpatients have a history of head injury (Davison and Bagley 1969). It must be recalled that DSM-III-R criteria for schizophrenia exclude those cases for which traumatic brain injury is the known etiology. The correct DMS-III-R diagnosis in such cases would be organic delusional syndrome or organic hallucinosis.

Aggression

In those patients who suffer brain injury, irritability and aggressiveness are a major source of disability to the victim and of stress to their families. In a review of 26 patients with severe traumatic closed head injury, 25 exhibited more than one agitated behavior in the acute period after trauma; 11 remained agitated during the rehabilitation phase (Rao et al. 1985). Even as long as 7 years after injury, 31 percent of patients stated that they often lost their temper, and 43 percent of relatives characterized them as impatient (Oddy et al. 1985). McKinlay et al. (1981) found that irritability and aggressiveness occur in as many as 70 percent of the people who suffer brain damage from blunt trauma. In reviewing the histories of 286 patients with recurrent attacks of uncontrolled rage, Elliott (1982) found that 94 percent had objective evidence of developmental or acquired brain defects, and many of these patients had a history of head injury.

Explosive and violent behavior have long been associated with focal brain lesions as well as with diffuse damage to the CNS (Elliott 1976). DSM-III classified the condition as intermittent explosive disorder and placed the category under disorders of impulse control not elsewhere classified. Other names for this syndrome include episodic dyscontrol syndrome, disinhibition syndrome, and explosive personality disorder. DSM-III maintained that "an underlying physical disorder, such as brain tumor or epilepsy, may in rare cases cause this syndrome" (p. 297). This is inconsistent with the broad range of clinical experience in which organic etiologies were the most common source of this condition. Thus DSM-III-R reflects this clinical reality and calls this syndrome organic personality disorder, explosive type, which is classified as an organic mental disorder. The authors submit that the most accurate label would be organic aggressive syndrome. Table 1 summarizes the suggested criteria for organic aggressive syndrome. The basic reason for proposing this diagnostic classification is that it more accurately describes the specific condition of dyscontrol of rage and violence secondary to the brain lesions and avoids reference to the variety of emotional and behavioral changes described in the DSM-III-R classification. The disadvantages of including these personality changes as has been proposed in the DSM-III-R schema is that these changes are largely related to injury to the prefrontal and frontal areas of the brain, whereas damage to many other cortical and subcortical structures (i.e., lesions in midbrain) may also lead to dyscontrol of aggression without the associated personality disturbances specified in DSM-III-R.

☐ TREATMENT

For the large number of people who are brain injured, there are many useful therapeutic approaches available. Although we propose a multifactoral and a multidisciplinary approach to treatment, we have, for purposes of exposition, divided treatment into psychopharmacologic, behavioral, psychological, and social interventions.

Psychopharmacologic Treatment

Psychopharmacologic treatments of brain injury are directed toward associated symptomatologies. The most important general principle is that patients with brain injury of any type are far more likely to be sensitive to the effects of medication than the non-brain-injured population. For example, disabling sedative and anticholinergic side effects from

TABLE 1. DIAGNOSTIC CRITERIA FOR ORGANIC AGGRESSIVE SYNDROME AS PROPOSED BY AUTHORS

- Persistent or recurrent aggressive outbursts, either of a verbal or physical nature
- The outbursts are out of proportion to the precipitating stress or provocation
- Evidence from history, physical examination, or laboratory tests of a specific organic factor that is judged to be etiologically related to the disturbance
- The outbursts are *not* primarily related to symptoms or disorders such as paranoia, mania, schizophrenia, narcissistic personality disorder, borderline disorder, conduct disorder, or antisocial personality disorder

thioridazine (Mellaril) or amitriptyline (Elavil and others) occur at doses much lower than those used in the non-brain injured. Included with anticholinergic side effects is memory impairment, which may be seen at relatively low doses of medications. In the brain-injured patient, doses of psychotropic medications must be raised and lowered in small increments over protracted periods of time.

Affective Illness. Affective disorder related to brain damage is common and destructive to a patient's rehabilitation and socialization. The published literature is sparse regarding the effects of antidepressant agents in the treatment of patients with brain damage and, specifically, traumatic brain injury. In a study examining the effects of antidepressants in the treatment of depression after minor closed head injury, amitriptyline and phenelzine were both ineffective, with no improvement detected in 10 patients (Saran 1985). In contrast, all 12 non-brain-injured control patients had an improvement in their depression. The depressed mood in the brain-injured patients was not worse in the morning, there was no significant weight loss, and there was no marked psychomotor agitation or retardation.

As a rule, patients with traumatic brain injury and depressed mood should have a therapeutic trial with antidepressants. Those antidepressants with the fewest sedative, hypotensive, and anticholinergic side effects are preferred. We suggest nortriptyline, with initial doses of 10 mg per day, or desipramine (10 mg three times a day), and a careful monitoring of plasma levels for the parent compound and its major metabolites. Should the patient become sedated, confused, or severely hypotensive, the dosage of these drugs should be reduced. Antidepressant benefit may be obtained with one-third to one-half of the standard treatment dose. Except for those patients with increased intracranial pressure and brain tumors, electroconvulsive therapy (ECT) remains a highly effective and underutilized modality for the treatment of patients with both depression and brain damage. In our experience, nondominant unilateral ECT—using pulsatile currents, increased spacing of treatments (2 to 3 days between each treatment), and fewer treatments in an entire course (4 to 6)—results in amelioration of depressive symptomatology without major memory deficit side effects.

Lithium has been reported to aggravate confusion in patients with brain damage (Schiff et al. 1982), as well as to induce nausea, tremor, ataxia, and lethargy. We limit the use of lithium to those patients with mania, and to patients with recurrent depressive illness that preceded brain damage. Carbamazepine (Tegretol) is effective in the treatment of patients with bipolar illness (Ballenger and Post 1980). However, the use of this medication to treat mania in patients with brain damage has yet to be examined.

Psychosis. In treating patients with psychosis resulting from brain injury, principles similar to those detailed for antidepressants should be followed. In addition to problems of hypotension, sedation, and confusion, psychotic patients with brain injury are particularly subject to severe dystonias, akathisias, and parkinsonian side effects when even relatively low doses of antipsychotic medications are used. If patients show agitation with psychosis, aliphatic phenothiazines such as chlorpromazine (in doses beginning at 5 mg three times a day) might be attempted. In this instance, therapeutic use is made of the sedative side effect of chlorpromazine in order to treat the agitation. In less agitated patients, piperazine phenothiazines such as fluphenazine (Prolixin 0.5 mg twice a day) or the butyrophenone haloperidol (Haldol 0.5 mg twice a day) may be tried.

Anxiety. Anxiety is a common symptom in patients with brain injury. We prefer to treat the anxiety of brain-injured patients with supportive psychotherapy and social interventions. When the symptoms are so severe that they require pharmacologic intervention, possible side effects of benzodiazepines such as sedation and amnesia need

to be kept in mind. Sleep patterns of patients with brain damage are often impaired; therefore, barbiturates, alcohol, and long-acting minor tranquilizers should be used with caution because of their interference with rapid eye movement (REM) and stage 4 sleep patterns. Short-acting benzodiazepines can be given if those agents are indicated. Clinicians should advise patients against using over-the-counter preparations for sleeping and for colds because of the prominent anticholinergic side effects of these remedies.

Aggression. Patients with organic aggressive syndrome are most often treated and, in the opinion of the authors, mistreated with antipsychotic medications. Antipsychotic drugs are appropriate for the management of aggressive disorders that are secondary to psychotic ideation, and are frequently the agents of choice for this condition. However, for aggression related to organic dyscontrol it is often the sedative side effects of these agents rather than their antipsychotic properties that are being utilized. The clinical result is the emergence of side effects, including oversedation, parkinsonian symptoms, and akathisias. Frequently, tolerance to the sedative effects of these agents occurs, and the doses are continuously increased. Of significant concern in utilizing antipsychotic agents in the management of chronic aggression is the possible emergence of tardive dyskinesia. In addition, many antipsychotic agents lower the seizure threshold and ultimately may exacerbate a patient's organic dyscontrol of rage and violence. Although others have suggested antipsychotic drugs such as haloperidol in the treatment of agitation with closed head injury (Rao et al. 1985), we recommend the use of antipsychotic agents only for the management of aggression stemming from psychotic ideation or for the intermittent management of brief aggressive events related to organic dyscontrol.

Sedatives and hypnotics have also been employed to manage aggression. This category includes barbiturates, antihistamines, benzodiazepines, and agents such as paraldehyde and chloral hydrate. Several of the agents in this category may lead to dependency and to aggravation of concomitant depression. The response of aggressive behavior to treatment with benzodiazepines is inconsistent. For example, both paradoxical induction of rage (Byrd 1985; Rosenbaum et al. 1984) and amelioration of aggression (Freinhar 1985) have been reported. If sedation is necessary in the management of the patient, agents such as paraldehyde, chloral hydrate, or diphenhydramine should be used in place of sedative antipsychotic agents. Intramuscular lorazepam has been suggested as an effective medication in the emergency treatment of the violent patient (Bick and Hannah 1986).

Several medications have been suggested for the chronic treatment of organic aggressive syndrome. There have been isolated case reports on the management of agitation after head injury with lithium carbonate (Haas and Cope 1985). As stated previously, however, some patients with brain damage tolerate lithium poorly (Schiff et al. 1982). Jackson et al. (1985) reported on the efficacy of amitriptyline for the treatment of agitation after head injury. Anticonvulsants such as carbamazepine have been suggested for the treatment of organic aggressive syndrome (Folks et al. 1982; Hakoloa and Laulumaa 1982; Luchins 1983; Mattes 1984; Mattes et al. 1984; Neppe 1982; Tunks and Demer 1977). In a review by Roy-Byrne et al. (1984), the recommended doses for the treatment of aggressive dyscontrol averaged 600 mg per day in divided doses of 200 mg.

Beta-adrenergic blocking agents have been advocated for the treatment of uncontrolled rage and violent outbursts secondary to brain damage (Elliott 1977; Greendyke et al. 1984; Mansheim 1981; Mattes 1984, 1985; Petrie and Ban 1981; Polakoff et al. 1986; Ratey et al. 1983, 1985, 1986; Schreier 1979; Silver and Yudofsky 1986; Williams et al. 1982; Yudofsky et al. 1981, 1984). Silver and Yudofsky (1985) reviewed 10 published reports comprising 59 patients whose uncontrolled outbursts responded to propranolol. In this literature, all patients had some form of brain damage and all reports were case studies or retrospective chart reviews. The doses of propranolol to which the patients responded were generally lower than 640 mg per day, with a median dosage of 100 mg per day. Response times vary from less than 2 days to more than 6 weeks. Since propranolol, when combined with thioridazine, may elevate thioridazine levels into the potentially toxic range, this drug combination should be avoided (Silver et al. 1986). Table 2 summarizes the clinical use of propranolol in the management of the aggressive patient.

Controlled treatment studies of organic aggressive syndrome are difficult due to the severe nature of the aggressive outbursts. Placebo-controlled prospective treatment studies have not been done. In addition, aggressive behaviors had not

TABLE 2. CLINICAL USE OF PROPRANOLOL

1. Conduct a thorough medical evaluation.
2. Exclude patients with the following disorders: bronchial asthma, chronic obstructive pulmonary disease, insulin-dependent diabetes mellitus, congestive heart failure, persistent angina, significant peripheral vascular disease, hyperthyroidism.
3. Avoid sudden discontinuation of propranolol (particularly in patients with hypertension, to avoid rebound hypertension).
4. Begin with a single test-dose of 20 mg per day in patients for whom there are clinical concerns about hypotension or bradycardia. Increase dose of propranolol by 20 mg per day every 3 days.
5. Initiate propranolol on a 20 mg tid schedule for patients without cardiovascular or cardio-pulmonary disorder.
6. Increase the dosage of propranolol by 60 mg per day every 3 days.
7. Increase medication until the pulse rate is reduced below 50 bpm, or systolic blood pressure is less than 90 mmHg.
8. Do not administer medication dose if severe dizziness, ataxia, or wheezing occurs. Reduce or discontinue propranolol if such symptoms persist.
9. Increase dose to 12 mg/kg or until aggressive behavior is under control.
10. Note that doses of greater than 800 mg are not usually required to control aggressive behavior.
11. Maintain the patient on the highest dose of propranolol for at least 8 weeks prior to concluding that the patient is not responding to the medication. Some patients, however, may respond rapidly to propranolol.
12. Utilize concurrent medications with caution. Monitor plasma levels of all antipsychotic and anticonvulsive medications.

been operationally defined or documented. Yudofsky et al. (1986) developed The Overt Aggression Scale to assist in the assessment and documentation of aggressive behaviors for research purposes. Table 3 provides a summary of the spectrum of aggressive events as abstracted from The Overt Aggression Scale.

Behavioral Treatments

Behavioral treatments are essential in the care of patients who have suffered traumatic brain injury. These programs require careful design and execution by a staff well-versed in behavioral techniques. One study has found the behavior modification approach 75 percent effective in dealing with disturbed behaviors after severe brain in-

TABLE 3. THE SPECTRUM OF AGGRESSIVE BEHAVIOR

Verbal Aggression
Makes loud noises, shouts angrily
Yells mild personal insults (e.g., "You're stupid")
Curses viciously, uses foul language in anger, makes moderate threats to others or self
Makes clear threats of violence toward others or self ("I'm going to kill you") or requests help to control self

Physical Aggression Against Objects
Slams door, scatters clothing, makes a mess
Throws objects down, kicks furniture without breaking it, marks the wall
Breaks objects, smashes windows
Sets fires, throws objects dangerously

Physical Aggression Against Self
Picks or scratches skin, hits self, pulls hair (with no or minor injury only)
Bangs head, hits fist into objects, throws self onto floor or into objects (hurts self without serious injury)
Small cuts or bruises, minor burns
Mutilates self, makes deep cuts, bites that bleed, internal injury, fracture, loss of consciousness, loss of teeth

Physical Aggression Against Other People
Makes threatening gesture, swings at people, grabs at clothes
Strikes, kicks, pushes, pulls hair (without injury to them)
Attacks others, causing mild or moderate physical injury (bruises, sprain, welts)
Attacks others, causing severe physical injury (broken bones, deep lacerations, internal injury)

Note. Abstracted from The Overt Aggression Scale (Yudofsky et al. 1986).

jury (Eames and Wood 1985). The reader is directed to text on behavior modification, as well as to specific articles on behavior techniques in the treatment of aggressive behaviors and other behavioral abnormalities (Liberman and Wong 1984).

Psychological and Social Interventions

In the broadest terms, psychological issues involving patients who incur brain injury revolve around four major themes: psychopathology that preceded the injury, psychological response to the traumatic event, psychological reactions to deficits of brain injury, and psychological issues related to potential recurrence of brain injury. In our experience, preexisting psychiatric illnesses are intensified by brain injury. Therefore, for example, the angry patient, the patient suffering from depression, or the

paranoid patient will exhibit an increase in these traits after brain injury. Although attention, concentration, and intellectual functions are often diminished in patients with brain injury, one must not underestimate the usefulness of psychological and psychotherapeutic approaches. The injured brain may often respond to traditional psychosocial approaches. Therefore, a thorough assessment of the capacity of a patient to benefit from psychological treatment is essential.

The events surrounding the traumatic experience often have far-reaching experiential and symbolic significance for the patient. Such issues as guilt, punishment, magical wishes, and fears crystallize about the nidus of the traumatic event. Patients retain complex psychological responses to brain injury. Tyerman and Humphrey (1984) assessed 25 severely head-injured patients for changes in self-concept and symptoms of anxiety and depression. Patients commonly had evidence of anxiety and depression. In addition, they viewed themselves as markedly changed after their head injury, but believed that they would return to their premorbid self within a year. The authors concluded that these unrealistic expectations may hamper rehabilitation and adjustment of both the patient and the relatives.

The psychiatrist should not neglect the psychological responses of the patient's family who also experience the shock of an adjustment to the brain injury of a loved one. Oddy et al. (1978) evaluated 54 relatives of patients with brain injury within 1, 6, and 12 months of the traumatic event. Approximately 40 percent of the relatives showed depressive symptomatologies within 1 month of the event; 25 percent of the relatives showed significant physical or psychological illness within 6 and 12 months of the brain damage. Mood disturbances, especially anxiety, and social role dysfunction are seen within this time (Livingston et al. 1985a, 1985b). By treating the psychological responses of relatives to the brain injury, the clinician can foster a supportive and therapeutic atmosphere for the patient.

A patient's reactions to being disabled by brain damage may have concrete as well as symbolic significance. When intense effort is required for a patient to form a word or to move a limb, frustration may be expressed as anger, depression, anxiety, or fear. Particularly in cases in which brain injury results in permanent impairment, a psychiatrist may experience countertransferential discomfort resulting in failure to discuss directly the patient's disabilities and limitations. Gratuitous optimism, collaboration with denial of the patient, and facile solutions to complex problems are rarely effective and can erode ongoing treatment. By gently and persistently directing the patient's attention to the reality of the disabilities, the psychiatrist may help the patient to begin the process of acceptance and adjustment to the impairment. Clinical judgment will help the psychiatrist in deciding whether explorations of the symbolic significance of the patient's brain injury should be pursued. The persistence of anxiety, guilt, and fear beyond the normative stages of adjustment and rehabilitation may indicate that psychodynamic approaches are required.

It is a distressing fact that many of the most severe types of brain injury recur. Trauma from accidents occurs more commonly in patients who have already suffered from such events than in those who have not. Therefore, patients' fears and anxieties about recurrence of brain injury are more than just efforts at magical control over terrifying situations. Therapeutic emphasis should be placed on those actions that will aid in preventing recurrence.

☐ PREVENTION OF BRAIN INJURY

Motor Vehicle Accidents

According to all responsible sources, the proper use of seat belts with upper torso restraints is 50 to 65 percent effective in the prevention of fatalities and injuries; this would translate to 12,000 to 16,000 lives saved per year (National Safety Council 1985). It is calculated that the installation of air bag safety devices in automobiles would save from 3,000 to 7,000 lives per year (National Safety Council 1985). Without specific legislation, car restraints are used infrequently (less than 10 percent) (Haddon and Baker 1981). The recent action by many state legislatures in mandating the use of car restraints has increased the use of safety belts.

Alcohol dependence is a highly prevalent and destructive illness. In addition, alcohol abuse is a common concomitant of affective and characterologic disorders. Alcohol intoxication is frequently seen in the patient who has suffered brain injury, whether from violence, falls, or motor vehicle accidents (Brismar et al. 1983). In the United States, it is estimated by the National Safety Council that

alcohol ingestion is implicated in more than 50 percent of all automobile-related fatalities (Haddon and Baker 1981). Drivers in fatal accidents have a more frequent history of alcohol use, previous accidents, moving traffic violations, psychopathology, stress, paranoid thinking, and depression. They often have had less control of hostility and anger, with a decreased tolerance for tension and a history of increased risk taking (Tsuang et al. 1985). Therefore, in all psychiatric and other medical histories, a detailed inquiry about alcohol use, seat belt use, and driving patterns is essential. Examples of driving patterns are accident records, violations, driving while intoxicated, speeding patterns, car maintenance, presence of distractions such as children and animals, hazardous driving conditions, and so forth. As of June 1985, 13 states had enacted legislation mandating the use of seat belts; 18 states have rejected those proposals (National Safety Council 1985). Initial seat belt use after enactment of those laws is high, but decreases with time. It is too early to assess the effectiveness of these laws. The use of illicit substances and medications that may induce sedation—such as antihistamines, antihypertensive agents, anticonvulsants, minor tranquilizers, and antidepressants—should also be assessed.

Clearly, motorcycle riding—with or without helmets—and bicycles for commuting purposes are associated with head injuries, even when safety precautions are taken and when driving regulations are observed. Significant preventive measures to reduce head trauma include counseling a patient about risk taking, the treatment of alcoholism and depression, the judicious prescription of medications and full explanations of sedation and other potentially dangerous side effects, and public information activities such as the proper use of seat belts, the dangers of drinking and driving, and automobile safety measures.

Prevention of Brain Injury in Children

Beyond nurturance, children rely on their parents or guardians for guidance and protection. Each year in the United States over 1,400 children under 13 years of age die as motor vehicle passengers; more than 90 percent of these children were not using car seat restraints (Insurance Institute of Highway Safety 1983). Child safety seats have been found to be 80 to 90 percent effective in the prevention of injuries to children (National Safety Council 1985).

In a sample of children younger than 4 years old who had suffered motor vehicle accident trauma, 70 percent had been unrestrained, 12 percent were restrained with seat belts, and 22 percent were restrained in child safety seats. In general, restrained children tended to sustain less serious injuries than the unrestrained children (Agran et al. 1985). Children less than 4 years old who are not restrained in safety seats are 11 times more likely to be killed in motor vehicle accidents (National Safety Council 1985). It is not safe for the child to sit on the lap of the parent, as the adult's weight can crush the child during an accident. Young children traveling with drivers who are not wearing seat belts are four times as likely to be left unrestrained (National Safety Council 1985). Legislation in Britain mandating the use of child safety seats has had a significant effect on decreasing fatal and serious injuries to children (Avery and Hayes 1985). In the United States, all 50 states and the District of Columbia have mandatory laws for child safety seats (National Safety Council 1985).

The clinician must always be alert to the possibility that patients may be neglectful, may utilize poor judgment, and may even be directly violent in their treatment of children. Unfortunately, it is not uncommon for head trauma to result from overt child abuse on the part of parents, other adults, and peers. We encourage direct counseling of patients who do not consistently use infant and child car seats for their children.

☐ CONCLUSION

Invariably, brain injury leads to emotional damage in the patient and in the family. In this chapter, we have reviewed the most frequently occurring psychiatric symptomatologies from traumatic brain injury. We have emphasized how the informed psychiatrist is not only effective but also essential in the prevention of brain injury and the treatment of its sequelae. We advocate, in addition to increased efforts devoted to the prevention of brain injury, a multidisciplinary and multidimensional approach to the assessment and treatment of psychiatric aspects of brain injury.

☐ REFERENCES

Adams RD, Victor M: Principles of Neurology, 3rd ed. New York, McGraw-Hill, 1985

Agran PF, Dunkle DE, Winn DG: Motor vehicle accident trauma and restraint usage patterns in children less than 4 years of age. Pediatrics 76:382–386, 1985

Amaducci LA, Fratiglioni L, Rocca WA, et al: Risk factors for clinically diagnosed Alzheimer's disease: a case control study of an Italian population. Neurology 36:922–931, 1986

American Psychiatric Association: Diagnostic and Statistical Manual of Mental Disorders, 3rd ed. Washington, DC, American Psychiatric Association, 1980

American Psychiatric Association: Diagnostic and Statistical Manual of Mental Disorders, 3rd ed, revised. Washington, DC, American Psychiatric Association, 1987

Avery JG, Hayes HRM: Death and injury to children in cars: Britain. Br Med J 291:515, 1985

Ballenger JC, Post RM: Carbamazepine in manic-depressive illness: a new treatment. Am J Psychiatry 137:782–790, 1980

Barth JT, Macciocchi SN, Giordani B, et al: Neuropsychological sequelae of minor head injury. Neurosurgery 13:529–533, 1983

Becker DP, Povlishock JT (ed): Central Nervous System Trauma Status Report 1985. Bethesda, MD, National Institutes of Health, National Institute of Neurological and Communicative Disorders and Stroke, 1985

Bick PA, Hannah AL: Intramuscular lorazepam to restrain violent patients. Lancet 1:206, 1986

Black DW: Mental changes resulting from subdural hematoma. Br J Psychiatry 145:200–203, 1984

Brismar B, Engstrom A, Rydberg U: Head injury and intoxication: a diagnostic and therapeutic dilemma. Acta Chir Scand 149:11–14, 1983

Brooks N (ed): Closed Head Injury: Psychological, Social, and Family Consequences. New York, Oxford University Press, 1984

Byrd JC: Alprazolam-associated rage reaction. J Clin Psychopharmacol 5:186–188, 1985

Cooper PR: Head Injury. Baltimore, Williams & Wilkins, 1982

Corkin S, Sullivan EV, Carr A: Prognostic factors for life expectancy after penetrating head injury. Arch Neurol 41:975–977, 1984

Crawford C: Social problems after severe head injury. NZ Med J 96:972–974, 1983

Davison K, Bagley CR: Schizophrenic-like psychoses associated with organic disorders of the central nervous system: a review of the literature, in Current Problems in Neuropsychiatry: Schizophrenia, Epilepsy, the Temporal Lobe. Edited by Herrington RN. Br J Psychiatry [special publication no. 4], 1969

Eames P, Wood R: Rehabilitation after severe brain injury: a follow-up study of a behavior modification approach. J Neurol Neurosurg Psychiatry 48:613–619, 1985

Elliott FA: The neurology of explosive rage. Practitioner 217:51–59, 1976

Elliott FA: Propranolol for the control of belligerent behavior following acute brain damage. Ann Neurol 1:489–491, 1977

Elliott FA: Neurological findings in adult minimal brain dysfunction and the dyscontrol syndrome. J Nerv Ment Dis 170:680–687, 1982

Folks DG, King LD, Dowdy SB, et al: Carbamazepine treatment of selective affectively disordered inpatients. Am J Psychiatry 139:115–117, 1982

Fordyce DJ, Roueche JR, Prigatano GP: Enhanced emotional reactions in chronic head trauma patients. J Neurol Neurosurg Psychiatry 46:620–624, 1983

Frankowski RF, Annegers JF, Whitman S: Epidemiological and descriptive studies part 1: the descriptive epidemiology of head trauma in the United States, in Central Nervous System Trauma Status Report. Edited by Becker DP, Povlishock JT. Bethesda, Md, National Institute of Neurological and Communicative Disorders and Stroke, 1985

Freinhar JP: Clonazepam treatment of a mentally retarded woman. Am J Psychiatry 142:1513, 1985

Greendyke RM, Schuster DB, Wooton JA: Propranolol in the treatment of assaultive patients with organic brain disease. J Clin Psychopharmacol 4:282–285, 1984

Gulbrandsen GB: Neuropsychological sequelae of light head injuries in older children 6 months after trauma. J Clin Neuropsychol 6:257–268, 1984

Haas JF, Cope N: Neuropharmacologic management of behavior sequelae in head injury: a case report. Arch Phys Med Rehabil 66:472–474, 1985

Haddon JW, Baker SP: Injury control, in Preventive and Community Medicine. Edited by Clark D, McMahn B. Boston, Little, Brown and Co, 1981

Hakoloa HP, Laulumaa VA: Carbamazepine in treatment of violent schizophrenics. Lancet 1:1358, 1982

Hartunian NS, Smart CN, Thompson MS: The incidence and economic cost of cancer, motor vehicle injuries, coronary heart disease and stroke: a comparative analysis. Am J Public Health 70:1249–1260, 1980

Hendrick EB, Harwood-Hash DCF, Hudson AR: Head injuries in children: a survey of 4465 consecutive cases at the Hospital for Sick Children, Toronto, Canada. Clin Neurosurg 11:46–65, 1965

Heyman A, Wilkinson WE, Stafford JA, et al. Alzheimer's disease: a study of epidemiological aspects. Ann Neurol 15:335–341, 1984

Hillbom E: After-effects of brain injuries. Acta Psychiatrica et Neurologica Scandinavica Supplement 142:1–195, 1960

Insurance Institute for Highway Safety: Children in Crashes. Washington, DC, Insurance Institute for Highway Safety, May 1983

Jackson RD, Corrigan JD, Arnett JA: Amitriptyline for agitation in head injury. Arch Phys Med Rehabil 66:180–181, 1985

Kraus JF, Black MA, Hessol N, et al: The incidence of acute brain injury and serious impairment in a defined population. Am J Epidemiol 119:186, 1984

Levin HS, Benton AL, Grossman RG: Neurobehavioral Consequences of Closed Head Injury. New York, Oxford University Press, 1982

Levin HS, High WM, Meyers CA, et al: Impairment of remote memory after closed head injury. J Neurol Neurosurg Psychiatry 48:556–563, 1985

Liberman RP, Wong SE: Psychiatric uses of behavioral analysis and therapy procedures related to seclusion and restraint, in The Psychiatric Uses of Seclusion and Restraint. Edited by Tardiff K. Washington DC, American Psychiatric Press, 1984

Lishman WA: Organic Psychiatry: The Psychological Consequences of Cerebral Disorder. London, Blackwell Scientific, 1978

Livingston MG, Brooks DN, Bond MR: Patient outcome in the year following severe head injury and relatives' psychiatric and social functioning. J Neurol Neurosurg Psychiatry 48:876–881, 1985a

Livingston MG, Brooks DN, Bond MR: Three months after severe head injury: psychiatric and social impact on relatives. J Neurol Neurosurg Psychiatry 48:870–875, 1985b

Luchins DJ: Carbamazepine for the violent psychiatric patient. Lancet 2:766, 1983

Mahoney WJ, D'Souza BJ, Haller JA, et al: Long-term outcome of children with severe head trauma and prolonged coma. Pediatrics 71:756–762, 1983

Mansheim P: Treatment with propranolol of the behavioral sequelae of brain damage. J Clin Psychiatry 42:132, 1981

Mattes JA: Carbamazepine for uncontrolled rage outbursts. Lancet 2:1164–1165, 1984

Mattes JA: Metoprolol for intermittent explosive disorder. Am J Psychiatry 142:1108–1109, 1985

Mattes JA, Rosenberg J, Mays D: Carbamazepine versus propranolol in patients with uncontrolled rage outbursts: a random assignment study. Psychopharmacol Bull 20:98–100, 1984

McKinlay WW, Brooks DN, Bond MR, et al: The short-term outcome of severe blunt head injury as reported by the relatives of the injured person. J Neurol Neurosurg Psychiatry 44:527–533, 1981

McLean A Jr, Dikmen S, Temkin N, et al: Psychosocial functioning at 1 month after head injury. Neurosurgery 14:393–399, 1984

Mortimer JA, French LR, Hutton JT, et al: Head injury as a risk factor for Alzheimer's disease. Neurology 35:264–267, 1985

Nasrallah HA, Fowler RC, Judd LL: Schizophrenia-like illness following head injury. Psychosomatics 22:359–361, 1981

National Safety Council: Accident Facts. Chicago, National Safety Council, 1985

Neppe VM: Carbamazepine in the psychiatric patient. Lancet 2:334, 1982

Oddy M, Humphrey M, Uttley D: Stresses upon the relatives of head-injured patients. Br J Psychiatry 133:507–513, 1978

Oddy M, Coughlan T, Tyerman A, et al: Social adjustment after closed head injury: a further follow-up seven years after injury. J Neurol Neurosurg Psychiatry 48:564–568, 1985

Petrie WM, Ban TA: Propranolol in organic agitation. Lancet 1:324, 1981

Polakoff SA, Sorgi PJ, Ratey JJ: The treatment of impulsive and aggressive behavior with nadolol. J Clin Psychopharmacol 6:125–126, 1986

Poleck DG: The body: what happens to it in a crash. Traffic Safety Magazine, April 1967

Rao N, Jellinek HM, Woolston DC: Agitation in closed head injury: haloperidol effects on rehabilitation outcome. Arch Phys Med Rehabil 66:30–34, 1985

Raphaely RC, Swedlow DB, Downes JJ, et al: Management of severe pediatric head trauma. Pediatr Clin North Am 27:715–727, 1980

Ratey JJ, Morrill R, Oxenkrug G: Use of propranolol for provoked and unprovoked episodes of rage. Am J Psychiatry 140:1356–1357, 1983

Ratey JJ, Mikkelsen EJ, Smith B, et al: β-blockers in the severely and profoundly mentally retarded. J Clin Psychopharmacol 6:103–107, 1986

Robinson RG, Szetela B: Mood change following left hemispheric brain injury. Ann Neurol 9:447–453, 1981

Rosenbaum JF, Woods SW, Groves JE, et al: Emergence of hostility during alprazolam treatment. Am J Psychiatry 146:792–793, 1984

Roy-Byrne PP, Uhde TW, Post RM: Carbamazepine for aggression, schizophrenia, and non-affective syndromes. International Drug Therapy Newsletter 19:9–12, 1984

Salazar AM, Jabbari B, Vance SC, et al: Epilepsy after penetrating head injury: I. clinical correlates: a report of the Vietnam head injury study. Neurology 35:1406–1414, 1985

Saran AS: Depression after minor closed head injury: role of dexamethasone suppression test and antidepressants. J Clin Psychiatry 46:335–338, 1985

Schiff HB, Sabin TD, Geller A, et al: Lithium in aggressive behavior. Am J Psychiatry 139:1346–1348, 1982

Schreier HA: Use of propranolol in the treatment of postencephalitic psychosis. Am J Psychiatry 136:840–841, 1979

Silver JM, Yudofsky SC: Propranolol for aggression: literature review and clinical guidelines. International Drug Therapy Newsletter 20:9–12, 1985

Silver JM, Yudofsky SC: Propranolol in the treatment of chronically hospitalized violent patients, in Biological Psychiatry (1985 ed). Edited by Shagass C, Josiassen RC, Bridger WH, et al. New York, Elsevier, 1986

Silver JM, Yudofsky SC, Kogan M, et al: Elevation of thioridazine plasma levels by propranolol. Am J Psychiatry 143:1290–1292, 1986

Sinanan K: Mania as a sequel to a road traffic accident. Br J Psychiatry 144:330–331, 1984

Stuss DT, Ely P, Hugenholtz H, et al: Subtle neuropsychological deficits in patients with good recovery after closed head injury. Neurosurgery 17:41–47, 1985

Thomsen IV: Late outcome of very severe blunt head trauma: a 10-15 year second follow-up. J Neurol Neurosurg Psychiatry 47:260–268, 1984

Tsuang MT, Boor M, Fleming JA: Psychiatric aspects of traffic accidents. Am J Psychiatry 142:538–546, 1985

Tunks ER, Demer SW: Carbamazepine in the dyscontrol syndrome associated with limbic dysfunction. J Nerv Ment Dis 164:56–63, 1977

Tyerman A, Humphrey M: Changes in self-concept following severe head injury. Int J Rehabil Res 7:11–23, 1984

Weddell R, Oddy M, Jenkins D: Social adjustment after rehabilitation: a two year follow-up of patients with severe head injury. Psychol Med 10:257–263, 1980

Williams DT, Mehl R, Yudofsky S, et al: The effect of propranolol on uncontrolled rage outbursts in children and adolescents with organic brain dysfunction. J Am Acad Child Psychiatry 21:129–135, 1982

Yudofsky SC, Williams D, Gorman J: Propranolol in the treatment of rage and violent behavior in patients with chronic brain syndromes. Am J Psychiatry 138:218–220, 1981

Yudofsky SC, Stevens L, Silver J, et al: Propranolol in the treatment of rage and violent behavior associated with Korsakoff's psychosis. Am J Psychiatry 141:114–115, 1984

Yudofsky SC, Silver JM, Jackson W, et al: The Overt Aggression Scale for the objective rating of verbal and physical aggression. Am J Psychiatry 143:35–39, 1986

Chapter 11

Neuropsychiatric Aspects of Cerebrovascular Disease

Robert G. Robinson, M.D.
Alfred W. Forrester, M.D.

CEREBROVASCULAR DISEASE REPRESENTS ONE of the major health problems in the United States, with an annual incidence for thromboembolic stroke estimated to be between 300,000 and 400,000 (Wolf et al. 1977). During the past few years, however, there has been a steady decline in the incidence of stroke, which is presumed to be related to the improved control of hypertension. Nevertheless, stroke remains behind heart disease and cancer as the third leading cause of mortality and morbidity in this country.

The neuropsychiatric complications of cerebrovascular disease include a wide range of emotional and cognitive disturbances. The major difficulty in providing a comprehensive review of this field is the relatively few empirical data that are known about individual neuropsychiatric disorders or their relationship to specific types of cerebrovascular disease. These data have begun to emerge only within the last few years; it is essential before we will have a firm empirical data base for our understanding of the clinical manifestations, treatments, and mechanisms of these disorders.

The other complicating factor in our understanding of neuropsychiatric disorders associated with cerebrovascular disease is the tendency of investigators to intermix different types of brain disorders when studying emotional problems in brain-injured patients. For instance, the early work of Babinski (1914) or Denny-Brown et al. (1952), as well as the systematic study of emotional disorders in brain-injured patients by Gainotti (1972), included patients with a variety of types of brain injuries such as traumatic, closed head injury; penetrating head injury; thromboembolic stroke; surgical incisions; and intracerebral hemorrhage. Although it is generally assumed that neuronal death produced by a variety of mechanisms will result in

The authors would like to thank Drs. Thomas R. Price, John R. Lipsey, Kenneth L. Kubos, Krishna Rao, and Godfrey Pearlson, and Ms. Lyn Book Starr, who participated in many of the studies described. This work was supported in part by the following National Institutes of Health grants: Research Scientist Development Award (RGR) MH00163, NS15178, NS18622, NS15080, and T32NH15330.

similar clinical symptoms, depending on the size and location of the lesion, that is not necessarily the case. Moreover, it is rare that two conditions producing brain injury will result in identical types of lesions. For instance, traumatic, closed head injury generally produces widespread brain injury with multiple small areas of shear or torsion injury, whereas cerebral embolism produces a focal lesion with an area of transient peripheral ischemia. Thus much of the early information about emotional disorders associated with cerebrovascular disease must draw on data obtained from a heterogeneous group of patients, some of whom had cerebrovascular disease and others of whom did not.

This chapter will be organized into four sections: the historical development of concepts in neuropsychiatry related to cerebrovascular disease; classification of types of cerebrovascular disease; description and classification of clinical psychiatric disorders associated with cerebrovascular disease; and a more in-depth discussion of poststroke depression, a disorder for which the most empirical data are available.

□ HISTORICAL PERSPECTIVE

The first reports of emotional reactions following brain damage (usually caused by cerebrovascular disease) were made by neurologists and psychiatrists in case descriptions. Meyer (1904) proposed a relationship between traumatic insanities and specific locations and causes of brain injury. Babinski (1914) noted that patients with right hemisphere disease frequently displayed the symptoms of anosognosia, euphoria, and indifference. Bleuler (1951) wrote that, following stroke, "melancholic moods lasting for months and sometimes longer appear frequently" (p. 230). Kraepelin (1921) recognized an association between manic depressive insanity and cerebrovascular disease when he wrote:

> The diagnosis of states of depression may, apart from the distinctions discussed, offer difficulties especially when the possibility of arteriosclerosis has to be taken into consideration. It may, at a time, be an accompanying phenomenon of manic depressive disease, but at another time may itself engender states of depression. (p. 271)

The emotional symptoms associated with brain injury have frequently been associated with aphasia. In the middle of the 19th century, Broca (1861) lo-

calized the process of speech production to the inferior left frontal lobe and deduced that the left brain was endowed with different functions than the right. Hughlings-Jackson (1915) regarded language as an extension of brain function existing in two basic forms: the intellectual (conveying content) and the emotional (expressing feeling). He suggested that these components may be separated by disease.

Goldstein (1939) was first to describe an emotional disorder thought to be uniquely associated with brain disease: the catastrophic reaction. The catastrophic reaction is an emotional outburst involving various degrees of anger, frustration, depression, tearfulness, refusal, shouting, swearing, and sometimes aggressive behavior. Goldstein ascribed this reaction to the inability of the organism to cope when faced with a serious defect in its physical or cognitive functions. In his extensive studies of brain injuries in war, Goldstein (1942) described two symptom clusters: those related directly to physical damage of a circumscribed area of the brain and those related secondarily to the organism's psychological response to injury. Emotional symptoms, therefore, represented the latter category, that is, the psychological response of an organism struggling with physical or cognitive impairments.

A second emotional abnormality, also thought to be characteristic of brain injury, was the indifference reaction described by Hecean et al. (1951) and Denny-Brown et al. (1952). The indifference reaction, associated with right hemisphere lesions, consisted of symptoms of indifference toward failures, lack of interest in family and friends, enjoyment of foolish jokes, and minimization of physical difficulties.

The first systematic study to contrast the emotional reactions of patients with right and left hemisphere brain damage was done by Gainotti (1972). He reported that catastrophic reactions were significantly more frequent among 80 left hemisphere brain-damaged patients, particularly those with aphasia, as compared to indifference reactions, which occurred more frequently among 80 right hemisphere brain-damaged patients. The indifference reaction was also associated with neglect for the opposite half of the body and space. Gainotti agreed with Goldstein's (1942) explanation of the catastrophic reaction: the desperate reaction of the organism confronted with severe physical disability. The indifference reaction, on the other hand, was not as easy to understand. Gainotti suggested that denial of illness and disorganization of the nonverbal type of synthesis may have been responsible for this emotional symptom.

Despite Meyer's (1904) and others' assertions that emotional disorder may be produced directly by focal brain injury, as indicated above, many investigators have tried to provide "psychological" explanations for the emotional symptoms associated with brain injury. Studies examining the emotional symptoms associated specifically with cerebrovascular disease began to appear in the early 1960s. Ullman and Gruen (1960) reported that stroke was a particularly severe stress to the organism, as Goldstein (1942) had suggested, because the organ governing the emotional response to injury had itself been damaged. Adams and Hurwitz (1963) noted that discouragement and frustration caused by disability could themselves impede recovery from stroke. Fisher (1961) described depression associated with cerebrovascular disease as reactive and understandable because "the brain is the most cherished organ of humanity" (p. 379). Thus depression was viewed as a natural emotional response to a decrease in self-esteem from a life-threatening injury and the resulting disability and dependence.

Systematic studies, however, led other investigators, who were impressed by the frequency of association between brain injury and emotional disorders, to hypothesize more direct causal links. In a study of 100 elderly patients with affective disorder, Post (1962) stated that the high frequency of brain ischemia associated with first episodes of depressive disorder suggested that the causes for arteriosclerotic disease and depression may be linked. Folstein et al. (1977) compared 20 stroke patients with 10 orthopedic patients. Even though the functional disability in both groups was comparable, more of the stroke patients than the orthopedic patients were depressed. They concluded that "mood disorder is a more specific complication of stroke than simply a response to motor disability" (p. 1018). Finkelstein et al. (1982) found that depression and failure to suppress serum cortisol after dexamethasone administration were more common among 25 randomly selected stroke patients than among a group of 13 control patients with equally disabling medical illnesses.

In conclusion, there have been two primary lines of thought in the study of emotional disorders that are associated with cerebrovascular disease.

One line of thought attributes emotional disorders to an understandable psychological reaction to the associated impairment; the other line of thought, based on a lack of association between severity of impairment and severity of emotional disorder, suggests a direct causal connection between cerebrovascular disease and neuropsychiatric disorder.

☐ CLASSIFICATION OF CEREBROVASCULAR DISEASE

There are many ways to classify the wide range of disorders that comprise the spectrum of cerebrovascular disease. On the one hand, cerebrovascular disease can be understood as an anatomic-pathologic process of the blood vessels that perfuse the central nervous system. This leads to a classification based on the etiologies of underlying anatomic-pathologic processes. Such a classification would include an extensive list of diseases, including infectious, connective tissue, neoplastic, hematologic, pharmacologic, and traumatic causes. Alternatively, one could examine the mechanisms by which these pathologic processes manifested themselves: for example, the interactive effects of systemic hypertension and atherosclerosis on the resilience of large arteries, integrity of vessel lumens, and production of end-organ ischemia; the formation of aneurysmal dilatations or vascular dissections; or the effect of cardiac arrhythmias on the propagation of thromboemboli.

From the perspective of schematizing the neuropsychiatric complications of cerebrovascular disease, however, probably the most pragmatic way of classifying cerebrovascular disease is not to focus on the anatomic-pathologic process or the interactive mechanisms but to examine the means by which parenchymal changes in the brain occur. The first of these, ischemia, may occur either with or without infarction of parenchyma, and includes transient ischemic attacks (TIAs), atherosclerotic thrombosis, cerebral embolism, and lacunes. The latter of these, hemorrhage, may cause either direct parenchymal damage by extravasation of blood into the surrounding brain tissue, as in intracerebral hemorrhage (ICH); or indirect damage by hemorrhage into the ventricles, subarachnoid space, extradural area, or subdural area. These changes result in a "common mode of expression," defined by

Adams and Victor (1985) "as a sudden, nonconvulsive, focal neurologic deficit" or stroke.

Expanding slightly on this categorization (i.e., the *means* by which parenchymal changes occur), there are four major categories of cerebrovascular disease (Table 1). These include atherosclerotic thrombosis, cerebral embolism, lacunes, and intracranial hemorrhage. In various studies of the incidence of cerebrovascular disease, the ratio of infarcts to hemorrhages has been shown to be about 4:1. Atherosclerotic thrombosis and cerebral embolism each account for approximately one-third of all strokes.

Atherosclerotic Thrombosis

Atherosclerotic thrombosis is often the result of a dynamic interaction between hypertension and atherosclerotic deposition of hyaline-lipid material in the walls of peripheral, coronary, and cerebral arteries. Risk factors in the development of atherosclerosis include hyperlipidemia, diabetes mellitus, hypertension, and cigarette smoking. Atheromatous plaques tend to propagate at the branchings and curves of the internal carotid artery at the carotid sinus, in the cervical part of the vertebral arteries and at their junction to form the basilar artery, in the posterior cerebral arteries as they wind around the midbrain, and in the anterior cerebral arteries as they curve over the corpus callosum. These plaques may lead to stenosis of one or more of these

cerebral arteries or to complete occlusion. TIAs, defined as periods of transient focal ischemia associated with reversible neurological deficits, almost always indicate that a thrombotic process is occurring. Only rarely is embolism or intracerebral hemorrhage preceded by transient neurologic deficits. Thrombosis of virtually any cerebral or cerebellar artery can be associated with TIAs.

TIAs, therefore, although not listed among the main causes of stroke, may precede, accompany, or follow the development of stroke or may occur by themselves without leading to complete occlusion of a cerebral or cerebellar artery. Most commonly, TIAs have a duration of 2 to 15 minutes, with a range from a few seconds to up to 12 to 24 hours. Whereas the neurologic examination between successive episodes of this thrombotic process is entirely normal, the permanent neurologic deficits of atherosclerotic thrombosis indicate that infarction has occurred. The progression of events leading to the completed thrombotic stroke, however, can be quite variable.

Cerebral Embolism

Cerebral embolism, which similarly accounts for approximately one-third of all strokes, is usually caused by a fragment breaking away from a thrombus within the heart and traveling up the carotid artery. Less commonly, the source of the embolism may be from an atheromatous plaque within the lumen of the carotid sinus or from the distal end of a thrombus within the internal carotid artery, or it may represent a fat, tumor, or air embolus within the internal carotid artery. The causes of thrombus formation within the heart can include cardiac arrhythmias, congenital heart disease, infectious processes (syphilitic heart disease, rheumatic valvular disease, endocarditis), valve prostheses, postsurgical complications, or myocardial infarction with mural thrombus. Of all strokes, those due to cerebral embolism develop most rapidly. In general, there are no warning episodes; embolism can occur at any time. A large embolus may occlude the internal carotid artery or the stem of the middle cerebral artery producing a severe hemiplegia. More often, however, the embolus is smaller and passes into one of the branches of the middle cerebral artery, producing infarction distal to the site of arterial occlusion, characterized by a pattern of neurologic deficits consistent with that vascular distribution, or producing a transient neurologic deficit that

---

TABLE 1. CLASSIFICATION OF CEREBROVASCULAR DISEASE

Ischemic phenomena   (85%)
  Infarction
    Atherosclerotic thrombosis
    Cerebral embolism
    Lacunes
    Other causes (arteritis, e.g., infectious or
      connective tissue disease; cerebral
      thrombophlebitis; fibromuscular dysplasia;
      venous occlusions)
  Transient ischemic attacks
Hemorrhagic phenomena   (15%)
  Intraparenchymal hemorrhage
    Primary (hypertensive) intracerebral hemorrhage
    Other causes (hemorrhagic disorders, e.g.,
      thrombocytopenia, clotting disorders; trauma)
  Subarachnoid or intraventricular hemorrhage
    Ruptured saccular aneurysm or arteriovenous
      malformation
    Other causes
  Subdural or epidural hematoma

resolves as the embolus fragments and travels into smaller, more distal arteries.

Lacunes

Lacunes, accounting for nearly one-fifth of strokes, are the result of occlusion of small penetrating cerebral arteries: they are infarcts that may be so small as to produce no recognizable symptoms; or, depending on their location, they may be associated with pure motor or sensory deficits. There is a strong association between lacunes and both atherosclerosis and hypertension, suggesting that lacunar infarction is the result of the extension of the atherosclerotic process into small diameter vessels.

Hemorrhage

Intracranial hemorrhage is the fourth most frequent cause of stroke. The main causes of intracranial hemorrhage that present as acute strokes include ICH, usually associated with hypertension; ruptured saccular aneurysms or arteriovenous malformations (AVMs); a variety of hemorrhagic disorders of assorted etiology; and trauma producing hemorrhage. Primary (hypertensive) intracerebral hemorrhage occurs within the brain tissue. The extravasation of blood forms a roughly circular or oval-shaped mass that disrupts and displaces the parenchyma. Adjacent tissue is compressed and seepage into the ventricular system usually occurs, producing bloody spinal fluid in more than 90 percent of the cases. Intracerebral hemorrhages can range in size from massive bleeds of several centimeters in diameter to petechial hemorrhages of a millimeter or less, most commonly occurring within the putamen, in the adjacent internal capsule, or in various portions of the white matter underlying the cortex. Hemorrhages of the thalamas, cerebellar hemispheres, or pons are also common. Severe headache is generally considered to be a constant accompaniment of intracerebral hemorrhage, but this occurs in only about 50 percent of cases. The prognosis for intracerebral hemorrhage is grave, with some 70 to 75 percent of patients dying within 1 to 30 days (Adams and Victor 1985).

Aneurysms and Arteriovenous Malformations

Ruptured aneurysms and AVMs are the next most common type of cerebrovascular disease after thrombosis, embolism, lacunes, and primary (hypertensive) intracerebral hemorrhage. Aneurysms are usually located at arterial bifurcations and are presumed to result from developmental defects in the formation of the arterial wall; rupture occurs when the intima bulges outward and eventually breaks through the adventitia. AVMs consist of a tangle of dilated vessels that form an abnormal communication between arterial and venous systems. They are developmental abnormalities consisting of embryonic patterns of blood vessels. Most AVMs are clinically silent but will bleed ultimately. Hemorrhage from aneurysms or AVMs may occur within the subarachnoid space, leading to an identifiable presentation as a bleeding vessel anomaly, or may occur within the parenchyma, leading to hemiplegia or even death.

Subdural and Epidural Hematomas

Although it could be contended that subdural hematomas (SDH) and epidural hematomas do not represent forms of cerebrovascular disease, nonetheless their behavior as vascular space-occupying lesions that produce many of the signs and symptoms of stroke warrants a brief description here.

Chronic SDHs are frequently (60 percent), but not exclusively, caused by head trauma, followed by a gradual progression of signs and symptoms during the subsequent days to weeks. Traumatic chronic SDH may be caused by tears of bridging veins in the subdural space. Nontraumatic causes include ruptured aneurysms or AVMs of the pial surface or rapid deceleration injuries. The most common symptom of chronic SDH is headache, with a variety of neuropsychiatric manifestations paralleling the gradual increase in intracranial pressure: confusion, inattention, apathy, memory loss, drowsiness, and coma. Chronic SDH is also one of the many conditions in the differential diagnosis of treatable causes of dementia. Fluctuations in the level of consciousness predominate over any focal or lateralizing signs, which may include hemiparesis, hemianopsia, cranial nerve abnormalities, aphasia, or seizures. Chronic SDH may continue to expand, if left unchecked, or may resorb spontaneously.

Acute SDH and epidural hematomas, while frequently manifested by similar changes in level of consciousness and focal neurologic deficits, as in chronic SDH, are associated with severe head trauma, may occur simultaneously or in combination with cerebral laceration or contusion, and progress rapidly over a period of a few hours to days, rather than days to weeks. Epidural hematomas usually follow a temporal or parietal skull fracture that causes a laceration or avulsion of the middle meningeal artery or vein or a tear of the dural venous sinus; acute SDH is usually caused by the avulsion of bridging veins or laceration of pial arteries. Both conditions produce loss of consciousness or a brief period of lucidity followed by a loss of consciousness; hemiparesis; cranial nerve palsies; and death, usually secondary to respiratory compromise, if the hematoma is not emergently evaluated.

Other Types of Cerebrovascular Disease

One of the other causes of cerebrovascular disease is fibromuscular dysplasia, which leads to narrowed arterial segments caused by degeneration of elastic tissue, disruption and loss of the arterial muscular coat, and an increase in fibrous tissue. Inflammatory diseases of the arterial system can also lead to stroke; these include meningovascular syphillis, pyogenic or tuberculous meningitis, temporal arteritis, and systemic lupus erythematosus.

There are many other, less common causes of cerebrovascular disease that have not been cited here due to lack of space. It appears obvious, however, that examining the many causes and types of cerebrovascular disease in relation to specific neuropsychiatric disorders is a very formidable task. Studies that have compared traumatic with thromboembolic stroke, or hemorrhagic versus ischemic infarcts (Robinson and Szetela 1981; Robinson et al. 1983b), have reported that the associated mood disorders are the same, depending on the size and location of the lesion and the time elapsed since injury. As indicated previously, however, the type or pattern of neuronal damage may be different, depending on the cause of the cerebrovascular disease. Resultant neuropsychiatric disorders must be systematically examined.

☐ CLINICAL SYNDROMES ASSOCIATED WITH CEREBROVASCULAR DISEASE

A wide variety of emotional disorders has been associated with cerebrovascular disease (Table 2). As indicated in the section on historical perspectives, Goldstein (1939) described the catastrophic

reaction in the 1930s and Hecaen et al. (1951) and Denny-Brown et al. (1952) described the indifference reaction in the early 1950s. In addition to these disorders, the authors of this chapter have described two types of depressive disorders associated with cerebrovascular disease (Robinson et al. 1984a). These depressive disorders are defined by DSM-III (American Psychiatric Association 1980) symptom criteria as either major depression or dysthymic depression.

There is also a group of disorders called the aprosodias in which patients have lost one of the affective components of language. This manifests itself as either an inability to express or comprehend emotion linguistically or to communicate emotions through the use of facial, limbic, or body gesturing. In addition, other less common emotional disorders occur, such as generalized anxiety disorder (Robinson et al. 1983a), organic hallucinosis (Peroutka et al. 1982), paranoid delusions (Benson 1976), and manic syndromes (Cummings and Mendez 1984).

Catastrophic Reaction

The catastrophic reaction, as defined by Goldstein (1939) and Gainotti (1972), consists of behavioral observations and verbal expressions of the patient. The symptoms and signs include restlessness, hyperemotionality, sudden burst of tears, irritation, or expressions of anger toward the examiner; cursing or other strong utterances; displacement of anxiety on extraneous events; sharp refusal to continue with the examination; and objection to the evaluation and a tendency to perform the test with bragging or anxious expectancy. Catastrophic reactions were reported more frequently among patients with left hemisphere lesions and aphasia, particularly those with Broca's type (Gainotti 1972).

Indifference Reaction

The indifference reaction consists of apparent indifference toward failures, lack of interest in events, tendency to joke in an unconcerned way, explicit denial of illness or lack of awareness of physical or mental impairments, and tendency to attribute physical or mental impairments to insignificant causes such as weariness or a lack of concentration. Robinson et al. (1983a) found that this syndrome also included patient self-reports of anxiety, slowness, and worrying. Indifference reactions were more often associated with neglect for the left half

TABLE 2. CLINICAL SYNDROMES ASSOCIATED WITH CEREBROVASCULAR DISEASE

Catastrophic reaction	Indifference reaction	Major depression	Minor depression	Aprosodias	
				Motor	Sensory
Clinical symptoms					
anxiety reaction	undue cheerfulness	depressed mood diurnal mood variation	depressed mood anxiety, restlessness, worry	poor expression of emotional prosody & gesturing	good expression of emotional prosody & gesturing
tears	jokes				
aggressive behavior	anosognosia	loss of energy	diurnal mood variation	good prosodic comprehension & gesturing	poor prosodic comprehension & gesturing
swearing	minimization	anxiety restlessness worry	hopelessness	denial of feelings of depression	difficulty empathizing with others
displacement	loss of interest	weight loss, decreased appetite	loss of energy		
refusal	apathy	early morning awakening	delayed sleep onset		
renouncement		delayed sleep onset	early morning awakening		
compensatory boasting		social withdrawal	social withdrawal		
		irritability	weight loss, decreased appetite		
Associated lesion location					
left hemisphere	right hemisphere	left frontal lobe	right or left posterior parietal and occipital regions	right hemisphere posterior inferior frontal lobe	right hemisphere posterior inferior parietal lobe and posterior superior temporal lobe

of the body in space and right hemisphere lesions. In a study of 48 patients with single lesions of the right or left hemisphere (Robinson et al. 1983a), this syndrome was found in 6 of 20 patients (30 percent) with single right hemisphere lesions and none of 28 patients with single left hemisphere lesions.

Aprosodias

The aprosodias have been described by Ross and Mesulam (1979) to be abnormalities in the affective components of language, encompassing prosody and emotional gesturing. Prosody can be defined as the "variation of pitch, rhythm and stress of pronunciation that bestows certain semantic and emotional meaning to speech" (p. 144).

Prosody can further be divided into four separate categories, two of which are combined with vocabulary and grammar to correspond to Hugh-lings-Jackson's (1915) concept of propositional speech. The latter two categories, emotional prosody and inarticulate prosody, which involve the emotional content and nonlinguistic aspects of communication, respectively, correspond to his concept of emotional speech. Together with the use of facial, limbic, and body gesture, the four categories of prosody are thought to be dominant linguistic features of the right hemisphere, with a functional-anatomic organization that mirrors that of propositional language in the left hemisphere.

Thus, motor aprosody consists of marked difficulty in spontaneous use of emotional inflection in language (e.g., an absence of normal prosodic variations in speech) or emotional gesturing, while comprehension of emotional inflection or gesturing remains intact. This is associated with posterior inferior lesions of the right frontal lobe. Sensory aprosody, on the other hand, is manifested by intact spontaneous emotional inflection in language and gesturing, while the comprehension of emotional inflection or gesturing is markedly impaired. It is associated with lesions of the right anterior parietal lobe. In a manner analogous to the organization of propositional language in the left hemisphere, both expression and comprehension of emotional inflection and gesturing are impaired in global aprosody. Repetition is impaired in conduction aprosody. Expression is impaired in transcortical motor aprosody, and comprehension is impaired in transcortical sensory aprosody; repetition remains intact in each of these conditions.

Defects in emotional expression or comprehension, then, might affect mental status findings by preventing either the understanding or the expression of emotion. Thus Ross and Rush (1981) hypothesized that patients who have impairments in emotional expression (motor aprosodia) may be depressed but unable to express their inner emotional state. Similarly, patients with posterior right hemisphere lesions who are unable to comprehend emotion would have difficulty in communicating or understanding the emotional intentions of others and might give false reports of their mental state or have marked difficulty in intimate relationships.

Depressive Disorder

By far, the most common emotional disorders associated with cerebrovascular disease, however, are depressions, which occur in between 30 and 50 percent of patients following acute stroke (Robinson et al. 1983b). In a study of 103 acute stroke patients, 26 percent met the DSM-III symptom criteria for major depression. The clinical symptoms found in more than half of the patients with major depression are shown in Table 2. In the same study, another 20 percent of the patients met the DSM-III symptom criteria for dysthymic depression. Depressed mood and anxiety symptoms, feelings of restlessness, and being worried were found in more than half of these patients. These disorders will be discussed in more detail in the section on poststroke depression.

Manic Syndrome

Among the infrequent emotional disorders subsumed into the category of organic affective disorders following acute stroke is secondary mania, or the "occurrence of manic symptoms . . . in the absence of a previous history of affective disturbance" (Cummings and Mendez 1984, p. 1084). In

the majority of reported cases of secondary mania, lateralized focal lesions were found in the right hemisphere involving regions of the basal ganglia, thalamic, or midbrain nuclei, or limbic portions of the frontal or temporal lobes. They were associated with vascular lesions (ischemic or hemorrhagic infarcts), neoplasms, or surgical resections. This manic syndrome generally consists of euphoric or irritable mood, hyperactivity, sleep disturbance, excessive and pressured speech, flight of ideas, grandiosity, and lack of judgment, in the absence of gross cognitive impairment. Associated symptoms may include unilateral neglect and anosognosia and other neurologic deficits that reflect the size and location of cerebrovascular compromise. Antimanic pharmacologic treatment (lithium and/or neuroleptic medications) usually leads to rapid resolution of the emotional symptoms and, typically, either partial or complete amnesia for events occurring during the manic period (Cummings and Mendez 1984).

Other Emotional or Cognitive Disorders

Less common mental disorders that occur following cerebrovascular disease include generalized anxiety disorder (Robinson et al. 1983a), organic hallucinosis (Peroutka et al. 1982), and paranoid-delusional states (Benson 1976). There are also large numbers of cognitive and language (aphasic) disorders associated with cerebral infarcts. Among patients who have suffered several cerebral infarcts over time, at least two syndromes of dementia have been identified: multiinfarct dementia (associated with cortical infarcts) and Binswanger's subcortical encephalopathy (associated with infarcts of the subcortical white matter). Space does not permit a full discussion of these interesting disorders here; readers are referred to Benson (1979) for a more in-depth discussion.

In summary, there are numerous emotional disorders associated with cerebrovascular disease, and they are probably intermixed to some degree (e.g., major depression and catastrophic reactions probably overlap). The only syndromes that have been studied in detail, however, are the major and dysthymic depressions.

□ POSTSTROKE DEPRESSION

Diagnosis

Although most studies of emotional disorders associated with cerebrovascular disease have not used strict diagnostic criteria, Robinson et al. (1984a) have used the symptom clusters defined by DSM-III to diagnose major and dysthymic (minor) depressions. DSM-III would categorize all mood disorders associated with brain injury that manifest certain signs and symptoms as organic affective disorders. Several investigations, however, have demonstrated that subdividing poststroke depression into major depression and dysthymic depression may be more accurate. As will be discussed in later sections, major depression is associated with left anterior brain injury and dysthymic disorder is associated with right or left posterior brain injury (Robinson et al. 1984a). In addition, major depression appears to have a natural course of approximately 1 year without treatment, while dysthymic disorder improved in only 30 percent of patients over 2 years' follow-up (Robinson et al., in preparation). Major depression is also associated with a "pseudo-dementia"; minor depression is not (Robinson et al. 1986).

Dexamethasone Suppression Test.
The dexamethasone suppression test (DST) (Carroll et al. 1981) has been investigated as a possible biologic marker for functional melancholic depression. Several studies have now demonstrated that, although there is a statistical association between poststroke depression and failure to suppress serum cortisol in response to administration of dexamethasone, the specificity of the test is insufficient to allow it to be useful diagnostically (Finkelstein et al. 1982; Lipsey et al. 1985). In a study of 65 patients whose acute strokes had occurred within the preceding year, 67 percent of the patients with major depression failed to suppress serum cortisol compared to 25 percent of patients with minor depression and 32 percent of nondepressed patients (Lipsey et al. 1985). The sensitivity of the DST for major depression was 67 percent, but the specificity was only 70 percent. False positive tests, found in 30 percent of patients, seemed to be related to large lesion volumes (Lipsey et al. 1985). The DST, therefore, does not presently appear to be useful diagnostically, but it may provide a research tool for examining more homogeneous groups of patients with cerebrovascular disease.

Duration and Prevalence

If poststroke depressions are to be clinically important entities, they must, in addition to being readily diagnosable, be found in a significant number of patients and last for prolonged periods of time. Transient depressions that rarely last for more than a few days or that reflect the clinical course of acute stroke would be much less clinically important than severe, prolonged depression occurring in a significant percentage of patients following acute stroke.

Longitudinal Studies.
The authors of this chapter have conducted two longitudinal investigations of stroke patients. One study was conducted in an outpatient stroke clinic; the other involved a prospective study of acute stroke patients. The outpatient study examined 103 patients attending the stroke clinic of an inner-city, major teaching hospital. Almost one-third of the patients were depressed (defined by a cutoff score of greater than 5 on the General Health Questionnaire) at the time of the initial interview (Robinson and Price 1982). At the time of follow-up evaluations, 67 percent of the patients who were depressed initially remained depressed for 8 to 9 months (Figure 1). By 1 year after the initial evaluation, however, none of the patients remained depressed.

In the second longitudinal study, acute stroke patients were prospectively studied over a 2-year

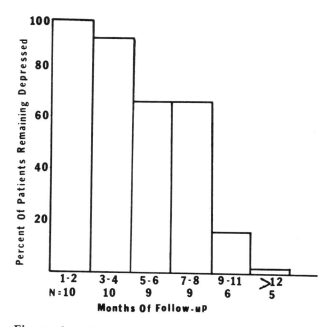

Figure 1. The percentage of patients who were depressed at the initial interview and who continued to be depressed at various time intervals following the initial interview. The number of patients evaluated at each time period is indicated. (From Robinson and Price 1982, reprinted with permission.)

course; depression was diagnosed according to DSM-III criteria for major or dysthymic depression (Robinson et al. 1984b). At the time of the initial in-hospital evaluation, 26 percent of 103 acute stroke patients had the symptom cluster of major depression; 20 percent had the symptom cluster of dysthymic depression (Robinson et al. 1983b). The diagnostic outcome for these patients with in-hospital diagnosis of major depression at 6-month, 1-year, and 2-year follow-up is shown in Table 3. Similarly, the outcome for patients with dysthymic depression or with no depression in-hospital is shown over 2 years follow-up in Table 3. Although both major and dysthymic depressive disorder following stroke lasted for prolonged periods of time, patients with major depression in-hospital recovered by 2 years poststroke. Patients with minor depression appeared to have a less favorable prognosis, with only 30 percent having recovered by 2 years poststroke. In addition, significant numbers of patients who were not depressed in-hospital became depressed after discharge.

In summary, the available data suggest that depression following cerebrovascular infarction is not a transient but a long-standing disorder with a natural course of approximately 1 year for major depression and of more than 2 years for dysthymic depression.

Determinants of Prevalence of Depression. The prevalence of clinically significant depression appears to vary depending primarily on two variables: the location of the cerebrovascular injury and the time elapsed since stroke. Several investigators have found that patients with left anterior hemisphere brain injury are more likely to develop se-

vere depressive or catastrophic symptoms than patients with any other lesion location (Gainotti 1972; Robinson et al. 1984a). In a study of 30 patients with single lesions of the right or left hemisphere, 6 of the 10 patients with left anterior brain injury had the symptoms of major depression and 1 had symptoms of minor depression (Table 4) (Robinson et al. 1984a). In addition, among these patients with left anterior brain injury, computerized axial tomography (CAT) scans showed a striking correlation between the proximity of the lesion to the left frontal pole and the severity of the depression (Figure 2). Among the patients with left anterior brain injury, the closer the anterior border of the lesion was to the *frontal* pole, the more severe the depression.

In contrast to patients with left hemisphere injury, only 2 of the 12 patients with single lesions of the right hemisphere had diagnosable depression during the acute poststroke period (Robinson et al. 1984a). During this period, patients with right anterior lesions tended to be apathetic and unduly cheerful; those with posterior lesions tended to have mild to moderate depressive symptoms. Among patients with right hemisphere injury, the severity of depression correlated with the proximity of the lesion to the posterior (occipital) pole (Figure 2).

Some investigators, however, have not found a differential effect of right versus left hemispheric brain injury and the occurrence of mood disorders. Those who have found relatively high prevalence of depression in patients with right hemisphere lesions have generally examined these patients after the acute poststroke period (Finkelstein et al. 1982; Folstein et al. 1977; Sinyor et al. 1986).

TABLE 3.   DIAGNOSTIC STATUS AT FOLLOW-UP FOR EACH IN-HOSPITAL DIAGNOSTIC GROUP, IN PERCENT

Percent having each in-hospital diagnosis (N = 103)	*Diagnosis at follow-up*	*6 month* (N = 50)	*1 year* (N = 37)	*2 year* (N = 48)
Major, 26	Major	77	20	0
	Minor	15	40	33
	Not depressed	8	40	67
Minor, 20	Major	44	28	40
	Minor	56	28	30
	Not depressed	0	43	30
Not depressed, 54	Major	11	8	19
	Minor	21	12	16
	Not depressed	68	80	66

TABLE 4. INTRAHEMISPHERIC LESION LOCATION AND PSYCHIATRIC DIAGNOSIS

Psychiatric diagnosis	Left hemisphere		Right hemisphere	
	Anterior (N = 10)	Posterior (N = 8)	Anterior (N = 6)	Posterior (N = 6)
Major depression	6	1	0	1
Minor depression	1	3	0	1
Hypomania[a]	0	0	5	1
None	3	4	1	3

Note. From Robinson et al. (1984a), reprinted with permission.
[a]Using the diagnostic criteria of the Present State Exam (PSE).

A study by Robins (1976) raised an even more fundamental issue: that is, whether stroke is more likely to produce depression than any other chronic medical illness. Robins compared stroke patients to patients disabled from spinal cord injury or orthopedic disorders within the preceding 5 years. No difference in severity of depression was found between the stroke and control patients, although both groups reported high levels of depression. Robins, however, did not take into account either the location of the stroke or the importance of extended time since injury.

In summary, although it is not certain which variables are responsible for the fact that some investigators have found correlations between hemispheric site of injury and mood disorders whereas others have not, the weight of evidence suggests that both inter- and intrahemispheric lesion location can interact in influencing the prevalence of poststroke depression.

The other variable that seems to be important in the prevalence of poststroke depression is time elapsed since stroke. Although some individual patients may improve or develop depression during the first 2 years following stroke, the overall prevalence of depression is fairly stable (Table 5). The outpatient follow-up study, however, found that after the first 2 years poststroke, there was a significant decrease in the prevalence of depressive symptoms (Robinson and Price 1982) (Figure 3). During the period from 2 to 10 years poststroke, the prevalence of depressive disorder remained relatively low, with an increase after 10 years. There is no clear explanation for this observation that patients who are more than 10 years poststroke seem to have an increase in depressive symptoms. Possible explanations include a relapse of a cyclical depressive disorder, recurrence of stroke, deterioration of medical condition, or withdrawal of social supports.

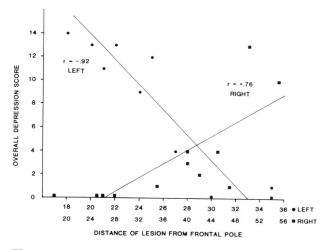

Figure 2. Relationship between overall depression score and distance of the anterior border of the lesion from the frontal pole for patients with either left anterior hemisphere infarcts or right hemisphere infarcts. The distance from the frontal pole is expressed as a percentage of the total anteroposterior distance. The correlation coefficients for the left ($p < .001$) and for the right ($p < .01$) are indicated. (From Robinson et al. 1984a, reprinted with permission.)

Relationship to Associated Impairments

As indicated earlier, there has been a tendency to explain depressive symptoms following stroke as understandable psychological reactions to the associated physical or intellectual impairments. If there has been one consistent finding from all studies of poststroke depression, however, it is that the severity of associated impairments is not an adequate explanation for the severity of depression (Finkelstein et al. 1982; Folstein et al. 1977; Robinson et al. 1984a; Sinyor et al. 1986). In the longitudinal

TABLE 5.   OVERALL PREVALENCE OF DEPRESSION OVER THE FIRST 2 YEARS POSTSTROKE, IN PERCENT

	In-hospital (N = 103)	3 months (N = 40)	6 months (N = 50)	1 year (N = 37)	2 years (N = 40)
Major depression	26	20	34	14	21
Minor depression	20	25	26	19	21
Not depressed	54	55	40	67	58

study of 103 stroke patients (Robinson and Price 1982), severity of depression was examined in relation to the severity of intellectual impairment as measured by the Mini-Mental State examination, physical impairment (activities of daily living) as measured by the Johns Hopkins Functioning Inventory, and social functioning as measured by the Social Functioning Exam. The Pearson *r* correlation coefficient between in-hospital depression scores and intellectual impairment scores was −.29; that between depression scores and physical impairment scores was .36; and that between depression scores and social functioning scores was .24 (Robinson et al. 1983a). These correlations suggest that

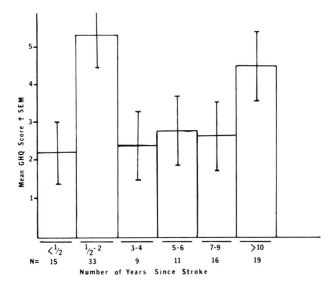

Figure 3.   Patients were divided into groups depending on the period of time since their stroke had occurred. The mean General Hospital Questionnaire (GHQ) score was significantly increased for the group 6 months to 2 years poststroke by analysis of variance ($F = 2.98$, 5/97 df, $p < .02$) and by *t*-test compared with the 0- to 5-month ($p < .01$), 3- to 4-year ($p < .05$), and 7- to 9-year ($p < .05$) groups. The greater than 10-year group did not differ significantly from any of the other groups. (From Robinson and Price 1982, reprinted with permission.)

between 6 and 13 percent of the variance in depression could be explained by severity of intellectual impairment, severity of physical impairment, or quality of available social supports.

In addition, there were no significant differences between patients with major depression, those with dysthymic depression, and those with no depression in their mean intellectual impairment, physical impairment, or social functioning scores. This also suggests the relatively low contribution of these impairments to the severity of depression. This is in contrast to the strong correlation between the proximity of the lesion to the frontal pole and severity of depression (.92) for left frontal lesions (Figure 2) (Robinson et al. 1984a) and highly statistically significant differences in depression scores between the three diagnostic groups of patients.

Similarly, Folstein et al. (1977) reported that 8 stroke patients who were matched with 8 orthopedic patients for comparable degrees of physical impairment in daily living and cognitive deficit had significantly higher levels of depression.

Although the relationship between severity of depression and severity of intellectual impairment is relatively weak, a question could nevertheless be raised as to whether intellectual impairment leads to depression or whether depression might lead to intellectual impairment. In a study of 36 patients with left hemisphere lesions (Robinson et al. 1986), patients with major depression had significantly smaller infarcts than nondepressed patients, although both groups had almost identical levels of intellectual impairment (Figure 4). Both lesion volume and depression were found to correlate significantly and independently with severity of intellectual impairment, and thus suggests that major depression can produce a "pseudo-dementia" (i.e., dementia of depression) in stroke patients, which may respond to treatment of the depression.

Thus, not only does intellectual impairment fail to explain severity of depression following stroke, but depression itself may contribute to intellectual

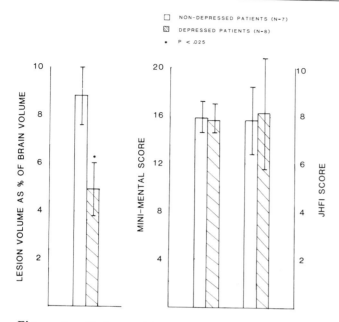

☐ NON-DEPRESSED PATIENTS (N=7)
▨ DEPRESSED PATIENTS (N=8)
• P < .025

Figure 4. Patients with Mini-Mental State scores below 23 were divided into depressed and nondepressed groups. Despite having comparable Mini-Mental State scores and Johns Hopkins Functioning Inventory (JHFI) scores (activities of daily living), depressed patients had a significantly smaller mean lesion volume than nondepressed patients.

impairment. This underlines the importance of recognizing and treating poststroke depression because of the possible impact on further recovery and rehabilitation. It is likely that there is a reciprocal, interactive relationship between depression and impairment. Once patients become depressed, they may not recover from their impairment as readily; those impairments may, in turn, exacerbate the depression. In addition, social functioning also seems not to produce depression, but once depression has occurred, it adversely affects social functioning (Robinson et al. 1985a).

Another impairment commonly found in stroke patients is aphasia. Because the diagnosis of depression requires a verbal interview, patients with severe comprehension deficits have been excluded from studies of cerebrovascular disease and depression. Patients with aphasia that does not significantly impair comprehension, however, have been examined. In the longitudinal study of 103 acute stroke patients (Robinson and Price 1982), the relationship between the existence of aphasia and depression was examined (Table 6). Among 15 patients with left hemisphere lesions and aphasia, 7 patients had major or minor depression, while 8

TABLE 6. APHASIA AND DEPRESSION IN PATIENTS WITH LEFT HEMISPHERE LESIONS (N = 48)

	Broca's aphasia	Wernicke's aphasia	Other aphasia	No aphasia
Major depression	2	0	2	9
Minor depression	1	1	1	7
None	4	1	3	17

Note. From Robinson et al. (1985b), reprinted with permission.

were not depressed. Among patients with left hemisphere lesions but without aphasia, 16 of 33 patients had diagnosable depression. Thus there was no significant difference between patients with aphasia and without aphasia in the frequency of their depression. In a study of patients with different types of aphasia (Robinson and Benson 1981), patients with Broca's aphasia were found to be more frequently depressed than patients with other types of aphasia. This probably represents an association between left frontal brain injury (where Broca's area is located) and depression. Thus aphasia and depression appear to be two independent outcomes of stroke that may coexist or occur independently, depending on the lesion size and location.

Mechanisms

It is likely that there are multiple etiologies of poststroke depression. Just as functional depression in nonbrain-injured patients is likely to arise from several possible mechanisms, poststroke depression is likely a composite of several depressive disorders. As discussed previously, the fact that major and dysthymic depression have different 2-year outcomes, different responses to dexamethasone administration, different relationships to anatomic lesion location, and different effects on intellectual function suggests that these two disorders have different etiologies.

Although the biologic mechanisms leading to poststroke depression are only speculative, the authors of this chapter have proposed a role for catecholamine-containing neurons in these disorders. The catecholaminergic neurons in the brain arise in the brain stem and project anteriorly into the frontal cortex. They then pass anterior to posterior within the deep layers of the cortex with arborizations throughout all cortical layers (Morrison et al. 1979) (Figure 5).

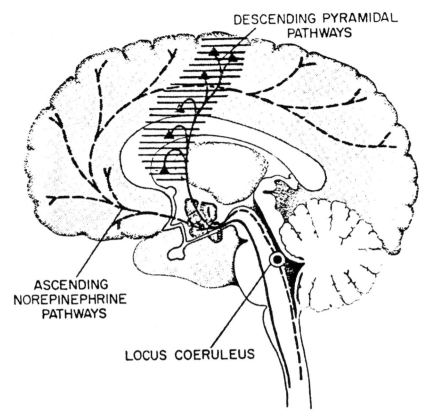

Figure 5. Schematic drawing of the anatomy of the ascending noradrenergic pathways. The cell bodies are located in the brain stem and send axonal projections through the median forebrain bundle and into the frontal pole. The fibers traverse the deep layers of cortex from frontal to occipital regions sending arborizing processes throughout the more superficial cortical layers. Lesions closer to the frontal pole would interrupt more of these cortical pathways than more posterior lesions. (From Robinson and Bloom 1977, reprinted with permission.)

Focal injury such as that occurring in stroke may cause partial damage to these catecholamine-containing neurons. Reis and Ross (1973) suggested that injured catecholaminergic neurons may switch from producing neurotransmitter to synthesizing protein for regeneration and sprouting, which leads to a precipitous decline in available transmitter throughout the injured as well as uninjured branches of the system. This may cause the entire catecholamine system in the brain to reduce neurotransmitter release drastically, with a resulting behavioral-emotional outcome of depressive disorder or indifference.

Several investigators have demonstrated that catecholamine concentrations are significantly altered following stroke in humans (Meyer et al. 1973). Using animal models of stroke, it has been shown that a focal cortical lesion can produce widespread depletions of biogenic amine neurotransmitters throughout uninjured as well as injured areas of the brain (Robinson et al. 1975; Zervas et al. 1974). In addition, the neurochemical response may be lateralized (Robinson 1979), that is, the degree of noradrenergic depletion depends on which hemisphere is injured. These findings are consistent with the suggestion that catecholamine depletion may be involved in some poststroke mood disorders and that differences in the emotional response to left anterior brain injury (major depression) as compared with right anterior brain injury (indifference and apathy) may be the result of differential biochemical responses to ischemia, depending on which hemisphere is injured. This hypothesis is also consistent with the extensive literature implicating depletions of catecholamines in the etiology of functional depression (Schildkraut 1965). In summary, laboratory findings using animal stroke models suggest that depletion of biogenic amines following injury to frontal brain regions may play a role in the production of depressive disorders or the indifference reaction.

The etiology of dysthymic depressions that appear to last for more than 2 years following stroke is uncertain. Dysthymic disorders do not appear to be related to a family history of depressive disorder or to a previous personal history of depressive disorder (defined as seeing a physician for treatment of depression). These depressions, however, might be related to premorbid personality vulnerabilities such as depressive or obsessional character traits or some other psychological or biologic process.

Treatment

Despite anecdotal reports of the efficacy of tricyclic antidepressants or stimulant medications in the treatment of poststroke depression, most depressed stroke patients do not receive treatment. Feibel and Springer (1982) reported that, in a series of 91 stroke patients seen at 6 months poststroke, only 5 (6 percent) had received treatment for depression, despite the fact that 24 (26 percent) of these patients displayed significant depressive symptoms. Feibel and Springer referred to the lack of treatment of poststroke depression as one of the great unmet needs of stroke victims.

Only one randomized double-blind treatment study on the efficacy of the antidepressant treatment of poststroke depression has been published (Lipsey et al. 1984). In this study, 14 patients were treated with nortriptyline and 20 patients with placebo. Half of the patients had major depressive symptoms; the other half had dysthymic depressive symptoms. No differences were noted between the placebo and nortriptyline treatment groups in terms of their demographic characteristics, severity of impairment, time elapsed since stroke, or size or location of stroke lesion. During the first week of treatment, patients received nortriptyline 20 mg per day, which was gradually increased over a 6-week period to 100 mg per day. Identical placebo was given to the control group. The 11 patients treated with nortriptyline who completed the study showed significantly greater improvement in their depression scores than did 15 placebo-treated controls (Figure 6). Although there was no difference between active and placebo treatment outcome during the first 2 weeks of the study, nortriptyline-treated patients continued to show improvement throughout the entire 6-week course;

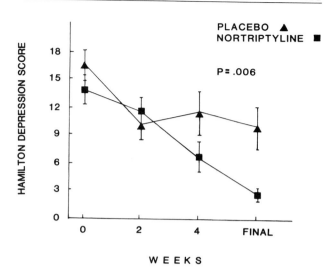

Figure 6. Mean Hamilton depression scores for depressed stroke patients given increasing doses of nortriptyline (squares) and 15 depressed stroke patients receiving identical placebo (triangles). The nortriptyline group improved significantly ($p = .006$) more than the placebo group. (From Lipsey et al. 1984, reprinted with permission.)

placebo-treated patients leveled off after the initial, expected placebo response. Successfully treated patients had serum nortriptyline levels between 50 and 150 ng/ml, which is the same range as that required for treatment of depression not associated with brain injury (Figure 7). These findings suggest that patients treated for poststroke depression need to have serum nortriptyline levels between 50 and 150 ng/ml and that the length of treatment should be at least 6 weeks before the maximum benefit of treatment can be assessed.

Patients with heart block or other severe cardiac conduction abnormalities, myocardial infarction within the past 6 months, significant prostatism, narrow angle glaucoma, or medications that might adversely interact with nortriptyline (e.g., monoamine oxidase inhibitors, guanethidine) were excluded. Given these medical contraindications to inclusion in this study, the frequency of adverse side effects, such as episodes of dizziness, hypotension, or recurrent stroke, was no greater among the nortriptyline-treated than among placebo-treated patients. Three of the nortriptyine-treated patients, however, developed delirium characterized by confusion, drowsiness, and sometimes agitation. These symptoms abated when the medication was discontinued, but these medical complications un-

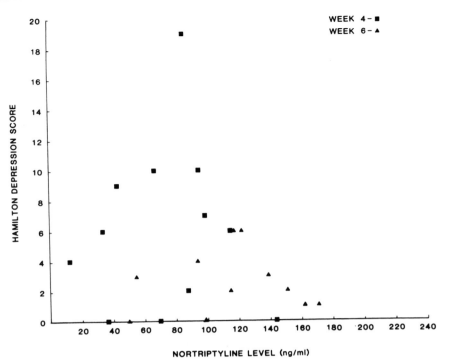

Figure 7. Hamilton depression scores related to serum nortriptyline concentrations for 11 patients after 4 weeks of treatment (70 mg for 1 week) and the same patients after 6 weeks of treatment (100 mg for 2 weeks). There appear to be both a dose-response effect, with patients whose serum concentrations were above 100 ng/ml having the lowest depression scores, as well as a length-of-treatment effect, with patients treated for 6 weeks having lower depression scores than patients treated for 4 weeks.

derline the fact that elderly stroke patients, who frequently have numerous medical problems, should be treated cautiously with any medication, including tricyclic antidepressants. Treatment of depression in patients requiring frequent close monitoring should probably be done in the hospital. Despite this caution, the demonstrated efficacy of nortriptyline in the treatment of poststroke depression indicates that these disorders are treatable, and every effort should be made to alleviate these depressive disorders.

☐ CONCLUSION

Despite the fact that clinicians have recognized the association between emotional disorders and cerebrovascular disease for more than 80 years, the relatively small amount of empirical research concerning the association between cerebrovascular disease and emotional disorders is surprising. A variety of neuropsychiatric disorders associated with cerebrovascular disease has been discussed. The

most common emotional disorder associated with cerebrovascular disease, however, is depression, of which at least two types have been recognized. Major depression has a natural course of approximately 1 year. Dysthymic depression has a more chronic course and a relatively unfavorable prognosis without treatment, although the depressive symptoms are milder than those of major depression. It is likely that the etiologies of these two disorders are different.

Although the mechanisms for these disorders remain to be identified, it is likely that at least some of these disorders have foundations in a neuropathological process initiated by stroke. It has been hypothesized that the biogenic amine neurotransmitters may be involved in the production or maintenance of some of these disorders, and the course of these disorders may reflect the underlying regenerative neurobiologic process.

Recent developments in the study of emotional disorders associated with cerebrovascular disease may have been propelled by advances in our ability to measure emotion more quantitatively as well as imaging techniques that allow discrete localization of lesions in living human brain. This, in addition to our increasing knowledge of specific neurotransmitter-mediated systems, has allowed formulations of brain-emotional relationships that may be mediated by specific neuronal pathways. These advances have created a scientific setting in which the relationship between cerebrovascular disease and emotional disorders can be more specifically investigated.

Despite these advances, we continue to be limited by several factors. These include our relatively primitive understanding of neuronal mechanisms of the brain, the enormous gulf between understanding functions of the mind and functions of the brain, and difficulties in interpreting the results of lesion studies. For instance, the fact that left frontal lesions are associated with major depression only indicates that this brain area plays some role in the production of depression; it does not mean that left frontal areas are primarily or even directly involved in human mood regulation.

Future research may delineate which neuronal systems or neurotransmitter pathways may be involved in the emotional disorders associated with cerebrovascular disease. In addition, an increased understanding of the nature of neuronal regeneration may help us to elucidate the natural course and dynamic nature of recovery from these emotional disorders. Finally, it is hoped that the study of specific emotional responses to cerebrovascular disease may help us to understand the production of emotional disorders in nonbrain-injured patients and the neuronal mechanisms that underlie mood regulation in normal individuals.

☐ REFERENCES

Adams GF, Hurwitz LJ: Mental barriers to recovery from strokes. Lancet 2:533–537, 1963

Adams RD, Victor M: Principles of Neurology (3rd ed). New York, McGraw-Hill, 1985, pp 569–640

American Psychiatric Association: Diagnostic and Statistical Manual of Mental Disorders, 3rd ed. Washington, DC, American Psychiatric Association, 1980

Babinski J: Contribution a l'etude des troubles mentaux dans l'hemiplegie organique cerebrale (Anosognosie). Rev Neurol (Paris) 27:845–848, 1914

Benson DF: Psychiatric aspects of aphasia. Br J Psychiatry 123:555–566, 1976

Benson DF: Aphasia, Alexia and Agraphia. New York, Churchill Livingstone, 1979

Bleuler EP: Textbook of Psychiatry. New York, Dover Publications, 1951, pp 230–242

Broca P: New finding of aphasia following a lesion of the posterior part of the second and third frontal convolutions. Bull de la Societe Anatomique 6:398–407, 1861

Carroll BJ, Feinberg M, Gredent JF, et al: A specific laboratory test for the diagnosis of melancholia: standardization, validation and clinical utility. Arch Gen Psychiatry 38:15–22, 1981

Cummings JL, Mendez MF: Secondary mania with focal cerebrovascular lesions. Am J Psychiatry 141:1084–1087, 1984

Denny-Brown D, Meyer JS, Horenstein S: The significance of perceptual rivalry resulting from parietal lesions. Brain 75:434–471, 1952

Feibel JH, Springer CJ: Depression and failure to resume social activities after stroke. Arch Phys Med Rehabil 63:276–278, 1982

Finkelstein S, Benowitz LI, Baldessarini RJ, et al: Mood, vegetative disturbance, and dexamethasone suppression test after stroke. Ann Neurol 12:463–468, 1982

Fisher SH: Psychiatric considerations of cerebral vascular disease. Am J Cardiol 7:379–385, 1961

Folstein MF, Maiberger R, McHugh PR: Mood disorder as a specific complication of stroke. J Neurol Neurosurg Psychiatry 40:1018–1020, 1977

Gainotti G: Emotional behavior and hemispheric side of lesion. Cortex 8:41–55, 1972

Goldstein K: The Organism: A Holistic Approach to Biology Derived from Pathological Data in Man. New York, American Books, 1939

Goldstein K: After-Effects of Brain Injuries in War. New York, Grune & Stratton, 1942

Hecean H, Ajuriaguerra J de, Massonet J: Les troubles visoconstructifs par lesion parieto occipitale droit. Encephale 40:122–179, 1951

Hughlings-Jackson J: On affections of speech from disease of the brain. Brain 38:106–174, 1915

Kraepelin E: Manic Depressive Insanity and Paranoia. Edinburgh, E & S Livingstone, 1921

Lipsey JR, Robinson RG, Pearlson GD, et al: Nortriptyline treatment of post-stroke depression: a double blind treatment trial. Lancet 1:297–300, 1984

Lipsey JR, Robinson RG, Pearlson GD, et al: Dexamethasone suppression test and mood following stroke. Am J Psychiatry 142:318–323, 1985

Meyer A: The anatomical facts and clinical varieties of traumatic insanity. American Journal of Insanity 60:373, 1904

Meyer JS, Stoica E, Pascu I, et al: Catecholamine concentrations in CSF and plasma of patients with cerebral infarction and hemorrhage. Brain 96:277–288, 1973

Morrison JH, Molliver ME, Grzanna R: Noradrenergic innervation of cerebral cortex: widespread effects of local cortical lesions. Science 205:313–316, 1979

Peroutka SJ, Sohmer BH, Kumar AJ, et al: Hallucinations and delusions following a right temporoparietooccipital infarction. Johns Hopkins Medical Journal 151:181–185, 1982

Post F: The Significance of Affective Symptoms in Old Age (Maudsley Monograph No. 10). London, Oxford University Press, 1962

Reis DJ, Ross RA: Dynamic changes in brain dopamine

B-hydroxylase activity during anterograde and retrograde reactions to injury of central noradrenergic axons. Brain Res 57:307–326, 1973

Robins AH: Are stroke patients more depressed than other disabled subjects? J Chronic Dis 29:479–482, 1976

Robinson RG: Differential behavioral and biochemical effects of right and left hemispheric cerebral infarction in the rat. Science 205:707–710, 1979

Robinson RG, Bloom FE: Pharmacological treatment following experimental cerebral infarction: implications for understanding psychological symptoms of human stroke. Biol Psychiatry 12:669–680, 1977

Robinson RG, Benson DF: Depression in aphasic patients: frequency, severity and clinical-pathological correlations. Brain Lang 14:282–291, 1981

Robinson RG, Price TR: Post-stroke depressive disorders: a follow-up study of 103 stroke out-patients. Stroke 13:635–641, 1982

Robinson RG, Szetela B: Mood change following left hemispheric brain injury. Ann Neurol 9:447–453, 1981

Robinson RG, Shoemaker WJ, Schlumpf M, et al: Effect of experimental cerebral infarction in rat brain on catecholamines and behavior. Nature 225:332–334, 1975

Robinson RG, Kubos KL, Starr LB, et al: Mood changes in stroke patients: relationship to lesion location. Compr Psychiatry 24:555–566, 1983a

Robinson RG, Starr LB, Kubos KL, et al: A two year longitudinal study of post-stroke mood disorders: findings during the initial evaluation. Stroke 14:736–741, 1983b

Robinson RG, Kubos KL, Starr LB, et al: Mood disorders in stroke patients: importance of location of lesion. Brain 107:81–93, 1984a

Robinson RG, Starr LB, Price TR: A two year longitudinal study of post-stroke mood disorders: prevalence and duration at six months follow-up. Br J Psychiatry 144:256–262, 1984b

Robinson RG, Bolduc PL, Starr LB, et al: Social functioning assessment in stroke patients: responses of patients and other informant and relationship of initial evaluation to six month follow-up. Arch Phys Med Rehab 66:496–500, 1985a

Robinson RG, Lipsey JR, Price TR: Diagnosis and clinical management of post-stroke depression. Psychosomatics 26:769–778, 1985b

Robinson RG, Bolla-Wilson K, Kaplan E, et al: Evidence for intellectual impairment related to depression in stroke patients. Br J Psychiatry 148:541–547, 1986

Robinson RG, Bolduc PL, Price TR: A two year longitudinal study of post-stroke mood disorders: diagnosis and outcome at one and two year follow-up. (in preparation)

Ross ED, Mesulam MM: Dominant language functions of the right hemisphere: prosody and emotional gesturing. Arch Neurol 36:144–148, 1979

Ross ED, Rush AJ: Diagnosis and neuroanatomical correlates of depression in brain damaged patients. Arch Gen Psychiatry 38:1344–1354, 1981

Schildkraut JJ: The catecholamine hypothesis of affective disorders: a review of supporting evidence. Am J Psychiatry 122:509–522, 1965

Sinyor D, Jacques P, Kaloupek DG, et al: Post-stroke depression and lesion location: an attempted replication. Brain 109:537–546, 1986

Ullman M, Gruen A: Behavioral changes in patients with strokes. Am J Psychiatry 117:1004–1009, 1960

Wolf PA, Dawber TR, Thomas HE, et al: Epidemiology of stroke, in Advances in Neurology, Vol. 16. Edited by Thompson RA, Green JR. New York, Raven Press, 1977, pp 5–19

Zervas NT, Hori H, Negora M: Reduction of brain dopamine following experimental cerebral ischemia. Nature 247:283–284, 1974

Chapter 12

Neuropsychiatric Aspects of Epilepsy and Epileptic Seizures

James M. Stevenson, M.D.
John H. King, M.D.

THE OCCURRENCE OF EPILEPSY and other seizure activity is not unusual in medical practice. Hauser and Kurland (1975) estimated that as many as one million individuals in the United States are subject to epilepsy, not including those who develop seizure activity as a manifestation of other illnesses. Epilepsy and any seizure activity frequently can affect cognitive, behavioral, sensory, and motor activity as well as emotional character. Epilepsy is predicted by a genetically predetermined vulnerability of neuronal tissue. Seizure activity per se can occur secondary to many pathophysiologic states. Psychiatric and neurologic practice often interfaces with clinical syndromes involving either primary or secondary seizure activity and with the more difficult to evaluate epileptic-like behavioral syndromes. This chapter will present briefly a classification of the seizures of epilepsy with a discussion of etiologic considerations. In addition, the motoric, sensory, emotional, and behavioral man-

ifestations of epilepsy and differential diagnostic considerations will be discussed. Treatment considerations will follow.

Epilepsy is a disturbance in central nervous system (CNS) function resulting from excessive neuronal discharge and manifested by recurrent stereotyped behavior. The seizure activity of the epileptic disturbance may develop anywhere in the cerebral cortex (or deeper). The specific phenomena demonstrated depend on the origin of the activity (focus) as well as where and how the sustained discharge spreads through CNS circuits. Seizure activity results from an abnormal electro-physiologic discharge at the cellular level secondary to neurochemical alterations. Those neurons affected are abnormal in their susceptibility to this activity either through genetic predisposition or secondary to trauma, infections, space-occupying lesions, toxic effects, or metabolic derangements among others. Normally the stability of brain function is maintained by a complex interaction of excitatory and inhibitory neurochemical and dependent physiologic mechanisms. Generally the resting cortex is in a state of inhibition. For a seizure to occur, a state of excessive excitation must be achieved. This state could result either from an increase in excitatory function or from a decrease in inhibitory mechanisms.

Acetylcholine (Ach) is a ubiquitous neurotransmitter found in the brain. It is the principal excitatory agent in the CNS, whereas gammaaminobutyric acid (GABA) is the principal inhibitory neurotransmitter. Theoretically, an excess of activity in the Ach system could lead to the required excitation necessary for seizure production, and there are pharmacologic models to support this possibility. However, these models of excesses in the neurochemistry of the excitatory system are not the predominantly accepted explanations for these abnormal discharges. The better pharmacologic evidence supports disinhibition (i.e., a decrease in GABA) as the major neurochemical mechanism in the production of seizure activity. Specifically, most drugs used to treat epilepsy facilitate the inhibitory system.

□ NORMAL BRAIN ELECTRICAL ACTIVITY AND THE ELECTROENCEPHALOGRAM

The electrical activity of the brain results from two different neuronal activities. There is activity at the dendrite where neurotransmitters polarize (GABA) or depolarize (Ach) the cell membrane through synaptic junctions. Polarizations are inhibitory; depolarizations are excitatory. When local excitatory potentials in the dendrite significantly override inhibitory potentials, a threshold may be reached, and an action potential may be generated. This action potential is an amplification of the electrical potential of the dendrite and is transmitted quickly down the axon to nerve terminals, with the consequent release of either inhibitory or excitatory neurotransmitters. Although the activities of these numerous electrical generators vary greatly in the normal state, enough are available to produce a significant, recordable impulse at the calvarium. This electrical activity occurs throughout the brain with some areas (centers) more active than others. Examples of active areas include the hippocampus,

the reticular activating system, and the forebrain. These areas can be referred to as the centrocephalic area.

Surface recordings by electroencephalogram (EEG) of this cortical electrical activity can be made to a depth of only 5 millimeters within cortical substance. Consequently, information supplied by these recordings reflects only surface activity. Significant neuronal firings within the deeper centers can be recorded if they are strong enough to be transmitted to the surface. A limitation results also from the difficulty involved in measuring certain cortical areas, such as those at the base of the brain encircling the brain stem (limbic area). These limbic areas are of particular interest because they are known to produce emotional and behavioral phenomena when stimulated, to have low seizure thresholds, and to be easily traumatized. Routine recording techniques fail to reflect limbic activity; consequently, knowledge regarding seizure activity within this highly important area is limited. Utilization of special nasopharyngeal recording electrodes is helpful in detecting electrical activity from some limbic cortex, although these recordings are limited because other limbic cortical areas remain remote to detection.

The ability to monitor intracranial stimulation assists immeasurably in the understanding of normal brain activity. The EEG was introduced in the 1930s for this purpose. Definitive characteristics of normal brain activity have been established by the EEG. Oscillations of electrical potential recorded by the EEG reflect activities generated from various brain centers. Several centers generate specific frequencies of electrical activity. Recordings of these predominant rhythms are complicated by the imposition of each on the other as well as imposition of the many minor frequencies generated by the brain. Spectral analysis by computers has determined the range of these normal frequencies to be from .5 to 50 cycles per second (cps). The alpha rhythm (Figure 1) is the basic resting rhythm of the brain and can be recorded well over the occipital area with the alert subject's eyes closed. The alpha rhythm has a frequency of 9 to 12 cps, which slows as the subject becomes drowsy or disappears if the subject's eyes open. On recording, alpha activity resembles a sine wave with slight irregularity. The alpha amplitude varies from 20 to 60 microvolts.

Beta activity (Figure 2) is usually a fast, low amplitude activity (less than 20 microvolts), seen most predominantly in recordings of central areas

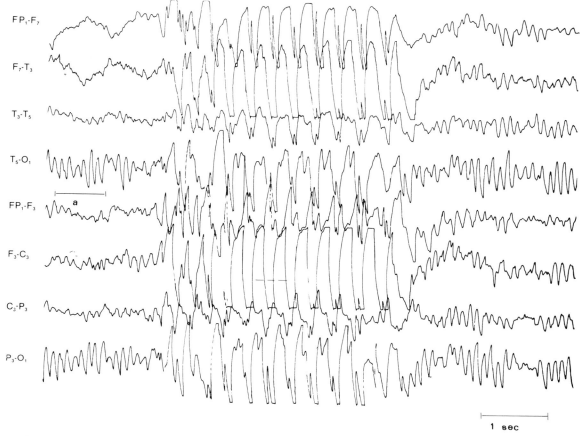

Figure 1. Alpha activity predominates at *a* as in other areas of the record. A 3-cps spike and wave activity of absence seizures dominates the center of the record in all eight leads.

of the cortex and with a frequency of 8 to 24 cps. The entire cortex has the potential to generate this activity; it is inconspicuous in the normal awake adult and is rarely a prominent rhythm. The slowest rhythms are theta and delta (Figure 3), with theta ranging from 4 to 7 cps and delta less than 4 cps. These rhythms are inconspicuous in the normal awake adult but become predominant during deeper stages of sleep. These rhythms usually are of high amplitude. Discussion of the EEG architecture during normal sleep can be found elsewhere in this text (Chapter 14).

Variations of normal brain-wave patterns occur with sleep deprivation and hyperventilation. After several days of sleep deprivation, alpha activity diminishes in amplitude yet becomes faster in frequency. Paradoxically, the activity can appear with open eyes and disappear on eye closing. With hyperventilation, slow activity becomes more prominent as alpha and beta rhythms are reduced.

Continued hyperventilation produces increases in amplitude and more pronounced slowing, and creates serial waves or bursts of high amplitude waves at 2 to 3 cps. Normalized breathing leads to a rapid return to a normal tracing.

At birth, low amplitude waves appear randomly. During the first 6 months, 4 to 6 cps rhythms become prominent over the frontal areas. At 12 months, high amplitude (5 to 7 cps) rhythms predominate. Temporal rhythms remain slow and rhythmic but the dominant activity becomes faster as the child matures. In old age, the faster waveforms start to dissipate and slow patterns dominate, particularly over the temporal area.

☐ CLASSIFICATION

Once brain-wave patterns had been determined for normal intracranial activity, measured alterations

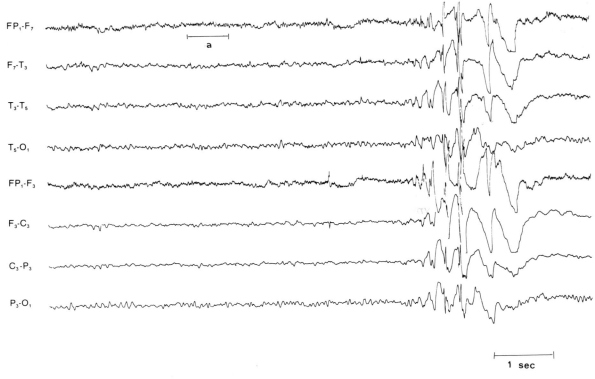

Figure 2.   Beta activity at *a*. Generalized spike and wave activity dominates all eight leads at the end of this record.

in these patterns took on new significance when coupled with clinical activity on the part of an individual. Thus abnormal phenomena may be explained in part by these changes in brain-wave patterns. Occasionally, if the increased electrical activity is generated from a specific source, locating that focus of irritation is possible. Combining the uses of EEGs and descriptive clinical medicine has led to a greater understanding of the generation of epileptic (seizure) activity and has assisted in the classification of the various forms of these illnesses.

Still, classification in the field of epilepsy presents great challenges. Epilepsy as a disorder may predict familial transmission, but the form of the

seizure activity predicts response to pharmacologic intervention. A specific classification of the epilepsies was organized in 1969 by the International League Against Epilepsy (ILAE). However, the classification of epileptic seizures that same year by the ILAE has gained widest acceptance for its practical contribution to management. A subsequent revision of this classification (ILAE 1981) is described in Table 1. In classifying seizure activity, it is necessary to consider both clinical and neurophysiologic characteristics that distinguish the various forms of seizures, recognizing the sustained patterns of discharge and spread for each seizure type; it is this pattern of discharge that de-

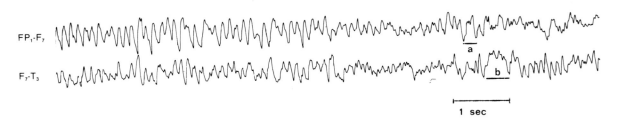

Figure 3.   Delta activity at *a*. Theta activity at *b*.

TABLE 1. EPILEPTIC SEIZURE CLASSIFICATION (ILAE 1981)

Partial (focal) seizures
  Simple partial seizures
    With motor signs
    With somatosensory or special sensory symptoms
    With autonomic symptoms or signs
    With psychic symptoms
  Complex partial seizures
    Simple partial onset followed by impairment of
      consciousness
    With impairment of consciousness at the onset
  Partial seizures evolving to secondarily generalized
    seizures
    Simple partial seizures evolving into generalized
      seizures
    Complex partial seizures evolving to generalized
      seizures
    Simple partial seizures evolving into complex
      seizures evolving to generalized seizures

Generalized seizures (convulsive or nonconvulsive)
  Absence seizures
    Impairment of consciousness only
    With mild clonic components[a]
    With atonic components[a]
    With tonic components[a]
    With automatisms[a]
    With autonomic components[a]
  Atypical absence, may have:
    More pronounced changes in tone
    Onset and/or cessation that is not abrupt
  Myoclonic seizures, myoclonic jerks (single or
    multiple)
  Clonic seizures
  Tonic seizures
  Tonic-clonic seizures (grand mal)
  Atonic seizures
  (Astatic combinations of the above can occur)

Unclassified epileptic seizures

[a]Alone or in combination.

termines clinical signs. This classification is a shift in emphasis from the diagnostic importance of foci in seizure activity. The focus, if located, may initiate the abnormal activity but does not determine this pattern of discharge nor the subsequent full clinical picture.

Partial Seizures

Simple Partial Seizures. Simple partial seizures are characterized by the onset of clinical and EEG activity that remains limited to a localized area in one cerebral hemisphere. Consciousness, there-

fore, is not affected. Early stages are recognized easily by motor signs or sensory symptoms. Several types exist. Focal motor or Jacksonian seizures are characterized by stereotyped movements, initially very limited but with progressive spread to the limbs or trunk. This type of seizure results from pathology in the motor areas within the frontal lobes of the contralateral hemisphere. Seizures arising from the parietal cortex are manifested by various paresthesias. Stimulation of specific areas of the temporal cortex results in auras reflecting the particular temporal functioning involved. Examples include the auditory or visual hallucinations seen if the association areas of auditory and visual cortex are involved. Additional symptoms from temporal lobe foci may include autonomic manifestations such as epigastric sensations, increased peristaltic activity, and sympathetic and respiratory phenomenon. The interictal (between seizures) EEG trait of partial epilepsies is a localized epileptiform spike. The most common ictal (seizure) pattern consists of localized, rhythmic, low voltage 16 to 30 Hz rapid potentials. In approximately half of these patients, seizures progress to develop secondary activity that is generalized with loss of consciousness; these are then called secondary generalized seizures.

Complex Partial Seizures. Complex partial seizures (Figure 4) are better known as temporal lobe, limbic system, or psychomotor seizures. This type of seizure may begin as a focus with simple symptomatology or may appear to begin as if both temporal lobes are involved spontaneously at the outset. The hallmark of this type of seizure is the impairment of consciousness. As the focal epileptic discharge associated with temporal aura spreads to involve the limbic system, various stages of impaired consciousness and loss of contact with the environment develop. Two subtypes of this classification exist. The first presents with focal onset and loss of consciousness later; the second type presents with loss of consciousness from the onset. Each type is subdivided further, depending on the presence of automatisms. Commonly, automatisms occur only after bilateral spread. Automatisms are movements that occur during temporal lobe and absence seizures. They are highly integrated and are unconscious to the patient, who is amnestic to them following the episode. Penry and Dreifuss (1969) classified these into three groups: (1) de novo automatisms from internal stimuli in-

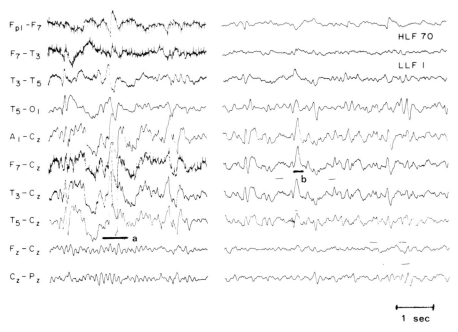

Figure 4.   Temporal lobe sharp waves occur frequently in the lead and are seen in multiple leads at *a* and *b*.

cluding chewing, lip smacking, swallowing, scratching, rubbing, kicking, fumbling, running, and disrobing; (2) de novo automatisms from external stimuli including drinking from a cup, chewing gum placed in the mouth, and resistance in response to restraint; and (3) perseverative automatisms (meaning the continuation of any complex act initiated prior to loss of consciousness) such as chewing food, using a fork or spoon, drinking, or walking. In temporal lobe seizures, these automatisms can be ictal or postictal events. The waveforms recorded by the EEG in partial complex seizures are similar to those described for partial seizures. The focus of complex partial seizures is limited to the temporal (limbic) structures solely; however, this activity does spread in one or to both temporal lobes.

Generalized Seizures

Nonconvulsive (absence) and convulsive (myoclonic and tonic-clonic) epilepsies are considered to be primary and generalized if the first clinical and EEG changes indicate spontaneous involvement of both cerebral hemispheres (see Figure 2 for generalized convulsive seizure example). Clinical features are generalized with bilateral motoric manifestations. There are no signs or symptoms related to an anatomic or functional system in a single hemisphere. Impaired consciousness may be the initial event. A more recent interpretation of pathophysiologic data contends that most generalized seizures, in fact, develop from a single, undetected focus followed by a rapid generalized spreading (Aird et al. 1984).

Tonic-Clonic (Grand Mal) Seizures.   Actually, the term *convulsion* is most applicable to the generalized seizure activity traditionally called *grand mal*. Other forms of grand mal epilepsy—clonic, tonic, tonic-clonic, and atonic seizures—are now recognized. Grand mal patients sometimes experience a vague, ill-described warning (aura). The majority lose consciousness without any premonitory symptoms. A sudden, sharp tonic contraction of muscles occurs, which may involve the respiratory muscles. Patients may fall to the ground in a tonic state. They may lie rigid, bite their tongue, and pass urine involuntarily. The tonic stage then gives way to clonic, convulsive movements. During both of these phases, the patients may develop respiratory inhibition and cyanosis. Following the clonic phase, repolarization occurs, and the muscles relax. The patient remains unconscious and often awakens feeling stiff and sore all over. Marked confusion with loss of memory surrounding the seizure event occurs. Frequently, the individual progresses to a deep sleep and, on awakening, may feel well, except for some soreness and perhaps a headache.

Generalized seizures may include specific disorders with major clonic or tonic features without the presence of the other. Atonic seizures are a third form of generalized seizures in which there is a sudden diminishing in muscle tone with slumping to the ground. These attacks may be brief and are often known as "drop attacks." If consciousness is lost, the loss is extremely brief.

Absence Seizures. Absence (*petit mal*) is marked by an abrupt loss of attention to the environment while remaining awake and maintaining posture, followed by an abrupt return of attention without residual confusion. The patient is unaware of the event. Clinical absence seizures recur and cluster from a few to several hundred times per day. Stereotyped or automatic behavior accompanies at least one attack in 88 percent of patients with absence. Motor automatisms are exhibited in 60 percent of all petit mal seizures. Loss of consciousness beyond 20 seconds is rare. Blank stare and stereotyped automatisms (lip smacking, chewing movements, and blinking) are characteristic, but there is no generalized convulsive activity. Some mild clonic, atonic, or tonic activity may occur. There are several variations to classic absence seizures. Myoclonic absence of childhood and adolescence are two subtypes that occur less frequently and may reflect a variant to the genetic pattern. Absence attacks are less frequent in these adolescents, are sporatic in occurrence, and nearly always have tonic-clonic seizures.

The absence attack starts with 4 to 6 Hz diffuse multispike and wave complexes and progresses to the distinctive 3 Hz (see Figure 1) spike and wave-per-second complexes.

Myoclonic Seizures. Myoclonic seizures or myoclonic jerks are sudden brief shock-like contractions that may be generalized or confined to the face and trunk, to individual muscles, or to groups of muscles. Myoclonic jerks may be rapidly repetitive or isolated. These occur predominantly at sleep or on awakening, and may be stimulated by volitional movement. Oftentimes myoclonic jerks are not classified as epileptic seizures. Myoclonic seizures may occur in certain spinal cord diseases, among other diseases. These seizures must be distinguished from supratentorial seizures. Juvenile

myoclonic epilepsy, also known as impulsive petit mal of Janz, is characterized by mild myoclonic jerks of the neck and shoulder flexor muscles and by tonic-clonic seizures shortly after awakening. Of patients who have myoclonic seizures, 37 percent also have absence attacks. The interictal EEG trait consists of the fast variety of spike and wave sequences of 4 and 6 Hz multiwave and spike complexes. During actual myoclonic seizures, diffuse rapid spikes form in both hemispheres at 16 to 24 Hz. EEG traits persist throughout life, although peak incidence of clinical activity occurs by age 13. It is important to separate this type of epilepsy from several others that have more severe consequences.

☐ EPIDEMIOLOGY

Historically precise epidemiologic figures have been difficult to obtain due to a lack of standard definitions of seizure types. Hauser and Kurland (1975) reported incidence figures showing that approximately half of patients with seizures have generalized tonic-clonic (grand mal) seizures; 15 percent generalized tonic-clonic and complex partial seizures; 10 percent generalized tonic-clonic and absence seizures; 15 percent complex partial only; 5 percent absence only; and 5 percent minor and partial. Caution should be used in extrapolating from this information as, undoubtedly, incidence varies greatly from one geographic region to another (Aird et al. 1984). Prevalence data varies from region to region as well. Difficulties in achieving uniformity in research protocols is a major factor in this confused picture. One good study (Baumann et al. 1978) revealed prevalence differences in neighboring counties in Kentucky; this is attributed to socioeconomic differences. Crombie et al. (1960) estimated the cumulative incidence of epilepsy through all ages to be 32/1,000. Over the same age range, prevalence figures reveal 4.2/1,000 cases. Woodbury (1978) pointed out that approximately 85 percent of patients who developed epilepsy in their lifetime either recovered or had remissions indistinguishable from recovery.

☐ ETIOLOGY

Etiologic factors in epilepsy include a panoply of disorders of a genetic, infectious, toxic, metabolic, or traumatic nature. Genetic predisposition is the time-honored explanation of epilepsy, as reflected in laws from the past that precluded marriage of afflicted individuals. Genetic predisposition remains the principal predictive factor in spontaneous epileptic activity. Although genetic transmission patterns have not been worked out, family studies leave little room to doubt their effects on epilepsy prevalence. Seizure activity accompanies physiologic derangements seen in certain inherited metabolic diseases also. Of the total number of epilepsies, this particular group represents perhaps no more than 2 percent (Aird et al. 1984). An example is the seizure activity seen in phenylketonuria, which can be ameliorated on determination soon after birth.

Precise estimations of genetic influence on the epilepsies is difficult. It has been established that the siblings of epileptic victims experience epilepsy at a rate 2.5 times that of siblings in a control group. Offspring of epileptic victims have an increased incidence of seizures nearly 7 times the occurrence in the control group. Febrile convulsions occur with increased frequency among family members of probands with febrile convulsions, but the mode of inheritance remains unclear. A family history of seizures is more frequent in patients with seizures associated with head trauma than in patients who have similar traumas but do not have seizures (Anderson et al. 1982). The concept of heterogeneity adds some clarity, at least theoretically, to this somewhat arbitrary situation. Heterogeneity encompasses the combination of factors (genetic in origin) necessary for maintenance of homeostasis within systems. This principle is assumed for neural transmission, where multiple systems determine the balance between excitation and inhibition. It is possible within genetically susceptible individuals for this homeostasis to be maintained under normal conditions, despite an inherent weakness for excessive activity. If a particular stressor is confronted (e.g., head trauma), this sensitivity is activated and irritability (e.g., epileptic firing) results. Such a view explains how two genetically unrelated individuals can react differently, given the same trauma.

The particular external stressors that induce the overt change necessary for seizure activity to be manifested can be defined (Table 2). Infections, toxic substances, trauma, circulatory and metabolic disorders, and neoplastic diseases are examples of such factors. Metabolic derangements that increase seizure susceptibility are varied and impede regular

TABLE 2.   FACTORS KNOWN TO PRODUCE SEIZURE ACTIVITY

Infections
Toxic substances (e.g., alcohol, heavy metals)
Trauma
Neoplasms
Circulatory disorders
Metabolic disorders (e.g., calcium, magnesium, sodium)
Pharmacologic agents (e.g., reserpine, chlorpromazine)
Febrile states

neuronal function at a molecular level. Oxygen, sodium, potassium, calcium, magnesium, and so on are necessary to maintain adequate cellular transport and membrane stability. Certain pharmacologic agents such as reserpine and chlorpromazine have the ability to alter the levels of excitatory and inhibitory neurotransmitters by affecting their synthesis, release, reuptake, and storage; or they can affect receptor sites. Febrile conditions, especially in children, likewise affect local metabolism, producing convulsive phenomenon in susceptible children. Inflammation of the brain associated with infectious processes, trauma, and perhaps some brain tumors can produce seizures. Precise mechanisms are not fully understood. However, alterations of cell membrane permeability are involved. Interest has been directed to the alterations of cell membrane permeability seen during the release of prostaglandins. These fatty acids, a part of the general inflammatory response, are capable of producing CNS excitation and seizures in animals. Studies of cerebrospinal fluid in humans with convulsive disorders have shown elevated prostaglandin levels (Aird et al. 1984).

Many exogenous toxic substances increase seizure susceptibility. These potential influences are too numerous to list extensively. Two examples include heavy metals and ethanol. Lead and arsenic are well-known examples of heavy metals that can induce seizures. Mercury has a powerful effect on neurons to depress protein synthesis. Although the exact mechanism for the production of withdrawal seizures in an alcoholic patient is unknown, it is recognized that serum magnesium levels drop during the alcohol withdrawal period. Magnesium deficiency is known to cause potent excitation. Consequently, it is plausible to explain the convulsions seen in alcohol withdrawal as secondary to the magnesium deficiency. A second explanation might involve the withdrawal of ethanol following chronic use, and the effect this withdrawal has on the GABA system and on disinhibition.

☐ PSYCHIATRIC MANIFESTATIONS

Under the section on classification, the general manifestations of the various seizures of epilepsy were described briefly. The generalized seizures were noted to affect sensory and motor functions globally, with dissolution of mental alertness or consciousness. Focal seizures were noted to affect local areas controlling motor activity, sensory perception, and emotional content or the association areas between these primary areas. Most interesting are epileptic seizures that arise between those primary areas, presenting with organized thought or behaviors that can mimic psychiatric illness. These seizures occur exclusively in the limbic areas of the human brain, including the cortical areas of the hippocampi, cingulate gyri, or fronto-orbital cortex.

The major association area is the temporal lobe; the epilepsy of these structures commonly is called temporal lobe epilepsy as mentioned previously. Important in temporal lobe epilepsy is the fact that this area is the most susceptible in the CNS to seizure activity because it has the lowest seizure threshold. Secondly, more epilepsies arise in this area in adults than in any other areas (although there is debate over this issue). An additional interesting feature is the high degree of connectivity between the various limbic structures and between the left and right temporal lobes. Commonly, the EEG spike and waveform indicating a seizure focus can arise from both temporal lobes at the same time. Alternatively, a seizure focus can start in one temporal lobe and only later develop an independent focus in the other.

The connectivity and low seizure threshold of the temporal lobes approximate an electrically continuous structure, with the spread of the epileptic focus nearly always bilaterally. A focus with an aura can initiate a temporal lobe seizure, but the full syndrome occurs with the spread bilaterally. Along with this spread is the typical picture of mental confusion and the subsequent postictal confused state. Additional manifestations of these temporal lobe seizures include features of the focus, its spread correlated to functions of the temporal lobe and associated deep limbic structures, and automatisms. Autonomic nervous system signs can be seen with involvement of the gastrointestinal tract, cardiovascular system, pulmonary system, and urogenital system. Common ictal emotional features include fear, depression, elation, anxiety, anger, and a sense of doom, in decreasing order of occurrence. Religiosity is well documented. Delusions, especially paranoid, can present with rage reactions or extreme fearfulness. Hallucinations are reported as well. Interestingly, memory can be affected, with extraneous memories being reproduced. Again, through the course of the epileptic disorder, these signs and symptoms are noted to be recurrent and stereotyped and are associated with the ictal and postictal confusion, amnesia, and automatisms characteristic of the temporal lobe seizure. It should be recognized that these temporal lobe seizures (psychomotor, partial complex) can evolve to generalized seizures (Cummings 1985).

The international classification considers that a focal disorder originating in the temporal lobe rarely remains localized and usually spreads bilaterally with ictal and postictal confusion and amnesia. Investigators point to evidence that, in rare instances, a localized focus may fail to generalize for a number of days or weeks. Psychiatric abnormalities may occur in this interim (interictal) period in patients known to be epileptic previously. EEG abnormalities may be found on routine examination, at times, but certainly not always. Controversy exists over ascribing interictal behavior changes to undetected foci because other investigators disagree on the existence (or necessity) of such lesions (Himmelhoch 1984). A new technique, the stereo EEG, which can localize foci within limbic areas previously remote to detection, has been developed. This is accomplished through the surgical introduction of fine wire electrodes into the brain. Although impractical for general application, this approach generates a much higher yield of EEG abnormalities in patients. Observations of epileptics over time combined with this technique can verify that episodes of atypical psychiatric disorders are related to abnormal electrical discharge within limbic cortex (Bancaud 1980).

Psychiatric syndromes and behavioral alterations can occur between seizure (interictal) events. These events may result from psychodynamic factors related to illness per se, from intermittent electrical discharge in the brain, or from direct injury to the brain with seizure and behavioral changes resulting. Cummings (1985) reported increased behavioral and psychiatric alteration in 10 to 80 percent of epileptics, greater than in patients with other chronic illnesses. Studies suggest that the most severe and highest rates of interictal psychiatric symptomatology occur among victims of complex partial seizures. These behavioral changes are manifest primarily as personality changes, schizophrenia-like syndromes, and affective disorders.

The "epileptic personality" described most frequently occurs in temporal lobe seizure patients and includes features of hyperreligiosity, hyposexuality, circumstantiality, and hypergraphia (Bear and Fedio 1977; Bear et al. 1982). Other features include elevated paranoia and schizophrenia scales on the Minnesota Multiphasic Personality Inventory, with more frequent occurrences of dissociative phenomena. These behavioral alterations can occur in other neuropsychiatric disturbances as well, however.

Interictal schizophrenia-like syndromes are well documented among seizure patients with temporal lobe pathology (Perez and Trimble 1980). Although a formal thought disorder is described in half of these patients, paranoid delusions and auditory hallucinations are the primary events. These patients fail to exhibit premorbid schizophrenic personality indicators and have no increased incidence of familial psychotic illnesses. Recent studies (Toone et al. 1982) suggested the prevalence of these alterations at 10 to 30 percent among the complex partial seizure patients. Generally the average onset of these events is 14 years after initial seizure activity.

Several types of interictal psychoses have been identified. Most common are those resembling schizophrenic psychosis and bipolar psychosis. These two clinical entities are distinguished by the fact that the schizophrenia-like syndrome is more often associated with left temporal lobe foci and alleviated by antipsychotic medications. These schizophrenia-like psychoses are atypical on the basis of their remissions and exacerbations (related to EEG abnormalities) and the fact that affect is maintained and social contacts persist. The bipolar-like syndrome is distinguished by the fact that a right temporal lobe focus predominates and the fact that this syndrome is resolved by electroconvulsive therapy (ECT) or by the occurrence of an epileptic seizure (Blumer 1984). An important feature for these focally stimulated disorders is that they fail to spread to both lobes immediately. There is no

resultant confusion or amnesia. The patient is conscious and is able then to plan behaviors based on extraneously derived thoughts, emotions, and motor activities. The implication is that deep, many times subclinical, electrical irritations in limbic areas might stimulate thoughts that lead to compensatory analysis and organized planning in a fully awake subject. The resultant behavior would appear as a highly organized, directed behavior in a seemingly intact individual. However, the motivating influences would be pathologic and based on the epileptic discharge. Necessarily, this situation would arise in a patient who had previously shown signs and symptoms of epilepsy. In fact, such a focus is usually known to terminate in partial complex seizures disorder ultimately.

Interictal depression occurs frequently; however, depression occurs ictally and postictally as well. Whether this interictal change results from the psychological stress of the illness or is induced by structural events is unknown. Recognizing depression in seizure patients is particularly important, however, as this population has an increased incidence of suicide (Mackay 1979).

Current literature rarely addresses the issue of psychological reactions to epilepsy. The general reaction is to a loss of health and the subsequent adjustment to a chronic illness process. In this regard, epilepsy is differentiated little from chronic illnesses with reactions that include depression, withdrawal, and isolation. Resistance to treatment reflected in compliance problems, especially in children (although not exclusively), may stimulate dynamic interpretation. Such an immature defense is maladaptive and often indicates an attempt to regain control of the environment, yet leads to a paradoxical worsening of symptoms and to a lessening of control.

In addition to these reactions, an additional stressor results from the negative stigma attached to the illness. Despite the fact that there have been descriptions in literature of the ancient belief that epileptics were "talking to the Gods" and that many prominent figures, good and evil, had epilepsy, the time-honored reaction by society toward persons affected with epilepsy has been that of repulsion and derision. At times the ancients believed these people to be possessed. Verbalizations were thought to be communications with demons. The reaction of an epileptic to these reigning sentiments might be akin to those experienced by persons badly disfigured. Powerful behavioral patterns of isolation and withdrawal and emotional features of depression and alienation may occur. The converse with overcompensation has been seen historically with figures such as Julius Caesar and the prophets Mohammed and Paul. The illness can vary greatly in severity, not always according to the severity of causative factors. For those afflicted who experience an overriding and disabling sense of inadequacy, supportive psychotherapy can be helpful. Central to this support is the education of family members to the medical and psychiatric concomitants of seizures. Education of the family can mediate compassionate communication and assistance in designing mature behavioral adaptations. The patient must deal with issues involving dependency on medications throughout life, with potential limitations both socially and vocationally as a result. Genetic counseling may be necessary at some point. Being restricted, and different, as a child may foster a negative self-concept and lead to further, self-imposed, restrictions intellectually and socially. The patient must learn to focus on realistic goals in an effort to gain mastery and competence as an individual. Once understanding of the physiology and psychology of the illness occurs, a more mature adaptation is possible.

☐ DIFFERENTIAL DIAGNOSIS

Accurate diagnosis requires careful consideration of disorders with similar features. The diagnosis of most epileptic seizures can be confirmed by serial EEG recordings. A much broader array of disorders must be investigated prior to making a diagnosis of temporal lobe epilepsy. Clearly the greatest diagnostic dilemma in epilepsy involves the category of seizure phenomena that includes complex partial or temporal lobe epilepsy. One study (Aird and Tsubaki 1958) revealed an 84 percent misdiagnosis of temporal lobe seizures. Of these patients, 55 percent were thought to suffer from grand mal or focal motor seizures because of dramatic motor presentations; 30 percent were misdiagnosed as absence because of the minor psychomotor activity identified. Additional diagnostic mistakes included various psychiatric conditions, behavioral disorders in childhood, brain tumors, and migraine. As a result, approximately 76 percent received inadequate treatment. Specific diagnosis, although difficult, is possible through careful clinical examination of the patient.

Temporal lobe epilepsy is currently a well-recognized seizure phenomenon. Temporal lobe symptoms followed by automatisms complete the diagnosis of temporal lobe epilepsy. An important fact to remember is the form of the aura that reflects temporal lobe function with occurrences such as hallucinations, psychic manifestations, automatisms, isolated fear, and autonomic and visceral manifestations. Affective manifestations of activity reflect deep temporal circuitry. Described above, interictal phenomena may be such that a primary psychiatric diagnosis appears evident. Confirmation by EEG of temporal lobe activity will alleviate doubt, but frequently cannot be obtained.

Important points to remember in considering a diagnosis of temporal lobe epilepsy include the following (Aird et al. 1984):

1. Minor spells are reflected in the patient by brief periods of missed conversation or reading lapses. The patient may be aware but, unless asked by the physician, may not report these spells.
2. Temporal aura precedes the seizure activity, which does not occur usually in either absence or grand mal.
3. Temporal automatisms last up to a minute or more. Absence events are shorter in duration and occur frequently in a given time period.
4. EEG findings include anterior temporal and low frontal foci, patterns not found in other forms.

Several systemic conditions—including hypoglycemia, transient cerebral ischemia, and hypoxic episodes—must be differentiated from temporal lobe epilepsy. Hypoglycemia is of particular interest. Hypoglycemia can induce seizure activity because the hippocampal area is known to be especially vulnerable to this metabolic state. Careful control of insulin therapy must be maintained as well as control of the primary seizure disorder, otherwise temporal activity will persist. Syncopal episodes may be confused with seizure activity, although rarely do EEG changes reflect electrical activity after these "fainting spells." It is important to consider the possibility of genetic vulnerability in a patient who does react to hypotensive episodes in an overdramatic way. Frequently a vague or minimal change in EEG activity in these people will occur; this should be followed carefully. Additional mechanisms that can produce hypoxic episodes and fainting and appear seizure-like include pulmonary conditions, arrhythmias, and cardiac abnormalities. Transient ischemic attacks in the elderly are a well-recognized phenomenon.

Several pain syndromes appear to accompany borderline seizure activity by EEG recordings. These episodic pain syndromes include an abdominal pain complex that occurs without stress or feeding complications. A variety of atypical migraine headaches has been described also. Unique to this headache is the mental slowing that may occur with failure to respond to ergotamine treatment. Rarely, chest pain may be reflective of borderline seizure activity. In all of these pain syndromes, associated cerebral symptoms are distinguishing. However, complete examinations and EEG studies are required for confirmation.

Differential diagnostic considerations of specific psychiatric phenomena such as psychosis and behavioral problems in childhood have been presented above. It is important to bear in mind their close relationship to temporal lobe activity. As stated, treatments often overlap. Functional disorders can complicate accurate diagnoses as well. These include hyperventilation and hysterical reactions. Hyperventilation is a common event in the practice of primary care, cardiology, and psychiatry. This syndrome is so common and recognizable that, on occasion, real seizure activity precipitated by hyperventilation is overlooked in a seizure-vulnerable person. A careful review of history and EEG findings can clarify this diagnostic issue, with treatment aimed at alleviating psychodynamic mechanisms as well as biologic mechanisms.

Finally, psychogenic or pseudoseizures (Table 3) are a well-recognized behavior that can mimic seizure activity to a high degree, depending on the sophistication of the patient. Rarely does incontinence occur during the episodes; consciousness, although clouded, is maintained. Response to pain may be of value in determining the level of awareness in these patients. The EEG is normal. Pseudoseizures frequently are events accompanying documented seizure disorders. Videotape examples of the patient's real seizure phenomenon as well as pseudoseizure activity is helpful in effecting a greater understanding in the patient of any volition employed in this reaction. The loss of control that many patients sense when subject to chronic illness may be heightened in these victims of pseudoseizures. Reassurance, support, and education are important to a successful resolution of this complicating behavioral form. Care should be taken in making this diagnosis because atypical seizures can occur without accompanying EEG changes. Conscientious attention to detail provides a clear diagnosis supporting successful treatment (Blumer 1984).

☐ CLINICAL EVALUATION

In attempting to delineate the treatment plan for epilepsy, the form of the seizure activity (classification) as well as etiologic factors must be considered. The work-up should include an extensive history, with the participation of a knowledgeable relative. Patients may have trouble providing important information as a result of changes in their level of consciousness. The history is important to

TABLE 3. DIFFERENTIATING FEATURES OF PSEUDOSEIZURES VERSUS EPILEPTIC SEIZURES

Feature	Epileptic seizure	Pseudoseizure
Clinical features		
Nocturnal seizure	Common	Uncommon
Stereotyped aura	Usually	None
Cyanotic skin changes during seizures	Common	None
Self-injury	Common	Rare
Incontinence	Common	Rare
Postictal confusion	Present	None
Body movements	Tonic and/or clonic	Nonstereotyped and asynchronous
Affected by suggestion	No	Yes
EEG features		
Spike and waveforms	Present	Absent
Postictal showing	Present	Absent
Interictal abnormalities	Variable	Variable

identify the clinical characteristic of the seizures and associated phenomena. Of particular importance are details from the patient suggesting focal abnormalities, such as motor signs or sensory symptoms and the observations of others regarding focal initiation and postictal manifestations. Past history may be helpful in documenting previous cerebral insult, such as head injury or infection. Birth history should also be elicited. Frequently, the patient's mother's perinatal history is of importance. Family history can reveal hereditary tendencies toward convulsive phenomena. The general physical examination and review of systems are of great primary value in detecting systemic mechanisms of significance. The principal goal of the neurologic examination is the determination of focal abnormalities.

Routine laboratory studies should include a blood count, urinalysis, serum chemistry, and electrolytes; certain X rays and an EEG are necessary. Described above, the EEG is of particular importance in determining the form of the seizure discharge and its locus. EEG abnormality is associated with approximately 90 percent of epileptic patients. Special activation procedures of the EEG accentuate the physiologic abnormalities of unstable portions of the cerebral cortex. These manipulations elicit activity from deep within the cerebrum; they include maneuvers such as hyperventilation, photic stimulation, sleep recording, and, in some cases, drug activation. When used properly, activation techniques add considerably to the identification of underlying abnormalities and to the understanding of mechanisms that precipitate seizures in an individual patient. The EEG must be correlated with the clinical data and other studies. A negative test by no means excludes epilepsy; commonly, epilepsy will have an EEG recording "within normal limits" on first examination.

The rapid advances in radiologic examination and computed tomography (CT) scanning techniques have revolutionized the field of neuroradiology. The principal advantage lies in the greater ability of the CT scanning device to detect lesions of the brain. The introduction of magnetic resonance imaging (MRI) is a major advance as computer analysis of intracranial detail allows even greater diagnostic accuracy. MRI technology promises increasing accuracy in providing structural detail in organ systems and hence detailing pathologies. The MRI is used to augment CT scans if clinical evidence demands further discrimination.

Currently, several centers are investigating the use of positron emission tomography (PET) scans. This procedure measures metabolic activity of tissues. The necessity of utilizing a cyclotron in the imaging process, however, limits practical use of such an instrument to date.

☐ TREATMENT CONSIDERATIONS

The accepted treatments of epilepsy include pharmacotherapy, surgical extirpation of a focus, and ECT. The most commonly applied is pharmacotherapy.

As with any other disorder, the correct diagnosis must be made before treatment decisions are made. This requires accurate information regarding the clinical description of the seizure activity. A thorough history confirmed by observers is crucial. Just as crucial is the clinician's ability to classify securely the seizure type that has been described. Finally, the diagnosis can be supported by the EEG; the conditions under which this test is done (sleep, photic stimulation, hyperventilation, nasopharyngeal leads) are important, and a decision to incorporate these activation procedures depends on the diagnostic classification of the seizure.

As a reliable diagnosis of a seizure disorder is made, the selection of pharmacotherapy becomes relatively easy. Table 4 is a listing of the first-choice anticonvulsants used for treatment. There are additional choices for each category of seizure if these first-line drugs fail. Appropriate management includes adequate dosages to provide therapeutic blood levels and caution regarding side effects (Table 5).

General guidelines for treatment include the following:

1. Barbiturates and benzodiazepines should be avoided whenever possible because of sedation and tolerance.
2. Phenytoin should be avoided because gingival hypertrophy, ataxia, and hirsuitism in females may occur.
3. Successful treatment depends on giving the specific drug for the specific seizure type at doses to produce adequate blood levels.
4. One drug should be used to control the seizures when possible. Each drug should be increased in dosage until seizures are controlled or untoward side effects are noted.

TABLE 4.   RECOMMENDED DRUGS FOR VARIOUS SEIZURE TYPES

Seizure type	Drugs[a]
Simple partial seizures	Phenytoin, carbamazepine, primidone, phenobarbital
Complex partial seizures	Carbamazepine, phenytoin, primidone, phenobarbital
Generalized tonic-clonic	Phenytoin, carbamazepine, phenobarbital, valproate
Absence	Ethosuximide, valproate, clonazepam, methsuximide
Myoclonic	Valproate, ethosuximide, clonazepam
Atonic	Valproate
Infantile spasms	ACTH, steroids, nitrarepam,[b] clonazepam

[a]In decreasing order of use.
[b]Not available in the United States.

5. Never withdraw a drug abruptly (unless dangerous side effects occur) because this can result in severe status epilepticus.
6. As one drug is being gradually reduced, another should be substituted slowly.
7. Multiple drugs can be used if no single drug can control seizures, but a multitude of side effects may result.
8. Blood levels of drugs are extremely important in monitoring treatment. Dosage frequency and drug interactions can affect blood levels. Patient compliance is problematic. Drug levels can help to monitor all of these possibilities.

Treatment failures commonly occur secondary to the complexity of the issues surrounding the management of epilepsy. It is imperative for the physician to communicate well with the patient, who sometimes can have difficulties in comprehension because of structural lesions of the brain or because of the sedating side effects of the medications. Compliance is a key issue. Verbal interventions including education and supportive and behavioral psychotherapies can be instrumental in obtaining control. Positive aspects of good control should be encouraged. Improvements in employment and in educational opportunities, social and family environment, and mental and physical health are reinforcing for the patient.

Noncompliance can lead to failure of control and negative repercussions in those areas previously mentioned. Occasionally, epileptic behavior is rewarding in itself. Psychotherapy supporting health and its rewards should overcome the rewards of any secondary gain. It is necessary for the therapist to educate while supporting family and friends in these complex situations.

There are two additional forms of treatment for epilepsy. The first is psychosurgery, used for patients who have intractable seizures. In this situation, a highly accurate localization of an uncontrollable seizure focus is made by EEG. This focus is then surgically removed, and the epilepsy cured. There are problems with this method of treatment. Many times multiple foci are present in epileptic

TABLE 5.   ANTIEPILEPTIC DRUGS

Name	Dosage (mg)	Blood level (mg/ml)	Side effects
Carbamazepine (Tegretol)	800–1200	4–12	Blood dyscrasias, leukopenia, dizziness, drowsiness, unsteadiness, nausea, vomiting, rash, hepatitis
Phenytoin (Dilantin)	100–500	10–20	Ataxia, gingival hypertrophy, hirsuitism, neuropathy, blood dyscrasias, rash
Phenobarbital	100–300	10–35	Lethargy, irritability, rash
Ethosuximide (Zarontin)	500–1500	40–100	Anorexia, nausea, fatigue, headache, blood dyscrasias, lupus, hepatitis
Primidone (Mysoline)	250–1000	5–11	Lethargy, irritability, impotence, rash
Valproic Acid (Depakene)	1500–3000	50–100	Nausea, weight gain, tremor, loss of hair, hepatitis
Clonazepam (Klonopin)	1.5–15	0.025–0.075	Lethargy, depression, tremor, headache, hair loss, nephritis, glaucoma
Methsuximide (Celontin)	300–1200	10–40	Nausea, ataxia, dizziness, weakness, rash, blood dyscrasias, nephritis

patients, and surgery is not a consideration. It can be difficult to locate a focus. Another problem is that many foci are not located in areas readily approached through surgery. Sometimes the epilepsy continues even though the focus has been removed. Finally, scarring from the surgery can produce new foci and new epileptic discharges.

ECT was mentioned previously as a form of treatment for complex partial epilepsies. In some of these patients, a temporal lobe focus is associated with psychosis. Many of these psychiatric symptoms worsen after a prolonged seizure-free period, yet resolve following the breakthrough of generalized seizure activity. On occasion, ECT has been used to provide this discharge and resultant seizure. Multiple ECTs may produce an even more positive effect.

☐ SPECIAL CONSIDERATIONS

Kindling

Kindling results from summation of low threshold electrical or chemical discharges to induce a full behavioral response over time (Goddard 1967). This phenomenon was first described in the mid-1960s and has resulted in the improved understanding of many confusing states of brain activity. For epileptologists, this means that seizure activity can result from subthreshold electrical irritations that seem to sensitize circuits over time to produce full-blown seizure activity, especially if there is genetic vulnerability. Poor control of seizures creates an opportunity for wider sensitization (by kindling) of CNS circuits by an existing focus. The primary seizure presentation becomes even more difficult to control. Victims of this course can demonstrate severe social and intellectual deterioration. Adequate seizure control should obviate kindling and its devastating consequences.

Kindling is a self-limited event in many. Although its end point may not be reached for years or decades, gradually the phenomenon subsides and the focus eventually fails to elicit electrical response and dissipates. At that point, treatment should be terminated.

☐ SUMMARY

Epilepsy and epileptic seizures result from a complex interaction of extrinsic factors on intrinsic conditions oftentimes predetermined genetically. The international classification of epileptic seizures has led to an increased understanding of etiology and treatment approaches. In addition to motoric, sensory, and cognitive effects, emotional and behavioral changes occur, especially in complex partial seizure disorders or temporal lobe epilepsy. Psychiatric changes are noted during seizure activity per se (ictally), as postseizure phenomena, and between seizure events (interictally). Particular personality characteristics are described frequently in seizure patients along with examples of schizophrenia-like and bipolar type psychoses. Depression occurs and recognition and treatment are extremely important. Utilization of the EEG is essential diagnostically, although deep foci are difficult to illicit. Treatment focuses on eradicating electrical seizure activity as well as on adjustment to the processes of experiencing a chronic illness.

☐ REFERENCES

Aird RB, Tsubaki T: Common sources of error in diagnosis and therapy of convulsive disorders. J Nerv Ment Dis 5:400–406, 1958

Aird RB, Masland MD, Woodbury DM: The Epilepsies: A Critical Review. New York, Raven Press, 1984

Anderson VE, Hauser WA, Penry JK, et al (eds): Genetic Basis of the Epilepsies. New York, Raven Press, 1982

Bancaud JC: Topographic relationship between cerebral lesions and seizure discharges, in Advances in Epileptology. Edited by Canger R, Angeleri F, Penry JK. New York, Raven Press, 1980, pp 103–109

Baumann RJ, Marx MB, Leonidakis MG: Epilepsy in rural Kentucky: prevalence in a population of school age children. Epilepsia 19:75–80, 1978

Bear DM, Fredio P: Quantitative analysis of interictal behavior in temporal lobe epilepsy. Arch Neurol 34:454–467, 1977

Bear D, Levin K, Blumer D, Ryder J: Interictal behavior in hospitalized temporal lobe epileptics: relationship to idiopathic psychiatric syndromes. J Neurol Neurosurg Psychiatry 45:481–488, 1982

Blumer D (ed): Psychiatric Aspects of Epilepsy. Washington, DC, American Psychiatric Press, 1984

Crombie DL, Cross KW, Fry J, et al: A survey of the epilepsies in general practice. Br Med J 2:416–422, 1960

Cummings JL: Epilepsy: ictal and interictal behavioral alterations, in Clinical Neuropsychiatry. New York, Edited by Grune & Stratton, 1985, pp 95–116

Goddard GU: Development of epileptic seizures through brain stimulation at low intensity. Nature 214:1020–1021, 1967

Hauser WA, Kurland LT: Epidemiology of epilepsy in Rochester, Minnesota, 1935 through 1967. Epilepsia 16:1–66, 1975

Himmelhoch JM: Major mood disorders related to epileptic changes, in Psychiatric Aspects of Epilepsy. Edited by Blumer D. Washington, DC, American Psychiatric Press, 1984, pp 271–294

International League Against Epilepsy Commission on Classification and Terminology: Proposal for revised clinical and electroencephalographic classification of epileptic seizures. Epilepsia 22:489–501, 1981

Mackay A: Self-poisoning: a complication of epilepsy. Br J Psychiatry 134:277–282, 1979

Penry TK, Dreifuss FE: Automatisms associated with absence of petit mal epilepsy. Arch Neurol 21:142–149, 1969

Perez MM, Trimble MR: Epileptic psychosis: diagnostic comparison with process schizophrenia. Br J Psychiatry 137:245–249, 1980

Toone BK, Garralda ME, Ron MA: The psychosis of epilepsy and functional psychoses: a clinical and phenomenological comparison. Br J Psychiatry 141:256–261, 1982

Woodbury L: Epidemiologic characteristics, in Plan for Nationwide Action on Epilepsy. Report of the Commission for the Control of Epilepsy and Its Consequences, Vol. IV (USDHEW Pub No NIH 78-279). Washington, DC, US Department of Health, Education and Welfare, 1978, pp 1–114

Chapter 13

Neuropsychiatric Aspects of Headache and Facial Pain

David Spiegel, M.D.

Reed J. Kaplan, M.D.

HEADACHE MAY BE THE MOST COMMON malaise in human experience. It is estimated that 1 in 3 of all Americans suffer from severe headaches at some stage in their lives. Approximately 30 million pounds of aspirin are ingested in the United States annually, most of it to relieve headache (Raskin and Appenzeller 1980).

Although the treatment of most headaches is relegated to home and over-the-counter remedies, headache may be the first sign of serious illnesses such as brain tumor, hypertension, meningoencephalitides, uremia, temporal arteritis (giant cell arteritis), pituitary tumor, and toxic ingestions, among others. Regardless of the cause, recurrent headache is a major reason for severe disability and discomfort. Estimates of the lifetime prevalence of

headache range between 80 and 90 percent (Waters and O'Connor 1975). In one study of presenting complaints at a university emergency department (Dhopesh et al. 1979), headache was the primary complaint of 64.9 percent of patients. Of these, approximately 40 percent of complaints were related to infection, 5 percent to hypertension, 1 percent to subarachnoid hemorrhage, less than 1 percent to meningitis, 9 percent to posttraumatic headache, almost 25 percent to tension and vascular (migraine), and 15 percent to miscellaneous causes. Of 41 patients admitted to the hospital, 27 percent were found to have headache associated with intercranial hemorrhage, viral meningitis, subdural hematomas, or tumor. The rest fell into the aforementioned categories. Four of five headache sufferers and one-half of those with migraines do not seek medical help (Ogden 1952). Estimates of socioeconomic loss sustained by absenteeism and medical cost associated with headache are approximately one-half billion dollars in the United States (Ekbom et al. 1978).

Headache is also a common problem among psychiatric patients. For example, the prevalence of migraine headaches has been found to be three times (9 percent) as high among a sample of psychotherapy patients than among age-matched controls (3 percent) (Schnarch and Hunter 1980). In a study of 229 psychiatry consultations for headache (Khouri-Haddad 1984), 19.2 percent were of the vascular type; 34.9 percent of the muscle contraction type; and 25.7 percent a combination of the two. The most common psychiatric diagnoses among this group of patients with headaches were depressive neurosis (dysthymic disorder), 22.7 percent; compulsive personality disorder, 13 percent; schizophrenia, 7 percent; and histrionic personality disorder, 6.5 percent.

MECHANISMS OF HEAD PAIN

The following cranial structures are sensitive to pain:

1. Skin, subcutaneous tissue, muscles, arteries, and periosteum of the skull
2. Delicate structures of eyes, ears, and nasal cavity
3. Intracranial venous sinuses and their tributary veins
4. Parts of the dura at the base of the brain and the arteries within the dura mater and pia arachnoid
5. The glossopharyngeal, trigeminal, vagus, and first three cranial nerves (Adams and Victor, 1981)

The pain of intracranial disease is generally referred to some part of the head within the territory supplied by the fifth, ninth, and tenth cranial nerves or the first three cervical nerves. There may be local tenderness at the site of referred pain. Dental and jaw pain may cause cranial pain in regions other than the immediate site of pathology. In general, except in systemic illness such as uremia, pain from other sites of pathology is not referred to the head. However, headache may be caused by other indirect means.

In landmark studies in the 1930s, Wolff (1963) demonstrated that spontaneous head pain may be attributed to one or more of the following mechanisms:

1. Distention, traction, and dilatation of intra- or extracranial vessels
2. Traction or displacement of large intracranial veins or the enveloping dura
3. Compression, traction, or inflammation of sensory cranial and spinal nerves
4. Voluntary or involuntary spasm and possibly interstitial inflammation of cranial and cervical muscles
5. Meningeal irritation and elevated intracranial pressure

Mass lesions cause pain by deforming, displacing, or exerting traction on vessels and dural structures. The location of the mass will cause pain referable to the nerve that innervates the deformed structures. Elevated cranial pressure generally causes bifrontal or occipital fluctuant pain, often exacerbated by changes in position, such as bending or lying down, and by maneuvers that physiologically raise intracranial pressure, such as coughing, sneezing, or straining during defecation. *Headaches that are worsened by changes in position, awaken patients from sleep (lying down for long periods), or are associated with vomiting are cause for aggressive investigation of a serious intracranial lesion.*

Inflammatory lesions, such as temporal arteritis, usually give rise to pain, often with tenderness in the region of inflamed vasculature, which later generalizes as the disease progresses. Another common cause of head pain is sinusitis, usually localized around the frontal regions of the eyes and forehead. This pain is sometimes intermittent within any one episode of sinusitis, due to fluctuant patterns of drainage from the sinuses. However, the diagnosis of sinusitis as a cause of *chronic* headache is much overused.

MIGRAINE

It is estimated that 20 to 25 percent of the population suffers with migraine headaches (Waters 1973, 1978; Waters and O'Connor 1975). There appears to be no association with intelligence, social class, or educational background (Markush et al. 1975; Waters 1971), although the female-to-male ratio is roughly 3:1 (Lance and Anthony 1966; Olesen 1978). There does appear to be a longitudinal pattern of inheritance. Migraine may affect children, adolescents, or adults for the first time, although age of onset and duration of the disorder do not bear a close relationship to the future course of the syndrome. However, the prodromata and intensity of pain may alter with time (Raskin 1980). Some people may begin having migraine in childhood, only to have it abate in adolescence and then recur later in adulthood. In some, headache begins in adult life and persists throughout life. However, the majority of "first attacks" occur during the first four decades of life.

Clinical Phenomenology

The usual pattern of onset for migraine is on awakening in the morning, although migraines may occur at any time during the day. The headache may at times awaken patients from sleep. When this is a new pattern, a space-occupying lesion or other source of raised intracranial pressure should be investigated and ruled out.

Migraine headache is usually gradual in onset and reaches peak intensity in minutes to several hours. There is usually a plateau phase, which lasts for hours to days, then a defervescence over several hours. The prototypic pain of migraine is often characterized as a dull throbbing unilateral headache, which varies in location between attacks. It may involve the entire hemicranium, remain confined to the occipital or frontal quadrant, or present in a combination of locations. A common place of presentation is at the vertex. Although the pain is not always pulsatile, this quality usually emerges after the onset of localized steady pain. This pulsatile pattern may be precipitated by changes in position, as in rapidly moving the head or in bending. Raskin and Schwartz (1979) reported that more than 30 percent of migraine patients experienced a superimposed sharp stabbing needle or knife-like pain, often at the orbit or temple. Movement of any sort may exacerbate the pain, and lying still in a quiet darkened room may help relieve it.

Co-occurring Symptoms and Signs

Nausea and vomiting are the two most common complaints with migraine, occurring in more than half of patients. Diarrhea and other gastrointestinal upsets are frequent, and may be part of an overall autonomic instability. The patient may experience these symptoms for a few hours or even days before the headache. They will then commonly continue through the course of the headache and subside as it does. Blurred vision, lightheadedness, and syncope are found in about 10 percent of patients (Barolin 1966; Weil 1962). Concurrent convulsive movements are sometimes apparent (Critchley and Ferguson 1933; Ely 1930). Approximately 70 percent of people have scalp tenderness with the migraine (Raskin and Appenzeller 1980), ranging from mild "odd sensations" to marked discomfort with pressure. Often the face may become pallid and cool, although facial flushing may be observed. Although not common, subconjunctival hemorrhages, epistaxis, and orbital ecchymoses have been reported (Sacks 1970). Fluid retention, which occurs in a majority of patients in the days and hours before a headache, may be a troublesome part of the migraine syndrome. Fluid retention can manifest as pitting edema or discomfort with tight-fitting clothes and jewelry. It may result in a weight gain of 5 pounds or more. There may also be concurrent or subsequent polyuria. About 10 to 20 percent of patients with migraine report nasal stuffiness, although this is more usually a prominent feature of cluster headaches. Symptoms of nasal stuffiness may lead to an erroneous diagnosis of sinusitis, which is rarely a cause of recurrent headache.

Of particular interest to the psychiatrist is the mood alteration seen with migraine, which may occur before, during, or after attacks. Mood alteration may include fatigue, lethargy, anxiety, irritability, and, at times, exhilaration. The intensity of the mood usually varies with the intensity of the headache. Raskin (1980) pointed out that "the exceptions to [this] generalization are striking, and render it unlikely that these changes are simply secondary to the acute headache pain" (p. 41).

Other somatic findings that often accompany migraine are autonomic variations that manifest as fever, tachycardia, and, specifically, paroxysmal atrial tachycardia. According to Perera (1971), 40 percent of patients with documented paroxysmal atrial tachycardia have classic migraine headaches.

Precipitants of Migraine

Common among the factors that may precipitate migraine are foodstuffs such as nitrites, tyramine, glutamates, and salt. Temperature and changes in weather, as in conditions before a storm, have been associated with incipient headache, as have such environmental and psychological events as fatigue, physical exertion, hunger, stress, and anxiety. Head trauma, menses, and oral contraceptives are associated with a higher incidence of migraine. Such diverse factors as hypervitaminosis A, nitroglycerine, histamine, steroid withdrawal, perfumes, naps, smoke, various industrial chemicals, fluorescent lighting, high altitudes, and allergic reactions have also been implicated (Raskin 1980).

Migrainous Syndromes

The most common cerebral disturbances accompanying migraine are bilateral visual hallucinations. These occur in more than 40 percent of patients (Hachinski et al. 1973) and usually take the form of simple monochromatic or polychromatic geometric patterns (most often stars, angles, and circles). The hallucinations may progress to more complicated forms, presumably as integrative structures in the visual systems are implicated in the attack. The hallucinations may shift in space (techopsias), shape (metamorphopsia), or luminance (scintillation). Some persons have actually experienced very complex visual hallucinations, which implies more extensive temporal lobe involvement. Total blindness is not common, but it may occur as a transient phenomenon, usually preceded by the aforementioned visual events. Blindness may be monocular, and then must be distinguished from central retinal occlusion, transient ischemic attacks, or embolic infarcts from the carotid circulation. Visual distortions in which objects appear to enlarge (macropsia) or diminish (micropsia) in size have been described. In addition, patients may have somatic hallucinations in which they experience a variation in their own size, extracorporeal experiences, and distortions of proprioceptive angles. Included among somatic hallucinations are deja vu and jamais vu phenomena.

When a headache occurs after these prodromata, as it most often does, it does so approximately 20 to 30 minutes after the prodrome. Paresthesias occur in about one-third of migraine patients. These show a predilection for the face and ipsilateral hand, lasting minutes to hours, and rarely days. Other distributions of paresthesias have been reported; these include both hands, feet, or all four limbs. Unlike transient ischemic attacks, these paresthesias often include internal oral structures.

Complicated Migraine

The definition of complicated migraine is controversial. Lance (1982) proposed the following definition: "cases in which the neurologic symptoms and signs outlast the headache for twenty-four hours or more, or in which permanent deficit develops because of retinal, cerebral, or brainstem infarction" (p. 128). This is not a complete definition; in some cases of complicated migraine, the pattern does not hold. This is true in hemiplegic migraine, in which the headache outlasts the hemiplegia.

Hemiplegic Migraine

This syndrome usually occurs in children and adolescents, rarely for the first time in adulthood. Hemiplegic migraine appears as a weakness on one side of the body, often the face and ipsilateral arm, rather than the leg. It may be accompanied by numbness and paresthesias. If the disturbance is on the dominant side of the body, a dysphasia (mixed type) or a global aphasia may be part of the symptom complex. The headache usually ensues about 20 to 30 minutes after the motor symptoms begin. Unlike the neurologic deficits of other complicated migraines, those in this syndrome rarely remain. Subsequent attacks may vary from side to side. There is an increased familial incidence of this syndrome, which appears to follow an autosomal dominant pattern of inheritance (Glista et al. 1975).

Basilar Migraine

Basilar migraine is of particular interest to the psychiatrist because of its quasipsychiatric presentation. The headache is usually in the occipital region and is steady or pulsating. In about 25 percent of patients, the only neurologic symptoms during the attack are referable to the territory of the basilar artery circulation. These symptoms include sudden and total blindness; alterations of consciousness, sometimes described as dream-like; agitated, aggressive, hysterical, or psychotic behavior; vertigo; tinnitus; ataxia; dysarthria; and distal or perioral paresthesias. These may occur in a variety of combinations. The patient may experience simple or vivid visual hallucinations prior to the onset of blindness. The onset of basilar migraine is usually in the second or third decade, with predominance among females.

Ophthalmoplegic Migraine

In ophthalmoplegic migraine, unlike the other migrainous headaches discussed, the headache usually *precedes* the neurologic symptoms. The pain is confined to the region of one eye, which is the same with each attack. It usually develops over the course of several hours, followed then by diplopia secondary to involvement of one of the oculomotor nerves, usually the third. Ipsilateral pupillary dilatation accompanies third nerve impairment. The headache usually abates within a few hours, but the ophthalmoparesis persists for a few days, even weeks. Permanent deficit is not frequent but may occur with successive incidents. Chronic lid droop and a sluggishly reactive pupil may also accompany the chronic ophthalmoparesis.

Sensory Migraine

Sensory migraine typically presents in young children or adults. It is characterized by tingling and numbness beginning in the hand, spreading over a period of minutes up the forearm, skipping the proximal arm, then involving the mouth, lips, cheek, and tongue. Variants may include scintillating scotoma, dysarthria, and mood disturbance. After usually 20 to 30 minutes, the sensory symptoms clear and a contralateral throbbing headache develops and persists for a few hours to days. The sensory symptoms typically clear prior to the onset of headache.

Migraine Equivalents

Migraine equivalents resemble transient ischemic attacks in that they yield associated neurologic deficits *without the concomitant or subsequent appearance of headache.* They are controversial as a clinical entity because they differ from all other migrainous phenomena in two ways. The first difference is that they typically first appear in middle age or later. The second is that they may occur in individuals with no prior or familial history of migraine.

Transient Migraine Accompaniments

Fisher (1980) hypothesized that transient migraine accompaniments explain transient neurological deficits in middle-aged individuals who have no evidence of occlusive vascular disease, cardiac disease, or other etiologies of thromboembolic disease. Patients typically have, in order of occurrence,

visual scintillations and other visual disturbance, paresthesias, dysphasia, dysarthria, and paralysis. They may be accompanied by brief (15- to 30-minute) headache, display a flurry of attacks in midlife, and usually follow a benign course. As already noted, they usually occur in individuals without a history of migraine, although it is more clinically reassuring when a migrainous history is obtained from the patient.

Ophthalmic Migraine

This disorder is probably a variant of transient migraine accompaniments, characterized by brief disturbances of vision either in one eye or visual field (i.e., retinal or cortical). It is usually thought of as "isolated visual auras." They may be seen as visual scintillations beginning in childhood, concurrent with headaches that then continue into adulthood. They may occur without headache. Or they may recur after a quiescent period, many years later in life. Distinction from more ominous entities such as embolic phenomena, central retinal artery occlusion, optic neuritis, or retinal detachment must be pursued.

Pathogenesis

The long-accepted concept of migraine pathogenesis has centered around the vasoconstriction-vasodilatation theory that the initial event in a migraine is intracranial vasoconstriction, causing the neurologic prodroma and subsequent extracranial vasodilation, resulting in the actual pain. This has been found to be a consistently observable phenomenon in migraine, and may, in fact, be true in tension headaches as well (Wolff 1963). The cranial vasoconstriction in the prodrome has been associated with serotonin release (Raskin and Appenzeller 1980). Further confirmation has come from the fact that vasodilators administered during the auras have abated them; vasoconstrictors administered during the headache have relieved and aborted the pain.

Recently, a group in Copenhagen (Olesen et al. 1981, 1982) challenged these hypotheses through experiments using quantitatively more accurate measures of cranial blood flow. In studying classic migraine, they observed that there was insufficient cerebral blood flow reduction to account for ischemic neurologic symptoms, that the regions of decreased blood flow were not in accordance with the symptoms, and that the initial event was a hyperperfusion, not hypoperfusion. This led to the unconventional conclusion that the vascular changes were secondary to a primary cerebral parenchymal event. In studying common migraine, they found *no alterations in blood flow.* Another interesting hypothesis proposed that migraine is initiated by efferent impulses from the trigeminal ganglion, which controls both cranial vasculature and pain phenomena in much of the cranium (Hardebo 1984). It has been proffered that this may be more explanatory of cluster headaches than migraine.

The hypothesis that patients vulnerable to migraine headaches have some disregulation of autonomic response received support from the study of Price and Clarke (1979), in which patients with migraines were unable to condition changes in digital pulse volume. The patients demonstrated a stereotypic response in which they constricted digital blood vessels in response to all stimuli rather than vasodilating in the appropriate conditioning situation. Since sympathetic discharge produces vasoconstriction, migraine patients demonstrated nonspecific sympathetic overreactivity.

☐ CLUSTER HEADACHES

Although cluster headaches are not an entity clearly different from migraine, they do display several distinguishing features. Cluster headaches do not always occur in families. They "cluster" in flurries of attacks lasting from a few minutes to a couple of hours (although not often days), with clear and protracted symptom-free periods between the clusters. The sex preponderance is the reverse of that in migraine: the female-to-male ratio is 2:3.

Cluster headaches, unlike migraines, have no known precipitants. Some cluster headaches occur at approximately the same time of day, or often at night and during rapid eye movement (REM) sleep. The frequency is 1 to 10 or more times per day. A further distinguishing feature is that there is little or no prodromal phase.

The onset of pain is rapid, severe, and unilateral. There is often an associated profound nausea and vomiting. Unilateral ptosis (lid drop), miosis (constriction of the pupil), and ipsilateral rhinorrhea make for a partial Horner's syndrome (there is no anhydrosis to complete the syndrome). Facial flushing is common. Bilateral or unilateral rhinorrhea and tearing may be observed. Extracranial vessels are usually engorged and tender. Unlike

migraine patients, patients with cluster headaches are usually agitated, and may even injure themselves by head banging in efforts to relieve the pain.

The cyclical character of cluster headaches has lead some authors to compare this entity to other cyclical illnesses (e.g., bipolar disorder).

☐ TENSION HEADACHES

Traditional approaches to headache have separated migraine and tension headaches into different clinical and etiologic entities. Later thought grouped the two together on a continuum, the tension–migraine model (Featherstone 1985). The boundaries between the two have since become even less distinct, with Raskin (1980) suggesting that—based on the phenomenology, studies of physiology, and response to similar treatments—they may, in fact, be the same entity. The arguments are too voluminous to review here, and the answer is still pending. For the sake of clarity, tension headache will be treated as a separate entity.

Tension headache is usually described as bilateral band-like sensations around the head or in specific muscle regions, such as occipital-nucchal, frontal, or temporal. *Dull, steady, full, tight,* and *stretching* are adjectives commonly used to describe the pain. Onset is usually more gradual and insidious than migraine, and certainly more so than cluster. The headache may last from hours to months, usually not disturbing sleep, although it may be present on awakening.

Tension headaches are more common in females. A distinguishing feature is that, unlike migraine, the headaches do not usually begin in childhood or adolescence; rather they have their onset in adulthood. Although local trauma may cause pain and tenderness in the area of injury, this pain is limited to the period of healing for tissue injury, and does not explain tension headache. Common analgesics are not usually effective in treatment, although agents useful for migraine often are effective.

☐ OTHER TYPES OF HEADACHES

Generalized Medical Illness and Headache

Half of patients with hypertension complain of headache, although no clear pathogenesis has been found (Adams and Victor 1981). Other systemic illnesses with headache as a prominent feature are carbon monoxide poisoning, uremia, chronic obstructive lung disease, hypothyroidism, Cushing's disease, fevers, steroid withdrawal, ergotism, nitrite ingestion, Addison's disease, adrenal tumors, pheochromocytoma, and anemia.

Space-Occupying Lesion

Intracranial space-occupying lesions (e.g., tumor, subdural hematoma) often give rise to steady, unilateral, or generalized pain, accompanied by other neurologic signs such as change in level of consciousness, confusion, irritability, giddiness, poor concentration, lability of emotion, motor and sensory changes, and signs of raised intracranial pressure (e.g., papilledema). Headache is a prominent symptom in about two-thirds of patients with brain tumor (Rooke 1968). With brain tumor, changes in head position typically may vary the intensity of pain, as sensitive intracranial structures adjacent to the tumor are stretched and irritated. As intracranial pressure rises, the patient may be awakened from sleep by headache and may display projectile vomiting.

Temporal Arteritis (Cranial Arteritis, Giant Cell Arteritis)

This source of headache, although not restricted to the elderly, is most commonly first seen in patients over the age of 60. In fact, when headache first appears after this age, temporal arteritis should be foremost in the differential diagnosis, as it is a medical emergency. The syndrome usually develops over weeks to months and is accompanied by a general malaise, engorgement of the superficial temporal artery with throbbing, and tenderness at its site. The illness may be seen in conjunction with polymyalgia rheumatica. Blindness and ophthalmoplegia are serious consequences of this illness if left untreated. Treatment consists of steroidal therapy, usually 60 mg per day of prednisone in divided doses, tapered over 2 weeks.

Cough and Exertional Headache

Cough and exertional headache is seen in immediate temporal relation to physical exertions such as bending, lifting, straining, stooping, coughing, laughing, sneezing, defecation, and the Valsalva maneuver. It is immediate to the activity, often

frontal in location, and lasts only minutes or hours. Although short-lived, the pain may be excruciating. These often occur for a period of years, then cease, never to return. Concomitant neurologic symptoms are absent. However, if neurologic symptoms are present, it is imperative to rule out serious intracranial pathology such as aneurysm, sources of bleeding or raised intracranial pressure.

Orgasmic Headache

Two types of headache associated with sexual activity have been described. One is a tension-type headache, occurring with sexual excitement. The other is a severe pounding explosive pain that occurs with orgasm. No neurologic sequelae develop with either. However, rupture of any intracranial vascular defect (e.g., aneurysm, arteriovenous malformation) should be considered and ruled out on the first appearance of the latter type of headache.

Temporomandibular Joint Syndrome

Temporomandibular joint syndrome is an increasingly widely recognized entity involving a dull constant ache, frequently worse in the morning, exacerbated by chewing, and frequently accompanied by limitations in jaw movement. Half of such patients also suffer bruxism. It has been commonly observed that these patients are anxious and prone to express psychological conflict in psychosomatic terms (Guralnick et al. 1978).

Trigeminal Neuralgia

Trigeminal neuralgia is seen in middle age and later. The pain is sharp, momentary, and lancinating, usually in the maxillary and mandibular distributions of the fifth cranial nerve. The pain may be so intense that it causes the patient to wince, thereby earning its other name, *tic douloureux*. A particularly distinguishing feature of this condition is the precipitation of pain by stimuli applied to so-called trigger zones. These are areas of the face, lips, tongue, or regions moved with talking and chewing. Although pains are typically paroxysmal, patients sometimes describe a continuous pain and sensitivity of the face.

Traumatic Headache

Traumatic headache is seen as part of a posttraumatic syndrome and is distinct from the pain consequent to the localizable injury (e.g., contusion, abrasion, laceration). It often lasts for days, weeks, or months, and may relate to the psychological profile of the individual and any pending litigation.

Psychogenic Headache

Psychogenic headache may be seen as a coincident or prominent feature of many psychiatric illnesses such as depression, generalized anxiety, panic disorder, obsessive-compulsive disorder, and somatization disorder. It may resemble migraine or tension headaches, although it often lacks the additional features that distinguish either. In general, any headache described as occurring "every day" for months or longer should be suspected of being of psychiatric etiology, and will usually subside with the treatment of the primary psychiatric disorder.

Psychogenic headache may fit the DSM-III-R (American Psychiatric Association 1987) criteria for idiopathic pain disorder: severe and prolonged pain that is in excess of or inconsistent with physical findings but is exacerbated by an environmental stimulus or results in avoiding unwanted activity or receiving social support. This may occur after a motor vehicle or work-related accident and therefore may involve the possibility of financial compensation.

The distinction between muscle contraction or tension headaches and psychogenic pain disorder headaches received reinforcement in a recent study (Haber et al. 1985), in which frontalis electromyogram (EMG) activity was examined. Patients suffering muscle contraction headaches showed significantly elevated EMG activity during headaches, whereas the psychogenic headache group showed no such elevation of EMG activity, either during or between headaches. The authors noted that patients with psychogenic headaches were twice as likely as patients with muscle contraction headaches to have been exposed to other individuals with headaches.

☐ PRINCIPLES OF DIAGNOSTIC EVALUATION

If systemic illness has been eliminated as the cause of headache, the following approach may be helpful in discriminating the type of headache, deter-

mining further investigations, and defining treatment:

1. Onset: When and what circumstances?
2. Duration?
3. Frequency?
4. Intensity?
5. Quality? Change in previous pattern?
6. Precipitating factors (work, food, activity, odors, chemicals, stress)?
7. Exacerbating and alleviating factors?
8. More than one type of headache?
9. Warning signs: aura, prodrome?
10. Associated symptoms (nausea, photophobia, paresis, sensory symptoms)?
11. Does pain interrupt activities?
12. Family history?

Investigations that may be of help include skull X rays, which may be useful in identifying bony lesions and pineal shifts. Sinus films may reveal fluid levels and inflammatory changes. Computed tomography (CT) can be of particular value in observing the intracranial contents for space-occupying lesions, vascular abnormalities, and hemorrhage. With evidence of localized neurologic signs or raised intracranial pressure, CT scanning is mandatory. Other radiologic tests have a low yield, unless specific abnormalities are found on previous examinations. Electroencephalograms (EEGs) generally reveal nonspecific (and non-useful) information. However, they are safe, noninvasive, and may be helpful as a screening test if a localized abnormality is suspected. Focal slow waves may suggest a space-occupying lesion.

Frequently co-occurring psychiatric problems are anxiety and dissociative disorders, psychogenic pain syndrome and other somatoform disorders, and, rarely, somatic delusions. It is therefore important to conduct a careful examination of mental status, with two principles in mind.

First, the initial diagnostic evaluation should be inclusive rather than exclusive. The clinician should initially presume that diagnoses of headache and psychiatric illness may co-occur rather than that the existence of one necessarily explains the other. Given evidence that the 6-month prevalence of DSM-III (American Psychiatric Association 1980) disorders ranges between 17 and 23 percent (Myers et al. 1984) and the high prevalence of headache symptoms, the two will frequently coexist simply by chance. Such an approach is more likely to uncover all relevant pathology, facilitate treatment, and avoid putting patients in the uncomfortable position of feeling that their headache complaint is "all in their head" in a functional rather than physical sense. It is important to patients to feel that their discomfort is taken seriously, and to emphasize that psychiatric treatment may be useful in treating the anxiety or depression that accompanies headache or makes it more difficult to tolerate. It is not useful to imply to the patient that the psychiatric syndrome necessarily causes the headache.

Second, use the history to delineate specific stressors that are associated with the onset or exacerbation of headache symptoms. Many patients with migraine and tension headaches experience them at certain times throughout the day, or in response to pressure at work or in the family. A careful history may guide the clinician in considering and suggesting psychotherapeutic strategies, ranging from family therapy to avoidance of work during certain hours to group therapy aimed at clarifying and improving interpersonal communication skills.

☐ TREATMENT

Pharmacotherapy of Headache

Pharmacotherapy may be divided into treatment of the acute attack and prophylactic therapy for persons plagued with frequent recurrent migraines.

Treatment of Acute Migraine.

As a general principle, the earlier in the attack a migraine is treated, the better. Patients with established migraines should be encouraged to receive benefit of treatment as soon as they perceive an attack beginning. The rapid use of a routine analgesic such as aspirin (650 mg every 3 to 4 hours), propoxyphene (65 mg every 4 hours), or codeine (30 to 60 mg every 4 hours) may be all that is needed to abort the episode. The latter two drugs are most often found in combination with other potentiating compounds such as aspirin and caffeine. For most patients, this approach will suffice. If the attack is not aborted by one of these medications, a repeat dose 30 minutes later may be taken. For some more severe migraines, stronger analgesics are recommended, such as meperidine (75 to 100 mg im or po every

3 hours), often in conjunction with a potentiating and antiemetic compound such as hydroxyzine hydrochloride (50 to 100 mg im). A combination of isometheptene, dichloralphenazone, acetominophen (2 capsules immediately, then 1 capsule every hour up to 5 capsules or until headache abates) may be necessary. Adjunctive benefit may be provided by the inhalation of 100 percent oxygen at high flow rates (8 to 10 liters) for up to an hour. These regimens will abort most acute migrainous attacks.

If a prodrome heralds a migraine, reasonable success may be achieved in preventing progression to more severe symptoms by the use of oral ergotamine compounds (2 mg ergotamine tartrate sublingual every half hour, as needed, but not to exceed 6 mg in any 24-hour period, or 10 mg in any 1 week). Experimentation with parenteral dihydroergotamine (DHE-45) is being conducted and is showing very promising results in the treatment of the seemingly most intractable migraine attacks. The dose is 0.5 mg iv with metaclopramide 10 mg, and an occasional additional dose when necessary. Repeated doses every 8 hours may be used. It is claimed (Edmeads et al. 1985) that this regimen terminated severe migraine episodes within 2 days in over 90 percent of patients.

Prophylactic Pharmacotherapy of Migraine.

Propranolol (40 to 60 mg po, four times per day) appears to be the most effective medication in the prophylaxis of migraine (Edmeads et al. 1985). Hypotension is a common side effect. In the class of compounds known as beta blockers, this medication clearly has been the drug of choice for this purpose. Other medications that have been tried with less success are other beta blockers such as nadolol (80 to 240 mg per day in four divided doses), timolol (50 to 100 mg per day in four divided doses), and atenolol (20 to 100 mg per day in four divided doses). Although the latter are less effective than propranolol, they may be preferred based on reduction in lethargy and depression as side effects. Calcium channel blockers are a new class of medications presently being looked at as migraine prophylactics. Of these, nimodipine and nifedipine are somewhat more effective although apparently more so in cluster headache than migraine.

Additional medications that have a place in migraine prophylaxis are amitriptyline, papaverine, cyproheptadine, ergotamine, phenelzine, and methysergide. Unfortunately, the most effective of these is methysergide, which has ominous side effects (e.g., fibrotic disorders, particularly retroperitoneal fibrosis, endocardial fibrosis, and pleuropulmonary fibrosis) and should be used only after careful consideration and under close supervision.

Pharmacotherapy of Cluster Headaches. The drug of choice in this condition is a rapidly absorbed (as the condition rapidly develops) ergotamine compound. For this purpose, ergotamine tartrate aerosol (.36 to 0.72 mg, 1 to 2 puffs, immediately) is generally used. With cluster headaches, 100 percent oxygen inhalation has also been reported to give dramatic results in preventing the progression of these headaches. Finally, methoxyflurane (10 to 15 drops inhaled from an absorbent cloth) inhalation has been observed to be effective in the acute attack.

Prophylaxis in chronically recurring cluster headaches is achieved with moderately high success by the use of lithium carbonate (600 to 1,500 mg per day in divided doses), prednisone (20 to 40 mg per day for 2 weeks, then tapered), and the already-mentioned calcium channel blocker, nifedipine (10 to 20 mg tid). Other medications that have shown some success are phenylpropanolamine (25 to 50 mg per day), naproxen (400 to 750 mg per day), indomethacin (75 to 150 mg per day), and carbamazepine (600 to 1,200 mg per day). Carbamazepine carries a 1 in 10,000 risk of potentially fatal aplastic anemia.

Pharmacotherapy of Tension Headaches. The most effective pharmacologic approach in the treatment of this condition is prophylactic, although aspirin, acetaminophen, and codeine are of limited value in treatment of acute attack. Stronger, narcotic analgesics should be avoided because of their addiction potential. Prophylactically, amitriptyline (50 to 75 mg per day; a therapeutic "window" probably exists, and higher doses are not indicated) has proven to be the most effective agent, usually in doses half of those used in the treatment of depression (Edmeads et al. 1985). Other agents shown to be effective are diazepam, chlordiazepoxide, imipramine, and a combination of ergotamine, belladonna, and phenobarbital.

Pharmacotherapy of Trigeminal Neuralgia. Anticonvulsant medications such as phenytoin (200 to 400 mg per day) and carbamazepine (600 to 1,600 mg per day) have been found effective in this con-

dition. In addition, clonazepam (2 to 8 mg per day) is a useful medication. Baclofen (60 to 80 mg per day) has been shown to be quite effective in treating patients refractory to other treatments.

Psychotherapeutic Treatment: General Principles

1. Disentangle etiology from treatment. Once it has been determined that the headache symptoms do not result from a developing medical emergency such as a tumor or hypertensive encephalopathy, it is important to assure the patient that the choice of treatment is based on efficacy, not etiology. From this point of view, treatments involving stress reduction, psychotherapy, or hypnosis do not indicate that there is no organic basis for the symptoms, nor does the use of medication or biofeedback necessarily imply that psychosocial factors are irrelevant. In general, vascular and muscle tension headaches are best described to patients as a special vulnerability to stress requiring a combined psychosomatic treatment approach.

Often factors that led to the development of a symptom differ from those that maintain it. For example, a particularly severe headache, which by chance occurred during a stressful period at work, may establish a classically conditioned relationship with subsequent work stress. The patient comes to expect work-associated headaches, and diverts cognitive resources formerly devoted to problem-solving at work to fending off the headache. Coping ability is thereby impaired and work stress is increased. This type of self-fulfilling prophecy is established and maintained and may be independent of the reasons for initial causation.

2. Use a rehabilitation model for symptom control. A rehabilitation approach has the advantage of taking the patient's current symptoms as a given while directing attention toward reducing them and minimizing associated disability. Thus this approach, which can be easily explained to the patient, serves to avoid a confrontation over the "reality" of the symptoms. "Getting better" need not imply that the headache pain was all in the patient's mind. This is a serious problem because many headache patients interpret referral to a psychiatrist as implying that they are thought to be confabulating symptoms. This puts them in the unenviable position of feeling dishonored if they improve, a kind of therapeutic double bind that hampers treatment. It is best to perform the necessary medical evaluation and institute treatment aimed at symptom control rather than confirmation of a theory of etiology.

3. Deal directly with secondary gain. If not addressed directly, the problem of secondary gain (i.e., the secondary benefits often associated with primary losses) can overshadow well-intended treatment attempts. Secondary gain may take the form of economic reinforcement for continued symptom-related disability as well as subtler social benefits, such as relief from onerous family duties provided by continued illness. As an example, posttraumatic headache occurring after a motor vehicle or work-related accident may involve the possibility of financial compensation. Early in an evaluation interview with such patients, before a great deal of information is elicited, it may be useful to point out that protracted litigation is usually destructive. To the extent that the patient is successful at rehabilitation, the party responsible for compensation will claim that the patient was not seriously injured in the first place. Thus, even the most honorable person is in a "double bind" in which the chance of compensation is undermined by improvement. Furthermore, the amount of emotional pain and loss of productive time endured through the years of litigation may not be compensated by any amount of money. Explaining this potential conflict at the beginning of the interview makes it clear to the patient that it is a statement of principle rather than a specific reaction to the individual's history or motivation. Often, with the patient's permission, a letter to the attorney underscoring the deleterious psychological effects of protracted litigation is helpful.

Some patients are less victims of systems of litigation than abusers of them. It is important for the clinician to understand a patient's motivation before attempting to relieve symptoms. Although, in general, headache patients suffer considerable distress and earnestly seek any available help, some embark on a ritual of seeking help to validate rather than ameliorate their symptoms. A therapist in such a situation should be no more interested in improvement than is the patient, or the treatment can degenerate into a situation in which the patient makes improvement the doctor's problem rather than the patient's problem.

4. Mobilize positive social reinforcement. The behavioral approach to pain control emphasizes an analysis of pain in terms of antecedents and consequences rather than causes and effects (Fordyce and Steger 1979). The behavioral literature distinguishes between operant and respondent pain, the latter being the commonly observed response to a noxious physical stimulus. Operant pain is defined as that which is under the control of social reinforcement of behavior related to pain. From this point of view, treatment is unlikely to be effective if there is little change made in the pattern of reinforcement for pain behavior. Some headache patients, for example, come to obtain much of their social support in the form of attention and sympathy as a result of their headaches and visible distress. Over time this can come to supplant social reinforcement for performing normal tasks at home and at work and makes the transition back to these usual tasks more difficult. In essence, relief from the headache will be perceived as resulting in a loss of social support. Reinforcement for change is thus negative, rather than positive.

Behavioral interventions emphasize self-observation and monitoring to increase patients' awareness of their current activity level associated with a symptom such as headache. A paradigm is established for stepwise gradual increases in activity level despite the symptom, with reinforcement built in for the increase in activity rather than for evidence of the symptom. Family members might be instructed to comment favorably on any increase in the headache patient's ability to work or do household chores but refrain from discussing the headache symptoms with the patient. On inpatient pain units, nursing staff are often encouraged to initiate conversations with pain patients at times other than those when pain medication is requested, thereby gradually dissociating social contact from the pain experience. Because many patients with severe headaches and other forms of chronic pain often become depressed and demanding, they alienate family and health care staff, who begin to avoid them. In turn, the patients sense this and come to rely increasingly on support offered grudgingly for pain, in what often becomes a descending spiral. The goal is to reverse this process by linking social support to normal functioning rather than to headache-related activity (Fordyce and Steger, 1979; Fordyce et al. 1973; Reuler et al. 1980).

5. Combine in vivo symptom control exercises such as progressive muscle relaxation or self-hypnosis with somatic treatments. There is evidence that such in vivo generalization of techniques such as biofeedback leads to an improvement in outcome (Blanchard et al. 1985). Patients benefit both from direct symptom relief and a sense of mastery. Having something to do when headache symptoms worsen reduces anxiety and muscle tension, which often exacerbates headache and other forms of pain.

Biofeedback and Hypnosis

Biofeedback and self-hypnosis approaches to the treatment of headache have much in common. Both techniques operate on the premise that an intense image reverses the presumed pathophysiologic vascular events and elicits actual somatic responses that partially reverse the pathophysiology (i.e., vasoconstriction of cranial arteries and vasodilation of vessels in the extremities). Relaxation training and cognitive restructuring are major techniques used to produce these responses.

Biofeedback. Migraine is thought to involve initial spasm and then excessive dilatation of one or more cerebral arteries. Patients, therefore, often experience uncomfortable warmth in their head and coolness in their hands and feet during an attack. Biofeedback treatment has been directed toward head cooling and extremity warming. Most commonly, a thermocouple is attached to a patient's finger, with the pitch of a repeated tone providing feedback as to the patient's ability to warm the finger. Patients can produce an average change of 1 to 2 degrees centigrade with training (Jessup et al. 1979). They may be instructed to imagine cooling their head at the same time. Temperature sensors have also been applied to the forehead, with feedback provided on head cooling.

The most common approach to muscle contraction headaches is the placement of EMG sensors on the frontalis muscle with visual or auditory feedback about the degree of relaxation of the muscle. Patients learn to produce relaxation in this and nearby muscle groups. A similar approach is used with temporomandibular joint syndrome, except that the electrodes are placed over the masseters.

Hypnosis. Hypnotizable migraine patients can be instructed in trance to imagine a giant block of ice settling down over their head with a hole in the front through which they can breathe. They are asked to feel the cold tingling numbness of the ice against their scalp, to allow the sensation to penetrate into their head, and to enjoy inhaling the icy

cool air, feeling their nose, mouth, and throat get cooler and cooler with each breath. They may initially concentrate on this icy cool numbness spreading throughout their head. Once this image is established, they are instructed to imagine that they have electric mittens on their hands and electric boots on their feet and that, when they throw an imaginary switch, heating coils like those in an electric blanket start to warm their hands as their head becomes cooler and cooler.

One patient who suffered migraine headaches as well as hysterical seizures associated with the headaches up to a frequency of 12 per day was instructed in this head and hand technique. Her antiseizure medications were discontinued, and she began a course of psychotherapy aimed at dealing in a concrete and supportive way with her conflicted late-adolescent relationship with her parents and her emerging sexuality. She practiced the self-hypnosis exercise several times a day for years. The hysterical seizures decreased in frequency to approximately three per year, usually at a time of some severe job-related stress. The headaches became fleeting and minor in contrast to their pretreatment course. Indeed, the headaches had been a prodrome for the seizures, and thus the headache treatment became the major preventive measure for controlling the conversion symptom.

Hypnotic procedures for treating muscle contraction headaches usefully involve different metaphors that take into account the more prominent anxiety-related components in these types of headaches. The major emphasis is on dissociating somatic tension from psychological stress. Thus, once in trance, these individuals are instructed to affiliate with a metaphor of floating, perhaps in a warm bath or a pool, and, using an imaginary screen, to picture some pleasant scene that, in itself, conveys relaxation. They are then asked to do problem solving on the screen while maintaining the physical sense of floating relaxation. They may mentally rehearse a discussion with an employer, think through alternative solutions to a problem, or establish priorities among problems. At times, specific images of warmth (e.g., a warm shower, a hot pad) or even reinforcement for less hypnotizable individuals with a physical change in temperature can be helpful.

Hypnosis has been used successfully in treating various kinds of atypical facial pain with metaphors, such as teaching the patient to use an imaginary or empty syringe without a needle to give an imaginary injection, mimicking the anesthetic effect produced earlier by a nerve block. Instructions include: "This anesthetic is screening a wall of numbness and taking the hurt out of the pain" (Swerdlow 1984, p. 107).

The most effective treatment of temporomandibular joint syndrome has been genuinely psychosomatic, combining local heat, the use of antiinflammatory analgesics and muscle relaxants such as diazepam, various psychotherapeutic interventions, and, occasionally, surgery. Psychotherapy includes a focus on identifying and resolving internal and intrapersonal conflicts. In addition, specific procedures, such as hypnosis and biofeedback, for dissociating psychological from somatic stress have been shown to be effective with generalization from the treatment environment to the patient's home environment (Carlsson and Gale 1977). The use of tricyclic antidepressants in selected patients with depressive components in addition to EMG biofeedback has also been shown to be effective (Gessel 1975). One advantage of procedures such as training in self-hypnosis is that generalization to the home environment is more natural because patients can practice self-hypnosis on their own without the need for equipment.

Treatment Outcome

There is good evidence that such techniques as biofeedback, hypnosis, and relaxation training can help a majority of headache patients. Migraine patients can learn voluntary control over superficial temporal artery blood flow volume and frontalis muscle tension, and there is a slight advantage for blood flow control (Bild and Adams 1980). Biofeedback may offer some specific advantage for patients with vascular headaches (Blanchard et al. 1982). Forehead cooling has some advantage over hand-warming (Jessup et al. 1979). In general, techniques applying biofeedback of one kind or another provide significant treatment effects that are not notably greater than simple relaxation training, such as Jacobson's progressive muscle relaxation (Jessup et al. 1979). Home relaxation training is an important component of good outcome (Budzynski et al. 1973). Thus the specific need for the equipment as opposed to the relaxation training and acquisition of voluntary control over automatic or autonomic functions has not been clearly demonstrated (Jessup et al. 1979; Thiebault et al. 1978).

There is evidence that hypnotized individuals are quite capable of changing body temperature (Grabowska 1971) and controlling vasoconstriction (Dubin and Shaprio 1974). Such relaxation procedures may work both by producing physiologic changes that result in changes in blood flow and muscle tension and by interrupting the cycle of physical discomfort and mental distress that tends to produce a snowball effect and worsen symptoms.

Andreychuk and Skriver (1975) demonstrated that biofeedback training for hand-warming and for alpha enhancement, and training in self-hypnosis were equally efficacious in reducing headache rates. Highly hypnotizable subjects were significantly more likely to reduce headaches than were patients with low hypnotizability, regardless of the treatment. This implies that hypnotizability is mobilized by treatments that do not formally employ hypnosis. This is understandable in light of the fact that many of the instructions given subjects in relaxation training or biofeedback are indistinguishable from a classic hypnotic induction. Finally, Andreychuk and Skriver found a significant correlation between hypnotizability and pretreatment headache symptoms, the more hypnotizable subjects being more symptomatic. Thus hypnotic concentration is a two-edged sword, potentially amplifying both symptoms and treatments.

Coexisting psychiatric disturbance, as indicated by elevated scores on the Depression, Psychasthenia, and Schizophrenia scales of the Minnesota Multiphasic Personality Inventory, predict poorer response to treatment; that is, the co-occurrence of psychopathology and headache makes for a poor outcome and indicates the importance of concurrent treatment of coexisting psychopathology (Blanchard et al. 1982).

The literature makes it clear that the various psychosomatic control techniques contain elements that are therapeutic. These include: specific somatic changes in blood flow, skin temperature, or muscle relaxation; nonspecific relaxation, the placebo effect, and an enhanced sense of mastery or control over the symptom; hypnotic analgesia; and a change in cognitive orientation toward the illness—that is, the development of new coping strategies, the acquisition of life management skills, and changes in motivation. These components can be mobilized by a variety of self-training techniques, including biofeedback, progressive muscle relaxation, training in self-hypnosis, and psychotherapy. The literature is clearer in showing that these treatments are effective than it is in demonstrating why they are effective. These techniques, in conjunction with pharmacotherapy and appropriate treatment of coexisting psychiatric and neurologic disorders, provide the clinician with an array of effective treatments for this common group of problems.

☐ CONCLUSION

Headache is a common and debilitating problem that often complicates psychiatric illnesses and is complicated by them. The majority of headaches can be found in the spectrum of vascular and muscle contraction types. Although headaches occasionally herald a medical emergency—such as temporal arteritis, a hypertensive crisis, or the growth of a space-occupying lesion—they more often are chronic and recurrent. Specific and effective pharmacologic programs are often effective, as are stress management techniques employing biofeedback and hypnosis. Psychotherapies directed at underlying intrapsychic or interpersonal conflicts are helpful in certain cases, as is attention to secondary gain. Rational selection among these treatment approaches will help reduce headaches for both the patient and the doctor.

☐ REFERENCES

Adams RD, Victor M: Principles of Neurology (2nd ed). New York, McGraw-Hill, 1981, pp 118–130

American Psychiatric Association: Diagnostic and Statistical Manual of Mental Disorders, 3rd ed. Washington, DC, American Psychiatric Association, 1980

American Psychiatric Association: Diagnostic and Statistical Manual of Mental Disorders, 3rd ed, revised. Washington, DC, American Psychiatric Association, 1987

Andreychuk T, Skriver C: Hypnosis and biofeedback in the treatment of migraine headache. Int J Clin Exper Hypn 23:172–183, 1975

Barolin G: Migraines and epilepsies—a relationship? Epilepsia 7:53–56, 1966

Bild R, Adams HE: Modification of migraine headaches by cephalic blood volume pulse and EMG biofeedback. J Consult Clin Psychol 48:51–57, 1980

Blanchard EB, Andrasik F, Neff DF, et al: Biofeedback and relaxation training with three kinds of headache: treatment effects and their prediction. J Consult Clin Psychol 50:562–575, 1982

Blanchard EB, Andrasik F, Appelbaum KA, et al: The efficacy and cost-effectiveness of minimal-therapist-contact, non-drug treatments of chronic migraine and tension headache. Headache 25:214–220, 1985

Budzynski EG, Budzynski T, Stoyva J, et al: EMG biofeedback and tension headache: a controlled outcome study. Psychosom Med 35:484–496, 1973

Carlsson SG, Gale EN: Biofeedback in the treatment of long-term temporomandibular joint pain. Biofeedback Self Regul 2:161–171, 1977

Critchley M, Ferguson FR: Migraine. Lancet 1:123–126, 1933

Dhopesh V, Anwar R, Herring C: A retrospective assessment of emergency department patients with complaint of headache. Headache 19:37–42, 1979

Dubin LL, Shapiro SS. Use of hypnosis to facilitate dental extraction and hemostasis in a classic hemophiliac with a high antibody titer to factor VIII. Am J Clin Hypn 17:79–83, 1974

Edmeads JG, Raskin NH, Rothner AD, et al (eds): Modern management of headache: mechanisms and therapeutics, in Annual Courses of the American Academy of Neurology, Vol. 2. Minneapolis, American Academy of Neurology, 1985, pp 1–132

Ekbom K, Rhlborg B, Schele R: Prevalence of migraine and cluster headache in Swedish men of 18. Headache 18:9–14, 1978

Ely FA: The migraine-epilepsy syndrome. Arch Neurol Psychiatry 24:943–949, 1930

Featherstone JH: Medical diagnosis and problems in individuals with recurrent idiopathic headaches. Headache 25:136–140, 1985

Fisher CM: Late life migraine accompaniments as a cause of unexplained transient ischemic attack. Can J Neurol Sci 7:9–17, 1980

Fordyce WE, Steger JC: Chronic pain, in Behavioral Medicine: Theory and Practice. Edited by Pomerleau OF, Brady JP. Baltimore, Williams & Wilkins Co, 1979, pp 125–153

Fordyce WE, Fowler RS, Lehman JR, et al: Operant conditioning in the treatment of chronic pain. Arch Phys Med Rehabil 54:399–408, 1973

Gessel AH: Electromyographic biofeedback and tricyclic antidepressants in myofascial pain-dysfunction syndrome: psychological predictors of outcome. J Am Dent Assoc 91:1048–1052, 1975

Glista GG, Mellinger JF, Rooke ED: Familial hemiplegic migraine. Mayo Clin Proc 50:307–311, 1975

Grabowska MJ: The effect of hypnosis and hypnotic suggestion on the blood flow in the extremities. Polish Medical Journal 10:1044–1051, 1971

Guralnick W, Kaban LB, Merrill RG: Temporomandibular-joint afflictions. N Engl J Med 299:123–129, 1978

Haber JD, Kuczmierczyk AR, Adams HE: Tension headaches: muscle overactivity or psychogenic pain. Headache 25:23–29, 1985

Hachinski VC, Porchowka J, Steele JC: Visual symptoms in the migraine syndrome. Neurology 23:570–579, 1973

Khouri-Haddad SE: Psychiatric consultation in a headache unit. Headache 24:322–328, 1984

Hardebo JE: The involvement of the trigeminal substance P neurons in cluster headache: an hypothesis. Headache 24:294–304, 1984

Jessup BA, Neufeld RWJ, Merskey H: Biofeedback therapy for headache and other pain: an evaluative review. Pain 7:225–270, 1979

Khouri-Haddad SE: Psychiatric consultation in a headache unit. Headache 24:322–328, 1984

Lance JW: Mechanisms and Management of Headache (4th ed). London, Butterworths, 1982, p 128

Lance JW, Anthony M: Some clinical aspects of migraine: a prospective survey of 500 patients. Arch Neurol 15:356–361, 1966

Markush RE, Karp HR, Heyman A, et al: Epidemiologic study of migraine symptoms in young women. Neurology 25:430–435, 1975

Myers JK, Weissman MM, Tischler GL, et al: Six-month prevalence of psychiatric disorders in three communities. Arch Gen Psychiatry 41:959–967, 1984

Ogden HW: Headache studies: statistical data. Allergy 23:58–75, 1952

Olesen J: Some clinical features of the acute migraine attack: an analysis of 750 patients. Headache 18:268–271, 1978

Olesen J, Larsen B, Lauritzen M: Progress in Neurology Series. London, Pitman Books, 1981, pp 41–42

Olesen J, Lauritzen M, Tfelt-Hassen P, et al: Spreading cerebral oligemia in classical and normal cerebral blood flow in common migraine. Headache 22:242–248, 1982

Perera GA: Paroxysmal arrhythmias and migraine. JAMA 215:488, 1971

Price KP, Clarke LK: Classical conditioning of digital pulse volume in migraineurs and normal controls. Headache 19:328–332, 1979

Raskin NH, Appenzeller O: Headache, in Major Problems in Internal Medicine. Edited by Smith LH. Philadelphia, WB Saunders Co, pp 115–160, 1980

Raskin NH, Schwartz RK: Icepick-like pain. Neurology 29:550, 1979

Reuler JB, Girard GE, Nardone DA: The chronic pain syndrome: misconceptions and management. Ann Intern Med 93:533–596, 1980

Rooke ED: Benign exertional headache. Med Clin North Am 52:801, 1968

Sacks OW: Migraine: The Evolution of a Common Disorder. Berkeley: University of California Press, 1970, pp 35–53

Schnarch DM, Hunter JE: Migraine incidence in clinical vs nonclinical populations. Psychosomatics 21:314–325, 1980

Swerdlow B: A rapid hypnotic technique in a case of atypical facial neuralgia. Headache 24:104–109, 1984

Thiebault EB, Williamson DA, Silver BV, et al: A controlled evaluation of temperature biofeedback in the treatment of migraine headaches. Arch Gen Psychiatry 35:581–588, 1978

Waters WE: Migraine: intelligence, social class and functional prevalence. Br Med J 2:77–81, 1971

Waters WE: The epidemiological enigma of migraine. Int J Epidemiol 2:189–194, 1973

Waters WE: The prevalence of migraine. Headache 18:53–54, 1978

Waters WE, O'Conner PJ: Prevalence of migraine. J Neurol Neurosurg Psychiatry 38:613–616, 1975

Weil AA: Observations on "dysrhythmic migraine." J Nerv Ment Dis 134:277–281, 1962

Wolff HG: Headache and Other Head Pain (2nd ed). New York, Oxford University Press, 1963

Neuropsychiatric Aspects of Sleep Disorders

Charles F. Reynolds III, M.D.
David J. Kupfer, M.D.

CHANGES IN SLEEP–WAKE ORGANIZATION are prominent in many psychiatric and neuropsychiatric disorders and, indeed, as a consequence of the aging process itself. Thus complaints of diminished sleep (with trouble initiating or maintaining nocturnal sleep) are frequent, particularly in depression and with advancing age. In other patients, however, increased time in bed or excessive daytime sleepiness is a problem (e.g., anergic depression). Bed partners may report disturbed behavior (e.g., confusional episodes) associated with sleep, as in patients with dementiform illnesses.

The objective measurement of changes in sleep–wake structure is being used increasingly in clinical psychiatry for diagnostic precision and treatment–response prediction. For example, a short rapid eye movement (REM) sleep latency is the most predictable and robust finding in the sleep of inpatients and outpatients with endogenous depressive disorders (Akiskal et al. 1982; Feinberg et al. 1982; Gillin et al. 1979; Kupfer et al. 1982a, 1982b; Reynolds et al. 1982a, 1982b; Rush et al. 1982). This finding, together with other REM sleep measures, has also been used to separate endogenous from nonendogenous depressives. It has also been used to support the distinction between primary depressives and other groups of patients, such as secondary depressives (Coble et al. 1976), patients with generalized anxiety disorder (Reynolds et al. 1983a), and patients with probable dementia of the

Supported in part by National Institute of Mental Health grants 00295, 37869 (Dr. Reynolds), 30915, 24652 (Dr. Kupfer), and by a grant from the John D. and Catherine T. MacArthur Foundation Research Network on the Psychobiology of Depression.

Alzheimer type (Reynolds et al. 1983b, 1985a). Prognostic studies have also made use of REM sleep latency to predict a patient's response to antidepressant chemotherapy (Kupfer et al. 1981, 1983) or to cognitive behavioral psychotherapy (Rush et al. 1982).

These studies suggest that when the patient's complaint of diminished, excessive, or otherwise disturbed sleep is measured objectively in the sleep laboratory (ideally as part of a comprehensive medical, neurologic, and psychiatric evaluation), it becomes apparent that not all sleep disturbance is alike. With respect to psychiatric disorders, for example, the altered or disturbed sleep seen in psychiatric states possesses varied features of sleep continuity, sleep architecture or composition, and REM sleep distribution.

Both clinical and electrophysiological heterogeneity is emphasized in the nosology of sleep and arousal disorders published by the Association of Sleep Disorders Centers (ASDC) (1979). This nosology sets forth the many types of disorders of initiating and maintaining sleep (i.e., the insomnias) associated with a variety of psychiatric and neuropsychiatric states, including depression. At the same time, it emphasizes the fact that some psychiatric patients, particularly those with anergic depression, may present with a disorder of excessive sleepiness. The nosology has been applied in a multicenter study of patients presenting with sleep complaints, and treatment prevalence data on more than 8,000 sleep disorder patients have now been published (Coleman et al. 1982). When one examines the distribution of medical, psychiatric, and psychophysiologic diagnoses of patients presenting to sleep disorders centers, a psychiatric condition, particularly anxiety and affective disorders, is the final diagnosis in 30 to 35 percent of patients presenting with a complaint of insomnia. The remaining two-thirds of diagnoses of insomnia include nocturnal periodic leg movements (or nocturnal myoclonus), 12 to 15 percent; sleep apnea syndromes (particularly central sleep apnea), 5 to 10 percent; persistent psychophysiologic (or "learned") insomnia, 15 percent; substance abuse disorders, 10 percent; subjective insomnia without objective findings, 5 to 10 percent; and a variety of primary medical disorders, 5 to 10 percent. In this same multicenter case series (Colemen et al. 1982), 43 to 50 percent of patients with a complaint of excessive daytime sleepiness received a final diagnosis of sleep apnea syndrome; 20 to 25 percent

received a diagnosis of narcolepsy. The remaining 25 to 30 percent of "sleepy" patients were diagnosed variously with nocturnal myoclonus, psychophysiologic or "learned" sleepiness, insufficient sleep, or idiopathic central nervous system (CNS) hypersomnolence.

After a brief review of normal sleep architecture, this chapter will consider the current classification of sleep disorders as this pertains to the differential diagnosis of insomnia and excessive daytime sleepiness, the two most common sleep–wake complaints. These differential diagnostic issues will be reviewed within the context of the effects of normal and deviant aging on sleep because differential diagnosis is greatly affected by the age of the patient. We will then turn to a brief review of the effects of different neuropsychiatric disorders on sleep–wake organization, including depression, schizophrenia, anxiety disorders, dementia of the Alzheimer type, and other neurologic conditions. After looking at the effects of neuropsychiatric disorder on sleep physiology, we will consider the neuropsychiatric aspects of primary sleep disorders, particularly narcolepsy and sleep apnea syndrome. We will conclude with a description of the management of sleep disorders, focusing particularly on etiologic-based diagnosis, nonpharmacologic treatment approaches, specificity of treatment, and indications for sleep laboratory referral.

☐ NORMAL SLEEP ARCHITECTURE

There are three principal operating states in the human central nervous system: waking; nonrapid eye movement (NREM) sleep; and REM sleep. These states are differentiated in the sleep laboratory by continuous monitoring of the electroencephalogram (EEG), the electrooculogram (EOG), and the submental or chin electromyogram (EMG).

NREM sleep consists of four different stages, the first of which (stage 1) is drowsiness and represents a usually brief transition between waking and sleeping. This stage is characterized by a low voltage, mixed theta and beta activity EEG pattern. The EOG shows characteristic slow eye movements (SEMs). As sleep deepens, stage 2 NREM becomes evident with the appearance on the EEG of sleep spindles—bursts of 12 to 14 cycles per second (cps) activity—and K-complexes (slow negative EEG deflections followed by a positive component). The deepest levels of NREM sleep, stages 3 and 4, are defined by an EEG recording showing at least 20 percent of delta waves (0.5 to 3 cps activity, with amplitude of greater than 75 μV). These stages are distinguished from one another according to the percentage of delta waves on the EEG (i.e., stage 3: 20 to 50 percent delta activity; stage 4: more than 50 percent delta activity); however, the two stages are generally termed *slow wave sleep*, the deepest level of sleep, from which subjects are most difficult to arouse.

REM sleep is signaled by the appearance of rapid, jerky, but symmetric eye movements that give this state its name; by an EEG pattern that is similar to the waking state; and by skeletal muscle atonia on the chin EMG. More than 80 percent of subjects awakened during REM sleep recall vivid dreams.

Essentially, sleep is a physiologically heterogeneous process, as demonstrated not only by these electrographic differences between NREM and REM sleep, but by other physiologic differences between these two states. For example, pulse and respiration rates are higher and more variable during REM than NREM sleep. Penile erections, which occur periodically at approximately 90-minute intervals, have been shown to coincide most frequently with REM sleep.

Sleep stages show an ultradian (< 24-hour) rhythm, with periods of REM and NREM alternating at 70- to 100-minute cycles throughout the night. The pattern and content of the REM–NREM cycles change over the course of a normal night's sleep: during the second half of the night, slow wave sleep decreases compared with the first half of the night, but REM periods become more frequent and prolonged.

Sleep also changes markedly with increasing age. Thus sleep efficiency (the ratio of sleep time to time in bed) remains relatively stable until about age 45, when it begins to decline. With advancing age, people stay in bed longer but sleep fewer hours. Sleep also becomes more fragmented with advancing age, with more awakenings during the night and greater difficulty returning to sleep. The duration of various sleep stages also changes over a lifetime. In particular, slow wave sleep (stages 3 and 4), which constitutes 15 to 20 percent of the night's sleep at about age 20, declines steadily with age. This decrease in slow wave sleep is more marked in men than in women. Conversely, NREM stage 1 increases with advancing age, reflecting

partly the increased number of arousals during the night.

These basic facts concerning the ultradian rhythm of NREM–REM sleep point to an active, rather than passive, regulation of sleep. The circadian rhythmicity of sleeping and waking appears to be endogenously driven, and influenced by the underlying circadian temperature rhythm. Further, sleep architecture (particularly in the amount of slow wave sleep and REM) is affected by temporal variables, such as age, length of time spent asleep, the time of day at which sleep occurs, and the duration of wakefulness preceding sleep. The ultradian rhythm of sleep architecture actively asserts itself following sleep deprivation, with both lengthened total sleep time and rebound of slow wave sleep on the first recovery night, and rebound of REM sleep thereafter.

☐ DIFFERENTIAL DIAGNOSIS OF INSOMNIA AND EXCESSIVE DAYTIME SLEEPINESS

The ASDC (1979) classification of sleep disorders, shown in Table 1, represents an attempt to systematize the differential diagnosis of chronic insomnia and excessive daytime sleepiness. The insomnias have been grouped under the rubric of disorders of initiating and maintaining sleep (DIMS). The hypersomnias have been classified as disorders of excessive daytime somnolence (DOES). There is also a group of dyssomnias associated with disruptions of the 24-hour sleep–wake cycle, such as those associated with shift work or jet lag. Finally, those dysfunctions associated with sleep, sleep stages, or partial arousal are grouped as parasomnias. These include such common clinical syndromes as sleepwalking, night terrors, and bedwetting. Parts of the ASDC classification of sleep disorders are being incorporated into DSM-III-R (American Psychiatric Association 1987).

In evaluating a patient with a chronic sleep–wake disturbance, one must first rule out several major primary sleep disorders, such as sleep apnea syndromes, narcolepsy–cataplexy, nocturnal myoclonus, and parasomnic disorders (e.g., nocturnal seizures). Suspicion of any of these warrants referral to a sleep disorders center for a full clinical investigation. The differential diagnosis of insomnia and hypersomnia will now be briefly reviewed, beginning with a consideration of some of the more

TABLE 1.   ASDC CLASSIFICATION OF SLEEP AND AROUSAL DISORDERS

A. Disorders of initiating and maintaining sleep (DIMS)—insomnias

1. Psychophysiologic
   a. Transient and situational
   b. Persistent
2. Associated with psychiatric disorders
   a. Symptoms and personality disorders
   b. Affective disorders
   c. Other functional psychoses
3. Use of drugs and alcohol
   a. Tolerance to or withdrawal from CNS depressants
   b. Sustained use of CNS stimulants
   c. Sustained use of withdrawal from other drugs
   d. Chronic alcoholism
4. Sleep-induced respiratory impairment
   a. Sleep apnea DIMS syndrome
   b. Alveolar hypoventilation DIMS syndrome
5. Sleep-related (nocturnal) myoclonus and "restless legs"
   a. Sleep-related (nocturnal) myoclonus DIMS syndrome
   b. "Restless legs" DIMS syndrome
6. Other medical, toxic, and environmental conditions
7. Childhood-onset DIMS
8. Other DIMS conditions
   a. Repeated REM sleep interruptions
   b. Atypical polysomnographic features
   c. Not otherwise specified
9. No DIMS abnormality
   a. Short sleeper
   b. Subjective DIMS complaint without objective findings
   c. Not otherwise specified

B. Disorders of excessive somnolence (DOES)

1. Psychophysiologic
   a. Transient and situational
   b. Persistent
2. Associated with psychiatric disorders
   a. Affective disorders
   b. Other functional disorders
3. Use of drugs and alcohol
   a. Tolerance to or withdrawal from CNS stimulants
   b. Sustained use of CNS depressants
4. Sleep-induced respiratory impairment
   a. Sleep apnea DOES syndrome
   b. Alveolar hypoventilation DOES syndrome
5. Sleep-related (nocturnal) myoclonus and "restless legs"
   a. Sleep-related (nocturnal) myoclonus DOES syndrome
   b. "Restless legs" DOES syndrome
6. Narcolepsy
7. Idiopathic CNS hypersomnolence
8. Other medical, toxic, and environmental conditions
9. Other DOES conditions
   a. Intermittent DOES (periodic) syndromes (e.g., Kleine-Levin syndrome, menstrual-associated syndrome
   b. Insufficient sleep
   c. Sleep drunkenness
   d. Not otherwise specified
10. No DOES abnormality
    a. Long sleeper
    b. Subjective DOES complaint without objective findings
    c. Not otherwise specified

C. Disorders of the sleep–wake schedule

1. Transient
   a. Rapid time zone change ("jet lag") syndrome
   b. "Work shift" change in conventional sleep–wake schedule
2. Persistent
   a. Frequently changing sleep–wake schedule
   b. Delayed sleep phase syndrome
   c. Advanced sleep phase syndrome
   d. Non-24-hour sleep–wake syndrome
   e. Irregular sleep–wake pattern
   f. Not otherwise specified

D. Dysfunctions associated with sleep, sleep stages, or partial arousals—parasomnias

1. Sleepwalking (somnambulism)
2. Sleep terror (pavor nocturnus, incubus)
3. Sleep-related enuresis
4. Other dysfunctions
   a. Dream anxiety attacks (nightmares)
   b. Sleep-related epileptic seizures
   c. Sleep-related bruxism
   d. Sleep-related head-banging (jactatio capitis nocturna)
   e. Familial sleep paralysis
   f. Impaired sleep-related penile tumescence
   g. Sleep-related painful erections
   h. Sleep-related cluster headaches and chronic paroxysmal hemicrania
   i. Sleep-related abnormal swallowing syndrome
   j. Sleep-related asthma
   k. Sleep-related cardiovascular symptoms
   l. Sleep-related hemolysis (paroxysmal nocturnal hemoglobinuria)
   m. Asymptomatic polysomnographic findings
   n. Not otherwise specified

important primary sleep disorders. For more detailed review, the reader should consult Guilleminault (1982), the major current reference in the field. Additional state-of-the-art information on the natural history, epidemiology, and long-term evolution of sleep–wake disorders is reviewed in a volume edited by Guilleminault and Lugaresi (1983).

Narcolepsy

Excessive daytime sleepiness in an otherwise healthy patient may suggest narcolepsy. Daytime sleepiness is usually the earliest sign of narcolepsy, with onset typically in the second or third decade of life. Symptoms worsen with time, leading to various social and psychiatric difficulties, as well as to accidents. Cataplexy (abrupt and reversible loss of muscle control) occurs in most cases of narcolepsy, usually in association with intense but specific emotional experiences (e.g., during sexual intercourse). The nocturnal sleep of narcoleptic patients is frequently disrupted by episodes of reversible paralysis, multiple arousals, vivid hallucinations, and nightmares.

Objective diagnostic confirmation of narcolepsy can be obtained only with a sleep study, which typically shows two or more sleep onset REM periods. The multiple sleep latency test (MSLT) is the most sensitive and specific approach to the diagnostic confirmation of narcolepsy. In this test, the patient has a series of four or five 20-minute naps, scheduled at 2-hour intervals (10 A.M., 12 noon, 2 P.M., 4 P.M., and, in some instances, 6 P.M.). Narcolepsy is confirmed by the presence of two or more sleep onset REM periods (Van den Hoed et al. 1981). In addition, narcoleptics typically fall asleep very rapidly during all naps, in less than 5 minutes. The MSLT should be performed as part of a comprehensive sleep evaluation, in which the preceding night's sleep was monitored in the laboratory for sleep apnea, cardiac arrhythmia, nocturnal myoclonus, and sleep continuity.

Treatment of narcolepsy includes attention to good sleep hygiene (Table 2) and the use of stimulant medications, most commonly methylphenidate, pemoline, and, occasionally, dextroamphetamine or codeine. Cataplectic attacks often respond at least partially to tricyclic antidepressants, including imipramine, clomipramine, or protriptyline. Tricyclics can frequently be prescribed for cataplexy on a prn basis, rather than as a maintenance drug. This reflects the waxing and waning

TABLE 2. RULES OF SLEEP HYGIENE

1. Sleep as much as needed to feel refreshed during the following day. Restricting the time in bed seems to solidify sleep, but excessively long times in bed seem related to fragmented and shallow sleep.
2. Get up at the same time each day, 7 days a week. (A regular awake time in the morning leads to regular times of sleep onset.)
3. Get a steady daily amount of exercise, which probably deepens sleep.
4. Insulate your bedroom against sounds (with carpeting, insulated curtains, closed doors).
5. Keep the room temperature moderate; excessively warm rooms may disturb sleep.
6. Have a light snack at bedtime; hunger may disturb sleep.
7. Avoid excessive liquids in the evening to minimize the need for nighttime trips to the bathroom.
8. Avoid caffeinated beverages in the evening.
9. Avoid alcohol in the evening. Although alcohol helps tense people fall asleep more easily, the ensuing sleep is then broken up.
10. Get up if you cannot fall asleep. People who feel angry and frustrated because they cannot sleep should not try harder and harder to fall asleep but should turn on the light, leave the bedroom, and do something different like reading a boring book. Do not engage in stimulating activity. Return to bed only when sleepy. Get up at your regular time the next day, no matter how little you slept.
11. Avoid tobacco; the chronic use of tobacco disturbs sleep.
12. Put the clock under the bed or cover it up if you find yourself waking up and looking at the clock.

nature of cataplectic symptoms. Pharmacologic approaches to narcolepsy–cataplexy are usually not entirely satisfactory, however. Most patients require social support and education, as is the case in other patients afflicted with chronic medical disorders.

An animal model of narcolepsy has been under study at Stanford and suggests cholinergic dysfunction as part of the neurochemical basis of this disorder (Baker and Dement 1985).

Sleep Apnea Syndromes

Sleep apnea is a frequent cause of both insomnia and, more often, excessive daytime sleepiness in all age groups.

Obstructive sleep apnea syndrome presents as excessive daytime sleepiness. The patient is usually a middle-aged, plethoric man with a history of hypertension. Bed partners report a history of very loud snoring. Other prominent symptoms include daytime automatic behaviors, personality changes (irritability, depression, organic mental syndromes), impotence, morning headache, bedwetting, and, on awakening, slurred speech, lack of coordination, and unsteady gait.

Diagnosis must be made in the sleep laboratory by the demonstrated absence of airflow at the mouth and nose despite persistent respiratory effort. Patients with obstructive sleep apnea syndrome may have hundreds of such episodes during the night, lasting 10 to 60 seconds or longer and representing 50 to 60 percent of total sleep time without effective airflow. These apneas are often associated with arterial oxygen desaturation to under 85 percent. Physiologic changes during sleep include hypoxia, hypercapnia, and cardiac arrhythmias.

A number of treatments for obstructive sleep apnea syndrome have been proposed, depending on the clinical and physiologic severity of the patient's illness. Behavioral approaches to sleep apnea syndrome are being developed and include position training during sleep, the use of a tongue-retaining device, and weight loss. Medical approaches to the treatment of sleep apnea syndrome include the use of continuous positive airway pressure (CPAP) or specific pharmacologic agents such as protriptyline. For more severe cases, the most effective treatment is surgical, involving a modified chronic tracheotomy with a value that can be closed during the day and opened at night. Tracheotomy effectively reverses all aspects of the syndrome. More recently, the use of uvulopalatopharyngoplasty (UPPP) has been advocated, particularly for the amelioration of loud snoring. Evaluation of the efficacy of UPPP in treating sleep apnea is currently under way in a number of sleep disorders centers.

In contrast to obstructive forms of sleep apnea, which typically present as excessive daytime sleepiness, central sleep apnea, which is defined by the absence of airflow at the nose and mouth *and* of respiratory effort (as measured by chest strain gauge, intercostal electromyogram (EMG), or intraesophageal balloon), often presents with a complaint of insomnia. Pharmacologic approaches such as the use of acetozolamide, theophylline, and imipramine may be of some help. Low flow nasal oxygen is also being investigated as a treatment.

Nocturnal Myoclonus and Restless Legs Syndrome

A complaint of chronic insomnia may be symptomatic of nocturnal myoclonus. Patients with this disorder complain of frequent arousals and aching leg muscles during the night and morning. Chronic fatigue and symptoms of depression are also characteristic. Bed partners may complain of being kicked during the night.

The disorder is characterized by repetitive myoclonic leg movements during sleep. The EMG of the anterior tibialis muscle shows a stereotyped, myoclonic discharge, occurring at 20- to 40-second intervals during NREM sleep. Episodes of repetitive myoclonic discharges last 5 to 30 minutes, and typically occur 5 to 7 times during the night. The EEG will show a K-complex or brief arousal during or directly after each myoclonic jerk. This finding probably accounts for subjective reports of disturbed sleep. Most sleep-disorder clinicians report that a short or long-acting benzodiazepine typically improves sleep continuity in these patients, without actually diminishing myoclonic activity per se.

Restless legs syndrome may occur independently or in association with nocturnal myoclonus. Patients complain of deep paresthesias in the lower leg muscles, with an irresistible urge to get up and walk, just as they are trying to fall asleep. Some physicians advocate the use of phenytoin, carbamazepine, or propoxyphene in patients with a primary diagnosis of restless legs. Others have found vitamin E, tryptophan, or tricyclic antidepressants to be helpful, but there is no proven effective treatment to date.

Age-Related Complaints of Insomnia

Complaints of chronic insomnia are almost always multiply determined and become more prevalent with advancing age. Chronic insomnia, particularly in middle-aged and older patients, often reflects the following factors: (1) age-dependent change in sleep; (2) increased prevalence of sleep apnea and nocturnal myoclonus with advancing age; (3) sleep phase alteration (i.e., redistribution of the main sleep period within the 24-hour day); (4) neuropsychiatric disorders (particularly depression and dementia); (5) pain and limitation of mobility; (6) poor sleep hygiene practices or negative conditioning; (7) drugs; (8) gastroesophageal reflux; and (9) adverse environmental factors, including excessive noise or uncomfortable room temperature.

Although the need for sleep does not diminish with advancing age, the ability to sleep apparently does, as evidenced by the age-dependent diminution in slow wave sleep (stages 3 and 4, the deepest levels of NREM sleep) and the age-dependent increase in the ability to consolidate and to maintain sleep (Miles and Dement 1980). In other words, the ability to achieve the deepest levels of sleep (stages 3 and 4) and to have long uninterrupted sleep is considerably diminished in older people (even healthy seniors) compared to young adults. There is also an increase in sleep pathologies with age, such as sleep apnea and nocturnal myoclonus. The reported prevalence of sleep apnea (usually defined as five or more apneas per hour of sleep) has ranged from 31 to 67 percent in elderly men and from 0 to 32 percent in elderly females (for review, see Smallwood et al. 1983). Thus the principal aim of clinical assessment is to establish the major correlates of the patient's complaints so that intervention can be targeted and precise.

☐ EFFECTS OF NEUROPSYCHIATRIC DISORDERS ON SLEEP

Affective Disorders

Approximately 90 percent of patients with major depressive illness experience some form of EEG-verified sleep disturbance. The most predictable sleep abnormalities of endogenous depression include: (1) sleep continuity disturbances (e.g., prolonged sleep latency, nocturnal awakenings, and early morning awakening); (2) diminished slow wave sleep (stages 3 and 4), with a shift of EEG delta activity from the first to the second NREM sleep period; (3) an abbreviated first NREM sleep period (i.e., REM latency) leading to more rapid appearance of the first REM sleep period; and (4) altered intranight temporal distribution of REM sleep, with increased REM sleep time and REM activity earlier in the night (Kupfer and Reynolds 1983; Reynolds and Shipley 1985).

Delusional depression represents a special subtype of endogenous depression, with a significantly poorer response rate to tricyclic antidepressants and often greater psychomotor disturbance. In a recent study of sleep in delusional depressives (Thase et al. 1986), comparison of pretreatment EEG sleep measures in delusional and nondelusional depressives indicated that the delusionals had significantly decreased generation of REM sleep time and REM activity (about 20 percent

less than nondelusionals) but higher frequency of sleep onset REM period (52 versus 31 percent of patients) than did nondelusional depressives, even after controlling for the effects of age, severity, and agitation.

Regarding the distinction between unipolar and bipolar affective disorders, sleep efficiency (the ratio of time spent asleep to total recording period) tends to be reduced in unipolar depressives but elevated in anergic bipolar depressives (Detre et al. 1972). The difference in sleep efficiency between unipolar and bipolar depressives may parallel differences between these groups in psychomotor activity levels because bipolar depressives tend to show lower levels of daytime and nocturnal activity than do unipolar depressives (Kupfer et al. 1974).

It is now clear that there are important interactions between age and disease in determining the sleep characteristics of major depressive disorders (Gillin et al. 1981; Kupfer et al. 1982b). Specifically, the sleep changes that characterize depression also occur, although to a lesser extent, during the course of normal aging itself. It is particularly the age-dependent increase in wakefulness after sleep onset and a decrease in slow wave sleep that characterize both normal aging and depressive illnesses. Moreover, in the course of normal aging, the tendency for REM sleep periods to become progressively longer during the night is significantly diminished. That is to say, the capacity to sustain REM sleep inhibition during the first half of the night appears to be diminished by advancing age and, to a much greater extent, by the presence of a depressive illness. This is evident in the shortening of REM sleep latency and the greater amounts of earlier REM sleep that seem most specifically to characterize the sleep of patients with endogenous depression (Vogel et al. 1980).

During the past 5 years, additional data on the sleep of childhood and elderly depressives have been published, lending support to the concept of an interaction between aging and disease in determining the sleep abnormalities of depression. For example, Puig-Antich et al. (1982) have reported few differences between the sleep of depressed prepubertal children and healthy controls matched for age, sex, and pubertal status. On the other hand, when the depressed children were studied during clinical remission, their REM latency showed a shortening compared to the controls (Puig-Antich et al. 1983). Lahmeyer et al. (1983) suggested that the sleep of adolescents with major depression is characterized by a constellation of findings similar to that of adult major depressives, particularly shortening of REM latency or first NREM sleep period. Studies of young adult and middle-aged depressives have shown a clear age-related decrease in EEG delta counts, particularly during the first two NREM periods, with a shift of delta activity counts from the first to the second NREM period. REM activity counts, by contrast, were increased in the middle-aged depressives, particularly during the first REM period (Kupfer et al. 1986). At the other end of the life cycle, it has been demonstrated that very short REM latencies, prolonged first REM periods, and extreme sleep maintenance difficulty reliably characterize the sleep of elderly endogenous depressives (Reynolds et al. 1985a). This same study also showed a high frequency of sleep onset REM periods in elderly endogenous depressives where approximately 43 percent of REM latency values were less than 10 minutes, in contrast to rates of 1.4 percent in healthy controls and 17 percent in nondepressed Alzheimer patients. Like middle-aged depressives, elderly depressed patients showed a shift of delta activity from the first to the second NREM period, whereas control and Alzheimer patients showed peak delta activity in the first NREM period (Reynolds et al. 1985b).

REM latency and other EEG sleep measures show little change over time in inpatients receiving placebo pharmacotherapy, in the absence of clinical change (Coble et al. 1981). Moreover, the findings of Hauri et al. (1974), Schulz et al. (1979), Cartwright (1983), and Rush et al. (1986) suggest that chronic sleep abnormalities, including reduced REM latency, may well persist beyond the clinically symptomatic period into remission. In other words, it appears that REM latency is reduced and stable in depression, in remission as well as during the acute clinical episode. This observation, if confirmed in larger samples, raises the question as to whether abnormal REM latency can be viewed as an indicator of continued vulnerability to depression, a consequence of depression that remits more slowly than the clinical episode itself, or as a potential predictor of depression in people who are unaffected but at risk.

A number of investigators have proposed that EEG sleep abnormalities might be helpful in understanding the pathophysiology of depression (for review, see Gillin and Borbely 1985; Reynolds and Shipley 1985). Several different explanatory models have been proposed, including neurochemical (McCarley 1982), chronobiologic (Borbely 1982; Wehr and Goodwin 1981), and developmental (Reynolds and Shipley 1985).

Schizophrenia

Numerous sleep physiologic studies in schizophrenia have been published during the past 30 years. For a comprehensive review of this area, readers are referred elsewhere (Feinberg and Hiatt 1978; Zarcone 1979). The EEG sleep findings most often reported in the literature include: (1) fragmentation of sleep and decrease in total sleep time; (2) decreased percentage of slow wave sleep, particularly of stage 4 sleep; (3) decreased as well as increased amounts of REM sleep; and (4) reduced REM compensation or rebound following REM deprivation. Some studies (e.g., Stern et al. 1969) reported finding a shortened latency to the first REM period in schizophrenics. Since shortened REM latency and increased density of REMs during the first REM period have been consistently found in patients with endogenous depression, the reports of short REM latency in schizophrenia have generated much controversy about the specificity of the latter finding for depressive illness. Unfortunately, methodologic shortcomings in both the positive and negative studies make it impossible to decide whether the weight of the evidence favors or rejects the idea that there are characteristic sleep abnormalities in schizophrenia. These shortcomings include the failure to use standardized diagnostic criteria and the failure to control for such potentially confounding variables as age, the effects of medication, and the effects of institutionalization. Hiatt et al. (1985) reexamined sleep in drug-free schizophrenics and found that stage 4 sleep was significantly reduced in schizophrenics and that this was most marked in the first NREM period of the night.

Ganguli et al. (in press) recently completed a study of EEG sleep in young, never-medicated nonschizoaffective schizophrenics, comparing the sleep of these patients to that of patients with major depressive disorders, both delusional and nondelusional, and to that of healthy controls. The schizophrenics had decreased sleep continuity comparable to delusional depressives, but percentage of slow wave sleep was similar to that seen in the healthy controls. The intranight temporal distribution of EEG delta activity was similar in schizophrenics and healthy controls, but different from nondelusional depressives. The latter showed a characteristic shift of NREM delta activity from first to second NREM period. In contrast, both groups of depressives showed diminished slow wave sleep compared to controls, greatly decreased delta activity (more so than did the schizophrenics), and an altered temporal distribution of delta activity. A most interesting, but preliminary, finding from the study was that minutes of slow wave sleep in the schizophrenics was inversely correlated with the presence of negative symptoms ($r = -.96$, $p < .0005$). When viewed in the historical context of sleep physiologic studies of schizophrenia over the past 30 years, these findings suggested that young, never-medicated schizophrenics did not show the characteristic constellation of abnormalities in the first NREM–REM cycle seen in patients with major depression. However, decreased slow wave sleep should be investigated as a possible marker for negative symptoms in schizophrenia.

Anxiety Disorders

Patients with generalized anxiety disorder appear to share with depressives some features of sleep continuity disturbance (difficulty falling asleep and maintaining sleep), as well as reduced percentage of slow wave sleep (Reynolds et al. 1983b). In contrast, reduction of percentage of REM sleep and an absence of short REM sleep latency appear to characterize the sleep of patients with generalized anxiety disorder, in contrast to the sleep of major depression.

Data on the sleep of patients with panic disorders are still sparse. In preliminary studies, it appears that some patients with panic disorders evidence diminished sleep continuity and slow wave sleep but do not appear as a group to show the severe REM sleep stigmata of major depression (Uhde et al. 1984). It seems likely, however, that the sleep of panic disorder patients will evidence considerable heterogeneity, perhaps related to a personal or family history of major depressive disorder, as is frequently the case in these patients. Thus it may be that panic disorder patients with a family history of major depression, or with a vulnerability to major depression, are more likely to evidence a short REM sleep latency than panic patients without such a personal or family history. Moreover, Dube et al. (1985) have suggested that

panic disorder patients with a history of major depression or a family history of depression are more likely to evidence cholinergic supersensitivity, as measured by arecoline REM induction responsivity.

A report of psychobiologic measures (including EEG sleep) in childhood obsessive compulsive disorder indicated that EEG sleep parameters in nine adolescents with primary obsessive compulsive disorder resembled those of young adults with primary depressive disorder (Rapoport et al. 1981). However, the authors reported that all subjects would have met DSM-III (American Psychiatric Association 1980) criteria for major depressive disorder at some time in their life. Insel et al. (1982) also found similarities between the sleep of adult obsessive compulsive patients and patients with major depression, suggesting a possible biologic link between obsessive compulsive disorder and affective illness.

Considerable additional research will be necessary in the area of sleep and anxiety disorders to establish whether the sleep of anxious and depressive patients differs. Given the heterogeneity of anxiety disorders, as evidenced in phenomenologic, family history, and treatment response studies, it is safe to predict that the sleep characteristics of different anxiety disorders will evidence similar neurophysiologic heterogeneity, and that this may be related in part to a personal or family history of affective disorder, or to a vulnerability to develop affective disorder.

Dementia

It is widely known that dysregulation of sleep–wake function is an important problem in normal aging and in the two most common neuropsychiatric disorders of old age: depression and dementia of the Alzheimer type. The belief is supported directly in the case of dementiform illnesses by such clinical phenomena as nocturnal or sleep-related confusion, episodic nocturnal wandering, increased time in bed, disorganization of the sleep–wake cycle (polyphasic sleep propensity), phase shifts, and excessive daytime sleepiness (Miles and Dement 1980). The limited observational data on the actual life-style and sleep–wake habits of the institutionalized elderly suggest also that many of these persons spend almost half of their time in bed, that their nocturnal sleep is fragmented, and that daytime naps are frequent.

There are a number of published EEG sleep studies of dementia of the Alzheimer type (Feinberg et al. 1967; Prinz et al. 1982; Reynolds et al. 1983b, 1985a, 1985b; Smirne et al. 1977). Compared with normative data from subjects of comparable age, patients with dementia of the Alzheimer type show a greater disruption of sleep continuity (with increased frequency and duration of awakenings), decreased REM sleep time and activity, and often decreased amounts of stages 3 and 4 sleep. Based on 72 hours of consecutive recording, Prinz et al. (1982) reported that dementing patients had very little slow wave sleep or REM sleep and that frequent daytime naps and nighttime periods of wakefulness occurred. Smirne et al. (1977) observed an absence of spindles, K-complexes, and vertex sharp activity in several demented patients. In our own comparative studies of sleep in Alzheimer disease and depression, we have suggested that the nocturnal sleep maintenance of patients with Alzheimer's disease is often not as impaired as in elderly depressives, although severely demented patients do develop a daily polyphasic pattern of sleep–wake activity (Figure 1). In contrast to depressives, demented patients tend to have lower REM sleep percentage, normal or prolonged REM sleep latencies, diminished intensity of REMs, and diminished numbers of spindles and K-complexes during stage 2 sleep. In our experience, the latter finding, which we have called "indeterminate NREM sleep," correlates significantly with the severity of dementia (Reynolds et al. 1985a) (Figure 2). In addition, we have reported that significantly more patients with Alzheimer's dementia (43 percent) have sleep apnea than do age- and gender-matched depressives (18 percent) and healthy controls (4 percent) (Reynolds et al. 1985c). The extent of apnea may be significantly correlated with the severity of dementia. This finding may support the concept of an interaction between sleep-disordered breathing and cognitive deterioration in dementia, one that could become more pernicious with the use of sleeping pills or other CNS depressants.

Data such as these suggest that there is a relation between changes in sleep and cognitive dysfunction. These and similar observations formed the basis of Feinberg et al.'s (1967) sleep-cognition hypothesis, which held that EEG sleep changes reflect the physiologic capacities of the brain, particularly to acquire and to process information. This hypothesis raises a very fundamental question: Does sleep loss in old age impede neurobiologic processes and thereby impair cognition; or are *both* sleep loss and cognitive decrements the result of some other underlying biologic changes, such as aging, decreased cholinergic activity, neuronal loss, or a decrease of cerebral blood flow? These and related issues have been explored elsewhere (Reynolds et al. 1983a).

Sleep in Other Neurologic Conditions

There are relatively few studies of sleep EEG changes in relation to acute brain syndromes or delirium. Feinberg et al. (1967) noted that 3 of 15 patients with dementia awakened repeatedly from REM sleep in delirium and showed "fixed ideas on which they attempted to act" (p. 133). They observed that aged normals and demented patients awakened more rapidly from all stages of sleep than did younger normals, returning to waking levels of function more rapidly. Gross and Hastey (1975) studied the EEG correlates of sleep disturbance and hallucinations in 4 subjects with delirium tremens. In the 2 subjects who slept, both showed high proportions of REM sleep. In a similar study, Greenberg and Pearlman (1967) found that 5 patients with delirium tremens tended to have higher levels of REM sleep than did 7 alcoholics who had been drinking but did not develop a withdrawal syndrome. It should be noted that not all alcoholics show REM rebound after an abrupt alcohol withdrawal and that the clinical course of delirium tremens and REM rebound are different.

Karacan et al. (1978) presented sleep EEG data on 5 patients with acute cerebral vascular disease. The patients ranged in age from 54 to 81 years and were in the first week of a stroke of either hemispheric or brain-stem origin. The 2 patients with the "worst" clinical outcome (exact meaning unknown) showed no sleep stage cycling and very little stage 2 spindle activity, and had poor correlation between left and right hemisphere delta activity as measured by the sleep-analyzing hybrid computer. By contrast, the 3 patients with somewhat better clinical outcomes showed diminished but recognizable REM and slow wave sleep, somewhat more spindling activity, and somewhat better interhemispheric correlations for delta activity.

Greenberg and Dewan (1969) reported similar findings to those of Karacan et al. (1978) in a group of 18 aphasic patients with varying rates of improvement and severity of aphasia, secondary to a vascular accident. The most severely aphasic pa-

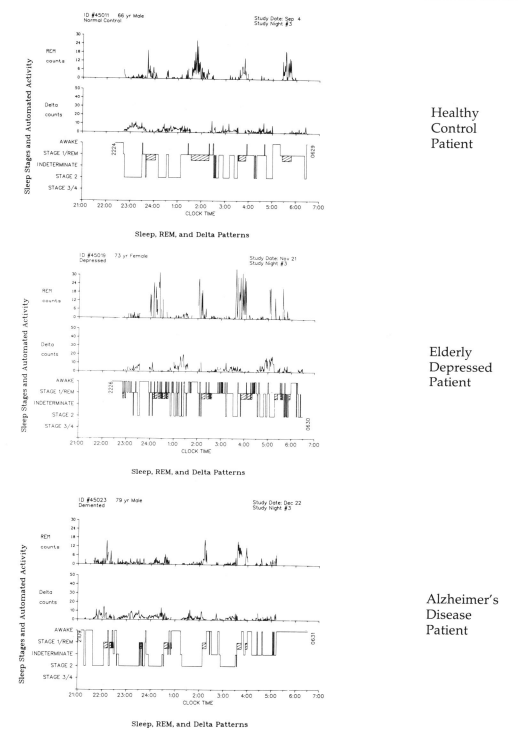

Sleep, REM, and Delta Patterns

Figure 1. EEG sleep structure in an elderly depressed patient (*center*) is characterized by extreme difficulty maintaining sleep, early-onset REM sleep, increased density of REM counts, and redistribution of EEG delta activity from the first to the second NREM period. By contrast, sleep maintenance difficulty is not as severe in the Alzheimer-demented patient (*bottom*), but REM time and REM counts are diminished. Some NREM sleep is also "indeterminate" (i.e., like stage 2, but with absence of stage 2 phasic events: spindles and K-complexes). Distribution of delta counts in the Alzheimer patient is similar to the healthy control (*top*).

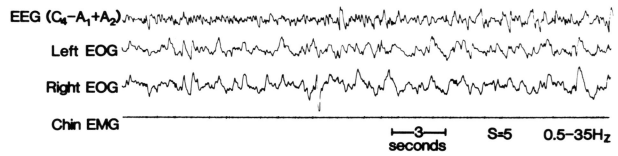

Figure 2. Appearance of indeterminate NREM sleep in a patient with probable Alzheimer's dementia. Sleep has a stage 2 appearance except for the absence of spindles and K-complexes.

tients tended to have less REM sleep time than less severely impaired patients. In addition, 2 patients who had severe language deficits, but who were showing improvement, had normal amounts of REM sleep. The authors speculated that recovery of function after brain damage requires "programming" indexed by REM sleep.

These studies are extremely interesting but equally inconclusive. The number of patients studied is small, and the effects of variables such as age and medication status were not well controlled. Additional studies of the sleep EEG are needed in specific neurologic syndromes, such as Huntington's and Parkinson's diseases, as well as in the early stages of Alzheimer's disease.

Finally, it can sometimes be difficult for the clinician to distinguish epileptogenic and nonepileptogenic forms of parasomnia. (The term *parasomnia* refers to specific disorders associated with partial arousal from sleep, such as an episode of sleepwalking occurring out of stage 4 sleep). For example, some sleepwalkers have an unusual form of epilepsy that is activated by sleep, which lowers the seizure threshold. These patients show episodic nocturnal wanderings often accompanied by screams or unintelligible vocalizations. In contrast to nonepileptogenic cases of sleepwalking, these patients generally have no family history of other parasomnia. In addition, seizure-related sleepwalking episodes often occur more than once a night (generally in the first and last hours of sleep) and are characterized by complex and, at times, violent behavior. Unlike patients with benign sleepwalking, patients with nocturnal epilepsy can be quite difficult to redirect. Many of these patients are found to have epileptiform abnormalities spe-

cifically activated by either NREM or REM sleep, originating particularly from the anterior or medial temporal lobe. Treatment with phenytoin or carbamazepine has been effective in some cases.

☐ NEUROPSYCHIATRIC ASPECTS OF PRIMARY SLEEP DISORDERS

Narcolepsy

Depression has been reported to be frequent in narcolepsy and has been considered to be variously a reaction to chronic sleepiness or an endogenous expression of the pathophysiology of narcolepsy (Broughton et al. 1981). Clinically, the two disorders have numerous symptoms in common. DSM-III notes "irritability, loss of energy, fatigue and interest" as features of major depression. The diagnostic classification of sleep disorders (ASCD 1979) states that narcoleptics may be considered "hostile, unmotivated, uninterested, or depressed" by others. In a recent study, we reported that 20 percent of a sample of narcoleptics met research diagnostic criteria for a past history of major or chronic intermittent depression; 12 percent for alcohol abuse, and 8 percent for generalized anxiety disorder (Reynolds et al. 1983c). Our observation of a concurrent or past psychiatric disorder in 40 percent of narcoleptic patients was similar to Roy's (1976) report of 40 percent and to Kales et al.'s (1982) report of 52 percent. We found quite distinctive REM latency distributions in the narcoleptics and outpatient depressives, with a much higher frequency of sleep onset REM periods in the narcoleptics. Further, compared with the outpatient depressives, the nocturnal sleep of narcoleptics was characterized by a shorter sleep latency, more wakefulness after sleep onset, a shorter mean REM latency, and greater stage 1 sleep percentage. These data suggested that the sleep of narcolepsy and depression differs significantly. Further, it seems premature to conclude that the depressive symptoms of narcolepsy represent an endogenous expression of its pathophysiology rather than a reaction to the disabling effects of sleepiness, particularly given these differences in sleep physiology. For additional current views on the pathophysiology and brain mechanisms of narcolepsy, the reader is referred to Baker and Dement (1985).

Sleep Apnea

Patients with sleep apnea syndromes often present with neuropsychiatric symptoms, including depression, anxiety, and organic mental syndrome. Guilleminault and Dement (1977) reported that 24 percent of patients with sleep apnea had seen psychiatrists for symptoms of anxiety and depression. Not infrequently, patients with sleep apnea syndrome (as well as patients with narcolepsy) can be discriminated from normal controls on the basis of elevated scores on the Depression scale of the Minnesota Multiphasic Personality Inventory. It seems reasonable to think that the occurrence and severity of depressive symptoms in sleep apnea may be related to the severity, chronicity, or disability caused by the disorder, or even to the treatment of its complications, including hypertension. In a sample of 25 consecutive male sleep apneics, 40 percent met research diagnostic criteria for affective disorder or for alcohol abuse (Reynolds et al. 1984a). Depression in the sleep apneic patients was significantly related to increasing age, increasing REM latency, and the presence of antihypertensive medication. Overall, the sleep apneic patients rated themselves as mildly to moderately depressed. The more depressed patients tended to complain of excessive daytime sleepiness, whereas the less depressed complained more often of insomnia. These findings suggested that diagnosable depressive psychopathology is an important aspect of sleep apnea syndromes.

Kleine-Levin Syndrome

Kleine-Levin syndrome is a disorder characterized by periodic attacks of hypersomnolence and megaphagia, usually with onset in adolescent males but occasionally later in life. Of interest to neuro-psychiatry is the frequent and periodic constellation of hypersomnia, gluttony, hypersexuality, and personality disturbances during the episode. Many studies of electrophysiologic changes during episodes of Kleine-Levin syndrome have been published, some employing continuous EEG recording during 24 hours or more, routine diurnal EEGs, all night polysomnography, and multiple sleep latency testing (for review, see Reynolds et al. 1984b). We recently reported MSLT findings in a case of Kleine-Levin syndrome. MSLT data indicated sleepiness as severe as in narcolepsy or obstructive sleep apnea as well as the occurrence of multiple sleep onset REM periods. This finding suggested the possibility that Kleine-Levin syndrome might be considered a form of periodic REM sleep disinhibition. While the conventional view has been that Kleine-Levin syndrome is a manifestation of hypothalamic dysfunction, the occurrence of multiple sleep onset REMs in a patient with Kleine-Levin suggests an important role of more caudal brain stem structures specifically activated during REM sleep.

☐ MANAGEMENT OF SLEEP DISORDERS

A basic tenet of modern sleep disorders medicine, as articulated at the National Institutes of Health Consensus Conference on Insomnia in 1984, is that the physician should attempt to establish the major (and possibly etiologic) correlates of the patient's complaint of disturbed sleep, with a goal of formulating a specific intervention. A more rational approach to the diagnosis and management of sleep disorders is now possible. An analogy with the prescription of analgesic drugs is useful: one would not consider it sound clinical practice to prescribe a narcotic analgesic without making a systematic attempt to ascertain the etiology of pain. Similarly, it is necessary, before prescribing sleeping pills, to make an etiologic diagnosis.

The first aim of clinical assessment is to establish the duration of the patient's complaint and its probable causes. For example, transient insomnia lasting less than 3 to 4 weeks is often situationally determined, whereas persistent insomnia (lasting more than 3 or 4 weeks) mandates evaluation for a variety of disorders. Sources of diagnostic information should include interviews with both the patient and bed partner and a sleep–wake diary (kept over a minimum of 14 days) to ascertain the distribution and quality of the patient's time in bed and sleep during the 24-hour day. A physical examination and portable screening (e.g., an audio cassette tape of the patient's breathing patterns during sleep, Holter monitoring for cardiac arrhythmia, or repeated oral temperature measurements to document circadian rhythm abnormalities) may also prove useful. Keeping in mind age-dependent changes in sleep–wake organization, the following factors should be assessed in the course of clinical investigation: (1) poor sleep hygiene practices (e.g., irregular sleep–wake schedule; excessive environmental temperature or noise; evening use of alcohol, nicotine, or caffeinated beverages); (2) adverse conditioning factors (e.g., obsessive fear about not sleeping, or use of the sleep setting for activities not conducive to sleep); (3) CNS depressant drug dependency; (4) phase advance or other temporal redistribution of the major sleep period; (5) heavy snoring or obstructed breathing during sleep, which may indicate sleep apnea; (6) periodic leg jerks or feelings of restlessness in the legs at sleep onset, which may indicate nocturnal myoclonus; (7) depression, dementia, or other neuropsychiatric disorders; (8) chronic pain (e.g., arthritis or nocturnal angina); and (9) gastroesophageal reflux, associated with hiatal hernia and possibly leading to laryngospasm. In addition, the use of sedating medication (hypnotics and some antihypertensives, antihistimines, and anxiolytics), their timing, and the dosage should be reviewed for potential adverse effects on sleep and daytime alertness.

Referral to a sleep disorders center is indicated if the physician suspects sleep apnea syndrome, nocturnal myoclonus, narcolepsy–cataplexy, nocturnal seizures, or sleep phase disturbance or irregularity. In addition, the physician should strongly consider referral of the patient to a sleep laboratory if routine treatment measures for persistent insomnia have not been effective. "Routine" treatment includes: (1) consistent attention to sleep hygiene (e.g., regulation of sleep–wake schedule and a comfortable sleep environment, with diminution of noise and excessive temperature); (2) reduction or omission of caffeine, nicotine, alcohol, and excessive liquid ingestion in the evening; (3) use of the bedroom for sleep and sex only; (4) careful attention to the timing of activity, meals, medication, and sleep periods; (5) CNS depressant or stimulant drug detoxification; (6) specific nonpharmacologic

treatment when indicated (e.g., circadian rhythm engineering or behavioral therapy); and (7) antidepressant medication for the treatment of an affective disorder.

Sleeping pills may have some place in the management of transient or situational sleep disturbance, in persistent psychophysiologic insomnia (e.g., sleep loss associated with negative conditioning or somatized tension anxiety factors), or in persistent insomnia associated with nonpsychotic psychiatric disorders. If the physician determines that a sleeping pill is indicated, the following practices are strongly advised:

1. Establish the smallest effective dose.
2. Tell the patient when to take the medication (generally 30 minutes before bedtime).
3. Monitor daytime sequelae, especially daytime sleepiness.
4. Follow the patient regularly.
5. Try to limit the use to less than 20 doses per month, for not more than 3 months.
6. Encourage the patient to increase reliance on nonpharmacologic approaches to sleep disturbance.

In summary, the consensus of sleep-disorders specialists concerning the management of sleep disturbances is that specific etiologic factors should be identified. This will often require clinical polysomnography or portable monitoring. Frequently, multiple factors are operating in the same patient to produce the sleep disturbance. In addition, physicians must recognize age-dependent changes, and patients must be told that their ability to sleep deeply and without interruptions diminishes with advancing age. The sleep–wake rhythm (i.e., entrainment) should be reinforced by strengthening time cues and enhancing stimulus control (e.g., using the bedroom only for sleep and sex). Physicians should attend to chronopharmacologic issues (e.g., timing of both psychotropic and nonpsychotropic drugs). Finally, the use of sleeping pills must be for specific indications, for limited periods of time using the minimum effective dosage, and with attention to possible effects on respiration during sleep.

☐ REFERENCES

Akiskal HS, Lemmi H, Yerevanian B, et al: The utility of the REM latency test in psychiatric diagnosis: a study of 81 depressed outpatients. Psychiatry Res 7:101–110, 1982

American Psychiatric Association: Diagnostic and Statistical Manual of Mental Disorders, 3rd ed. Washington, DC, American Psychiatric Association, 1980

American Psychiatric Association: Diagnostic and Statistical Manual of Mental Disorders, 3rd ed., revised. Washington, DC, American Psychiatric Association, 1987

Association of Sleep Disorders Centers: Classification of sleep and arousal disorders. Sleep 2:1–153, 1979

Baker TL, Dement WC: Canine narcolepsy-cataplexy syndrome: evidence for an inherited monoaminergic-cholinergic imbalance, in Brain Mechanisms of Sleep. Edited by McGinty DJ, Drucker-Colin R, Morrison A, et al. New York, Raven Press, 1985

Borbely AA: A two-process model of sleep regulation. Hum Neurobiol 1:155–204, 1982

Broughton R, Ghanem Q, Hishikawa Y, et al: The socio-economic and related life-effects in 180 patients with narcolepsy from North America, Asia, and Europe compared to matched controls, in Psychophysiological Aspects of Sleep. Edited by Karacan I. New Jersey, Noyer Medical Publications, 1981

Cartwright RD: REM sleep characteristics during and after mood-disturbing events. Arch Gen Psychiatry 40:197–201, 1983

Coble PA, Foster FG, Kupfer DJ: Electroencephalographic sleep diagnosis of primary depression. Arch Gen Psychiatry 33:1124–1127, 1976

Coble PA, Kupfer DJ, Shaw DH: Distribution of REM latency in depression. Biol Psychiatry 16:453–466, 1981

Coleman RM, Roffwarg HP, Kennedy SJ, et al: Sleep-wake disorders based on a polysomnographic diagnosis: a national cooperative study. JAMA 247:997–1003, 1982

Detre TP, Himmelhoch J, Swartzburg M, et al: Hypersomnia and manic-depressive disease. Am J Psychiatry 128:1303–1305, 1972

Dube S, Kumar N, Ettedgri E, et al: Cholinergic REM induction response: separation of anxiety and depression. Biol Psychiatry 20:408–418, 1985

Feinberg I, Hiatt JF: Sleep patterns in schizophrenia: a selective review, in Sleep Disorders: Diagnosis and Treatment. Edited by Williams RC, Karacan I. New York, Wiley, 1978

Feinberg I, Koresko RL, Heller N: EEG sleep patterns as a function of normal and pathological aging in man. J Psychiatr Res 5:107–144, 1967

Feinberg M, Gillin JC, Carroll BJ, et al: EEG studies of sleep in the diagnosis of depression. Biol Psychiatry 17:305–316, 1982

Ganguli R, Reynolds CF, Kupfer DJ: Sleep in young never-medicated non-schizoaffective schizophrenics: a comparison with delusional and non-delusional depressives and with healthy controls. Arch Gen Psychiatry (in press)

Gillin JC, Borbely AA: Sleep: a neurobiological window in affective disorders. Trends in Neuroscience 8:537–542, 1985

Gillin JC, Duncan W, Pettigrew KD, et al: Successful separation of depressed, normal, and insomniac subjects by EEG sleep data. Arch Gen Psychiatry 36:85–90, 1979

Gillin JC, Duncan WC, Murphy DL, et al: Age-related changes in sleep in depressed and normal subjects. Psychiatry Res 4:73–78, 1981

Greenberg R, Dewan EM: Aphasia and rapid eye movement sleep. Nature 223:183–184, 1969

Greenberg R, Pearlman C: Delirium tremens and dreaming. Am J Psychiatry 124:133, 1967

Gross MM, Hastey JM: A note on REM rebound during experimental alcohol withdrawal in alcoholics, in Advances in Experimental Biology and Medicine. Edited by Gross MM. New York, Plenum Press, 1975

Guilleminault C (ed): Sleep and Waking Disorders: Indications and Techniques. Reading, Mass, Addison-Wesley, 1982

Guilleminault C, Dement WC: Sleep apnea syndrome due to upper airway obstruction. Arch Intern Med 137:296–300, 1977

Guilleminault C, Lugaresi E (eds): Sleep-Wake Disorders: Natural History, Epidemiology, and Long-Term Evolution. New York, Raven Press, 1983

Hauri P, Chernik D, Hawkins D, et al: Sleep of depressed patients in remission. Arch Gen Psychiatry 31:386–391, 1974

Hiatt JF, Floyd TC, Katz PH, et al: Further evidence of abnormal non-rapid-eye-movement sleep in schizophrenia. Arch Gen Psychiatry 42:797–802, 1985

Insel TR, Gillin JC, Moore A, et al: The sleep of patients with obsessive compulsive disorder. Arch Gen Psychiatry 39:1372, 1982

Kales A, Soldatos CR, Bixler EO, et al: Narcolepsy-cataplexy. II. Psychosocial consequences and associated psychopathology. Arch Neurol 39:169–171, 1982

Karacan I, Dervent A, Ambuehl RA, et al: Cerebrovascular disease: on some correlations between clinical and electroencephalographic evidence. Sleep Research 7:260, 1978

Kupfer DJ, Reynolds CF: Neurophysiologic studies of depression: state of the art, in The Origins of Depression: Current Concepts and Approaches. Edited by Angst J. Berlin, Springer-Verlag, 1983

Kupfer DJ, Weiss BL, Foster FG, et al: Psychomotor activity in affective states. Arch Gen Psychiatry 30:765–768, 1974

Kupfer DJ, Spiker DG, Coble PA, et al: Sleep and treatment prediction in endogenous depression. Am J Psychiatry 138:429–434, 1981

Kupfer DJ, Foster FG, Coble PA, et al: The application of EEG sleep for the differential diagnosis of affective disorders. Am J Psychiatry 135:69–74, 1982a

Kupfer DJ, Reynolds CF, Ulrich RF, et al: EEG sleep, depression and aging. Neurobiol Aging 3:351–360, 1982b

Kupfer DJ, Spiker DG, Rossi A, et al: Recent diagnostic and treatment advances in REM sleep and depression, in Treatment of Depression: Old Controversies and New Approaches. Edited by Clayton P, Barrett J. New York, Raven Press, 1983

Kupfer DJ, Reynolds CF, Ulrich RF, et al: Comparison of automated REM and slow wave sleep analysis in young and middle-aged depressed subjects. Biol Psychiatry 21:189–200, 1986

Lahmeyer HW, Poznanski EV, Bellur SN: Sleep in depressed adolescents. Am J Psychiatry 140:1150–1153, 1983

McCarley RW: Sleep and depression: common neurobiological control mechanisms. Am J Psychiatry 139:565–570, 1982

Miles LE, Dement WC: Sleep and aging. Sleep 3:119–220, 1980

Prinz P, Peskind E, Vitaliano P, et al: Changes in the sleep and waking EEG's of nondemented and demented elderly subjects. J Am Geriatr Soc 30:86–93, 1982

Puig-Antich J, Goetz R, Hanlon C, et al: Sleep architecture and REM sleep measures in prepubital children with major depression. Arch Gen Psychiatry 39:932–939, 1982

Puig-Antich J, Goetz R, Hanlon C, et al: Sleep architecture and REM sleep measures in prepublital major depressives. Arch Gen Psychiatry 40:187–192, 1983

Rapoport J, Elkins R, Langer DH, et al: Childhood obsessive-compulsive disorder. Am J Psychiatry 138:1545–1554, 1981

Reynolds CF, Shipley JE: Sleep in depressive disorders. Psychiatric Update 4:78–88, 1985

Reynolds CF, Coble PA, Kupfer DJ, et al: Application of the multiple sleep latency test in disorders of excessive sleepiness. Electroencephalogr Clin Neurophysiol 53:443–452, 1982a

Reynolds CF, Newton TF, Shaw DH, et al: EEG sleep findings in outpatients with primary depression. Psychiatry Res 6:65–75, 1982b

Reynolds CF, Shaw DH, Newton TF, et al: EEG sleep in generalized anxiety disorder: a preliminary comparison with primary depression. Psychiatry Res 8:81–89, 1983a

Reynolds CF, Spiker DG, Hanin I, et al: EEG sleep, aging, and psychopathology: new data and state of the art. Biol Psychiatry 18:139–155, 1983b

Reynolds CF, Christiansen CL, Taska LS, et al: Sleep in narcolepsy and depression: does it all look alike? J Nerv Ment Dis 171:290–295, 1983c

Reynolds CF, Kupfer DJ, McEachran AB, et al: Depressive psychopathology in male sleep apneics. J Clin Psychiatry 45:287–290, 1984a

Reynolds CF, Kupfer DJ, Christiansen CL, et al: Multiple sleep latency test findings in Kleine-Levin Syndrome. J Nerv Ment Dis 172:41–44, 1984b

Reynolds CF, Kupfer DJ, Taska LS, et al: EEG sleep in elderly depressed, demented and healthy subjects. Biol Psychiatry 20:431–442, 1985a

Reynolds CF, Kupfer DJ, Taska LS, et al: Slow wave sleep in elderly depressed, demented and healthy subjects. Sleep 8:155–159, 1985b

Reynolds CF, Kupfer DJ, Taska LS, et al: Sleep apnea in Alzheimer's dementia: correlation with mental deterioration. J Clin Psychiatry 46:257–261, 1985c

Roy A: Psychiatric aspects of narcolepsy. Br J Psychiatry 128:562–565, 1976

Rush AJ, Shaw BF: Failures in treating depression by cognitive behavior therapy, in Failures in Behavior Therapy. Edited by Foa EB, Emmelkamp PMG. New York, Wiley, 1983, pp 217–228

Rush AJ, Erman MK, Giles DE, et al: Polysomnographic findings in recently drug-free and clinically remitted depressed patients. Arch Gen Psychiatry 43:878–884, 1986

Rush AJ, Giles GE, Roffwarg HP, et al: Sleep EEG and dexamethasone suppression findings in outpatients with unipolar major depressive disorders. Biol Psychiatry 17:327–341, 1982

Schulz H, Lund R, Cording C, et al: Bimodal distribution of REM sleep latencies in depression. Biol Psychiatry 14:595–600, 1979

Smallwood RG, Vitiello MV, Giblin EC, et al: Sleep apnea: relationship to age, sex, and Alzheimer's dementia. Sleep 6:16–22, 1983

Smirne S, Come G, Franceschi M, et al: Sleep in presenile dementia, in Communications in EEG. International Federation of Societies for Electroencephalography and Clinical Neurophysiology, 9th Congress, 521–522, E271, 1977

Stern M, Fram D, Wyatt R, et al: All night sleep studies of acute schizophrenics. Arch Gen Psychiatry 20:470–477, 1969

Thase ME, Kupfer DJ, Ulrich RF: EEG sleep in psychotic depression: a valid subtype? Arch Gen Psychiatry 43:886–893, 1986

Uhde TW, Roy-Byrne P, Gillin JC, et al: The sleep of patients with panic disorders: a preliminary report. Psychiatry Res 12:251–259, 1984

Van den Hoed J, Kraemer H, Guilleminault C, et al: Disorders of excessive daytime somnolence: polygraphic and clinical data for 100 patients. Sleep 4:23–37, 1981

Vogel GW, Vogel F, McAbee RS, et al: Improvement of depression by REM sleep deprivation. Arch Gen Psychiatry 37:247–253, 1980

Wehr TA, Goodwin FK: Biological rhythms and psychiatry, in American Handbook of Psychiatry, Vol. 7. Edited by Arieti S, Brode HRH. New York, Basic Books, 1981, pp 46–74

Zarcone VP: Sleep and schizophrenia. Psychiatric Annals 9:29–40, 1979

Chapter 15

Neuropsychiatric Aspects of Degenerative Diseases

Maurice J. Martin, M.D.
John L. Black, M.D.

THIS CHAPTER DISCUSSES A HETEROGENOUS GROUP of disorders we categorize under the term *degenerative disease*. Many of the diseases described here are degenerative. Others—such as Wilson's disease, Friedreich's ataxia, Guillaine-Barré syndrome, and myesthenia gravis—are not degenerative but are metabolic, hereditary, or autoimmune in nature. These disorders will be discussed in order of descending frequency in the population.

The practicing psychiatrist needs to be familiar with these conditions and their range of manifestations because these disorders do not always present in a straightforward fashion. Frequently, patients with poorly understood illnesses, those with vague complaints, or those with atypical presentations are suspected of having a psychiatric condition and are referred to the psychiatrist. The psychiatrist can often be of most service to these patients by encouraging proper diagnosis by sug-

gesting a possible diagnosis and recommending specific tests when possible.

Many of the disorders discussed in this chapter also have psychiatric sequellae. Psychiatrists who consult to the patients of generalists, internists, neurologists, and psychologists will be asked to care for such patients.

☐ PARKINSON'S DISEASE

Parkinson's disease was first described in 1817 by James Parkinson. It has since come to be recognized as a common cause of neurologic morbidity.

Clinical Features

Parkinsonian syndromes can be categorized as to whether they are a primary disorder, a genetic dis-

257

order, or secondary to some other condition, medication, or toxin (Table 1).

Patients with idiopathic Parkinson's disease exhibit tremor, rigidity, and bradykinesia, as well as disturbances of posture, gait, and autonomic functions (Figure 1). Tremor is the initiating symptom in 60 to 70 percent of patients with Parkinson's disease and is present in 90 percent of cases during the course of the disease (Hoehn and Yahr 1967). The tremor is classically described as a "pill rolling," alternating motion of the thumb and forefinger, which occurs at rest and has a frequency of 4 to 7 Hz. However, the tremor often affects other areas of the body; the frequency and amplitude may vary.

Rigidity, present in 90 percent of patients, progresses from initially mild and restricted rigidity to a more severe and generalized symptom (Hoehn and Yahr 1967). The rigidity contributes to feelings of weakness, limited range of motion, bradykinesia (ranging to akinesia), and probably contributes to the postural changes that these patients exhibit. On examination, cogwheeling is a manifestation of rigidity.

The postural abnormality is typified by the head bowed, trunk bent forward, shoulders drooped, arms and knees flexed, and the hands held anteriorly. The patient walks with a festinated gait whereby small steps are taken in a shuffling fashion while the patient leans forward.

One of the most disturbing symptoms is the inability to perform volitional motor tasks easily.

TABLE 1.   PARKINSONIAN SYNDROME

Primary
  Idiopathic Parkinson's disease

Secondary
  Antipsychotic drugs
  Other degenerative neurologic conditions
    Striatonigral degeneration
    Shy-Drager syndrome
    Arteriosclerotic parkinsonism
  Postencephalitic infections
  Toxins
    Carbon monoxide
    1-Methyl-4-phenyl-1,2,3,6-tetrahydropyridine
    Heavy metal exposure
  Tumor
  Trauma

Genetic
  Familial (rare)
  Parkinson-dementia complex of Guam

Figure 1.   Patient with idiopathic Parkinson's disease. Note posture and position of hands and arms.

This results from the bradykinesia, which varies and is so severe at times as to cause akinesia. This symptom can be capricious; occasionally even severely restricted, unmedicated patients will suddenly be able to move in an amazingly normal fashion.

The autonomic dysfunction of Parkinson's disease causes sialorrhea, hypotension (especially postural hypotension), hyperhidrosis, bowel and bladder dysfunction, and thermoregulatory instability. Seborrheic dermatosis frequently occurs on the forehead (Yahr 1984).

Drug-induced parkinsonism is probably the type with which psychiatrists are most familiar. Any agent that causes dopamine D2 receptor blockade (as do all modern-day antipsychotics) can cause parkinsonism. However, those antipsychotics with high antimuscarinic receptor-blocking potential cause less of this side effect for the reasons explained below. This side effect occurs in about 13 percent of all patients placed on a neuroleptic and usually develops within the first 72 days of treatment. It is common to all age groups but affects women twice as often as men (Ayd 1983). In contrast to idiopathic Parkinson's disease, antipsychotic-induced parkinsonism is transient in that it tends to lessen with several months' exposure, it is infrequently associated with a pill-rolling tremor, the extrapyramidal symptoms (cogwheel rigidity, bradykinesia, gait disturbance, mask-like facies) are bilateral, and the side effect resolves nearly entirely with anticholinergic agents (Hausner 1983). Discontinuation of the antipsychotic is followed by remission from parkinsonism features within 10 to 60 days.

Some toxins can cause parkinsonism. Carbon monoxide poisoning, such as that due to a suicide attempt by breathing automobile exhaust, may cause irreversible parkinsonism. A recent finding is that 1-methyl-4-phenyl-1,2,3,6-tetrahydropyridine (MPTP) exposure can cause a severe, irreversible parkinsonism. Drug abusers sometimes take drugs contaminated with the agent, underscoring the importance of asking about drug use in parkinsonian patients with atypical demographic characteristics (Lang and Blair 1984; Yahr 1984).

Other types of parkinsonism include the parkinsonism-dementia complex of Guam, which is indigenous to the Chamorro population of Guam and which appears to be genetic; postencephalitic parkinsonism, which resulted from the epidemic of encephalitis lethargica (von Economo encepha-litis) between 1919 and 1926; parkinsonism due to striatonigral degeneration; and parkinsonism secondary to multiple infarcts (arteriosclerotic parkinsonism), head trauma, brain tumor, infection, and heavy metal exposure. For a more complete discussion of the symptoms of these parkinsonian syndromes, the reader is referred to Yahr (1984).

Most forms of parkinsonism, except antipsychotic-induced types, are progressive. In idiopathic Parkinson's disease, prior to the advent of treatment with levodopa, the disease could be expected to cause severe disability or death in 25 percent of patients within 5 years of onset, 65 percent within 10 years of onset, and 80 percent within 15 years of onset (Hoehn and Yahr 1967). Since levodopa therapy became available, morbidity and mortality from this disease have lessened, even though this treatment probably does not alter the underlying pathophysiology of the illness (Yahr 1984). Death in Parkinson's disease is usually due to heart disease, bronchopneumonia, malignant neoplasm, vascular lesions of the central nervous system (CNS), urinary tract infection, or hypertensive cardiovascular disease (Hoehn and Yahr 1967).

Psychiatric Manifestations

Dementia of a subcortical subtype occurs in an estimated 25 percent of patients with Parkinson's disease (Brown and Marsdew 1984). This may be due to interruption of dopamineric mesocortical and mesolimbic projections, although the role of these tracts in memory function is speculative. The dementia is frequently mild and is characterized by memory loss, with preservation of higher-order associative functions. Hence, aphasia, agnosia, and apraxia are not common (Huber and Paulson 1985). These patients frequently appear apathetic. The bradykinesia, sialorrhea, and masked facies that parkinsonism causes, however, tend to give the false impression of advanced dementia. Alzheimer's dementia and Parkinson's disease are both frequent occurrences in the elderly. Coexistence of these diseases occurs, sometimes causing a picture consistent with cortical dementia. Whatever the cause of the dementia that a particular patient exhibits, these patients may exhibit nocturnal confusion, increased sensitivity to the psychotogenic effects of drugs used to treat parkinsonism, impulsivity, combativeness, and deterioration of personal appearance in advanced stages.

A major psychiatric sequela to Parkinson's disease is the occurrence of depression in approximately 38 percent of patients (Mayeux et al. 1984). The subjective experience of loss at the onset of this illness is tremendous; loss of independence, loss of control of volitional movement, and sometimes loss of intellectual capacity can contribute to adjustment difficulties. The depression may take on major depressive proportions. Frequently, however, this diagnosis is difficult to confirm because many of the features of Parkinson's disease look like the neurovegetative symptoms of major depression. Dysthymic disorders also occur with Parkinson's disease. All depressions associated with Parkinson's disease are usually mild to moderate in severity; patients are rarely suicidal. Depression is not related to the severity of disease or the patient's age or sex. Depression may precede or develop just after the onset of Parkinson's disease in 15 to 25 percent of cases (Mayeux et al. 1984).

Psychiatrists are sometimes asked to evaluate patients with Parkinson's disease by physicians who do not understand that the bradykinesia of Parkinson's disease can intermittently markedly lessen, allowing the patient to move about freely, or that "on-off" effects of medication can occur. Unfortunately, such patients may be labeled as unmotivated, passive-aggressive, malingerers, or said to be displaying factitious illnesses.

Epidemiology and Etiology

Parkinson's disease is a leading cause of neurologic morbidity. It usually begins insidiously between the ages of 50 and 65. The prevalence rate of Parkinson's disease is estimated to be 200 per 100,000, and the annual incidence rate is about 20 per 100,000 (Kurland et al. 1973). Males and females are affected equally, and the disease is prevalent in all races throughout the world. There is little to suggest a genetic link in most cases, except in the parkinsonism-dementia complex of Guam and in rare familial forms of the disease (Yahr 1984).

Parkinsonism is caused by an imbalance between dopaminergic inhibition and cholinergic excitation in the basal ganglion. In parkinsonism, dopamine stores are either depleted or dopamine D2 receptors are blocked, preventing normal dopaminergic transmission. Other neurotransmitters such as gamma-aminobutyric acid (GABA), serotonin, noradrenalin, and various neuropeptides are also present in the basal ganglion and may be im-

plicated in the pathogenesis of this disease with future research (Yahr 1984).

Pathology

In idiopathic Parkinson's disease, neuronal loss and depigmentation occur in the substantia nigra, locus ceruleus, and dorsal vagal nucleus of the brain stem (Figure 2). These areas develop intracellular inclusion bodies called Lewy bodies. The neostriatum is depleted of dopamine.

Neuroleptic-induced parkinsonism is not associated with pathologic changes. Carbon monoxide poisoning has been found to cause bilateral basal ganglion necrosis and calcification. 1-Methyl-4-phenyl-1,2,3,6-tetrahydropyridine (MPTP) exposure causes severe loss of dopaminergic substantia nigra neurons and may cause Lewy bodies (Davis 1979).

Diagnosis

Routine examinations of blood, cerebrospinal fluid (CSF), and urine, as well as electroencephalograms

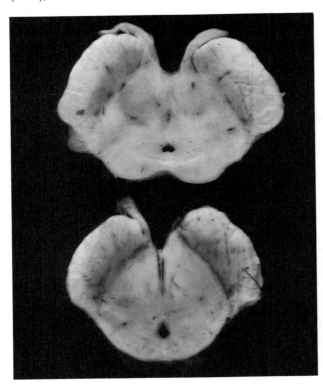

Figure 2.   Substantia nigra of patients with Parkinson's disease (top) compared to normal (bottom). Note depigmentation of the diseased patient's substantia nigra. From Okazaki (1983); reprinted with permission.

(EEGs), skull radiographs, isotope brain scans, and computed tomography (CT) scans are normal, except in arteriosclerotic parkinsonism and disease secondary to some toxins, brain tumors, or trauma. CSF homovanillic acid levels have been reported to be decreased in idiopathic Parkinson's disease, but few centers routinely run this test. The diagnosis of Parkinson's disease is usually based on history, physical examination, and, occasionally, nationality. In idiopathic Parkinson's disease, a hyperactive glabellar reflex and a positive palmomental reflex are commonly present in addition to the classic clinical features of the disease. A Babinski sign may be present.

Treatment

Treatment of all forms of parkinsonism centers on attempts to rebalance the dopamine/acetylcholine imbalance that is responsible for the disorder. An attempt to find an underlying cause should be made but, in most situations, correction will be impossible. For neuroleptic-induced parkinsonism, treatment consists of the use of anticholinergic agents such as benztropine, biperiden, diphenhydramine, or trihexyphenidyl. Amantadine or a switch to a more anticholinergic antipsychotic such as chlorpromazine, mesoridazine, or thioridazine is usually beneficial, as is a decreased dosage of the antipsychotic medication used. Because tolerance to the parkinsonian side effect of antipsychotics often occurs, attempts to taper and discontinue anticholinergic agents or amantadine may be possible with time (Black et al. 1985).

Essentially all other forms of parkinsonism, whether primary, secondary, or of genetic origin, are controlled with anticholinergic agents, amantadine, levodopa/carbidopa, bromocriptine, or L-deprenil. The reader is referred elsewhere (Lang et al. 1984; Yahr 1984) for more information on the medical management of parkinsonism. Two important treatment side effects, however, will be discussed.

Levodopa/carbidopa combinations and bromocriptine can cause a continuum of psychiatric symptoms. Disturbed sleep may occur, with motor restlessness and calling out, for which the patient has no memory and which may progress to illusions and hallucinations while the patient is fully awake. This may develop into a psychotic state with paranoia and hallucinations. The demented

patient suffers from these side effects most (Lang et al. 1984).

The "on-off" ("wearing-off") phenomenon is another side effect of long-term levodopa/carbidopa therapy. The on state is characterized as a state of activation in which the patient can move about freely. The off state is a state of severe parkinsonism where the patient is immobilized. Mood is often described as euphoric during the on state and depressed during the off state. The transition from on to off can be rapid and is believed to be associated with declining blood levels of levodopa, but these may occur in a seemingly random fashion that may actually be precipitated by changes in the emotional state. Initially, this symptom is controlled by shortening the interval between doses or by giving the medications between meals to ensure sustained blood levels and reliable absorption. If the phenomenon is unpredictable, it undermines patients' confidence in their ability to function with any degree of autonomy.

Surgical destruction of the ventrolateral nucleus of the thalamus is occasionally used on selected patients. Physical therapy can be used to maintain joint mobility and muscle strength and to provide gait training in advanced cases of Parkinson's disease.

Patients with Parkinson's disease can often benefit from psychotherapeutic interventions, especially when the disease is progressive and is beginning to interfere with social and occupational functioning. Most likely the patient will present with a differential diagnosis of adjustment disorder with depressed mood versus dysthymic disorder or major depressive disorder. Psychotherapy will center on issues of loss of idealized body image and loss of control. Patients have reported that psychotherapy aimed at exploring such issues has led to more reasonable self-expectations, better medication compliance, and better response to the medications (Todes 1983).

Medications are useful in some depressed patients. Patients with newly diagnosed Parkinson's disease who are depressed may experience improved parkinsonism and mood with levodopa/carbidopa therapy. Antidepressants, particularly the more anticholinergic agents (amitriptyline, doxepin, protryptiline, and trimipramine), are not only useful in the treatment of depression, but also block the uptake and storage of dopamine, thus making more dopamine available to the dopamine D2 receptor and lessening the parkinsonian symptoms. In addition, anticholinergic activity helps to rebalance the dopamine/acetylcholine imbalance (Mayeux et al. 1984). If tolerated, these drugs should be used in full therapeutic dosages (150 to 200 mg daily in divided dosages).

Sometimes the patient appearing depressed ultimately proves to be demented. Even this condition may respond somewhat to antidepressant medications. An important point is that demented patients can be depressed, particularly early in subcortical dementia, where insight remains and recognition of impairment and intellectual deterioration occurs (Huber and Paulson 1985).

In advanced cases of dementia, behavior may become quite disorganized, particularly when a patient suffering on-off phenomena is in the on state. Patients with advanced dementia are more sensitive to the anticholinergic agents, which are known to cause memory disturbance and delirium. Behaviorally disorganized, demented patients may improve if these agents are reduced, but the parkinsonism may worsen. Other factors that may be contributing to the patient's deterioration should be sought and corrected. Good sleep habits, stimulation, and attempts to orient the patient during the day by family and attendants will help with this condition. If all else fails, antipsychotic agents can be used, but this must be done with extreme caution as described below.

An occasional patient with Parkinson's disease will also suffer from functional psychosis. Before giving a diagnosis of functional psychosis, however, attempts should be made to seek and correct organic factors that may be responsible for the psychotic symptoms. This is especially true of antiparkinsonian drug therapy. The dosage of levodopa/carbidopa or bromocriptine should be decreased to see if the psychosis clears. If not—and if other psychotropics or treatment modalities such as lithium carbonate for mania; tricyclic antidepressants for psychotic depression; or electroconvulsive therapy for mania, psychotic depression, or schizophreniform psychosis are inappropriate or impractical—a neuroleptic can be used with caution. The best policy is to use the lowest effective dose of a highly anticholinergic antipsychotic such as chlorpromazine, mesoridazine, or thioridazine (Black et al. 1985; Hausner 1983).

☐ MULTIPLE SCLEROSIS

Multiple sclerosis is a chronic disease characterized pathologically by areas of demyelination of the CNS. It is marked by exacerbations and remissions over many years and often has both emotionally and organically induced psychiatric manifestations.

Clinical Features

This chronic disease appears in previously healthy young adults, females more than males. The onset is highly variable and may be sudden or subacute. The symptoms depend on the site of demyelination. The most common symptom is muscle weakness but ocular symptoms such as diplopia, visual field defects, or blurring of vision with a loss of visual acuity are also common. Urinary disturbances may involve incontinence of urine. Although peripheral nerves are not affected by the pathologic demyelination, paresthesias and gait disturbance due to CNS involvement are common. A wide variety of other less common symptoms may be present at any time during the course of the disease. These include dysarthria with a scanning speech, pain, vertigo, dysphagia, impotence, decreased hearing, tinnitus, convulsions, and a variety of mental symptoms.

Psychiatric Manifestations

Since many of the initial symptoms of multiple sclerosis are nonspecific and may be subjective, there is often concern that a somatoform disorder is present. The consulting psychiatrist, therefore, may become involved early in the progression of the disease. Many patients who are eventually shown to have multiple sclerosis are felt to have a hysterical disorder. When the symptoms progress and a correct diagnosis is made, the patient may develop a mood disturbance. One study showed a significantly increased rate of depressive diagnoses among the population with multiple sclerosis as compared with patients with temporal lobe epilepsy and amyotrophic lateral sclerosis (Schiffer and Babigian 1984). Euphoria may occur and be confused with the *la belle indifférence* of hysteria. It is unclear whether this type of mood disturbance is related to an organic process. Acute psychotic states have been reported with multiple sclerosis. They may be confusional states or they may mimic a schizophrenic disorder.

More characteristic changes due to anatomic lesions frequently occur. Memory disturbances and various cognitive defects may be found. These problems occasionally progress to dementia. Remission of severe cognitive defects is unusual. Since multiple sclerosis usually begins during productive years, the impact of the disease with its unpredictable course manifest by sudden exacerbations may produce serious difficulties in coping. The lack of specific treatment and long-term prognosis adds to this difficulty. Emotional support from family, friends, and co-workers is essential. Occasionally the frustrations of an uncertain diagnosis early in the course of the disease will provoke acting-out or rebellious behavior and altered career goals. There is no published evidence for an increased incidence of suicide in patients with multiple sclerosis.

Epidemiology and Etiology

The cause of multiple sclerosis is unknown. The two major theories currently are divided between a slow virus causation and alterations in the immune system. Since the disease occurs most frequently in northern latitudes of Europe and North America, it would appear that some environmental factor was present. The disease does not occur in native-born Africans, but the incidence rate is equal in all races in natives of the northern United States. Both the incidence and clinical characteristics of the disease vary from one location to another. The incidence is lower in Asia and often has a more acute onset. Kurland et al. (1973) have summarized extensive epidemiologic data concerning this disease.

There is a higher prevalence in women (60:40 in the United States), and the disease rarely begins after age 50. The majority of the cases in the United States develop clinical symptoms between the ages of 20 and 40 (Poser et al. 1984).

Pathology

There are scattered losses of myelin sheath in the white matter throughout the CNS. These areas of discoloration, called plaques, may be scattered throughout the brain and spinal cord. Occasionally, atrophy of the cerebral convolutions appears with involvement of the cerebral cortex. The lesions are usually discrete, and the brain may have a modeled appearance. A high concentration of immunoglobulin G has been demonstrated in plaque tissue. The role of this substance is not clear.

Diagnosis

The diagnosis of multiple sclerosis is usually difficult and requires months or even years of follow-up to confirm the presence of the disease. The presence of a neurologic abnormality in a previously healthy young person in a temperate climate raises suspicion of multiple sclerosis. All physicians should be wary of making a presumptive diagnosis of multiple sclerosis based on a single neurologic symptom. Unnecessary anxiety may be provoked in a patient who may not have a demyelinating disease or who may have a remission of many years. On the other hand, a hasty diagnosis of hysteria based on bizarre neurologic symptoms may interfere with proper follow-up and the correct diagnosis of multiple sclerosis. There are no specific diagnostic tests; however, the most consistent abnormality is an elevation of the CSF gamma globulin. There may also be mild elevation of CSF protein and slight lymphocytic pleocytosis. Magnetic resonance imaging or CT frequently show the plaques of multiple sclerosis (Figure 3).

Treatment

There is no specific treatment for multiple sclerosis. Adrenocorticotropic hormone (ACTH) has been used for acute exacerbations of the disease, but controlled studies question the value of this form of treatment. Various drugs have been used for the treatment of muscle spasticity that often occurs. Intellectual loss, personality change, and mood disorders usually do not respond to psychopharmacologic agents. Emotional support in the form of supportive psychotherapy is indicated, especially during times of the inevitable exacerbation of the disease.

Prevention

Until more information is available concerning the etiology of multiple sclerosis, there are no preventive measures. There is no evidence of contagiousness of this disease.

☐ AMYOTROPHIC LATERAL SCLEROSIS

Amyotrophic lateral sclerosis (ALS), also called Lou Gehrig's disease, is a progressive motor neuron disease.

Clinical Features

ALS is a progressive disease of the spinal cord and brain characterized by degeneration of both the up-

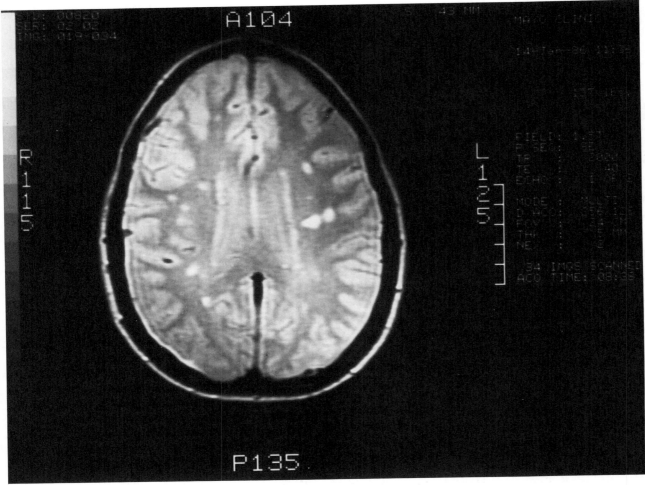

Figure 3.   Magnetic resonance image of a patient with multiple sclerosis. Note asymmetrically located plaques. (Courtesy of David B. Kispert, M.D.)

per and lower motor neurons. The symptoms include muscular abnormalities and hyperactivity of deep tendon reflexes with spasticity. There is retention of normal extraocular movement and maintenance of bladder and bowel continence. The sensory system and the autonomic nervous system are uninvolved.

Abnormalities of the muscular system include symptoms of fatigue, cramping, and fasciculations that are initially asymmetric. Often the patient does not present to the physician with these complaints until substantial weakness and atrophy involving muscles essential for day-to-day activity have occurred (Figure 4). The disease occasionally begins in the tongue, lips, or throat; weakness in the arms or legs develops later. In all cases, repeated ex-

aminations over time will show progressive weakness and atrophy.

The deep tendon reflexes are hyperactive, especially in atrophied limbs. Interestingly, despite the hyperactive reflexes, plantar reflexes are usually flexor. In patients with bulbar symptoms, a hyperactive jaw jerk with sucking reflex is common. As the disease advances, respiratory impairment occurs, ultimately leading to respiratory decompensation, rendering the patient dependent on a ventilator.

Several forms of ALS exist. The most commonly identified form is the sporadic form. Familial forms have been identified, as has a Guamanian form common to the Chamorros of Guam (Munsat 1984).

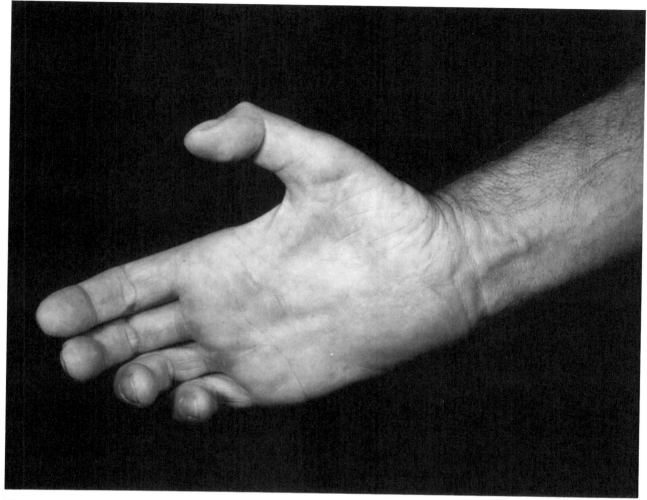

Figure 4. Muscle wasting of amyotropic lateral sclerosis. (Courtesy of Mehrsheed Sinaki, M.D.)

ALS is a chronically progressive neurologic condition that results in the death of the patient in 5 to 10 years; rarely it may extend as long as 30 or more years. According to Mulder (1982), 50 percent of patients die in 3 years, 20 percent live for 5 years, and 10 percent live for 10 years. Very few live for as long as 20 years after the onset of symptoms.

Psychiatric Manifestations

Intellectual impairment does not occur frequently in ALS. In fact, some diagnostic schemes would exclude patients with dementia from the diagnosis of ALS. Nonetheless, some cases of dementia have been described in sporadic ALS (Wikström et al. 1982) and familial ALS (Burnstein 1981). The Gua-

manian form of ALS is often associated with the Parkinson-dementia complex; hence, the finding of dementia is not uncommon in this form of the disorder.

Patients with bulbar symptoms often describe the inability to modulate their emotional responses of laughter and crying appropriately. This emotional incontinence is typical of patients with pseudobulbar palsy-type symptoms.

The presence of psychosis in patients with ALS has been described but is not a consistent feature of the disease (Burnstein 1981). In one study that cross-referenced with the Monroe County Psychiatric Register (Schiffer et al. 1984), patients with ALS had few psychiatric contacts when compared to patients with temporal lobe epilepsy and multiple sclerosis. Nonetheless, sporadic cases of psychosis occurring with ALS have been described since the late 1880s. These cases were primarily of a paranoid psychotic state resembling a schizophreniform disorder or schizophrenia. Burnstein (1981) detailed familial ALS, dementia, and psychosis, but it was impossible to tell whether these illnesses were interrelated or merely chance occurrences in a family.

As with any chronic neurologic condition, especially those where intellect and insight are retained, patients must adjust to a number of losses. Adjustment difficulties should be anticipated and treated accordingly (Rabin 1982).

Epidemiology and Etiology

Sporadic ALS has a mean age of onset of approximately 55 years. Occasionally, the disease develops in the third decade of life. Males are affected slightly more frequently than females, and there is no significant racial or ethnic pattern. The prevalence is 4 to 6 per 100,000, and the incidence is 0.8 to 1.2 per 100,000, with a death rate of about 50 per 100,000. The etiology of this illness remains unknown. The familial form of ALS occurs quite infrequently; inheritance is usually autosomal dominant. Guamanian ALS occurs among the Chamorros of Guam. This ethnic group has an incidence rate 50 to 100 times the incidence elsewhere in the world (Munsat 1984).

Pathology

Degeneration of motor neurons of the spinal cord, the brain-stem nuclei, and the cerebral cortex are responsible for the upper and lower motor neuron findings on clinical examination. Brain-stem nuclei that innervate ocular muscles are spared.

Diagnosis

The diagnosis of ALS can be made on the basis of clinical findings and some laboratory abnormalities. Occasionally patients will present early enough in their disease that it is impossible to make a diagnosis without repeated neurologic evaluations over time. Electromyogram (EMG) findings will vary with the stage of the disease and the degree of lower motor neuron damage. With increasing lower motor neuron damage, signs of denervation become prominent. Muscle biopsy also provides evidence of denervation. Other laboratory tests such as routine screening labs, the EEG, and the CSF examinations are usually within normal limits. However, in rapidly progressive forms of the disease, serum creatinine kinase and CSF cell and protein content may be slightly elevated (Mulder 1982; Munsat 1984).

Treatment

No treatment prevents the progression of this neurologic disorder. The spasticity may be controlled using baclofen or diazepam, but diazepam tends to cause sedation. Supportive measures such as braces, walkers, and wheelchairs will provide for continued mobility of the patient through part of the illness (Janiszewski et al. 1983). Ultimately, patients become bedridden and require mechanical ventilation if they are to survive. Whether to place a patient on mechanical ventilators poses a difficult ethical question. Sometimes patients can help make this decision, providing them with some control over their illness and ultimately the amount of suffering that they will sustain.

Psychiatric disturbances appear sporadically in this disorder and should be treated on a case-by-case basis. There is no contraindication to the use of tricyclic antidepressants in patients with major depressive disorders. In fact, sialorrhea is a common occurrence in this disorder and may be improved if an antidepressant with sufficient anticholinergic activity is selected. Patients with the Guamanian form of ALS with concomitant parkinsonism and dementia who require an antipsychotic should be treated as discussed in the section on Parkinson's disease.

Perhaps the psychiatrist can do the most good by helping patients deal with the chronicity and progression of their disease. Supportive or insight-oriented psychotherapy can help patients understand their reactions to their illness and help them place more realistic expectations on themselves. The patient's family may also benefit from supportive interventions because they suffer along with the patient throughout the decline. It is important that the patient be supported by visitations from not only family, friends, clergy, and co-workers but also from the psychiatrist and other physicians participating in the care of the patient. An understanding, supportive, and skilled physician can often significantly lessen the severity of suffering endured by the patient and the family.

☐ MYASTHENIA GRAVIS

Myasthenia gravis is a disease at the neuromuscular junction that is characterized by fluctuating muscle weakness.

Clinical Features

The fluctuating nature of myasthenic weakness is unique. It varies greatly from one time to another. There may be prolonged remissions. Patients do not complain of fatigue or rapid tiring, but specific muscle weakness that usually involves ocular muscles at some time during the disease. Diplopia and ptosis occur frequently. Dysarthria, dysphagia, and weakness of facial muscles occur commonly. Weakness of extremities or neck muscles is common, but almost always occurs in conjunction with cranial nerve weakness. The weakness of the involved muscles is restored with rest. A myasthenic "crisis" occurs with respiratory or oral pharyngeal muscle weakness. This is manifest by difficulty breathing with inadequate ventilation and a threat to life. Physical examination during an attack reveals weak muscles; if the face and eye muscles are involved, there is a characteristic expressionless face. Sensation and the reflexes are normal, even though muscle weakness may be extensive.

Psychiatric Manifestations

Emotional problems secondary to the presence of a chronic but not progressive illness are sometimes seen. Psychiatrists most often see patients with myasthenia gravis before the diagnosis is confirmed. It is important not to mistake the weakness of myasthenia gravis for a functional disorder. Occasionally, subjective weakness that may occur as a part of a somatoform disorder is misdiagnosed and treated as myasthenia gravis. A psychiatric study of 25 patients revealed that 7 described psychic stress at the time of onset of their disease (MacKenzie et al. 1969). Twelve patients demonstrated exacerbation of weakness following emotional upheaval. Anger was the most common precipitant. Such historical facts can be misleading to the diagnostician.

Epidemiology and Etiology

It has been established that myasthenia gravis is due to a defect of neuromuscular transmission due to antibodies to the acetylcholine receptor (Engel et al. 1977). The origin of these antibodies is unknown, but viral infection is suspected. The antibodies may be generated in the thymus gland. The disease occurs more commonly in young women, but there is no difference in the incidence between the sexes after age 40.

Pathology

Most adults who have myasthenia gravis have a hypertrophied thymus gland. Antibodies can be demonstrated on synaptic folds.

Diagnosis

Weakness and fatigue are frequent complaints of patients with depression and somatoform disorders. It is essential for the physician to distinguish between the two symptoms. The actual muscle weakness of myasthenia gravis has dramatic improvement following the injection of neostigmine (Prostigmin) or edrophonium (Tensilon). This maneuver is usually diagnostic.

Treatment

Anticholinesterase drug therapy is usually helpful. Thymectomy is considered good treatment for the patients with generalized myasthenia. Assisted ventilation may be imperative during a crisis.

☐ GUILLAIN-BARRÉ SYNDROME

The Guillain-Barré syndrome is the most frequently acquired demyelinative neuropathy.

Clinical Features

Guillain-Barré syndrome is an illness that begins a few days to 4 weeks after a viral upper respiratory infection, immunization, or surgery. It is characterized by cranial and peripheral nerve derangements. The initial symptoms are usually muscle weakness, paresthesias, or radicular pain (Beghi et al. 1985). The weakness is usually symmetrical and begins in the legs, with progression to other regions such as the trunk and arms. Weakness usually progresses from distal to proximal and progresses to flaccid paralysis. Facial weakness occurs in half of patients and is often bilateral but asymmetrical. Extraocular muscle palsies sometimes occur. Half of patients develop dysphagia and dysarthria. Involvement of the respiratory muscles causes some patients to require mechanical ventilation. Hyporeflexia or areflexia is present at some point during the illness. Sensory abnormalities include loss of joint position, vibratory sense, nociception, and thermoreception. The sensory impairment may occur in a stocking and glove distribution. Pain varies from a dull aching to burning sensations of the skin. Other, less common, symptoms include papilledema, sensory ataxia, transient extensor plantar responses, or autonomic dysfunction. Variants of this illness exist (Pleasure and Schotland 1984; Swash 1979).

The typical case of Guillain-Barré syndrome can be divided into three phases. The progressive phase is marked by progressive neurologic impairment and loss of function. This phase lasts up to 3 weeks. The plateau stage occurs next and is characterized by no further loss of function. Pain sometimes develops or worsens during this phase. This phase lasts a variable length of time. The recovery phase is completed in 85 percent of cases within 6 months and is characterized by recovery of function and normalization of sensation in most cases (Eisendrath et al. 1983; Swash 1979). However, about 35 percent of patients have permanent deficits (hyporeflexia, paresis of facial muscles, or weakness and atrophy of distal musculature); 3 to 10 percent relapse during the recovery phase, and about 2 to 3 percent have a recurrence of the illness after a full recovery (Pleasure and Schotland 1984; Swash 1979).

Death is unusual since the advent of mechanical ventilation. Presently, deaths are most frequently due to aspiration pneumonia, pulmonary embolism, infection, or autonomic dysfunction.

Psychiatric Manifestations

Patients suffering from Guillain-Barré syndrome frequently suffer anxiety, depression, hallucinations, and delirium.

During the progressive stage, patients suffer a marked sense of vulnerability because they are forced to go from independent functioning to dependence on strangers and often machines. The adjustment difficulties associated with these changes can cause anxiety, depression, irritability, or behavioral difficulties. During the plateau stage, depression may again continue. Patients may have feelings of de-

personalization and may experience a loss of ego boundaries. Visual hallucinations associated with disorientation are common, especially in ventilator-bound patients in the intensive care unit (ICU). Pain control may become a major issue for these patients, and drug-seeking behavior and interpersonal dependency may be pronounced. Depression is again a major issue during the recovery phase because the patient realizes that function returns slowly and there is considerable pain with rehabilitation. How the patient handles convalescence depends on the patient's personality, occupation, and expectations. For example, sedentary people not requiring much strength or physical stamina may tolerate this phase better than those who require manual dexterity, endurance, and activity. Anxiety will be prominent when a patient has been ventilator-dependent and the time comes to be weaned from the ventilator. In addition, as patients improve and are transferred from the ICU to other floors, they become anxious about being cared for by new staff and grieve the loss of previous care givers (Eisendrath et al. 1983).

Epidemiology and Etiology

The incidence of Guillain-Barré syndrome ranges from 0.8 to 3.2 cases per 100,000, depending on age. Incidence figures increase gradually with age. Males are stricken nearly twice as often as females (Beghi et al. 1985). Patients with Hodgkin's disease or other lymphomas are at higher risk.

The cause of Guillain-Barré syndrome is unknown but may be due to an autoimmune phenomenon whereby antibodies are formed against various antigens on the peripheral nerve. The frequent close temporal relationship to viral infections suggests viral invasion of the peripheral nerve, but no evidence of this has been found (Pleasure and Schotland 1984).

Pathology

In Guillain-Barré syndrome, the cranial nerves, peripheral nerves, and nerve roots exhibit widely scattered focal segmental demyelination. Diffuse endoneuronal infiltrates of mononuclear cells are present. Occasional axonal degeneration may also be present. On recovery, the peripheral nerve is remyelinated, but mononuclear infiltrates may remain for some time.

Diagnosis

Guillain-Barré syndrome is diagnosed by the history, the typical features of the disease, the EMG findings, and CSF studies. The EMG shows evidence of a segmental demyelinating process with reduced conduction velocity and prolonged sensory and motor latencies. The CSF examination classically shows elevated protein with a normal cell count.

Other causes of subacute polyneuropathy should be excluded, such as systemic lupus erythematosus, Refsum's disease, acute diphtheric neuropathy, poliomyelitis, porphyric neuropathy, toxic neuropathies, and tick paralysis (Pleasure and Schotland 1984).

Occasionally, patients with Guillain-Barré syndrome are misdiagnosed as having conversion disorder. This is more likely to occur in patients with a previous psychiatric history or a concurrent psychiatric condition. The early symptoms of weakness, clumsiness, or falling with associated subjective paresthesias can resemble a conversion disorder. The differential diagnosis can be made by repeated neurologic examinations to watch for progression of the disease. The Minnesota Multiphasic Personality Inventory (MMPI), although rarely diagnostic, may also help rule out conversion (Drake 1984; Edelsohn 1982).

Treatment

The treatment of the medical aspects of this illness is mainly supportive. Patients may require mechanical ventilation in cases involving the respiratory musculature. Patients are at risk for aspiration if the oropharyngeal muscles are affected. In cases where facial diplegia is present, measures must be taken to prevent exposure keratitis of the cornea. For pain, narcotics can be used in a regular dosing regimen to minimize discomfort and drug-seeking behavior. Patients may respond to hypnotherapy for pain control. The use of corticosteroid agents does not change prognosis or speed recovery. The role of plasmaphoresis is being investigated.

The psychiatrist can be helpful in the management of these patients. During the progressive phase, anxiety can be countered by educating the patient and family about the nature of the illness and by empathically listening to the patient if the patient can speak. For those who cannot speak, setting up a communication system and taking time

to use it will serve to reassure the patient (Henschel 1977). Patients will be less anxious if the same care givers are involved consistently and if family frequently visits and talks to the patient.

During the plateau phase, depression and anger can be managed by encouraging communication about feelings, concerns, and needs. When the patient stabilizes, family and friends may become less interested because "the crisis" seems to have passed. Family, friends, chaplains, and volunteers should be encouraged to visit and support the patient. The hallucinations that frequently occur during this phase are usually multifactorial and resemble "ICU psychosis." In such cases, the medical status of the patient should be evaluated for correctable precipitants. Normalization of sleep patterns, proper environmental stimuli, and orienting environmental cues (e.g., window, clock, calendar, television, radio, newspaper) should be provided. Small doses of an antipsychotic such as haloperidol 1 to 5 mg prn can be given, but the physician must be alert to the possibility of extrapyramidal side effects.

During the recovery phase, individuals who place a high premium on physical activity, endurance, or manual dexterity will need the most support. Often the psychiatrist can be a person with whom the patient can ventilate anger or sadness with regard to the recovery process. If a patient has been ventilator-dependent, weaning from the mechanical ventilator will occur during this phase. This will be an anxiety-provoking time for the patient because the patient may experience dyspnea and fear death. In addition, patients with severe illness who were in the ICU will be transferred to other floors for care during this phase as their condition improves. The patient will experience attendant feelings of anxiety and sadness about leaving the trusted care givers. The psychiatrist can serve not only as a common link between the ICU and the other floor, but can also help the patient grieve the loss of the other care givers (Eisendrath et al. 1983).

The use of antidepressants may be considered if a major depressive illness is identified. However, depressive symptoms are usually secondary to adjustment difficulties, and antidepressants may not be indicated. Support groups have been formed in some centers to help such patients cope (Streinberg 1984). Anxiolytics can be used to treat anxiety, particularly when it is caused by an upcoming procedure or worsening in condition. Anxiolytics use should be short term (under 10 days) and should not occur during weaning from the ventilator for fear of causing depression of respiratory drive.

□ NORMAL PRESSURE HYDROCEPHALUS

Normal pressure hydrocephalus was first described by Adams et al. (1965).

Clinical Features

Normal pressure hydrocephalus is a disease that gradually develops over weeks to months. The classic progressive triad of this disease is gait ataxia, urinary incontinence, and dementia. Headaches and symptoms of increased intracranial pressure such as papilledema are absent. The gait of these patients is described as being ataxic and wide based. Patients usually take short steps and require support when walking. The urinary difficulties patients complain of are urgency, enuresis, and incontinence (Prockop 1984).

Psychiatric Manifestations

The dementia of normal pressure hydrocephalus is characterized by poor memory with confabulation, inertia, and apathy, sometimes to the point of akinetic mutism. Constructional apraxia and visual-spatial impairments occur. These abnormalities are said to be secondary to frontal lobe impairments. The frontal lobe impairment is believed to be due to diminished cerebral blood flow to this area, which gives rise to relative ischemia, or to edema of the periventricular tissue secondary to the hydrocephalus (Berglund et al. 1979; Caltagirone et al. 1982).

Other psychiatric conditions that have been described in normal pressure hydrocephalus include psychosis and depressive disorders (Lying-Tunell 1979; Tsuang et al. 1979). From the descriptions provided in the literature, it is difficult to know if the psychosis, which was usually paranoid in nature, was secondary to the ongoing dementia or functional in nature. In addition, the accurate diagnosis of depression in a patient exhibiting the apathy frequently associated with dementia can be difficult.

Epidemiology and Etiology

Peak incidence of this disorder is in the fifth decade of life. Most cases of normal pressure hydrocephalus are idiopathic, but some cases occur after head injury, meningitis, or subarachnoid hemorrhage. The pathogenic mechanism appears to be decreased absorption of the CSF by the arachnoid villi due to either diminished CSF circulation in the subarachnoid space or decreased absorption of subarachnoid fluid into the venous sinuses. It has been hypothesized that there is a transient elevation in CSF pressure early in normal pressure hydrocephalus. This causes the ventricles to dilate. Once the ventricles are dilated, it takes less pressure to maintain them in a dilated condition, so that when the CSF pressure decreases, the ventricles remain dilated. There is no evidence of a genetic predisposition to normal pressure hydrocephalus (Briggs et al. 1981; Prockop 1984).

Pathology

Brains of patients with normal pressure hydrocephalus show enlargement of the ventricles without cortical atrophy. The exit foramina remain patent, and the gray matter is preserved at the expense of the white matter.

Diagnosis

The diagnosis of normal pressure hydrocephalus is based on the finding of the classic triad of gait ataxia, urinary incontinence, and dementia. CT scans of patients with normal pressure hydrocephalus show enlargement of the ventricles without cortical atrophy (Figure 5). A lumbar puncture reveals CSF pressures of less than 200 mm of mercury. Patients have diminished cerebral blood flow to the frontal lobes.

The main differential diagnosis to normal pressure hydrocephalus is Alzheimer's disease. In patients with Alzheimer's disease, the CT scan may show enlargement of the ventricles with cortical atrophy. In Alzheimer's disease, CSF circulation is normal, whereas it is decreased in normal pressure hydrocephalus. CSF circulation can be measured using lumbar isotope cisternography or quantitative isotope ventriculography, thus helping differentiate between these two disorders. It has been suggested that one can confirm the diagnosis of normal pressure hydrocephalus by performing a lumbar puncture and withdrawing 30 cc of spinal fluid. Patients with normal pressure hydrocephalus will show a transient improvement in their clinical status after this test (Briggs et al. 1981; Prockop 1984). Before a shunt is placed, it is proper to get

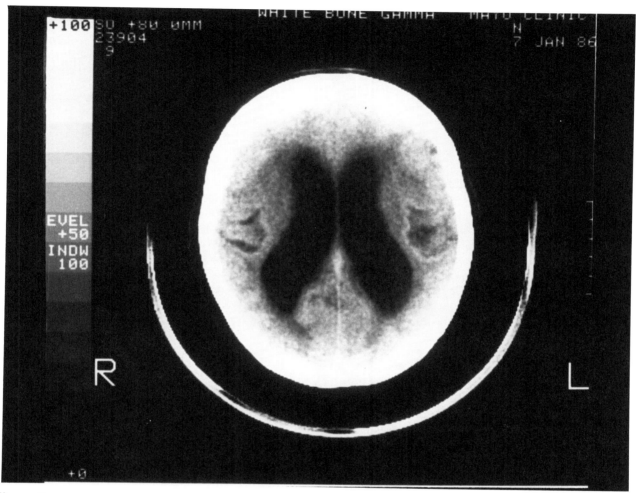

Figure 5. Computed tomographic scan of the brain of a patient with normal pressure hydrocephalus. (Courtesy of David B. Kispert, M.D.)

baseline psychometrics so that one can measure improvement or deterioration after the procedure is performed.

Treatment

It is important to consider the diagnosis of normal pressure hydrocephalus in demented patients because this condition represents a potentially correctable cause of dementia. Of all newly diagnosed dementia patients, 7 percent will ultimately prove to have normal pressure hydrocephalus. One-fourth of all treatable dementias are due to normal pressure hydrocephalus (Briggs et al. 1981). The treatment of choice for normal pressure hydrocephalus is a ventricular shunt. Patients with recent onset of the classic triad of symptoms do best. Although

60 percent of these patients improve, complications such as infection, hemorrhage, and shunt blockage are common (Prockop 1984). It has been shown that urinary incontinence and the gait disturbance improve first and the dementia last (Meyer et al. 1985). The psychiatric conditions of paranoia and depression may respond to shunting in some cases. In other cases, the use of neuroleptics, antidepressant drugs, or electroconvulsive therapy (ECT) can be considered (Lying-Tunell 1979; Tsuang et al. 1979).

☐ SYRINGOMYELIA

Clinical Features

Syringomyelia is a chronic, progressive disorder affecting the spinal cord. The disorder causes sensory loss, muscle weakness and amyotrophy, and skeletal abnormalities. The clinical presentation of a patient with syringomyelia depends on the location of the syringomyelic cavity (syrinx), which is most commonly encountered in the lower cervical region and at the base of the posterior horn. The lesion tends to interrupt spinothalamic fibers as they decussate, causing impairment of pain and temperature sensation with preservation of other sensations early in the disease. If the syrinx is located in the cervical cord, impairment of sensation usually occurs in the arm ipsilateral to the lesion. Pain frequently occurs and is described as aching in quality. It usually involves the neck and shoulders but may be found in a radicular pattern as well.

The syrinx extends with time. Eventually the posterior columns can be affected, with associated loss of proprioception and vibratory sense in the feet. Extension into the anterior horn region of the cord causes motor neuron loss, resulting in atrophy of the small muscles of the hand and, in a progressive fashion, the forearms and then the shoulder girdle muscles. The amyotrophy is asymmetric in distribution and is associated with weakness and fasciculations of the affected muscles. Stretch reflexes of the arms are lost. With extension of the syrinx into the lateral columns of the cord, spasticity of the legs occurs; ultimately, paraparesis results. Hyperreflexia and extensor plantar reflexes can be expected in the lower extremities. Respiratory impairment can occur. Impairment of bowel and bladder function occurs late. Scoliosis is frequently seen, as are neurogenic arthropathies.

Although the syrinx is most commonly located in the lower cervical cord, it may be located at any level of the spinal cord. Extension of the syrinx into the medulla or higher has been recorded (Mancall 1984).

Psychiatric Manifestations

Syringomyelia does not predispose patients to psychiatric disturbances other than adjustment disorders or depression. Sporadic cases of other psychiatric disturbances have been recorded in the medical literature, but these are probably incidental and not causally related (Jefferson and Cohen 1982). The disease is progressive, and the patient sustains loss as progression occurs. Depression can occur as can a sense of urgency to live one's life before time runs out (Anderson 1984). Patients may feel

lonely, vulnerable, fearful, and panicky as they notice their disease progress and their capacity to function diminish. The disease does not cause dementia so there is no doubt that respirator-bound patients suffer in their isolation. Some patients may opt to commit suicide when they reach the point in their incapacity where they feel they will lose charge of their lives.

Epidemiology and Etiology

Syringomyelia is a disease that usually begins in the third or fourth decade of life. This disease is slowly progressive; the course of the disease may span many years. The incidence rate of this disorder is estimated to be about 3 per 1,000,000, and the prevalence rate is 3 to 9 per 100,000 (Kurland et al. 1973). Men are affected more frequently than women. Some cases appear to be familial in nature. Syringomyelia may develop after spinal cord trauma, meningitis, subarachnoid hemorrhage, or birth trauma, but the etiology of most cases of syringomyelia is unknown (Mancall 1984).

Pathology

Syringomyelia is caused by the development of a cavity usually beginning within the cervical cord region and extending over many segments. The syrinx is usually found at the base of the posterior horn, may communicate with the central canal, and contains fluid similar to CSF. The lesion enlarges with time to involve so much of the cord that, in advanced cases, very little cord parenchyma can be identified histologically. The syrinx may be lined by ependymal cells. In a small number of cases, an ependymoma or astrocytoma may be encountered. Surrounding the syrinx is dense gliosis (Mancall 1984).

Diagnosis

The diagnosis of syringomyelia is usually made on the basis of the neurologic findings, metrizamide-CT myelography, or magnetic resonance imaging (Figure 6). Metrizamide-CT myelography frequently shows an expanded or collapsed cord. Frequently, metrizamide enters the syrinx from the subarachnoid space, causing enhancement of the lesion.

Examination of the CSF does not reveal specific information in the diagnosis of syringomyelia, al-

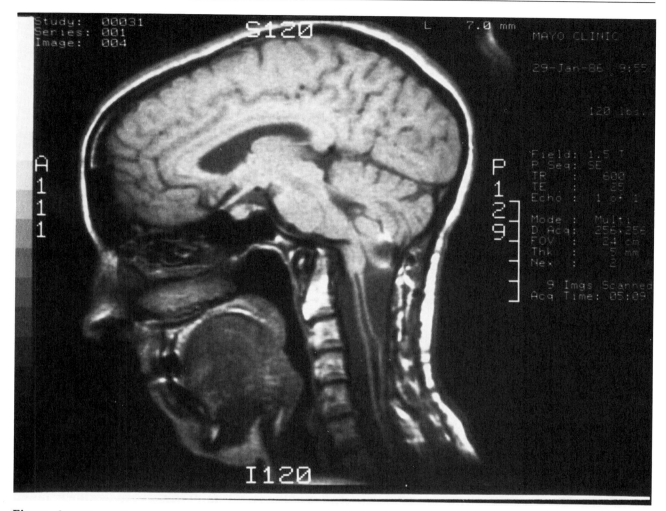

Figure 6. Magnetic resonance imaging of a patient with syrinx involving the cervical cord. Patient also has Arnold-Chiari malformation. (Courtesy of David B. Kispert, M.D.)

though the pressure is sometimes elevated, and the cell count may be slightly elevated. The CSF protein is normal unless there is a subarachnoid block, in which case it becomes quite elevated. Cervical spine films may show widening of the cervical spinal canal with erosion of the pedicles. Myelography usually demonstrates a wide cord in the cervical region and, sometimes a subarachnoid block (Mancall 1984).

Treatment

As with many progressive neurologic conditions, there exists no specific therapy for syringomyelia. Radiation therapy may be helpful in the case of a spinal cord tumor or in an effort to relieve pain. Various surgical interventions have been proposed but their effectiveness remains in question. In cases with co-existent hydrocephalus, a ventricular shunting procedure should be done (Mancall 1984).

From a psychiatric point of view, much can be done to aid patients suffering from this disease. Supportive or insight-oriented psychotherapy can help patients cope with and understand their reactions to this progressive illness and the losses that it incurs. Patients can be helped to place more realistic expectations on themselves in view of their illness. The psychiatrist can be an important advocate for patients whose illness prevents effective communication. For example, the psychiatrist can remind staff and family to spend time with and to talk to the patient. An effective means of nonverbal communication can be established before verbal communication is lost so that the patient will not feel cut off from the rest of the world by the illness. Psychotropic medications can be used should a clear indication arise.

☐ HUNTINGTON'S DISEASE

Huntington's disease is an autosomal dominant hereditary disorder that is characterized by dementia and choreiform movements. The condition was described in 1872 by Huntington, and is sometimes called Huntington's chorea or chronic progressive chorea.

Clinical Features

The onset of the disease is insidious, but the clinical course is gradually progressive, with increased choreiform movements and dementia. Huntington's disease may begin at any age, but most often becomes clinically evident during late middle life. Death may occur 10 to 20 years after the onset. Depression and suicide sometimes occur, but the disease most often has a steady progression, with dementia and the eventual need for custodial care. Seizures may be part of the clinical picture when the onset occurs in childhood. Early in the course of the disease, patients are usually aware of their cognitive difficulties. Many note a change in temperament and are often withdrawn. They may have difficulty planning and organizing, with diminished detailed memory that may be noted when attempting to give the history of the disease. Furthermore, many patients lack spontaneity, a problem that worsens as the dementing process continues. Caine et al. (1978) suggested that patients with Huntington's disease demonstrate a loss of cortical "executive" functions similar to those found in classic frontal lobe patients.

Psychiatric Manifestations

Although a rare disease, Huntington's disease is of importance to psychiatrists because when the quick, purposeless movements are first noted, they are often misinterpreted as habit spasms or tics.

Most patients will disguise the chorea by associated voluntary movements. Because of this and the frequent antecedent psychiatric problems, diagnosis may be difficult. In a study of 102 patients, Dewhurst et al. (1970) noted that only 38 had been correctly diagnosed initially; 46 had a psychiatric diagnosis, and only 10 did not have some associated psychiatric symptoms prior to the onset of Huntington's disease. Most patients were diagnosed as having an anxiety state. Dewhurst et al. also found that the earliest presenting symptom of the disease was a psychiatric symptom in 57 cases, a neurologic symptom in 16 cases, and mixed psychiatric and neurologic symptoms in the remaining 29 cases. Psychiatrists may also be involved in the management of the associated dementia that inevitably develops as the disease progresses (Wells and Duncan 1980). Psychiatric help is often sought to deal with the issues of genetic counseling, and at-risk relatives sometimes seek psychotherapy to help them deal with anxiety that may be present in those who anticipate the 50:50 odds of eventually acquiring the disease. Psychiatrists may also be involved in family counseling or dealing with the effects of separation. Dewhurst et al. noted that 38 percent of 82 patients were either divorced or separated, mostly due to the social and intellectual deterioration caused by the disease. Dewhurst et al. (1970) also noted a high incidence of abnormal sexual behavior of various types. Of the 102 patients, 19 (12 males) manifested hypersexual behavior at some point in their illness.

Epidemiology and Etiology

Recent work in gene structure indicates the possibility of a clinical test to ascertain the development of Huntington's disease in a genetically at-risk individual. Such a development would pose a dilemma for the children of a person with Huntington's disease. Knowledge that the possibility of developing the condition was remote would allay much anticipatory anxiety; however, learning that one is almost certain to develop the disease given a normal life span would strain the coping abilities of most people. Consequent anxiety and depression could be formidable, especially if the potential victim had seen a parent or other close relative suffer with the disease. Ethical concerns regarding presymptomatic testing for Huntington's disease have been of recent interest (Bird 1985).

Pathology

The brain, especially the frontal lobes, becomes atrophied; this accounts for the dementia. There is atrophy with a loss of small cells in the caudate and putamen nuclei (Figure 7). Klawans (1970) suggested that affected cells in these nuclei are abnormally sensitive to normal amounts of dopamine.

Diagnosis

The triad of choreiform movements, dementia, and a family history of the disease will confirm the di-

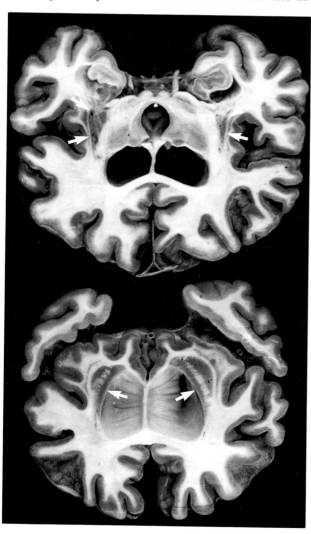

Figure 7. Gross specimen of patient with Huntington's disease showing degenerative changes of the caudate (top photo) and putamen (bottom photo). From Okazaki (1983); reprinted with permission.

agnosis. Usually, the diagnosis is uncertain early in the course of the disease when the movement disorder is poorly defined or when the first symptoms resemble those of a psychiatric disorder. Dementia often appears later. Furthermore, the presence of chorea in the patient or a family history of mental illness may be vague or denied. A careful genetics history is indicated when Huntington's disease is considered. Only time and the development of a progression of choreiform or dementia-like symptoms will allow for a definitive diagnosis of the disease.

Huntington's disease must be differentiated from Sydenham's chorea, but this problem usually has an onset at an earlier age and is self-limited without associated psychiatric disorders. Tardive dyskinesia may be confused with Huntington's disease, but patients with tardive dyskinesia have usually been on long-term therapy with neuroleptics and commonly have oral-buccal-lingual movements and a normal gait. Most patients with Huntington's disease eventually develop an abnormal gait. Dementia from other causes, such as the dementia of the Alzheimer type, must be considered in the differential diagnosis, but the dementia associated with Huntington's disease usually does not produce language difficulties until later in the course of the disease. Choreiform movements are unusual in other forms of dementia. The tics associated with Gilles de la Tourette syndrome are stereotyped and accompanied by verbal outbursts. Huntington's disease must be differentiated from senile chorea, which presents later in life and is not associated with a positive family history.

Treatment

There is no satisfactory treatment for the disease. The course is progressive and no drugs have been found that will significantly alter the course. Theoretically, phenothiazines and other drugs that block dopamine should be effective in controlling the choreiform movements. While drugs in these categories will often produce symptomatic improvement, there is usually little change in the course of the disease.

Prevention of the transmission of the responsible gene is the only effective way of curtailing the disease. Genetic counseling should be obtained for the offspring of all patients with this preventable disease.

☐ WILSON'S DISEASE

Wilson's disease, also referred to as hepatolenticular degeneration, is an inborn error of copper metabolism that is associated with cirrhosis of the liver and degenerative changes in the basal ganglia. If untreated, it leads to progressive deterioration and death.

Clinical Features

Although there are no classic features of this disease, most patients develop tremors and rigidity. The onset usually occurs in adolescence or early adulthood. The tremor is commonly bizarre and may be localized to the arms, producing a "wing-beating" effect. This tremor develops when the arms are extended; the movements are often of a flailing or violent nature. Rigidity similar to that of parkinsonism is frequently present, and the facies appear flat with a fixed open-mouth smile. Hepatic symptoms include jaundice and ascites and may occur at any stage of the disease. Characteristic intracorneal pigmentation around the periphery of the cornea called Kayser-Fleischer rings occurs in most patients with Wilson's disease. These rings may be seen on careful physical examination of the eyes or may be seen only with slit-lamp examination. For further details of the clinical features, the reader is referred elsewhere (Dobyns et al. 1979).

Psychiatric Manifestations

Many cases of Wilson's disease simulate a functional psychosis. The early onset, bizarre behavior, and flattened affect may lead to a presumptive diagnosis of a schizophrenic disorder. Occasionally, behavioral problems, including acting out, will cause parents and an unwary physician to suspect adolescent turmoil. Neurologic signs usually occur prior to the onset of psychiatric problems. Dobyns et al. (1979) found psychiatric difficulties in 19 of their series of 53 cases.

Epidemiology and Etiology

Wilson's disease is a hereditary disease transmitted as an autosomal recessive with a high rate of consanguinity in parents of the affected patient. It occurs in all races but has a higher incidence in areas where there is a high rate of inbreeding.

Pathology

The disordered copper metabolism results in markedly low serum ceruloplasmin concentrations. Radioactive copper studies have shown abnormal copper transfer from the serum to protein fractions. As a result, serum copper levels are increased, and copper excretion through the liver is decreased. Copper is deposited in the liver, kidney, cornea, and basal ganglia of the brain. Reddish pigmentation is noted on gross examination, with degeneration especially in the putamen with a loss of neurons. Copper deposits are also seen in the pericapillary areas in the cerebral cortex.

Diagnosis

The presence of progressive extrapyramidal symptoms in adolescence or early adulthood, especially when associated with hepatic disease and the characteristic Kayser-Fleischer ring, leads to a diagnosis (Figure 8). Almost all cases have abnormally low serum ceruloplasmin levels. A family history of hepatic or neurologic disease is helpful. The psychiatrist must be aware of the possibility of Wilson's disease when evaluating young people with tremor, rigidity, or other extrapyramidal signs.

Treatment

The goal of treatment is to prevent tissue accumulation of copper. A low copper diet and the use of a chelating agent, penicillamine, to promote urinary excretion of copper has been shown to be

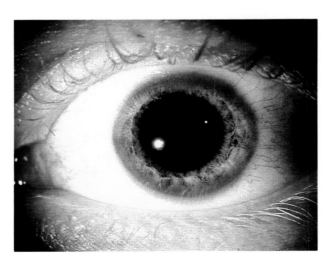

Figure 8. Kayser-Fleischer ring of Wilson's disease.

quite effective. With adequate treatment, the neurologic, hepatic, and psychiatric signs and symptoms may improve.

Prevention

Genetic counseling of affected individuals and avoidance of consanguineous marriages are the only preventive measures.

☐ DYSTONIA

Dystonic movement disorders include a group of conditions of various causes that usually appear on action. Because of similarities, they will be discussed together. A form of dystonia that begins in childhood and seems to be inherited is called dystonia musculorum deformans. Adult onset dystonia affects various muscle groups and may be referred to as spasmodic torticollis when neck muscles are involved; writer's cramp, which involves the arms; Meige syndrome of blepharospasm and oromandibular dystonia; and spastic dysphonia, when muscles that control the vocal cords are affected.

Clinical Features

Dystonia musculorum deformans presents with a wide variety of twisting, writhing, and spastic movements that may involve all muscle groups, but usually begins in the legs and prevents normal walking. When the disease progresses, the movements involve the trunk, neck, and arms and may occur at rest. Torticollis usually becomes a prominent feature of the disease, along with facial grimacing and speech difficulties. The body is contorted to extreme degrees.

Adult onset dystonia usually remains limited to the affected areas. Spasmodic torticollis, the most common, is manifest by involuntary contraction of the sternocleidomastoid and adjacent muscles on one side of the neck so that the head twists and turns to the opposite side of the contracted muscles. The neck muscles are tense; there is usually associated facial distortion. Many patients develop dystonic movements in other parts of the body. Spastic dysphonia may have a sudden onset and results in a strained speech that produces fatigue and frustration in the patient.

Psychiatric Manifestations

Mental functions usually remain normal in most patients with dystonia. Dystonia musculorum deformans has a devastating influence on the life of the patient, rendering normal activities impossible. Rarely, the bizarre movements will be confused with hysteria, especially in early stages.

Adult onset dystonias may have a lesser effect on the individual's ability to function, but may destroy careers. Writer's cramp, blepharospasm, and spastic dysphonia have been considered emotionally induced because the onset may occur at the time of stress. For example, one of the authors saw a man who developed spastic dysphonia when shouting for help during a fire. However, dysphonia secondary to spastic muscles is quite different from the voiceless aphonia of hysteria. Occasionally, patients afflicted with dystonia will become depressed; some have committed suicide (including the patient noted above).

Epidemiology and Etiology

Dystonia musculorum deformans is a hereditary disease that seems to be autosomal recessive. It is common among Ashkenazi Jews. The etiology of the adult onset dystonias is unknown, and there is little current evidence that psychosocial factors are contributory. There are no prevalence studies of these disorders.

Pathology

Dystonic symptoms arise from a dysfunction in the basal ganglia and may involve biochemical changes No gross or microscopic changes have been found.

Diagnosis

Dystonic movements in childhood, with bizarre gait and varied spasms and grimacing, especially in an Ashkenazi Jew, lead to the diagnosis of dystonia musculorum deformans. Wilson's disease and the extrapyramidal side effects of pharmacologic agents should be excluded. Hysteria is usually ruled out by the development of additional neurologic defects.

Adult dystonia is more easily confused with hysteria. The associated muscle spasm usually helps differentiate dystonic disorders from hysteria. The spasms associated with these disorders are not inhibited voluntarily, as are habit spasms or tics.

Treatment

The use of muscle-relaxing drugs may be helpful, but lasting effects are limited. Sensory biofeedback, nerve stimulation, and surgical procedures have had mixed results. Adult dystonias of all types have been treated with psychotherapy and hypnosis with limited benefit.

☐ FRIEDREICH'S ATAXIA

Friedreich's ataxia is the most common hereditary ataxia.

Clinical Features

The typical presentation of Friedreich's ataxia is that of a child or adolescent with ataxia, sensory loss, altered reflexes, clubfoot deformity, and kyphoscoliosis. Ataxia of gait is usually the first symptom to appear. With time, the ataxia progresses to include the arms and later the trunk. The ataxia results from a loss of proprioceptive sense and from cerebellar asynergia. Speech is affected, becoming slurred and ultimately unintelligible. Intention tremor may be present. Muscle weakness is commonly seen, with distal muscle atrophy being apparent in some cases.

Sensory changes are primarily due to involvement of the posterior funiculi of the spinal cord, causing poor proprioception and loss of vibratory sense. Loss of pain and temperature and tactile sensations may be noted, usually only in advanced cases. In most cases, reflex changes include loss of tendon reflexes and extensor plantar response.

The skeletal abnormalities are clubfoot deformity and kyphoscoliosis, present in 75 and 80 percent of cases, respectively. Foot abnormalities may be present from infancy or may not develop until late in the disease. The spinal abnormalities usually develop quite late in the disease and progress slowly. Cardiomyopathy and diabetes mellitus occur in some patients.

Abortive forms of this disease are fairly common and may be associated with a nearly normal life span. In such cases, only a couple of the typical characteristics of the disease are present. Rarely, spontaneous remissions of otherwise typical cases of Friedreich's ataxia occur. For most patients, the disease is progressive and leads to death or inca-

pacity by age 20. Patients usually die from infections (Rosenberg 1984).

Psychiatric Manifestations

There is controversy regarding the effects of Friedreich's ataxia on the psyche and intellectual capacity of individuals suffering from it. Sporadic cases of schizophreniform psychosis (formerly called Friedreich's psychosis), major depressive episodes, and personality disorders have been reported, but probably are not overrepresented in this patient population. Some reported cases may have actually been organic mental disorders (Davies 1949b). Adjustment disorders are possible, especially when disease progression leads to impairment.

Although this has been a controversial subject, there is little evidence that Friedreich's ataxia causes mental retardation or results in dementia (Davies 1949a; Fehrenbach et al. 1984). Patients with this disease tend to exhibit deficiencies in tasks of spatial reconstruction, however. This abnormality can be explained by "lack of training" caused by a lengthy illness characterized by severe motor and somatosensory handicaps. It has been hypothesized that the cerebellum participates in cognitive functions that analyze spatial relationships and that the pathologic changes of this disorder interfere with this process (Fehrenbach et al. 1984).

Epidemiology and Etiology

Friedreich's ataxia is a disease with onset in the first or second decade of life. Some cases are not recognized until the third decade. It is an autosomal recessive disease that is found in all races and tends to affect males slightly more than females. The prevalence rate is estimated to be 1 per 100,000 (Kurland et al. 1973); incidence data are not available. The biochemical abnormality is under investigation, and several hypotheses exist (Barbeau 1982).

Pathology

Degenerative changes are found in the posterior funiculi, lateral corticospinal tracts, and the dorsal and ventral spinocerebellar tracts of the spinal column. These changes rarely extend above the medulla. The cerebellum may exhibit loss of Purkinje cells and atrophy of the dentate nuclei (Rosenberg 1984). The cerebral cortex has been said to be atrophied in up to 17 percent of these patients, but this finding is controversial (Claus and Aschoff 1980).

Diagnosis

Laboratory studies are usually unremarkable and not diagnostic. An electrocardiogram (EKG) may show abnormalities where cardiomegaly is present. An elevated serum glucose is found in patients with diabetes mellitus. Diagnosis is usually made on the basis of the clinical findings. There is usually a positive family history.

Treatment

Unfortunately, no specific treatment exists for this disease. Orthopedic procedures may relieve spinal and foot deformities, and physical therapy helps to maintain function.

Psychiatric disturbances in this disease should be treated as they would in otherwise normal patients. Organic etiologies should be sought and corrected if possible. Appropriate psychotropic agents or psychotherapy should be administered. Patients with this disorder have sometimes been described as psychosocially and psychosexually immature. This is probably because physical deformities and disability have prevented normal interaction with peers and significant others.

☐ PROGRESSIVE SUPRANUCLEAR PALSY

This disorder was first described by Steele et al. (1964).

Clinical Features

The hallmarks of this disorder are paralysis of vertical gaze (especially downward gaze), gait abnormality, and mental disturbance. Other, less frequent, ophthalmologic findings include decreased blinking, photophobia, lateral gaze palsy, internuclear ophthalmoplegia, diplopia, and decreased corneal reflexes. Pseudobulbar symptoms occur with associated dysarthria, dysphagia, hyperactive gag reflex, speech abnormalities, and gait disturbances due to dysequilibrium. Patients may develop symptoms resembling Parkinson's disease. For this reason, Parkinson's disease is frequently misdiagnosed. Dystonic rigidity and hyperextension of the neck and upper trunk are common. The findings of a mental disturbance, paralysis of vertical gaze, and gait abnormalities in a patient previously diagnosed as having Parkinson's disease are highly suspicious for progressive supranuclear palsy if there is preservation of ocular movement on oculocephalic maneuvers.

Sleep disorders, particularly sleep apnea, occur as the disease advances. Death usually occurs in 2 to 12 years as a result of intercurrent infection, not infrequently secondary to aspiration or complications of sleep apnea (Duvoisin 1984; Steele et al. 1964).

Psychiatric Manifestations

Patients with progressive supranuclear palsy may exhibit depression, pseudobulbar affective changes, and subcortical dementia (Duvoisin 1984; Steele 1964).

The depression resembles that seen in Parkinson's disease and may be related to adjustment difficulties relative to the onset of early physical symptoms or memory impairment. Depression may also result from neuronal loss or changes in absolute numbers and balance of neuroreceptor types, although this is by no means understood. Patients suffering from prominent pseudobulbar symptoms often exhibit "emotional incontinence" such as exaggerated emotional responses or involuntary laughing and crying that is associated with emotions incongruous with the affect being displayed. The subcortical dementia ranges from mild to severe and is progressive. The symptoms are memory loss, with preservation of higher-order associative functions. Aphasia, agnosia, and apraxia do not occur or do so only in very advanced dementia (Huber and Paulson 1985). These patients frequently exhibit flat affect, apathy, mask-like facies, infrequent blinking, poverty of speech, and slowness of thinking resembling a major depressive episode. In fact, depression may occur in addition to the dementia because patients retain the insight to recognize that their memory is deteriorating. As the dementia progresses, behavioral disorganization in the form of irritability, combativeness, deterioration of personal appearance, impulsivity, and episodes of superimposed delirium become more likely. However, irritability and poor general functioning have been noted in individuals with progressive supranuclear palsy who are not demented (Janati and Appel 1984).

Epidemiology and Etiology

Progressive supranuclear palsy usually begins in the sixth or seventh decade of life. The etiology and incidence are unknown. There is no evidence of genetic transmission; the search for an infectious agent has been unsuccessful to date.

Pathology

Neurofibrillary tangles and neuronal loss occur in the substantia nigra, pontine tegmentum, periaqueductal gray matter, and pallidum as well as other areas, depending on the progression of the disease at death. Even the anterior horn cells of the spinal cord have been affected in some cases.

Diagnosis

Routine laboratory investigations will be normal unless there is some other coexisting disorder. EEGs often show slowing without localizing features. CSF exams are unremarkable. The CT scan may show atrophy of the brain stem, especially of the pons and midbrain.

Because laboratory findings are nonspecific, this diagnosis is made mainly on the grounds of the history and physical examination (Duvoisin 1984; Steele et al. 1964).

Treatment

No specific treatment is available. The response to antiparkinsonian drugs has been inconsistent and unreliable. Anticholinergic antiparkinsonian drugs, bromocriptine, levodopa/carbidopa, amantadine, and methysurgide may reduce the parkinsonism and pseudobulbar signs, but abnormalities of extraocular movements improve infrequently. The use of bromocriptine and levodopa/carbidopa may be limited by the psychotogenic effects of these drugs, especially in those who are demented. None of these drugs halts the progression of the disease.

The treatment of depression may include a combination of an antidepressant and psychotherapy (Janati and Appel 1984). Highly anticholinergic tricyclic antidepressants such as amitriptyline, doxepine, protriptyline, and trimipramine may be used. The dosage utilized should be based on what the patient can tolerate, but certainly not in excess of manufacturer's recommendations. The anticholi-

nergic properties of these tricyclics may improve rigidity, tremor, and bradykinesia, but there is a risk that these agents may cause memory impairment and delirium, particularly in the demented. ECT has been used in the treatment of depression with progressive supranuclear palsy, with evidence of at least partial effectiveness (Steele et al. 1964).

For the behavioral disorganization associated with advanced dementia, the use of an antipsychotic agent is possible but runs the risk of superimposing drug-induced parkinsonism.

If an antipsychotic is used, the lowest effective doses of a highly anticholinergic agent such as chlorpromazine, mesoridazine, or thioridazine should be employed. The use of other sedating agents such as various benzodiazepines may also be helpful in the lowest effective dose, but these drugs run the risk of causing paradoxical excitement, confusion, or somnolence in the demented. In addition, tolerance to these agents and the need for higher dosages will occur unless the drug is tapered and stopped periodically.

☐ SHY-DRAGER SYNDROME

Shy and Drager (1960) described this degenerative disorder of the CNS.

Clinical Features

Shy-Drager syndrome is a disease of middle-aged patients characterized by the insidious onset of autonomic dysfunction and the degeneration of the cerebellum, basal ganglia, and spinal motor neurons.

Autonomic manifestations of Shy-Drager syndrome include dizziness and syncope secondary to orthostatic hypotension in 95 percent, impaired sweating in 11 percent, urinary dysfunction in 65 percent, bowel dysfunction in 51 percent, and impotence and impaired libido in 30 percent of patients suffering from the disease according to Thomas (1970).

Degeneration of other systems include the corticobular and corticospinal tracts with attendant hyperreflexia, extensor toe signs, dysarthria, and sucking reflex; the basal ganglion with symptoms not unlike parkinsonism such as masked facies, rigidity, cogwheeling, and resting tremor; and the cerebellum with symptoms including intention tremor, ataxia of gait, and ataxic or dysarthric speech. Atrophy of the iris and impaired eye movements also occur (Barr 1979; Cote 1984).

Psychiatric Manifestations

If a patient with Shy-Drager syndrome manifests any psychiatric disturbance, it is usually depression or dementia. The frequency of these sequelae is unknown, however.

Depression can be due to adjustment difficulties or a major depressive disorder. Shy-Drager syndrome imposes many losses on those suffering from it. For example, the orthostatic hypotension can prevent patients from being able to carry out normal social and occupational obligations. Thus rewards and benefits derived from such activities are lost. In addition, loss of control over one's body as manifest by impaired libido with erectile dysfunction or impaired sphincter control, for example, can make it difficult for these patients to tolerate their illness. Exactly where an adjustment disorder leaves off and major depressive disorder begins is not always clear in clinical practice; frequently the patients receive antidepressant medications (Kwentus et al. 1984).

The dementia of Shy-Drager syndrome is not a consistent finding, and it is usually mild and slowly progressive. If it does develop, it is a dementia of the subcortical variety where there may be mild memory impairment, but higher level associative functioning remains intact. Patients with subcortical dementia frequently exhibit apathy, mask-like facies, decreased blinking, and flatness of affect, which resemble major depressive disorder. Emotional lability is common late in the disease (Cote 1984; Kwentus et al. 1984).

Epidemiology and Etiology

Shy-Drager syndrome is a rare illness of unknown incidence. The prevalence and the etiology are unknown. There is no evidence of a genetic predisposition. It is a disease of middle age, with age of onset averaging 55 years. The male to female ratio is 3:1. Death occurs on the average 7 to 8 years after symptoms begin, but ranges from 3 to 33 years. Death is usually secondary to bronchopneumonia, aspiration pneumonia, pulmonary embolism, or cardiac arrhythmias (Barr 1979; Thomas 1970).

Pathology

At autopsy of Shy-Drager, patients show diffuse degenerative changes in the Purkinje layer of the cerebellum, substantia nigra, striatum, dorsal motor nucleus of the vagus, and locus ceruleus. Degeneration also occurs in the intermediolateral column and anterior horn cells of the spinal cord, the pontine nuclei, and the olivopontocerebellar tracts (Barr 1979).

Diagnosis

The diagnosis of Shy-Drager syndrome is based on the history, clinical findings of severe orthostatic hypotension with syncopal episodes, and other signs of autonomic instability. Other findings may include hyperreflexia, extensor toe signs, parkinsonian symptoms, gait ataxia, and speech abnormalities.

Routine laboratory studies are within normal limits. EEG studies, lumbar punctures, and CT scans show nonspecific changes. The EMG often shows fasciculation of distal limb muscles and other evidence of anterior horn cell degeneration.

Treatment

The treatment of Shy-Drager syndrome involves a combination of the use of mechanical vasoconstriction such as Jobst half-body leotards, plasma, extracellular fluid volume expanders such as 9-alpha-fluorohydrocortisone plus sodium chloride, and pressor drugs such as ephedrine. Vasopressin is also used because of its pressor and volume expansion characteristics (Barr 1979; Cote 1984).

Patients with Shy-Drager syndrome frequently become depressed and, in fact, may present with depression as an initial complaint (Kwentus et al. 1984). Unfortunately, the use of antidepressants is limited by their propensity to cause orthostatic hypotension and other manifestations of autonomic dysregulation. It appears that blockade of the alpha-1 adrenergic, the histamine H_1, and possibly the antimuscarinic receptors is responsible for the orthostatic hypotension seen with antidepressant use (Richardson and Richelson 1984). Hence, it is best to select a drug that has low activity at these sites if an antidepressant is to be used at all. Desipramine and trazodone are probably the drugs of choice here and should be used in doses dependent on patient tolerance. Supportive psychotherapy has a role in the management of depression in these patients.

The dementia that occurs with Shy-Drager syndrome, if present, is mild and appears late in the course of the disease. In most cases, behavioral dyscontrol will not occur due to dementia. In instances where it does occur, the use of antipsychotic agents for the control of behavior is fraught with complications. Blockade of dopamine D2 receptors will worsen parkinsonian symptoms if present. In addition, it is difficult to balance the dopamine D2 receptor blockade versus antimuscarinic receptor blockade because of the possible effects of antimuscarinic activity on blood pressure and the observation that drugs with high antimuscarinic activity tend to block α_1 adrenergic and H_1 histaminic receptors strongly as well. Agents such as chlorpromazine, mesoridazine, and thioridazine, which would normally be used in parkinsonian patients, are rendered inappropriate (Black et al. 1985). In patients with Shy-Drager syndrome with secondary dementia and behavioral abnormalities, treatment must be conservative. An underlying cause should be sought and corrected. The use of sedatives such as various benzodiazepines can be considered but should be on a time-limited basis only.

The management of parkinsonian symptoms in these patients can be difficult. These symptoms should be treated as per Parkinson's disease, except that anticholinergic agents should probably be avoided (Barr 1979; Kwentus et al. 1984).

☐ SENILE CHOREA

Clinical Features

Senile chorea is a choreiform movement disorder that begins insidiously in the limbs and progresses to form a generalized symmetrical movement disorder not associated with mental deterioration. Some clinicians believe that the lingual-facial-buccal dyskinesia sometimes seen in the elderly is the earliest sign of senile chorea (Weiner and Klawans 1973). As a rule, the disorder is mild and usually does not require pharmacologic intervention.

Psychiatric Manifestations

Psychiatric disturbances are not a common clinical feature of this disorder. It is important, however, to differentiate it from Huntington's disease in which psychiatric and cognitive dysfunction is the rule (Fahn 1984).

Epidemiology and Etiology

Senile chorea is a disease of the elderly in that it usually develops after age 60. The etiology of the illness is unknown, as is its incidence. It has been suggested that the disease is due to an abnormality of the dopamine receptors, but this abnormality has not been typified yet.

Pathology

Like Huntington's disease, senile chorea is associated with degeneration of the cells of the caudate nucleus and putamen. The changes in senile chorea, however, are less extreme than in Huntington's disease. In addition, there is an absence of degenerative changes of the cerebral cortex of patients with senile chorea.

Diagnosis

Differentiation between Huntington's disease and senile chorea is critical. A misdiagnosis of Huntington's disease causes needless worry not only for the patient but also for all the patient's relatives. Senile chorea usually presents later in life than Huntington's disease and is not associated with a positive family history of chorea.

Another important differential is between senile chorea with a primarily lingual-facial-buccal presentation and tardive dyskinesia. In this case, the absence of a history of exposure to neuroleptics helps secure the proper diagnosis.

Unless a coexisting illness exists, laboratory studies are within normal limits. A CT scan will probably not be sensitive enough to show degeneration of the caudate nucleus and putamen.

Treatment

Generally, no treatment is required for this condition. The use of neuroleptics may produce control of the syndrome, but it is uncertain as to what the long-term consequences of neuroleptic treatment are for these patients. Reserpine and tetrabenazine, sometimes useful in Huntington's disease, may also be helpful. No medication is capable of curing patients of this syndrome (Fahn 1984).

☐ BENIGN ESSENTIAL TREMOR

This common condition is characterized by a postural tremor that usually affects both hands, but may also affect the head and voice. It is also called familial tremor or, in older people, senile tremor.

Clinical Features

This tremor usually has a gradual onset in adult life and begins in the hands. It diminishes at rest. It is a coarse tremor with a frequency of 8 to 10 Hz. Although the tremor may remain static for many years, it usually increases in severity and may involve the head with rhythmic bobbing. The voice is affected when the tremor involves the thorax and diaphragm. The tremor is most severe on arising in the morning. Like most tremors, it is accentuated by anxiety.

Psychiatric Manifestations

A benign tremor often causes embarrassment. Patients learn to mask the tremor, and, if the head is involved, a tilting may occur. This sometimes leads to muscle-contraction headaches. Many laypersons misinterpret the tremor as "nervousness."

Epidemiology and Etiology

Benign essential tremors tend to run in families and seem to be transmitted as an autosomal dominant trait. A carefully done prevalence study of people 40 years and older showed a rate of 414.6 per 100,000, with a higher prevalence among women and members of the caucasian race (Haerer et al. 1982). The prevalence increases with advancing age.

Pathology

There are no known pathologic findings. The mechanism of the tremor is not understood.

Diagnosis

Parkinsonism is easily excluded in the differential diagnosis of benign essential tremor because rigidity and bradykinesia of parkinsonism are absent. The diagnosis may be based on a history of many years of hand tremor without other neurologic signs. There is often a family history of the same disorder. Hyperthyroidism, lithium intoxi-cation, chronic alcoholism, and anxiety are easily excluded because of the absence of associated features in benign essential tremor.

Treatment

A correct diagnosis with appropriate reassurance concerning the lack of a serious, progressive neurologic disease may be helpful. Although benzodiazepine tranquilizers have been used with mixed success, the treatment of choice when the problem is severe enough to require drug treatment is the beta-blocker propranolol. This drug, in small doses, often reduces the amplitude of the tremor and does not produce chemical dependency.

☐ STIFFMAN SYNDROME

Stiffman syndrome is a rare entity first described by Moersch and Woltman (1956).

Clinical Features

Stiffman syndrome begins with fleeting episodes of aching and tightness of the axial musculature, which progresses to involve the limb girdles. These symptoms progress over the ensuing weeks to years to cause tightness and board-like rigidity, involving limbs, trunk, and neck musculature and hindering volitional movements. Patients complain of awkwardness and slowness of gait and other movements. Superimposed on the rigidity are episodes of paroxysmal muscle spasms that may last for several minutes and can be precipitated by sudden movements, sensory stimulation, or emotions. The episodic spasms may be so severe as to cause rupture of the muscle involved, fracture bones, or induce joint deformities or dislocations. Without treatment, this disease may slowly progress or become stable (Layzer 1984; Warneke 1974).

Psychiatric Manifestations

Since this disorder was typified, various authors have suggested that it is a psychosomatic condition. This is probably because the early symptoms of the disease are nonspecific and variable in nature and may be associated with symptoms of depression, irritability, and anxiety. Heiligman and Paulson (1977) reviewed a single case of stiffman syndrome and the psychiatric literature regarding this disease. Patients were found to have overly dependent personalities, childhood domination by an authoritarian parent, inadequate and unfulfilled psychosexual adjustment, and a tendency to gamble and to achieve specific secondary gains from the illness that helped the patient to avoid adult sexual responsibility. Three of the cases discussed improved with psychotherapy or hospitalization, but two subsequently had recurrence of their symptoms. It is not unusual for patients with stiffman syndrome to have a psychiatric disturbance that antedates the onset of the stiffness (Cobb 1974; Heiligman and Paulson 1977). One case of stiffman syndrome was associated with dementia (Drake 1983).

Epidemiology and Etiology

Stiffman syndrome can occur in all ages but is most frequently seen between the ages of 29 and 59. Stiffman syndrome is a very rare disorder. The incidence and cause are unknown. A familial form inherited in an autosomal dominant fashion has been identified. This form of the disease is manifest by muscular rigidity in newborns, which gradually lessens after early childhood (Layzer 1984).

Pathology

No pathologic abnormality has been identified on examination of the brain or spinal cord.

Diagnosis

The diagnosis of this disease is made primarily on its clinical manifestations. On neurologic examination, passive muscle stretching sometimes promotes powerful reflex contraction lasting several seconds. Despite patients' complaints of awkwardness and weakness, muscle strength is within normal limits. Babinski sign has been present in some cases. Otherwise, the neurologic examination is normal.

EMG recordings from stiff muscles show a pattern of persistent tonic contraction as manifested by a continuous discharge of motor unit potentials not responsive to the patient's attempt to relax the muscle. Muscle activity is not inhibited by voluntary contraction of antagonistic muscles.

Sleep, anesthesia, and peripheral nerve block abolish the rigidity as do succinylcholine, curare, and tubocurarine (Layzer 1984; Warneke 1974).

Treatment

Treatment of choice in this disorder is diazepam, often in very high doses. The use of this medication often produces complete control of the physical symptoms within days. The use of the GABA agonist baclofen or the anticonvulsant phenytoin is sometimes helpful as adjunctive therapy (Layzer 1984).

The psychiatric symptoms sometimes seen with this disorder may continue to be present after the physical symptoms resolve. Pharmacotherapy and psychotherapy should be employed as indicated.

□ CONCLUSION

In this chapter we have attempted to discuss the clinical description, psychiatric sequelae, and treatment of various neurologic conditions grouped under the category of degenerative disorders. By being knowledgeable about these conditions, the psychiatrist can help patients not only in the diagnosis of their illness but by assuring proper treatment of their condition.

□ REFERENCES

Adams RD, Fisher CM, Hakim S, et al: Symptomatic occult hydrocephalus with "normal" cerebrospinal fluid pressure: a treatable syndrome. N Engl J Med 273:117–126, 1965

Anderson AD: A collection of poetry by a physician with progressive neurological disease. J Chronic Dis 37:863–868, 1984

Ayd FJ: Early onset neuroleptic induced extrapyramidal reactions: a second survey, 1961–1981, in Neuroleptics: Neurochemical, Behavioral and Clinical Perspectives. Edited by Coyle JT, Enna SJ. New York, Raven Press, 1983, pp 75–92

Barbeau A: Friedreich's disease 1982: etiologic hypothesis: a personal analysis. Can J Neurol Sci 9:243–263, 1982

Barr AN: The Shy-Drager syndrome, in The Handbook of Clinical Neurology, Vol. 38. Edited by Viken PJ. New York, North-Holland, 1979, pp 233–256

Beghi E, Kurland LT, Mulder DW, et al: Guillian-Barré syndrome: clinicoepidemiologic features and effect of influenza vaccine. Arch Neurol 42:1053–1057, 1985

Berglund M, Gustafson L, Hagberg B: Amnestic-confabulatory syndrome in hydrocephalic dementia and Korsakoff's psychosis in alcoholism. Acta Psychiatr Scand 60:323–333, 1979

Bird SJ: Presymptomatic testing for Huntington's disease. JAMA 253:3286–3291, 1985

Black JL, Richelson E, Richardson JW: Antipsychotic agents: a clinical update. Mayo Clin Proc 60:777–789, 1985

Briggs RS, Castleden CM, Alvarez AS: Normal pressure hydrocephalus in the elderly: a treatable cause of dementia? Age Ageing 10:254–258, 1981

Brown GR, Marsdew CD: How common is dementia in Parkinson's disease? Lancet 2:1262–1265, 1984

Burnstein MH: Familial amyotrophic lateral sclerosis, dementia and psychosis. Psychosomatics 22:151–157, 1981

Caine ED, Hunt RD, Weingartner H, et al: Huntington's dementia: clinical and neuropsychological features. Arch Gen Psychiatry 35:377–384, 1978

Caltagirone C, Gainotti G, Masullo C, et al: Neurophysiological study of normal pressure hydrocephalus. Acta Psychiatr Scand 65:93–100, 1982

Claus D, Aschoff, JC: Computer-tomographie bei atrophien in Bereich der hinteren Schadelgrube. Archiv für Psychiatrie und Nervenkrankheiten 229:179–187, 1980

Cobb J: Stiffman syndrome: is the lesion of the spinal cord or brain stem level. Proceedings of the Royal Society of Medicine 67:1065–1066, 1974

Cote LJ: Neurogenic orthostatic hypotension, in Merritt's Textbook of Neurology (7th ed). Edited by Rowland LP. Philadelphia, Lea & Febiger, 1984, pp 617–621

Davies DL: The intelligence of patients with Friedreich ataxia. J Neurol Neurosurg Psychiatry 12:34–38, 1949a

Davies DL: Psychiatric changes associated with Friedreich ataxia. J Neurol Neurosurg Psychiatry 12:246–250, 1949b

Davis GC, Williams AC, Markey SP, et al: Chronic parkinsonism secondary to intravenous injection of meperidine analogues. Psychiatry Res 1:249–254, 1979.

Dewhurst K, Oliver JE, McKnight AL: Socio-psychiatric consequences of Huntington's disease. Br J Psychiatry 116:255–258, 1970

Dobyns WB, Goldstein NP, Gordon H: Clinical spectrum of Wilson's disease (hepatolenticular degeneration). Mayo Clin Proc 54:35–42, 1979

Drake ME: Stiffman syndrome and dementia. Am J Med 74:1085–1087, 1983

Drake ME: Depression and conversion hysteria in chronic inflammatory polyradiculoneuropathy. J Fam Pract 19:679–682, 1984

Duvoisin RC: Progressive supranuclear palsy, in Merritt's Textbook of Neurology (7th ed). Edited by Rowland LP. Philadelphia, Lea & Febiger, 1984, pp 537–539

Edelsohn G: Guillain-Barré misdiagnosed as a conversion disorder. Hosp Community Psychiatry 33:766–767, 1982

Eisendrath BJ, Matthay MA, Dunkel NA, et al: Guillain-Barré syndrome: psychosocial aspects of management. Psychosomatics 24:465–475, 1983

Engel AG, Lambert EH, Howard FM: Immune complexes (IgG and C3) at the motor end-plate in myasthenia gravis. Mayo Clin Proc 52:267–280, 1977

Fahn HS: Huntington's disease and other forms of chorea, in Merritt's Textbook of Neurology (7th ed). Edited by Rowland LP. Philadelphia, Lea & Febiger, 1984, pp 517–521

Fehrenbach RA, Wallesch CW, Claus D: Neuropsychologic findings in Friedreich ataxia. Arch Neurol 41:306–308, 1984

Haerer AF, Anderson DW, Schoenberg BS: Prevalence of essential tremor. Arch Neurol 39:750–751, 1982

Hausner RS: Neuroleptic-induced parkinsonism and Parkinson's disease: differential diagnosis and treatment. J Clin Psychiatry 44:13–16, 1983

Heiligman R, Paulson MJ: The stiffman syndrome: a psychiatric disease? Int J Psychiatry Med 7:363–371, 1977

Henschel EO: The Guillaine-Barré syndrome: a personal experience. Anesthesiology 47:228–231, 1977

Hoehn MM, Yahr MD: Parkinsonism: onset, progression and mortality. Neurology 17:427–442, 1967

Huber SJ, Paulson GW: The concept of subcortical dementia. Am J Psychiatry 142:1312–1317, 1985

Janati A, Appel AR: Psychiatric aspects of progressive supranuclear palsy. J Nerv Ment Dis 172:85–89, 1984

Janiszewski DW, Caroscio JT, Wisham LH: Amyotrophic lateral sclerosis: a comprehensive rehabilitation approach. Arch Phys Med Rehab 64:304–307, 1983

Jefferson TD, Cohen C: Familial syringomyelia with mental impairment. J R Army Med Corps 128:42–42, 1982

Klawans HL Jr: A pharmacologic analysis of Huntington chorea. Eur Neurol 4:148–163, 1970

Kurland LT, Kurtzke JF, Goldberg ID: Epidemiology of Neurologic and Sense Organ Disorders. Cambridge, Harvard University Press, 1973

Kwentus JA, Auth TL, Foy JL: Shy-Drager syndrome presenting as depression: a case report. J Clin Psychiatry 45:137–139, 1984

Lang AE, Blair RDG: Parkinson's disease in 1984: an update. Can Med Assoc J 131:1031–1037, 1984

Layzer RB: Cramps and stiffness, in Merritt's Textbook of Neurology (7th ed). Edited by Rowland LP. Philadelphia. Lea & Febiger, 1984, pp 590–592

Lying-Tunell U: Psychotic symptoms in normal pressure hydrocephalus. Acta Psychiatr Scand 59:415–419, 1979

MacKenzie KR, Martin MJ, Howard FM: Myasthenia gravis: psychiatric concomitants. Can Med Assoc J 100:988–991, 1969

Mancall EL: Syringomyelia, in Merritt's Textbook of Neurology (7th ed). Edited by Rowland LP. Philadelphia, Lea & Febiger, 1984, pp 552–556

Mayeux R, Williams JBW, Stern Y, et al: Depression and Parkinson's disease. Adv Neurol 40:241–250, 1984

Meyer JS, Kitagawa Y, Tanahashi N, et al: Evaluation of treatment of normal pressure hydrocephalus. J Neurosurg 62:513–521, 1985

Moersch F, Woltman H: Progressive fluctuating rigidity and spasm (stiffman syndrome). Proceedings of the Staff Meetings of the Mayo Clinic 31:421–422, 1956

Mulder DW: Clinical limits of amyotrophic lateral sclerosis. Adv Neurol 36:15–22, 1982

Munsat TL: Adult motor neuron diseases, in Merritt's Textbook of Neurology (7th ed). Edited by Rowland LP. Philadelphia, Lea & Febiger, 1984, pp 548–552

Okazaki H: Fundamentals of Neuropathology. New York, Igaku-Shoin Medical Publishers, 1983, pp 158–159

Pleasure DE, Schotland DL: Acquired neuropathies, in Merritt's Textbook of Neurology (7th ed). Edited by Rowland LP. Philadelphia, Lea & Febiger, 1984, pp 484–498

Poser CM, Alter M, Sibley WA, et al: Demyelinating disease, in Merritt's Textbook of Neurology (7th ed). Edited by Rowland LP. Philadelphia, Lea & Febiger, 1984, pp 593–611

Prockop LD: Hydrocephalus, in Merritt's Textbook of Neurology (7th ed). Edited by Rowland LP. Philadelphia, Lea & Febiger, 1984, pp 199–206

Rabin D: Compounding the ordeal of ALS: isolation from my fellow physicians. N Engl J Med 307:506–509, 1982

Richardson JW, Richelson E: Antidepressants: a clinical update for medical practitioners. Mayo Clin Proc 59:330–337, 1984

Rosenberg RN: Hereditary ataxias, in Merritt's Textbook of Neurology (7th ed). Edited by Rowland LP. Philadelphia, Lea & Febiger, 1984, pp 499–506

Schiffer RB, Babigian HM: Behavioral disorders in multiple sclerosis, temporal lobe epilepsy, and amyotrophic lateral sclerosis: an epidemiological study. Arch Neurol 41:1067–1069, 1984

Shy GM, Drager GA: A neurologic syndrome associated with orthostatic hypotension. Arch Neurol 2:511–527, 1960

Steele JC, Richardson JC, Olszewski J: Progressive supranuclear palsy. Arch Neurol 10:333–359, 1964

Streinberg JS: Guillaine-Barré syndrome support group. (letter) Heart Lung 13:455, 1984

Swash M: Clinical aspects of Guillain-Barré syndrome: a review. Royal Society of Medicine 72:670–673, 1979

Thomas JE, Schirger A: Idiopathic orthostatic hypotension: a study of its natural history in 57 neurologically affected patients. Arch Neurol 22:289–293, 1970

Todes C: Inside parkinsonism: a psychiatrists' personal experience. Lancet 1:977–978, 1983

Tsuang MT, Tidball JS, Geller D: ECT in a depressed patient with shunt in place for normal pressure hydrocephalus. Am J Psychiatry 136:1205–1206, 1979

Warneke L: Stiffman syndrome. Can Psychiatr Assoc J 19:399–403, 1974

Weiner WJ, Klawans HL: Lingual-facial-buccal movements in the elderly: II: pathogenesis and relationship to senile chorea. J Am Geriatr Soc 1:318–320, 1973

Wells CE, Duncan GW: Neurology for Psychiatrists. Philadelphia, FA Davis Co, 1980, pp 173–174

Wikström J, Paetau A, Palo J, et al: Classical amyotrophic lateral sclerosis with dementia. Arch Neurol 39:681–683, 1982

Yahr MD: Parkinsonism, in Merritt's Textbook of Neurology (7th ed). Edited by Rowland LP. Philadelphia, Lea & Febiger, 1984, pp 526–537

Chapter 16

Neuropsychiatric Aspects of Metabolic Diseases

Lawrence S. Gross, M.D.

THE POTENTIAL CAUSES OF metabolic nervous system disease are multitudinous. The central nervous system (CNS) is often prominently affected in metabolic disturbances that can arise from nutritional deficiencies, underlying illnesses, or as the result of iatrogenic treatments. This chapter will address neuropsychiatric manifestations in selected acquired (exogenous) and inherited metabolic diseases.

A selected list of exogenous causes of metabolic brain disease can be found in Table 1. Certain illnesses that could be included here are described in other chapters of this text; the reader is referred to those chapters for the relevant discussions. This chapter will address a few of the more commonly encountered clinical entities with a well-established metabolic pathogenesis.

☐ FLUID, ELECTROLYTE, AND ACID-BASE DISORDERS

Cerebral dysfunction is one of the most sensitive findings in patients with disturbances of fluid, electrolyte, and acid-base balance. However, common clinical measurements that assess blood concentrations of electrolytes may not reflect the more important CNS electrolyte environment, namely that of the cerebrospinal fluid (CSF) and the brain itself. Similarly, pH adjustments in CSF occur faster than those in blood, and compensatory mechanisms in the brain are more rapid than either CSF or blood (Arieff and Schmidt 1980). CNS changes in acid-base disorders are thought to be more closely linked to CSF pH than to blood pH. Because carbon dioxide rapidly crosses the blood-brain barrier, neu-

TABLE 1. SOME CAUSES OF ACQUIRED METABOLIC BRAIN DISEASE

Hypoxia (impaired cerebral oxygenation)
  Pulmonary disease
  Alveolar hypoventilation
  High altitude
  Anemia
  Carbon monoxide poisoning
  Methemoglobinemia

Ischemia (impaired cerebral blood flow)
  Cardiac disease
    Myocardial infarction
    Congestive heart failure
    Cardiac arrhythmias
  Pulmonary embolism
  Syncopy/hypotension
  Hypertensive encephalopathy

Cofactor deficiency
  Thiamine
  Niacin
  Pyridoxine
  Folate
  Vitamin B12

Hyperfunction/hypofunction of endocrine organs
  Pituitary
  Thyroid (thyrotoxicosis/myxedema)
  Parathyroid (hyperparathyroidism and
    hypoparathyroidism)
  Adrenal (Cushing's disease, Addison's disease,
    pheochromocytoma)
  Pancreas (hypoglycemia/diabetes)

Diseases of nonendocrine organs
  Liver (hepatic encephalopathy)
  Kidney (uremic encephalopathy)
  Lung (CO_2 narcosis)

Other systemic diseases
  Cancer
  Sepsis

Exogenous poisons and drug intoxications
  Ethanol and other sedative drugs

Acid poisons or poisons with acidic breakdown
  products
    Paraldehyde
    Methanol
    Ethylene glycol
Psychotropic drugs
  Tricyclic antidepressants/anticholinergic drugs
  Amphetamines/stimulants
  Lithium
  Phenothiazines
  LSD/mescaline/phencyclidine
  Monoamine oxidase inhibitors
Others
  Anticonvulsants
  Steroids
  Cardiac glycosides
  Cimetidine
  Heavy metals
  Organic phosphates
  Cyanide
  Salicylates

Abnormalities of fluid, electrolyte, or acid-base balance
  Acidosis (metabolic and respiratory)
  Alkalosis (metabolic and respiratory)
  Water and sodium (hyperosmolarity and
    hypoosmolarity/hypernatremia and hyponatremia)
  Potassium (hyperkalemia and hypokalemia)
  Calcium (hypercalcemia and hypocalcemia)
  Magnesium (hypermagnesemia and
    hypomagnesemia)
  Phosphorus (hyperphosphatemia and
    hypophosphatemia)

Disorders of temperature regulation
  Hypothermia
  Hyperthermia (heat stroke/fever)

Miscellaneous causes
  Ethanol and other sedative drug withdrawal
  Postoperative delirium

Note. Adapted from Posner (1985).

rologic symptoms in respiratory alkalosis and acidosis are much more dramatic than in metabolic disturbances of the same degree (Epstein 1980).

Metabolic Acidosis

Metabolic acidosis results from bicarbonate depletion or acid accumulation within the body. It can occur in renal disease, severe diarrhea, ingestion of certain diuretics and acidifying salts, hyperalimentation, lactic acidosis, ketoacidosis, and certain toxic states (e.g., salicylates, paraldehyde, methanol, ethylene glycol). Diagnosis is made by analysis of serum electrolytes and, if necessary, arterial blood gases. Hyperventilation is a clinical hallmark but may be difficult to detect if the metabolic acidosis

is chronic. Characteristic deep sighing respiration known as Kussmaul breathing is present in severe acute acidosis. There is progressive impairment in consciousness, with lethargy, disorientation, and stupor. Mild degrees of metabolic acidosis may be accompanied by loss of appetite, nausea, headache, and apathy.

Metabolic Alkalosis

Metabolic alkalosis may be initiated by loss of hydrogen ion (acid) from the body, but the condition is maintained by increased renal reabsorption and/or generation of bicarbonate. This can occur in states of gastric acid loss (e.g., vomiting, gastric suction), potassium loss, salt wasting (e.g., diuretics, Bartter's syndrome), mineralocorticoid excess, bicarbonate loading, delayed conversion of accumulated organic acids, and alkali loading (e.g., milk-alkali syndrome). There are no signs and symptoms specific for this disorder. Severe metabolic alkalosis can lead to cardiac arrhythmias and hypoventilation. Muscular weakness and hyporeflexia are often seen when the condition is chronic (Andreoli 1985). Diagnosis can be inferred from serum electrolyte measurements and confirmed by arterial blood gases. Hypokalemia is usually present.

Respiratory Acidosis

Respiratory acidosis occurs from impaired alveolar ventilation. Acute respiratory acidosis can occur in sudden depression of the medullary respiratory center (e.g., anesthesia, narcotic overdose), paralysis of the respiratory muscles (e.g., hypokalemia, neuromuscular diseases), airway obstruction, chest trauma, or an acute insult superimposed on chronic hypercapnia. Chronic respiratory acidosis usually occurs in association with chronic pulmonary disease.

Clinically, symptoms depend on the severity and rate of development of the acidosis. Severe uncompensated respiratory acidosis results in a characteristic syndrome called CO_2 narcosis. Early symptoms are fatigue and weakness, which are followed by irritability, confusion, and lethargy. Headache is common, at times with blurred vision. Mental changes can include depression, anxiety, and delirium. Characteristic electroencephalogram (EEG) changes include abundant slow frequency activity, prominent theta waves, and slow alpha activity with increased or decreased voltage. Tremors, jerking, and clonic movements may be present; asterixis is common. CSF pressure is often increased, and papilledema with engorged retinal vessels may be seen. CO_2 is a cerebral vasodilator, and signs and symptoms of peripheral vasodilation occur in systemic acidosis of any type (Epstein 1980).

Treatment consists of adequate ventilation and treatment of the underlying disorder. The possibility of drug abuse and drug overdose should be investigated in an otherwise healthy patient with acute onset of respiratory depression. Naloxone (Narcan) therapy should be considered in the emergency treatment of comatose patients with no identifiable cause for respiratory depression. In patients with chronic pulmonary disease who develop sudden increased hypercapnia, any superimposed

pulmonary pathology should be identified and treated. Caution should be exercised with oxygen therapy in these patients because sudden correction of hypoxemia may cut off their only remaining respiratory drive.

Respiratory Alkalosis

Hyperventilation leads to decreased arterial pCO_2 and increased pH, resulting in respiratory alkalosis. The classic hyperventilation syndrome is usually associated with severe anxiety, but acute respiratory alkalosis also occurs in salicylism, fever and sepsis, and damage to the respiratory centers, and in diseases such as pneumonia, pulmonary emboli, and congestive heart failure. Chronic respiratory alkalosis occurs at high altitudes, in advanced hepatic insufficiency, and during pregnancy; it may be clinically asymptomatic. The acute hyperventilation syndrome consists of light-headedness, paresthesias, circumoral numbness, and tingling of the extremities; tetany may occur in severe cases. Emotional support and rebreathing into a paper bag generally terminate the acute hyperventilation syndrome, which is frequently associated with extreme anxiety and apprehension, often in histronic patients.

Hyperosmolarity and Hypernatremia

Etiology. Hyperosmolarity results when the ratio of solutes to total body water is increased. Sodium is the principal extracellular fluid (ECF) cation; all hypernatremic states are hypertonic, but in some disorders the increase in ECF osmolarity is due to solutes other than sodium (e.g., uncontrolled hyperglycemia). Hyperosmolar states can arise as the result of inadequate water intake, osmotic diuresis, and excessive water losses from either renal or extrarenal causes. Alteration in osmoregulatory centers secondary to CNS pathology may result in a syndrome of "essential hypernatremia." Ectopic pinealomas within the hypothalamus may be associated with hypernatremia from loss of thirst. Children and the elderly often exhibit the most significant symptomatology, which varies with the degree and rate of development of the hypertonicity. Gastroenteritis with diarrhea is the most common cause of hypernatremia in infants; in the elderly it results from infirmity and the inability to obtain water (Arieff and Guisado 1976).

Symptomatology. Most infants with chronic hypernatremia have evidence of dehydration; about two-thirds have CNS symptoms including irritability, high-pitched crying, and varying degrees of increased muscle tone, twitching, and hyperactive reflexes. Seizures are common in acute hypernatremia, in which infants also exhibit emesis, fever, respiratory distress, spasticity, and a variety of focal neurologic abnormalities. Symptoms in adults are much less straightforward due to the presence of associated severe medical conditions. Seizures are unusual in chronic hypernatremia but may be present in up to 40 percent of patients after the initiation of therapy (Arieff and Guisado 1976). Depression of sensorium is present to varying degrees in all hypernatremic patients and may progress from lethargy and confusion to coma, respiratory paralysis, and death. Hypernatremic dehydration has significant morbidity and mortality in both infants and the elderly. Permanent brain damage may result from severe hypernatremia, especially in children; this may represent sequelae of complications such as subdural effusions, subarachnoid hemorrhages, and intracerebral bleeding (Epstein 1980). Nervous system symptoms are thought to be related to brain shrinkage from the osmotic movement of water from brain cells into the ECF. Chronic hypertonicity generally produces fewer symptoms because of adaptive osmotic mechanisms within the brain.

Diagnosis. In acute hyperosmolar states, symptoms generally appear when the effective ECF osmolality exceeds 320 to 330 milliosmol per kilogram of water; coma and respiratory arrest may occur above 360 to 380 milliosmol per kg water (Andreoli 1985). CSF in hypernatremic infants may demonstrate elevated protein without pleocytosis. The EEG in hypernatremia is usually normal or shows minor slowing of background frequencies. Some patients may have generalized slow wave activity, and about 7 percent may demonstrate epileptic activity. EEG changes usually return to normal within 4 to 6 weeks of successful therapy (Arieff and Guisado 1976).

Treatment. In addition to the correction of the underlying cause, treatment of hypernatremic dehydration involves fluid therapy with dilute solutions calculated for administration over about 48 hours. More rapid correction is hazardous because of the risk of cerebral edema, seizures, brain damage, and death (Arieff and Guisado 1976).

Hypoosmolarity and Hyponatremia

Etiology. Hyponatremia and hypotonicity develop when water intake exceeds renal and extrarenal water losses. In addition to dilution from excess water, hyponatremia may also occur as the result of depletion of body sodium stores. A number of pathologic conditions are associated with hyponatremia. Starvation and beer potomania (ingestion of large quantities of beer as the major dietary constituent) result in reduced solute intake and a reduction in renal urinary dilution capacity. Hyponatremia secondary to impaired renal free water clearance is seen in Addison's disease, hepatic cirrhosis, congestive heart failure, and the syndrome of inappropriate antidiuretic hormone production (SIADH). SIADH can occur secondary to a variety of illnesses such as pulmonary disease, CNS trauma and infection, and neoplasms (most notably pancreatic and oat cell lung carcinomas). Numerous drugs may also cause hyponatremia via stimulation of antidiuretic hormone (ADH) secretion; these include clomipramine, amitriptyline, thioridazine, thiothixene, tranylcypromine, carbamazepine, morphine, barbiturates, nicotine, and others (Nanji 1983). Increased plasma ADH without hyponatremia or hypoosmolarity has been reported in untreated psychotic patients compared to controls; ADH level was positively correlated with degree of psychosis (Raskind et al. 1978).

Of particular interest psychiatrically is hyponatremia that results from water intoxication as a complication of primary, or psychogenic, polydipsia. The prevalence of compulsive water drinkers in mental hospital populations has been reported to range from 6.6 percent (Jose and Perez-Cruet 1979) to 17.5 percent (Blum et al. 1983), with a significant percentage of these patients showing signs of water intoxication. Most compulsive water drinkers have schizophrenic disorders. Previously thought to be a relatively straightforward problem of increased water intake that exceeds a normal kidney's ability to excrete free water, recent evidence that self-induced water intoxication may be associated with SIADH has led to controversy concerning the cause of the syndrome (Vieweg et al. 1985a). Response to fluid deprivation in these patients has suggested a reset osmostat or ADH response to nonosmotic stimuli, which tended to sustain hyponatremia (Hariprasad et al. 1980).

Symptomatology. The clinical manifestations of hypoosmolar states depend on the etiology, magnitude, and acuteness of the condition. Chronic hypoosmolar states usually involve a combination of sodium depletion and water ingestion. Symptom severity is related to the degree of serum sodium reduction. Experimental reduction of serum sodium levels from 147 to 131 meq/l was associated with thirst, anorexia, muscle cramps, impaired taste, fatigue, apathy, mental slowness, and dyspnea on exertion (McCance 1936); these nonspecific subjective complaints in mild hyponatremia may be confused with depression. Lightheadedness and headaches may be prominent. Other neuropsychiatric features appear as the hyponatremia worsens. These include progressive weakness, lethargy, restlessness, confusion, delirium, psychosis, tremors, and muscle twitches that often lead to focal or generalized seizures. Coma and death may follow. A variety of focal and diffuse neurologic signs have been described (Epstein 1980).

Symptoms of acute water intoxication may be somewhat different from sodium depletion, possibly related to the rapidity of the development of hyponatremia. Symptoms are usually not observed until sodium levels have fallen below 125 meq/l and include nausea, vomiting, muscle twitching, grand mal seizures, and coma. Acute water intoxication, in which serum sodium levels of 125 meq/l or less develop within 24 hours, has substantial morbidity from brain damage and a mortality rate of about 50 percent (Arieff and Guisado 1976). This is contrasted with more gradual development of significant hyponatremia over several days to weeks, in which patients are usually much less symptomatic at comparably reduced serum sodium levels. The underlying pathology appears to be initially related to the development of cerebral edema from the osmotic flow of water from the hypotonic ECF into the brain cells; with hyponatremia lasting longer than a few hours, adaptive osmotic changes within the brain cells may further impair brain function and be partly responsible for the encephalopathy as well (Arieff and Guisado 1976).

Although patients with psychogenic polydipsia generally develop mild, asymptomatic hyponatremia, significant morbidity and mortality may occur. In a recent review of patients who died prior to age 53 in a state mental hospital, Vieweg et al. (1985a) reported that 27 (45 percent) of the 60 deaths between 1974 and 1981 were in patients with a schizophrenic disorder; and 5 (18.5 percent) of those 27 died of complications of self-induced water intoxication. Clinical, laboratory, and autopsy fea-

tures of those 5 patients plus 5 cases obtained from the literature included psychosis, polydipsia, polyuria, severe hyposthenuria (specific gravity 1.003 or less), hyponatremia (serum sodium 120 meq/l or less), seizures, coma, and cerebral and visceral edema. Because of the lack of pathognomonic tissue changes, self-induced water intoxication must be kept in mind as a potential cause of death in schizophrenic patients.

Diagnosis. The diagnosis of hyponatremia is made from appropriate blood and urine chemistries; in addition, investigations should be carried out to identify the underlying cause. CSF pressure is often elevated, and papilledema may be present, but CSF protein is usually normal (Epstein 1980). EEG changes are common but nonspecific; most often seen are loss of normal alpha activity and irregular discharges of high amplitude theta (4–7 Hz) activity. The severity of EEG abnormalities tends to increase with lower serum sodium levels, and the EEG usually returns to normal with correction of the hyponatremia (Arieff and Guisado 1976). Severe hyposthenuria, with a urine specific gravity of 1.003 or less, may be a marker for the syndrome of self-induced water intoxication and schizophrenic disorders (Vieweg et al. 1984).

Treatment. Cases of acute hyponatremia in which serum sodium levels below 120 to 125 meq/l are accompanied by neurologic abnormalities, particularly seizures, have a high mortality if untreated and require active measures to raise the serum sodium. Hypertonic saline solutions are usually used, although furosemide may be used in combination with normal or hypertonic saline, depending on the hydration status of the patient (Andreoli 1985). Concomitant intravenous dexamethasone has been used to reduce cerebral edema, along with phenytoin for seizure coverage (Daggett et al. 1982). Treatment should be designed to achieve a serum sodium level no higher than 120 to 125 meq/l; more rapid or higher serum corrections can cause CNS damage from brain shrinkage, complicating the brain's internal compensatory osmotic regulation (Andreoli 1985). Rapid correction can also precipitate congestive heart failure and cerebral hemorrhage (Arieff and Guisado 1976). In addition to these acute treatment measures, efforts should be directed to the identification and correction of the underlying cause of the hyponatremia.

Chronic mild asymptomatic hyponatremia usually responds to treatment of the underlying disorder and fluid restriction. Chronic hyponatremia associated with SIADH is often corrected by fluid restriction, although lithium and demeclocycline have been effective in many, but not all, patients. Demeclocycline has also been reported to be helpful in the management of hyponatremia in a patient with psychosis, psychogenic polydipsia, and episodic water intoxication (Nixon et al. 1982). Because of the difficulty maintaining water restriction in the long-term management of schizophrenic patients with water intoxication, oral sodium chloride supplementation has been used effectively for short-term prevention of seizures (Vieweg et al. 1985b).

Calcium

For discussions of hypercalcemia and hypocalcemia, the reader is referred to Chapter 17.

Potassium

Potassium is the principal intracellular fluid (ICF) cation, with only about 2 percent of the body's potassium located extracellularly. Serum concentrations are usually between 3.5 and 5.0 meq/l. Regulation of serum potassium not only depends on external potassium balance (dietary intake versus renal output) but also on potassium exchange between the ICF and ECF compartments. The balance between ECF and ICF potassium is vital in the regulation of the resting membrane potential of nerve, heart, and muscle; clinical consequences of hyperkalemia and hypokalemia are generally reflected in changes in the electrical excitability of these tissues.

Hypokalemia

Etiology. Hypokalemia occurs whenever renal and extrarenal potassium losses exceed potassium intake. This may result from inadequate intake, excessive renal loss (e.g., mineralocorticoid excess, diuretic therapy, chronic metabolic alkalosis, renal tubular acidosis), gastrointestinal losses such as severe vomiting and diarrhea, and potassium shifts from the ECF to the ICF in such conditions as acute alkalosis, hypokalemic periodic paralysis, and therapy with insulin and vitamin B12 (Andreoli 1985). Numerous drugs can cause hypokalemia, including certain antibiotics, L-dopa, thiazide diuretics, and furosemide. Laxative abuse can lead to excessive gastrointestinal losses, and lithium carbonate overdose can produce hypokalemia by causing a rapid influx of potassium into the cells (Nanji 1983).

Symptomatology. Symptoms of hypokalemia may be evident in various organ systems. Changes in cardiac excitation are evidenced by arrhythmias and characteristic electrocardiogram (EKG) changes. Long-standing potassium deficiency may lead to a hypokalemic nephropathy from renal tubular damage. A paralytic ileus may result from the effect of reduced potassium on gastrointestinal tract smooth muscle. Large potassium losses from skeletal muscle can lead to rhabdomyolysis and myoglobinuria (Andreoli 1985).

Neuromuscular symptoms are common in severe potassium depletion but are usually not seen until the serum potassium level has dropped to 2.5 meq/l. Some degree of muscle weakness and pain is common and most prominent in the legs; muscular tenderness and paresthesias may be present. Deep tendon reflexes are usually preserved. However, severe potassium depletion may lead to an areflexic paralysis, which can compromise the muscles of respiration and result in death from respiratory failure. Chvostek's and Trousseau's signs, indicating latent tetany, may be present with severe potassium deficiency in the absence of hypomagnesemia and hypocalcemia (Epstein 1980).

Hypokalemic periodic paralysis is a predominantly familial disorder affecting mostly males. The usual inheritance is autosomal dominant. Acute shifts of potassium from the ECF to the ICF are thought to be responsible for the periodic symptoms, which may range in severity from mild weakness, usually of the extremities, to paralysis lasting from a few hours to several days. Attacks tend to occur every few weeks and decrease in frequency with age. Acute attacks may respond to potassium replacement; supplemental potassium with a low-carbohydrate, low-salt, high-potassium diet may prevent attacks if potassium alone is not effective. Another form of hypokalemic periodic paralysis, predominantly in young Asian males, has been associated with thyrotoxicosis. Potassium chloride reverses the symptoms of the attacks, which are prevented by treating the hyperthyroidism (Adams and Victor 1985).

Cerebral dysfunction in hypokalemia can be evidenced neuropsychiatrically by fatigue, drowsiness, lethargy, apathy, confusion, irritability, dysphoria, nervousness, and, occasionally in the elderly, as an organic brain syndrome. Coma, delirium, and hallucinations are less common. A case of psychotic decompensation associated with diuretic-induced hypokalemia has been described in a 60-year-old schizophrenic woman (Hafez et al. 1984).

Diagnosis. Characteristic EKG changes are usually present with serum potassium levels less than 3.0 meq/l; these include ST segment depression, T wave flattening or inversion, accentuated U wave, and variable conduction defects. Cardiac arrhythmias may be present in severe hypokalemia. The EEG in hypokalemia is usually normal, although abnormalities have been described. Both the EKG and EEG changes are completely reversible with treatment of the potassium deficit (Epstein 1980).

Treatment. Treatment of hypokalemia involves replacement therapy with potassium salts along with identification and correction of the underlying disorder.

Hyperkalemia

Etiology. Hyperkalemia occurs when potassium intake or potassium shifts from the ICF to ECF exceed the rate of renal plus extrarenal potassium loss. Increased intake may be from exogenous (e.g., diet, salt substitutes, medications) or endogenous (e.g., hemolysis, gastrointestinal bleeding, catabolic states) sources. Decreased renal potassium excretion is the cause for hyperkalemia in acute and chronic renal failure, in Addison's disease, and in the use of potassium-sparing diuretics. Extrarenal causes of hyperkalemia usually result from potassium shifts from the ICF to ECF, as seen in such conditions as chronic acidosis, diabetic hyperglycemia, exercise, periodic paralysis, tissue damage, and the use of certain drugs. Factitious causes include laboratory error and pseudohyperkalemia, a condition in which potassium is released from erythrocytes, leukocytes, and platelets during the clotting process. The causes of hyperkalemia are extensively reviewed elsewhere (DeFronzo et al. 1982). Drug-induced rhabdomyolysis with associated hyperkalemia has been implicated with barbiturates, heroin, phencyclidine, amphetamines, and other sedatives and narcotics (Nanji 1983).

Symptomatology. Clinically, the most significant effects of potassium excess are cardiac. Significant

changes usually do not occur at serum levels below 7.0 meq/l but are almost always present above 8.0 meq/l. The initial EKG change is the appearance of high, peaked T waves, particularly in the chest leads. With higher levels the PR interval becomes progressively longer, followed by disappearance of the P waves and prolongation of the QRS complex. Arrhythmias and complete heart block may appear. At potassium levels above 9 or 10 meq/l, the QRS eventually merges with the T wave in a continuous sine wave appearance that may progress to ventricular fibrillation and cardiac standstill. The EKG changes of hyperkalemia do not directly correlate with serum levels and are exaggerated by hyponatremia, hypocalcemia, acidosis, and hypermagnesemia (Epstein 1980).

Neuropsychiatrically, weakness leading to a rapidly progressive bilateral ascending flaccid paralysis and quadriplegia has occurred with hyperkalemia and azotemia in cases of renal failure and Addison's disease. Associated features included stocking distribution of sensory loss with burning pain and paresthesias in the lower extremities, dysphagia, dysarthria, and respiratory failure (Bull et al. 1953). Confusion, clouding of consciousness, and disorientation may be present, but this could be due to the underlying disorder rather than the hyperkalemia per se.

Hyperkalemic periodic paralysis is an autosomal dominant disorder characterized by transient attacks of paralysis and hyperkalemia that may be precipitated by exercise, cold exposure, and potassium administration. Renal, adrenal, and pancreatic function are normal; during an attack, however, potassium is released from muscle cells, resulting in a shift of potassium extracellularly and causing muscle paralysis. A high-carbohydrate diet has been used to prevent the attacks, and thiazides and acetazolamide have been effective in decreasing the frequency of attacks. Salbutamol, a β_2 agonist, has been useful in treating and preventing attacks (DeFronzo et al. 1982).

Diagnosis. An increased serum potassium level above 5.0 meq/l and characteristic EKG changes (described above) can be useful diagnostically. As in other electrolyte disturbances, it is essential to investigate and identify the underlying cause of the hyperkalemia.

Treatment. Treatment of acute hyperkalemia includes the administration of sodium bicarbonate or glucose plus insulin to promote the transfer of potassium from the ECF to ICF; this lowers the blood level but does not remove potassium from the body. If extreme cardiotoxicity is present, the administration of calcium gluconate will help counteract the hyperkalemic effects on cardiac excitability and may be lifesaving, but it does not alter the serum potassium concentration. The use of ion exchange resins, such as Kayexalate, promotes gastrointestinal loss of potassium; diuretics can increase renal potassium loss. Dialysis may be useful in cases of acute renal failure or continuous release of potassium into the ECF, as in extensive burns or rhabdomyolysis (Andreoli 1985).

Treatment of chronic hyperkalemia involves reduction of dietary potassium, removal of other exogenous sources of potassium, and discontinuation of predisposing drugs. Acidosis and hypovolemia should be corrected if present, and underlying causes of hyperkalemia should be identified and treated (DeFronzo et al. 1982).

Magnesium

Magnesium, like potassium, is present in much higher concentration intracellularly than extracellularly. Only about 1 percent of the body's magnesium is in the ECF, with 31 percent in the cells and 67 percent in bone. Normal serum concentration is 1.6 to 2.1 meq/l. Magnesium has a structural role in bone. Intracellular magnesium is important in cell physiology and catalyzes several enzyme reactions involved in energy metabolism. Magnesium absorption in humans occurs mainly in the jejunum and ileum; magnesium balance in the body is primarily regulated by the kidney via glomerular filtration and tubular reabsorption. Neuropsychiatric symptoms may be associated with both magnesium deficiency and excess.

Hypomagnesemia

Etiology. Routine serum magnesium determinations in inpatient medical populations have shown the prevalence of hypomagnesemia to be as high as 11 percent (Whang et al. 1984). Magnesium deficiency may result from gastrointestinal disorders such as malabsorption syndromes, bowel and biliary fistulas, prolonged nasogastric suction, parenteral hyperalimentation, excessive vomiting, diarrhea, malnutrition, and alcoholic cirrhosis. Endocrine disorders such as hyperparathyroidism,

hypoparathyroidism, hyperthyroidism, primary hyperaldosteronism, and diabetic ketoacidosis have been associated with hypomagnesemia. Chronic renal disease may lead to magnesium wasting. Alcoholics are particularly prone to magnesium deficiency from inadequate dietary intake, starvation ketosis, diarrhea, vomiting, and increased urinary excretion. It has been estimated that 30 percent of all alcoholics and 86 percent of patients with delirium tremens have hypomagnesemia during the first 24 to 48 hours after hospital admission (Cronin and Knochel 1983). Drug-induced magnesium deficiency can result from increased urinary (e.g., aminoglycoside antibiotics, carbenicillin, amphotericin B, polymixin B, digitalis, diuretics) or gastrointestinal (e.g., purgatives, laxative abuse) losses (Nanji 1983).

Symptomatology. Magnesium deficiency results in changes in potassium, calcium, and phosphorus balance; this has led some investigators to question whether symptoms are specific for hypomagnesemia (Cronin and Knochel 1983). Cardiac manifestations may include tachycardia, arrhythmias, and T wave flattening or inversion (Epstein 1980). Patients are often anorectic, with nausea, vomiting, and poor intestinal motility that may lead to a paralytic ileus (Smith 1985a).

The most prominent symptoms of hypomagnesemia are neuropsychiatric. Lethargy, weakness, and muscle irritability may progress to classic signs of tremors and seizures. Seizures are usually generalized but may be focal; the EEG is usually abnormal but nonspecific. Signs of tetany, such as Chvostek's and Trousseau's signs, may be present, but Trousseau's is less common. Hyperreflexia is usual, with or without clonus; muscle fasciculations are common, and abnormal movements of the face and extremities may occur. Less common features include vertigo, ataxia, rigidity and cogwheeling, carpopedal spasm, nystagmus, and dysarthria (Epstein 1980). Psychiatrically, patients may exhibit depression, restlessness, irritability, and marked agitation progressing to hallucinations, disorientation, confusion, and coma. An acute organic brain syndrome has been described (Hall and Joffe 1973).

Diagnosis. Serum magnesium and 24-hour urinary magnesium excretion are useful in evaluating possible magnesium deficiency. Muscle and bone biopsies have been used to assess total body magnesium (Cronin and Knochel 1983). The occurrence of hypomagnesemia in a significant percentage of patients with either hypokalemia, hyponatremia, hypophosphatemia, or hypocalcemia has led to the recommendation of serum magnesium determination in patients discovered to have a deficiency of one of these more routinely measured electrolytes (Whang et al. 1984).

Treatment. In mild deficiencies, body stores can often be quickly replenished by a high-magnesium diet (meat, seafoods, green vegetables, cereals, and dairy products); oral magnesium supplementation may also be used. In more severe losses, parenteral magnesium salts are safe and effective, especially in patients with symptomatic hypomagnesemia or malabsorption; caution must be used in cases of renal disease. Most neuromuscular signs respond quickly to magnesium replacement (Cronin and Knochel 1983). It has been reported that psychiatric manifestations may be among the first signs to appear and may take longer than other CNS symptoms to resolve following treatment (Hall and Joffe 1973).

Hypermagnesemia

Etiology. Because of the normal kidney's ability to excrete a magnesium load, hypermagnesemia occurs almost exclusively either in patients with severe renal failure or in patients with milder degrees of renal impairment accompanied by treatment with magnesium-containing salts or antacids. Excess ionized magnesium is thought to block neuromuscular transmission by decreasing acetylcholine release at the neuromuscular junction (Epstein 1980).

Symptomatology. Mild magnesium elevations may be associated with variable nonspecific symptoms (e.g., low blood pressure, facial flushing, nausea, vomiting). Cardiac effects usually become apparent at magnesium levels above 10 meq/l. These include peripheral vasodilatation leading to hypotension, generalized depression of cardiac conduction, bradyarrhythmias, and asystole, with cardiac arrest in diastole associated with extremely high levels greater than 25 meq/l (Smith 1985a).

Neuropsychiatrically, symptoms of lethargy, dysarthria, and drowsiness appear when the serum magnesium level reaches 5 to 7 meq/l, progressing to coma at 15 meq/l. Magnesium exerts a curare-

like effect at the neuromuscular junction, leading to the usual loss of deep tendon reflexes when the serum level reaches about 7 meq/l; further increases in serum magnesium lead to progressive weakness and paralysis that may be counteracted by physostigmine. Depression of the respiratory center with progressive respiratory distress occurs at magnesium levels greater than 10 meq/l; because deep tendon reflexes disappear before respirations are depressed, the presence of knee jerks has been suggested as a reliable sign that the hypermagnesemia is not life-threatening (Epstein 1980).

Diagnosis. In addition to serum and 24-hour urinary magnesium measurements, renal status and exogenous sources of magnesium must be investigated. EKG at higher serum levels may show bradycardia, QT interval prolongation, and depressed atrioventricular and intraventricular conduction (Epstein 1980).

Treatment. Removal of the exogenous source is usually sufficient to treat mild forms of hypermagnesemia. In the presence of cardiac or respiratory depression, emergency treatment includes ventilatory support and the intravenous administration of calcium, a pharmacologic antagonist of magnesium, and of glucose and insulin to promote temporary magnesium influx intracellularly. Patients with severe renal impairment or life-threatening hypermagnesemia should receive hemodialysis with a magnesium-free solution (Parfitt and Kleerekoper 1980).

Phosphorus

Phosphorus is the principal intracellular anion. About 80 percent of the body's phosphorus is in bone, 9 percent is in skeletal muscle, and the rest is distributed in the soft tissues. A small proportion is found in the ECF, where normal concentrations are in the range of 2.7 to 4.5 mg/dl in adults and 4.0 to 7.1 mg/dl in children (Knochel 1977). Phosphorus is mainly absorbed in the intestine in the form of phosphate. Phosphate balance is maintained by the kidney through a combination of glomerular filtration and tubular reabsorption. Parathyroid hormone (PTH) decreases proximal tubular reabsorption of phosphate.

Phosphorus is essential for the structural and functional integrity of all cells. It is an integral constituent of bone, and, as part of phospholipids, it is necessary for the structure of all cell membranes. It is a component of nucleotides and nucleic acids. Phosphorylated adenine and guanine nucleosides are involved in the storage and transformation of energy, vital to all anabolic and catabolic cellular processes. Phosphorus is a urinary buffer and is a cofactor in a variety of enzyme reactions. By regulating the level of 2,3-diphosphoglycerate (2,3-DPG) in erythrocytes, it has an important effect on oxygen delivery to tissues. Inorganic phosphorus regulates the rate of glycolysis. Clinically, because hyperphosphatemia has few neuropsychiatric effects, this discussion will focus on hypophosphatemia.

Hypophosphatemia

Etiology. Because phosphorus is present in widespread abundance in foods, phosphorus deficiency is rare under normal conditions. Symptoms may occur, however, with a selective dietary deficiency and ingestion of large quantities of phosphate-binding antacids. Moderate hypophosphatemia (serum levels between 1.0 and 2.5 mg/dl) can be caused by conditions resulting in (1) transcellular shifts of phosphorus, as occurs with salicylate poisoning, sepsis, acute gout, and parenteral administration of insulin, glucose, or fructose; (2) increased urinary excretion, as seen in hyperparathyroidism, renal tubular defects, and the administration of steroids, diuretics, bicarbonate, and glucagon; and (3) decreased intestinal absorption from starvation, vitamin D deficiency, and malabsorption syndromes (Janson et al. 1983). Interestingly, starvation rarely causes significant hypophosphatemia, and hyperparathyroidism is seldom associated with phosphorus concentrations below 1.5 mg/dl (Knochel 1977). Conditions associated with further depletion of serum phosphorus levels below 1.0 mg/dl include uncontrolled diabetes (treatment of ketoacidosis and hyperosmolar nonketotic coma), chronic alcoholism and alcohol withdrawal, phosphate-binding antacids, prolonged respiratory alkalosis, rapid nutritional recovery from malnutrition, and recovery from severe burns (Janson et al. 1983).

Symptomatology. Symptoms of hypophosphatemia are associated with severe deficiencies (serum levels below 1.0 mg/dl). Chronic hypophosphatemia commonly leads to changes associated with metabolic bone disease. More acute depletions are associated with hematologic abnormalities (erythrocyte, leukocyte, and platelet dysfunctions), impaired myocardial performance, hepatic dysfunction, muscle weakness, rhabdomyolysis and CNS impairment (Knochel 1977; Smith 1985b).

Early nonspecific symptoms of phosphorus depletion include anorexia, weakness, and bone pain. Severe hypophosphatemia has been associated with neuropsychiatric symptoms consistent with a metabolic encephalopathy: irritability, apprehension, muscular weakness, tremor, numbness, paresthesias, dysarthria, confusion, obtundation, seizures, and coma. Hyperventilation and respiratory failure from advanced respiratory muscle weakness have been described. The EEG may show diffuse slowing. Postulated mechanisms for the development of CNS symptoms include impaired brain glucose utilization and reduced 2,3-DPG-dependent brain cell oxygenation (Knochel 1977; Janson et al. 1983).

Diagnosis. Diagnostic investigations include identification of the underlying cause of the hypophosphatemia in addition to appropriate serum and urine chemistries. Because phosphorus is primarily an intracellular anion, hypophosphatemia does not necessarily indicate phosphorus depletion; conversely, serious phosphorus depletion may exist with normal or even elevated serum inorganic phosphorus concentrations (Knochel 1977).

Treatment. Chronic, asymptomatic, moderate hypophosphatemia (levels between 1.0 to 2.5 mg/dl) can be treated by reduction or removal of offending agents (e.g., diuretics, antacids) and increased ingestion of phosphorus with low-fat milk or oral phosphate salts. Severe phosphate depletion (serum levels below 1.0 mg/dl), particularly when accompanied by serious neurologic complications, requires parenteral treatment with either potassium or sodium phosphate solutions (Janson et al. 1983). Contraindications to the use of phosphate salts and the potential hazards of phosphate therapy are discussed elsewhere (Knochel 1977).

☐ RENAL FAILURE

Uremic Encephalopathy

The clinical signs and symptoms of end-stage renal disease comprise the uremic syndrome. Multiple organ systems are affected, and normally the adult patient is unaware of the advancing condition until the glomerular filtration rate has decreased to 20 ml/minute (Kokko 1985). Acute renal failure may result in a variety of neuropsychiatric presentations, usually secondary to underlying physical illnesses or fluid and electrolyte abnormalities (Marshall 1979). Chronic renal failure, however, is associated with a continuum of CNS dysfunctions.

Symptomatology. Early behavioral symptoms of renal failure include apathy, fatigue, drowsiness, dysarthria, lethargy, and social withdrawal. Mood changes may range from constriction of affect to irritability and emotional lability, with demanding behavior and angry outbursts. Early intellectual deficits are episodic and include inability to concentrate, decreased attention span, and impaired recent and long-term memory. Psychological testing has shown impairment in higher cortical functioning and deterioration in nonverbal intelligence. Selective cortical dysfunctions have been demonstrated in patients with advanced renal failure that were qualitatively different from deficits in controls with neurologic or medical/psychiatric disorders (Souheaver et al. 1982).

As uremia progresses, anorexia, weight loss, and decreased sexual interest may lead the patient to be diagnosed as depressed. Total or partial impotence is common in patients with chronic uremia; autonomic nervous system dysfunction has been suggested to be important etiologically (Campese et al. 1982). Further progression of the uremic syndrome leads to the development of a classic delirium. Confusion, hallucinations, delusions, disorientation, and stupor may be present. Clouding of the sensorium is often associated with a variety of motor disturbances, including peripheral neuropathy, myopathy, gait abnormalities, tremor, multifocal myoclonus, and asterixis. Characteristic muscle twitches and jerking may appear, often associated with seizures and sometimes referred to as the uremic twitch-convulsive syndrome (Adams and Victor 1985). More advanced renal failure may result in focal neurologic deficits, coma, and death. As is common in delirium, the symptoms tend to fluctuate in intensity. Patients occasionally progress to stupor and coma without delirium (Marshall 1979).

Diagnosis and Pathophysiology. The EEG in patients with mild renal failure may be normal or of low voltage. As uremia worsens, there is loss of

normal alpha activity followed by progressive background slowing, eventually leading to diffuse slowing with spiking; paroxysmal bursts of slow waves may occur without clinical evidence of seizures (Marshall 1979). The cause of EEG abnormalities in uremia has not been definitely established but may be related to the effect of elevated PTH on the brain; routinely measured indicators of renal failure have not correlated with the presence of encephalopathy. Cerebral edema is absent. Animal studies have shown increased permeability to organic acids, impaired energy utilization with decreased metabolic rate, and alterations in cerebral oxygen consumption in the uremic brain (Arieff and Schmidt 1980).

Treatment. Treatment of uremic encephalopathy is related to the nature of the renal disease. In reversible renal failure, restoration of renal function may correct the neurologic syndrome, but the prognosis is poor in progressive renal failure without dialysis or renal transplantation. Seizures respond to relatively low concentrations of anticonvulsants (Adams and Victor 1985). There is a lag period in the response of neuropsychiatric symptoms to dialysis (Marshall 1979). Dialysis is associated with a host of psychological factors that will not be addressed in this discussion; however, two dialysis-related metabolic conditions—dialysis disequilibrium syndrome (DDS) and dialysis dementia—deserve inclusion here.

Dialysis Disequilibrium Syndrome

DDS is a symptom complex, more common in younger patients, that usually occurs late during the course of, or soon after, hemodialysis. Formerly called the reverse urea syndrome, its exact cause has not been established, although consistent findings of elevated CSF pressure and brain swelling in patients dying with the disorder have led to the postulation of cerebral edema as the primary pathogenic factor (Arieff and Schmidt 1980). Early symptoms include restlessness, mild drowsiness, and headache progressing to nausea, vomiting, blurred vision, and hypertension. Sensorium changes vary from lassitude and apathy to agitation and disorientation. Increasing muscle irritability may lead to generalized seizures; without treatment, coma and death may follow. The EEG frequently becomes abnormal during the disequilibrium period but returns to predialysis status within 48 hours.

Prophylactic anticonvulsants can be used to prevent seizures. The syndrome may be avoided by slower dialysis over a longer period, by more frequent but shorter dialysis periods, or by a slower alteration in osmolality with dialysis against a high glucose concentration. The syndrome tends to be self-limited and reversible if the biochemical changes are not extreme (Marshall 1979).

Dialysis Encephalopathy (Dialysis Dementia)

Alfrey et al. (1976) initially described a progressive, fatal encephalopathy in patients on long-term dialysis. Clinical features include a mixed dysarthria-apraxia of speech, asterixis, myoclonus, dementia, and focal seizures. Characteristic EEG changes consist of generalized slowing with multifocal bursts of delta activity and spikes. The dementia is global, with confusion, disorientation, and memory impairment; behavioral symptoms may include personality changes, paranoid ideation, hallucinations, and bizarre behavior (Marshall 1979). Increased aluminum content in the brains of patients who died of this syndrome led Alfrey et al. to postulate aluminum intoxication from dialysate and aluminum-containing gels as the etiologic mechanism; this remains the commonly accepted theory. Interrupting aluminum intake early in the syndrome may reverse the symptoms of the encephalopathy. The incidence of the syndrome has been reduced in recent years, largely due to improved purification procedures that have resulted in less aluminum in dialysate water. Once thought to be uniformly fatal, gradual although not necessarily complete recovery can occur following renal transplantation early in the disease. Because transplantation late in the course of the encephalopathy does not halt the downhill progression to coma and death, early recognition is important (Parkinson et al. 1981).

Uremic Polyneuropathy

Polyneuropathy is probably the most common complication of renal failure, occurring to some degree in up to 70 percent of patients starting or continuing dialysis (Adams and Victor 1985). It usually presents with gradually progressive symmetrical muscle weakness and atrophy of the legs and then the arms, with loss of reflexes and variable sensory involvement. A severe rapidly progressive neuropathy has been reported in four patients with end-stage renal disease associated with accelerated hypertension and sepsis (McGonigle et al. 1985).

The cause of uremic polyneuropathy is unknown. Pathologically, there is nonspecific axonal degeneration with secondary segmental demyelination. Long-term hemodialysis may prevent further progression of the neuropathy, but peritoneal dialysis has been more successful than hemodialysis in causing any improvement in the symptoms. Successful renal transplantation may lead to a rapid resolution of symptoms over weeks to months. The postulated mechanism is the "middle molecule" theory, in which nondialyzable uremic neurotoxins that accumulate during renal failure are removed by the transplanted kidney (Adams and Victor 1985). In a study from Greece, nine uremic patients undergoing chronic hemodialysis showed marked improvement in encephalopathy and peripheral neuropathy within 3 months of the initiation of treatment with oral biotin, 10 mg tid (Yatzidis et al. 1984).

Complications of Renal Failure and Its Treatments

Subdural hematoma and cerebral hemorrhage may occur in dialysis patients as a result of anticoagulant therapy to maintain the patency of arterovenous shunts or because of abnormal bleeding associated with advanced renal failure. Nutritional depletion in uremic patients has been associated with findings of Wernicke-Korsakoff disease and central pontine myelinolysis. Immunosuppression following renal transplantation predisposes to the development of systemic infections that may involve the CNS (Adams and Victor 1985).

☐ LIVER FAILURE

Hepatic Encephalopathy

Hepatic encephalopathy, also known as portal-systemic encephalopathy (PSE), is seen in patients with severe hepatic insufficiency secondary to acute liver failure or chronic hepatocellular disease with or without portal systemic shunting of blood. It is commonly considered to arise secondary to the extracellular accumulation of toxic products that have not been metabolized by the liver. Hyperammonemia has been most implicated, but accumulations of potentially toxic amino acids and their metabolites (e.g., glutamine, alpha-ketoglutarate, methionine, mercaptans, tryptophan, and other aromatic amino acids) have been demonstrated. Other mechanisms that may be involved include changes in the blood-brain barrier, alterations in fatty acid metabolism, abnormal neurotransmitter balance, disturbed cerebral metabolism, and impaired neuronal membrane function (Fraser and Arieff 1985; Hoyumpa et al. 1979). The encephalopathy can also be seen in children with congenital urea-cycle enzyme defects and rarely in patients with surgical porta-caval shunts without prior parenchymal liver disease (Hoyumpa et al. 1979).

Etiology. In addition to liver failure from primary liver pathology (e.g., hepatitis, cirrhosis, liver cancer), other factors may precipitate or aggravate hepatic encephalopathy. These include azotemia (spontaneous or diuretic-induced), drugs (e.g., sedatives, tranquilizers, anesthetics, analgesics), gastrointestinal bleeding, metabolic alkalosis, infection, constipation, excess dietary protein, heart failure, hypoxia, hypokalemia, and fluid and electrolyte disturbances (Fraser and Arieff 1985; Hoyumpa et al. 1979).

Symptomatology. Neuropsychiatrically, hepatic encephalopathy involves varying degrees of neurologic dysfunction with alterations in state of consciousness, intellectual function, personality, and behavior. The severity and extent of symptoms are related to the acuteness and extent of liver failure as well as to the presence of complicating factors. Presentations may vary widely. The encephalopathy often consists of a derangement of consciousness in which initial confusion with psychomotor agitation or retardation gives way to progressive drowsiness, stupor, and coma.

Criteria may be used for grading mental status changes, as described by Conn and Lieberthal (1979): Grade 0 is considered normal. Grade I is characterized by mild lack of awareness, euphoria, or anxiety; shortened attention span; and impairment in simple calculations. Grade II shows apathy, lethargy, disorientation to time, obvious personality change, and inappropriate behavior. Patients with grade III encephalopathy are somnolent or semistuporous, but respond to stimuli and show confusion and gross disorientation. Grade IV is characterized by stupor progressing to coma. Fetor hepaticus, a characteristic odor thought to be produced by mercaptans, is believed to be present in all patients in stage IV hepatic coma (Fraser and Arieff 1985). Although staging may be useful, patients often do not show an orderly progression of mental status changes.

Characteristic neurologic signs early in the encephalopathy may include asterixis, myoclonus, facial grimacing, blinking, and hyperactive deep tendon reflexes, as well as primitive suck, snout, and grasp reflexes. As the encephalopathy progresses, extensor toe responses, clonus, and decerebrate or decorticate posturing may be present; areflexia and generalized flaccidity may occur preterminally (Scharschmidt 1985). Focal or generalized seizures may occur.

The course of hepatic encephalopathy may be quite variable. It often evolves over days to weeks and terminates fatally. Some patients may not progress beyond mild neuropsychiatric deficits; others may show intermittent or chronic fluctuating disturbances that are reversible with appropriate therapy. Another group of patients may develop irreversible symptoms of mild dementia and persistent neurologic dysfunction with gait ataxia, tremor, rigidity, dysarthria, grimacing, and choreoathetosis (Adams and Victor 1985). Encephalopathy with chronic liver disease may present as single or recurrent episodes of coma, chronic cerebral degeneration, or occasionally as a spastic paraparesis (Hoyumpa et al. 1979).

The EEG in hepatic encephalopathy shows generalized slowing accompanied by high voltage and slow wave forms. Paroxysmal bursts of triphasic waves and paroxysms of delta waves are commonly present; these findings are characteristic but not specific for PSE (Fraser and Arieff 1985).

The primary neuropathologic finding in the brains of patients with PSE is the presence of increased size and number of protoplasmic astrocytes called Alzheimer Type II cells; Alzheimer Type I astrocytes are also present. A less clear-cut feature is the degeneration of nerve cells and myelin sheaths in the deeper layers of the cerebral cortex and subadjacent white matter (particularly the parietal lobes), the basal ganglia, and the cerebellar cortex (Conn and Lieberthal 1979). Like the EEG features, spongy degeneration and Alzheimer Type II astrocytosis are characteristic but not specific for hepatic encephalopathy. These morphologic changes are not present in patients with acute fulminant hepatic failure, which develops most commonly as a complication of viral hepatitis but may also occur following exposure to certain drugs or hepatotoxins. The major finding in the brains of these patients is cerebral edema, which is often severe enough to be the cause of death (Fraser and Arieff 1985).

Diagnosis. The diagnosis of hepatic encephalopathy is clinical, with a history and physical examination suggestive of liver failure and a neurologic examination demonstrating neuromuscular dysfunctions and mental status changes. Routine blood chemistries and liver function tests are helpful to assess the severity of hepatic disease and to rule out other causes of metabolic encephalopathy. Jaundice is usually present in acute liver failure but may not be present in chronic cirrhosis. Because hyperammonemia occurs in many but not all patients with hepatic encephalopathy, the use of the blood ammonia level to diagnose the disorder is unreliable; it may be more useful in monitoring the clinical course of individual patients. CSF glutamine is usually elevated in PSE and may be more specific than blood ammonia levels, except when complicating renal failure alters the levels of both compounds (Fraser and Arieff 1985).

Treatment. The therapy of hepatic encephalopathy is designed to reduce the amounts of toxic metabolites in the blood. Factors that precipitate or aggravate the encephalopathy should be identified and corrected. The mainstay of therapy is the administration of either lactulose or neomycin. In a double-blind crossover investigation, both were shown to be effective in lowering serum ammonia levels and improving clinical symptoms in chronic PSE (Conn et al. 1977). Bowel cleansing with cathartics and enemas is a valuable adjunctive treatment. Less well-established therapies reported to be of some benefit in PSE include protein restriction, use of branched-chain amino acid supplements or ketoanalogs of essential amino acids, and administration of metronidazole, bromocriptine, lactose, or L-dopa (Fraser and Arieff 1985).

Encephalopathy in acute fulminant hepatic failure usually reflects the severe nature of the underlying liver injury. In addition to the previously mentioned general treatments, therapy must also be directed toward the treatment of potential complications of fulminant hepatic failure, such as hypoglycemia, hyponatremia, hypokalemia, azotemia, hypovolemia, bleeding, disseminated intravascular coagulation, sepsis, pulmonary edema, respiratory alkalosis, and cerebral edema (Scharschmidt 1985). Once thought to be beneficial, corticosteroid therapy has not been effective and is no longer

recommended in the treatment of fulminant hepatic failure or associated cerebral edema (Hoyumpa et al. 1979).

Reye Syndrome

Reye syndrome is a special type of nonicteric hepatic encephalopathy characterized by acute brain swelling and fatty infiltration of the viscera, especially the liver. Most cases occur in childhood, usually following a viral infection. There is rapid progression to stupor and coma, often with focal and generalized seizures. The CSF pressure is usually increased, as are serum glutamic oxaloacetic transaminase (SGOT) and ammonia levels; the EEG shows diffuse arrhythmic delta activity. The main pathologic findings are cerebral edema and infiltration of hepatocytes with fine fat droplets; the pathogenesis is unknown. In the past, the mortality rate was quite high once the child became comatose, but early diagnosis and initiation of treatment prior to the onset of coma have reduced the fatality rate to 5 to 10 percent. Treatment, designed to correct the metabolic derangements and reduce the intracranial pressure, includes temperature and ventilatory control, maintenance of blood glucose and fluid and electrolyte balance, neomycin enemas, and the control of intracranial pressure by continual monitoring and the use of hypertonic solutions. Cerebral function is normal after recovery unless there was deep and prolonged coma (Adams and Victor 1985).

☐ HEAVY METALS

Lead Intoxication

Perhaps the best studied of the trace metal poisonings, lead toxicity is a well-recognized complication of acute and chronic lead exposure in both children and adults.

Etiology. Exposure may occur from a variety of environmental sources, both domestic and occupational. The abnormal ingestion (pica) of lead-based paints found in old houses is probably the most common cause of lead intoxication in children. Ingestion of other lead-containing objects, as well as contaminated food, water, air, dust, and soil, can contribute to pediatric lead toxicity (Chisolm and Barltrop 1979). Lead is widely used in industry, with significant risk of exposure in a variety of occupations where it is used in manufacturing and processing. Nonoccupational sources of lead poisoning include ingestion of lead-pipe distilled moonshine, inhalation of gasoline fumes, and retention of bullets and lead shot (Cullen et al. 1983).

Symptomatology. Clinically, lead toxicity in adults can cause hematologic, gastrointestinal, rheumatologic, renal, endocrine, and neurologic impairments (Cullen et al. 1983). Neuropsychiatrically, presentation of lead toxicity in children is often different than in adults. Largely as the result of increased public awareness, effective screening programs, and early treatment, the incidence of acute lead encephalopathy, the most severe form of lead poisoning, has been greatly reduced. Children are much more likely to develop encephalopathy than adults. Early nonspecific CNS symptoms of lead intoxication include anorexia, apathy, irritability, abdominal pain, vomiting, headache, emotional lability, incoordination, sleep disturbance, and memory lapses. Continued lead exposure leads to the rapid development of signs of encephalopathy such as disorientation, psychosis, ataxia, syncope, focal neurologic signs, delirium, and lethargy progressing to stupor, seizures, and coma. This syndrome most commonly occurs during the summer months in children under 3 years of age. Pathologically, the brain shows massive edema with vascular changes. Chelation therapy has reduced the mortality to under 5 percent, but, when the therapy is begun after the symptoms of acute encephalopathy appear, 25 to 50 percent of survivors show permanent neuropsychiatric sequelae such as seizures and mental retardation (Chisolm and Barltrop 1979). Atypical presentations of lead encephalopathy in children may be confused with other conditions (Selbst et al. 1985). Most of the infrequent adult cases of encephalopathy have been associated with illicit whiskey. Seizures are the most common symptom, but obtundation, confusion, focal motor deficits, papilledema, headaches, and optic neuritis have also been described. Chelation therapy has been reported to be helpful, but the outcome was complicated by coexisting alcoholism in most cases (Cullen et al. 1983).

Considerable debate has been focused on the "subclinical" effects of lead in children found to have increased lead absorption with no symptoms or with only mild nonspecific symptoms of lead

toxicity. While some reports implicate lead exposure in the etiology of neuropsychologic deficits that may interfere with classroom performance (Needleman et al. 1979), others suggest that the causative contribution of lead is small relative to other influencing factors such as social background (Winneke and Kraemer 1984). Adults with subclinical CNS effects associated with lead absorption may show nonspecific symptoms such as fatigue, irritability, insomnia, nervousness, headache, and weakness as well as abnormalities in neuropsychological testing (Cullen et al. 1983).

In contrast to encephalopathy, peripheral neuropathy associated with lead toxicity rarely occurs in children and is uncommon but more likely to be described in adults. The neuropathy is typically motor and primarily affects the upper extremities, with weakness and decreased motor nerve conduction velocities associated with heavy intoxications. The appearance of clinical neuropathy seems to be related to the severity and duration of lead exposure. Sensory and cranial nerve involvement and a syndrome similar to amyotrophic lateral sclerosis have been less frequently described (Cullen et al. 1983).

Psychiatrically, organic affective illness has been associated with lead intoxication (Schottenfeld and Cullen 1984). Common subtle nonspecific presenting signs of chronic lead intoxication may be confused with depression (Cullen et al. 1983). Organic lead intoxication from inhaling gasoline fumes containing tetraethyl and tetramethyl lead additives can cause insomnia, irritability, nervousness, euphoria, delusions, hallucinations, and convulsions. Controversies surrounding the behavioral effects of increased lead absorption in children have been previously described, and the association between increased lead absorption and hyperactivity in children remains unclear (Chisolm and Barltrop 1979).

Diagnosis. Often the most important diagnostic factor is identifying a history of lead exposure. Whole blood lead levels of 30 μg/dl or more in children and 40 μg/dl or more in adults are generally considered evidence of excessive lead absorption (Louria 1985). Levels in this range have been associated with subclinical symptoms (see above); higher reference levels established for lead toxicity in children and adults must be evaluated in the context of symptomatology at lower levels. Delta-aminolevulinic acid and coproporphyrin levels are increased in the urine.

Treatment. It is critical to remove the patient from further lead exposure. Chelating agents such as dimercaprol (BAL), calcium disodium edetate (EDTA), and penicillamine are used to bind lead and promote tissue excretion. Initial improvement from reduction in blood lead levels may be followed by reemergence of symptoms necessitating further treatment as lead is mobilized from bone, its principal storage reservoir. Although treatment response in both acute and chronic lead poisoning has been favorable, complete resolution has only been shown for gastrointestinal and hematologic effects (Cullen et al. 1983). Because neuropsychiatric manifestations often improve slowly and incompletely, early recognition and treatment are important to minimize permanent damage.

☐ INHERITED METABOLIC BRAIN DISEASE

The Hepatic Porphyrias

Porphyrias are a rare group of disorders characterized by abnormalities in heme production. They may be classified as either erythropoietic or hepatic, depending on the major site of the metabolic abnormality. This discussion will be limited to the hepatic porphyrias, which have prominent neuropsychiatric findings.

Etiology. The hereditary hepatic porphyrias result from enzyme deficiencies in the biosynthetic pathways of heme. Acute intermittent porphyria (AIP) results from a reduction in uroporphyrinogen-I synthetase (porphobilinogen [PBG] deaminase) activity. In variegate porphyria (VP), there is a partial deficiency of protoporphyrinogen oxidase. Hereditary coproporphyria (HC) has reduced levels of coproporphyrinogen oxidase. All of these disorders have autonomal dominant inheritance patterns. The different enzyme defects result in differing patterns of heme precursor excretion in these disorders, but because the neuropyschiatric symptoms are indistinguishable, they will be considered as a group in this discussion.

The hallmark of the porphyrias is the acute attack resulting from an increased demand for heme synthesis secondary to endogenous (e.g., infection, fasting) or exogenous factors. A number of drugs may precipitate attacks, including barbiturates, chlordiazepoxide, estrogens, ethanol, griseo-fulvin, hydantoins, imipramine, meprobamate, methyldopa, and sulfonamides (Bissell 1985).

Symptomatology. Neurologic symptoms are common in the acute attack, which can have a variable presentation; generalized seizures, psychosis, or confusion may be the initial symptoms. Abdominal pain is the most frequent symptom and is thought to be due to an autonomic neuropathy; accompanying fever and leukocytosis may initially confuse the diagnosis. Other features possibly related to autonomic dysfunction include tachycardia, labile hypertension with postural hypotension, urinary retention, and diaphoresis (Bloomer 1976). Anorexia, nausea, vomiting, and constipation are frequent. Peripheral neuropathy is often present, with both motor and sensory involvement reported. The course may vary from slowly progressive paresthesias and weakness to a rapidly developing flaccid paralysis with bulbar involvement leading to quadriplegia, respiratory failure, and death. Although generally regarded as reversible, the neuropathy may result in residual weakness lasting years after the acute attack. Both demyelination and axonal degeneration have been described (Becker and Kramer 1977). Conduction velocity studies have shown an association between slight peripheral neuropathy and latent hereditary hepatic porphyria, even in patients who had never experienced symptoms (Mustajoki and Seppalainen 1975).

Psychiatric manifestations in the hepatic porphyrias are also common and may precede neurologic symptoms. An organic brain syndrome with restlessness, disorientation, and hallucinations frequently occurs. Seizures may be present. Psychosis, depression, and hysteria have also been described and may be related to cerebral disturbances. Hypothalamic involvement has been suggested as the cause of associated hyponatremia. The relationship between the hepatic biochemical abnormality and neuropsychiatric manifestations remains unclear; postulated mechanisms include a decrease in heme-containing compounds in the nervous system or potential neurotoxicity from overproduction of porphyrin precursors (Becker and Kramer 1977).

Carriers of these metabolic defects may complain of body aches and mood swings in the absence of acute attacks; the diagnosis of these vague symptoms as being related to porphyria is often difficult to establish because the excretion of heme precursors varies widely among asymptomatic carriers.

Diagnosis. Urinary PBG is elevated during acute attacks in all three porphyrias and remains elevated while symptoms persist; delta-aminolevulinic acid is also elevated. Elevation of urinary PBG is characteristic in AIP, fecal coproporphyrin in HC, and fecal protoporphyrin in VP; these tests can also be used to identify the asymptomatic carrier state (Bissell 1979). However, urinary PBG may be within normal limits in 20 to 30 percent of carriers of AIP; in these cases, measurement of erythrocyte PBG deaminase is used for carrier identificaton (Bissell 1985). The urine in patients with AIP may darken when exposed to light from conversion of PBG to porphobilin. Cutaneous symptoms associated with porphyrin overproduction may be seen in HC and VP but are absent in AIP, in which porphyrin precursors accumulate.

Treatment. Identification and education of families at risk is important in the prevention of attacks.

Carriers should be identified via the appropriate screening procedure; conditions or drugs that may precipitate acute attacks should be avoided. In the acute attack, offending drugs should be removed, carbohydrate should be given to reverse the fasting state, electrolyte abnormalities should be corrected, and other complications should be treated symptomatically. Seizures generally respond to parenteral diazepam; propranolol may be helpful in controlling tachycardia. Chlorpromazine and meperidine have been used for analgesia. If acute manifestations fail to respond within 48 hours, treatment with hematin is recommended to compensate for the impairment in endogenous heme synthesis. Hematin and modern critical care have significantly reduced the mortality of acute attacks. Neurologic deficits may require months or years to resolve, but recovery often occurs. Mental abnormalities usually do not persist after acute attacks. Most carriers remain asymptomatic without an effect on longevity if they avoid offending drugs (Bissell 1985).

TABLE 2.   SELECTED INHERITED METABOLIC DISEASES AFFECTING THE NERVOUS SYSTEM

Neonatal metabolic disease (Birth to 1 month)
  Pyridoxine dependency
  Galactosemia
  Inherited-hyperammonemic syndromes
  Disorders of branched-chain amino acids (maple
    syrup urine disease and variants)

Diseases of early infancy (1–12 months)
  Tay-Sachs disease (Gm$_2$ gangliosidosis)
  Infantile Gancher's disease
  Infantile Neimann-Pick disease
  Infantile GM$_1$ (type I) generalized gangliosidosis
  Krabbe disease (globoid-body leukodystrophy)
  Farber disease (lipogranulomatosis)
  Pelizaeus-Merzbacher/sudanophilic leukodystrophies
  Spongy degeneration (Canavan-Van Bogaert disease)
  Alpers disease
  Alexander disease
  Leigh disease (subacute necrotizing
    encephalomyelopathy)
  Congenital lactic acidosis

Late infancy/early childhood (1–4 years)
  Disorders of amino acid metabolism
    (aminoacidurias)
    Phenylketonurias
    Hartrup disease
    Homocystinuria
  Progressive cerebellar ataxias of early childhood
    Refsum disease
    Ataxia-Telangectasia
  Metachromatic leukodystrophy

Neuroaxonal dystrophy (degeneration)
Late infantile and early childhood Gaucher and
  Neimann-Pick disease
Late infantile/childhood GM$_1$ gangliosidosis
Mucopolysaccharidoses
  Hurler disease
  Scheie disease
  Hunter disease
  Sanfilippo disease
  Sly disease (β-glucuronidase deficiency)
Mucolipidoses and other diseases of complex
  carbohydrates

Late childhood/adolescence
  Bassen-Kornzweig acanthocytosis
    (abetalipoproteinemia)
  Parkinsonian/extrapyramidal symptoms
    Wilson's disease (hepatolenticular degeneration)
    Hallervorden Spatz disease
    Juvenile Huntington's chorea
  Dystonia/generalized chorea and athetosis
    Lesch-Nyhan syndrome/hyperuricemia
    Familial calcification of vesselsin basal ganglia and
     cerebellum (Fahr syndrome)
  Familial polymyoclonias
    Lafora-body polymyoclonus
    Juvenile cerebroretinal lipofuscinosis
  Familial leukodystrophies
    Sudanophilic leukodystrophy
    Orthochromic leukodystrophy
    Cerebrotendinous xanthomatosis
  Fabry disease

Note. Adapted from Adams and Victor (1985).

Inborn Errors of Metabolism

Recent advances in biochemistry have resulted in the discovery of a consistently growing number of enzyme deficiencies, usually of autosomal recessive inheritance, in which a metabolic defect disturbs cellular function. This may occur either due to the accumulation of a harmful metabolite or to the lack of an essential substrate. The nervous system is particularly vulnerable to these metabolic insults because of its protracted growth and development that continues after birth. The symptoms vary according to the nature of the defect and the level of maturation of the nervous system when the disease strikes. Both the gray matter and white matter can be involved. Many of these diseases become apparent early in life, with a rapid downhill course if unrecognized and untreated. Table 2 is a partial list of these disorders based on the typical age at expression of the illness. Clinical symptoms may include failure to thrive, mental retardation, failure of neurologic and physical development, seizures, blindness, and weakness progressing to paralysis and terminal decerebration (Solomon 1985). Prenatal diagnosis and newborn screening tests have led to earlier recognition and treatment of some of these disorders; detection of a carrier state permits genetic counseling.

Because discussions of each of these illnesses is beyond the scope of this chapter, the reader is referred to standard texts of neurology, medicine, or metabolic diseases.

☐ REFERENCES

Adams RA, Victor M: Principles of Neurology. New York, McGraw-Hill, 1985

Alfrey AC, LeGendre GR, Kaehny WD: The dialysis encephalopathy syndrome: possible aluminum intoxication. N Engl J Med 294:184–188, 1976

Andreoli TE: Disorders of fluid volume, electrolyte, and acid-base balance, in Cecil Textbook of Medicine. Edited by Wyngaarden JB, Smith LH Jr. Philadelphia, WB Saunders Co, 1985

Arieff AI, Guisado R: Effects on the central nervous system of hypernatremic and hyponatremic states. Kidney Int 10:104–116, 1976

Arieff AI, Schmidt RW: Fluid and electrolyte disorders and the central nervous system, in Clinical Disorders of Fluid and Electrolyte Metabolism. Edited by Maxwell MH, Kleeman CR. New York, McGraw-Hill, 1980

Becker DM, Kramer S: The neurological manifestations of porphyria: a review. Medicine 56:411–423, 1977

Bissell DM: Haem metabolism and the porphyrias, in Liver and Biliary Disease. Edited by Wright R, Alberti KGMM, Karran S, et al. London, WB Saunders Co, 1979

Bissell DM: Porphyria, in Cecil Textbook of Medicine. Edited by Wyngaarden JB, Smith LH Jr. Philadelphia, WB Saunders Co, 1985

Bloomer JR: The hepatic porphyrias: pathogenesis, manifestations and management. Gastroenterology 71:689–701, 1976

Blum A, Tempey FW, Lynch WJ: Somatic findings in patients with psychogenic polydipsia. J Clin Psychiatry 44:55–56, 1983

Bull GM, Carter AB, Lowe KG: Hyperpotassaemic paralysis. Lancet 2:60–63, 1953

Campese VM, Procci WR, Levitan D: Autonomic nervous system dysfunction and impotence in uremia. Am J Nephrol 2:140–143, 1982

Chisolm JJ Jr, Barltrop D: Recognition and management of children with increased lead absorption. Arch Dis Child 54:249–262, 1979

Conn HO, Lieberthal MM: The Hepatic Coma Syndromes and Lactulose. Baltimore, Williams & Wilkins Co, 1979

Conn HO, Leevy CM, Vlahcevic ZR, et al: Comparison of lactulose and neomycin in the treatment of chronic portal-systemic encephalopathy. Gastroenterology 72:573–583, 1977

Cronin RE, Knochel JP: Magnesium deficiency. Adv Intern Med 28:509–533, 1983

Cullen MR, Robins JM, Eskenazi B: Adult inorganic lead intoxication: presentation of 31 new cases and a review of recent advances in the literature. Medicine 62:221–247, 1983

Daggett P, Deanfield J, Moss F: Neurological aspects of hyponatremia. Postgrad Med J 58:737–740, 1982

DeFronzo RA, Bia M, Smith D: Clinical disorders of hyperkalemia. Annu Rev Med 33:521–554, 1982

Epstein FH: Signs and symptoms of electrolyte disorders, in Clinical Disorders of Fluid and Electrolyte Metabolism. Edited by Maxwell MH, Kleeman CR. New York, McGraw-Hill, 1980

Fraser CL, Arieff AI: Hepatic encephalopathy. N Engl J Med 313:865–873, 1985

Hafez H, Strauss JS, Aronson MD, et al: Hypokalemia-induced psychosis in a chronic schizophrenic patient. J Clin Psychiatry 45:277–279, 1984

Hall RCW, Joffe JR: Hypomagnesemia: physical and psychiatric symptoms. JAMA 224:1749–1751, 1973

Hariprasad MK, Eisinger RP, Nadler IM, et al: Hyponatremia in psychogenic polydipsia. Arch Intern Med 140:1639–1642, 1980

Hoyumpa AM Jr, Desmond PV, Avant GR, et al: Hepatic encephalopathy. Gastroenterology 76:184–195, 1979

Janson C, Birnbaum G, Baker FJ: Hypophosphatemia. Ann Emerg Med 12:107–116, 1983

Jose CJ, Perez-Cruet J: Incidence and morbidity of self-induced water intoxication in state mental hospital patients. Am J Psychiatry 136:221–222, 1979

Knochel JP: The pathophysiology and clinical characteristics of severe hypophosphatemia. Arch Intern Med 137:203–220, 1977

Kokko J: Chronic renal failure, in Cecil Textbook of Medicine. Edited by Wyngaarden JB, Smith LH Jr. Philadelphia, WB Saunders Co, 1985

Louria DB: Trace metal poisoning, in Cecil Textbook of Medicine. Edited by Wyngaarden JB, Smith LH Jr. Philadelphia, WB Saunders Co, 1985

Marshall JR: Neuropsychiatric aspects of renal failure. J Clin Psychiatry 40:81–85, 1979

McCance RA: Experimental sodium chloride deficiency in man. Proceedings of the Royal Society of Medicine 119:245–268, 1936

McGonigle RJS, Bewick M, Weston MJ, et al: Progressive, predominantly motor, uremic neuropathy. Acta Neurol Scand 71:379–384, 1985

Mustajoki P, Seppalainen AM: Neuropathy in latent hepatic porphyria. Br Med J 2:310–312, 1975

Nanji AA: Drug-induced electrolyte disorders. Drug Intell Clin Pharm 17:175–185, 1983

Needleman HL, Gunnoe C, Leviton A, et al: Deficits in psychologic and classroom performance of children with elevated dentine lead levels. N Engl J Med 300:689–695, 1979

Nixon RA, Rothman JS, Chin W: Demeclocycline in the prophylaxis of self-induced water intoxication. Am J Psychiatry 139:828–830, 1982

Parfitt AM, Kleerekoper M: Clinical disorders of calcium, phosphorus, and magnesium metabolism, in Clinical Disorders of Fluid and Electrolyte Metabolism. Edited by Maxwell MH, Kleeman CR. New York, McGraw-Hill, 1980

Parkinson IS, Ward MK, Kerr DNS: Dialysis encephalopathy, bone disease, and anaemia: the aluminum intoxication syndrome during regular haemodialysis. J Clin Pathol 34:1285–1294, 1981

Posner JB: Disturbances of consciousness and arousal, in Cecil Textbook of Medicine. Edited by Wyngaarden JB, Smith LH Jr. Philadelphia, WB Saunders Co, 1985

Raskind MA, Weitzman RE, Orenstein H: Is antidiuretic hormone elevated in psychosis? Biol Psychiatry 13:385–390, 1978

Scharschmidt BF: Acute and chronic hepatic failure with encephalopathy, in Cecil Textbook of Medicine. Edited by Wyngaarden JB, Smith LH Jr. Philadelphia, WB Saunders Co, 1985

Schottenfeld RS, Cullen MR: Organic affective illness associated with lead intoxication. Am J Psychiatry 141:1423–1426, 1984

Selbst SM, Henretig FM, Pearce J: Lead encephalopathy. Clin Pediatr (Phila) 24:280–285, 1985

Smith LH Jr: Disorders of magnesium metabolism, in Cecil Textbook of Medicine. Edited by Wyngaarden JB, Smith LH Jr. Philadelphia, WB Saunders Co, 1985a.

Smith LH Jr: Phosphorus deficiency and hypophosphatemia, in Cecil Textbook of Medicine. Edited by Wyngaarden JB, Smith LH Jr. Philadelphia, WB Saunders Co, 1985b

Solomon S: Clinical neurology and neuropathology, in Comprehensive Textbook of Psychiatry, Vol. 4. Edited by Kaplan HI, Sadock BJ. Baltimore, Williams & Wilkins Co, 1985

Souheaver GT, Ryan JJ, Dewolfe AS: Neuropsychological patterns in uremia. J Clin Psychol 38:490–496, 1982

Vieweg V, Rowe W, David J, et al: Hyposthenuria as a marker for self-induced water intoxication and schizophrenic disorders. Am J Psychiatry 141:1258–1260, 1984

Vieweg WVR, David JJ, Rowe WT, et al: Death from self-induced water intoxication among patients with schizophrenic disorders. J Nerv Ment Dis 173:161–165, 1985a

Vieweg WVR, Rowe WT, David JJ, et al: Oral sodium chloride in the management of schizophrenic patients with self-induced water intoxication. J Clin Psychiatry 46:16–19, 1985b

Whang R, Oei TO, Aikawa JK, et al: Predictors of clinical hypomagnesemia; hypokalemia, hypophosphatemia, hyponatremia, and hypocalcemia. Arch Intern Med 144:1794–1796, 1984

Winneke G, Kraemer U: Neuropsychological effects of lead in children: interactions with social background variables. Neuropsychobiology 11:195–202, 1984

Yatzidis H, Koutsicos D, Agroyannis B, et al: Biotin in the management of uremic neurologic disorders. Nephron 36:183–186, 1984

Chapter

17

Neuropsychiatric Aspects of Endocrine Disorders

William A. Rafuls, M.D.

Irl Extein, M.D.

Mark S. Gold, M.D.

Frederick C. Goggans, M.D.

INCREASING EVIDENCE HAS ACCUMULATED for an important complex relationship between the endocrine and nervous systems that includes the control and modulation of emotions and motivated behavior (Haskett and Rose 1981). In recent years there have been remarkable advances in the field of neuroendocrinology, which encompasses the neurologic control of endocrine secretion and hormonal effects on the nervous system. Neurophysiologic and neuroendocrine research has shown that the neuronal networks that are responsible for changes in behavior, mood, cognition, and perception are

activated by certain hormones (Martin et al. 1977). Hormones can influence brain function in many different ways. Some hormones act by disturbing the constancy and internal milieu that are necessary for normal functioning of neural cells; others act more directly on neurons to influence, for example, electrolyte flux and electric properties of cell membranes or synapses and rate of biosynthesis and turnover of central biogenic amines. Certain hormones affect the growth and differentiation of nerve cells and synapses; others react with specific receptors and neurons to activate genetically reprogrammed patterns of behavior and drive (Martin et al. 1977). Neuroendocrine mediators are critical both in maintaining homeostasis and in coordinating hormonal neuronal responses to environ-

Part of this chapter is reproduced with revisions from Groggans et al. (1986); reprinted with permission.

mental stimuli such as the stress response. The hypothalmic-pituitary-adrenal (HPA) axis appears to play a critical role in the coordination of the mammalian stress response.

The relationship between the endocrine system and mental functioning is a complex one. Stress can cause changes in many hormone levels. *Stress* is a vague term that has been used to refer both to environmental inputs and to endocrine response. The stress response can be defined as a behavioral and endocrine response to a stress—for example, Walter Cannon's term *fight or flight* (Martin et al. 1977). At the level of the hypothalamus, monoamine transmitters control the release of corticotropin-releasing factor (CRF) and other stress hormones. Hormones that are responsive to stressor stimuli include CRF, adrenocorticotropic hormone (ACTH), cortisol, vasopressin, prolactin, growth hormone, epinephrine, norepinephrine, and endorphins. In addition, the sympathetic nervous system becomes activated by stress.

Many reports of endocrine changes accompanying altered mental states have appeared during the past 30 years and have been reviewed several times (Haskett and Rose 1981; Leigh and Kramer 1984). Psychiatric symptoms are obvious findings of some endocrine disorders—the anxiousness of some hyperthyroid patients, the depression of hypothyroid patients, and the weakness and fatigue of patients with Addison's disease. Disturbances of certain physiologic parameters such as the level of calcium, steroid hormones, glucose, and thyroid hormones result in psychiatric symptoms. Many of these symptoms are reversed by correcting the underlying abnormality. The psychiatric symptoms of an endocrine disorder in any patient may result from, or be associated with, other factors, such as underlying personality disturbances and vulnerability of the individual, chronicity of the disorder, circumstances in which the illness occurs, and abnormalities in brain function (Martin et al. 1977). When psychiatric symptoms form a predominant part of the presenting disturbance, it is imperative for the evaluating clinician to have a high index of suspicion for endocrinopathy.

Psychiatric disorders are often seen in patients with primary disorders of the neuroendocrine system. These patients may either present with undiagnosed endocrinopathy directly to a psychiatrist or be referred to the consultation liaison service for treatment of a psychiatric illness that has complicated the course of a known endocrine disorder.

Hall et al. (1981) conducted a prospective study of 100 committed state hospital patients. The study revealed that 46 percent of the patients had a previously unrecognized and undiagnosed physical illness that was specifically related to their psychiatric symptoms and either caused these symptoms or substantially exacerbated them. In another study, Hall et al. (1978) investigated the etiologic role of medical illness in patients presenting with psychiatric symptoms. In a study of 658 outpatients, 9.1 percent proved to have a medical disorder that explained a presenting psychiatric complaint and 46 percent had a previously undiagnosed medical illness (Leigh and Kramer 1984).

Endocrine disorders present frequently with psychiatric symptoms. Of those endocrine disorders causing psychiatric symptoms, hypothyroidism has been found to be responsible for a large percentage. In the study by Hall et al. (1981), 8 percent of the patients showed hypothyroidism and 6 percent showed hyperthyroidism. The next most frequent are disorders of glucose regulation, with the most common being diabetes mellitus. Diabetes was found in 5 percent of the patients and hypoglycemia was found in 4 percent. In addition to thyroid disorders and disorders of glucose regulation, 1 percent of the patients had either Addison's disease or hyperparathyroidism. The total of endocrine disorders was 29 percent (Gold et al. 1984a; Hall et al. 1981).

☐ HYPOGLYCEMIA

Hypoglycemia occurs in many disorders in addition to diabetes mellitus. It is seen in alcoholism, barbiturate abuse, insulinomas, some gastrointestinal disorders, and other endocrine diseases (Marks and Rose 1965). Hypoglycemia may result from overutilization of glucose seen with insulin-secreting tumors, thyrotoxicosis, massive connective tissue sarcomas, and growth hormone deficiency. Deficiency in glucose production is seen with glycogen storage disease, extensive liver damage, and adrenal corticol or glucagon deficiency. During hypoglycemia attacks, patients may relapse into coma or behave in an abnormal way and, on recovery, have no memory of the attack. Some degree of organic brain syndrome is seen in 20 to 40 percent of hypoglycemic patients, with mild delirium occurring at serum glucose levels below 30 mg/100 ml, and coma occurring at levels below 10 mg/100 ml (Leigh and Kramer 1984). The rate of fall of serum glucose is more important than the absolute level.

Hypoglycemia can be manifested in various ways. Repeated episodes in any given patient are usually similar in symptomatology but may vary in severity. These symptoms may be divided into two groups. One group represents the stimulation of the sympathetic nervous system and includes pallor, weakness, palpitations, sweating, hunger, and tremor. The other set of symptoms is secondary to cerebral hypoglycemia; this includes mental disturbances of slow cerebration, aggressiveness, and impairment of speech and gait. More severe hypoglycemia causes somnolence alternating with agitation. Increased deep tendon reflexes, positive Babinski sign, and incoordination of the eye muscles can be observed. A further increase in severity causes coma with flaccidity or decerebrate rigidity, shallow respiration, cool moist skin, and hypothermia (Levin 1968). Marks and Rose (1965) separated cerebral hypoglycemia into three types: acute neuroglycopenia, subacute neuroglycopenia, and chronic neuroglycopenia. Acute neuroglycopenia is exemplified by an overdose of exogenous insulin. An acute episode includes anxiety, panic, detached feelings, hunger, palpitations, restlessness, tachycardia, facial flushing, diaphoresis, and unsteady gait. Subacute neuroglycopenia occurs with sustained periods of hypoglycemia. Increasing somnolence occurs, but consciousness can be retained for a variable rate. The behavior pattern is somewhat like that of an alcoholic with poor performance of habitual tasks. In its subacute form, symptoms of acute neuroglycopenia (autonomic type) are mild, if present at all. Chronic neuroglycopenia occurs after repeated episodes of prolonged hypoglycemia; this is typically the case in insulinoma. The obvious changes present in acute and subacute forms are not predominant in this type. Instead, insidious personality changes with decreasing memory, psychosis with paranoid features, and a mental deterioration leading to dementia are observed (Marks and Rose 1965).

One of the most common types of hypoglycemia is reactive. This occurs 2 to 3 hours after food intake. Symptoms resemble those of anxiety. This condition is thought to result primarily from epinephrine produced by hypoglycemia. Reactive hypoglycemia is common after subtotal gastrectomy, in early onset of diabetes mellitus, and following ingestion of galactose, fructose, or amino acids in

sensitive individuals. The epinephrine response to low serum glucose levels exactly mimics the anxiety syndromes seen in pure psychiatric disorders (Smith et al. 1972). Anxiety states occur in 20 to 40 percent of patients with hypoglycemia of varying etiology (Ettigi and Brown 1978). Hypoglycemic episodes may suggest or mimic conditions such as convulsive disorders, brain tumors, psychosis, or hysteria.

Hypoglycemic symptoms such as psychomotor retardation, poor performance of routine tasks, depersonalization, altered states of consciousness, perseverative thoughts and speech patterns, and confusion may appear as a part of a psychotic syndrome (Leigh and Kramer 1984). Chronic hypoglycemia may result in syndromes that closely resemble depression and dementia, especially in the absence of such overt signs or symptoms of epinephrine excess such as tachycardia, sweating, pallor, or anxiety (Sachs 1973). Chronic hypoglycemia of any etiology may present as depression. Elderly patients are more susceptible to hypoglycemic attacks, with neuropsychiatric symptoms that may be the first evidence of medical illness.

Insulinoma is one cause of hypoglycemia. Insulinoma is a rare tumor occurring more often in women and in the older age range. A single benign tumor usually less than or equal to 2 centimeters in diameter and located with about equal frequency in body, head, or tail of the pancreas is present in 80 percent of patients with insulinoma. Patients with this type of insulinoma may be cured by surgery. About 10 percent of patients with insulinoma have multiple tumors; in this group, there is a high incidence of multiple endocrine neoplasia type 1 syndrome. The remaining 10 percent of patients have metastatic malignant insulinoma. In all categories of insulinoma, symptoms are intermittent, recur at irregular intervals in food-deprived states over a median of 1.5 years, and arise from varying degrees of neuroglycopenia. Symptoms resulting from insulinoma often lead to misdiagnoses as neurologic or psychiatric disorders. Transient neurologic deficits and electroencephalogram (EEG) abnormalities may be present during hypoglycemia. Diagnosis of insulinoma requires repeated demonstration of hypoglycemia (i.e., glucose less than or equal to 40 mg/100 ml), relief with ingestion of carbohydrates, simultaneous hyperinsulinemia, and absence of insulin antibodies (Service et al. 1976). In a review of 60 patients with insulinoma, the diagnosis was suspected at the time of initial evaluation in most cases, but neurologic or psychiatric disorder was the initial diagnosis in 12 instances (Service et al. 1976).

☐ HYPERGLYCEMIA

High blood glucose levels are characteristically detected in untreated or poorly treated diabetics and occasionally in extremely stressed individuals. High plasma glucose levels cause hyperosmolarity, which may result in the gross encephalopathy seen in patients with renal failure. Hyperosmolarity is frequently fatal, but, if recovery should occur, patients show impaired intellectual function because of irreversible neuronal damage. Diabetics may suffer considerable intellectual deterioration secondary to their illness or to its treatment (Wilkinson 1981). Bale (1973) found that 17 of 100 insulin-dependent diabetics with a duration of illness of 15 years scored in the brain-damaged range on a new word learning test, whereas no matched controlled subject performed in this range. Test scores correlated with the apparent severity of previous hypoglycemic episodes and not with age, duration of illness, or obvious cerebral vascular disease. Accelerated cerebral atherosclerosis in diabetes may resemble a schizophrenic disorder. Controversy abounds regarding the relationship between manic-depressive illness and diabetes. Of the manic-depressive population, 10 percent were also diabetic compared to less than 4 percent of patients with other psychiatric diagnoses and 2 percent of national normative prevalence studies (Lilliker 1980).

☐ PANCREATIC CARCINOMA

There is consistency in the description of the affective disorder seen with pancreatic carcinoma as reviewed by Leigh and Kramer (1984). Depression and anxiety are frequently the presenting symptoms and may precede physical signs and symptoms by 6 months to several years. In a review of patients with pancreatic disease, 40 percent of those with pancreatic carcinoma presented with delirium; at least 10 percent of pancreatic cancer patients have an associated psychiatric disorder of significant proportions. Depression, anxiety, insomnia, and a feeling of impending doom are noted characteristically. The sensorium is clear, but weight loss of more than 5 pounds per month and com-

plaints of pain are seen to variable extents. The depression is mild to moderate, without psychotic features. A psychiatric syndrome was noted prior to physical complaints in 50 percent of patients with pancreatic carcinoma. The insomnia tends to be resistant to sleep medication, and the depression is usually unresponsive to antidepressant medications.

☐ HYPOPARATHYROIDISM

Hypoparathyroidism results from a deficit of circulating parathyroid hormone. It generally is the inadvertent result of surgery (thyroidectomy), but it may be an idiopathic disorder or condition termed *pseudohypoparathyroidism*. Laboratory findings in hypoparathyroidism are hypocalcemia and hyperphosphatemia. The decrease in blood calcium levels results in neural hyperirritability.

Since the calcium ion is necessary for neuronal membrane function and synaptic transmission, hypocalcemia may lead to a variety of brain dysfunctions. The most frequent neuropsychiatric problem associated with hypoparathyroidism is intellectual impairment; this occurs in 33 percent of the patients with this disorder (Denko and Kaelbling 1962).

Hypoparathyroidism can cause a myriad of psychologic and neurologic signs and symptoms. Tetany, seizures, nervousness, dizziness, fainting spells, personality changes, and decreased intellect are often present (Smith et al. 1972). Increased respiration leading to respiratory alkalosis tends to exacerbate symptoms. Tetany is characterized by muscle twitchings, carpopedal spasm, laryngeal stridor, muscle cramps, and choreiform movements. Contractions of facial musculature on percussion of the facial nerve anterior to the ear and the induction of carpalspasm by ischemia of the arm are classic phenomena in hypocalcemia. Psychiatric disorders are prominent in studies of hypoparathyroidism. In a review of 267 cases of hypoparathyroidism (Denko and Kaelbling 1962), organic brain syndrome was recorded in 36.5 percent, mental deficiency in 7.1 percent, functional psychosis in 9.1 percent, and unclassified psychiatric disorders in 54.5 percent. Emotional lability, impairment of memory, delusions, hallucinations, and mental retardation were prominent. Psychiatric symptoms may coexist with impaired motor coordination. Calcification may occur in the basal ganglia, the dentate nuclei, and other regions of the brain. Psychiatric disturbances are sometimes the first and only manifestations of disease observed with carpopedal spasm (Denko and Kaelbling 1962; Leigh and Kramer 1984).

The psychiatric manifestations of hypoparathyroidism are usually more varied than the neurologic. Denko and Kaelbling (1962) established five categories of mental disturbance associated with hypoparathyroidism: (1) intellectual impairment; (2) organic brain syndrome; (3) functional psychosis, including schizophrenia and affective states; (4) pseudoneurosis, or hysteric, hypochondriacal, or "neurotic"; and (5) psychiatric symptoms, such as depression, nervousness, or irritability. More than 40 percent of patients with hypoparathyroidism have an organic brain syndrome, which may include dementia or delirium in the absence of tetany or seizures (Ettigi and Brown 1978). In a review of all available reports meeting stringent criteria, Denko and Kaelbling (1962) noted that, in idiopathic hypoparathyroidism, intellectual impairment occurred in 30 percent of patients and organic brain syndrome in 25 percent. Psychosis was detected in 9 of 178 patients with idiopathic hypoparathyroidism; this improved either spontaneously or with specific therapy.

According to Leigh and Kramer (1984), depression is a consistent feature in many patients with hypoparathyroidism. Manic-depressive pictures with well-defined mood swings have been noted in surgical hypoparathyroidism, but not in the idiopathic form. Anxiety syndromes are more than likely to occur in idiopathic hypoparathyroidism compared to surgically induced hypoparathyroidism. Seizures secondary to hypoparathyroidism are often misdiagnosed as hysterical because of their atypical presentations, involvement of emotions, and the difficulty in their management—even by therapeutic levels of anticonvulsants. Abnormalities in EEG have been described in hypoparathyroidism, but the changes are not specific. Idiopathic hypoparathyroidism is marked by such symptoms as obsessions, phobias, and tics.

Pseudohypoparathyroidism, a disease in which hypocalcemia is due to tissue unresponsiveness to parathyroid hormone, has a high incidence of encephalopathy, behavior disturbance, seizures, tics, and athetoid movements (Ettigi and Brown 1978).

Because of the variety of psychological manifestations of hypocalcemia, it is recommended that calcium be measured in all initial psychiatric evaluations.

☐ HYPERPARATHYROIDISM

Abnormalities in the function of the parathyroid glands may also produce psychiatric changes. Changes are directly related to disorders of calcium and homeostasis but not to any direct effects of the parathyroid hormone on the brain (Petersen 1968; Smith et al. 1972). Hyperparathyroidism is one cause of hypercalcemia, and changes in mental status have been correlated with the degree of elevation in serum calcium (Petersen 1968; Smith et al. 1972). Parathyroid hormone plays a key role in regulating the level of circulating calcium and inorganic phosphate. Increased amounts of parathyroid hormone associated with hyperparathyroidism result in the cardinal feature of the disorder, hypercalcemia and associated hypophosphatemia. Parathyroid hormone controls the serum inorganic phosphate levels by regulating its reabsorption by the renal tubules. Lack of the hormone allows increased reabsorption, whereas excessive amounts of parathyroid hormone inhibits reabsorption (Lichtenstein 1980). Calcium is an essential ion in the normal function of muscle and it has been suggested that it is stored in the sarcoplasmic reticulum, released during excitation, and stored during relaxation (Lichtenstein 1980; Martin et al. 1977).

Psychiatric symptoms occur in about half of the patients with primary hyperparathyroidism, and the symptoms may include confusion, mental depression, stupor, and organic types of psychosis (Lichtenstein 1980). The general symptoms of hyperparathyroidism are anorexia, weakness, dysphasia, nausea, vomiting, and headache. The acute symptoms are the result of hypercalcemia and are characterized by headache, restlessness, disorientation, lethargy, and, finally, coma. An identical syndrome can occur with vitamin D overdosage in which hypercalcemia occurs. Nausea and vomiting may be the first symptoms of hypercalcemia. Hellstrom and Ivemark (1962) studied 138 patients with hyperparathyroidism and found that 11 (8 percent) manifested nervous disorders and depression as subsidiary symptoms. In 343 patients, the primary clue to diagnosis of endocrine disorder was reported to be fatigue (Cope 1960). Personality changes were considered diagnostic clues in 3 percent of 460 patients with hyperparathyroidism (Cope 1960; Keynes 1961). Hyperparathyroidism should be considered when depression, thirst, and lack of initiative appear during a prolonged, slowly developing, and diagnostically unclear change of personality.

In another study, 65 percent of patients with hyperparathyroidism had psychiatric symptoms (Petersen 1968); this study clearly relates the level of hypercalcemia to severity of psychiatric symptoms. At levels of calcium below 16 mg/100 ml, the symptoms are principally those of a depression with lowered mood, fatigue, loss of interest, and irritability. Less frequently there is memory impairment and difficulty concentrating at this level of calcium. At levels of about 16 mg/100 ml, the clinical features resemble an organic delirium or psychosis with confusion and perceptual aberrations that proceed to coma in the most severe cases. Return of serum calcium to normal levels coincides with rapid reversal of the psychiatric disturbances, despite persistence of elevated parathyroid hormone levels. Thus psychic changes are associated directly with the calcium level rather than the parathyroid hormone level.

A psychosis with predominant hallucinations and delusions has been consistently reported in the range of 5 to 20 percent of patients with hyperparathyroidism (Leigh and Kramer 1984). When calcium levels rise rapidly, psychosis may abruptly appear and dominate the presentation. In hyperparathyroidism, depression is noted in 5 to 20 percent of patients; anxiety and irritability have been noted in up to one-third of patients (Leigh and Kramer 1984). The clinical symptoms of fatigue and muscular weakness, particularly of the proximal muscles of the lower extremities with preserved or hyperactive deep tendon reflexes, are physical clues of hyperparathyroidism. Long-standing fatigue, weakness, anorexia, and personality changes may form a pseudo-neurosis syndrome in primary hyperparathyroidism with serum calcium levels in the 12 to 16 mg/100 ml range (Leigh and Kramer 1984).

☐ NEUROENDOCRINE REGULATION

Harris (1948) first suggested that the brain, via the limbic system, controls the secretion of pituitary hormones. Abnormalities in the dynamics of the particular endocrine system, as might result from limbic system pathology, appear to be more precisely identified by studies of endocrine regulation (Carroll and Mendels 1976). Carroll and Mendels showed that the levels of cortisol in cerebrospinal fluid (CSF), plasma, and urine were all increased in depressed patients. The levels were highest in

patients with psychotic depression, wherein levels averaged four times those of controlled subjects.

The principal anatomic substrates of neuroendocrine regulation are the basal forebrain, limbic system, midbrain, hypothalamus with its medium eminence portal capillary system, and the anterior and posterior pituitary (Figure 1). Neuroendocrine mediators include monoamines, traditional peptide hormones, and an array of more recently characterized peptides. Each peptide may act in one or more of the following roles: (1) as classic hormones released by endocrine tissues, (2) as hormones secreted by neurons, (3) as hypophysiotropic-releasing hormones, and (4) as neurotransmitters within the central nervous system (CNS). Many of these peptides are also found within the gastrointestinal tract. The classic neurotransmitters such as monoamines, acetylcholine, and amino acids appear to account for only 40 percent of the synapses in the CNS.

The hormones of the posterior pituitary or neurohypophysis are the classic neurosecretory hormones (i.e., hormones secreted into systemic circulation by neurons). Vasopressin and oxytocin are produced in neurons of the supraoptic and paraventricular nuclei of the hypothalamus. The axons of these cells transport these two hormones to the median eminence in the posterior pituitary. Hormone release is mediated by depolarization of the neurosecretory neurons regulated by excitatory and inhibitory inputs from higher centers. The hormones are released into the systemic circulation and probably also into the portal capillary system to reach the anterior lobe. The best-known function of vasopressin is in the regulation of fluid or electrolyte balance. The hormones of the anterior pituitary are under both stimulatory and inhibitory control. The most important stimulatory inputs are the neuronally secreted hypothalamic-releasing hormones such as thyrotropin-releasing hormone (TRH), gonadotropin-releasing hormone (GNRH), CRF, and growth-hormone-releasing hormone (GHRH). Inhibition secretion is controlled both by hypothalmic inhibitory hormones and by negative feedback by end-organ hormones. Two hypothalamic inhibitory hormones have been identified: one a peptide, somatostatin, which inhibits release of growth hormone, and the other a monoamine, dopamine, which inhibits secretion of prolactin. The hypophysiotropic and inhibitory hormones are released by hypothalamic neuroterminals in the median eminence of the hypothalamus where they

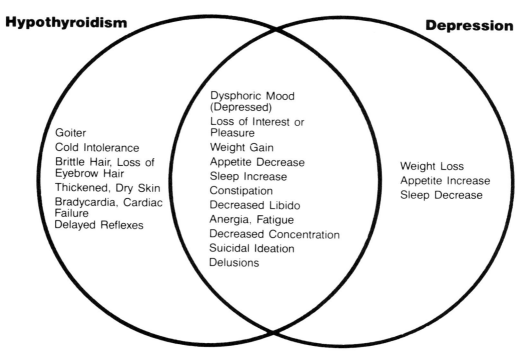

Figure 1. Neuroendocrine regulation

enter a plexus of fenestrated capillaries in the hypothalamic-pituitary portal system and are transported to a secondary plexus within the substance of anterior pituitary gland. The hypophysiotropic neurosecretory cells of the hypothalamus are under neurotransmitter regulation from higher centers. A variety of neurotransmitters have excitatory and inhibitory effects on the neurosecretion of each of the releasing factors, with resulting effects on the release of pituitary hormones. These transmitters are involved in control of the complex patterns of secretion of the releasing factors, including basal release and various patterns of pulsatile release, usually with circadian rhythmicity and stress-mediated release. Patterns of release are critical to end-organ effects of hormone.

The dopaminergic pathways involved in neuroendocrine regulation arise mainly in the arcuate nucleus of the hypothalamus and descend into the median eminence, where they are involved in the control of anterior pituitary secretions. The noradrenergic pathways that effect pituitary secretion arise outside of the hypothalamus in brain-stem nuclei. The specific fibers involved in neuroendocrine regulation arise in areas adjacent to locus caeruleus

and ascend to the hypothalamus. Serotonergic projections to the hypothalamus ascend from the brain-stem raphe nuclei.

The HPA axis is a major component of the neuroendocrine system. The major hormones for the HPA axis are CRF, ACTH, and cortisol. CRF is the major releasing hormone for ACTH. ACTH is a pituitary hormone that is a major tropic and releasing factor for the adrenalcortical cells that produce glucocorticoids. There is a striking integration of the stress response involving the HPA axis and the adrenal medulla. Cortisol, elaborated by the adrenal cortex, induces two of the enzymes in the pathway for epinephrine release by the neighboring adrenal medulla.

☐ HYPOCORTISOLISM

Even since Addison first described adrenal cortisol deficiency, significant changes in personality and behavior have been invariably demonstrated in patients with this condition (Ettigi and Brown 1978). Adrenal cortisol insufficiency as originally described by Addison is frequently accompanied by depressive symptoms. These include apathy, loss of interest, fatigue, poverty of thought, irritability, and negativism.

The severity of the mental disability parallels the severity of the physical disorder. A mild-to-moderate chronic organic brain syndrome with memory impairment is a frequent presentation of hypocortisolism. Early psychiatric symptoms of adrenalcortical deficiency are apathy, depression, fatigue, poverty of thought, and lack of initiation. Patients are often seclusive, irritable, and negativistic. In its more severe form, Addisonian encephalopathy, the patient presents a typical organic psychosis or delirium characterized by memory deficit and clouding of consciousness, progressing to stupor or coma. The incidence of organic brain syndrome patients with Addison's disease is 5 to 20 percent (Leigh and Kramer 1984). The EEG, which shows waves with high amplitudes and slow activity, further helps to confirm the presence of brain disturbance in Addison's disease. Psychosis develops in 20 to 40 percent of patients with Addison's disease. The psychosis is not exclusively indicative of impending or actual Addisonian crisis and may include seclusiveness, negativism, poor judgment, agitation, hallucinations, and delusions with bizarre and catatonic posturing. Seclusiveness, irritability, apathy, and negativism are seen in over half of the cases of Addison's disease. The psychosis may persist for several months following adequate treatment.

The affective syndrome might predate physical signs and does not necessarily coincide with physical findings. Some 20 to 40 percent of patients with Addison's disease exhibit depression manifested by apathy or sad affect, fatigue, poverty of thought, or lack of initiative (Leigh and Kramer 1984). A mild, shallow cheerfulness appearing as euphoria occasionally emerges in Addison's disease, which is chronically present, but manic episodes and elation are otherwise rare in this endocrinopathy.

Adrenal cortisol insufficiencies are also associated with profound perceptual dysfunction. Detailed testing has revealed lowered thresholds of sensitivity to taste, smell, touch, and hearing; ability to recognize stimuli is also impaired (Ettigi and Brown 1978). This diminished sensory threshold with increased difficulty interpreting sensory input is noted in Addisonian patients; for example, vague, dull, deep back pain may be misinterpreted as hysterical in or-

igin (Leigh and Kramer 1984). Patients with Addison's disease are extremely hypersensitive to sedatives, particularly barbiturates.

☐ HYPERCORTISOLISM

Cushing's syndrome is an endocrine disorder strongly associated with severe psychiatric disturbance. Estimates of the incidence of severe psychiatric disorder in Cushing's syndrome vary from 15 to 30 percent (Reus and Berlant 1986). The most common picture of psychiatric disorder is a depressive illness; this may be severe, with delusions and mental retardation. Cushing's syndrome is the endocrinopathy with the highest frequency of mental status changes (Leigh and Kramer 1984). Although depression and psychosis are the prototypic psychiatric manifestations, organic brain syndrome occurs in 20 to 40 percent of patients (Ettigi and Brown 1978). The variety of psychiatric symptoms seen in this disorder may be explained by the varying effects of increased CRF, ACTH, and cortisol on the brain. The largest percentage of all mental status changes in Cushing's syndrome has been seen in adrenocortical hyperplasia secondary to pituitary tumor or an ACTH-secreting neoplasm (Leigh and Kramer 1984). Cushing's syndrome of hypothalamic or pituitary origin has been recently studied and shown to be associated more often with mood disturbances than when this disorder originates from an adrenal-adenoma or ectopic ACTH-producing neoplasm (Ettigi and Brown 1978). This seems to suggest that the diencephalic abnormality may be the cause of both neuroendocrine and mood disturbance in these patients. The syndrome of hyperadrenalcortical secretion can be of three types: primary adrenal gland dysfunction, ectopic ACTH dysfunction, or primary hypothalamic or pituitary dysfunction. When the disease is due to primary adrenal dysfunction, adrenal hormone (cortisol) is increased in the blood, but pituitary hormone (ACTH) levels and presumably hypothalamic hormone (CRF) levels are low. If the disease is due to ectopic production of ACTH, both adrenal hormone and pituitary hormone levels are high. Finally, if it is due to primary hypothalamic dysfunction, levels of all three hormones (adrenal, pituitary, and hypothalamic) are elevated.

Most investigators have found abnormal behavioral symptomatology in anywhere from 40 to 90 percent of Cushing's syndrome patients (Reus et al. 1986). An exaggeration of personality traits or the appearance of behavioral disturbances are common complaints from the family of the patient with an early stage of endocrine disorder. In general, euphoria and increased activity are observed early in the course of illness, and depression, insomnia, fatigue, loss of libido, emotionability, and cognitive impairment are more pronounced in later stages (Reus et al. 1986). Both agitated and retarded depressions are the most common psychiatric syndromes in patients with Cushing's syndrome, with occurrences in more than 50 percent and suicide attempts in more than 10 percent of patients studied (Leigh and Kramer 1984). Other features include irritability, difficulty in concentration, insomnia, paranoid delusions, and hallucinations. These features have been reported to predate the onset of other obvious signs of the disorder, such as obesity, development of moon facies, stria, and muscle wasting. In a prospective study, increased levels of cortisol and ACTH were associated with impairment of affect, decreased concentration, diminished memory capacity, decreased libido, and insomnia (Whelan et al. 1980). In a series of 29 patients, 25 (86 percent) were significantly depressed, and there was a family history of depression or suicide in half of the cases (Cohen 1980). The majority of patients with Cushing's syndrome show mental status changes. Cushing (1932) reported changes in the mentation in some of his patients. Most reports have underscored prominent changes in affect and cognition.

Psychotic symptomatology and schizophrenia-like symptoms characterized by auditory and visual hallucinations, severe confusion, paranoia, or mania are evident in 10 to 20 percent of patients with Cushing's syndrome, and suicidal ideation or action is common (Leigh and Kramer 1984). Acute episodes of anxiety are also common; these may be misinterpreted to be hysterical in origin (Leigh and Kramer 1984).

Steroids given for the treatment of other medical conditions may also cause psychological changes. Patients treated with pharmacologic doses of glucocorticoids may show euphoria and cheerfulness (Martin et al. 1977). These symptoms, observed in 75 percent of such patients, are often accompanied by increased appetite and increased libido. Although steroid depression is less prevalent than endogenous depression, it may be as severe. A significant number of patients attempt suicide. Severe psychotic states may also be seen—often with an affective component and a mixture of organic symptoms such as confusion and disorientation. Direct steroid effects on the sensitive regions of the CNS are the probable cause of the mood alteration. Steroid therapy suppresses pituitary and hypothalamic secretions, and this may explain the behavioral changes observed in drug-induced Cushing's syndrome. Steroid hormones have a profound influence on nervous system function, and steroid-induced euphoria—often with increased appetite and libido—occurs in at least 20 to 40 percent of patients receiving these medications. However, euphoria has been noted in less than 5 percent of those patients with endogenous Cushing's syndrome (Leigh and Kramer 1984). Von Zerssen (1976) summarized the literature and stated that attempts to demonstrate an antidepressant effect of glucocorticoid compounds have failed.

Nearly all of the HPA abnormalities in Cushing's syndrome can occur in patients with major depression, including increased plasma and CSF cortisol, increased nocturnal cortisol secretion, increased plasma ACTH, decreased circadian variation of cortisol release, and dexamethasone suppression test nonsuppression (Reus et al. 1986). A study utilizing ovine CRF infusion indicated that this test may be useful in differential diagnosis (Gold et al. 1984b). Patients with primary psychiatric diagnoses were found to have a blunted ACTH and cortisol response to the CRF in comparison to Cushing's syndrome patients who were noted to have augmented responses.

Thyroid disorders are probably the most common of the endocrinopathies that present with psychiatric manifestations (Gold et al. 1981; Hall et al. 1981). Both hyperthyroidism and hypothyroidism have been associated with clinical syndromes such as dementia, depression, anxiety, mania, and psychosis (Ettigi and Brown 1978). However, clinicians usually consider hyperthyroidism primarily in the differential diagnosis of anxiety disorders or agitated behavior states such as mania, whereas hypothyroidism is included in the workup of dementia and depressive disorders.

☐ HYPOTHYROIDISM

Hypothyroidism, in contrast to thyrotoxicosis, is a common disorder that seems to occur at a relatively greater prevalence in psychiatric populations (Goggans et al. 1986; Gold et al. 1981). Indeed, early hypothyroidism may be the most common medical disorder to present as a depressive syndrome (Gold et al. 1981; Hall et al. 1981). As will be discussed below, however, the most commonly used tests of thyroid function—such as the serum thyroxine (T4) level and the triiodothyronine (T3) uptake test (T3U)—will not detect the vast majority of patients with psychiatrically relevant but "subclinical" hy-

pothyroidism. These patients have few, if any, gross physical findings typical of the myxedema syndrome (Gold et al. 1981).

It has long been recognized that many signs and symptoms of thyroid illness overlap with those of major depressive disorder (Gold et al. 1981; Lidz and Whitehorn 1949) (Figure 2). These signs and

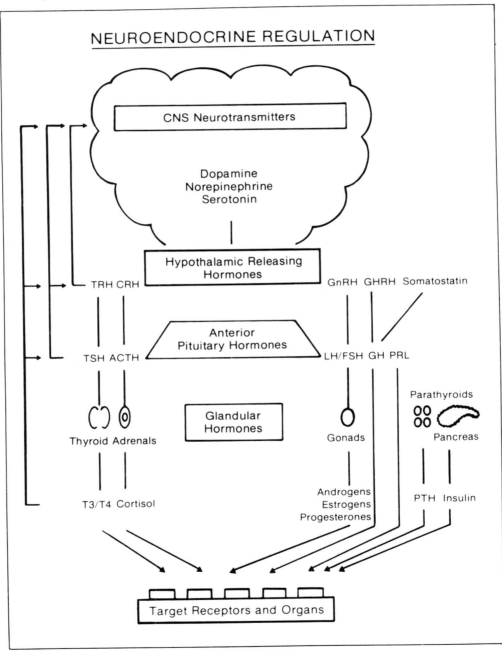

Figure 2. Signs and symptoms of hypothyroidism and depression. Reprinted with permission from Goggans et al. (1986).

symptoms include dysphoric mood, decreased energy, weakness, impaired cognitive ability, anhedonia, and other neurovegetative problems. Because both depression and hypothyroidism are disorders associated with effective although different therapies, it is obviously important to diagnose each accurately. Psychiatric diagnostic systems such as the Research Diagnostic Criteria (RDC) and the DSM-III-R (American Psychiatric Association 1987) emphasize careful differential diagnoses among the psychiatric syndromes and stress the importance of excluding organic etiologies. Yet it is clear that because there is a wide overlap between the signs and symptoms of hypothyroidism and depression, laboratory testing has an important role in the diagnostic process. Screening tests for thyroid illness are most likely to be limited to the measurement of T4 and T3U when the possibility of this diagnosis is considered (Gold et al. 1982). These tests will certainly detect patients with advanced hypothyroidism but may not identify milder degrees of the illness. Interestingly, depression is not the only medical disorder that has been recognized as a clinical variant presentation of early hypothyroidism. Anemia, coagulopathy, myopathy, and inflammatory arthritis have all been described as due to autoimmune thyroiditis at a stage when T4 and T3 resin reuptake (T3RU) values were normal and the myxedema syndrome was absent (Klein and Levey 1984). These patients did, however, have abnormal thyroid-stimulating hormone (TSH) levels and thyrotropin-releasing hormone (TRH) stimulation tests. Thus it has been increasingly recognized that there is a spectrum of emerging thyroid dysfunction, and a system has been created to divide this spectrum into three grades (Evered et al. 1973) (Table 1).

Grade one, or overt hypothyroidism, is characterized by the classic picture of myxedema and completely abnormal laboratory findings: de-creased T4, increased TSH, and an exaggerated TRH test response. Grade two, or mild hypothyroidism, is associated with fewer clinical symptoms and a normal T4, but with an increased baseline (TSH) and an exaggerated TRH test score. Grade three, or subclinical hypothyroidism, is without any obvious "thyroid" symptoms other than decreased energy or depression. T4 and TSH levels are normal in grade three, but the TRH test shows an exaggerated response.

The finding that some depressed patients manifested laboratory evidence for thyroid dysfunction when TSH levels and TRH stimulation tests were performed stimulated interest in the actual prevalence of this disorder in psychiatric patients with symptoms of depression. Efforts first focused on hospitalized patients. In an initial study of 250 patients, 20 (8 percent) showed some degree of hypothyroidism on comprehensive clinical evaluation and laboratory tests (Gold et al. 1981). Two patients had overt hypothyroidism with positive clinical findings and typical laboratory findings. Eight had clinical evidence of mild hypothyroidism such as fatigue, weight gain, and dry skin along with normal T4 levels, mildly elevated TSH levels, and an increased delta score on the TRH test. Another 10 patients had no clinical symptoms of hypothyroidism other than complaints of diminished or depressed mood; they had normal T4 and TSH levels but increased TRH test scores. These findings were confirmed in a study of 270 similar patients admitted to inpatient care in hospitals in New Jersey, Georgia, and Texas, where 12 percent of the patients showed evidence of hypothyroidism; 94 percent of these hypothyroid patients had either the grade two or grade three types, and their condition would not have been detected by measurement of serum T4 alone (Dackis et al. 1983).

These findings suggest that the prevalence of hypothyroidism in depressed patients is much higher than previously thought. To examine whether this finding occurs solely in the inpatient setting, outpatient studies were done. In one study of 44 consecutive outpatients meeting RDC for major unipolar depression, 6 (14 percent) showed laboratory evidence for either grade two or grade three hypothyroidism (Sternbach et al. 1983). Although the study was small, the result agreed with the inpatient studies and suggests that the increased incidence of hypothyroidism is not limited to inpatients. Furthermore, it indicated that a full DSM-III syndrome of depression can be produced by

TABLE 1. GRADES OF HYPOTHYROIDISM

I. Overt	Classic symptoms	T4 low, TSH ↑, TRHST ↑
II. Mild	Few clinical symptoms	T4 normal, TSH ↑, TRSH ↑
III. Subclinical	Depression, anergia	T4 normal, TSH normal, TRHST ↑

early hypothyroidism and that routine thyroid tests cannot exclude the possibility of organic dysfunction as required by the DSM-III. "Routine" thyroid testing would have only identified less than 10 percent of these patients. Taken together, these studies make it clear that thyroid dysfunction is by far the most likely condition to present as depression to the psychiatrist.

Another study showed that of 156 patients who were admitted to a psychiatric inpatient service, 22 (14 percent) showed evidence of some degree of hypothyroidism; 16 of these patients were diagnosed as having an affective disorder rather than other psychiatric diagnoses ($\chi^2 = 8.43$, $p < .01$) (Goggans et al. 1986). The depressed patients with hypothyroidism had a mean age of 39 years; 81 percent were women. There were no significant differences in symptom profiles, Carroll and Hamilton rating scale scores, or between the euthyroid and the hypothyroid subgroups among the patients with major depression in the entire sample. There was a predominance of women in the hypothyroid subgroup and one-third of the hypothyroid patients with depression had a positive family history of thyroid disorder. This was most frequently seen in a first-degree female relative (Goggans et al. 1986).

Etiologies of primary hypothyroidism are diverse, but autoimmune illness is currently considered the most common cause. Other causes include lithium therapy, prior thyroid surgery or radiation treatment, and discontinuation of prescribed thyroid hormone. Another study of 100 inpatients that identified 15 patients with evidence of hypothyroidism included screening for antithyroid antibodies (Gold et al. 1982). Of these patients, 60 percent had significant titers of antimicrosomal antibodies. This suggests that active autoimmune thyroiditis was present. In patients without other evidence of thyroid disease, the term *symptomless autoimmune thyroiditis* has been proposed for persons with increased TSH responses to TRH infusion in the presence of circulating antithyroid antibodies (Gold et al. 1982). However, emerging thyroid dysfunction that is symptomless to the internist looking for gross physical dysfunction may appear as depression if a detailed psychiatric interview is accomplished.

A question that remains is that of therapeutics. Those few patients with grade one hypothyroidism who present to psychiatrists should certainly be treated with complete thyroid replacement. Patients with grade two or three hypothyroidism tend

to be poor responders to antidepressants alone. Patients actually seem to worsen on antidepressants because they are sensitive to the sedative and anticholinergic side effects of these medications. It is our impression that such patients tend to convert to responders when T3 or other thyroid hormone replacement is added to the antidepressant program (Targum et al. 1984).

There are some reports that patients with mild hypothyroidism are at increased risk for cardiac disease and myocardial dysfunction; there are also proven beneficial cardiac responses to thyroid replacement in patients with grade two hypothyroidism (Cooper et al. 1984). Many internists who treat patients with thyroid replacement for overt hypothyroidism require the laboratory normalization of TSH levels or the TRH stimulation test before accepting that treatment is adequate. A double-blind, placebo-controlled study of nondepressed patients with grade two hypothyroidism reported that T4 replacement was beneficial in terms of improving mild clinical symptoms and improving objective measures of cardiac function (Cooper et al. 1984). It is also possible that many grade two and three patients with psychiatric symptoms may respond to thyroid replacement alone, although this has not been proven in large studies. In a small open study, 8 of 10 patents with grade two or three hypothyroidism who met RDC criteria for either major or minor depression responded to thyroid replacement alone over a 1-month period (Dackis et al. 1983). After a 1-year follow-up, only 1 of the responders had relapsed. That patient was the only person in the study who had an abnormal dexamethasone suppression test at the time of initial evaluation, and he subsequently responded to the addition of an antidepressant to the thyroid replacement program.

In another open study, 9 patients with grade two hypothyroidism and either major or minor depression were followed for 6 months on an average daily dose of 100 μg of T4 (Goggans et al. 1986). Patients were given enough thyroid replacement to suppress their baseline TSH levels below 4.0 μIU/ml and were judged to have recovered if their Carroll and Hamilton rating scale scores both dropped below 10 from pretreatment means of 23.4 and 18.6, respectively. During the treatment period, 2 of 5 patients with major depression and all 4 patients with major depression subsequently responded with the addition of either electroconvulsive therapy (ECT) or tricyclic antidepressants.

All 3 of these patients had previously failed to respond to antidepressants alone.

Given the proven medical benefits, we recommend initial treatment with thyroid hormone for all patients with grade two hypothyroidism and the addition of antidepressants if the response, in terms of mood and energy, is poor after 2 months. The treatment of patients with grade three hypothyroidism is less certain and should be individualized. An adjunctive trial of thyroid replacement should be considered if the patient has not responded to prior treatment with antidepressants; these patients are, in our experience, particularly responsive to T3 potentiation. Thyroid replacement should be sufficient to return TSH and TRH values into the normal laboratory range. For most individuals, this is accomplished by an eventual dose of 75 to 150 μg of T4 daily. Elderly patients should be advanced more slowly than younger patients and seldom require more than 100 μg daily. All patients with grade three hypothyroidism who are not treated with thyroid replacement should be closely followed for the possibility of progressive thyroid failure, especially if they are treated with medications such as lithium.

The finding that early thyroid failure is the most common medical condition to mimic depression is probably not a chance phenomenon. Whybrow and Prange (1981) hypothesized a close relationship between thyroid function and the responsiveness of central catecholamine receptors. Thyroid hormones increase beta-adrenergic receptor sensitivity; noradrenergic activity would therefore be enhanced or diminished by corresponding levels of thyroid in the CNS. Hence, either a thyroid deficit or a primary noradrenergic neurotransmitter deficit would be expressed the same as decreased effective beta-adrenergic activity. According to the monoamine hypothesis of depressive illness, this would be expected to result in clinical depression.

Ms. A., a 27-year-old executive, was referred to the hospital from the intensive care unit of a general hospital following an overdose of amitriptyline. This was the second overdose of an antidepressant within 6 months. Ms. A. had been in psychotherapy with a psychologist for 12 months prior to this admission and had been followed concurrently by a psychiatrist for 9 months for purposes of medication provision. Her chief complaint was that she wanted to commit suicide twice, so "I guess that means that I am depressed." She had no prior history of psychiatric hospitalization nor was there any family history of affective disorder. The patient complained of depressed mood, decreased energy, increased need for sleep (which seemed to worsen following administration of amitriptyline), anhedonia, impaired concentration and memory, progressive feelings of hopelessness, and a desire to withdraw socially. At the time of admission, the patient expressed a feeling of disappointment that her second suicide attempt had been unsuccessful and stated that she would probably try again. Her Beck Depression Inventory score was 28; her Hamilton Rating Scale for Depression score was 22. General physical examination was within normal limits. General medical screening tests were also normal. The T4 was 6.5 (normal, 4–12); the T3U was 26.0 (normal, 24–36); the free T4 index was 5.6; the TSH level was 4.8 (normal, 1–7). A TRH stimulation test revealed a delta score of 27.1 (normal, 7–20). Antithyroid antibodies were not present. A 6-point dexamethasone suppression test showed normal suppression at all time points. The patient was diagnosed as having grade three hypothyroidism. She was treated with thyroid replacement alone because she had not previously tolerated the side effects of antidepressants and had also used them destructively. After 1 month, the patient was markedly improved on thyroid replacement alone. The Beck Depression Inventory score was 3 and the Hamilton score was 2. The T4 was 11.2, the T3U was 28.8, and the TSH was less than 1. Following discharge from the hospital, the patient has continued to take sodium T4 (Synthroid) 125 μg daily for a period of 2.5 years. She has not received any other medications. She has remained free of depression and anergia and has continued to be productive in both her professional and personal life.

Thyroid Workup. The psychiatrist must screen all patients for physical illness. Not only is this consistent with the role of the psychiatrist as a physician but also many authors have documented the high percentage of patients with physical disorders that either cause or contribute to the clinical problem for which psychiatric care is sought. In evaluating patients with suspected thyroid disease, the clinician needs to rely on history, physical examination, and laboratory testing. The fact that the patient has a full depressive syndrome does not exclude secondary depression, particularly in the case of thyroid disorder. All patients presenting with lack of energy and depression should have their T4, T3U, and TSH levels measured. This panel of tests will pick up all patients with overt and mild hypothyroidism. One-third of patients in the above-described studies would have been detected with this panel. We recommend that all patients who are suspected to have subclinical hypothyroidism on the basis of family history of thyroid disorder, failure to respond to or tolerate antidepressants, and depression of the severity to require inpatient care should have a TRH infusion test. If that test score is abnormally increased, antithyroid antibodies should also be measured.

☐ HYPERTHYROIDISM

Of euthyroid patients who are admitted to psychiatric hospitals in a state of acute stress and behavioral crisis, 5 to 10 percent will show elevation of the serum T4 and free T4 levels (Cohen and Swigar 1979). Repeat thyroid testing after 1 week of psychiatric stabilization and general supportive care usually reveals complete normalization of these parameters. This stress-related phenomenon, sometimes referred to as "pseudohyperthyroidism," should not be mistaken for acute thyrotoxicosis. Clinicians should delay more expensive and complex thyroid investigations such as thyroid scans in patients with few clinical findings of hyperthyroidism until a second set of basic thyroid parameters, drawn after 1 week's time, has been reviewed.

True hyperthyroidism, by contrast, is a relatively uncommon finding in psychiatric populations, and is probably not more prevalent in such patients relative to the general population. The prevalence rate is less than 1 percent in each of these groups (Lidz and Whitehorn 1949). Most hyperthyroid patients complain of anxiety or "nervousness" and are overtly restless, hyperactive, or tremulous. Generally the physical examination will distinguish hyperthyroidism from anxiety because of the more obvious clinical features such as exophthalmos, diffuse goiter, prominent and sustained tachycardia, sweating, weight loss despite preservation of appetite, and other indicators of a hypermetabolic state. Rarely hyperthyroidism may present as an apathetic depression in the elderly.

☐ HYPOPITUITARISM

In hypopituitarism, the psychiatric symptoms are related to the rapidity of onset of the disease process and the degree of the pituitary insufficiency regarding the specific hormone deficiencies. The psychiatric symptoms may be the dominant clinical feature. Confusion, disorientation, and drowsiness were among the most common psychiatric complaints in a series of 101 patients with pathologically verified disease (Smith et al. 1972). Hypopituitarism leads to features seen in other glandular failures such as hypoparathyroidism, Addison's disease, and hypogonadism. Hypopituitarism is often mentioned in the differential diagnosis of anorexia nervosa (Leigh and Kramer 1984). Psychiatric symptoms associated with hypopituitarism include lethargy, malaise, depression, loss of libido, and amenorrhea. Severe metabolic crisis with coma and delirium may occur. Such crisis may result in brain damage, which is slow to reverse.

☐ HYPERPROLACTINEMIA

Prolactin is one of the few hormones that has been found to act directly on the brain and that has been definitely identified in the CSF (Fava et al. 1981). Unique among the pituitary hormones, prolactin secretion is controlled by a predominantly inhibitory influence from the hypothalamus. Evidence suggests that dopamine is a primary prolactin inhibitory factor. Several substances found in the hypothalamus stimulate prolactin secretion. Neurotransmitters, including serotonin, are among these substances. Hyperprolactinemia occurs under a variety of circumstances (i.e., physiologic, pathologic, and pharmacologic). Physical and emotional stress are reported to increase the secretion of prolactin (Martin et al. 1977). Acute psychological stress appears to lead to significant increase in the plasma prolactin level of only "neurotic" females; it does not have this effect on "normal" controls (Fava et al. 1981).

Women with hyperprolactinemia have been found to be more distressed and more hostile than other women (Fava et al. 1981; Kellner et al. 1984). Findings suggest that the syndrome of depression, hostility, and anxiety in a woman with amenorrhea, especially if associated with decreased libido and galactorrhea, may be a manifestation of hyperprolactinemia. Lability of mood, irritability, and depression may occur before menstruation in some women, and women with premenstrual tension syndrome have been found to have higher prolactin levels throughout the menstrual cycle, especially premenstrually, than other women (Fava et al. 1981). The association of hyperprolactinemia and depression is known, but it is uncertain whether or not excessive prolactin secretion causes the symptoms.

It has been observed that patients with hyperprolactinemia amenorrhea complain of depression and personality changes that remit when they are treated with bromocriptine. Bromocriptine is effective in lowering serum prolactin levels in most patients (Fava et al. 1981). A double-blind, placebo-controlled, crossover study of bromocriptine in 8 hyperprolactinemia patients rated distress (Buckman and Kellner 1985). The distress decreased and well-being increased parallel with the fall in prolactin levels. The differences were significant for the majority of measures. In an uncontrolled study of patients with hyperprolactinemia, the distress was reduced with bromocriptine (Fioretti et al. 1978). With bromocriptine treatment, the serum prolactin levels of all patients fell. Six patients' levels reached a normal range, and the other two patients' levels decreased substantially. Prolactin levels are significantly lower with bromocriptine than with placebo. These results suggest that, in the treatment of hyperprolactinemia patients, bromocriptine diminishes depression, anxiety, and hostility; increases well-being; improves libido; and substantially decreases serum prolactin concentrations (Buckman and Kellner 1985; Fava et al. 1981; Fioretti et al. 1978).

Prolactinomas are the most common type of pituitary tumors seen in clinical practice (Martin et al. 1977). The cardinal signs of hyperprolactinemia in women are amenorrhea and galactorrhea. They occur in more than 90 percent of women with established prolactinomas. In contrast, only 10 to 20 percent of men with prolactinomas have galactorrhea. Only 20 to 30 percent of such men have gynecomastia (Martin et al. 1977). Symptoms induced by a prolactinoma are due either to hormonal effects or to local effects of an intracranial, space-occupying lesion. These symptoms may be sex specific. Patients may often, however, be endocrinologically asymptomatic despite tremendously high serum prolactin levels (Wagner and Weitzman 1980). Kraft and Fanby (1967) noted a 1 percent prevalence of pituitary adenomata in 2,200 neuropsychiatric patients. It has been reported that 5 to 10 percent of all pituitary glands show evidence of prolactin-secreting adenomata on autopsy (Martin et al. 1977). A chart review of 16 male patients with prolactin-secreting pituitary adenomas revealed the frequent presence of four neuropsychiatric signs and symptoms: apathy, asexuality, adiposity, and headache (Cohen et al. 1984). This symptom constellation may be easily mistaken for that of an affective disorder. Men displaying these four signs and symptoms should be referred for endocrinologic consultation.

☐ MALE HORMONAL DYSFUNCTION

Gonadal hormones have major effects on brain function. These effects vary at different stages of a patient's development. The onset of puberty is heralded by certain changes in gonadal secretion. In the male, increased levels of androgenic hormones at puberty are required for normal libidinal drive and potency (Ettigi and Brown 1978). In many species of animals, androgens exert an organizing effect on brain mechanisms very early in life, and determine characteristic male patterns of gonadotropin regulation of sexual behavior. Analogous with the rhesus monkey, a critical time for brain androgenization in humans is approximately at the end of the first trimester of pregnancy.

Increased androgenic activity also affects other aspects of the personality besides increasing libido and sex drive. In a study of a young (20–25 years) male criminal population, a high plasma testosterone level correlated with a history of violent crimes in adolescence but not with continued aggressiveness (Kreus and Rose 1972). Lowered testosterone levels are seen in hypogonadism from a variety of causes as well as in Klinefelter's syndrome. Klinefelter's syndrome is a 47XXY chromosome abnormality that is manifested as aspermatism, gynecomastia, increased excretion of follicle-stimulating hormone (FSH), hypogonadism evident at puberty, and decreased libido (Ettigi and Brown 1978). This syndrome in its classic form consists of small testes, infertility, gynecomastia, and variable degrees of underandrogenization, sometimes with mild retardation, antisocial behavior, or both, as the consequence of the addition of an extra X to the male complement 47. Other chromosomal variations seen are XXYY, XXXY, and XXXXY. These patients have a male habitus under the influence of the Y chromosome, and they often have gender disturbances (e.g., transsexualism, homosexuality, and transvestism). In addition to diminished libido, these men show marked poverty of ideation, apathy, hypokinesia, timidity, diminished drive and general vigor, and a higher than normal incidence of psychoneurotic symptoms (Ettigi and Brown 1978). Neurologic dysfunction is manifested by EEG abnormalities and neuropsychologic test deficits.

Diminished libido and impaired arousal can occur due to CNS depression, general debility, androgen deficiency, or an affective disorder. Kinsey (1948) demonstrated that the male sexual drive reaches a peak during the second decade of life and gradually declines progressively thereafter. This decline is not due to androgen deficiency; normal testosterone levels are maintained until the sixth decade. Normal decline in male sexual vigor has been attributed to maturation and aging of neural and gonadal structures involved in sexual behavior (Ettigi and Brown 1978). In men under 50, this decline may be due to other factors, such as psychosocial issues, depression, poor health, fatigue, and fear of erectile failure. After the age of 50, men tend to show elevated plasma levels of luteinizing hormone (LH) and FSH; this suggests a reduced feedback signal from the testes. A proportion of these men lose libido and manifest autonomic and nervous changes, a situation that is improved by treatment with testosterone.

Hypothyroidism, Cushing's syndrome or Addison's disease, hypopituitarism, hypogonadism, acromegaly, and diabetes may present with sexual dysfunction. Hypothalamic pituitary gonadal dysfunction produces potentially reversible impotence (Leigh and Kramer 1984). Pituitary adenomas may present with diminished libido, galactorrhea, and impotence secondary to hyperprolactinemia in men. Loss of libido has been noted in up to 60 percent of acromegalic patients (Leigh and Kramer 1984). Alcohol and cannabis have antiandrogenic effects.

☐ FEMALE HORMONAL DYSFUNCTION

Alterations in gonadal function have been known to produce physiologic and psychologic changes in women not only at puberty and menopause but during different periods of the menstrual cycle. Withdrawal of estrogen not only produces physical signs such as vaginal mucosal atrophy, osteoporosis, hot flashes, headache, and backache, but also depressive symptoms ranging from a mild feeling of blues to inability to work and a sense of hopelessness (Ettigi and Brown 1978). These are common features observed during menopause, antiestrogen therapy, and hypopituitarism. It has been shown that androgen and not estrogen is a major determinant of sexual behavior in human females

(Ettigi and Brown 1978). In some women, adrenalectomy or hypophysectomy has resulted in a complete loss of libido and sex drive, which is reversed by treatment with testosterone (Ettigi and Brown 1978).

Psychological disturbances have been correlated with menstruation and characteristic hormone changes during the menstrual cycle. Estrogen levels begin to rise during the follicular phase, peak in the ovulatory phase, remain high in the progesterone phase, and drop rapidly in the premenstrual phase. Progesterone rises only after ovulation and drops together with estrogen in the premenstrual phase. Several workers have studied the mood changes during the menstrual cycle (Ettigi and Brown 1978). Most women experience a decline in sexual feeling at the end of the luteal phase of the cycle, when estrogen levels seem to be low. It is during the luteal phase that some women experience mood changes, increased irritability, lethargy, and somatic complaints such as headache, breast swelling and tenderness, edema, and weight gain. This cluster of symptoms recurring in the luteal phase is called premenstrual tension syndrome (Ettigi and Brown 1978). The syndrome begins when estrogen and progesterone begin to fall rapidly from the postovulatory peak and is most severe when the hormone levels are approaching their nadir. The exact mechanism of this syndrome is not clear. The rate or pattern of fall in the sex steroids is not different in patients with premenstrual tension syndrome from normal subjects (Ettigi and Brown 1978). These patients have been reported to have elevated plasma prolactin levels during the luteal phase of their cycle; this has been implicated as a possible cause of the syndrome. Treatment with bromocriptine, a drug that suppresses secretion of prolactin, has been reported to significantly reduce the symptoms (Ettigi and Brown 1978). The prevalence of premenstrual tension syndrome in adult women has been estimated at greater than 25 percent (Leigh and Kramer 1984). The depression is short-lived and improves abruptly in days. However, in a small percentage of severe cases, suicidal ideation or even psychotic features may be present and may be distinct from the irritable, anxious, and hostile symptoms some women report. An increase in violent crimes, industrial illness, and acute psychiatric medical and surgical admissions has been attributed to the premenstrual tension syndrome (Martin et al. 1977). Hypotheses regarding etiology of premenstrual tension syndrome include vitamin

TABLE 2. PSYCHIATRIC DISTURBANCES IN NEUROENDOCRINE DISEASES

	Delirium	Dementia	Anxiety	Apathy	Depression	Irritability	Euphoria	Psychosis	Insomnia	Personality changes
Hypoglycemia	X	X	X		X					X
Hyperglycemia	X	X			X					X
Pancreatic cancer	X		X		X				X	X
Hypoparathyroidism	X		X		X	X	X	X		X
Hyperparathyroidism	X	X	X		X	X		X		X
Hypocortisolism	X	X		X	X	X				X
Hypercortisolism			X		X	X	X	X	X	X
Hypothyroidism		X			X			X		X
Hyperthyroidism			X		X	X	X		X	X
Hypopituitarism	X	X	X	X	X	X		X		X
Hyperprolactinemia			X		X	X				X

B6 deficiency, direct action of the renin-angiotensin-aldosterone system, and abnormalities in CNS monoamine oxidase activity. Bromocriptine has been reported to bring about improvement in physical and behavioral symptoms with consistency in a number of studies; this may be a promising agent for the treatment of premenstrual tension syndrome (Leigh and Kramer 1984).

□ DISCUSSION

An understanding of neuroendocrinology is becoming increasingly important in psychiatry. Firstly, "psychiatric" signs and symptoms may be manifestations of primary neuroendocrine disease. For some neuroendocrine diseases, the earliest manifestations may be psychiatric. Therefore, neuroendocrine illnesses need to be part of the differential diagnosis of changes in behavior, mood, or thinking (Table 2). Secondly, neuroendocrine tests are beginning to be used as diagnostic and prognostic markers for primary psychiatric disorders, particularly for depression. Thirdly, and perhaps most intriguing of all, the line between primary neuroendocrine disease is becoming increasingly blurred as we learn more about the brain's role as the master of the endocrine system as well as an end-organ for multiple hormonal effects.

□ REFERENCES

American Psychiatric Association: Diagnostic and Statistical Manual of Mental Disorders, 3rd ed, Revised (DSM-III-R). Washington, DC, American Psychiatric Association, 1987

Bale RN: Brain damage in diabetes mellitus. Br J Psychiatry 122:337, 1973

Buckman MT, Kellner R: Reduction of distress in hyperprolactinemia with bromocriptine. Am J Psychiatry 142:242–244, 1985

Carroll BJ, Mendels J: Neuroendocrine regulation in affective disorders, in Hormones, Behavior and Psychopathology. Edited by Sachar EJ. New York: Raven Press, 1976, pp 193–224

Cohen KL, Swigar ME: Thyroid function screening in psychiatric patients. JAMA 242:254–257, 1979

Cohen LM, Greenberg DB, Murray GB: Neuropsychiatric presentation of men with pituitary tumors (the "four A's"). Psychosomatics 25:925–928, 1984

Cohen SI: Cushing's syndrome: a psychiatric study of 29 patients. Br J Psychiatry 136:120–124, 1980

Cooper DS, Halpern R, Wood LC, et al: L-thyroxine therapy in subclinical hypothyroidism. Ann Intern Med 101:18–24, 1984

Cope O: Hypoparathyroidism: diagnosis and management. Am J Surg 99:394–403, 1960

Cushing H: The basophil adenomas of the pituitary body and their clinical manifestations (pituitary basophilism). Bulletin of the Johns Hopkins Hospital 50:137–195, 1932

Dackis CA, Goggans FC, Bloodworth R, et al: The prevalence of hypothyroidism in psychiatric populations, in Abstracts of Scientific Proceedings of the American Psychiatric Association Annual Meeting, New York, 1983

Denko JD, Kaelbling R: The psychiatric aspects of hypoparathyroidism. Acta Psychiatr Scand 38:7–70, 1962

Ettigi PG, Brown GM: Brain disorders associated with endocrine dysfunction. Psychiatr Clin North Am 1:117, 1978

Evered DC, Ormston BJ, Smith PA, et al: Grades of hypothyroidism. Br Med J 1:657–662, 1973

Fava GA, Fava M, Kellner R, et al: Depression, hostility and anxiety in hyperprolactinemia amenorrhea. Psychother Psychosom 36:122–128, 1981

Fioretti P, Corsini GU, Murru S, et al: Psychoneuroendocrinological effects of 2-alpha-bromoergocriptine therapy in cases of hyperprolactinemia amenorrhea, in Clinical Psychoneuroendocrinology in Reproduction. Edited by Carenza L, Pancheri P, Zichella L. London, Academic Press, 1978

Goggans FC, Allen RM, Gold MS: Primary hypothyroidism and its relationship to affective disorders, in Medical Mimics of Psychiatric Disorders. Edited by Extein I, Gold MS. Washington, DC, American Psychiatric Press, 1986, pp 93–109

Gold MS, Pottash ALC, Extein IL: Hypothyroidism in depression: evidence from complete thyroid function evaluation. JAMA 245:1919–1922, 1981

Gold MS, Pottash ALC, Extein IL: "Symptomless" autoimmune thyroiditis in depression. Psychiatry Res 6:261–269, 1982

Gold MS, Lydiard RB, Carman JS: Advances in Psychopharmacology: Predicting and Improving Treatment Response. Boca Raton, FL, CRC Press, 1984a

Gold P, Chrousos G, Kellner C, et al: Psychiatric implications of basic and clinical studies with cortiocotropin releasing factor. Am J Psychiatry 141:619–627, 1984b

Hall RCW, Gardner ER, Stickney SK, et al: Physical illness presenting as psychiatric disease. Arch Gen Psychiatry 35:1315, 1978

Hall RCW, Gardner ER, Popkin ER, et al: Unrecognized physical illness prompting psychiatric admission: a prospective study. Am J Psychiatry 138:629, 1981

Harris GW: Electrical stimulation of hypothalamus and mechanisms of neural control of adenohypophysis. J Physiol (Lond) 197:418, 1948

Haskett RF, Rose RM: Neuroendocrine disorders and psychopathology. Psychiatr Clin North Am 4:239–252, 1981

Hellstrom J, Ivemark BI: Primary hyperparathyroidism. Acta Chir Scand [Suppl] 294:5–113, 1962

Kellner R, Buckman MT, Fava GA, et al: Hyperprolactinemia, distress and hostility. Am J Psychiatry 141:759–763, 1984

Keynes WM: The symptoms of hyperparathyroidism. Br Med J 1:239–242, 1961

Kinsey AC: Sexual Behavior in the Human Male. Philadelphia, WB Saunders Co, 1948

Klein I, Levey GS: Unusual manifestations of hypothyroidisms. Arch Intern Med 144:123–128, 1984

Kraft E, Fanby N: Endocrinologic features of skull and hand roentgenograms in psychiatric patients. Clin Radiol 18:272–275, 1967

Kreus LE, Rose RM: Assessment of aggressive behavior and plasma testosterone in a young criminal population. Psychosom Med 34:321, 1972

Leigh H, Kramer SI: The 1984 Year Book. New Haven, CT, Year Book Medical Publishers, 1984

Levin ME: Endocrine syndromes associated with pancreatic islet cell tumors. Med Clin North Am 52:295–312, 1968

Lichtenstein BW: Nervous and mental manifestations of parathyroid and thyroid disorders: hyperparathyroidism, hypoparathyroidism, hyperparathyroidism, and hypothyroidism. Otolaryngol Clin North Am 13:137–145, 1980

Lidz T, Whitehorn JC: Psychiatric problems in a thyroid clinic. JAMA 139:698–701, 1949

Lilliker SL: Prevalence of diabetes in a manic-depressive population. Compr Psychiatry 21:270, 1980

Marks V, Rose FC: Hypoglycemia. Oxford, Blackwell Scientific Publications, 1965

Martin JB, Reichlin S, Brown GM: Clinical Neuroendocrinology. Philadelphia, FA Davis Co, 1977

Petersen P: Psychiatric disorders in primary hyperparathyroiditis. J Clin Endocrinol 28:1491, 1968

Reus VI, Berlant JR: Behavioral disturbances associated with disorders of the hypothalamic-pituitary-adrenal system, in Medical Mimics of Psychiatric Disorders. Edited by Extein I, Gold MS. Washington, DC, American Psychiatric Press, 1986, pp 111–130

Sachs W: Disorders of glucose metabolism in brain dysfunction, in Biology of Brain Dysfunction, Vol. 1. Edited by Guall GE. New York, Plenum, 1973

Service FJ, Dale AJD, Elveback LR, et al: Insulinoma: clinical and diagnostic features of 60 consecutive cases. Mayo Clin Proc 51:417–429, 1976

Smith CK, Barish J, Correa J, et al: Psychiatric disturbance in endocrinologic disease. Psychosom Med 34:69–86, 1972

Sternbach HA, Gold MS, Pottash ALC, et al: Thyroid failure and protirelin test abnormalities in depressed outpatients. JAMA 249:618–620, 1983

Targum SD, Greenberg RD, Harmon RL, et al: Thyroid hormone and the TRH test in refractory depression. J Clin Psychiatry 45:345–346, 1984

Von Zerssen D: Psychotropic Action of Hormones. New York, Spectrum Publications, 1976

Wagner D, Weitzman E: Neuroendocrine secretion and

biological rhythms in man. Psychiatr Clin North Am 3:223–250, 1980

Whelan TB, Schteingart DE, Starkman MN, et al: Neuropsychological deficits in Cushing's Syndrome. J Nerv Ment Dis 168:753–757, 1980

Whybrow PC, Prange HA: A hypothesis of thyroid-catecholamine-receptor interaction: its relevance to affective illness. Arch Gen Psychiatry 38:106–113, 1981

Wilkinson DG: Psychiatric aspects of diabetes mellitus. Br J Psychiatry 138:1, 1981

Chapter 18

Neuropsychiatric Aspects of Vitamin Deficiency States

Lawrence S. Gross, M.D.

CERTAIN VITAMIN DEFICIENCY STATES have long been associated with a variety of physical, psychological, and neurologic symptoms. In underdeveloped areas of the world, severe chronic protein-calorie malnutrition remains a major cause of these dietary syndromes. With the improvement in general nutritional status in the economically developed nations of Western society, vitamin deficiency is unusual but must still be considered in certain populations. These include the mentally retarded, the chronically mentally ill, the economically disadvantaged, and the elderly. Alcoholism, chronic medical illness, malabsorption syndromes, and postoperative status are also associated with vitamin deficiency states.

These deficiencies can result from impaired intake, absorption, or metabolism of vitamins, which, in turn, act as cofactors in metabolic reactions. Neuropsychiatric symptoms are mostly associated with depletion of B-complex vitamins—particularly thiamine, niacin, pyridoxine, folic acid, and vita-

min B12. Typically, poor diet results in multiple vitamin deficiencies. The similarity of early nonspecific symptoms, as well as the common substrates for many B vitamins, may prevent the emergence of the classic single vitamin deficiency syndromes to be described. Vitamins are currently used not only for the prevention and treatment of these deficiency states but more recently as pharmacologic agents in the management of certain inborn errors of metabolism independent of nutritional status.

☐ THIAMINE

Biochemistry and Physiology

Thiamine's primary biochemical role is as the precursor of thiamine pyrophosphate (TPP), a coenzyme in carbohydrate metabolism. TPP is a cofactor in the oxidative decarboxylation reactions of the

Krebs cycle and in the transketolase reactions of the hexose monophosphate shunt pathway for glucose metabolism. This transketolase reaction is used as a measure of thiamine nutritional status. TPP and particularly thiamine triphosphate have been postulated to play a role in peripheral nerve conduction.

Absorption of dietary thiamine occurs in the small intestine by passive diffusion at high concentrations and by active transport at low concentrations. Folate deficiency reduces thiamine absorption. Most body stores are in muscle in the form of TPP. Thiamine has a high turnover rate and is not stored in the body in large quantities for long periods of time. Reduced intake can lead to clinical deficiency in as little as 2 to 3 months (Moran and Green 1979a). Cooking and processing of foods destroys thiamine.

Nutritional Requirements and Sources

The recommended dietary allowance (RDA) for thiamine is 1.2 to 1.5 mg/day in adult males and 1.0 to 1.1 mg/day in adult females (depending on age), with a 50 percent increase during pregnancy and lactation. The allowance is usually expressed relative to caloric intake as 0.5 mg/1,000 kcal, although it is recommended that thiamine intake not be less than 1.0 mg/day even with daily caloric reduction below 2,000 kcal (Rivlin 1985). Although thiamine is widely distributed in foods, its content is low in most foods. The best dietary sources are pork, whole grains, enriched cereal grains, nuts, and beans (Gubler 1984).

Deficiency

Several factors are known to influence thiamine status and may predispose to deficiency states. Foods high in refined carbohydrates have often undergone processing that removes much of the thiamine. Certain foods, including raw fish, coffee, and tea, are believed to contain thiamine-destroying substances that reduce the amount of available thiamine. Disease states can affect thiamine status by (1) decreasing the intake (e.g., anorexia, gastrointestinal distress, dietary restrictions); (2) preventing normal absorption (e.g., diarrhea, colitis, alcoholism); (3) interfering with utilization (e.g., liver disease); and (4) increasing requirements (e.g., fevers, infection, diuresis). Intestinal parasites and drugs can also decrease available thiamine. Alco-

holics are particularly at risk not only from decreased dietary intake but also from ethanol's interference in thiamine absorption (even in healthy individuals) and decreased utilization, particularly associated with liver disease (Gubler 1984).

Beriberi, the classic thiamine deficiency syndrome, is mostly seen today in the Orient where polished white rice is the dietary staple. Clinical manifestations vary with abruptness of onset, age, duration, and severity of the deficiency. Infantile beriberi is a syndrome of acute onset with an often fulminating course that may lead to death from heart failure in a matter of hours. It is typically seen in 2- to 6-month-old breast-fed infants of mothers who may or may not show signs of mild thiamine deficiency. These infants often have a characteristic cry, changing from loud to weak or even inaudible (aphonia) prior to death (Gubler 1984).

Symptoms of early thiamine deficiency include anorexia, irritability, and weight loss. Advanced thiamine deficiency involves the cardiovascular system (wet beriberi) and the central and peripheral nervous system (dry beriberi). Cardiac beriberi presents with signs of right-sided heart failure, including cardiomegaly, exertional dyspnea, tachycardia, and peripheral edema, which may mask associated tissue wasting.

Nervous system manifestations predominate in deficiency states associated with alcoholism, the primary cause of thiamine deficiency in Western societies. Central nervous system involvement most often results in the Wernicke-Korsakoff syndrome, described in detail elsewhere in this book. Peripheral nervous system involvement is evidenced by a polyneuropathy with varying degrees of symmetrical motor, sensory, and reflex impairment. Limbs are more severely affected distally, with the lower extremities affected earlier and more extensively than the arms. Associated paresthesias and dysesthesias result in the classic "burning feet" syndrome. Neuropathologicly, there is axonal degeneration with destruction of both axon and myelin sheath (Adams and Victor 1985).

In both naturally occurring and experimental thiamine deficiency in humans, various emotional disturbances have been encountered. These include intolerance to noise, poor concentration, anxiety, depression, irritability, and insomnia (Gubler 1984). In a study of 154 general hospital psychiatric inpatients with a history of poor diet, 58 had abnormally low thiamine levels; it was felt that these findings were probably associated with malnutrition rather than etiologically related to psychiatric diagnosis (Carney et al. 1979).

Diagnosis. Thiamine status is most accurately assessed by measuring the activity of whole blood or erythrocyte transketolase, an enzyme requiring TPP as a cofactor. In general, an increase in enzyme activity of greater than 16 percent following addition of exogenous TPP is indicative of thiamine deficiency (Moran and Greene 1979a). Urinary thiamine can also be measured, but it may be falsely elevated if there has been recent thiamine intake or diuretic use. In the absence of laboratory confirmation, a therapeutic trial of thiamine with rapid improvement of symptoms (within hours) supports the diagnosis of thiamine deficiency.

Treatment. In cases of suspected thiamine deficiency, treatment should begin immediately with large doses of thiamine—50 to 100 mg im or iv for the first few days, often with dramatic improvement in cardiovascular symptoms and in the ophthalmoplegia associated with Wernicke's syndrome. Treatment is continued with 5 to 10 mg/day po until adequate dietary intake is resumed (Rivlin 1985).

Several inborn errors of metabolism have responded to pharmacologic doses of thiamine. These include thiamine responsive megaloblastic anemia, lactic acidosis, and branched-chain ketoaciduria, as well as subacute necrotizing encephalomyelopathy (Leigh's disease), an autosomal recessive condition in which thiamine triphosphate is deficient in the brain.

☐ NIACIN

Biochemistry and Physiology

Niacin refers to two compounds, nicotinic acid and nicotinamide, which serve as precursors of two coenzymes, nicotinamide adenine dinucleotide (NAD) and nicotinamide adenine dinucleotide phosphate (NADP), used in a wide variety of oxidation-reduction reactions. Niacin is stable to light and heat. It is almost completely absorbed from the gastrointestinal tract by diffusion. In addition, niacin can be synthesized by the liver from the amino acid tryptophan, with about 1.5 percent of dietary tryptophan being converted to niacin. Only small amounts of the vitamin are stored in the body; clinical signs can develop after as little as 8 to 10 weeks of dietary deficiency (Moran and Greene 1979b).

Nutritional Requirements and Sources

The RDA for niacin varies with age: in adult males it is 16 to 19 mg/day; in adult females it is 13 to 14 mg/day, with an additional 2 mg/day during pregnancy and 5 mg/day during lactation (Food and Nutrition Board 1980). Liver, meat, poultry, fish, and peanuts are good dietary sources of niacin. Animal proteins from meat, milk, and eggs have high tryptophan content for endogenously generated niacin. Niacin in wheat grains and corn has reduced absorption and limited bioavailability.

Deficiency

Dietary niacin deficiency can result from general malnutrition and food fadism. It is common in areas of the world where corn is a dietary staple. Prolonged alcoholism may result in reduced niacin intake as well as impaired absorption and metabolism. Because pyridoxine and riboflavin are cofactors for the conversion of tryptophan to niacin, deficiencies of these vitamins increase requirements for dietary niacin. Conversion of tryptophan to niacin may also be impaired in Hartnup's disease (hereditary impairment in tryptophan absorption), carcinoid syndrome (diversion of tryptophan from niacin to serotonin synthesis), and treatment with isoniazid (INH) (via pyridoxine deficiency). Malabsorption syndromes and numerous other metabolic diseases may affect niacin status.

Clinically, early symptoms of niacin deficiency may be fluctuating and nonspecific, with patients complaining of malaise, anorexia, weight loss, weakness, poor concentration, insomnia, and nervousness. Irritability, emotional lability, and depression may be prominent (Lishman 1978). As the deficiency progresses, symptoms of the classic syndrome of pellagra begin to develop. These include: (1) oral lesions with sore tongue and stomatitis, (2) cutaneous lesions of exposed skin surfaces, (3) gastrointestinal involvement with diarrhea and malabsorption, and (4) nervous system involvement.

Neuropsychiatrically, a peripheral neuropathy indistinguishable from that of thiamine deficiency and spinal cord involvement of the posterior columns and corticospinal tract have been described, but most nervous system involvement is cerebral (Adams and Victor 1985). A nicotinic acid deficiency encephalopathy in which progressive cerebral deterioration occurred in elderly alcoholics with poor nutritional status has been reported. Mortality was reduced with large doses of nicotinic acid, but patients often had residual organic memory deficits (Jolliffe 1941). This syndrome was postulated to represent an acute form of nicotinic acid deficiency, but it has not been reported in recent years.

As niacin deficiency becomes more advanced, florid neuropsychiatric manifestations may appear with or without dermatologic, gastrointestinal, or prodromal emotional symptoms. Acute disorientation, confusion, and memory impairment may appear with significant depression, violent outbursts, and frank psychosis. Delirium may ensue and progress to coma and death in advanced cases. Occasionally chronic untreated pellagra may present as a slowly progressive dementia (Lishman 1978). The popular association of pellagra with the "Four Ds"—dermatitis, diarrhea, dementia, and death (Rivlin 1985)—may be amended to include delirium and depression as well.

Diagnosis. The most practical and widely used index of niacin status is the measurement of a urinary metabolite, N-methylnicotinamide. Low levels in the urine are indicative of niacin deficiency.

Treatment. Dosage regimens have been somewhat empirical for replacement therapy in niacin deficiency. Oral doses in the range of 50 to 500 mg/day are used to treat the acute manifestations of pellagra (Danford and Munro 1980). This is usually supplied in the form of nicotinamide until adequate dietary intake has resumed. Similar dosage regimens are used to treat niacin deficiency associated with Hartnup's disease and the carcinoid syndrome. Psychotic and behavioral symptoms may respond dramatically, although chronic severe mental changes may require high-dose parenteral niacin therapy and show a less complete response.

Because of its lipid-lowering effect, large doses specifically of nicotinic acid, in the range of 3 g/day or more, have been used in the treatment of hypertriglyceridemia, hypercholesterolemia, and types II, IV, and V hyperlipoproteinemia. Although it may reduce the recurrence rate of nonfatal myocardial infarction, nicotinic acid has not

been shown to increase survival of patients with prior history of myocardial infarction. The subject of much controversy in the past, large doses of nicotinic acid have not been shown to be effective in the treatment of schizophrenia or other psychiatric disorders, except for those related to pellagra. Large doses of nicotinic acid (3–10 g/day) for prolonged periods of time have been associated with significant toxic effects, including vasodilation, flushing, sensation of heat, gastrointestinal distress (nausea, vomiting, abdominal pain), skin pigmentation, hyperuricemia, and liver disturbances (Moran and Greene 1979b).

☐ VITAMIN B6 (PYRIDOXINE)

Biochemistry and Physiology

Vitamin B6, or pyridoxine, is used to refer to three active compounds: pyridoxol, pyridoxal, and pyridoxamine. These compounds are widely distributed in tissues, but none is stored. As little as 3 or 4 weeks of deficiency has been associated with the appearance of signs and symptoms (Moran and Greene 1979a). The liver converts vitamin B6 into its metabolically active form, pyridoxal phosphate (PLP), an important coenzyme in amino acid metabolism and heme biosynthesis. Pyridoxal and pyridoxamine are generally found in animal products; pyridoxol is the form obtained from plant sources. Absorption takes place by passive diffusion, mainly in the jejunum but also in the ileum.

Nutritional Requirements and Sources

The RDA for vitamin B6 is 2.2 mg/day for adult males and 2.0 mg/day for adult females, with an increase of 0.6 mg/day in pregnancy and 0.5 mg/day during lactation (Food and Nutrition Board 1980). High protein intake increases the requirement for vitamin B6, which is widely distributed in both plant and animal sources. Liver, meats, whole-grain cereals, beans, and nuts are good sources. Reduction of bioavailability of the vitamin occurs in the cooking and processing of foods.

Deficiency

Because of its widespread food sources, dietary deficiency of pyridoxine is unusual but may occur with multiple deficiencies in severe malnutrition or malabsorption syndromes. Vitamin B6 deficiency associated with increased PLP degradation has been observed in uremic patients and in patients with liver disease. Age and stress may also alter vitamin B6 status (Driskell 1984).

A number of drugs have been associated with pyridoxine deficiency. Isoniazid (INH), used in the treatment of tuberculosis, and the antihypertensive agent hydralazine probably interfere with vitamin B6 metabolism by complexing with pyridoxal to form inactive hydrazones. Slow inactivators of isoniazid are particularly at risk for B6 deficiency, which causes a peripheral neuropathy characterized by paresthesias and burning pain of the feet and legs (hands are less affected), followed by weakness and loss of ankle reflexes (Adams and Victor 1985). Concomitant administration of pyridoxine with isoniazid prevents the development of the neuropathy, which occurs after weeks to months of isoniazid therapy. Children taking isoniazid are less likely to develop neuropathy; they more commonly show diarrhea, pyridoxine-responsive anemia, and seizures. Hydralazine-induced neuropathy responds to discontinuation of the drug and administration of pyridoxine (Adams and Victor 1985). Another hydrazine compound, the monoamine oxidase inhibitor phenelzine, has also been associated with pyridoxine deficiency responsive to concomitant administration of pyridoxine without discontinuation of the antidepressant (Stewart et al. 1984a). Other drugs associated with pyridoxine deficiency include cycloserine, penicillamine, and L-dopa. Oral contraceptives have been associated with pyridoxine-responsive abnormalities in tryptophan metabolism that may or may not represent a B6 deficiency syndrome. Pyridoxine deficiency is common in alcoholism and is associated with reduced dietary intake, impaired absorption, and increased PLP degradation. Associated liver disease may impair PLP synthesis as well.

General clinical features of pyridoxine deficiency include stomatitis, dermatitis, and glossitis. Symptoms of marked deficiencies in adults may include hypochromic microcytic anemia, gastrointestinal distress, weight loss, weakness, irritability, peripheral neuropathy, depression and confusion followed by seizures, and EEG changes. B6 deficiency has been implicated in carpal tunnel syndrome (Ellis et al. 1979). Low levels of vitamin B6 have been found in medically cleared depressed

outpatients (Stewart et al. 1984b). Pyridoxine deficiency in depressed inpatients has been suggested to be of possible etiologic significance (Carney et al. 1979).

In addition to the previously described deficiency symptoms, vitamin B6-dependent syndromes have been described in which tissue levels of the vitamin are normal but pharmacologic doses of pyridoxine are needed for treatment of the biochemical abnormalities. If treatment is delayed, irreversible alterations in brain function may occur, leading to mental retardation (Driskell 1984). Pyridoxine-dependent convulsions usually begin within the first 2 weeks of life and do not respond to standard anticonvulsant regimens. Resolution of seizures has occurred after administration of 5 to 10 mg of pyridoxine; treatment must be continued indefinitely (Moran and Greene 1979a). Other rare metabolic vitamin B6-dependency syndromes include pyridoxine-responsive microcytic hypochromic anemia, xanthurenic aciduria, cystathioninuria, and homocystinuria.

Diagnosis. Measurement of plasma PLP levels and PLP-stimulated erythrocyte transaminase activity are considered to be the best indicators of clinical pyridoxine status (Driskell 1984). Other tests include direct assay of vitamin B6 in blood (normal levels greater than 50 ng/ml) or urinary excretion of its main metabolite, 4-pyridoxic acid (excretion of less than 1.0 mg/day suggests deficiency) (Rivlin 1985).

Treatment. Dietary pyridoxine deficiency can be treated with oral doses in the range of 2 to 10 mg/ day; pregnancy may require dosages of 10 to 20 mg/day. Peripheral neuropathy of pyridoxine deficiency associated with B6-antagonizing drugs requires higher doses of approximately 100 mg/day. Since iatrogenic pyridoxine deficiency is preventable, concomitant B6 therapy can be initiated with these drugs, particularly if prolonged treatment is anticipated. B6 is now routinely prescribed for patients receiving isoniazid; treatment with high doses of the vitamin is contraindicated in patients receiving L-dopa because of possible interference with the efficacy of the drug (Rivlin 1985). Much higher doses of vitamin B6, up to 1,500 mg/day, may be required to treat the pyridoxine-dependent syndromes. Although routine prophylactic pyridoxine administration has not been established for patients receiving phenelzine, they should be observed for symptoms of B6 deficiency with addition of pyridoxine if symptoms appear (Stewart et al. 1984a). Pyridoxine, 40 mg/day, was reported to be effective in the treatment of women with B6 deficiency and depression secondary to the use of estrogen-containing oral contraceptives; depressed contraceptive users without B6 deficiency did not respond to pyridoxine (Larsson-Cohn 1975). B6 deficiency was also correlated with pyridoxine-responsiveness in patients with associated carpal tunnel syndrome. A crossover study with pyridoxine and placebo demonstrated complete resolution of symptoms of both B6 deficiency and carpal tunnel syndrome with pyridoxine 100 mg/day for 9 to 11 weeks (Ellis et al. 1979). This is contrasted with pyridoxine's generally regarded ineffectiveness in the treatment of schizophrenia, autism, childhood hyperactivity, and peripheral neuropathies without known vitamin B6 deficiency (Rivlin 1985). A sensory neuropathy has been described in patients receiving pyridoxine 2 g/day or more, raising the question of megavitamin toxicity (Schaumburg et al. 1983).

☐ VITAMIN B12

Biochemistry and Physiology

Vitamin B12 (cyanocobalamin) and its analogue hydroxocobalamin are precursors of active coenzymes methylcobalamin and 5-deoxyadenosylcobalamin, which are essential for cell growth and replication and the maintenance of normal myelin in the nervous system. Methylcobalamin is a required cofactor in the synthesis of methionine from homocysteine. Vitamin B12 deficiency may serve to trap folic acid (another substrate in this pathway) in a metabolically unavailable form. The resultant reduction in deoxyribonucleic acid (DNA) synthesis, most notably in cells with rapid turnover rates, may account for the hematologic abnormalities associated with vitamin B12 deficiency. 5-Deoxyadenosylcobalamin is involved in lipid and carbohydrate metabolism; impairment in lipid synthesis may affect the integrity of the myelin sheath and contribute to the neurologic symptoms seen in B12 deficiency (Hillman 1980).

Peptic enzymes in the acidic gastric juices release dietary vitamin B12 from ingested proteins. B12 is then bound to intrinsic factor, a glycoprotein

produced by gastric parietal cells essential for vitamin B12 absorption. Absorption takes place at specific receptor sites in the ileal microvilli. Absorbed B12 is then bound to proteins called transcobalamins and transported via the circulation to the liver where most of the body's B12 is stored. Enterohepatic circulation occurs with 3 to 8 μg of the vitamin excreted daily into the bile and reabsorbed in the ileum (Hillman 1980).

Nutritional Requirements and Sources

The RDA for vitamin B12 for adult males and females is 3.0 μg/day. An additional 1.0 μg/day is recommended during pregnancy and lactation (Food and Nutrition Board 1980). With total body stores of the vitamin estimated at 2 to 5 mg in an adult male, it takes years for signs and symptoms of deficiency to develop. As the vitamin is only synthesized by certain microorganisms that grow in soil, sewage, or intestines, the best sources are the tissues and organs of host animals. Good sources of vitamin B12 are meats, fish, eggs, and milk.

Deficiency

B12 deficiency can occur from decreased ingestion, decreased absorption, increased requirements, and impaired utilization. Because vitamin stores greatly exceed daily requirements, dietary deficiency is rare but has occurred in strict vegetarians who avoid dairy products and eggs. The most common cause of vitamin B12 deficiency is pernicious anemia, in which a gastric mucosal defect decreases intrinsic factor production, thereby reducing B12 absorption. Lack of intrinsic factor is also responsible for decreased cyanocobalamin absorption in gastrectomy and cases of destruction of gastric mucosa by ingestion of corrosive agents. Blind loops, strictures, anastamoses, and diverticuli can result in overgrowth of intestinal flora that compete for available B12. In addition, competitive utilization from fish tapeworm infestation as well as ileal defects can lead to decreased absorption of the vitamin despite adequate amounts of intrinsic factor. Drugs can impair B12 absorption (e.g., colchicine, neomycin) and metabolism (e.g., nitrous oxide) (Ellenbogen 1984). An association between reduced vitamin B12 and the use of psychotropics is unclear (Carney and Sheffield 1978). Enzyme deficiencies and reduced or abnormal binding proteins can result in impaired cyanocobalamin utilization.

Pernicious anemia classically affects fair-complected northern Europeans over the age of 40, but a notable exception is the report of higher than expected incidence and younger age of onset in American black women (Carmel and Johnson 1978). The frequent presence of serum binding or blocking antiintrinsic factor antibodies suggests an underlying autoimmune process, which often occurs in association with thyrotoxicosis, Hashimoto's thyroiditis, hypogammaglobulinemia, vitiligo, rheumatoid arthritis, and gastric carcinoma (Beck 1985).

Clinically, vitamin B12 deficiency impacts the hematopoietic and nervous systems. Hematologic abnormalities are often the first symptoms to appear, but neurologic or psychiatric manifestations may be the initial or sole presentation. Megaloblastic anemia is classically of slow onset. Because of the underlying DNA defect, megaloblastosis occurs in varying degrees in all proliferating body cells, particularly in the bone marrow where erythrocyte precursors are usually most severely affected. Red blood cell (RBC) survival is decreased; ineffective erythropoesis can lead to hemolysis, both in the marrow and in the peripheral circulation. Other changes include reduced reticulocyte counts, hypersegmentation of neutrophils, and varying degrees of leukopenia, thrombocytopenia, and normochromic macrocytic anemia.

Neurologic symptoms frequently begin with general weakness and paresthesias, often described as tingling or "pins and needles" feelings. The paresthesias are usually constant and progressive, symmetrically affecting the distal parts of all extremities, although sometimes the legs are affected first and more extensively. Gait becomes unsteady, with worsening stiffness, weakness, and ataxia that may progress to spastic paraplegia if the disease is not treated (Adams and Victor 1985).

Objective signs may be absent initially if only paresthesias are present. However, as the disease progresses, evidence of the involvement of the posterior and lateral columns of the spinal cord becomes evident—hence the term *subacute combined degeneration*. Loss of vibration sense is the most consistent sign; this usually affects the legs more extensively than the arms and may involve the trunk as well. Impairment of position sense also usually occurs. Motor signs are often limited to the lower extremities and include loss of strength, spasticity, reflex changes, clonus, and extensor plantar responses. Nervous system involvement in subacute

combined degeneration is relatively symmetrical; the presence of persistent asymmetrical motor or sensory changes should cast doubt on the diagnosis. Occasionally, visual impairment may be the initial or only manifestation. The cerebrospinal fluid (CSF) is usually normal, although protein may be moderately increased (Adams and Victor 1985).

Neuropathologically, the process involves diffuse although uneven white matter degeneration of the spinal cord and less commonly the brain. Early swelling of myelin sheaths progresses to demyelination and axonal degeneration with pronounced gliosis in chronic lesions. These changes begin in the posterior columns of the lower cervical and upper thoracic segments of the cord and spread up and down the cord as well as to the lateral and anterior columns. Visual involvement is evidenced by foci of spongy degeneration in the optic nerves and chiasm (Adams and Victor 1985).

Low vitamin B12 levels have been documented in patients with a variety of psychiatric diagnoses (Carney and Sheffield 1970). Many psychiatric symptoms, including depression, mania, paranoid states, confusion, and dementia, have been described in pernicious anemia (Shulman 1967). As in other vitamin deficiencies, nonspecific symptoms such as anorexia, weight loss, weakness, palpitations, lightheadedness, syncope, and headache may result in a psychiatric presentation.

Despite its presence in psychiatric populations, low vitamin B12 has not been clearly related etiologically to functional psychiatric disorders. In the case of affective disorders, it may simply be an associated feature in predisposed individuals (Shulman 1967). However, there is evidence for a causal link between vitamin B12 deficiency and cerebral dysfunction, particularly memory deficits and organic psychosis (Carney and Sheffield 1978). Electroencephalogram (EEG) abnormalities have been shown in a significant percentage of pernicious anemia patients; these changes do not correlate with the severity of the anemia and are reversible to varying degrees with B12 replacement (Walton et al. 1954; Wallace and Westmoreland 1976). Scheinberg's (1951) study of cerebral blood flow and metabolism in pernicious anemia suggested that a disturbance in cerebral metabolism produced by the vitamin deficiency state (not the anemia) was responsible for the neuropsychiatric symptoms. Cerebral lesions that are identical to spinal cord lesions in subacute combined degeneration have been described in pernicious anemia; as with cord lesions, because delays in diagnosis and B12 replacement can lead to irreversible damage, vitamin B12 deficiency should be considered in the differential diagnosis of all patients with unexplained confusional states and dementia (Shulman 1967).

Since the presence of neuropsychiatric symptoms is not well correlated with hematologic abnormalities, there is growing evidence that, in some cases, organic psychiatric manifestations may be the initial clinical presentation of vitamin B12 deficiency. Because these symptoms are potentially reversible with replacement, the consideration of B12 deficiency and serum B12 determination in all patients with organic psychiatric symptoms has been recommended (Evans et al. 1983).

Diagnosis. Demonstration of a reduced serum vitamin B12 level is diagnostic of deficiency. Normal plasma contains 175 to 725 pg/ml of the vitamin (range varies with method and laboratory), with clinical signs generally appearing when the serum level is below 80 to 100 pg/ml (Beck 1985). Gastric achlorhydria following histamine stimulation and an abnormal Schilling's test are diagnostic in pernicious anemia. Serum folate is often elevated when serum B12 is reduced unless there is coexisting folate deficiency. Because both deficiencies may present with similar manifestations of megaloblastic anemia, levels of vitamin B12 and folate should always be measured together. Methylmalonic aciduria, response to physiologic doses of B12, and lack of response to physiologic doses of folic acid are specific indicators of B12 deficiency.

Treatment. Parenteral administration of vitamin B12 is used to supply the daily requirement and to replenish depleted body stores of the vitamin. Doses greater than 100 μg lead to rapid excretion of unbound vitamin, yet the general dosage given is in excess of need. Treatment begins with 500 to 1,000 μg im daily for 2 weeks, followed by the same dose twice weekly for 4 weeks or until the hematocrit returns to normal, and then the same dose once a month for the lifetime of the patient. For patients with neurologic symptoms, 500 to 1000 μg every 2 weeks for 6 months is recommended. Neurologic abnormalities lasting longer than 12 to 18 months are usually irreversible (Beck 1985).

Patients with B12 deficiency often report an increased sense of well-being within 24 hours after the start of replacement therapy. Hematologic abnormalities begin to correct within days, the length of time to complete recovery depending on the duration and severity of the deficiency. The same is true for organic and neurologic symptoms. Memory and orientation can show dramatic improvement with treatment, although full recovery of mental and neurologic function may take months or may never occur (Hillman 1980). A partial hematologic response in B12 deficiency may follow large (pharmacologic) doses of folic acid, but neurologic symptoms will be unchanged and the abrupt onset of neurologic abnormalities may be precipitated in previously asymptomatic patients.

No toxicity has been demonstrated from megadoses of vitamin B12. Despite its use in the treatment of various disorders without evidence of deficiency (e.g., various dermatologic, neurologic, and psychiatric disorders; allergies; and as an appetite or growth stimulant), the effectiveness of vitamin B12 in these conditions has not been established and is not recommended. With the rare exception of hereditary methylmalonic aciduria, the only valid indication for B12 therapy is vitamin B12 deficiency of whatever etiology (Beck 1985).

☐ FOLIC ACID

Biochemistry and Physiology

Folic acid is the commonly used name for pteroylmonoglutamic acid, the reduced form (5,6,7,8-tetrahydrofolic acid) of which is active in a variety of enzyme reactions, including amino acid metabolism, purine synthesis, and synthesis of thymidylate, a rate-limiting step in DNA synthesis. Impairment in thymidylate synthesis with folic acid deficiency reduces DNA production, with resulting megaloblastic transformation (Beck 1985). The reduction of folate to its metabolically active form is dependent on dihydrofolate reductase, a single enzyme linked to NADPH (a reduced form of NADP).

Most folate is absorbed in the duodenum and jejunum. Dietary folates are predominantly polyglutamate derivatives that are hydrolyzed to monoglutamate forms for absorption from the gut and transport to the tissues. There they are taken up and metabolized intracellularly to polyglutamate forms that are retained in the cells. Folates are widely distributed in tissues, with normal body stores estimated at 5 to 10 mg, half of which is in the liver (Brody et al. 1984). Supplies of folates are maintained both by diet and by an enterohepatic circulation that may provide as much as 200 μg or more of folic acid each day for recirculation to tissues (Hillman 1980).

Nutritional Requirements and Sources

The RDA for folic acid for adult males and females is 400 μg/day, with an additional 400 μg/day in pregnancy and 100 μg/day during lactation (Food and Nutrition Board 1980). Folic acid requirements in infants may be relatively greater than those of adults, presumably due to the demands of active cell growth and division in infants (Sullivan 1970). Good dietary sources of folate include fresh green vegetables, particularly asparagus, broccoli, spinach, and lettuce. Liver and yeast are also rich in folates. Protracted cooking, especially with large amounts of water, can destroy much of the folic acid contained in foods.

Deficiency

Folic acid deficiency is most commonly the result of poor dietary intake often associated with alcoholism, poverty, and food fadism. Malabsorption diseases of the small bowel (e.g., tropical and nontropical sprue, Crohn's disease involving the jejunum) impair folate absorption. Drugs that inhibit dihydrofolate reductase (e.g., methotrexate, trimethoprim) or interfere with absorption or tissue storage of folate (e.g., certain anticonvulsants, oral contraceptives) can lead to a deficiency state (Hillman 1980). In addition to the dietary deficiency associated with alcoholism, alcohol interferes with folate metabolism; the toxic effect of alcohol on hepatic parenchymal cells may interfere with the enterohepatic circulation and liver storage of the vitamin. Certain disease states characterized by rapid cell turnover, such as hemolytic anemias and neoplastic diseases, increase folate requirements. As previously mentioned, this also occurs in pregnancy, lactation, and periods of increased growth.

Pernicious anemia and nutritional vitamin B12 deficiency can be associated with symptoms of folate deficiency. Similar physical symptoms may occur in both vitamin deficiencies, including glossitis, anorexia, diarrhea, hyperpigmentation, hepatomegaly, splenomegaly, and general features of anemia (Sullivan 1970).

Clinically, the megaloblastic anemia of folate deficiency is indistinguishable from that of B12 deficiency; this is not surprising considering the metabolic interrelationships of the two vitamins. The anemia of B12 deficiency may actually be due to

the impaired retention and utilization of cellular folates due to decreased activity of the B12-requiring enzyme methionine synthetase (Brody et al. 1984). However, due to limited body stores of folic acid, the onset of the anemia in folate deficiency is much more rapid. In Herbert's (1962) classic description of symptoms following reduction of dietary folate intake to 5 μg/day, the earliest indication of deficiency was a fall in serum folate below normal levels after only 3 weeks of deprivation. Hypersegmentation of neutrophils was noted after 7 weeks of reduced folate intake, but macrocytosis did not appear until after 18 weeks. Anemia was first noted after 4.5 months of folate deprivation.

Despite similarities in hematologic symptoms in folate and B12 deficiencies, folate deficiency is much less frequently associated with neurologic abnormalities. In a study of 50 patients with B12 deficiency and 34 patients with folate deficiency presenting with megaloblastosis in a general hospital, peripheral neuropathy was the most common neurologic finding in B12 deficiency and was three times more common than in folate deficiency; subacute combined degeneration of the cord was an uncommon finding limited to B12-deficient patients (Shorvon et al. 1980). Conversely, 10 folate-deficient patients with normal B12 levels who exhibited neurologic disease indistinguishable from subacute combined degeneration were reported; the neuropathy completely resolved in 3 patients and significantly improved in 5 others following folate treatment (10 mg tid) (Manzoor and Runcie 1976). There was no relationship between hematologic and neurologic abnormalities in either study.

Folate deficiency has been described in association with various psychiatric diagnoses. Surveys of inpatient populations have shown the incidence of low serum folate to be as high as 20 to 30 percent (Carney and Sheffield 1978; Thornton and Thornton 1978), commonly associated with epilepsy, depression, and organic psychosis (Carney 1967). There is a question whether this high figure reflects true folate deficiency due to the presence of drugs and other factors. Antifolate activity of psychotropics is unclear, but disturbances of folate and B12 metabolism by anticonvulsants may play a role in the production of the schizophrenia-like psychoses of epilepsy (Reynolds 1967).

The association between folate deficiency and mood and organic disturbances is well documented, mostly by British investigators. Of particular interest is the relationship between folic acid deficiency and depression. In the previously cited study of patients with megaloblastosis (Shorvon et al. 1980), the most common neuropsychiatric abnormality in folate-deficient patients was an affective disturbance (present in 56 percent). This was almost three times more common than in B12-deficient patients. In another study (Reynolds et al. 1970), 24 percent of depressed inpatients had low serum folate concentrations associated with significantly higher depression inventory scores on admission and discharge compared to patients with equivocal or normal serum folates. This was postulated to be due to either a dietary deficiency secondary to severe depression or to a possible causal influence of folate deficiency in depression by interference in hydroxylation of tyrosine and tryptophan in central nervous system catecholamine and 5-hydroxytryptamine synthesis. Some investigators believe that folic acid deficiency depression may be a distinct clinical entity (Ghadirian et al. 1980). Others consider depression to be the result of prolonged fatigue and lassitude associated with the vitamin deficiency and describe a syndrome of "distractibility, fatigue, and perplexity as mild signs of diffuse incipient organic brain damage" (Botez et al. 1984, p. 434). In his original description of experimental deficiency, Herbert (1962) reported gradually progressive sleeplessness, forgetfulness, and irritability that disappeared within 48 hours of the initiation of oral folic acid therapy. Encephalopathy and dementia have also been associated with folic acid deficiency (Manzoor and Runcie 1976). Psychiatric manifestations may precede or occur in the absence of hematologic and neurologic abnormalities. The widespread incidence of affective disorders makes routine screening impractical, but folate deficiency should be considered in those patients with coexisting evidence of organicity and/or neuropathy, particularly in the presence of poor diet, malabsorption, or megaloblastic anemia.

Diagnosis. Measurement of serum folate has been widely used as an index of folate status. Levels less than 3 ng/ml indicate folate deficiency, levels between 3 and 6 ng/ml indicate marginal deficiency, and levels above 6 ng/ml indicate adequate folate status. Caution should be used in the interpretation of serum levels in that they will reflect any recent dietary intake. RBC folate levels reflect body folate stores at the time of red cell formation and thus may be a more accurate measure of tissue folate status than plasma levels. RBC levels of less than 140 ng/ml packed cells are indicative of folate de-

ficiency, levels between 140 and 160 ng/ml suggest marginal deficiency, and levels greater than 160 ng/ml indicate normal folate status (Brody et al. 1984). Folic acid is concentrated in the CSF, and there is a positive correlation between serum and CSF folate activity; thus the CSF folate level may most accurately reflect the folate status of the nervous system (Wells and Casey 1967).

Treatment. Therapy of the patient with megaloblastic anemia who is acutely ill may need to be instituted before a definitive diagnosis is reached and may necessitate intramuscular injections of both vitamin B12 (described above) and folic acid (1–5 mg). Prior to any treatment, serum levels of both vitamins should be obtained to establish an accurate diagnosis and to avoid neurologic complications from folate treatment of occult B12 deficiency.

Following the initial treatment, oral therapy is begun with 1 to 2 mg/day, which is adequate for most patients and will usually replenish body stores after 4 or 5 weeks of therapy. Treatment is continued until diet or underlying problems are corrected; in certain cases of chronic illness, such as malabsorption, treatment must be continued indefinitely. No toxicity has been reported from large doses of folic acid.

The hematologic response to folic acid is predictable and identical to that in the B12 treatment of B12 deficiency. Within 48 hours of the initiation of appropriate therapy, megaloblastic erythropoesis disappears. Reticulocyte count begins to rise on the second or third day and peaks on the fifth or sixth day; hematocrit starts to rise during the second week (Hillman 1980).

Neuropsychiatric symptoms have also shown response to folate therapy. In the previously cited study of folate-responsive neuropathy (Manzoor and Runcie 1976), improvement in mood was noted in all patients within 2 weeks of starting treatment. Mental status changes included dramatic resolution of psychosis in 2 of 3 patients and improvement in 4 of 5 cases of pretreatment confusion; improvement in mood preceded neurologic improvement by weeks to months. Low-folate inpatients with endogenous depression, schizophrenia, and organic psychoses who were treated with folic acid in addition to conventional treatments were discharged sooner and in a better state than those who did not receive folate (Carney and Sheffield 1970). Improvement has been reported in depressive and organic symptoms following folate supplementation in patients with low serum and CSF folic acid concentrations (Botez et al. 1984). Despite the association between reduced folate levels and neuropsychiatric symptoms, any etiologic significance remains unclear and needs further investigation. For a comprehensive review of folic acid, the reader is referred elsewhere (Botez and Reynolds 1979).

☐ OTHER VITAMIN DEFICIENCIES

Pantothenic acid deficiency has been implicated in the "burning feet" syndrome observed in prisoners and malnourished subjects in the Far East during World War II; it responded to pantothenic acid preparations and not to other B vitamins (Moran and Greene 1979b). A peripheral sensory neuropathy has been reported from experimental dietary deficiency of another B vitamin, riboflavin (Cooperman and Lopez 1984). Deficiencies of vitamins A, C, D, E, and K have not been clearly related to neuropsychiatric syndromes.

☐ REFERENCES

Adams RD, Victor M: Diseases of the nervous system due to nutritional deficiency, in Principles of Neurology. New York, McGraw-Hill, 1985

Beck WS: Megaloblastic anemias, in Cecil Textbook of Medicine. Edited by Wyngaarden JB, Smith LH Jr. Philadelphia, WB Saunders Co, 1985

Botez MI, Reynolds EH (eds): Folic Acid in Neurology, Psychiatry, and Internal Medicine. New York, Raven Press, 1979

Botez MI, Botez T, Maag U: The Wechsler subtests in mild organic brain damage associated with folate deficiency. Psychol Med 14:431–437, 1984

Brody T, Shane B, Stokstad ELR: Folic acid, in Handbook of Vitamins. Edited by Machlin LJ. New York, Marcel Dekker, 1984

Carmel R, Johnson CS: Racial patterns in pernicious anemia. N Engl J Med 298:647–650, 1978

Carney MWP: Serum folate values in 423 psychiatric patients. Br Med J 4:512–516, 1967

Carney MWP, Sheffield BF: Associations of subnormal serum folate and vitamin B12 values and effects of replacement therapy. J Nerv Ment Dis 150:404–412, 1970

Carney MWP, Sheffield BF: Serum folic acid and B12 in 272 psychiatric in-patients. Psychol Med 8:139–144, 1978

Carney MWP, Williams DG, Sheffield BF: Thiamine and pyridoxine lack in newly-admitted psychiatric patients. Br J Psychiatry 135:249–254, 1979

Cooperman JM, Lopez R: Riboflavin, in Handbook of Vitamins. Edited by Machlin LJ. New York, Marcel Dekker, 1984

Danford DE, Munro HN: Water-soluble vitamins, in The Pharmacological Basis of Therapeutics. Edited by Gilman AG, Goodman LS, Gilman A. New York, Macmillan, 1980

Driskell JA: Vitamin B6, in Handbook of Vitamins. Edited by Machlin LJ. New York, Marcel Dekker, 1984

Ellenbogen L: Vitamin B12, in Handbook of Vitamins. Edited by Machlin LJ. New York, Marcel Dekker, 1984

Ellis J, Folkers K, Watanabe T, et al: Clinical results of a cross-over treatment with pyridoxine and placebo of the carpal tunnel syndrome. Am J Clin Nutr 32:2040–2046, 1979

Evans DL, Edelsohn GA, Golden RN: Organic psychosis without anemia or spinal cord symptoms in patients with vitamin B12 deficiency. Am J Psychiatry 140:218–221, 1983

Food and Nutrition Board, National Research Council: Recommended Dietary Allowances (9th rev ed). Washington, DC, National Academy of Sciences, 1980

Ghadirian AM, Ananth J, Engelsmann F: Folic acid deficiency and depression. Psychosomatics 21:926–929, 1980

Gubler CJ: Thiamin, in Handbook of Vitamins. Edited by Machlin LJ. New York, Marcel Dekker, 1984

Herbert V: Experimental nutritional folate deficiency in man. Trans Assoc Am Physicians 75:307–320, 1962

Hillman RS: Vitamin B12, folic acid, and the treatment of megaloblastic anemias, in The Pharmacological Basis of Therapeutics. Edited by Gilman AG, Goodman LS, Gilman A. New York, Macmillan, 1980

Jolliffe N: Treatment of neuropsychiatric disorders with vitamins. JAMA 117:1496–1500, 1941

Larsson-Cohn U: Oral contraceptives and vitamins: a review. Am J Obstet Gynecol 121:84–89, 1975

Lishman WA: Organic Psychiatry. London, Blackwell Scientific Publications, 1978

Manzoor M, Runcie J: Folate-responsive neuropathy: report of 10 cases. Br Med J 1:1176–1178, 1976

Moran JR, Greene HL: The B vitamins and vitamin C in human nutrition, I: general considerations and 'obligatory' B vitamins. Am J Dis Child 133:192–199, 1979a

Moran JR, Greene HL: The B vitamins and vitamin C in human nutrition, II: 'conditional' B vitamins and vitamin C. Am J Dis Child 133:308–314, 1979b

Reynolds EH: Schizophrenia-like psychoses of epilepsy and disturbances of folate and B12 metabolism induced by anticonvulsant drugs. Br J Psychiatry 113:911–919, 1967

Reynolds EH, Preece JM, Bailey J, et al: Folate deficiency in depressive illness. Br J Psychiatry 117:287–292, 1970

Rivlin RS: Disorders of vitamin metabolism: deficiencies, metabolic abnormalities, and excesses, in Cecil Textbook of Medicine. Edited by Wyngaarden JB, Smith LH Jr. Philadelphia, WB Saunders Co, 1985

Schaumburg H, Kaplan J, Windebank A, et al: Sensory neuropathy from pyridoxine abuse, a new megavitamin syndrome. N Engl J Med 309:445–448, 1983

Scheinberg P: Cerebral blood flow and metabolism in pernicious anemia. Blood 6:213–227, 1951

Shorvon SD, Carney MWP, Chanarin I, et al: The neuropsychiatry of megaloblastic anemia. Br Med J 281:1036–1038, 1980

Shulman R: Vitamin B12 deficiency and psychiatric illness. Br J Psychiatry 113:252–256, 1967

Stewart JW, Harrison W, Quitkin F, et al: Phenelzine-induced pyridoxine deficiency. J Clin Psychopharmacol 4:225–226, 1984a

Stewart JW, Harrison W, Quitkin F, et al: Low B6 levels in depressed outpatients. Biol Psychiatry 4:613–616, 1984b

Sullivan LW: Differential diagnosis and management of the patient with megaloblastic anemia. Am J Med 48:609–617, 1970

Thornton WE, Thornton BP: Folic acid, mental function and dietary habits. J Clin Psychiatry 39:315–322, 1978

Wallace PW, Westmoreland BF: The electroencephalogram in pernicious anemia. Mayo Clin Proc 51:281–285, 1976

Walton JN, Kiloh LG, Osselton JW, et al: The electroencephalogram in pernicious anemia and subacute combined degeneration of the cord. Electroencephalogr Clin Neurophysiol 6:45–64, 1954

Wells DG, Casey HJ: Lactobacillus casei CSF folate activity. Br Med J 3:834–836, 1967

Chapter 19

Neuropsychiatric Aspects of Infectious and Inflammatory Diseases of the Central Nervous System

Jean Lud Cadet, M.D.
James B. Lohr, M.D.

THE INVASION OF THE CENTRAL NERVOUS SYSTEM (CNS) by bacteria and viruses can cause severe neuropsychiatric symptoms and some of the most marked disabilities associated with medical illnesses. Although modern therapeutic approaches have significantly altered the course of these disorders, there remain many cases where treatment is mainly palliative. The identification of some causative infectious agents was made possible by the development of modern immunologic techniques and the realization that viral illnesses may present with quite variable tempos. For example, herpes simplex encephalitis has an abrupt onset that may be associated with focal or generalized seizures, whereas Creutzfeldt-Jakob disease has a more gradual onset accompanied by cognitive and movement disturbances.

Recent advances in molecular biology are revolutionizing the field further. This approach promises to enhance the understanding of the interaction between the immune system and the brain and their relationship to behavior. Thus neuropsychiatric aspects of infections are additionally important insofar as they might provide another window through which to gaze at the complexities of the brain–mind dilemma.

The purpose of this chapter is to discuss briefly several infectious diseases of the CNS that are known to affect behavior early in their course and that may leave residual psychiatric symptoms often difficult to distinguish from idiopathic psychiatric disorders such as schizophrenia and manic-depressive psychosis. The chapter will be divided into three parts: bacterial, viral, and other inflammatory diseases.

☐ GENERAL PRINCIPLES IN CNS INFECTIONS

The anatomy of the brain and of the spinal cord and their relationship to other structures such as blood vessels and the meninges influence the presentation and the course of CNS infections. Most infections of the brain usually arise from any focus of colonization elsewhere in the body and thus may arrive there through a number of ways. These include the blood, skull fractures, or peripheral nerves. The most common route of infection, however, is via hematogenous spread. There are both humoral and anatomic barriers that prevent the CNS from getting infected more often despite the significant number of organisms that may invade other peripheral tissues.

The reticuloendothelial system (RES) and the host's humoral and cellular immune response are very efficient systems that clear the blood of viruses and bacteria. The brain itself is suspended in cerebrospinal fluid (CSF) and is protected by the meninges, which are made of the pia mater, the arachnoid, and the dura mater. Infants and patients with immune deficiency diseases are particularly prone to infections of the CNS because the delay involved in mounting an effective immune response may allow the infection to reach the CNS of these individuals. The brain has a limited armamentarium against infections. For example, it does not have a lymphatic system and depends, during an infection, on the increase in capillary permeability that allows the entry of immune agents from the periphery.

As in other disorders of the CNS, when approaching a patient with an infection, the clinician attempts to localize the site of the lesion. The functional specialization of various neuroanatomic regions are often involved in such a way as to produce characteristic neurologic signs and symptoms. Surrounding edema, hemorrhage, and associated hydrocephalus can cause significant disability in patients with CNS infections. Tests, such as computed tomography (CT), can help to localize a lesion but do not provide a diagnosis or identify the organism as, for example, in a brain abscess. A working knowledge of the functional anatomy of the brain and of some of the characteristic syndromes that can be caused by pathologic involvement may help to raise the clinician's level of suspicion, help to localize the lesion, and encourage neurologic consultation if indicated.

☐ ACUTE BACTERIAL INFECTIONS

Acute bacterial meningitis is a medical emergency that requires prompt diagnostic and therapeutic interventions. The death rate without medical intervention is very high, but treatment with the proper antibiotic can lower it significantly. A rapid determination of the pathogenic organism is required so that the appropriate antibiotics can be prescribed to prevent complications, which may include lactic acidosis and disseminated intravascular coagulation.

Bacterial meningitis is usually caused by one of three organisms: *Pneumococcus*, *Haemophilus*, or *Meningococcus*. Predisposing factors include pneumonia, recent or old head trauma, sinusitis, and alcoholism. These infections cause significant meningeal inflammation, accumulate over the convexity of the brain, and may lead to hydrocephalus. Involvement of cortical structures may lead to characteristic neurologic signs and symptoms.

Clinical Presentation

The manifestations of acute bacterial infections are the results of the interaction of the inflammatory process and the host's anatomy and immune response. The tempo may be quite variable in that the infection may develop abruptly (acute) or over a few days (subacute). The patient appears to be acutely ill, perhaps presenting with generalized malaise, fever, chills, and vomiting. The patient may also complain of having a terrible headache. Involvement of cortical structures may lead to lethargy, confusion, or delirium. Seizures, stupor, or coma may also develop. Neuropsychiatric symptoms such as changes in mood or hallucinatory phenomena are not prominent.

The presence of petechiae or purpuric rashes indicates meningococcal meningitis. Brudzinski's sign (flexion of knees and hips following the flexion of the head on the chest) and Kernig's sign (flexion of the knees following gentle flexion of the thigh with the leg in extension) are very prominent on examination.

Laboratory Findings

The blood reveals a high white count with neutrophilic preponderance. Radiographic studies may reveal another site of infection or a skull fracture. In patients who have signs of increased intracranial

TABLE 1.   CSF FINDINGS IN INTRACRANIAL INFECTIOUS DISEASES

Infections	Pressure	Cell Count	Glucose	Protein (g/100 ml)
Acute meningitis	elevated	leukocytosis (100–10,000/mm³)	decreased	elevated (100–500)
Tuberculous meningitis	elevated	lymphocytosis (<500/mm³)	decreased	elevated (100–300)
Syphilitic meningitis	elevated	lymphocytosis	decreased	elevated (50–200)
Brain abscess	elevated	lymphocytosis	normal	elevated (100–500)
Viral meningitis	elevated	lymphocytosis	normal	elevated (50–100)
Systemic lupus erythematosus	normal or elevated	lymphocytosis	normal	elevated (50–150)
Acquired immune deficiency syndrome	normal or elevated	lymphocytosis	normal	elevated (50–100)

pressure such as papilledema, an emergency CT scan is indicated to rule out a brain abscess before a spinal tap is performed. The spinal fluid shows decreased blood glucose, elevated protein, and high polymorphonuclear cell counts (Table 1). The fluid should be gram stained to get an early hint to the identity of the causative agents. A knowledgeable interpretation of the gram stain will help to start the patient on an antibiotic to which the organism might be susceptible while awaiting the results of the cultures.

Treatment

The choice of an agent that enters the CNS and achieves high enough concentration to bacteriostatic or bacteriocidal is mandatory. Early on, treatment is aimed at eradicating all possible agents that may be encountered in a given age group. Because pneumococci, meningococci, and streptococci are often the pathogenic agents, the drug of choice is usually penicillin (100,000–500,000 units/kg of body weight/day). In a case of penetrating head injury, a penicillin plus an aminoglycoside are indicated.

Complications

Some of the complications associated with acute bacterial infections include cranial nerve palsies, focal brain lesions, hydrocephalus, adrenal hemorrhage, disturbances in cognition, and personality changes. Modern treatment modalities have caused a significant decrease in the prevalence of sequelae associated with acute bacterial infections.

☐   SUBACUTE INFECTIONS

Meningitis may sometimes present as a more slowly progressive disease, with signs and symptoms referring to the cognitive function of the patient. It may be difficult to arrive at the proper diagnosis under these circumstances if the clinician does not have a high degree of suspicion. A number of infectious agents may present with such a course. These include *Myobacterium tuberculosis*, *Trepenoma pallidum*, and *Cryptococcus* (Table 2).

TABLE 2.   POSSIBLE CAUSES OF SUBACUTE MENINGITIS

Behçet's meningitis
Brucellosis
Coccidiodomycosis
Cryptococcosis
Cysticercosis
Echinococcosis
Histoplasmosis
Leptospirosis
Mollaret's meningitis
Sarcoidosis
Syphilis
Tuberculosis

☐ TUBERCULOUS MENINGITIS

Because the incidence of tuberculous meningitis has decreased during the past several years, it is often not considered in the differential diagnosis until late in the course of an infectious process. It often results from the rupture of a subependymal tubercle into the CSF (Auerbach 1954). A substantial number of patients have other extrapulmonary involvements of the disease process.

Clinical Presentation

The clinical presentations of CNS tuberculosis (TB) may vary considerably. These may consist of chronic headache, vague complaints of personality changes, irritability, listlessness, chronic fatigue, and changes of cognitive function (Kocen and Parsons 1970; Oatey et al. 1981). There is no other clinical evidence of involvement of an infectious process anywhere else in a great percentage of these patients.

Laboratory Findings

The diagnosis of CNS TB is made by the examination of the CSF, which shows increased white cell counts ($100–500/mm^3$) with a lymphocytic preponderance, increased protein, and decreased glucose levels. Because results of mycobacterial cultures are usually not back until 2 to 6 weeks, examination for other organ involvement on chest X ray, culture of sputum, and urine is mandatory. The intermediate-strength purified protein derivative (PPD) may be negative in patients who are suffering from overwhelming infections, malnutrition, or acquired immune deficiency diseases.

The CT scan has supplemented the diagnostic armamentarium and has also helped to enlarge the conceptual approach to tuberculous meningitis. There have been cases of patients who presented with miliary TB and no clinical evidence of tuberculous meningitis but who turned out on CT studies to have tuberculomas of the brain (Witham et al. 1979). The lesions disappeared with successful treatment of the infectious process.

Treatment

Isoniazid is the cornerstone to the treatment of TB meningitis. Doses of 10 mg/kg are used. Rifampin may be added to the regimen in cases that may require two drugs. Both drugs cross the blood-brain barrier and reach concentrations much higher than their minimal inhibitory concentration for mycobacterial TB.

Complications

Hydrocephalus, infarctions, and basilar pachymeningitis are reported complications of tuberculous meningitis. Several patients may be left with hemiplegia, cranial nerve abnormalities, psychomotor retardation, and chronic cognitive deficits.

☐ NEUROSYPHILIS

The sexually transmitted spirochete, *Treponema pallidum*, can cause significant abnormalities in many organ systems. When it affects the CNS, the symptom complex at the time of presentation can vary substantially. At times, symptoms referable to the CNS appear rather early. At other times, it may take several decades after the initial peripheral infection before the CNS is involved. Because of the diversity of the neuropsychiatric symptoms, the clinical diagnosis may be difficult to make.

Clinical Presentation

The major presentation of primary syphilis is the genital chancre. The spirochetes then migrate through the bloodstream and infect other areas of the body. When invasion of the CNS develops, the patient may be either symptomatic or not. The symptomatic patients may present with meningovascular syphilis, tabes dorsalis, or general paresis, which is a rare condition at the present time.

In meningovascular syphilis, the patient presents with complaints of headaches. Further progression of the illness may lead to thromboses of the cerebral vasculature, with subsequent progressive neurologic impairments and cerebrovascular accidents (CVAs). This entity should be a consideration in a young patient who develops a CVA. The presentation of general paresis is more variable. There may be complaints of irritability, nervousness, and insidious personality changes. The most common presenting symptom is dementia associated with memory loss, labile and inappropriate affect, disorientation, and significant impairment of judgment. Some patients may present with symptoms that are reminiscent of an affective diathesis. These include marked depression, fatigue, sleep disturbances, forgetfulness, psychomotor retardation, and somatic preoccupations. Patients have also presented with full-blown manic episodes. Other symptoms appear to be similar to those seen in schizophrenic illness. Burke and Schaberg (1985) reported that 11 of 30 patients with neurosyphilis had symptoms of dementia, mania, or paranoia. A significant number of these patients had concomitant symptoms of taboparesis. Some patients have presented with dysarthria, which appears to be similar to symptoms secondary to drug intoxication. These patients often show significant decline in their social interaction with others. Some reports have suggested that the clinical presentation of general paresis may be different from the preantibiotic era (Heathfield 1976; Hooshmand 1972).

The symptoms of tabes dorsalis usually progress very slowly. The clinical examination reveals that the patient manifests decreased position and vibratory sensation. The gait is broad based. The patients complain of sharp, burning pain in the legs or other areas of the body. Although the Argyll-Robertson pupillary abnormalities (small, irregular pupils that react on accommodation but not to light) are classically written about, other ophthalmologic abnormalities include unilateral fixed dilated pupils, unilateral myotonic pupil, optic neuritis, visual field defects, and ocular nerve palsies. Often when a patient presents with a neuropsychiatric symptom complex, it is the development of the ophthalmologic abnormalities that help the clinician in clinching the diagnosis.

Laboratory Findings

The blood cell count is usually normal. The CSF examination shows lymphocytic preponderance, elevated protein, and normal glucose. The diagnosis is made by documenting a positive VDRL test in the CSF. The serum VDRL may be positive in a number of illnesses such as the connective tissue diseases; however, the CSF is almost never positive in these disorders. The electroencephalogram (EEG) is abnormal in general paresis and shows mild to moderate slowing.

Treatment

Patients are treated with benzathine penicillin 2.4 million units im every week for 3 weeks or with penicillin G 600,000 units im daily for 15 days. Some prefer to admit patients in cases of general paresis.

During the initial part of treatment, the status of some patients may deteriorate because of the Jarisch-Herxheimer reaction, which consists of fever and leukocytosis. The course of treatment is followed by watching the CSF protein, cell counts, and VDRL titer.

Adequate treatment, if started early, usually leads to arrest of the disease process. When treatment is started too late, the CNS abnormalities may progress relentlessly and lead to a demented state. The treatment of neurosyphilis caused a revolution in the treatment of some psychiatric patients in the early part of this century and led to the emptying of many asylums during that time.

Complications

Complications may include palsies of the sixth and seventh cranial nerves, ptosis, and even CVAs. The advent of specific antibiotic treatment has significantly decreased the prevalence of these complications.

☐ BRAIN ABSCESS

Abscess results from localized infection of the CNS and often causes signs and symptoms that are similar to tumors that affect similar areas of the brain. The regions of the brain that are invaded depend on the site of origin of the primary infection: ear infections affect the temporal lobe, whereas sinus infections may cause abscess in the frontal lobe (De Louvois et al. 1977; Ingham et al. 1977). The presenting signs and symptoms depend on which areas of the brain are involved in the infectious process. After the organisms invade the CNS, they lead to softening, edema, and petechial hemorrhages in the brain parenchyma.

Patients with pulmonary, dental, and cyanotic heart disease and those with recent head traumas are more prone to developing brain abscesses.

Clinical Presentation

The initial presentation may consist of recurrent headaches, personality changes, memory loss, and confusion. Fever may or may not be present. The absence of fever and of focal neurologic signs may often delay the diagnosis for weeks. As the disease progresses, the development of hemiparesis, seizures, stupor, and even coma often lead to the correct diagnosis.

To rule out brain abscess as a possible cause of a patient neuropsychiatric symptoms, the psychiatric consultant on an infectious disease service should look for possible signs of predisposing factors such as the ones listed above.

Laboratory Findings

When a brain abscess is suspected, a lumbar puncture is not advisable. A CT scan should be performed first to localize the focus of infection. The scan usually shows a ring (capsule of abscess)–enhancing lesion after the infusion of dye. Radionuclide scans have been reported to show the early stages of abscess formation better than the CT scan (Crocker et al. 1974). The identification of the offending organism is made by growing it from pus obtained during neurosurgical intervention.

Treatment

Once the diagnosis is suspected and there is radiographic evidence of an encapsulated mass in the brain, therapy should start with broad spectrum antibiotics. Several of the drugs (e.g., the penicillins and chloramphenicol) that enter the CNS easily often have difficulty penetrating brain abscess. Sulfamethoxazole and metronizadole penetrate abscess very well and are effective against anaerobes, which are the most common causes of brain abscesses (Morgan et al. 1973). Several groups have reported the effective treatment of brain abscess with antibiotic alone, and these cases were followed by serial CT scan (Berg et al. 1978; Heineman et al. 1971).

Complications

Complications may include aphasia, hemiparesis, and cranial nerve palsies depending on the areas of the brain affected. Recent antibiotic treatment has helped to reduce these complications.

☐ VIRAL INFECTIONS

Symptoms similar to those seen in major affective and schizophrenic disorders may antedate or follow the onset of neurologic signs in patients who suffer from viral encephalitides. A large number of the patients who suffered from influenza in the 1920s presented with a psychotic-like illness. These symptoms have been reported with many viruses (e.g., measles, polio, Epstein-Barr virus) (Table 3). The most common cause of viral illnesses presenting as psychosis is herpes simplex virus. Chronic neurodegenerative diseases may be secondary to so-called slow viruses that invade the CNS and live there in an indolent form for many years until the patient develops a deteriorating neurologic illness from which the patient may not recover. The clearest example of such an entity is Creutzfeldt-Jakob disease (Gajdusek 1978).

Viral encephalitides presenting as "functional" psychoses might be more common than usually assumed. As discussed below, a significant number of patients who suffer from viral encephalitis may often present with a psychotic-like disorder. Thus it is important that the neuropsychiatrist be aware of the possibility that patients who develop acute psychiatric symptoms may be suffering from viral illnesses, which, in some cases (e.g., herpes encephalitis), may be treatable.

Clinical Presentation

Torrey (1986) reviewed the literature on viral causes of psychoses published since 1970. All the patients had a comparatively abrupt onset of their illness, varying between a few days to 5 weeks. Delusions and auditory hallucinations are the most common presenting symptoms. Patients may present with other subtle signs of personality changes, including irritability, bizarre behavior, and depressed feelings. Other patients may show significant behavior disturbances, including thought disorder, inappropiate affect, mutism, and catatonic behavior. It may be difficult to differentiate this last symptom from the neuroleptic malignant syndrome, which is often fatal if not recognized in time. Several of these patients were diagnosed as either schizophrenic or manic-depressive and received neuroleptic treatment in an attempt to control their behavior abnormalities.

TABLE 3. VIRUSES THAT MAY PRESENT WITH PSYCHIATRIC SYMPTOMS

Coxsackievirus	Influenza virus
Cytomegalovirus	Measles virus
Enterovirus	Rabies virus
Epstein-Barr virus	Togavirus
Herpes simplex virus	Poliovirus

In the course of their illness, the patients may develop other neurologic signs and symptoms that may help the clinician to make the diagnosis. These include headaches, seizure-like activities, syncopal episodes, and other flu-like symptoms.

Laboratory Findings

Although the CSF may be normal, it often reveals pleocytosis with increases in lymphocyte count, elevated protein, normal glucose level, and normal pressure. Repeat taps may be necessary before the organism responsible for the viral diathesis can be grown. Other diagnostic tests include immunofluorescence, IgM-specific serology that may be elevated in the acute phase of the illness. For the diagnosis to be made, the demonstration of an increase of the viral titer with a subsequent fall must be demonstrated. Other standard tests include cultures of sputum, nasopharyngeal aspirates, and serum. The EEGs may show localized slowings, but diffuse abnormalities are the most common findings.

Treatment

In most cases, therapy is supportive. Several agents have been developed for the treatment of acute encephalitides but these are mostly in the experimental stages.

Complications

The course of viral encephalitis is usually benign. However, severe cases may be associated with aphasia, hemiplegia, and chronic cognitive deficits.

☐ SYSTEMIC LUPUS ERYTHEMATOSUS

Systemic lupus erythematosus (SLE) is a common collagen vascular disease that is characterized by multisystem involvement, remissions, and exacerbations. It is the cause of significant morbidity among young women (Rubin et al. 1985). The disorder is idiopathic but is believed to involve genetic as well as environmental factors. The high degree of mortality that may be associated with untreated cases and the high frequency of neuropsychiatric symptoms as the initial manifestations of the disorder underlie the importance of SLE to the psychiatrist.

After rheumatoid arthritis (RA), SLE is the most common vasculitis. The disease is nine times more common in women than in men, with a prevalence of 143 per 100,000. Black women have a significantly higher incidence of the disease (Fessel 1974). The diagnosis of SLE is made according to the criteria of the American Rheumatological Association (Cohen et al. 1971).

Clinical Presentation

The most common presenting features of SLE are arthritic complaints and fever (Grigor et al. 1978). Nonneuropsychiatric manifestations include nonspecific erythemas, dermatitis, malar rash, palmar and plantar rashes, urticaria, and discoid lesions. The patients may show periungual telangectasia and digital gangrene. Pulmonary manifestations include pneumonitis, pulmonary hemorrhage, lymphocytic interstitial pneumonia, pulmonary hypertension, and sometimes significant weakness of the diaphragm. Kidney involvement may be manifested by the nephrotic syndrome, which is associated with diffuse proliferative and membranous glomerulonephritis. Pericarditis, diffuse lymphadenopathy, and splenomegaly are also seen in SLE.

The neuropsychiatric manifestations of SLE are protean (Abel et al. 1980; Feinglass et al. 1976; Hall et al. 1980; Johnson and Richardson 1968; Stern and Robbins 1960). These include affective and psychotic symptoms, subtle personality changes, and even dementia. The affective disturbances may include depression, hypomania, or full-blown manic episodes. There may be reports of auditory or visual hallucinations, bizarre delusions, and other psychotic symptoms. It may be very difficult to differentiate such patients from those who are suffering from a typical idiopathic schizophrenic syndrome. However, in contrast to most schizophrenics, these patients may recognize the hallucinations as being inappropriate. There have also been reports of catatonic reactions (Feinglass et al. 1976; Kronfol et al. 1977). Demented patients show memory disturbances, problems with calculations, difficulty orienting themselves, and confusion. These may progress to delirium and even stupor and coma.

Seizure disorders have also been seen in patients with SLE. These are usually of the grand mal variety, but other types have also been reported.

Even though they usually occur toward the end of the course of the illness, they may be the presenting manifestation. A significant number of SLE patients complain of migraine and may report fortification spectrum in the visual field. Chorea may also be a significant problem. It is more often reported in much younger patients in whom it may be mistaken for Sydenham's chorea (St. Vitus' Dance).

Laboratory Findings

Because a number of vasculitic diseases need to be differentiated from SLE (Table 4), researchers have attempted to develop several immunologic tests that might increase the accuracy of diagnosis by supplementing the mostly clinical criteria of the ARA.

The most widely used test is the antinuclear antibody (ANA). It is very sensitive but highly nonspecific. SLE patients have antibodies (Abs) to a wide variety of antigens, including nuclear or membranous substances. For example, lupus patients may have Abs against native double-stranded DNA, nuclear ribonucleic acid (RNA), or anti-smooth muscle Abs. Because SLE is the prototype immune complex disease, several tests were developed to assess the status of the complement system in SLE. These include CH_{50}, C_3, C_4, and other immune complexes that contain IgG, IgA, or complement. A low level of C_3 is thought to correlate with disease activity (Valentijn et al. 1985).

A number of researchers have been studying the relevance of brain-specific antigens in patients with CNS lupus (Bresnihan et al. 1977; Temesvari et al. 1983; Williams et al. 1981). Patients with cerebral involvement are more likely to show antineuronal antibodies than those without such signs and symptoms. Inoue et al. (1982) reported the occurrence of antineuronal Abs in the brain of a patient who had died with cerebral lupus.

CT scan studies correlate well with focal lesions of the CNS, but more often show diffuse atrophy or nonspecific ventricular dilatation (Gonzalez-Scarano et al. 1979). The EEG shows diffuse or focal abnormalities in about 70 percent of cases but is often abnormal during clinical remission. The CSF may show pleocytosis, elevated protein, elevated red blood cell counts, and xanthochromia if there is subarachnoid hemorrhage. It is important to do a lumbar puncture in patients with SLE to rule out infections to which this population is particularly prone.

The diagnosis of CNS lupus is mostly clinical. The development of more specific immunologic and more sensitive radiologic tests such as nuclear magnetic resonance (NMR) may help in following the natural course of the illness.

Treatment

The mainstay of therapy is corticosteroid treatment. These agents have provided significant benefit to SLE patients. It is felt that the introduction of steroids and the early recognition of serious illness have altered the mortality rate associated with SLE (Rubin et al. 1985). However, the mortality rate due to vascular accidents has increased because of the lengthier course of the illness.

The psychiatric symptoms may respond to typical psychiatric agents such as antidepressants, antipsychotics, or anxiolytics. The presence of steroid-induced psychosis may be a confounding variable in the long-term treatment of these patients since either a reduction or an increase in the steroid dosage may lead to an exacerbation of the symptoms. In any case, in a patient who develops significant neuropsychiatric symptoms while on steroids, it is advisable that the dose of the drug be reduced slowly to evaluate the relationship of the psychosis to the illness or the drug treatment.

Complications

As mentioned above, there is significant morbidity associated with SLE. The short-term outcome for improvement in the psychiatric symptoms is better than in the past because of the higher degree of suspicion among physicians who take care of these patients. It has been reported that suicide is a significant cause of early death among SLE patients (Dubois et al. 1974).

☐ ACQUIRED IMMUNE DEFICIENCY SYNDROME

The acquired immune deficiency syndrome (AIDS) consists of significant abnormalities in cell-mediated

---

TABLE 4. VASCULITIDES WITH POSSIBLE NEUROPSYCHIATRIC MANIFESTATIONS

Rheumatoid arthritis	Polyarteritis nodosa
Scleroderma	Wegener's granulomatosis
Sjogren's syndrome	Giant cell arteritis
Cogan's syndrome	Henoch-Schonlein purpura

immunity that render the patients highly susceptible to opportunistic infections. The disorder is very virulent and affects a young population of homosexual individuals, hemophiliacs, drug abusers, recent Haitian immigrants, and, more recently, heterosexual individuals via blood products or sexual relationship with bisexuals. The disorder has reached epidemic proportion, has caused significant psychiatric morbidity, and has a high death rate. Even though the hallmark of the disorder is multiple infections and malignancies, there is a significantly high rate of patients who present with neuropsychiatric symptoms. This syndrome is thus important to the psychiatrist from several vantage points because these patients need to be diagnosed as early as possible so that they may be provided with the appropriate medical care. Furthermore, the psychological needs of this population of patients whose life-styles may result in specific psychosocial problems must be addressed as early as possible during the illness.

Clinical Presentation

AIDS varies in its clinical presentation and may present some difficulties in making the initial diagnosis. The most common presenting complaints are those of nonspecific malaise, low-grade fever, and generalized lymphadenopathy, which are often the harbinger of other significant infections in several organ systems in the body (Mildvan et al. 1981; Waterston 1982). *Pneumocystis carinii* pneumonia is the opportunistic infection most commonly reported. However, these patients are highly susceptible to other infectious agents such as viruses, fungi, mycobacteria, and various parasites. *Toxoplasma gondii*, papovavirus, *Mycobacterium avium intracellulare*, and cryptococcus are some infectious agents to which the CNS is particularly vulnerable. The same type of infections have been reported in patients with various malignancies and in patients who have been treated chronically with steroids (Hooper et al. 1982). These patients also may present with Kaposi's sarcoma, which is a very common disorder in certain African countries.

Neuropsychiatric symptoms have been a common accompaniment of AIDS since the early reports of the disorder. Initially, these abnormalities were thought to be either secondary to the psychosocial disorders that might have preceded the AIDS or the psychological response to an overwhelming illness that is almost always fatal. These views have had to be modified somewhat because

the human T-cell lymphotropic virus-type III (HTLV-III) has been shown to be highly toxic to cells of the CNS (Gallo et al. 1984). Thus neuropsychiatric changes may also be the result of brain lesions inherent to the syndrome.

It has been recognized that the natural history of patients who suffer from AIDS is often replete with signs and symptoms that are often of a psychiatric nature before other neurologic changes emerge (Perry and Jacobsen 1986). About one-third of patients who have AIDS have neurologic complaints at the time of presentation (Levy et al. 1985). The most common neurologic complication is subacute encephalitis (Levy et al. 1985; Snider et al. 1983). These patients often develop generalized malaise, lethargy, social withdrawal, lack of interest in daily activities, and sometimes significant depression. They often exhibit progressive dementia, confusion, agitation, seizures, and coma. Some patients have also been reported with myoclonus.

In addition, several patients may present with symptoms that could be considered to be of a purely psychiatric nature. These individuals often have a long history of social withdrawal, lack of energy, apathy, and a significant lack of concern in their daily activities before the more common medical symptoms appear. More significant, however, are the symptoms of depression and of acute psychosis that the patients may present with or may develop during the course of their illness (Perry and Jacobsen 1986; Price et al. 1986). They may complain of dysphoria, fatigue, loss of appetite, personality changes, and significant sleep disturbances. Often these individuals have no cognitive changes that might lead the clinician to suspect an organic basis of the psychiatric symptoms. The psychotic symptoms include suspiciousness, grandiosity, delusions, and hallucinations that may involve all the senses. Some patients have been reported with full-blown manic episodes (Perry and Jacobsen 1986). These patients are often very difficult to treat because they may be more sensitive to the side effects of the drugs used in the therapy of these psychiatric disorders. For example, Perry and Jacobsen (1986) reported the case of a 33-year-old lawyer who presented with a manic episode after the death of his lover who was suffering from AIDS. His mania was controlled with chlorpromazine but he subsequently developed significant depression accompanied by suicidal ideation. Treatment with imipramine, 75 mg daily, caused him to become very disorganized. Subsequent treatment with trazodone failed to cause any improvement; the patient remained withdrawn and refused to participate in daily activities on the ward. A few weeks later the patient developed symptoms consistent with the diagnosis of AIDS and died within a period of 4 weeks despite antibiotic treatment.

Laboratory Findings

It is very difficult to diagnose AIDS-related psychiatric illness during the early stages of the illness when there may be no other systemic signs of an ongoing infectious process. Often repeated laboratory examinations fail to detect any abnormalities in the CSF of these patients until late in the illness.

The diagnosis of AIDS is made by documenting the HTLV-III antibodies in the serum of a patient who has severe derangement in cell-mediated immunity, which has led to the development of opportunistic infections or unusual neoplasms. AIDS-related mental changes should be suspected in all patients who fall in a high-risk group for the development of the disorder. Despite the best efforts of the clinician, however, it is often virtually impossible to establish the diagnosis definitively before the full development of the other complications of the illness.

CSF findings may vary from being normal to showing significant lymphocytosis, increased protein, and increased immunoglobulins. The most common CT scan finding is nonspecific atrophy in patients who present with mostly neuropsychiatric symptoms. However, several patients who had seizures, significant progressive dementia, or myoclonus showed atrophy as the only finding on CT scan (Snider et al. 1983). In cases where demonstrable neurologic deficits are prominent, the CT reveals enhancing intracerebral mass lesions with surrounding edema (Levy et al. 1985; Snider et al. 1983). The EEG may be normal or diffusely abnormal and does not correlate well with the neuropsychiatric status of the patient. A significant abnormality on the EEG rules out an idiopathic psychiatric diagnosis such as schizophrenia or manic-depressive illness. The magnetic resonance image (MRI) may provide more information than the CT scan. When AIDS-related neuropsychiatric symptoms are suspected, serial CT scans or MRI should be done to watch for or to follow the development of possible CNS lesions that may be medically treatable.

Neuropathologic studies have revealed axonal swelling, ischemic changes, or spongiform degeneration in the CNS of patients who died of AIDS-related complications.

Treatment

The treatment of AIDS focuses mostly on controlling the many opportunistic infections that these patients develop. It includes the use of antifungal, antibacterial, and possible antiviral agents, depending on which infections are more prominent. These infections tend to be quite virulent and the mortality rate is high.

Treatment of the neuropsychiatric symptoms is complicated because they are mostly secondary to an unremitting neurodegenerative process. Attempts to treat these patients with the usual psychiatric armamentarium have not met with a high degree of success. As with all organically caused psychiatric symptoms, psychotropic drugs should be started at much lower dosages than usual, especially in the case of neuroleptics that might be used to control agitation. For example, if haloperidol is chosen, it should be started at .5 mg and increased very slowly to avoid motor side effects that may complicate the care of these patients. An attempt should always be made to correct any neurologic infections that may be the cause of these symptoms before psychotropic medications are used.

The psychosocial component of the treatment of AIDS patients is probably one of the most difficult problems facing modern medicine at present. AIDS patients are often rejected by family and friends who are afraid of catching the virus. Many medical staff members may be adamant about not taking care of these individuals. The liaison psychiatrist may be an important member of the treatment team, and may help the staff express their fears about contracting AIDS or their prejudices toward people with homosexual orientation. It is especially incumbent on the consultation-liaison psychiatrist to become very familiar with the pathophysiology of AIDS, the approaches to its treatment, and the special social and psychiatric needs of the people who are afflicted with this devastating illness.

Complications

Despite the increasing number of investigators who have become involved in AIDS research and the discovery of the pathogenic relationship of the HTLV-III virus to the illness, no recent discovery has been made that is curative. The patients usually die from the progressive involvement of all systems by the virus. In the CNS, there is a progressive multifocal encephalopathy that involves the cerebral cortex, the cerebellum, and the brainstem.

☐ CONCLUSION

In this chapter, we have attempted to review briefly several infectious and immunologic disorders to help the clinician stay aware of many possible infectious causes of subtle psychiatric changes in previously healthy individuals. This chapter illustrated the role that the immune system may play in the interaction between the brain and behavior. As was demonstrated during the early part of this century, it was the treatment of an infectious process (neurosyphilis) that emptied the asylum. It is thus possible that the advances in research in AIDS and SLE-related neuropsychiatric complications might help to pave the way to a better understanding of other psychiatric illnesses such as schizophrenia and manic-depressive illnesses by using recently developed molecular biologic techniques.

☐ REFERENCES

Abel T, Gladman D, Grocertz MB: Neuropsychiatric lupus. Journal of Rheumatism 7:325–333, 1980

Auerbach O: Tuberculous meningitis: correlation of therapeutic results with pathogenesis and pathological changes: general considerations and pathogenesis. American Review of Tuberculosis 64:408, 1951

Berg B, Franklin G, Cuneo R, et al: Nonsurgical cure of brain abscess: early diagnosis and follow-up with computerized tomography. Ann Neurol 3:474, 1978

Bresnihan B, Oliver M, Gigor R, et al: Brain reactivity of lymphocytotoxic antibodies in systemic lupus erythematosus with and without cerebral involvement. Clin Exp Immunol 30:333–337, 1977

Burke JM, Schaberg DR: Neurosyphilis in the antibiotic era. Neurology 35:1368–1371, 1985

Cohen AS, Reynolds WE, Franklin EC, et al: Preliminary criteria for the classification of systemic lupus erythematosus. Bull Rheum Dis 21:643, 1971

Crocker EF, Mclaughlin AF, Morris JG, et al: Technitium brain scanning in the diagnosis and management of cerebral abscess. Am J Med 56:192, 1974

De Louvois J, Gortvai P, Hurley R: Bacteriology of the central nervous system: a multicentre prospective study. Br Med J 2:981, 1977

Dubois EL, Wierzchowiecki M, Cox MB, et al: Duration and death in systemic lupus erythematosus: an analysis of 249 cases. JAMA 227:1399, 1974

Feinglass EJ, Arnett FC, Dorsch CA, et al: Neuropsychiatric manifestations of systemic lupus erythematosus: diagnosis, clinical spectrum and relationship to other features of the disease. Medicine 55:323, 1976

Fessel WJ: Systemic lupus erythematosus in the community. Arch Intern Med 134:1027, 1974

Gajdusek DC: Slow infections with unconventional viruses. Harvey Lecture Series 72:283–353, 1978

Gallo RC, Salahuddin SZ, Popovic M, et al: Frequent detection and isolation of cytopathic retroviruses (HTLV-III) from patients with AIDS. Science 224:500–503, 1984

Gonzales-Scarano F, Lisak RP, Bilariuk LT, et al: Cranial computed tomography in the diagnosis of systemic lupus erythematosus. Ann Neurol 5:158, 1979

Grigor R, Edmond J, Keukonia R, et al: Systemic lupus erythematosus: a prospective analysis. Ann Rheum Dis 37:121, 1978

Hall RCW, Stickney SK, Gardner ER, et al: Psychiatric symptoms in patients with systemic lupus erythematosus. Psychosomatics 22:15–24, 1981

Heathfield KW: The decline of neurolues. Practitioner 217:753, 1976

Heineman HS, Braude AI, Osterholm JL: Intracranial suppurative disease: early presumptive diagnosis and successful treatment without surgery. JAMA 218:1542, 1971

Hooper DC, Pruitt AA, Rubin RH: Central nervous system infection in the chronically immunosuppressed. Medicine 61:166–188, 1982

Hooshmand H: Neurosyphilis: a study of 241 patients. JAMA 219:726, 1972

Ingham HR, Selkon JB, Roxby CM: Bacteriological studies of otogenic bacterial abscesses: chemotherapeutic role of metronizadole. Br Med J 2:991, 1977

Inoue T, Okamura M, Amatsu K: Antineuronal antibodies in brain tissue of a patient with systemic lupus erythematosus (letter). Lancet 1:852, 1982

Johnson RT, Richardson EP: The neurological manifestations of systemic lupus erythematosus: a clinical-pathological study of 24 cases of review of the literature. Medicine 47:337, 1968

Kocen RS, Parsons M: Neurological complications of tuberculosis. Q J Med 39:17, 1970

Kronfol Z, Schlesser M, Tsuang MT: Catatonia and systemic lupus erythematosus. Diseases of the Nervous System 38:729, 1977

Levy RM, Bredesen DE, Rosenblum ML: Neurological manifestations of the acquired immunodeficiency syndrome (AIDS): experience at UCSF and review of the literature. J Neurosurg 62:475–495, 1985

Mildvan D, Mathur U, Enlow RW, et al: Opportunistic infections and immune deficiency in homosexual men. Ann Intern Med 96:700–704, 1981

Morgan H, Wood M, Murphey F: Experience with 88 consecutive cases of brain abscess. J Neurosurg 38:698, 1973

Oatey P, Blumberg PC, Burrow D, et al: Test your diagnostic skills: tuberculoma of the central nervous system. Med J Aust 2:68, 1981

Perry S, Jacobsen P: Neuropsychiatric manifestations of AIDS-spectrum disorders. Hosp Community Psychiatry 37:135–142, 1986

Price RW, Naira BA, Cho E: AIDS encephalopathy. Neurol Clin 4:285–301, 1986

Rubin LA, Mourtz MB, Gladman DD: Mortality in systemic lupus erythematosus: the bimodal pattern revisited. Q J Med 216:87–98, 1985

Snider WD, Simpson DM, Nielsen S, et al: Neurological complications of acquired immune deficiency syndrome: analysis of 50 patients. Ann Neurol 14:403–418, 1983

Stern M, Robbins FS: Psychoses in systemic lupus erythematosus. Arch Gen Psychiatry 3:205–212, 1960

Temesvari P, Oenburg J, Benburg S, et al: Serum lymphocytotoxic antibodies in neuropsychiatric lupus: a serial study. Clin Immunol Immunopathol 28:243–251, 1983

Torrey EF: Preencephalitic psychoses. Integrative Psychiatry (in press)

Valentijn RM, Van Overhagen H, Hazevoet HM, et al: The value of complement and immune complex determinations in monitoring disease activity in patients with systemic lupus erythematosus. Arthritis Rheum 28:904, 1985

Waterston AP: Acquired immune deficiency syndrome. Br Med J 286:743–746, 1982

Williams GW, Bluestein HG, Stemberg AD, et al: Brain reactive lymphocytotoxic antibodies in the cerebrospinal fluid of patients with systemic lupus erythematosus: correlation with central nervous system involvement. Clin Immunol Immunopathol 18:126–132, 1981

Witham RR, Johnson RH, Roberts DL, et al: Diagnosis of miliary tuberculosis by cerebral computerized tomography. Arch Intern Med 139:479–480, 1979

Chapter 20

Neuropsychiatric Aspects of Brain Tumors

James B. Lohr, M.D.

Jean Lud Cadet, M.D.

TUMORS ASSOCIATED WITH THE central nervous system, including meninges, vessels, and bone, account for approximately 10 percent of all neoplasms and almost 2 percent of all cancer-related deaths (Gilroy and Holliday 1982). The average annual incidence of brain tumors, both primary and metastatic, is 30 per 100,000 population, with 20 per 100,000 being either primary malignant neoplasms or metastatic tumors (Kurtzke 1984). The point prevalence of tumors is 80 per 100,000, with 60 per 100,000 being benign tumors, 15 per 100,000 metastatic tumors and 5 per 100,000 primary malignant tumors (Kurtzke 1984). Although not the most common of focal neurologic conditions, neoplasms may nevertheless present the greatest diagnostic difficulties in neuropsychiatry. Because of the im-

portant psychiatric manifestations of many cerebral neoplasms, a number of investigators have commented that psychiatrists and other mental health care workers should possess greater "tumor consciousness" (McIntyre and McIntyre 1942). In this chapter, we address some of the clinical characteristics of brain tumors, the classification of brain tumors, important psychiatric features, and psychiatric aspects of treatment.

□ CLINICAL CHARACTERISTICS OF BRAIN TUMORS

The most characteristic clinical effect of cerebral neoplasms is that they cause a progression of neurologic and psychiatric signs and symptoms. Rapidly growing, malignant neoplasms may result in a sudden appearance of clinical symptomatology and a rapid decline in social and psychological

---

The authors acknowledge the artistic gifts of Mr. Jeffrey Aarons, who created the figures for this chapter.

351

functioning. In the case of benign, slow-growing tumors, however, progression of clinical signs may only take place over the course of years to decades. Although the clinical presentation of cerebral neoplasms may be quite variable, a number of characteristic signs and symptoms alert one to the possible presence of brain tumors. Apart from the signs and symptoms listed below, mental changes are quite common, and these are discussed in detail later.

Headache

Headache is a frequent accompaniment of brain tumors and is the initial symptom in 25 to 35 percent of patients with tumors. By the time the tumor is diagnosed, headaches may be present 60 to 85 percent of the time (Lance 1978; Redlich et al. 1948). Characteristic locations of head pain have been described for tumors in different areas of the brain. For example, supratentorial tumors may be more associated with frontal, temporal, or ocular pain (especially over the region of the tumor); infratentorial tumors may be more associated with ipsilateral occipital or neck pain (Saper 1983). Tumors in the region of the sella turcica are sometimes associated with pains described as "a nail driven into my forehead between my eyes." Frontal, temporal, and ocular pains are also common. With enlargement of tumors in different brain areas and with an increase in intracranial pressure, the head pain tends to become bilateral in the frontal and occipital regions. In general, there is wide variation in the location of pain produced by similar neoplasms among different patients.

The type of pain is also highly variable. There is often a postural component, especially in posterior fossa tumors. Often the pain has more of a deep, unremitting nature than in other causes of headache, although intermittent forms of headache are also described. The pain may be sharp or dull, mild or severe. Some symptoms, such as pain awakening a patient from sleep, have been considered to be more specific characteristics of tumor headache, but such symptoms also occur in other types of head pain as well. The mechanism of headache is unknown in the early stages of tumor growth. In later stages, the pain is believed to be due to increased intracranial pressure.

Nausea and Vomiting

Vomiting occurs in approximately one-third of patients with brain tumors, perhaps more commonly in patients with posterior fossa tumors (Adams and Victor 1981). Vomiting may occur along with nausea; in some cases patients may suddenly and unexpectedly vomit with great force, called projectile vomiting. Vomiting does not usually appear to be associated with food intake, and it may occur shortly after rising in the morning.

Seizures

Seizures occur in between 20 and 50 percent of patients with cerebral neoplasms (Adams and Victor 1981). The occurrence of seizures in previously healthy adults should always signal the possible presence of a tumor. Focal motor (jacksonian) or sensory seizures may be of localizing value. Patients with slow-growing tumors may only have occasional seizures separated by weeks, months, or even years. The pattern of seizures in more malignant tumors is quite variable.

Visual Loss

The visual pathways in the brain extend across much of the cerebrum. Thus tumors frequently affect some aspect of vision, and visual field examination is crucial in any patient with suspected tumor. In many cases of tumor presenting with psychiatric symptomatology, visual field changes have been the only initial neurologic sign present. The pattern of visual field loss is often of localizing significance. For example, patients with tumors of the sella turcica often have temporal field cuts, progressing to bitemporal quadrantanopia (usually a superior bitemporal quadrantanopia in the case of pituitary adenoma and chordoma and an inferior bitemporal quadrantanopia in the case of craniopharyngioma), and later to bitemporal hemianopia. Because the optic radiations carrying information from the upper temporal fields (Meyer's loop) pass through the temporal lobes, tumors of the temporal lobe may result in congruous or homonymous (i.e., identical in both eyes) visual-field defects in the contralateral upper quadrant. Similarly, information from the contralateral visual field passes through the parietal lobe. Tumors of this cortical area may produce a congruous inferior quadrantanopia (although it is more common for these lesions to produce a hemianopia than a quadrantanopia). In both parietal lobe and temporal lobe tumors, the shape of the visual-field defect may be quite irregular. Occipital lesions may cause a hemianopia that either includes or excludes the macular region (depending on whether or not the primary visual cortex is involved). The visual pathways along with the visual-field cuts that accompany specific lesions are shown in Figure 1.

Papilledema

Papilledema is a sign of increased intracranial pressure that occurs in only a small percentage of patients with tumors at the time of diagnosis. It often takes weeks of increased intracranial pressure before papilledema occurs. Its absence, therefore, does not necessarily indicate the absence of increased pressure. This is particularly important in cases in which a lumbar puncture is being considered because the absence of papilledema does not rule out the possibility of herniation with lumbar puncture or with electroconvulsive therapy (ECT). In general, papilledema begins with an increase in venous caliber and tortuosity, followed by pinkening of the disc, disappearance of the vessels on the disc, blurring of disc margins (usually at the nasal edge), and elevation of the disc with disappearance of

vessel origins. In its final stages, papilledema is accompanied by perivenous hemorrhages. Exudates, however, are uncommon in papilledema that is secondary to raised intracranial pressure.

Neurologic Signs and Symptoms

There are many neurologic signs that are helpful in determining the location of a brain tumor. Some of these are listed in Table 1.

☐ CLASSIFICATION OF BRAIN TUMORS

Brain tumors are often divided into primary tumors that arise in the brain itself and secondary tumors that are metastatic from other parts of the body. Neoplasms of the central nervous system may be further classified according to topography (i.e., the location of the neoplasm) and histology (i.e., the cellular makeup of the neoplasm).

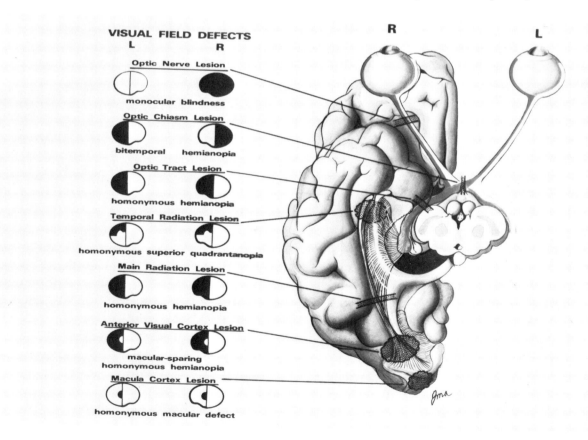

Figure 1. Primary visual pathways along with the visual-field defects that occur following lesions at various locations.

TABLE 1.   NEUROLOGIC FINDINGS OF LOCALIZING VALUE IN PATIENTS WITH BRAIN TUMORS

Brain region	Neurologic finding
Frontal Lobes	
Prefrontal	Contralateral grasp reflexes
Dorsolateral surface	Impaired ability to sustain gaze to side opposite tumor, Broca's aphasia (dominant hemisphere)
Olfactory groove	Ipsilateral optic atrophy and anosmia with contralateral papilledema (Foster-Kennedy syndrome)
Precentral gyrus	Partial motor and jacksonian seizures, hemiparesis
Temporal lobes	Partial complex seizures, contralateral homonymous superior quadrantanopia, Wernicke's aphasia
Parietal lobes	Partial sensory seizures, agraphesthesia, astereognosis, anosognosia, autotopagnosia, contralateral homonymous inferior quadrantanopia, Gerstmann's syndrome (agraphia, acalculia, finger agnosia, right-left confusion)
Occipital lobes	Partial sensory seizures with simple or elementary visual phenomena, homonymous hemianopia
Corpus callosum	Callosal apraxia (mainly left-hand)
Thalamus	Contralateral hemisensory loss, pain
Basal ganglia	Contralateral choreoathetosis, rigidity, dystonia
Pituitary and hypothalamus	Bitemporal hemianopia, optic atrophy, precocious puberty, amenorrhea, galactorrhea, hypopituitarism, diabetes insipidus, hypothyroidism
Pineal	Loss of upward gaze (Parinaud's syndrome)
Cerebellopontine angle	Hearing loss, ataxia, facial pain and weakness, tinnitus, dysarthria
Cerebellum	Ipsilateral hypotonia, ataxia, dysmetria, intention tremor, nystagmus toward side of tumor
Brainstem	
Midbrain	Pupillary and extraocular muscle abnormalities, contralateral hemiparesis
Pons	Sixth and seventh nerve involvement (diploplia, ipsilateral facial paralysis), contralateral hemiparesis, and hemisensory loss

Topographic Classification

Tumors of the central nervous system may be divided into those that occur within the cranial vault (intracranial) and those that occur within the spinal canal (intraspinal). Intracranial tumors are further separated into those arising above the tentorium cerebelli (supratentorial) and those below (infratentorial or posterior fossa). The relative frequency of location of intracranial tumors is depicted in Figure 2. Intraspinal tumors are usually subdivided into those that occur inside (intradural) or outside (extradural) of the dura. Intradural tumors are further divided into those that occur within the spinal cord proper (intramedullary) and those that occur outside the cord (extramedullary). Further topographic subclassification of tumors is offered in Table 2. The importance of the topographic distribution of tumors is twofold. First, certain histologic types of tumors are more likely to occur in certain areas

of the brain (shown in Table 2). Second, tumors in specific locations are likely to give rise to specific patterns of neurologic and psychiatric dysfunction.

Histologic Classification

Basically, the histologic classification of tumors is made according to the histologic elements from which the tumors derive. Primary tumors may be broadly divided into those that arise from neural tube derivatives (glial cells and neurons), from neural crest derivatives (Schwann cells, arachnoidal cells, and melanocytes), from embryonal remnants (notochord, germ cells), and from other tissues (connective tissue, adenohypophyseal cells, and others) (Escourolle and Poirier 1978).

Neural Tube Derivatives.   The most common tumors in this category are gliomas, which are tumors of glial cells. Glial cells include astrocytes, oligo-

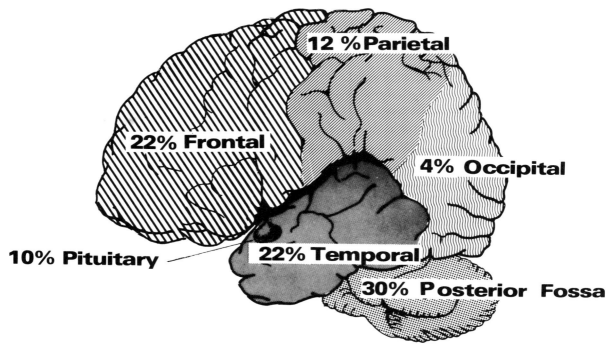

Figure 2. Relative frequency of intracranial brain tumors according to location in the adult. (From Escourolle and Poirier 1978 and Patten 1981).

dendrocytes, and ependymocytes; these give rise to astrocytomas, oligodendrocytomas, and ependymomas, respectively. Astrocytomas have been classified into four grades dependent on their malignancy; the most malignant astrocytomas (grades III and IV) are often called glioblastomas. In contrast with tumors of glial cells, tumors of neurons are relatively rare and tend to occur more commonly in children. These include medulloblastomas, ganglioneuromas, and gangliogliomas. Pinealocytes are also derivatives of the neural tube and may give rise to pinealocytomas and pinealoblastomas, which are also quite rare.

Neural Crest Derivatives. Tumors arising from neural crest tissues include meningiomas (from arachnoidal cells), schwannomas and neurofibromas (from Schwann cells), and melanomas (from melanocytes).

Embryonal Remnants. Tumors in this group include craniopharyngiomas and cholesteatomas (from embryonal ectodermal tissue), germinomas (from germ cells), lipomas (from adipose cells), chordomas (from notochord), and teratomas (from all three germ layers).

Derivatives of Other Cells. Tumors arising from other cells include pituitary adenomas (from adenohypophyseal cells), sarcomas (from connective tissue), hemangioblastomas (possibly from vascular cells), and glomus jugulare tumors (from glomus jugular cells).

In addition to the above histologic classification scheme, primary neoplasms of the brain have been divided according to whether they are benign (such as most astrocytomas, oligodendrogliomas, ependymomas, pituitary adenomas, and meningiomas) or malignant (such as glioblastomas and medulloblastomas).

The most common histologic types of tumors are presented in Tables 2 through 4 (Escourolle and Poirier 1978; Gilroy and Holliday 1982; Russell and Rubinstein 1977). In both adults and children, primary tumors account for approximately 80 percent of all brain tumors, with the remaining 20 percent being metastases. The frequency of different types of primary intracranial tumors is dependent on whether the population in question consists of adults or children.

In adults, approximately 70 percent of all intracranial tumors are supratentorial; the great ma-

TABLE 2. TOPOGRAPHIC CLASSIFICATION OF CENTRAL NERVOUS SYSTEM NEOPLASMS AND THE MOST COMMON HISTOLOGIC TYPES OF TUMORS

Topographic location	Common histologic types
Intracranial	
Supratentorial	Astrocytomas, glioblastomas
Cerebral lobe	Meningiomas
a. frontal	Metastases
b. temporal	
c. parietal	
d. occipital	
Subcortical	
a. lateral ventricle	
b. basal ganglia	
Midline	
a. sella turcica	Pituitary adenomas, craniopharyngyomas
b. corpus callosum	
c. third ventricle	
d. pineal	
Infratentorial	Meningiomas, hemangioblastomas, metastases
Cerebellar lobe	Astrocytomas[a]
Brain stem	Brain-stem gliomas
Midline	Medulloblastomas,[a] ependymomas[a]
a. vermis	
b. fourth ventricle	
Extraparenchymatous	
a. cerebellopontine angle	Acoustic schwannomas
b. Gasserian ganglion	
Intraspinal	
Extradural	
Spinal	Vertebral metastases, bone tumors
Intraspinal	Epidural metastases
Intradural	
Extramedullary	Meningiomas, schwannomas, neurofibromas
Intramedullary	Ependymomas, astrocytomas, glioblastomas

Note. Adapted from Escourolle and Poirier 1978.
[a]Common in children

TABLE 3. COMMON HISTOLOGIC TYPES OF TUMORS AND THEIR RELATIVE FREQUENCIES

Tumor type	Frequency (%)
Primary	
Gliomas	40–50
astrocytomas	10–15
glioblastomas	20–25
others	10–15
Meningiomas	10–20
Pituitary adenomas	10
Neurilemmomas (mainly acoustic neuromas)	5–8
Medulloblastomas and pinealomas	5
Miscellaneous primary tumors	5
Metastatic	15–25

TABLE 4. COMMON TYPES OF METASTATIC TUMORS TO THE BRAIN AND THEIR RELATIVE FREQUENCIES

Tumor	Frequency (%)
Lung	35–45
Breast	10–20
Kidney	5–10
Gastrointestinal tract	5–10
Melanoma	2–5
Others (including thyroid, pancreas, ovary, uterus, prostate, testes, bladder, sarcoma)	25–30

jority of these are astrocytomas, glioblastomas, meningiomas, pituitary adenomas, and metastases. Of the 30 percent of intracranial tumors that occur in the posterior fossa, about 8 percent are acoustic schwannomas (also called acoustic neuromas or acoustic neurinomas) and 5 percent are medulloblastomas.

In children, approximately 70 percent of all intracranial tumors are infratentorial, and consist primarily of cerebellar astrocytomas (30 percent), cerebellar medulloblastomas (30 percent), and fourth ventricle ependymomas (10 percent) (Escourolle and Poirier 1978). The 30 percent of intracranial tumors that are supratentorial are a miscellaneous group.

☐ PSYCHIATRIC FEATURES OF BRAIN TUMORS

Brain tumors are important from a psychiatric point of view in two ways. First, some patients presenting with psychiatric problems have undetected neoplasms. Second, patients with known neoplasms often develop psychiatric symptomatology. We will address each of these in turn.

Occult Brain Tumors in Psychiatric Patients

It has been estimated that somewhere between 40 and 100 percent of patients with brain tumors have psychiatric symptoms (Jameison and Henry 1933; Soniat 1951). Of these patients with psychiatric symptoms, some are mistakenly thought to have primary psychiatric disorders. Based on autopsy studies of patients admitted to mental hospitals, it has been estimated that 2 to 4 percent of institutionalized mental patients have brain tumors (Benson and Geschwind 1975; Hunter et al. 1968). This estimate is based on autopsy data from institutionalized patients, however, and it is likely to be inflated because of the higher mortality rate of patients with neoplasms. This estimate is possibly higher than the prevalence of tumors in general hospital settings, which has been reported to be in the range of 1 to 2 percent (Zulch 1957). Other investigators have reported that the prevalence of brain tumors in patients admitted to acute psychiatric hospitals is in the range of .2 to .3 percent (Hobbs 1963; Rubert and Remington 1963). Even this statistic may not be truly representative of the number of patients presumed to have mental illness who actually suffer from cerebral neoplasms because it does not take into account lesser degrees of psychopathology in patients who are not hospitalized. Finally, it is not clear if all the brain tumors reported in mental patients contribute to psychopathology or are merely incidental findings. Nevertheless, it appears that perhaps as many as 1 or 2 percent of patients with primary psychiatric diagnoses may have undetected cerebral neoplasms.

Meningiomas are probably the most common tumors that may present predominantly with psychiatric symptoms such as depression, personality changes, anxiety, and psychosis (Direkze et al. 1971; Hunter et al. 1968; Sachs 1950; Selecki 1965). Meningiomas may be very slow growing, and present with psychopathology many years before the tumor is discovered. Certain tumor locations appear more likely to mimic primary or "functional" psychiatric disorders. These include tumors of the prefrontal lobes, midline tumors (such as third ventricle tumors), tumors of the olfactory groove and temporal lobe, and limbic system tumors (Burkle and

Lipowski 1978; Hobbs 1963; Malamud 1967; Pool and Correll 1958). If there is the slightest suspicion of brain tumor, a computed tomography (CT) scan should be performed. It should be remembered that patients on neuroleptics may have a suppression of vomiting. In addition, a number of psychiatric patients, especially those with psychosis, are unable to communicate adequately complaints such as headache.

Psychiatric Symptoms in Patients with Brain Tumors

Psychopathology associated with cerebral neoplasms may be divided according to the location of the neoplasm and the type of neoplasm.

Location of Tumor. Tumors of all areas of the brain may be associated with psychiatric symptoms. In general, however, tumors of the frontal and temporal lobes and midline tumors are more commonly accompanied by psychiatric symptoms.

Frontal lobe tumors. Somewhere between 60 and 90 percent of patients with tumors of the frontal lobe have psychiatric symptoms (Direkze et al. 1971; Frazier 1936; Keschner et al. 1938). Personality, affective, and intellectual changes each occur in approximately half of patients with frontal lobe tumors. In one-quarter of patients, mental changes, especially memory loss, may be the presenting symptoms.

Personality changes include apathy, irresponsibility, childishness, inappropriate behavior, and *Witzelsucht* (a tendency to make light of everything) (Frazier 1936).

The most common affective changes are depression and inappropriate affect. Depression has been especially associated with vascular damage to the left fronto-temporal and right parieto-occipital region (Robinson et al. 1984), and this appears to be true for tumors as well (J. B. Lohr and D. V. Jeste, unpublished observations).

Disturbance in memory is the most common cognitive impairment (Hécaen and de Ajuriaguerra 1956). Patients may also show difficulty in coordinating tasks and may be especially impaired in those tasks that require that the patient follow a set of internalized instructions (Luria 1966). In such cases, perseveration is likely to occur. Hallucinations and delusions may occur in 5 to 20 percent of patients (Frazier 1936; Hunter et al. 1968; Keschner et al. 1938; Levin 1949; Rubert and Remington 1963). Occasionally, a syndrome resembling catatonia may be seen, including waxy flexibility, mutism, and stereotypies.

It has been suggested that dorsolateral frontal lobe damage may cause more "negative" symptoms such as apathy and dementia, whereas lesions of the orbitofrontal cortex are associated more with excitement, disinhibition, and irritability (Hunter et al. 1968). Frontal lobe tumors are most commonly mistaken for dementia, depression, and, to a lesser extent, schizophrenia.

Temporal lobe tumors. Psychiatric symptoms are very common in patients with temporal lobe tumors, possibly occurring in greater than 90 percent of such patients (Keschner et al. 1938). Anxiety and depression are common early accompaniments of temporal lobe neoplasms (Mulder and Daly 1952). Hallucinations are also fairly common, occurring in as many as one-third of patients (Keschner et al. 1938). The most frequently observed hallucinations appear to be olfactory and gustatory hallucinations, followed by auditory and visual hallucinations, which are often of a complex nature (e.g., music, voices, and scenes from the past). Other perceptual changes include dream-like states, depersonalized states, deja vu (the feeling that someone has been somewhere or done something before), jamais vu (the feeling that a certain familiar situation or environment becomes suddenly strange and alien), and micropsia, macropsia, and metamorphopsia (when the environment appears to shrink, enlarge, or change shape, respectively). Tumor involvement of the bilateral medial temporal lobes can produce an amnesic state marked by loss of recent memory (Smith and Smith 1966). The mental symptoms of temporal lobe tumor are usually paroxysmal in nature. There is some evidence suggesting that patients with dominant temporal lobe tumors may have more psychopathology, especially intellectual and affective changes, than those with nondominant tumors; this remains, however, to be convincingly demonstrated (Bingley 1958).

Temporal lobe tumors are most commonly mistaken for schizophrenia, affective disorders, and personality disorders (especially paranoid, schizotypal, and borderline personality disorders) (Bingley 1958; Lishman 1978; Malamud 1967; Mulder and Daly 1952).

Parietal lobe tumors. Psychiatric symptoms are less commonly associated with parietal lobe tumors than with frontal or temporal lobe tumors (Lishman 1978). Affective disturbances such as depression

may be seen; this may be more associated with nondominant parietal lobe pathology (Lohr and Jeste unpublished observations; Robinson et al. 1984). Hallucinations, especially of the tactile nature, also occur. Personality disturbances appear to be rare.

As Lishman (1978) points out, the variety of cognitive disturbances seen in parietal lobe tumors (such as anosognosia, autotopagnosia, apraxias, and aphasias) may be mistaken for hysterical disorders.

Occipital lobe tumors. Occipital lobe tumors probably cause less psychopathology than those in any other cerebral area. Dementia, affective changes, and hallucinations may occur. Tumors primarily involving the occipital lobe may present with visual hallucinations that are usually confined to one-half of the visual field, and are often described as stars, simple patterns, zigzags, spots, or fire (Benson and Geschwind 1975). Occasionally, more complex visual problems are present, especially when there is additional involvement of parietal and temporal lobes; these include alexia without agraphia, Anton's symptom (in which an individual with bilateral occipital lobe damage denies being blind), and simultagnosia (in which the individual elements of a picture cannot be assembled into a meaningful whole). These may be mistaken for hysteria. Personality changes in occipital lobe tumors are rare (Lishman 1978).

Midline tumors. Tumors of the floor and walls of the third ventricle, especially colloid cysts, are likely to produce a syndrome of anterograde amnesia (Burkle and Lipowski 1978; Cairns and Mosberg 1951). Corpus callosum tumors, especially of the rostrum and splenium, are associated with a high incidence of psychopathology (90 percent in one series), especially amnesia, apathy, akinesia, and other signs and symptoms of depression and dementia (Nasrallah and McChesney 1981; Schlesinger 1950). Although psychotic symptoms have been reported as well, they appear to be less common. A high incidence of psychopathology (including amnesia, personality disturbances, and apathy) has also been reported for tumors of the pituitary and hypothalamus (Lishman 1978). In addition, there are reports of hypothalamic tumors presenting as anorexia nervosa (Heron and Johnston 1976; White and Hain 1959) and rage attacks (Reeves and Plum 1969). Disturbances in sexual functioning, including impotence, sterility, loss of libido, and, more rarely, hypersexuality, also occur with hypothalamic and pituitary pathology (Benson and Geschwind 1975). In many cases of tumors of the corpus callosum, pituitary, and hypothalamus, however, it is difficult to say what proportion of the psychiatric symptoms is due to tumor compression of adjacent structures, such as the frontal and temporal lobes, rather than to direct tumor effects.

Subcortical tumors. In recent years, subcortical dementia has been described in patients with pathologic processes involving the thalamus and basal ganglia (Huber and Paulson 1985). Basically, subcortical dementia differs from cortical dementia in that it is characterized more by forgetfulness, apathy, depression, and slowing of mental processes and less associated with aphasia, agnosia, apraxia, lack of insight, and amnesia. Although the concept of subcortical dementia was originated for conditions such as progressive supranuclear palsy, Huntington's disease, and Parkinson's disease, tumors of subcortical nuclei also appear to be associated with this symptom complex.

Infratentorial tumors. Tumors of the cerebellum are less commonly associated with psychopathology than tumors of other locations. Frequently, the symptoms are nonspecific, including memory loss, confusion, and slowness of thought and speech, probably due to increased intracranial pressure (Assal et al. 1975; Lishman 1978). Visual phenomena such as hallucinations may occur, presumably because of transtentorial effects on the occipital lobes (David et al. 1955).

Type of Tumor. Of all tumors, gliomas are most commonly associated with mental changes, but usually these are accompanied by clear-cut neurologic signs (Soniat 1951). Meningiomas are more commonly associated with relatively pure mental changes, without focal neurologic signs or symptoms. There is evidence that more rapidly growing tumors, such as metastatic tumors or glioblastomas, cause a more rapid development and progression of psychiatric symptoms (Direkze et al. 1971).

Psychiatric Aspects of the Treatment of Brain Tumors

The treatment of brain tumors includes the use of agents to reduce intracranial pressure such as corticosteroids and osmotic drugs, along with surgery, radiation, and chemotherapy (Marshall and Greco 1982). It is important to remember that some forms of treatment may be associated with mental changes.

For example, corticosteroids are associated with a syndrome of delirium and psychosis. Some antineoplastic drugs such as lomustine (CCNU) may cause disorientation and lethargy.

When to Suspect a Brain Tumor in Patients with Psychiatric Symptoms

In patients demonstrating an acute or progressive change in sensorium, affect, or personality, a brain tumor should be suspected. In patients with psychiatric problems or mental changes, any of the following accompanying conditions should also alert one to the possible presence of a brain tumor.

1. Frequent or unremitting headaches, especially at night and on awakening. Headaches are more common in psychiatric conditions due to tumors than in primary psychiatric illnesses (Blustein and Seeman 1972; Carlson 1977).
2. Vomiting.
3. Seizures.
4. Any visual complaints or findings, including loss of vision or visual-field defects.
5. Any other focal neurologic findings (e.g., grasp reflexes, paresis, sensory loss).

It should be remembered that headache, vomiting, seizures, visual-field defects, papilledema, and focal findings often do not occur in the early stages of tumors.

☐ THE DIAGNOSTIC WORKUP

The workup of a patient with a possible brain tumor includes a physical examination and a variety of radiologic procedures.

Physical Examination

Any patient suspected of having a brain tumor should receive a full neurologic and psychiatric examination. Neurologic signs associated with tumors of certain brain areas are presented in Table 1. The psychiatric examination should include a detailed mental status evaluation. Despite a rigorous physical examination, a number of tumors may not be detected, including tumors of the anterior frontal lobes, nondominant temporal lobe, corpus callosum, and posterior fossa.

Radiologic Procedures

CT Scan. Obtaining a CT scan is very important because most tumors can be detected with this procedure. In addition to demonstrating many tumors directly, CT scans often indirectly reveal the possible presence of a tumor through midline shift, cerebral edema, ventricular compression, or hydrocephalus due to obstruction. CT scans should be obtained before a lumbar puncture is performed; lumbar punctures are contraindicated in the presence of asymmetrical mass lesions because of the possibility of herniation of the brain through the foramen magnum. Patients with possible brain tumors should have CT scans both with and without intravenous contrast material because this greatly increases the sensitivity of detecting neoplasms. CT scans fail to demonstrate some tumors, however, especially tumors in the posterior fossa, isodense gliomas, and meningeal carcinomatosis.

Skull X Rays. Skull films are usually no longer necessary for the evaluation of most intracranial tumors. However, X ray tomograms of the sella turcica are still of importance in detecting pituitary tumors, craniopharyngiomas, or the "empty sella." Skull X rays may also better demonstrate bone metastases than CT scans.

Metrizamide-CT Cisternography. This is currently the most widely employed technique for evaluating the ventricular system and subarachnoid cisterns, which is useful for determining the presence of intraventricular and pituitary tumors.

Cerebral Angiography. This technique, occasionally helpful diagnostically, can demonstrate the vascular structure of tumors before surgery.

Lumbar Puncture. Lumbar puncture is rarely helpful in the diagnosis of brain tumor. Although certain nonspecific findings such as increased opening pressure and elevated cerebrospinal fluid (CSF) protein may be seen, the procedure is potentially dangerous, especially as regards asymmetrical mass lesions. In certain cases of suspected meningeal carcinomatosis and leukemia, however, an examination of the CSF is important for making the diagnosis.

☐ PSYCHOPHARMACOLOGIC AND PSYCHOSOCIAL TREATMENT

The psychiatric symptoms accompanying brain tumors often remit following treatment of the tumor, especially when a complete extirpation of the neoplasm can be made. However, many tumors do not respond satisfactorily to treatment. In other cases, psychiatric symptoms may remain after the tumor has been removed. In these cases, the psychiatric symptoms themselves may be a focus for psychopharmacologic and psychosocial treatment.

Psychopharmacologic Treatment

Treatment of psychopathology associated with brain tumors follows general principles of psychotropic medication administration, with certain caveats.

Neuroleptic Medications. Psychosis and delirium should be treated with neuroleptic medications. In general, lower doses should be used first, because patients with cerebral neoplasms may be quite sensitive to the sedative and extrapyramidal side effects of these medications. Also, neuroleptics reduce the seizure threshold, which is an important consideration in patients already prone to develop seizures. In this regard, there is evidence that molindone and possibly haloperidol and fluphenazine may be safer in terms of their seizure-producing effects than chlorpromazine (Baldessarini and Lipinksi 1976; Oliver et al. 1982; Remick and Fine 1979). Finally, age is an important factor in neuroleptic treatment. Older patients generally require much less neuroleptic medication for antipsychotic effect. Whereas the dosage of a drug such as haloperidol can be begun at 1 or 2 mg and increased as necessary in patients middle-aged or younger with brain tumors, elderly patients may show improvement after only 0.25 to 0.5 mg. Administration of higher doses of neuroleptics may cause such severe subjective distress (such as akathisia) that the patient may be mistakenly thought to require more neuroleptic.

Extrapyramidal side effects of neuroleptics may be treated with anticholinergic drugs such as benztropine, trihexyphenidyl, and orphenadrine. Again, because these medications may precipitate delirium and cause memory loss, caution is warranted. Drugs such as benztropine should be started in doses of 0.5 mg once or twice a day, and raised as necessary.

Antidepressant Medications. Tricyclic antidepressants may be useful in treating depression secondary to brain tumors. Doses similar to those used in the treatment of major affective disorders may be required. Again, however, it is safer to start with reduced doses in the range of 10 mg twice a day for tricyclics such as imipramine, amitriptyline, and nortriptyline, increasing the dosage gradually. Significant antidepressant effects may be achieved with only 25 to 50 mg/day. Although reduction of the seizure threshold occurs with tricyclic and tetracyclic antidepressants, there are few reports of convulsions. An exception is the tetracyclic antidepressant maprotiline, which has been reported to cause grand mal seizures (Molnar 1983; Atri and Julius 1984; Northrup et al. 1984) and which we believe should not be used in cases of depression accompanying brain tumors. Monoamine oxidase inhibitors should not be used because of the possibility of increasing blood pressure and intracranial pressure.

Lithium. Mania accompanying brain tumors is relatively rare (Krauthammer and Klerman 1978). To our knowledge, there have been only nine cases of mania reported with brain tumors (Table 5). Only 3 of these patients were reported to have been treated with lithium; of these 3, 2 patients were responsive

to lithium at a level of 1.0 to 1.2 mEq/liter (Jamieson and Wells 1979; Oyewumi and Lapierre 1981) and the third became lethargic on a combination of lithium and haloperidol (Greenberg and Brown 1985). Patients with mania secondary to organic brain syndromes other than brain tumor have been reported to respond to lithium with serum levels in the range of 0.8 to 1.2 mEq/liter, including following hematoma (Cohen and Niska 1980), hemispherectomy (Forrest 1982), and stroke (Cummings and Mendez 1984; Rosenbaum and Barry 1975). Therefore, we would recommend the use of lithium in patients with mania secondary to brain tumor, beginning at doses of 300 mg/day, gradually increasing the dose over several weeks until the lithium level is in the range of 0.8 to 1.2 mEq/liter. If the patient responds well to this regimen, the lithium dose may be reduced and possibly discontinued after several months.

Antianxiety Agents. Drugs such as benzodiazepines are useful in the treatment of certain patients with brain tumors and anxiety, regardless of whether the anxiety is a response to having the tumor or a direct effect of the neoplasm. However, care should be taken in using these drugs, as they may precipitate confusional states in some patients, particularly the elderly. Also, some patients with brain tumors may have a paradoxical reaction to benzodiazepines, manifesting as increased anxiety occasionally accompanied by agitation and hostility.

TABLE 5. REPORTS OF MANIA IN ASSOCIATION WITH BRAIN TUMOR

Reference	Lesion	Lithium response[a]
Stern and Dancey 1942	Spongioblastoma polare of right posterior diencephalon	NS
Oppler 1950	Right parasagittal meningioma	NS
Waggoner and Bagchi 1954	Ependymoma of fourth ventricle	NS
Pool and Correll 1958	Left sphenoid meningioma	NS
Bourgeois and Campagne 1967	Benign neoplasm of left spheno-occipital region	NS
Malamud 1967	Craniopharyngioma on floor of third ventricle	NS
Avery 1971	Left olfactory groove meningioma	NS
Jamieson and Wells 1979	Metastatic tumors in right cerebral hemisphere	+
Oyewumi and Lapierre 1981	Intraventricular tumor on floor of fourth ventricle	+
Greenberg and Brown 1985	Right metastatic mesencephalic tumor extending into posterior thalamus	−

[a]NS = not stated.

ECT. Brain tumors used to be considered an absolute contraindication for ECT because of reports of deterioration in clinical condition and because of several fatalities in patients with brain tumors simulating major depression who received ECT (Gassel 1960; Gralnick 1945; Pool and Correll 1958; Rond 1957; Shapiro and Goldberg 1957; Waggoner and Bagchi 1954). More recently, however, investigators have questioned whether the presence of brain tumor in the absence of elevated intracranial pressure represents an absolute contraindication to ECT (Dressler and Folk 1975). Current guidelines have been offered by the recent National Institute of Mental Health Consensus Development Conference on Electroconvulsive Therapy (1985), which states that "ECT is contraindicated for increased intracranial pressure, while space-occupying lesions in the brain, a recent history of myocardial infarction, and large aneurysms are relative contraindications for ECT" (p. 2106).

Psychosocial Treatment

Many patients with brain tumors, even those of a more benign nature, are greatly concerned about dying, permanent physical disability, and a loss of mental functioning. They are often unwilling to bring these subjects up spontaneously, and should, in many instances, be encouraged by the physician to express these concerns. Patients have differing abilities to cope with brain tumors, to a large extent predicted by their previous ability to handle stressful situations. Some patients may react with depression, others with denial. In cases of severe malignant tumors, death and dying issues should be addressed early.

Patients who are cured of their tumors may continue to demonstrate need for psychiatric intervention. It is difficult to determine whether their continuing psychiatric problems are the result of direct effects of the previous tumor or surgery, or of other problems such as the sudden immersal into a role of dependency. Some patients are reluctant to engage in normal activities and fear redevelopment of symptoms or loss of abilities. Supportive therapy may be helpful in these cases. There are no general rules regarding disclosure of the lethality of different tumors. For patients with more severe tumors, supportive therapy is also helpful, but it should be remembered that therapy should be tailored to the cognitive and emotional abilities of the patient. Insight-oriented therapy and other therapies requiring abstracting abilities may not only be of little value, but may precipitate distress as patients are confronted with tasks that they once were able to perform, but no longer can.

☐ CONCLUSION

Brain tumors are commonly associated with psychiatric symptoms and, in some cases, may be mistaken for primary psychiatric disorders. Psychiatric patients with acute or progressive changes in mental state—especially if accompanied by headache, seizures, visual changes, or any focal neurologic signs or symptoms—should be worked up for brain tumor, including obtaining a CT scan and other radiologic procedures. Psychiatric symptoms vary according to the location of the tumor, with frontal lobe, temporal lobe, and midline tumors being associated with the greatest amount of psychopathology. Psychiatric symptoms also vary with the type of neoplasm—with rapidly growing neoplasms (such as glioblastomas and metastatic tumors) causing a more sudden and rapidly progressive development of mental symptoms, and slow growing tumors (such as astrocytomas and meningiomas) causing a more slowly progressive development of mental symptoms. Although gliomas are more commonly associated with mental changes accompanied by neurologic findings, meningiomas are more likely to be mistaken for primary psychiatric illnesses without focal neurologic signs. Treatment should involve both psychopharmacologic agents (which in general should be used in lower doses and increased more slowly than in primary psychiatric conditions) and psychosocial intervention.

☐ REFERENCES

Adams RD, Victor M: Principles of Neurology (2nd ed). New York, McGraw-Hill, 1981

Assal G, Zander E, Hadjiantoniou J: Les troubles mentaux au cours des tumeurs de la fosse posterieure. Arch Suiss Neurol Neurochir Psychiatrie 116:17–27, 1975

Atri PB, Julius DA: Maprotiline hydrochloride associated with a clinical state of catatonic stupor and epileptic encephalogram. J Clin Psychopharmacol 4:207–209, 1984

Avery TL: Seven cases of frontal tumour with psychiatric presentation. Br J Psychiatry 119:19–23, 1971

Baldessarini RJ, Lipinski JF: Toxicity and side effects of antipsychotic, antimanic and antidepressant medications. Psychiatric Annals 6:484–493, 1976

Benson DF, Geschwind N: Psychiatric conditions associated with focal lesions of the central nervous system, in American Handbook of Psychiatry, Vol. 4, (2nd ed). Edited by Reiser MF. New York, Basic Books, 1975, pp 208–243

Bingley T: Mental symptoms in temporal lobe epilepsy and temporal lobe gliomas. Acta Psychiatrica et Neurologica Scandinavica Supplement 120:1–151, 1958

Blustein J, Seeman MV: Brain tumors presenting as functional psychiatric disturbances. Canadian Psychiatric Association Journal Supplement 17:59–63, 1972

Bourgeois M, Campagne A: Maniaco-depressive et syndrome de Garcin. Ann Med Psychol (Paris) 125:451–460, 1967

Burkle FM, Lipowski ZJ: Colloid cyst of the third ventricle presenting as psychiatric disorder. Am J Psychiatry 135:373–374, 1978

Cairns H, Mosberg WH Jr: Colloid cyst of the third ventricle. Surg Gynecol Obstet 92:545–570, 1951

Carlson RJ: Frontal lobe lesions masquerading as psychiatric disturbances. Canadian Psychiatric Association Journal 22:315–318, 1977

Cohen MR, Niska RW: Localized right cerebral hemisphere dysfunction and recurrent mania. Am J Psychiatry 137:847–848, 1980

Cummings JL, Mendez ML: Secondary mania with focal cerebrovascular lesions. Am J Psychiatry 141:1084–1087, 1984

David M, Hecaen H, Mamo H: Photopsies, hallucinations visuelles et états de rêve au cours de l'évolution de tumeurs de la fosse cérébrale postérieure, angle ponto-cérébelleux en particulier. Neurochirurgie (Stuttg) 1:414–423, 1955

Direkze M, Bayliss SG, Cutting JC: Primary tumours of the frontal lobe. Br J Clin Pract 25:207–213, 1971

Dressler DM, Folk J: The treatment of depression with ECT in the presence of brain tumor. Am J Psychiatry 132:1320–1321, 1975

Escourolle R, Poirier J: Manual of Basic Neuropathology (2nd ed). (Translated by Rubinstein LJ.) Philadelphia, WB Saunders, 1978

Forrest DV: Bipolar illness after right hemispherectomy: a response to lithium carbonate and carbamazepine. Arch Gen Psychiatry 39:817–819, 1982

Frazier CH: Tumor involving the frontal lobe alone: a symptomatic survey of one hundred and five verified cases. Arch Neurol Psychiatry 35:525–571, 1936

Gassel MM: Deterioration after electroconvulsive therapy in patients with intracranial meningioma. Arch Gen Psychiatry 3:504–506, 1960

Gilroy J, Holliday PL: Basic Neurology. Macmillan, New York, 1982

Gralnick A: A fatality incident to electroshock treatment: review of subject and autopsy report. J Nerv Ment Dis 102:483–495, 1945

Greenberg DB, Brown GL: Mania resulting from brain stem tumor. J Nerv Ment Dis 173:434–436, 1985

Hécaen H, de Ajuriaguerra J: Troubles Mentaux au cours des Tumeurs Intracraniennes. Paris, Masson, 1956

Heron GB, Johnston DA: Hypothalamic tumor presenting as anorexia nervosa. Am J Psychiatry 133:580–582, 1976

Hobbs GE: Brain tumours simulating psychiatric disease. Can Med Assoc J 88:186–188, 1963

Huber SJ, Paulson GW: The concept of subcortical dementia. Am J Psychiatry 142:1312–1317, 1985

Hunter R, Blackwood W, Bull J: Three cases of frontal meningiomas presenting psychiatrically. Br Med J 3:9–16, 1968

Jameison GR, Henry GW: Mental aspects of brain tumors in psychotic patients. J Nerv Ment Dis 78:333–353, 500–518, 1933

Jamieson RC, Wells CE: Manic psychosis in a patient with multiple metastatic brain tumors. J Clin Psychiatry 40:280–282, 1979

Keschner M, Bender MB, Strauss I: Mental symptoms associated with brain tumor. JAMA 110:714–718, 1938

Krauthammer C, Klerman GL: Secondary mania: manic syndromes associated with antecedent physical illness or drugs. Arch Gen Psychiatry 35:1333–1339, 1978

Kurtzke JF: Neuroepidemiology. Ann Neurol 16:265–277, 1984

Lance JW: Mechanisms and Management of Headache (3rd ed). London, Butterworth, 1978

Levin S: Brain tumors in mental hospital patients. Am J Psychiatry 105:897–900, 1949

Lishman WA: Organic Psychiatry: The Psychological Consequences of Cerebral Disorder. Oxford, Blackwell, 1978

Luria AR: Higher Cortical Functions in Man. New York, Basic Books, 1966

Malamud N: Psychiatric disorder with intracranial tumors of limbic system. Arch Neurol 17:113–123, 1967

Marshall LF, Greco CM: Primary and secondary tumors of the central and peripheral nervous systems, in Therapy for Neurologic Disorders. Edited by Wiederholt WC. New York, Wiley, 1982, pp 217–244

McIntyre HD, McIntyre AP: The problem of brain tumor in psychiatric diagnosis. Am J Psychiatry 98:720–726, 1942

Molnar G: Seizures associated with high maprotiline serum concentrations. Can J Psychiatry 28:555–556, 1983

Mulder DW, Daly D: Psychiatric symptoms associated with lesions of temporal lobe. JAMA 150:173–176, 1952

Nasrallah HA, McChesney CM: Psychopathology of corpus callosum tumors. Biol Psychiatry 16:663–669, 1981

National Institute of Mental Health Consensus Development Conference on Electroconvulsive Therapy: Electroconvulsive therapy. JAMA 254:2103–2108, 1985

Northrup L, Reed G, McAnalley B, et al: Seizures due to maprotiline overdose. Ann Intern Med 13:468–470, 1984

Oliver AP, Luchins DH, Wyatt RJ: Neuroleptic-induced seizures: an in vitro technique for assessing relative risk. Arch Gen Psychiatry 39:206–209, 1982

Oppler W: Manic psychosis in a case of parasagittal meningioma. Archives of Neurology and Psychiatry 64:417–430, 1950

Oyewumi LK, Lapierre YD: Efficacy of lithium in treating mood disorder occurring after brain stem injury. Am J Psychiatry 138:110–112, 1981

Patten J: Neurological Differential Diagnosis. New York, Springer-Verlag, 1981

Pool JL, Correll JW: Psychiatric symptoms masking brain tumour. J Med Soc NJ 55:4–9, 1958

Redlich FC, Dunsmore RH, Brody EB: Delays and errors in the diagnosis of brain tumor. N Engl J Med 239:945–950, 1948

Reeves AG, Plum F: Hyperphagia, rage and dementia accompanying a ventromedial hypothalamic neoplasm. Arch Neurol 20:616–624, 1969

Remick PA, Fine SH: Antipsychotic drugs and seizures. J Clin Psychiatry 40:78–80, 1979

Robinson RG, Kubos KL, Starr LB, et al: Mood disorders in stroke patients: importance of location of lesion. Brain 107:81–93, 1984

Rond PC: Pontine tumor uncovered with electroshock. Am J Psychiatry 113:1118–1119, 1957

Rosenbaum AH, Barry MJ Jr: Positive therapeutic response to lithium in hypomania secondary to organic brain syndrome. Am J Psychiatry 132:1072–1073, 1975

Rubert SL, Remington FB: Why patients with brain tumors come to a psychiatric hospital: a 30-year survey. Psychiatr Q 37:253–263, 1963

Russell DS, Rubinstein LJ: Pathology of Tumours of the Nervous System, 4th ed. London, Edward Arnold, 1977

Sachs E Jr: Meningiomas with dementia as the first and presenting feature. J Ment Science 96:998–1007, 1950

Saper JR: Headache Disorders: Current Concepts and Treatment Strategies. Boston, John Wright/PSG, 1983

Schlesinger B: Mental changes in intracranial tumours, and related problems. Confina Neurologica 10:225–263, 322–355, 1950

Selecki BR: Intracranial space-occupying lesions among patients admitted to mental hospitals. Med J Aust 1:383–390, 1965

Shapiro MF, Goldberg HH: Electroconvulsive therapy in patients with structural disease of the central nervous system. Am J Med Sci 233:186–195, 1957

Smith RA, Smith WA: Loss of recent memory as a sign of focal temporal disorder. J Neurosurg 24:91–95, 1966

Soniat TLL: Psychiatric symptoms associated with intracranial neoplasms. Am J Psychiatry 108:19–22, 1951

Stern K, Dancey TE: Glioma of the diencephalon in a manic patient. Am J Psychiatry 98:716–719, 1942

Waggoner RW, Bagchi BK: Initial masking of organic brain changes by psychic symptoms: clinical and electroencephalographic studies. Am J Psychiatry 110:904–910, 1954

White LE, Hain RF: Anorexia in association with a destructive lesion in the hypothalamus. Archives of Pathology 68:275–281, 1959

Zulch KJ: Brain Tumors, Their Biology and Pathology. New York, Springer, 1957

Chapter 21

Neuropsychiatric Disorders of Childhood and Adolescence

Daniel T. Williams, M.D.

Richard Pleak, M.D.

Helen Hanesian, ED.D.

WHILE THE INTEGRATION OF NEUROLOGIC and psychiatric perspectives is inherent in this volume, the clinician dealing with children and adolescents must be additionally prepared to integrate developmental considerations in evaluating and treating patients. Some neurologically based syndromes such as the Tourette syndrome and torsion dystonia tend to have their onset characteristically at these early periods of life and consequently usually have a major impact on formative life experiences and on personality development. Other syndromes, such as epilepsy, may occur at any point in the life cycle, but tend to have particularly augmented cognitive, emotional, and behavioral effects if beginning and persisting during these early periods of development.

Clearly, the issue of whether a syndrome is static in its neurologic sequelae, as is generally the case, for example, with cerebral palsy or lead encephalopathy, is quite different in its psychiatric implications from a progressive disorder, such as muscular dystrophy or the various neurodegenerative diseases commonly diagnosed initially in childhood. Whether intellectual impairment in the form of learning disabilities or frank mental retardation is the concomitant of a primary neurologic disorder will clearly make a substantial difference in the patient's coping capacities, independent of other neurologic or psychiatric limitations. The impact of neurologic or psychiatric treatment, including the balance of pharmacologic and other benefits versus side effects, is yet another factor that can markedly influence the manifestations of the patient's primary condition. Thus, the array of variables that can impact on normal development is vast, making difficult a cohesive discussion of the neuropsychiatric disorders of childhood and adolescence.

There are some common themes, however, that are pertinent to clinical management. Prominent among these is the issue of self-esteem, which is often more closely tied to a basic sense of physical and cognitive intactness in childhood and adolescence than at other times of life. Related to this is the more openly and often abrasively competitive nature of peer-group interaction at these stages, perhaps fostered by a performance-oriented educational system. Being deficient in a readily observable way (such as commonly occurs in neuropsychiatric illness) clearly leaves one vulnerable to the damaging effects of persistent teasing and scapegoating or even to more subtle invidious comparisons with one's more intact peers.

The Isle of Wight study documented that children with brain injury suffered a significantly greater rate of psychiatric impairment than children with comparable degrees of physical disability not involving the central nervous system (CNS) (Shaffer 1985). Thus, beyond the psychological sequelae of impaired physical functioning, the clinician needs to consider the potential direct neurophysiologic impact on emotional, cognitive, and behavioral capacities engendered by central nervous system dysfunction. In this context, therefore, the appearance of secondary anxiety or depression in a patient with primary CNS disorder needs to be explored with a view to elucidating both exogenous and endogenous contributants.

Another common and more clearly psychological theme occurring throughout the spectrum of neuropsychiatric disorders in childhood and adolescence is the problem of dependency and its many permutations. While some degree of augmented parental solicitude and support is a natural and, indeed, healthy response to the sequelae of a chronic neurologic dysfunction in a child, frequently this pattern becomes exaggerated as a by-product of features of anxiety, guilt, or demoralization in the patient, the parents, or both. One route of expression of this tendency can be the development of secondary somatoform disorders, factitious disorders, or malingering, superimposed on the patient's primary neurologic deficit (Williams 1985). In effect, the patient can be tempted, either unconsciously or consciously, to exploit the sick role with its associated dependency gratifications when feeling overwhelmed by ongoing life stresses.

Perhaps the most useful way to address some of these salient themes amid the vast array of neuropsychiatric disorders commonly encountered in childhood and adolescence is to select a few representative syndromes and delineate some of their characteristic neuropsychiatric features in more detail. It is hoped that the perspective thus generated can be readily applied to other neuropsychiatric syndromes commonly encountered at these formative periods.

☐ TICS AND THE TOURETTE SYNDROME

Tics and the Tourette syndrome (TS) constitute a paradigm of the spectral nature of neuropsychiatric disorders of childhood and reflect the interaction among genetic, neurophysiologic, behavioral, and environmental factors that change in their expression during the course of development (Cohen et al. 1982). Tics are rapid, rhythmic, involuntary movements of individual muscle groups that serve no apparent purpose. The *Diagnostic and Statistical Manual of Mental Disorders*, Third Edition (DSM-III; American Psychiatric Association 1980) and Third Edition, Revised (DSM-III-R; American Psychiatric Association 1987) note the need to distinguish tics from other movement disorders, including choreiform, dystonic, athetoid, myoclonic, and other movements. Although different formats of classification have been proposed, it seems useful to outline that delineated in DSM-III-R, in which the categories subsumed under the heading of Stereotyped Movement Disorders are summarized in Table 1.

Some authors have proposed that tic phenomena should be regarded as a continuum, subsuming the three major categories in Table 1 (Corbett and Turpin 1985). For example, in contrast to the usual lifelong persistence of symptoms, albeit with waxing and waning, characteristics of TS, transient tic disorder is generally considered to be a self-limited disorder that most often remits by early adulthood. Furthermore, chronic motor tic disorder generally has a chronic and usually unremitting course. Klawans and Barr (1985), however, described 4 patients who had histories of multiple tics in childhood, complete absence of tics throughout most of their adult lives, and a recurrence of tics in late adult life. Clinically, it is useful to concep-

TABLE 1.   DSM-III-R DIAGNOSTIC CRITERIA FOR TIC DISORDERS

Tourette's Disorder
A. Both multiple motor and one or more vocal tics have been present at some time during the illness, although not necessarily concurrently.
B. The tics occur many times a day (usually in bouts), nearly every day or intermittently throughout a period of more than one year.
C. The anatomic location, number, frequency, complexity, and severity of the tics change over time.
D. Onset before age 21.
E. Occurrence not exclusively during psychoactive substance intoxication or known central nervous system disease, such as Huntington's chorea and postviral encephalitis.

Chronic Motor or Vocal Tic Disorder
A. Either motor or vocal tics, but not both, have been present at some time during the illness.
B. The tics occur many times a day, nearly every day, or intermittently throughout a period of more than one year.
C. Onset before age 21.
D. Occurrence not exclusively during psychoactive substance intoxication or known central nervous system disease, such as Huntington's chorea and postviral encephalitis.

Transient Tic Disorder
A. Single or multiple motor and/or vocal tics.
B. The tics occur many times a day, nearly every day for at least two weeks, but for no longer than 12 consecutive months.
C. No history of Tourette's or chronic motor or vocal tic disorder.
D. Onset before age 21.
E. Occurrence not exclusively during psychoactive substance intoxication or known central nervous system disease, such as Huntington's chorea and postviral encephalitis.

Specify: *single episode* or *recurrent*

tualize the tic-Tourette domain of phenomenology as a continuum, with the subtypes of diagnostic categories being understood primarily for descriptive convenience in delineating course and severity.

In comparison with TS, patients having transient tic disorder usually have only mild symptoms that do not interfere with school performance or social relationships and usually do not require pharmacologic treatment. The psychiatrist's role here is most suitably directed to educating and reassuring the patient and family, while addressing any independent psychiatric issues that merit consideration. In keeping with the diagnostic continuum notion outlined above, however, one needs to be aware that what initially presents as a transient tic disorder may subsequently evolve into a more chronic or complex variant, including TS. Because there is no evidence that early pharmacologic treatment influences the long-term prognosis of the symptoms longitudinally, and because all existing pharmacologic treatments are associated with potentially significant side effects, it is most judicious in mild and early instances of tic disorder to withhold medication in favor of supportive monitoring.

The polymorphous motor and phonic tics of TS can be characterized by their frequency, complexity, and the degree to which they cause impairment or disrupt the patient's ongoing activities and life. Further, the above-noted diagnostic criteria do not adequately convey the full range of behavioral difficulties observed in TS patients, including attentional problems, hyperactivity, obsessions, compulsions, emotional irritability, lability, and echophenomena. These symptoms may greatly impair school work as well as interfere with normal peer interaction. Self-destructive physical compulsions may also be observed in some patients. Other clinical features of TS will be discussed below.

Epidemiology, Genetics, and Etiology

The prevalence of transient tic disorder is estimated to be as high as 10 to 15 percent among boys 5 to 9 years of age, with a significantly lower incidence among girls (Leckman and Cohen 1985). This disorder seems to occur more often in families in which other family members have a history of a tic disorder, including TS.

TS has been described in all major racial groups and appears to have a comparable pattern of manifestation in different cultures (Friedhoff and Chase 1982). Although definitive epidemiologic studies are unavailable, estimates of the lifetime prevalence range from 0.1 to 1.0 per 1,000 population. Boys are more commonly affected than girls, with estimates of the sex ratio ranging from 3:1 to 9:1. Socioeconomic factors have not been found to influence the prevalence of TS.

Although the etiology of TS has not been established, both hereditary and environmental factors have been identified in the pathogenesis of the disorder.

The familial propensity to TS has been multiply documented, and the pattern suggests some form of vertical transmission. Some but not all pedigrees suggest a dominant mode of transmission at a single locus. The continuum notion linking tics and TS is supported by the finding that families with TS also have a high rate of transient and chronic tic disorders among first-degree relatives.

A recent study of 30 monozygotic twin pairs, in which at least one twin had TS, indicated only a 53 percent concordance for TS and a 76 percent concordance for TS or another tic disorder (Price et al. in press). Concordant twin pairs were also frequently found to show varying degrees of symptom severity. Furthermore, although genetics appear commonly to exert a powerful influence on the etiology of TS, a positive family history is not found in all patients. These findings point to the role of both genetic and environmental factors in the genesis of the spectrum of tic–TS disorders.

Although the vulnerability to stereotyped movement disorders appears to involve genetic and/or neurophysiologic predisposition, clinical experience and pilot epidemiologic studies suggest that periods of increased anxiety and emotional stress can produce a worsening of symptoms (Jagger et al. 1982).

Another factor known to worsen symptoms of TS is exposure to stimulant medication, including D-amphetamine, methylphenidate, and pemoline (Golden 1983). These medications have been reported to be associated with both the de novo appearance of tics in children with no prior history, as well as with the exacerbation of preexisting tics. Since many children who develop TS often manifest attention deficit disorder symptoms as one of the early manifestations of the disorder, however, it is often unclear whether the use of stimulants was an actual precipitant or a coincidental influence in the development of the syndrome (Erenberg et al. 1985).

Neurochemistry, Neurophysiology, and Neuropsychology

Although a number of neurochemical systems have been implicated in TS, the strongest evidence supports the role of dopaminergic systems in the pathophysiology of TS (Cohen et al. 1984). Pharmacologically, the beneficial suppressant effects of dopamine-blocking agents such as haloperidol, pimozide, or other neuroleptics in 60 to 80 percent of patients requiring treatment supports the role of dopamine mechanisms. So also does the detrimental role of stimulant medications, direct dopamine agonists, and dopamine precursors on the symptoms of TS.

Cohen et al. (1984) posited that the manifestations of TS may involve several neurotransmitter systems operating in a cascading or reinforcing manner. Various aspects of the disorder may involve different neurotransmitters or a balance between them. Thus motor symptoms might express dopaminergic overactivity, whereas difficulties with inhibition (e.g., distractability, coprolalia) might represent involvement of noradrenergic or serotonergic mechanisms.

Several investigators have reported abnormal electroencephalograms (EEGs) in 27 to 86 percent of TS cases (Shapiro et al. 1978), markedly higher than in the general population. This, together with the reportedly high incidence of attentional deficits and neurologic soft signs, has led to the presumption of an underlying neurophysiologic dysfunction. Nonlocalized sharp waves and slowing are the most frequently encountered EEG abnormalities; epileptiform activity is uncommon. Volkmar et al. (1984) found that TS patients with abnormal EEGs have a significantly younger age at onset. Otherwise, the EEG does not appear to be of either clinical or prognostic significance.

Neuropsychologic testing of patients with TS has most often disclosed a normal distribution of intelligence, evidence of visual-motor integration impairments, and a significant decrease on coding subtests of the Wechsler Intelligence Scale for Children (WISC) (Friedhoff and Chase 1982). Older patients, who have had TS symptoms longer, tend to have more impairments.

Clinical Features

Cohen and his associates (Cohen et al. 1984, 1985; Leckman and Cohen 1985) enhanced our appreciation of the breadth of phenomenology encompassed by TS and emphasized the evolutionary quality of its natural history. Attentional problems and difficulties with hyperactivity and impulse control frequently appear before motor and phonic tics. Motor tics, with a mean age of onset of 7 years, usually involve the face and head first, then proceed to involve the trunk and/or the extremities. Simple motor tics are usually rapid and meaningless muscular movements, such as eye blinking, grimacing, and nose twitching. Complex motor tics are slower, seemingly more purposeful, and may have a camouflaged quality. Often they include repetitive grooming behaviors, but can involve myriads of others (e.g., touching objects, others, or oneself; snapping one's fingers; clapping; writhing). A small minority of patients develop self-abusive, complex motor tics of biting or hitting, which can result in serious injuries.

Simple phonic tics, with a mean age of onset of 11 years, generally involve linguistically meaningless noises and sounds, such as sniffing, coughing, hissing, barking, or a variety of others. Complex phonic tics involve the sudden forced expression of inappropriate words or phrases. TS patients may also suddenly change the pitch or volume of their speech or mimic the speech of others (echolalia).

The most socially distressing complex phonic symptom is coprolalia, the explosive utterance of foul words or more extended sexual or aggressive statements. Although occurring in only a minority (variably reported) of TS patients, it is a widely recognized symptom of TS. The symptom may evolve over time from mental coprolalia (appearing in thought but unverbalized) to camouflaged mumblings of parts of words, to shouting curse words randomly, to more elaborate hostile or sexual insults directed at others. Sometimes obscene gestures may also appear (copropraxia). As more mild TS cases have been diagnosed with greater physician and public awareness, the overall incidence of coprolalia has dropped from 60 to 33 percent (Shapiro and Shapiro 1982).

The waxing and waning of symptoms over time is another cardinal feature of TS. This waxing and waning, together with the multiplicity of symptoms potentially involved, leads to a wide array of clinical manifestations of TS. Historically, prior to the advent of controlled studies, this extensive variety of symptoms made for great difficulty in evaluating treatment interventions because spontaneous wanings of symptoms coincident with behavioral or psychotherapeutic interventions could easily be misconstrued as a positive treatment response.

As previously noted, a variety of behavioral symptoms that may be clinically more significant than the pathognomonic motor and phonic symptoms are often encountered in TS patients. These include restlessness, impulsivity, reduced frustration tolerance, argumentativeness, impaired concentration, obsessions, and compulsions. The obsessive-compulsive behaviors usually appear later

in the developmental course (mean age, 11 years); they may become severe and disabling, preventing decision making and daily functioning.

Because of the frequently encountered impairment of social, educational, and vocational adaptation of TS patients, it is understandable that minor and major depression are reported by several workers in this area (Cohen et al. 1985; Friedhoff and Chase 1982). Exact figures about the incidence of depression in TS are not currently available. The spectrum of adult adaptation of TS patients may range from quite adequate functioning to severe incapacitation or even suicide. Factors affecting prognosis include intelligence; attentional capacity; school achievement; family support; the severity of motor, phonic, and other behavioral symptoms; and the patient's response to treatment.

Diagnostic Assessment

Because there are no laboratory or other tests diagnostic of TS, a careful review of the history, assessment of the patient, and interviews with parents are needed to substantiate this clinical diagnosis. As previously noted, the differential diagnosis of tics includes choreiform, dystonic, athetoid, myoclonic, and other movement disorders. Although rarely confused with TS, patients with amphetamine intoxication, cerebrovascular accident, seizures, Wilson's disease, Sydenham's and Huntington's chorea, multiple sclerosis, and other organic mental disorders may present with abnormal movements. Consequently, every patient being considered for a diagnosis of TS should have a physical and neurologic examination and appropriate laboratory tests, including an EEG. Practically speaking, careful history taking and observation generally yield the diagnosis because no other disorder exactly mimics the characteristic features of TS.

It is important in history taking to determine the onset, progression, waxing and waning, and specific factors (including medication) that have ameliorated or worsened the manifestation of motor and phonic tics. If possible, it is useful to monitor symptoms for a period of time before initiating medication to assess symptom severity and fluctuation, impact on the family, and the mode of the child's and family's adaptation. This monitoring can be aided if the family keeps records or uses standard rating forms (Harcherik et al. 1984). Furthermore, in addition to motor and phonic tics, it is important to inquire about associated problems, including attention deficit disorder, hyperactivity, specific or pervasive developmental disorders, retardation, and obsessive-compulsive symptoms. A full family history, specifically inquiring about tics, attentional problems, and compulsions, should be obtained to help elucidate pertinent genetic risk factors. Previous medications should be reviewed in detail, particularly with reference to stimulants and prior medications used to treat TS symptoms.

Multiple areas of functioning—including school performance and relationships with family members and peers—clearly merit careful assessment. Any child experiencing difficulty in school should have a complete evaluation of cognitive functioning and academic performance.

Treatment

Although currently available treatment modalities are symptomatically palliative rather than curative, the majority of patients with TS stand to benefit from appropriate treatment (Bruun 1984). As previously noted, if the patient is not severely symptomatically distressed at the time of initial evaluation, there is merit to conducting an ongoing assessment that permits some baseline monitoring before initiating medication. If there is ongoing use of a stimulant, it should be discontinued to evaluate the effects on both the behavioral symptoms for which it was prescribed as well as on the TS symptoms. During the period of baseline assessment, the establishment of a therapeutic relationship and provision of clarification and support to the patient and family are clearly important. A factual review of the current state of knowledge regarding etiologic factors, treatment options, and prognosis geared to the patient's and family's level of understanding is advisable. Because medications are the most effective means of suppressing symptoms for the majority of patients, they are the mainstay of treatment.

Haloperidol.
The efficacy of haloperidol in treating TS was recognized in the 1960s; it continues to be the drug of choice of many, but not all, physicians. By virtue of having been found effective in many clinical studies, haloperidol has been approved by the Food and Drug Administration (FDA) for use in treating TS symptoms (Bruun 1984). Although originally used in rather high doses (occasionally over 100 mg/day), haloperidol is now recognized as being most effective at low doses. It

is generally recommended to begin at 0.5 mg/day po and not to raise the dose more rapidly than 0.5 mg every 3 to 7 days. This allows evaluation of the extent of symptom control at a given dose and prevents overtreating by virtue of overly rapid titration. Higher doses are more likely to engender unwanted side effects, including dysphoria, depression, phobias, sedation, cognitive dulling, excessive weight gain, parkinsonian symptoms, akathesia, and dystonic reactions. There is rarely a benefit in exceeding 5 mg/day. Even when it is effective in controlling TS symptoms, only a minority of patients choose to remain on haloperidol for more than a year because of side effects (Leckman and Cohen 1985). Prolonged use of haloperidol carries a risk of inducing tardive dyskinesia.

Pimozide.
Because of the above-noted side-effect problems with haloperidol, pimozide, a potent neuroleptic with possibly a more favorable clinical and side-effect profile, has been introduced for the treatment of TS symptoms (Shapiro and Shapiro 1984). The dosage is usually begun at 1 mg/day and increased by 1 mg every 3 to 7 days until symptoms abate. Maximum doses are 6 to 10 mg/day (0.2 mg/kg) for children and 20 mg/day for adults. When side effects are encountered, they are similar to those described for haloperidol. Pimozide also causes electrocardiogram (EKG) changes in up to 25 percent of patients, which include T-wave inversion, U waves, QT prolongation, and bradycardia. With pimozide use, careful cardiac monitoring should be instituted, with a baseline EKG and follow-up at regular intervals.

Clonidine.
After the neuroleptics, clonidine is the most widely used agent to treat TS in this country (Cohen et al. 1985). Clonidine preferentially stimulates α-adrenergic receptors and results in the decreased release of norepinephrine at the synapse. Thus far, clonidine has been approved by the FDA only for use in hypertension. However, clinicians can prescribe it without special government approval as long as they share the basis for their recommendations with and gain consent from the patient and family. A number of open and blind trials have suggested that from 50 to 70 percent of TS patients may benefit from its use. Many physicians are now using clonidine as the first drug for TS because of its relative safety and the low incidence of side effects. A period of 2 to 3 months may be needed for the full benefit of clonidine to

be evident. Dosage is started at 0.05 mg/day and slowly titrated over several weeks to 0.15 to 0.30 mg/day. At low doses, side effects include fatigue (which usually subsides after several weeks) and dry mouth. At higher doses, orthostatic hypotension and increased emotional irritability can occur. A baseline EKG should be done before starting clonidine.

Psychosocial Interventions. Psychotherapy has not been demonstrated to be effective in reducing tics (Shapiro et al. 1978). However, psychotherapy and other supportive measures may be useful in helping the patient and family to adjust more effectively to living with TS and to deal with its consequences. Special education may be needed if a child's symptoms are disruptive in a regular classroom setting. Homebound instruction, with its consequent social isolation from developmentally important peer interaction, should be avoided.

Prevention

Although effective prevention is not yet possible because of uncertainties regarding pathogenesis, genetic counseling may well be indicated if multiple family members are affected with TS or related conditions (Pauls et al. 1984). The question of whether exposure to stimulant medication increases the likelihood of expression in genetically vulnerable individuals is still controversial and unsettled (Comings and Comings 1984). It seems judicious, however, to avoid the use of stimulants in children and adolescents who have close family members with TS or other tic disorders. The use of sympathomimetics (as in cold preparations) should also be minimized in such individuals. Finally, there is evidence suggesting that when such individuals do present with symptoms of the attention deficit disorder–hyperactivity spectrum, clonidine may be effective and hence the preferred treatment (Hunt et al. 1985).

☐ EPILEPSY

Epilepsy is a condition characterized by sudden, recurrent, and transient disturbances of mental functions or body movements that result from excessive discharging of groups of brain cells (Goldensohn et al. 1984). As such, epilepsy does not refer to a specific disease but rather to a group of symptoms that have many different causes in different individuals. In some individuals, the underlying causes are static, and in others they are progressive. All of the underlying causes of epilepsy have in common the quality of causing cerebral neurons to become excessively excited. The statistically more common causes of this neuronal hyperexcitability generally involve either structural abnormality of the brain or biochemical aberrations of a metabolic, infectious, or other physical etiology. Nevertheless, a review of the literature on the psychogenic precipitants of neurogenic seizures (Williams 1982) clarifies that numerous studies in both experimental animals and in patients have substantiated the capacity of emotional stress to precipitate neurogenic seizures. Hence there is an important role for the psychiatrist, not only in helping patients and their families to cope with the troubling psychiatric consequences of epilepsy, but also in potentially intervening in some cases with regard to influencing pathogenesis.

The signs and symptoms of epilepsy are manifold. The most common manifestations include episodes of partial or complete loss of consciousness, localized or generalized muscular spasms or jerks, or apparently purposeful behavior performed while awareness is depressed. The multifaceted modes of clinical manifestation, and the fact that EEG recordings are not always diagnostic, lead to the frequently encountered problem of pseudoseizures as another major diagnostic and therapeutic challenge at the neuropsychiatric interface.

Epidemiology and Genetics

Estimates based on epidemiologic studies indicate that up to 1 percent of the population in the United States have epilepsy and that new cases appear at an annual rate of 40 per 100,000 (Hauser et al. 1983). Furthermore, the rate is highest in children younger than 5, with another peak of incidence at the age of puberty. Thus it is clear that children and adolescents merit special consideration with regard to developmental issues that interact with the psychiatric complications of epilepsy.

There is evidence that socioeconomic factors play an important role in the development of epilepsy. For example, the incidence was found to be higher in black children (1.96 percent) than in white children (0.95 percent) living in New Haven, Connecticut (Hauser et al. 1983). Yet the cause of this difference is uncertain; the relative importance of

perinatal factors, trauma, nutrition, other environmental influences, or genetics is unknown.

In this context, the role of inheritance in epilepsy is controversial. It is often difficult to distinguish social and economic factors from primary
genetic predisposition; poor nutrition and inadequate perinatal care, for example, frequently run
in families. However, several studies indicate that,
in patients with generalized epilepsy, close relatives have a two-to-fourfold increase in incidence
of convulsive disorders, strongly suggesting a genetic component of vulnerability.

Classification

Classification of epileptic seizures is discussed in
Chapter 12. Space limitations preclude more detailed consideration of these clinical subtypes here,
but it clearly behooves the psychiatrist working with
a seizure patient to be cognizant of the specific
seizure manifestations, associated clinical and
prognostic features, and specific medication requirements connoted by the patient's specific seizure type.

Psychological and Psychiatric Assessment

Cognitive Functioning.   A review of several studies in this area indicated that although many children with epilepsy function normally at school,
proportionately more of them have learning problems compared with nonepileptic children (Stores
1981). In the Isle of Wight study, for example, which
concentrated on 9- to 11-year-olds, over twice as
many of those with epilepsy showed serious specific reading retardation compared with nonepileptic children (Shaffer 1985).

Developmental considerations appear pertinent here. O'Leary et al. (1981) administered a neuropsychological test battery to 48 children ages 9
to 12 with tonic-clonic seizures. The children with
seizures of early onset (before age 5) were significantly impaired relative to the children with later
onset on 8 of the 14 measures in the battery. The
deficits were seen on tasks whose requirements
included attention and concentration, memory,
complex problem solving, and motor coordination.

Seizure type, duration, and degree of seizure
control also seem pertinent. Farwell et al. (1985)
did detailed neuropsychological testing of 118 epileptic children, ages 6 to 15 and a control group of
100 children without seizures. The WISC full-scale

IQ of seizure patients was significantly lower than
that of controls and was related to seizure type.
Children with minor motor or atypical absence seizures had the lowest average full-scale IQ. All seizure types except classic absence alone were
associated with below-control intelligence. Intelligence was also correlated with degree of seizure
control. A highly significant inverse correlation between years with seizures and intelligence was
found. Finally, children with seizures had been
placed in special education or had repeated a grade
in school almost twice as frequently as controls,
and their academic achievement was behind grade
placement more often than in controls.

Anticonvulsant drugs, especially in combination, have been shown in recent years to interfere
in significant ways with cognitive function, including attention, concentration, memory, motor and
mental speed, and mental processing (Reynolds
1985). These sometimes subtle effects are easily
overlooked, but may accrue to the point of substantial impairment, particularly for children in
learning situations.

Recent studies have shown that most epileptic
patients can be controlled on single drug therapy,
and that there is very little difference in antiepileptic efficacy between the major antiepileptic drugs
within designated seizure categories (Reynolds
1985). Consequently, the relative influence of each
drug on cognitive function may prove to be a most
important factor in the choice of an anticonvulsant
drug. In this regard, it should be noted that several
studies have shown significant associations between long-term use of phenytoin and of phenobarbital and cognitive deterioration in children
(Corbet et al. 1985). By contrast, carbamazepine has
been noted to be markedly less prone to contribute
to cognitive impairments in both short- and long-
term use in both normal volunteers and seizure
patients.

From the above, it can readily be discerned that
primary attention should be given to periodic formal monitoring of the cognitive functioning of seizure patients, with particular view to picking up
signs of progressive cognitive impairment that might
otherwise be overlooked. It is certainly within the
purview of a psychiatrist treating such a patient to
ascertain that such monitoring has occurred, to ascertain that therapeutic serum anticonvulsant levels have been documented, and to discuss with the
treating neurologist the possible need for a change
in anticonvulsant regimen when indicated by the
patient's level of cognitive functioning.

Behavior and Personality. The literature on personality changes in epilepsy has been prolific, long-standing, and controversial (Trimble 1985a, 1985b). According to some estimates, for example, 30 to 40 percent of patients with temporal lobe epilepsy (complex partial seizures) experience persistent psychiatric symptoms that, more frequently than uncontrolled seizures, become the most incapacitating aspect of the illness (Baer et al. 1984). Multiple clinical reports of adult patients with temporal lobe seizures have delineated characteristic features, including deepened emotions, changes in sexual function, aggressivity, development of intense religious or philosophic interests, circumstantiality, and interpersonal viscosity. One fascinating neuropsychiatric correlate in this regard was the finding in adults of a different constellation of personality features in patients with right versus left temporal lobe seizures (Baer and Fedio 1977).

A study of this issue in children with unilateral temporal-lobe-seizure foci failed to disclose characteristic differences in cognitive or personality features between patients with right and left temporal lobe seizures (Camfield et al. 1984). Yet, when the two groups of unilateral seizure patients were combined, 10 (5 with left, 5 with right focus) of 27 patients were seen to have personality maladjustment on formal assessment. Futhermore, the group as a whole showed significantly lower neuropsychological test functioning than normally adjusted children.

Developmental considerations may help understand the evolution of certain psychopathologic correlates of the seizure state over time. Flor-Henry (1983) studied severe psychopathologic syndromes (psychosis) seen in adult seizure patients. He found that schizophreniform psychosis in these patients was related to pathology in the dominant hemisphere, whereas depressive psychosis (and neurosis) related to pathology of the nondominant hemisphere. In relation to this, Lindsay et al. (1979) did a long-term outcome study of 100 children with temporal lobe seizures. In childhood, mental deficiency, the hyperkinetic syndrome, and cataclysmic rage outbursts were prominent. Indeed, only 15 of the 100 probands were wholly free from psychological problems in childhood. Yet follow-up indicated that the occurrence of overt psychiatric disorder in adult life was relatively low: of those survivors who were not gravely mentally retarded, 70 percent were regarded as psychiatrically healthy. Overt schizophreniform psychoses developed in 10 percent of the survivors. Males with continuing epilepsy and left-sided foci were at special risk: 30 percent of such patients became psychotic. In consonance with the above-noted findings of Flor-Henry and others, no patient coded as having a right-sided focus in childhood became psychotic by the time of follow-up 13 years later. Lindsay et al. emphasized the surprising and hopeful change from the overwhelming presence of psychopathology in the childhood sample to the predominance of relative psychological intactness by adulthood. They noted that the majority of their patients received psychiatric intervention in their early years and emphasized the importance of providing such service in the appropriate management of epileptic children.

Further indications of the probable role of CNS dysfunction in the psychiatric vulnerabilities of patients with epilepsy are reflected in a study by Hoare (1984a). Two groups of epileptic children, one newly diagnosed and one with chronic epilepsy, were contrasted with two comparable groups of diabetic children and with a nonpatient sample to evaluate the development of psychiatric disorder. The results confirmed previous findings that children with chronic epilepsy are significantly more disturbed than children with chronic physical illness not involving the CNS and than children in the general population. Children with newly diagnosed epilepsy were also significantly more disturbed than those with newly diagnosed diabetes and than children in the general population. In both groups of epileptic children, those with focal EEG abnormalities and/or complex partial seizures were particularly vulnerable to psychiatric disturbance. The development of inappropriate dependency was also greater in the two epileptic groups of children than in the comparison groups (Hoare 1984b).

Psychogenically Precipitated Neurogenic Seizures and Pseudoseizures

Based on the substantial evidence pointing to the enhanced cognitive and emotional vulnerability of youngsters with epilepsy, it is not surprising that one manifestation of this vulnerability would be a worsening of their presenting seizure symptoms under circumstances of emotional stress. What is important in this regard, however, is the need for the clinician to be thoughtful and sensitive in exploring this area because of the many complexities that abound regarding differential diagnosis and treatment.

Williams (1982) reviewed several studies pointing to the role of environmental stress and emotional experiences as precipitants of psychogenically precipitated neurogenic seizures. These included reports of the emotional activation of the EEG in patients with convulsive disorder, particularly those with sensory (simple partial) and complex partial seizures. Furthermore, the direct emotional activation of seizures has been documented in several animal species when seizure-prone animals were exposed to various forms of environmental stress.

In contrast to the above, the term *pseudoseizures* has been used to designate seizure-like phenomena of purely psychological origin that are produced by patients with varying degrees of conscious or unconscious intentionality and for a vast array of psychological motivations. Although reviewed in detail elsewhere (Williams and Mostofsky 1982), brief notation is made here of the general categories of diagnostic classification to be considered in the process of assessment. These include somatoform disorders, factitious disorders, and malingering (Williams 1985).

It may sometimes be extremely difficult for the clinician (e.g., neurologist, psychiatrist), even after a thorough review of the history, physical exam, and laboratory findings, to be certain about the distinction between neurogenic seizures, whether psychogenically precipated or not, and pseudoseizures. This is so not only because of the protean manifestations of epileptic phenomena, but also because of the frequently artful capacity of many patients to mimic neurogenic seizures on a conscious or unconscious basis.

Simultaneous videotape and EEG recording has been a significant aid in the differential diagnosis of epilepsy and pseudoseizures (Feldman et al. 1982). The procedure focuses one camera on the patient, who is wired with electrodes connected to an EEG, while a second camera is focused on the EEG write out. The picture of the patient and the simultaneous EEG tracing appear on a split-screen video-monitor. This combined recording is stored on the videotape for future analysis and interpretation. Studies using this technique have disclosed that, even in patients with clearly documented pseudoseizures, there may be a coexisting neurogenic seizure disorder in from 10 percent (Lesser et al. 1983) to 37 percent (Krumholz and Niedermayer 1983) of patients.

In light of the above, the psychiatrist should be sensitive and thoughtful in approaching a youngster with a seizure disorder in which emotional precipitants have been observed or suspected. It is wise to explain supportively to both the patient and family that emotional stress factors often worsen seizure symptoms, just as they play a role in many other physical disorders. With such a nonconfrontational beginning, one can engage the youngster and family in an exploration of existing life stresses and characteristic patterns of individual and family response. Generally, this is best accomplished with a series of sessions that include seeing the youngster alone, the parents alone, and the family together. If evidence is elicited further supporting a hypothesis of emotional precipitants of seizures, the psychiatrist is then in a position to utilize the existing therapeutic relationship to implement an appropriate treatment plan. Implicit in the above is the psychiatrist's stance of seeing the patient as a victim of the illness, of which the emotional stress factors are a part. The psychiatrist's role thus is defined as helping the youngster and family to delineate more effective coping methods to deal with existing life stresses that have been contributing to the seizures. Only after meticulous and exhaustive application of the above approach, or the emergence of clear evidence documenting a factitious disorder of malingering, should a more confrontational approach be considered. It should be emphasized that errors in diagnosis are common in the distinction between uncomplicated neurogenic seizures, psychogenically precipitated neurogenic seizures, and pseudoseizures. Often, ongoing assessment of the patient and family over time and close collaboration between the neurologist and mental health professional are needed to clarify the issue.

Epilepsy, Aggression, and Violence. There is controversy in the literature regarding the association between epilepsy on the one hand and aggression and violence on the other. One well-controlled study of 83 children with epilepsy found an association between the presence of anterior temporal lobe epileptiform spike activity and increased aggression scores on the Achenbach Child Behavior Checklist (Whitman et al. 1982). The authors noted, however, that such biologic variables predictive of behavioral disorder accounted for only small amounts of the variance in their comparison of children with temporal lobe and generalized epilepsies. In this regard, they recommended that more consideration be given to delineating the "situation-centered" variables predictive of behavioral disorder in children with epilepsy.

Using a different research strategy, clinical studies of violent incarcerated adolescents by Lewis et al. (1982, 1983) have suggested that epilepsy, especially psychomotor (complex partial, temporal lobe) epilepsy is more prevalent in young offenders than in the general population. Furthermore, psychomotor epilepsy in this population was particularly associated with violence. In a clinical study of 97 incarcerated boys, 11 had psychomotor seizures and an additional 8 were thought most probably to have psychomotor seizures. Of the 11 boys with definite seizure disorders, all had been seriously assaultive; 5 had committed acts of violence during seizures as well as at other times. The authors reviewed some of the diagnostic difficulties inherent in establishing the diagnosis of psychomotor seizures in an individual where such a clinical diagnosis may interact with the perception of legal responsibility for a violent act. Despite some of the imprecision inherent in diagnosing psychomotor seizures, however, added circumstantial support for the diagnosis was lent by the very frequent history of severe CNS trauma such as perinatal difficulty, CNS infection, head injury, or a history of frank grand mal seizures. Of note also was the frequent association of a number of psychotic symptoms, as well as the frequent association of a history of severe physical abuse in the histories of these youngsters. The latter association, in particular, certainly addresses the probable role of situational variables in fostering violence in youngsters biologically at risk by virtue of a greater predisposition to impulsivity and aggression. Most importantly, the authors emphasized that a clinician called on to evaluate a violent delinquent may render a valuable service in identifying potentially treatable neuropsychopathology so that appropriate intervention can occur.

Treatment

In view of the generally acknowledged enhanced psychological vulnerability of epileptic patients, particularly to the effects of anxiety and depression (Betts 1981), it is clearly advisable to provide appropriate intervention when such symptoms are in evidence. In this regard, the elevated risk of suicide in epileptic patients is noteworthy (Barraclough 1981). Psychotherapeutic interventions in such patients should be geared to the nature of the pre-

senting symptomatology, while taking note of the relevance of the patient's epileptic condition. Consideration of psychopharmacologic agents requires attention to a potential impact on seizure threshold, as noted below.

A somewhat unique psychotherapeutic challenge in this population is that of treating psychogenically precipitated neurogenic seizures and pseudoseizures. There are many reports of successful psychotherapeutic or psychobiologic treatment interventions for purposes of seizure control (Mostofsky and Balaschak 1977; Williams and Mostofsky 1982; Williams et al. 1978, 1979). It should be emphasized that appropriate differential diagnostic assessment is a prerequisite to effective treatment planning in this area. The various treatment approaches utilized may be summarized under the following broad headings: conditioning techniques, psychodynamic approaches, relaxation, hypnosis, and biofeedback. Often several such approaches may be usefully integrated in the service of maximizing therapeutic impact to facilitate symptom relinquishments and to foster improved adaptation by the patient.

A particularly noteworthy consideration with youngsters is the importance of taking into account the issue of secondary gain in treating emotionally precipitated seizures. Since the secondary gain inherent in the special attention, solicitude, and avoidance of ongoing responsibilities at home and competitive pressures at school is generally mediated by the parents, it is crucial to help the parents recognize this inadvertent contribution to the seizure problem. Similarly, the parents' cooperation is essential to minimizing or eliminating these secondary gain factors and implementing other essential aspects of the treatment plan.

Special psychopharmacologic considerations are also noteworthy in this area. Already noted has been the need for the clinician to be aware of potentially cognitive impairing effects of various anticonvulsants, particularly phenytoin and phenobarbital. Additionally, the frequently observed capacity of phenobarbital to generate hyperactivity, irritability, and aggressivity in children should be borne in mind. Consequently, it is clearly important to advocate the lowest reasonable dose of the least toxic anticonvulsant consonant with good seizure control. Carbamazepine has been reported in a number of studies to manifest mood stabilizing as well as anticonvulsant properties (Post et al. 1986). It may thus be advisable in a patient being treated with another anticonvulsant who is experiencing disturbance of mood or behavior to consider switching to carbamazepine if anticonvulsant efficacy is comparable.

Another developmentally important consideration in children and adolescents is their different rates of metabolizing anticonvulsants. Children generally require higher doses of anticonvulsants (per kg of body weight) than do adults by virtue of their metabolizing the drugs more efficiently. There is a shift toward the adult rate in early adolescence. Consequently, an anticonvulsant dose that had yielded therapeutic blood levels in late childhood may insidiously be transformed into a toxic level in early adolescence if not monitored closely. An associated consideration is the advisability of immediately checking a youngster's serum anticonvulsant level if there is any sudden change in cognitive, emotional, or behavioral functioning or a worsening of seizure control.

In many epileptic patients, however, even when the anticonvulsant regimen is optimized, there may still be indications for the additional use of psychotropic medication. Benzodiazepines have a valid place in this regard when minor tranquilization is needed. Because the value of intravenous diazepam in status epilepticus is well known, there is clearly no danger of its lowering the seizure threshold; the capacity to enhance sedation by interaction with coexisting anticonvulsants, however, should be noted.

Major tranquilizers do have a place in the treatment of interictal psychoses in patients with epilepsy (Trimble 1985a, 1985b). It should be noted, however, that several neuroleptics, particularly chlorpromazine, have a significant capacity to lower the seizure threshold and to induce seizures. Of the neuroleptics currently available, molindone appears to be the safest in this regard.

Most antidepressants also have the capacity to lower the seizure threshold and induce seizures. A study by Luchins et al. (1984), however, noted a marked variability between various antidepressants in the capacity to lower the seizure threshold. This study used an in vitro technique involving drug influence on spike activity in perfused guinea pig hippocampal slices. Imipramine, amitriptyline, nortriptyline, maprotiline, and desipramine tended to increase spike activity in a descending order of effect. Doxepine increased spike activity at lower concentrations, but reduced it at higher concentra-

tions; protriptyline and trimipramine reduced spike activity with increasing concentrations.

It is noteworthy that imipramine, the prototypic tricyclic antidepressant, and its main active metabolite, desmethylimipramine, both have shorter half-lives in children than in adults. Children are also relatively more susceptible to cardiotoxic effects of tricyclic antidepressants than are adults. Both of the above considerations favor a divided daily dosage format of administration. Further, children are also likely to need a higher weight-corrected tricyclic antidepressant dose than do adults when used for the same indication. In view of possible interactive effects between tricyclic antidepressants and anticonvulsants, monitoring blood levels of both is advisable when they are used concomitantly.

In epileptic patients with uncontrolled aggressive outbursts that have not been controlled by optimal anticonvulsant medication adjustment, there is clinical evidence of the potential benefit of adding propranolol to their medication regimen (Williams et al. 1982; Yudofsky et al. 1980). Although this has not yet been subjected to a controlled study, open clinical experience to date suggests that a significant proportion of such patients demonstrate improved behavioral control of aggressive behavior and irritability. As long as titration is gradual with appropriate monitoring of EKG, pulse, and blood pressure, and with cognizance of the relevant contraindications to using β-adrenergic-blocking medication, side effects are minimal and well tolerated.

Prevention

Efforts at prevention of epilepsy itself are best addressed to the most common and remediable etiologies. These would include improved perinatal care, genetic counseling of individuals with family histories of epilepsy, and early intervention with those infectious, traumatic, or metabolic aberrations that are known to predispose to epilepsy. Efforts at prevention of the psychiatric complications of epilepsy include judicious use of anticonvulsant medications to minimize adverse side effects as well as appropriate education of the patient and family to enable early recognition and appropriate early treatment of psychiatric complications should they arise. Finally, educating the public about epilepsy is important to minimize the unwarranted stereotypic stigmatization and discrimination that have long burdened these patients and their families.

☐ THE MUSCULAR DYSTROPHIES

The muscular dystrophies are a group of inherited degenerative diseases of skeletal muscle characterized by progressive symmetrical muscle weakness and atrophy. The biochemical etiology is still unknown, but most likely involves disturbances in the muscle fiber (particularly the membranes), rather than the nervous system. Sensation and cutaneous reflexes remain intact. The various types of muscular dystrophies are divided on the basis of clinical and genetic criteria, and many classification systems have been proposed (Adams and Victor 1985). The major types affecting children will be discussed here.

Duchenne muscular dystrophy (pseudohypertrophic type or severe generalized muscular dystrophy of childhood) is X-linked recessive, thus occurring almost exclusively in males. It is the most common muscular dystrophy of childhood, with an incidence of 13 to 33 per 100,000 male births (Adams and Victor 1985). Symptoms begin between 2 and 4 years of age with delays in major motor milestones. The pelvic girdle is affected first, with difficulty walking, running, and climbing stairs and with frequent falls. A typical waddling gait is seen. Early in the disease, infiltration of fat into the gastrocnemii make the calves appear hypertrophic (pseudohypertrophy). Winged scapulae and lordosis are also observed. Later, as more muscle groups become involved, the child cannot raise his arms above his head nor lift heavy objects, and arises from the supine by "climbing up his own trunk" with his arms (Gowers sign) (Roses 1984, p. 575). Contractures develop; confinement to a wheelchair by adolescence is the rule. Death occurs in adolescence or in the third decade, usually from respiratory weakness and pneumonia. Laboratory examination shows elevated serum creative phosphokinase (CPK). Female carriers also may show mild CPK elevation. Abnormal R and Q waves are seen on the EKG due to cardiac fiber loss. Mental retardation has often been reported.

Becker type or variant is another X-linked recessive form but with later onset than Duchenne. It is less common (3 to 6 per 100,000 male births). The onset is usually between 5 and 11 years of age; the progression is much slower, with wheelchair confinement in the third to fourth decade and death in the fifth. There is usually no cardiac involvement.

Facioscapulohumeral muscular dystrophy (Landouzy-Dejerine or restricted type) is autosomal dominant, occurs between 6 to 20 years of age, and often presents with difficulty raising the arms above the head. Common features are winging of the scapulae and facial weakness with protruding lips. This type is very slowly progressive, often with long periods of arrest. CPK elevation is slight to moderate.

Myotonic muscular dystrophy (Steinert's) is also autosomal dominant, with a great variation in age of onset (infancy to adulthood). It primarily involves distal muscles as well as facial muscles, resulting in a characteristic transverse smile (Herskowitz and Rosman 1982). Other characteristics are cataracts, gonadal atrophy, mental retardation, and myotonia (sustained contraction). The congenital form (myotonia congenita or Thomsen's) is not associated with cataracts, gonadal atrophy, or mental retardation.

Congenital muscular dystrophy (not myotonia) is present at birth, with much variation in its severity of proximal muscle weakness and contractures. The inheritance appears to be autosomal recessive. Mental retardation may be associated.

Neuropsychiatric Aspects

Varying degrees of mental retardation have been reported in Duchenne, myotonic, and congenital muscular dystrophies, but less so in Becker, facioscapulohumeral, or myotonia contenita types. Because the muscular dystrophies are supposedly disorders of muscle, the etiology of mental retardation in these children is unclear. Indeed, there has been controversy over the nature and progression of this retardation: increasing, decreasing, and static intellectual impairment have all been noted with increasing age and physical disability. Most recent reports show that IQ deficits in young Duchenne patients are primarily on tasks requiring language and attentional-organizational skills, but not on visual-motor tasks (Sollee et al. 1985). Furthermore, these deficits improve with age so that older Duchenne boys have average IQ scores. Similar language deficits have been reported in Becker and facioscapulohumeral muscular dystrophies (Karagan and Sorensen 1981). Schorer (1964) suggested the language defect may represent both a failure in social development and the underlying muscular disease.

The psychological impact of muscular dystrophy is typical of that seen in both children with chronic illness and those with terminal illness. Social isolation, depression, and prolonged grief reactions are commonly found in the children; parents exhibit preoccupation with their affected children, difficulty responding to death issues, guilt over the genetic transmission of the disease, and marital stress (Buchanan et al. 1979; Witte 1985).

Treatment and Prevention

Treatment of the muscular dystrophies focuses on maintaining ambulatory status as long as possible and on prevention and treatment of contractures, fractures, cardiac decompensation, and pneumonia. Symptoms of myotonia may be lessened by phenytoin, procainamide, or quinine, although the mechanisms of these empirical treatments are unclear. Supportive psychotherapy and counseling with the entire family may be very beneficial and should involve early education about the disease, reassurance, encouragement, assistance with school placement, orientation to present-day activities, and outlets for the parents, especially introduction to muscular dystrophy associations (Buchanan et al. 1979). Genetic counseling should be provided for families with children or relatives who have muscular dystrophy.

☐ DOWN SYNDROME

Down syndrome (Mongolism, trisomy 21) is characterized by mental retardation associated with disordered growth of the skeletal system and other physical abnormalities. Manifest physical signs are a small and rounded skull; flattened face; slanting of the eyes, often with epicanthal folds (especially in the young child); whitish specks in the iris (Brushfield spots); lenticular opacities; strabismus; small ears; flat nasal bridge; enlarged and protruding tongue; shortened and broad neck; shortened extremities, especially the phalanges (the fifth finger is shortest and also curves inward); a single transverse (simian) palmar crease; an increased space between the first and second toes; average size at birth but later dwarfed stature; and frequent congenital cardiac malformation (primarily septal defects) (Adams and Victor 1985). Diagnosis is usually evident at birth.

Epidemiology and Genetics

The syndrome occurs in approximately 1.5 to 2 per 1,000 births, with a slightly greater incidence in the male. Most cases are due to a triplication of chromosome 21; the mother is often over 35 years of age. Occasionally the cause is a translocation of chromosome 21; these mothers are under 35 years of age, and some of these cases are inherited. More rarely, mosaicism of normal and trisomic cells is found; these patients are generally less severely affected. Many Down syndrome children die in infancy, and most die in the first or second decade from cardiac defects and infections. Few live beyond 40 years of age.

Neuropsychiatric Aspects

The brain in Down syndrome is small, with shortened frontal and temporal poles; there is less convolution, myelination, and cortical cellular differentiation. After the age of 30, typical Alzheimer changes are seen (neurofibrillary tangles and neuritic plaques), clinically manifested by dementia, seizures, gait disturbance, and pathologic release reflexes (Lott and Lae 1982). The degree of mental retardation is usually severe to moderate, the IQ ranging from 25 to 50 and occasionally up to 70. Motor milestones are delayed, with walking occurring at around 3 to 4 years of age and speech by age 5. Children with Down syndrome are generally noted for being docile, good tempered, and easily managed; however, some challenge this stereotype. There is less separation and stranger anxiety at 2 to 3 years of age (Sigman 1985), although these children, when in institutions, show greater social competence and less maladaptive behavior (tantrums and aggression) than other institutionalized children (Silverstein et al. 1985).

In the past, most of these children were institutionalized; however, it is now common for them to be raised at home. The majority of parents wish to be informed of the diagnosis as early as possible and counseled as to keeping their affected child at home (Pueschel 1985). As with other chronic illnesses, marital disharmony often develops.

Treatment and Prevention

The risk of having a child with Down syndrome is strongly correlated to maternal age, being about 0.05 percent for mothers younger than 25 but rising to 1 percent by age 40. Most centers advise prenatal diagnostic procedures when the mother is 35 or older and/or if the family already has a Down syndrome child. Amniocentesis is the most frequently performed of these procedures, generally done at 15 to 16 weeks of gestation. An abdominal ultrasound is usually done first to establish location of the placenta or presence of twins. Then 15 to 20 ml of amniotic fluid is withdrawn by syringe via transabdominal (usually suprapubic) aspiration. The amniotic fluid cells (sloughed fetal cells) are cultivated and cytogenically analyzed for chromosomal abnormalities, which takes 2 to 3 weeks. Risks of amniocentesis are very small but include damage to the fetus, placental puncture, laceration of umbilical vessels, stimulation of uterine contraction, premature labor, amnioitis, and maternal sensitization to fetal blood, all possibly leading to fetal death. Chorionic villi sampling (CVS) is a recently developed procedure in which villi cells are aspirated by catheter transcervically, between 9 to 12 weeks of gestation. Because these cells are actively dividing, chromosomal analysis can be performed within hours. CVS thus allows for much earlier diagnosis and decisions than amniocentesis; however, the procedure is less well developed, is not as widely available, and is riskier (approximately 2 to 6 percent risk for spontaneous abortion) (Garver and Marchese 1986). With more experience, CVS may become the preferred method of prenatal diagnosis. The family is counseled regarding the results of amniocentesis or CVS, and regarding the decision of whether or not to terminate the pregnancy.

Treatment of children with Down syndrome is entirely symptomatic, with education being foremost. The child requires and can do quite well in specialized educational settings that utilize behavior modification and appropriate vocational rehabilitation. Most will be able to read, but will not develop abstract thinking. There is evidence that early parent education and support leads to better family and child adjustment. Parents should be cautioned to avoid infantilization and overprotection of the child.

☐ CEREBRAL PALSY

Cerebral palsy primarily denotes a nonprogressive CNS motor deficit. Clinically, however, cerebral palsy is one component of a broader brain damage syndrome which may include not only neuromotor dysfunction, but also psychological dysfunction, convulsions, and behavior disorder of organic origin (Scherzer and Tscharnuter 1982).

Etiology and Prevalence

The underlying static encephalopathy of cerebral palsy has many possible causes that should be considered in differential diagnosis. Denhoff (1976) proposed an etiologic classification based on time of onset and cause of the cerebral malformation or injury. These factors are (1) prenatal—hereditary, chromosomal abnormality and congenital (acquired in utero), maternal illnesses or disorders affecting the fetus; (2) perinatal—asphyxia, trauma, consequences of "small-for-date" babies, isoimmunization hemolytic disorders, and obstetrical complications; and (3) postnatal/early infancy—trauma, infections, toxins, and nutritional and metabolic factors. Cerebral palsy may have its origin exclusively in any one of the periods listed above, or may be secondary to a combination of factors occurring in more than one period.

In an international review of population studies since 1950, data on the prevalence of cerebral palsy indicated an estimate of 2.0 per 1,000 school-age children; only 10 percent of these cases were estimated to be of postnatal origin (Paneth and Kiely 1984). Research of the 1950s reported that perinatal insults were a predominant cause of cerebral palsy, but more recent investigations revealed prematurity and prenatal causes as prominent factors (Holm 1982).

Classification

Classification of cerebral palsy is difficult because there is no single cause of the disorder nor a characteristic course. More important, the description of the motor disability may not give any insight into associated cognitive and emotional dysfunctions. The basic classification of clinical types adopted by the American Academy of Cerebral Palsy include spasticity, athetosis, rigidity, ataxia, tremor, and atonia (Minear 1956). These types are followed by the topographic involvement of monoplegia, paraplegia, hemiplegia, triplegia, quadriplegia, diplegia, and double hemiplegia. Along with the neuromuscular deficit, there are often other disabilities present. Although investigators differ as to the prevalence of related disabilities, Scherzer and

Tscharnuter (1982) noted that associated dysfunctions appear frequently:

> These include abnormalities of vision (twenty-five percent), hearing and speech (greater than fifty percent), seizure disorders (one-third), mental retardation (fifty to seventy-five percent depending on motor severity), learning disabilities among the vast majority, and frequent, social, emotional, and interfamily problems. In every sense, therefore, the term conveys the concept of a multiple handicapping condition (p. 8).

Eighty-eight percent of cerebral palsied youngsters have three or more disabilities.

Assessment

The multiple dysfunctions of youngsters with cerebral palsy require comprehensive assessment of a transdisciplinary nature. Various disciplines of medicine including physical, occupational, speech therapies, and dentistry, as well as psychiatry, psychology, social service, and education are integral elements of an effective program. Although the motor deficit is often the most obvious disability, it may not be the predominant handicap.

Cognitive Functioning. The most common associated deficit of cerebral palsy is cognitive dysfunction. Mental retardation occurs in approximately 50 to 75 percent of patients, while more subtle problems such as learning disabilities are also present (Scherzer and Tscharnuter 1982). Results from the Isle of Wight study (Rutter et al. 1970) indicated that children with cerebral palsy tended to be retarded readers even when their intelligence was average.

Cognitive abilities are difficult to assess in the cerebral palsy child who may, for example, have a quadriplegic motor dysfunction and be nonvocal due to neuromuscular involvement. Because of the multiple deficits, this youngster is at a serious disadvantage in a standard psychological evaluation which would probably place the child's functioning within the profound range of mental retardation. The severe deficits may further give the child a label of "untestable." It is understandable, therefore, that a solely quantitative psychometric approach to these youngsters is inappropriate. Two primary principles of psychological evaluation for the multiple-handicapped are necessary: (1) adaption and understanding of standard measurement and (2) sys-

tematic/naturalistic observation of the child in the test situation and in the classroom environment (Diller et al. 1977).

Social/Emotional Development. Children with cerebral palsy are at high risk for development of emotional and behavioral disturbance. In a systematic, extensive study of brain-injured children (including cerebral palsy) on the Isle of Wight, Rutter et al. (1970) reported psychiatric disorder to be five times higher in children with cerebral palsy than in the general population, and three times higher than in children who had physical disorders not involving the brain. The specific types of psychiatric problems were similar to those found in any group of youngsters with psychiatric disorder and no known organic brain dysfunction. The majority of these cases showed neurotic and antisocial behaviors. Using the same measures in a 3-year longitudinal study of physically handicapped 15-year-olds (approximately 75 percent with cerebral palsy), Anderson et al. (1982) found a preponderance of depression, fearfulness, lack of self-confidence, and worry, with anxiety related to school and effects of the handicap. Emotional problems were also manifested by general irritability, with some cerebral palsy adolescents showing tantrums or rages.

In addition to the direct effects of brain injury, factors that may lead to development of secondary emotional disorders in cerebral palsied children range from physical and cognitive limitations to environmental and societal circumstances. In the course of growing up, the child—due to restricted movement, disturbances in perception, and ability to react—may fail to engage in normal interactions with objects in the environment, which results in delays in cognitive development. Social interactions may also be less frequent and meaningful than those of other children due to factors such as parental overprotection and sporadic school attendance. This may result in diminished and distorted interpersonal feedback such that the child's social development is impoverished, superficial, and immature. A pattern of passivity may unwittingly be imposed on the child from the earliest years.

For the adolescent with cerebral palsy, emotional problems are usually greater and more serious than in children. Normal developmental concerns of peer-group acceptance, relationships with the opposite sex, and striving for independence are compounded by the multiple disabilities. This is further complicated by conflicts deriving from parental inclination toward overprotection on the one hand, and their concern for the disabled youngster's potential for independence in adult life on the other.

Treatment

The concept of cerebral palsy as a multiple-handicapping condition in need of a transdisciplinary approach has led to legislation for provision of services. These laws, which grant rights to handicapped persons and their families, not only mandate services, but, as importantly, reflect public acceptance of responsibility for the disabled.

Early intervention programs beginning with children as early as 2 months of age are increasingly available. For those of school age (3–21 years old), the 1975 Education for All Handicapped Children Act, Public Law 94-142 requires that every child with a handicapping condition receive an appropriate education. Under these regulations, the child is entitled to related services in addition to special education. Within this orientation, psychotherapeutic intervention is an integral part of treatment.

It has been reported that family stress related to the handicapped youth may be expected during periods of transition—such as time of diagnosis, entrance to school, change in school placement, puberty, graduation, and transition to adult life (Anderson et al. 1982). The problems were found to be even greater for those mothers from lower socioeconomic background. To meet the complex psychosocial needs of young people with cerebral palsy, many schools and medical facilities offer a variety of services, including individual and peer-group therapy, family counseling, and group work for siblings and parents. Other interventions that have been helpful include behavior modification, hypnotic imagery, and provision of respite care (which allows parents time away from their handicapped child). Appropriate psychopharmacologic intervention, where indicated, is often effective and must be considered.

☐ CONCLUSION

Neuropsychiatric evaluation of a child or adolescent with a primary neurologically based syndrome requires an understanding of the physical, cognitive, emotional, and behavioral effects directly engendered by that syndrome as well as its secondary psychiatric complications in a particular patient and family. Developmental considerations as they impact both on the patient and family need to be evaluated, as do the family resources that can be mobilized in the service of effective treatment. The importance of maintaining open channels of communication between the neurologist, the mental health practitioner, the patient, and the family to assure appropriate psychobiologic treatment integration cannot be overemphasized.

☐ REFERENCES

Adams RD, Victor M: Principles of Neurology (3rd ed). New York, McGraw-Hill, 1985

American Psychiatric Association: Diagnostic and Statistical Manual of Mental Disorders, 3rd ed. Washington, DC, American Psychiatric Association, 1980

American Psychiatric Association: Diagnostic and Statistical Manual of Mental Disorders, 3rd ed, revised (DSM-III-R). Washington, DC, American Psychiatric Association, 1987

Anderson EM, Clarke L, Spain B: Disability in Adolescence. London, Methuen, 1982

Baer D, Fedio P: Quantitative analysis of interictal behavior in temporal lobe epilepsy. Arch Neurol 34:454–467, 1977

Baer D, Freeman R, Greenberg M: Behavior alterations in patients with temporal lobe epilepsy, in Psychiatric Aspects of Epilepsy. Edited by Blumer D. Washington, DC, American Psychiatric Press, 1984, pp 197–227

Barraclough B: Suicide and epilepsy, in Epilepsy and Psychiatry. Edited by Reynolds E, Trimble M. Edinburgh, Churchill Livingstone, 1981, pp 72–76

Betts T: Depression, anxiety and epilepsy, in Epilepsy and Psychiatry. Edited by Reynolds E, Trimble M. Edinburgh, Churchill Livingstone, 1981, pp 60–71

Bruun R: Gilles de la Tourette's syndrome: an overview of clinical experience. J Am Acad Child Psychiatry 23:126–133, 1984

Buchanan DC, LaBarbera CJ, Roelofs R, et al: Reactions of families to children with Duchenne muscular dystrophy. Gen Hosp Psychiatry 1:262–269, 1979

Camfield P, Gates R, Rowen G, et al: Comparison of cognitive ability, personality profile, and school success in epileptic children with pure right versus left temporal lobe EEG foci. Ann Neurol 15:122–126, 1984

Cohen D, Detlor J, Shaywitz B, et al: Interaction of biological and psychological factors in the natural history of Tourette syndrome, in Advances in Neurology. Edited by Friedhoff A, Chase T. New York, Raven Press, 1982, pp 31–40

Cohen D, Riddle M, Leckman J, et al: Tourette's syndrome, in Neuropsychiatric Movement Disorders. Edited by Jeste D, Wyatt R. Washington, DC, American Psychiatric Press, 1984, pp 19–52

Cohen D, Leckman J, Shaywitz B: The Tourette syndrome and other tics, in The Clinical Guide to Child

Psychiatry. Edited by Shaffer D, Ehrhardt A, Green-hill L. New York, Free Press, 1985, pp 3–28

Comings D, Comings B: Tourette's syndrome and attention deficit disorder with hyperactivity: are they genetically related? J Am Acad Child Psychiatry 23:138–146, 1984

Corbett J, Turpin G: Tics and Tourette's syndrome, in Child and Adolescent Psychiatry: Modern Approaches. Edited by Rutter M, Hersov L. Oxford, Blackwell Scientific Publications, 1985, pp 516–525

Corbett J, Trimble M, Nicol T: Behavioral and cognitive impairment in children with epilepsy: the long term effects of anticonvulsant therapy. J Am Acad Child Psychiatry 24:17–23, 1985

Denhoff E: Medical Aspects, in Cerebral Palsy: A Developmental Disability (3rd ed). Edited by Cruickshank WM. Syracuse, New York, Syracuse University Press, 1976

Diller L, Hanesian H, Gordon M, et al: Response patterns in brain damaged children and teaching style. JSAS Catalog of Selected Documents in Psychology, 7 August 1977

Erenberg G, Cruse R, Rothner A: Gilles de la Tourette syndrome: effects of stimulant drugs. Neurology 35:1346–1348, 1985

Farwell J, Dodrill C, Batzel L: Neuropsychological abilities of children with epilepsy. Epilepsia 26:395–400, 1985

Feldman R, Paul N, Cummins-Ducharme J: Videotape recording in epilepsy and pseudoseizures, in Pseudoseizures. Edited by Riley T, Roy A. Baltimore, Williams & Wilkins, 1982, pp 122–131

Flor-Henry P: Cerebral Basics of Psychopathology. Boston, John Wright-PSG, 1983

Friedhoff A, Chase T: Gilles de la Tourette Syndrome. New York, Raven Press, 1982

Garver KL, Marchese SG: Genetic counseling for clinicians. Chicago, Year Book Medical Publications, 1986

Golden G: Tics in childhood. Pediatric Ann 12:821–824, 1983

Goldensohn E, Glaser G, Goldberg M: Epilepsy, in Merritt's Textbook of Neurology. Edited by Rowland L. Philadelphia, Lea & Febiger, 1984, pp 629–649

Harcherik D, Leckman J, Detlor J, et al: A new instrument for clinical studies of Tourette's syndrome. J Am Acad Child Psychiatry 23:153–160, 1984

Hauser W, Annegers J, Anderson V: Epidemiology and genetics of epilepsy. Res Publ Assoc Res Nerv Ment Dis 61:267–294, 1983

Herskowitz J, Rosman NP: Pediatrics, Neurology, and Psychiatry: Common Ground. New York, Macmillan, 1982

Hoare P: The development of psychiatric disorder among schoolchildren with epilepsy. Dev Med Child Neurol 26:3–13, 1984a

Hoare P: Does illness foster dependency? A study of epileptic and diabetic children. Dev Med Child Neurol 26:20–24, 1984b

Holm VA: The causes of cerebral palsy: a contemporary perspective. JAMA 247:1473–1477, 1982

Hunt R, Minderaa R, Cohen D: Clonidine benefits children with attention deficit disorder and hyperactivity:

report of a double-blind placebo-crossover therapeutic trial. J Am Acad Child Psychiatry 24:617–629, 1985

Jagger J, Prussoff BA, Cohen DJ, et al: The epidemiology of Tourette's syndrome: a pilot study. Schizophr Bull 8:267, 1982

Karagan NJ, Sorensen JP: Intellectual functioning in non-Duchenne muscular dystrophy. Neurology 31:448–452, 1981

Klawans H, Barr A: Recurrence of childhood multiple tic in late adult life. Arch Neurol 11:1079–1080, 1985

Krumholz A, Niedermeyer E: Psychogenic seizures: a clinical study with follow-up data. Neurology 33:498–502, 1983

Leckman J, Cohen D: Tourette's disorder and other stereotyped movement disorders, in Psychiatry, Vol. 2 (No. 38). Edited by Michels R, Cavenar J. Philadelphia, JB Lippincott Co, 1985, pp 1–8

Lesser R, Leuders H, Dinner D: Evidence for epilepsy is rare in patients with psychogenic seizures. Neurology 33:502–504, 1983

Lewis DO: Neuropsychiatric vulnerabilities and violent juvenile delinquency. Psychiatr Clin North Am 6:707–714, 1983

Lewis D, Pincus J, Shanok S, et al: Psychomotor epilepsy and violence in a group of incarcerated adolescent boys. Am J Psychiatry 139:882–887, 1982

Lindsay J, Ounsted C, Richards P: Long-term outcome in children with temporal lobe seizures, III: psychiatric aspects in childhood and adult life. Dev Med Child Neurol 21:630–636, 1979

Lott IT, Lai F: Dementia in Down's syndrome: observations from a neurology clinic. Appl Res Ment Retard 3:233–239, 1982

Luchins D, Oliver P, Wyatt R: Seizures with antidepressants: an in vitro technique to assess relative risk. Epilepsia 25:25–32, 1984

Minear W: A classification of cerebral palsy. Pediatrics 18:841, 1956

Mostofsky D, Balaschak B: Psychological control of seizures. Psychol Bull 84:723–750, 1977

O'Leary D, Seidenberg M, Boll T: Effects of age of onset of tonic-clonic seizures on neuropsychological performance in children. Epilepsia 22:197–204, 1981

Paneth N, Kiely J: The frequency of cerebral palsy: a review of population studies in industrialized nations since 1950, in The Epidemiology of the Cerebral Palsies. Edited by Stanley F, Alberman E. Philadelphia, JB Lippincott Co, 1984

Pauls D, Kruger S, Leckman J, et al: The risk of Tourette's syndrome and chronic multiple tics among relatives of Tourette's syndrome patients obtained by direct interview. J Am Acad Child Psychiatry 23:134–137, 1984

Post R, Uhde T, Roy-Byrne P, et al: Antidepressant effect of carbamazepine. Am J Psychiatry 143:29–34, 1986

Price RA, Kidd KK, Cohen DJ, et al: A twin study of Tourette syndrome. Arch Gen Psychiatry 42:815–820, 1985

Pueschel SM: Changes of counseling practices at the birth of a child with Down syndrome. Appl Res Ment Retard 6:99–108, 1985

Reynolds E: Antiepileptic drugs and psychopathology, in The Psychopharmacology of Epilepsy. Edited by

Trimble M. New York, John Wiley & Sons, 1985, pp 49–64

Roses A: Progressive muscular dystrophies, in Merritt's Textbook of Neurology, 7th ed. Edited by Rowland L. Philadelphia, Lea & Febiger, 1984, pp 573–581

Rutter M, Graham P, Yule W: A Neuropsychiatric Study in Childhood. Clinics in Development Medicine Nos. 35/36. London, Heinemann Spastics International Medical Publications, 1970

Scherzer AL, Tscharnuter I: Early Diagnosis and Therapy in Cerebral Palsy: A Primer on Infant Development Problems. New York, Marcel Dekker, 1982

Schorer CE: Muscular dystrophy and the mind. Psychosom Med 26:5–13, 1964

Shaffer D: Brain damage, in Child and Adolescent Psychiatry, Modern Approaches. Edited by Rutter M, Hersov L. Oxford, Blackwell Scientific Publications, 1985, pp 129–151

Shapiro A, Shapiro E: An update on Tourette syndrome. Am J Psychother 36:379–389, 1982

Shapiro A, Shapiro E: Controlled study of pimozide vs. placebo in Tourette's syndrome. J Am Acad Child Psychiatry 23:161–173, 1984

Shapiro A, Shapiro E, Buun R, et al: Gilles de la Tourette Syndrome. New York, Raven Press, 1978

Sigman M (ed): Children with Emotional Disorders and Developmental Disabilities: Assessment and Treatment. New York, Grune & Stratton, 1985

Silverstein AB, Ageno D, Alleman AC, et al: Adaptive behavior of institutionalized individuals with Down syndrome. Am J Ment Defic 89:555–558, 1985

Sollee ND, Latham EE, Kindlon DJ, et al: Neuropsychological impairment in Duchenne muscular dystrophy. Journal of Experimental Neuropsychology 7:486–496, 1985

Stores G: Problems of learning and behavior in children with epilepsy, in Epilepsy and Psychiatry. Edited by Reynolds E, Trimble M. Edinburgh, Churchill Livingstone, 1981, pp 33–48

Trimble M: Psychosomatic aspects of epilepsy. Adv Psychosom Med 13:133–150, 1985a

Trimble M: The psychoses of epilepsy and their treatment, in The Psychopharmacology of Epilepsy. Edited by Trimble M. New York, John Wiley & Sons, 1985b, 83–94

Volkmar F, Leckman J, Cohen D, et al: EEG abnormalities in Tourette's syndrome. J Am Acad Child Psychiatry 23:352–353, 1984

Whitman S, Hermann B, Black R, et al: Psychopathology and seizure type in children with epilepsy. Psychol Med 12:843–853, 1982

Williams D: The treatment of seizures: special psychotherapeutic and psychobiological techniques, in Epilepsy: A Handbook for the Mental Health Professional. Edited by Sands H. New York, Brunner/Mazel, 1982, pp 58–74

Williams D: Somatoform disorders, in The Clinical Guide to Child Psychiatry. Edited by Shaffer D, Ehrhardt A, Greenhill L. New York, Free Press, 1985, pp 192–207

Williams D, Mostofsky D: Psychogenic seizures in childhood and adolescence, in Pseudoseizures. Edited by Riley T, Roy A. Baltimore, Williams & Wilkins, 1982, pp 169–184

Williams D, Spiegel H, Mostofsky D: Neurogenic and hysterical seizures in children and adolescents. Am J Psychiatry 135:82–86, 1978

Williams D, Gold A, Shrout P, et al: The impact of psychiatric intervention on patients with uncontrolled seizures. J Nerv Ment Dis 167:626–631, 1979

Williams D, Mehl R, Yudofsky S, et al: The effect of propranolol on uncontrolled rage outbursts in children and adolescents with organic brain dysfunction. J Am Acad Child Psychiatry 21:129–135, 1982

Witte, RA: The psychological impact of a progressive physical handicap and terminal illness (Duchenne muscular dystrophy) on adolescents and their families. Br J Med Psychol 58(Pt 2):179–187, 1985

Yudofsky S, Williams D, Gorman J: Propranolol in the treatment of rage and violent behavior in patients with chronic brain syndromes. Am J Psychiatry 138:218–220, 1980

Section
IV

Treatment Issues
in Neuropsychiatry

Chapter 22

Psychosocial Treatment in Neuropsychiatry

David V. Forrest, M.D.

To DISCUSS THE PSYCHOSOCIAL ASPECTS of treatment in neuropsychiatry in a separate chapter is not to imply that it should be separated in our minds from the neurologic and pharmacotherapeutic aspects of care. Indeed, psychiatrists will frequently rely on their medical background to help patients interpret the real meaning of a neuropsychiatric disorder, to translate diagnostic jargon into emotionally relevant human meaning, and to help fine-tune complex treatment regimens. All psychiatrists could well spend some time on neurologic rounds to refresh their knowledge of the burgeoning pharmacopeia in use there. Just as contact with patients with gross neurologic impairment helps us assess subtle neurologic abnormalities in psychiatric patients, our familiarity with the needs of more impaired psychiatric patients, especially those with schizophrenia, organic mental disorders, and substance use disorders, can help us frame a psychotherapeutic approach that is tailored to the cognitive and affective needs of neurologic patients. According to Woods and Short (1985), 50 percent of patients with psychiatric disorders have neurologic abnormalities. According to Schiffer (1983), 42 percent of neu-

rology patients have psychiatric disorders. In formulating an approach to neuropsychiatry patients, the psychiatrist cannot be content with vague homilies about the necessity of support and outreach, but must interact effectively with other professionals, especially neurologists and neurosurgeons. The psychiatrist's knowledge of psychodynamics, personal warmth, and kindness are also not sufficient. Empathic medical psychotherapy techniques must be adapted to the specific neurologic features of the patient.

☐ PSYCHODYNAMIC ASPECTS OF THE MENTAL EXAMINATION

Today's state-of-the-art psychiatrist will find it valuable to expand the traditional mental status examination to include components of the neurologic exam. A good outline helps. Although brief ones like the Mini-Mental State (Folstein 1975) may suffice as a routine ritual, from time to time one will wish to employ a more extensively elaborated paradigm such as elaborated in Chapter 1. But structured examinations and formal neuropsychological testing, such as the Halstead-Reitan battery and computerized neuropsychological tasks, do not obtain the information necessary to formulate a comprehensive treatment plan and only crudely hint at the difficulties that will be encountered as the psychiatrist adjusts the treatment to individual difficulties. Instead, a psychodynamically oriented interview with ample open-ended questions will enable the psychiatrist to appreciate the unique personality and affective qualities of each patient. Such an interview should include information about the patient's personality, including hereditofamilial, constitutional, developmental, experiential, and interpersonal aspects. The interview should also summarize major developmental traumata and conflicts. The impact of the illness is assessed similarly and placed in the context of the person's longitudinal history. The psychiatrist goes beyond assessing the elements of function, as in physical medicine, and is interested in the operational aspects of how the patient will fare at home and at work, as in rehabilitation medicine. Employment of any structured mental examination, whether systematic and of great length or limited to a few tests of attention (such as serial 7s) marks a shift away from a psychotherapeutic relatedness with the patient to an evaluative mode that always has a distancing effect and is sometimes experienced as threatening or outrageous by the patient. The analogy with the physical exam is not accurate because the patient's very ability to make sense of the proceedings is being questioned. The mental status exam is a time for great compensatory warmth and reassurance on the part of the examiner, who thereby elicits the patient's best performance. The patient may experience self-loathing and humiliation, depending on the deficits present and the degree of investment in the integrity of those functions.

The examining psychiatrist must ensure that a methodologic approach is not mistaken for scorn or that the psychiatrist's supplying of correct answers (which are of little interest to the patient) is not taken for an air of superiority. Seemingly "playing to the crowd" at the patient's expense, whether before assembled family or one's residents and medical students, is to be scrupulously avoided. Sympathetic recognition of all deficits should be directed first to the patient. For instance, the psychiatrist may comment: "Exercises such as this seem to exaggerate the difficulty. I wonder if you've noticed any trouble keeping your attention on the task." Even deficits in complex concepts such as constructional ability can be conveyed to the patient in an empathic manner. For instance, the psychiatrist may respond: "Has it been difficult lately to plan your day, or grasp the overall picture in complicated situations?"

☐ IMPAIRED CAPACITY FOR PSYCHOTHERAPEUTIC CONTACT

On first entering the patient's room, the psychiatrist should be aware that impairments in the patient's hierarchy of capacities listed in Table 1 are likely to impede the therapeutic alliance and may require adaptations and compensations in psychotherapeutic technique. Each capacity in the checklist is dependent on the integrity of those that precede it.

With regard to the more complex function of demarcation of the self, projection with splitting or fusion are not regressions to a normal infantile state, but rather pathologic formations to be understood as part of the repertory of defenses available to the injured brain.

A neuropsychiatric patient who was previously capable of mature love and appreciation of other persons may display shallow relatedness comparable to that displayed by some patients with sociopathic personality disorders or with substance use disorders, who tend to see others, including the psychiatrist, merely as vending machines. Such a situation may be indicative of a deficit in the neuropsychiatric function of relation. The psychiatrist should guard against showing anger toward the patient for such atavistic relatedness and, while maintaining greatest empathy for family members, should avoid siding against the patient.

☐ DEFENSES: THE NEUROPSYCHODYNAMIC CONTINUUM

The psychiatrist well-trained in psychodynamic psychotherapy brings to the study of defense mechanisms in neuropsychiatry a relevant but incomplete knowledge base. Defenses in psychoanalytic terms have been classified on a dimension from the most mature to the most immature. The most mature defenses are viewed as the healthiest ones (e.g., sublimation, suppression, and laughter). Less mature defenses (e.g., reaction forma-

TABLE 1. HIERARCHY OF CAPACITIES FOR PSYCHOTHERAPEUTIC CONTACT THAT MAY BE IMPAIRED IN NEUROPSYCHIATRIC PATIENTS

Capacity	Adaptations in Psychiatric Technique
Consciousness	Adopt reassuring manner. Avoid agitation by avoiding overstimulation. Limit time of visit. Assess changing tolerance for interventions. Keep affect positive even if patient is not fully conscious.
Attention	Eliminate distractions. Keep contacts one on one. Speak clearly and simplify language. Use brief syntax. Make sure your presence is noted. Note perceptual impairments, such as field cuts or hearing deficits, and position self helpfully.
Retention	Repeat from time to time. Simplify. Break down communications into simple steps. Reinforce with other channels and modalities (e.g., writing, diagrams). Practice mnemonics with the patient. Identify yourself at each visit and keep your appearance constant.
Orientation	Remind patient as needed as to the time, place, person, and situation. Keep a calendar and clock in view. Visit at the same time daily.
Recognition	Tailor your approach to compensate for specific impairments of any of the many parallel brain processors: trouble with simple geometric perceptions, lack of facial recognition, and difficulty with complex perceptual components. Adapt communication to circumvent dysphasic deficits through reassurance when verbal reception is poor.
Construction	Assist in putting together cause and effect, spatial and temporal connections. Help the patient to see how necessary activities will fit into the day. Offer structure.
Emotion	Assess underlying drives of anxiety, aggressiveness, and sexuality. Do not stress patient's difficulty with control. Identify for the patient when the patient experiences joy, fear, anger, shame, guilt, or sadness. Name more specific emotions under these headings to increase the sense of being understood.
Conation	Help the patient build on fragile will and find his or her way during periods of confusion. Do not be overbearing because you may cause automatic obedience or opposition, echopraxia, echolalia, or cataplexy.
Motivation	Facilitate positive incentives by behavioral manipulation and remove negative influences. Help the patient identify latent longings for improved adaptation. Help the patient guard against helplessness. Look for prosocial intention in actions.
Proposition	Understand that, for the patient, the first stage of recovery is usually opposition, as with a child in the "terrible twos." Respect the inherent positive energy, but set limits. Encourage half-baked initiatives and help structure only after they get going. Do not discourage the patient or complicate things.
Demarcation	Help the patient see the origins of affects in oneself or from others. Use patient projections as clues to self-concepts. Handle excessive blame taking as a failure of demarcation from family or as anger or disappointment about the patient's not being sufficiently restored to normal.
Relation	Note quality of and changes in relations with significant others. The patient's caring about the needs of others is an extremely good sign that social function will recover and psychotherapy will be helpful. Balance looking out for the patient's needs against validating reasonable needs of the spouse and family on whom the patient is dependent.

tion, rationalization, displacement, and isolation) are believed to be characteristic of a neurotic level of function. The most immature defenses (e.g., denial, splitting, merging, projection, and projective identification) are considered the sickest, typifying psychotic functioning. But "healthy" people in sufficiently desperate or emotional circumstances may also employ "immature" or "sick" defenses (Forrest 1980; Stern 1985). Although psychoanalytic theory originally recognized a somatic contribution to the mental defenses (Freud 1966), it did not specify which mental defenses are associated with or-

TABLE 2.   NEUROPSYCHIC DEFENSE CONTINUUM

Condition	Mental Defenses	Neuropsychic Defenses	Cortical Reactions
Nonrecognition	Denial of damage, avoidance, disavowal; or conscious caring for paralyzed limb	Neglect of body part or side with preservation of the concept of a damaged limb[a]	Hemi-inattention because of diminished cortical representation
Misdirection	Circumstantiality, tangentiality	Overinclusion, ellipsis	Inattention, distractibility
Nondenotation	Metaphor, metonymy, symptom and symbol formation circumlocution, poetic language and logic	Rhyming, clang associations, neologism, substitution	Aphasic paraphasias, jargon, dysnomia
Nonrecall or nongrasp	Obsessive ordering, hysterical evasion, paranoid reductiveness, schizoid invention, sociopathic approximate answers	Confabulation, structure by constant talking, compensatory grandiloquence, ignore what one cannot structure, repeating and quoting self	Amnestic or state-dependent lapses, failure of processing with information overload
Referential loss	Delusions of reference and influence	Delusions of loss, impoverishment, metaphorical substitution of time, feces, money, or other measurable things for unacceptable and incomprehensible loss of brain function	Diminished capacity for construction proposition, planning
	Helplessness, hopelessness; compensation or plaintive self-denigration with realization of deficit	Beneficence toward or degradation of self without recognition of deficit	Apathy
Regression	Ontogenic regression to a less mature state with diminished object constancy, tantrums, or catastrophic reactions to stress[b]	Stereotypy and complex innate primitive patterns such as touching one's face in Huntington's, regression to silly humor or puns	Phylogenetic regression to neural reactions characteristic of lower mammalian and vertebrate predecessors (e.g., grasp, snout)

ganic impairment, or how the defenses are related to organic processes. Indeed, it may be incorrect to assume that "sicker" or "more primitive" defenses are consistently associated with worse organic disease, and that "healthier" defenses are associated with milder impairment. Much depends on the level of distress.

In approaching defenses in neuropsychiatry, parallels might be sought between the mental mechanisms of defense and defensive brain (or cortical) reactions. Despite Freud's (1953) contributions to aphasiology, the two domains—mental defenses and cortical reactions—have not been meaningfully interrelated. At the very least, the confused patient and baffled family could be helped to see which defensive reactions are exacerbations of characterologic armor (and amenable to interpretation), and which are primitive, automatic defenses of an injured brain that may be compensated for by tolerant understanding and environmental manipulation. Between these two extremes are neuropsychic defenses that are rooted in both psyche and brain.

Certain analogic comparisons may be made

TABLE 2. (Continued)

Condition	Mental Defenses	Neuropsychic Defenses	Cortical Reactions
Kindling or temporolimbic hyperconnection	Hypermoralism, religiosity, and proselyting; a sense of urgency and mission; anger and remorse, graphomania	Viscosity, emotional deepening, sensations of imminence, transcendence, divine presence and thought insertion	Organic sensations of otherness, bodily intrusion; hyposexuality
Impaired world view	"My relationship to the world has changed"	"The world is bigger, harder to deal with, more confusing"	"The world has been changed, reduplicated, substituted"
Impaired view of others	Transference reactions: "It's I who changed, my perceptions differ because I'm injured"; interpersonal shallowness and manipulativeness	Misidentification: "People have changed, have been replaced by imposters"; splitting and projective identification	Prosopagnosia: state-dependent change in cognition of people in relation to self
Sex object shift	Avoidance of parental object to preserve ties to family	Splitting objects, failing to integrate affects and sexuality	Failure to differentiate sexual objects (Klüver-Bucy syndrome) or own gender
Impaired ego boundary	Creativity, regression in the service of the ego	Disturbing nightmares and other vulnerabilities to internal and external processes and schizophrenia[c]	Diminished stimulus barrier
Impairment of conation	Identification with the aggressor; introjection, incorporation in health, neurosis, and depression	Made cognition, made volition, command hallucinations in schizophrenia	Echolalia, echopraxia, involuntary reflect activity in brain injury
Impaired movement or spatial play	Disorientation, agoraphobia, diminished sense of mastery and mobility of bodily feedback and control, lowered confidence in actions	Vestibular defensiveness, fear of moving, fear of falling or of whirling; incoordination, clumsiness	Vertigo, motor or proprioceptive impairment, incoordination, poor eye tracking, ataxia, tremor

[a]Weinstein and Friedland (1977).
[b]Goldstein (1942).
[c]Hartmann (1984).

among cortical defenses, mental defenses, and neuropsychic defenses. In Table 2, parallels are drawn among defensive structures that are (1) mental defenses of the psyche, (2) neuropsychiatric defenses clearly influenced by the neurologic state, and (3) cortical reactions.

☐ THE STRESS OF BRAIN DAMAGE

Hamburg (unpublished manuscript) discussed cognitive and defensive approaches to stress situ-

ations, whether life threatening, psychosocial, or psychobiologic. Ideally, a sequence of steps (Table 3), anchored in human support networks, answers the need for adaptation. By employing such comfortably sequenced mechanisms, patients may convert unfamiliar to the familiar, removing the sense of strangeness that Hamburg noted is such a powerful stimulus to the adrenal responses of fear and aggression.

But consider how the person stressed with brain damage is deprived of these optimal mental and psychosocial mechanisms of mastery. The stress

TABLE 3. IDEAL SEQUENCE OF COGNITIVE DEFENSES AGAINST A THREAT

1. Regulate the timing and dosage of threat.
2. Deal with stresses one at a time.
3. Seek information from multiple sources.
4. Formulate expectations.
5. Delineate manageable goals.
6. Rehearse coping strategies and practice in safe situations.
7. Test coping strategies in situations of moderate risk.
8. Appraise feedback from those situations.
9. Try more than one approach, keeping several options open.
10. Commit to one approach.
11. Develop buffers against disappointment and develop contingency plans.

arises from within and cannot be eliminated by avoidance or flight. The organic disease cannot be viewed at a distance from the self because it is in the very organ's self-perception. On the other hand, the cognitively distorted perceptions of a paralyzed limb involve highly metaphorical removals from the self and illustrate the difficulty one has in grasping an illness of one's own brain. The virtual impossibility of clearly grasping the disease of the perceiving organ itself renders the regulation of the timing, dosage, and sequence of multiple threats (Table 3) as formidable problems for psychotherapy. Formulation of expectations and delineation of goals are frequently impossible when the requisite cognitive skills are absent. "Safe" and "moderate risk" situations are lacking for the patient haunted by a global sense of impairment that intrudes into every pleasurable aspect of life, especially the seemingly simple pastimes that, when we analyze them neuropsychiatrically, are brain tests of one sort or another. For instance, think of the faculties required for reading novels, playing cards, crocheting, taking a drive, model building, tennis, golf, billiards, or appreciation of ballet. Even the taste of food is frequently altered; network television, despite its simplicity, may seem confusing. Finally, the choice of multiple options, the use of feedback from situations, and the possibility of contingency plans are all techniques that may be quite unreachable for the brain-damaged patient.

The task of psychotherapy with the brain-damaged patient is to assess the patient's capability for each step of the cognitive sequence of defenses, to help break down difficult steps into subroutines, and to assist in bridging gaps with the psychiatrist's own analytic functions.

☐ TECHNIQUES FROM PSYCHOTHERAPY OF SCHIZOPHRENIA

Schizophrenia is a symptom formation that is more complex than an organic deficit, but it may serve as a model for psychiatric work with less familiar neurological conditions. All of the dysfunctional features previously catalogued for schizophrenia (Forrest 1983) may be variably present in neurological patients with brain impairment (especially those with mesolimbic involvement) and require sensitive adjustments of technique. One avoids overstressing the particular brain mechanism, aids the patient to detour around it, and explains what is happening to the patient in the immediate situation. The psychiatrist uses his own evaluative ego processes as a splint in helping the patient to accomplish impaired functions and to calibrate affective responses against the psychiatrist's own in shared experiences.

The mechanisms that occur both in schizophrenia and in neurological patients with disordered brain function include undifferentiated "catastrophic" reactions to stresses by becoming overwhelmed, originally described in brain-injured patients (Goldstein 1942); incapability of moving among levels of abstraction, especially regarding interpersonal relations; fear of novel situations (neophobia); segmentalization and deautomatization of previously automatic sequences of emotional response (such as shaking hands on meeting a person); slow habituation and extinction of reactions to stimuli; and probabilistic incapacity (poor ability to evaluate the likely outcome of actions and events).

Frequently there is an additional feature of language disturbance not present in schizophrenia. While the schizophrenic person almost always exhibits an impairment of language in a larger sense, that is, in its consensual or interpersonal use, and in the attachment of affects to language and thought, other patients with impaired brain function usually have some difficulty *accessing* language. This is typically absent in schizophrenia, despite what seem at times paraphasic substitutions of uncommon phrases that are reminiscent of fluent posterior or jargon aphasias. Sufficiently lengthy contact with the schizophrenic person will usually dispel the impression of impediment and reveal instead *increased* access to elements of thought and language that are improperly freighted with affect. The crucial pragmatic difference is that emotions in most neurological patients are recruited to overcome cognitive and linguistic problems and to make interpersonal sense, and therefore are salutary and ego syntonic; in schizophrenia, cognitive and linguistic elements—often exaggerated and fanciful—are recruited to compensate for poor command of affects that have become terrifying and ego dystonic, and the result frustrates interpersonal sense.

PSYCHOSOCIAL INTERVENTIONS IN SPECIFIC CONDITIONS

Brain Injury

Childs (1985) stated that the most difficult sequelae of head injury to treat are psychosocial disabilities and that physical abilities are the least difficult.

Additionally, the family suffers most severely from the disruption of emotions and object relations, next most severely from the intellectual impairments, and least from the physical impairments (Oddy et al. 1978).

The family's optimism that full recovery will occur, based on successes in physical rehabilitation, turns to disappointment when the patient's impulse control worsens. As a result, the physician often bears the transferred brunt of family anger. Additionally, unconscious or unacknowledged family anger at the patient for being injured contributes to the patient's internalized anger within the family system and must be addressed to decrease severe self-loathing and possible suicidal trends as the protection of denial wears off. Regression in the patient's mental processes may parallel neurologic regression, and both mental and neuropsychic defenses (discussed previously) parallel pathologic brain reactions. Often an organic personality disorder results, which comprises an array of symptoms roughly paralleling functional personality syndromes (Childs 1985). Family and friends should be interviewed to determine the effects of injury on the patient's premorbid personality.

Psychosocial interventions optimally begin soon after hospitalization and are crucial to successful recovery. Childs (1985) placed a high priority on the reestablishment of object constancy in cognitively impaired patients by staff members, carefully selected for their lack of personal tension and anger, who work one-to-one all day with the patient. This familiar and consistent other person assists in cognitively retraining the patient's regressively lost relational skills through the use of a soothing voice

and touch, limitation of talk to familiar subjects, and the restriction of stimulation to a single communication channel (i.e., no conflicting conversations or television in the background). Later, active exercises include practice in following directions requiring progressively more sequential steps (1 to 5) (Luria 1973), problem solving, and movement from the concrete to the abstract, a process that retraces Piaget's developmental steps. Newcombe (1983) reviewed such developing techniques as the use of imagery and other memory aids (e.g., cooking buzzers, electronic diaries, alarm clocks, calendars) for the left-hemisphere-damaged patient, and maps and drawing exercises for nonverbal visuospatial and constructional defects. Cognitive rehabilitation is reviewed in Chapter 24.

Other psychosocial measures include the following, adapted from Berry (1984):

1. Identify the affective quality of the grieving stage the family is undergoing (denial, anger, grief resolution). Prepare them to expect fluctuations of improvement and regression, and incomplete resolution of grief when the condition is chronic in nature.
2. Structure events each day for internalization by the cognitively impaired. Reestablish circadian rhythms as soon as possible by helping the patient to experience bodily cycles (e.g., meals, sleep) at the same time each day.
3. Establish positive rewards to reinforce responsible behavior. Structure behavioral feedback with a point-scoring system for each daily activity. For example, a patient would win points for completing a program of hygiene that could be "spent" on a favorite snack or activity.
4. Treat disabilities as difficulties to overcome, never as excuses for misbehavior. Consequently, the patient will seek help with such problems as clumsiness, anxiety, irritability, inattention, and expressive dysphasias, and will give his or her best effort cheerfully rather than express anger by breaking something or becoming intoxicated.
5. Individualize treatment goals to reflect the patient's specific problems. For instance, withdrawn patients would earn rewards for initiation of conversation, and aggressive patients would earn rewards by not reacting in situations of interpersonal stress. Individualize rewards to what the patient likes.
6. Regard irresponsible behaviors as maladaptive habits that are to be broken by vigilance and restraint. Motivation often follows rather than

precedes the elimination of irresponsible behavior so that the patient internalizes the role of self-therapist.

7. Orient the family extensively as to the current level of structure that is necessary for satisfactory home treatment.

Self Expectations, Language, and Other Psychosocial Correlates. Tyerman et al. (1984) studied expectations about recovery in 25 severely head-injured patients. Typically, the patients expected the return of their premorbid self within a year. The authors concluded that while unrealistic expectations may emotionally protect and motivate the profoundly disabled individual at first, eventually such expectations can work against rehabilitation and adjustment. Consequently, it helps if the psychiatrist immediately understands the probable limitations of the patient's prognosis without becoming discouraged and adversely affecting the patient's outcome. Follow-up at 2 years after severe head injury (Tyerman et al. 1984), as compared with at 7 years (Oddy et al. 1985) or at 10 to 15 years (Thomsen 1984), demonstrated the same cognitive and physical defects, although social and work function improved over time. Data such as these suggest two things to the psychiatrist: that at some point the patient must have come to terms with the loss of the premorbid state of functioning, and that there is more to a person's recovery for the psychiatrist to address than measurable cognitive deficits. Van Zomeren and van den Burg (1985) found that the severity of posttraumatic amnesia and difficulty resuming previous work were related at 2 years to "impairment complaints" of forgetfulness, slowness, poor concentration, and inability to divide attention over two simultaneous activities. Other complaints, such as anxiety or intolerance of noise, glaring light, or bustle, were not related to posttraumatic amnesia or resumption of previous work. In their study, "very severe" closed head injury was defined as having a posttraumatic amnesia of 1 week or more.

Agitation on emergence from coma was present in 25 of 26 patients with severe traumatic head injury in the series of Rao et al. (1985); 11 of these patients required haloperidol. Since this medication is a typical pharmacotherapeutic intervention, it is noteworthy that although they did not differ in demographics, length of coma, and success of rehabilitation outcome, the duration of posttraumatic amnesia was significantly longer (median of

8 vs 4 weeks) in the haloperidol-treated group (median dose 4 mg/day for 35 days) than in the untreated group. Although the causal relationship of haloperidol is not clearly established here, posttraumatic amnesia has emerged as a predictor of recovery after head injury (Artiola et al. 1980).

Verbal impairment to some degree is found in all closed head-injury patients referred to a rehabilitation medicine center. In a study by Sarno (1980), 32 percent of patients had classic aphasia, 38 percent had motor dysarthria, and 30 percent had no discernible aphasic deficit in spontaneous speech but clear evidence of verbal deficit on testing. Dysarthric patients without exception showed subclinical linguistic effects. Since psychotherapy depends on the use of language, the psychiatrist should be alert to subtle evidence of dysarthria and adapt psychotherapeutic techniques to the deficit.

Sexual Disturbances after Brain Injury. Sexual disturbance may follow brain injury, especially damage to the limbic system (e.g., following rupture of aneurysms of the Circle of Willis at the base of the brain). Weinstein (1974) suggested several useful generalizations about these organic sexual problems. First and foremost, he has stated that, in humans, "sex is not only a drive or emotion but a vital component of identity, a means of social relatedness and a form of communication" (p. 10), and that "changes in sexual behavior observed in brain-damaged patients are often abnormal by reason of the [inappropriate] circumstances in which they occur, rather than their intrinsic nature" (p. 16). It is often helpful to make it clear to the family that the patient is not a "sex maniac" when the patient's drives appear to become amplified due to brain injury and that their loved one is just enacting normal sexuality in the wrong context because of a more general disorder of judgment. Another principle is that sexual behavior in brain-damaged individuals is usually marked by a loss of specificity as to objects or forms of excitation. Although specific behavior such as fetishism has been linked to temporal lobe seizure activity, preexisting personality disorders are more likely the cause. Verbal seductiveness frequently occurs in a situation of stress, such as when patients are asked about their illness or when they are being tested. Often patients classify their disabilities in sexual terms, which may be a useful sign that sexual behavior will be acted out later. Some patients seek relatedness through physical contact, which may "put off" visitors or staff.

Another feature of brain injury noted by Weinstein (1974) is the interesting phenomenon of an unusually strong, stereotyped male-female dichotomy. Weinstein stated that this stereotypic sexism (in psychoanalytic terms, splitting) is common in brain-injured abusers of children. A general tendency toward stereotyping or forming judgments of other people on the basis of superficial criteria is characteristic of these patients and may lead to projective splitting of the ward staff into "good" and "bad" individuals.

Stroke

As in head injury, the psychiatrist should be aware of prognostic parameters in stroke patients when communicating with the patient and family. In a study of 154 survivors of 255 stroke patients, no difference in outcome was found between subarachnoid hemorrhage patients and infarction patients when matched for age (Kotila et al. 1984). Major negative influences on outcome were old age, hemiparesis, impairment of intelligence and memory, visuoperceptual deficits, inadequate emotional reactions, and living alone. Clear improvement could be expected from the acute stage to 3 months and continuing to a lesser degree to 12 months. At 12 months, 78 percent were living at home and 68 percent were independent in activities of daily living. Of those gainfully employed before their stroke, 55 percent had returned to work after 12 months. The authors emphasized that emotional reactions as well as neurologic deficit influenced outcome and should be considered in estimating prognosis.

Stevens (1984) found that the Type A behavior pattern is found more frequently (71 percent) than the Type B patterns (29 percent) in those who had carotid artery atherosclerosis on Doppler ultrasonography. Nondiseased individuals were equally divided: Type A (53 percent) and Type B (47 percent). This premorbid personality classification suggests that Type A personality factors, such as an intolerance of disability and recuperation requirements, may be frequent in stroke patients and may benefit from psychiatric intervention. A stroke is unwelcome at any age, but Goodstein (1983) has remarked that for the older patient a stroke activates preexisting fears of losing control, becoming insane, dying, and becoming impaired physically or sexually. The elderly are also more insecure about sudden recurrences, long stays away from home, and running out of retirement funds. Goodstein emphasized that therapeutic endeavors should address these subtle mental syndromes that are often associated with cerebrovascular accidents.

Management of Defenses after Mild Stroke. A case of minor cerebrovascular event that tipped the balance into neuropsychiatric dysfunction is illustrative of the management problems for these patients. Mr. A is a right-handed 73-year-old retired businessman who, 5 years previously, survived a full episode of delirium tremens, including a coma, with no apparent residual. Recently, he sustained an episode of hemiparesis lasting only 5 minutes and leaving no motor residual. Neurologic workup, including computerized tomography (CT) scan, was negative, and he soon returned home. Yet it was clear he was very changed. He became preoccupied with the amount of his bowel movements and anal cleanliness, greatly reduced his food intake, and lost 20 pounds. He greatly resisted each stage of daily living, from getting dressed to going out. He repeated that he was an "old guy," that he would die soon, and there was little hope for him. Cleared by his neurologist, he was referred for neuropsychiatric assessment by his family internist. On examination he showed intact comprehension and production of language, could read and assess newspaper articles (although he thought the events had not happened), and was physically robust. Furthermore, his mood was not depressed nor was there evidence of restricted or flat affect. He was often cheerful and could joke in a nettling way. He was not consistently angry, but at times was quite verbally abusive of his family and doctors for bothering with such a hopeless case in which he was "uninterested." His main difficulties were his reflexive nay saying and a need to make image-tarnishing statements. Underlying these problems was a profound inability to construe his own reduced position in the world, based on his negative statements and neurologic defenses. This deficiency was demonstrated by his conviction that any given time interval would be insufficient to accomplish a given goal in daily living, whether it be going to the barber or obtaining clothes for the next winter. Money and electricity were handled in the same conserving way as calories and feces. He tore up checks his wife tried to write, was convinced he was poor, refused to carry his billfold for fear it would be stolen, and went about turning off lights.

Attempts by his family to contradict such statements resulted in stubborn resistance. The behaviors, which were regressive and symbolically retentive, were not discussed as such but were interpreted as expressive of his legitimate fear that he had lost some mental capacity to deal with the world. His family was encouraged to praise the strength of his negative behavior as evidence of the preservation of his willpower, and they were told that his opposition period would, hopefully, improve. Also encouraged and praised as a promising sign was the patient's concern for his wife's medical problems, which were felt to be evidence of a preserved capacity for loving object relations. If the capability for empathic, loving relatedness is lost, as it frequently is in a variety of degenerative and other organic brain states such as Parkinson's disease, the patient may not be able to invest the spouse with emotion. The tragic result may be a lack of appreciation of the spouse's loving care, with alienation or demoralization of the most important caretaker, whose needs the psychiatrist must also address.

Postdischarge Planning. A number of studies have underscored the importance of social support in the patient's adjustment to physical deficits from a stroke. Evans and Northwood (1983) related the wide variation in individual differences in adjustment to expressed interpersonal needs for social support. Labi et al. (1980) studied long-term stroke survivors and found that a significant proportion manifested social disability despite complete physical restoration. In this study, the parameters of social function were socialization inside and outside the home, hobbies, and interests. Much of the disability could not be accounted for by age, physical impairment, or specific neurologic deficits. The distribution of documented functional disabilities suggested that, in addition to organic deficits, psychosocial factors were major determinants of outcome. Many times the psychiatrist will be laboring at the border of neurologic and reactive-interpersonal problems, and be required to keep a balance between the two. But passive resignation is appropriate neither to neurologic deficits in view of the new views of neuroplasticity nor, of course, to interpersonal disability, although the latter, including rigidities of character, may be harder to change. Davidson and Young (1985) emphasized the importance of outpatient management after the patient completes a formal rehabilitation program. They

found that so much of the patient's energy is consumed with activities of daily living that "complex planning and timing were necessary to continue a few pleasurable activities." Smith-Brady (1982) noted that because most of the patient's spontaneous improvement occurs before discharge, inpatient rehabilitation programs should attempt to increase postdischarge compliance, including the patient's comprehension of the disease, its physical limitations, and prescribed therapy. In addition to educating the patient, Smith-Brady also recommended "interpersonal contracts." For recalcitrant patients, who are noncompliant, Jain (1982) recommended using operant conditioning techniques. For example, good performances in activities of daily living are rewarded with small privileges; good performance in therapies are rewarded with tokens worth weekend passes.

The psychiatrist should also be aware that poststroke patients may have problems driving an automobile (Wilson and Smith 1983). For example, they may have special difficulty in entering and leaving highways, handling traffic at traffic circles, and parking their cars accurately on the right. Many of these problems are predictable from the clinical examination, and the patient should be warned. In addition to these deficits, problems with diminished vision, personality change, the prominence of denial and projection as mental defenses, and alcoholism are likely to increase the risk associated with driving. The decreased tolerance of society for impaired drivers should make psychiatrists cautious in encouraging poststroke patients to assume the liability of taking the wheel once more. Even if driving is a major source of self-esteem and independence, ego-building substitutes often should be found.

Defenses and Object Relations in Hemiplegia. Critchley's (1979) discussion of patients' reactions to hemiplegia, which he calls "misoplegia, or hatred of hemiplegia," contains observations of a variety of defensive maneuvers that epitomize the possibilities of "neurologizing" the dynamic defenses of psychiatry. In the loss of the sensation and control of parts of the body, the most remarkable change occurs in relatedness to those parts, which Critchley called "personification of the paralyzed limbs." This change develops after a initial period of anosognosia and may be an overcompensation. The patient becomes a detached onlooker and the limb a foreign body. Some patients refer to the paralyzed limb as an object such as a pet or a plaything: a "poor little withered hand" that the patient would kiss, or a "little monkey" the patient would like to feed. Sometimes personality traits are attributed to the paralyzed limb, as in "the curse," "lazy bones," "old useless," "the delinquent," or "the dummy." Illusions about the appearance of the limb ("like the hand of a mummy"), aversion of gaze from it, striking it, or screaming abuse at it are what Critchley called "misoplegia in the highest degree."

Critchley (1979) summarized four hypotheses to explain the misoplegia: (1) that it is a specific focal neurologic manifestation of involvement of the parietal lobe on the nondominant side of the brain; (2) that it is an organic repression or denial syndrome present in varying degrees in every victim of brain damage and especially in damage to nonparietal areas; (3) that the lack or presence of insight into the effects of a cerebral lesion depends almost entirely on the nature of the premorbid personality; and (4) that it is an iatrogenic product of the interpersonal relationship between the doctor and a suggestible patient. When we evaluate the patients' communications in light of such psychodynamic defenses as splitting and projective identification, and of transference phenomena, we see these mechanisms are apparent in and affected by neurologic impairments. For instance, splitting and lateralization into good and bad sides of the body, which usually require a much more "fragile" personality structure to be manifested in the absence of neurologic disease, becomes readily accessible defenses against the impaired representation of the damaged body part in the mind.

Spinal Cord Injury

Premorbid personality traits may also be relevant to the prevention and postinjury care of patients with spinal cord injuries, but the issue is controversial. In a study of 56 patients 16 to 50 years old, Ditunno et al. (1985) found no correlations between a scale designed to measure sensation-seeking behavior and the dimension of prudence-imprudence in the incidents causing spinal cord injuries. Sensation-seeking scores were no higher for the spinal cord-injured patients than for a comparable normal population.

Cord patients, insofar as they are brain intact, may exhibit emotional reactions similar to those of mourning in the death of a loved one or other situations of severe loss (Bracken and Shepard 1980).

Therefore, it is not surprising that premorbid personality and the influence of significant others play a central role in coping with injury. Bodenhamer et al. (1983) added a "positive outlook" scale to scales that measured anxiety, depression, and social discomfort, and found that spinal cord-injured patients reported less depression and more anxiety and optimism than their care givers predicted. The authors concluded that "traditional theoretical models of adjustment to disability have provided very limited predictive utility for professionals in understanding individual responses to spinal cord injury."

Manifest depression is not an inevitable psychological sequel of spinal cord injury. Howell et al. (1981) found diagnosable depression in only 5 of 22 patients with spinal cord injuries of less than 6 months duration. Palmer (1985), reviewing depressions and adrenocortical function following spinal cord injury, noted that while depression is frequent (presumably amenable to psychotherapy), endogenous depression (presumably amenable to pharmacotherapy) is infrequent and the dexamethasone suppression test is of questionable validity because of spinal cord injury-related changes in adrenocortical regulation. Malec and Neimeyer (1983) found that measures of distress and depression administered at admission predicted the duration of inpatient rehabilitation and the patient's accomplishment of critical bladder and skin-care behaviors after discharge.

The best predictor of future self-care was past self-care behavior. Green et al. (1984), studying persons who had had spinal cord injuries at least 4 years previously, administered the Tennessee Self Concept Scale and found, in comparison with scale norms, that the respondents had significantly higher personal self, moral-ethical self, and social self scores and significantly lower physical self scores. The higher-than-normal self-concept scores were related to perceived independence, provision of one's own transportation, assistance needed, and living arrangements. These findings suggest the possibility of enhanced self-concepts through mastery of handicaps. From another perspective, Wool et al. (1980) studied learned helplessness theory: that experiences of failure breed feelings of helplessness and depression, while experiences of self-controlled success produce feelings of competence and industriousness. Results obtained from studying 24 recent spinal cord-injured patients using standard learned helplessness tasks suggested that the psychiatrist might "immunize" spinal cord-injured patients "against debilitating emotional reactions to paralysis with a success-oriented rehabilitation regime during the initial stages of recovery."

Bracken et al. (1981) considered the coping and adaptation of 190 spinal cord-injured patients in an acute care hospital. Affective reactions that persisted at discharge were correlated with the severity of motor disability and, to a lesser degree, with sensory disability. Affective reactions were also associated with negative coping reactions that could interfere with rehabilitation therapy. This indicated a need for intensive psychotherapeutic intervention prior to discharge. In a longitudinal study, Rosenstiel and Roth (1981) found that their best-adjusted spinal cord-injured patients predominantly employed the defenses of rationalization and denial, which are more "primitive" defenses in psychoanalytic terms. Other traits that facilitated adjustment were the avoidance of worrying what their life would be like, the thinking about goals after leaving the rehabilitation center, and the employment of internal forms of mental rehearsal in anticipating going home. On a phenomenologic level of prediction, DeJong et al. (1984) found that the best predictors of independent living were marital status, education, transportation barriers, economic disincentives, and the severity of disability.

Sexual Therapy for the Spinal Cord-Injured Patient. Sexual therapy for the spinal cord-injured patient, like sexual counseling for other patients, requires that the psychiatrist be comfortable and specially trained in such work. Schuler (1982) described techniques from five programs. The myth that the spinal cord injured are asexual should be dispelled, and the patients require help to derive satisfaction from their sexual relationships. Emphasis should be placed on resolving marital discord, which is quite frequent in these patients. Avoid provoking guilt in the spouses with homilies about mutual responsibility, but give close attention to the spouse's role in the vital area of sexuality. Educate the couple about how the level of the lesion affects whether reflexive, psychogenic, or no orgasms can be expected, and encourage female patients to learn about phantom orgasms. Ovulation occurs in women, and testicular atrophy is avoidable in many men with excellent care. Attitudes toward sexuality may be changed with the exploration of neglected erogenous zones in each partner, and sexuality should be redefined as any activity

that is mutually stimulating. New techniques that utilize mechanical devices for stimulation and the expanded use of fantasy may be introduced. The psychiatrist should be sensitive to embarrassment in patients and should be willing to spend sufficient time to discuss the topics. A psychosexual history may be used to obtain information that initially may be too controversial (e.g., prosthetic devices, oral sex, masturbation). Disabled males and their spouses must be helped to overcome any rigid sex-role stereotypes of male domination and female passivity. Romano and Lassiter (1972) provide much specific information pertinent to sexual activity by the spinal cord injured, such as the necessity of foreplay, the use of certain positions, and the emptying of the bladder beforehand to prevent spasms. Communication is improved and made more specific by introducing colloquial language while conducting the counseling (Romano 1973). Groups of mixed gender are strongly recommended.

The Family Model in Spinal Cord Injury. Members of the family are affected differently by the spinal cord-injured patient. Children must be prepared for their first confrontation with their parent's disability (Romano 1976), especially dealing with fantasies of divine punishment. Children and other family members who construe human relationships in overly corporeal terms may also fear that with paralysis the disabled parent has lost all effectiveness as an authority. Questions about the meaning of suffering almost always arise after severe injury in persons with strong religious beliefs; often persons whose religiousness is less than mature have fantasies that they or their entire families are being punished for their intrinsic badness. Steinglass et al. (1982) considered the suddenness of the impact of spinal cord injury on families and how an overemphasis on short-term stability of family life may lead patients to sacrifice family needs for growth and development. Prescription of a 1-day group meeting for patient and family improves family involvement with the rehabilitation process and decreases feelings of anxiety, helplessness, and isolation (Rohrer et al. 1980).

Epilepsy

General Therapeutic Principles. In formulating psychotherapy, the neuropsychiatrist may consider the functional context (Sands 1982) in which epilepsy occurs. Differing age-related needs and tasks may be delayed or arrested at each stage of life by seizures, which usually have a regressive, exhibitionistic, and inferiority-producing effect on the patient. In the preschooler, consider the impact on the affective climate of the family and whether the family reaction manifests enlightenment or neurotic enmeshment. In the school-age child, consider the effects of peer acceptance or scapegoating on medication compliance. In the adolescent, explore issues related to epilepsy and driving, dating, sexuality, employability, and substance abuse. Also determine if there is any relationship between menstruation and seizure occurrence and, if so, what the teenage girl's ideas about this relationship may be. In the young adult, consider the degree of autonomy as opposed to inhibition of independence. Travel becomes relevant as well as issues regarding the pursuit of a career, and the acceptance of seizures by employers, prospective mates, or the patient's own family. In the older adult, consider the patient's ability to be helped to accept any necessary limitations on living alone or to face such issues as forced retirement or placement in nursing homes.

The following case illustrates how a psychiatrist may constructively interpret for a patient the functional context of epilepsy.

> A 35-year-old government official with recently diagnosed idiopathic epilepsy also was experiencing mild to moderate depression about work advancement and marital difficulties. He omitted his medication on two occasions and experienced grand mal seizures at work, about which he seemed surprisingly indifferent. Gains from this behavior were considered in psychotherapy, from the primary gain of an electroconvulsive therapy-like effect of the seizures on his depression to such secondary gains as the dramatic expression of repressed anger and self-punishment derived from career frustrations. The psychiatrist was able to help the patient achieve greater self-understanding and compliance through interpretations and discussion of these issues.

Neuropsychiatric Management. Further principles of neuropsychiatric management in epilepsy include:

1. Educate the patient based on the patient's ethnic and social background. The family should be asked (in appropriate language) about possible mythical, demonic, or punitive ideas of their peer group about epilepsy.

2. Teach the patient and family to keep detailed records about moods, situations, mental conflicts, and activities that precede episodes of seizure activity. This will help to identify and study avoidable triggering factors.

3. Be pragmatic. The woman humiliated by incontinence during a seizure on the job does not necessarily need psychoanalysis of the earliest sources of shame. She could be advised to limit overconsumption of fluids, wear incontinence underpants, or keep a towel and deodorant in her desk drawer (Sands 1982).

4. Formulate behavior in psychodynamic and developmental terms specific for the patient's personality rather than assuming fixed concepts such as "the epileptic personality" or "narcissistic regression."

5. Avoid encouraging dependency and allow regressive transference states during treatment only with the greatest care because epilepsy already fosters dependency. Encourage the patient's active role in observing the improved handling of seizures. Intensive psychotherapy should seek specific goals and limits, with maintenance or as-needed visits afterward.

6. Employ marital or family therapy when indicated with other family members and group therapy for shame, shyness, and other social problems, ideally in groups including nonepileptic patients.

Behavioral Conditioning Techniques. Much evidence suggests that seizures have a psychosomatic contribution and therefore can respond (by decreased severity or frequency) to measures that affect the mental state. Sometimes patients feel that they have a surprising amount of conscious control over their seizures. This possibility always warrants a line of open-minded questioning by a good psychiatric interviewer to elicit any useful techniques from the patient to decrease the incidence of seizures. Whether or not the patient can supply control techniques, the psychiatrist can suggest or structure patients in both inpatient and outpatient settings. Williams (in Sands 1982) recommended the following behavioral conditioning techniques.

1. Deny rewards for a seizure by avoiding a display of care, concern, or attention following a seizure. Treat a seizure like a tantrum and largely ignore the seizure, especially in children.

2. Institute penalty programs for hospital or home use by asking the patient to enter a "time-out room" where reinforcement is absent. Take away privileges or favorite activities until the patient "will no longer be in danger."

3. Undertake relief or avoidance programs in a conditioning lab with an aversive stimulus, such as photic stimulation during a spike-and-wave electroencephalogram (EEG) pattern, until the seizure activity is reduced.

4. Try punishment programs using a noxious stimulus such as annoying shock or light immediately following a seizure.

5. Consider overt reward programs suitable for home use when seizures are decreased or absent during a time period.

6. Institute overt reward programs for patients with psychogenic seizures: visualization during relaxation of seizure-provoking scenes followed by imagined, rewarding scenes.

7. Institute habituation or extinction programs using classical deconditioning of the seizure-evocative stimuli (e.g., light, music, reading, touch, voice). If this seems to help in the lab or office, further applications and reinforcement at home may extend the effect.

Management of Interictal Behavioral and Personality Changes. Techniques for the management of behavior and personality changes associated with temporal lobe epilepsy interictal states, and which may occur in other seizure states, should be considered:

1. Viscosity or stickiness to a subject in conversation by a laborious, detailed, and emphatic conversation on the way out of the psychiatrist's office may be worked with if the psychiatrist is neither rejecting nor overly passive.

2. Deepened emotionality is associated with a hyperreligious preoccupation with righteousness. Cheerful hypermoralism alternates with briefer episodes of explosive verbalized anger, followed by remorse or denial. The patient may lack insight but will benefit from the psychiatrist's explaining how others may avoid the patient because of this deepened emotionality. Patients may also be coached to drop the proselyting mode and to switch mental sets, removing themselves physically from entanglements.

3. Hyposexuality is seldom complained of, but further isolates temporal lobe epileptics, especially males. Although the hyposexuality may be drug-

responsive, the psychiatrist should address the isolation and the needs of the spouse and encourage closeness.

4. Mood swings, especially those that build up over several days prior to a seizure, may be difficult for relatives, who try to avoid outbursts.

5. Schizophrenia-like psychosis may occur after many years. Adapt your treatment approach to specific features, as with schizophrenic patients. Psychosis may diminish when anticonvulsants are discontinued for a few days.

6. Memory disorders, related in severity to seizure severity and bitemporality, occur retrograde and anterograde during postictal confusion. Having the patient write notes at the first sign of an aura may help. Psychomotor automatisms are also a postictal phenomenon to be identified and explained to the patient.

Organic Brain Syndrome

Cummings (1985a, 1985b) described four classifications of organic delusions, which occur most commonly in older patients with limbic or basal ganglial toxic-metabolic disorders. Simple persecutory delusions usually occur in more impaired patients, but respond to medical treatment. Complex persecutory delusions require the patient to have more cognitive integrity and are relatively resistant to treatment. Grandiose delusions have traditionally been thought to reflect greater deterioration and less insight than persecutory ones. The fourth category includes delusions associated with specific neurologic defects such as anosognosia or reduplicative paramnesia. Patients with this type of delusion may act on their delusional beliefs, including taking excessive security measures, refusing food or medications, or attempting suicide.

Families tend to overestimate the prognostic severity of acute organic brain syndromes in medically ill neuropsychiatric patients. In these situations, when their loved one is so delirious or confused that no serious psychotherapeutic work can be done, the psychiatrist can be of great help to the family. Delirious patients frequently may be transferred among hospital clinical services, and the psychiatrist may provide emotional continuity for terrified and overwhelmed family members who do not understand the fragmented medical reports about their loved one's condition. For example, delirium developed in a 79-year-old man who had previously tolerated the drug propranolol. The pa-

PSYCHOSOCIAL TREATMENT IN NEUROPSYCHIATRY

tient's inertness and verbal unresponsiveness during the day and wild agitation at night mimicked a cerebrovascular accident and convinced his greatly aggrieved family that he was about to die. The psychiatrist was called by the patient's private internist because of his agitation and depression, and to help deal with the family, who had found psychiatrists helpful in bringing the patient out of retarded depression over a decade ago. The psychiatrist considered the patient's psychiatric history and potential adverse effects of propranolol and informed the medical staff that propranolol was the most likely cause of the delirium. The psychiatrist explained to the family that the usually acute nature of the delirium was a hopeful sign. When the propranolol was discontinued, the patient returned to a normal mental status. However, the medical staff still doubted that propranolol had been the cause of the delirium and restarted it, with a return of the delirium. The delirium completely cleared again when the drug was stopped. The patient recalled some of the content of his hallucinations and numerous things said to him when the staff thought him unconscious. Each time the family was helped to weather the delirium by explanations that its acuteness suggested reversibility and treatability.

Alzheimer's Disease

The neuropsychiatrist should approach the patient with Alzheimer's disease and the patient's family in a way that is comprehensive yet sensitive to the stage of the disease. As is often the case, in this condition in which "nothing can be done," there is much that the psychiatrist can do. The following suggestions are adapted and amplified from Aronson (1984), Jenicke (1985), and Rabins et al. (1982).

Because attention and memory are impaired, a dyadic psychotherapeutic learning process is usually impossible. However, in speaking with the patient and family together, the psychiatrist may convey that the patient is valued by the psychiatrist. Also, the psychiatrist's attitude toward the patient will serve as a model for the family members. The patient faces a loss in status and evaluation by the family and needs comforting while coming to terms with these changes. The single overriding principle for treatment of the family unit of the Alzheimer patient is the maintenance of family homeostasis and equilibrium despite the great changes in roles that result. Both patient and family benefit most if the family can preserve its function

as a holding environment for all its members and a social entity in which the members can feel loved and love others.

Sleep is the first consideration in home care. The family members cannot care for the patient and will resent the patient if they are suffering from sleep deficits caused by the patient's reversed sleep cycle. A strict diurnal schedule is prescribed as with any insomnia, with sufficient daily activity and exercise so that the characteristically physically vigorous patient does not have an ususual amount of leftover energy during the night.

Quality-of-life considerations for the family should be immediately addressed. Such discussions will tend to counter irrational feelings of guilt and responsibility taking, family shame, and punitive self-denial, all of which may lead to resentment and abuse of the patient. Additionally, the physician must prescribe family fun with and without the patient.

Financial planning based on clinical reality is addressed as soon as possible after diagnosis. Early consultation with a social worker to access available care resources and legal advice about the shifting of financial responsibility can help avoid bankrupting the family. The psychiatrist neither ignores relevant financial concerns nor takes sides in financial disputes. Aspects of the clinical condition may require the psychiatrist to testify in court, and the psychiatrist should, as always, keep detailed notes of the patient's clinical condition. The family should also be encouraged to keep a log of the patient's incapacity to accomplish routine tasks of daily living. A consultation with a colleague to determine competency may preserve the treating psychiatrist's relationship with both patient and family in the event either is unhappy with the subsequent determination.

Care of the patient, a newly added dependent, will require help from the whole family, but children may find it especially taxing and be less than helpful because of their own unanswered needs for support and their inability to tolerate a family situation that does not conform with ideal expectations. This is especially difficult when the Alzheimer patient is a role model for a teenager. Exhibition of sexual inappropriateness, incontinence, or abusive hitting will humiliate an adolescent thoroughly. Encouragement of substitute role models is vital.

Certain practical measures are directly applicable to the patient's condition and thereby indirectly helpful to the family. The psychiatrist should assist the family to avoid situations that are stressful to the patient's diminished information-processing ability. Just as a person with cardiac failure should not be physically overtaxed, a person with brain failure should not be pressed to evaluate multiple inputs or negotiate complex interpersonal situations. Catastrophic reactions may be prevented or minimized by directing the patient's attention away from stressful tasks and capitalizing on distractibility and poor memory.

The family should also be encouraged to eliminate dangerous choices for the patient. Just as one childproofs a house, one should Alzheimer-proof it. Weapons, dangerous tools, or substances that could erroneously be ingested must be locked away. Outside door locks that cannot be opened at night need to be installed. Keys to the car should be made unavailable. The knobs should be removed from stoves and matches should be hidden. The patient should not be left alone with minors vulnerable to molestation. On the positive side, favorite radio or television shows can be set on a timer in the patient's room. Secondary systems of memory enhancement may be employed, such as posted signs, arrows on walls, daily schedules, and identifying labels on objects or clothes. Finally, simple syntax should be used in all conversations so that memory and attention are not taxed.

Frank fear in the patient should be investigated as a possible index of victimization by the family. As Rathbone-McCuan and Goodstein (1985) pointed out, "a disoriented aged person generally exhibits serenity in a familiar setting unless there is a sense of threat" (p. 337). Abuse of the elderly may require social support for the abusers in much the same way that child abuse does.

The psychiatrist should employ knowledge of predictable functional assessment stages in the progressions of Alzheimer's disease (Reisberg 1985) to judge the patient's performance and to determine possible treatable conditions. For example, incontinence should only occur late in Alzheimer's disease or there may be a treatable infection. Loss of the ability to dress properly never precedes loss of the ability to choose clothing properly, and may be a symptom of misbehavior. However, skills that were present yesterday may be gone today, and the family should be helped to accept the deterioration.

Research progress with Alzheimer's, although promising, does not diminish the emotional suffering of patient and family. It is an emotional reality that families may mourn the loss of the personality of the Alzheimer patient before the patient's death and devalue what is left of the person. Often the patient is protected by the disease from awareness of this, but at times the caring doctor remains the last real representative of other people.

Parkinson's Disease

In describing the "shaking palsy" as a purely motor rather than mental degeneration, Parkinson himself referred to depression and terminal delirium. Reflecting the more recent recognition of concomitant mental involvement, Mayeux and Stern (1983) described some of the specific mental processes that are impaired. Building on such observations, the psychiatrist may make a more educated psychotherapeutic approach to the patient with this syndrome.

Because the degree of intellectual impairment tends to increase as the severity of motoric symptoms increases (Mayeux and Stern 1983), the psychiatrist should also assume that the patient will have greater impairment in the ability to make therapeutic contact if motor ability is more impaired. Furthermore, the psychiatrist should not conclude that all psychopathology is reactive to impairment, or that the constriction of the patient's life is due solely to motoric limitations. The types of motor impairments tell us much about the patient's quality of thought, insight, and ability to relate to the therapist. Mayeux and Stern (1983) and Hallet (1979) noted that the activities that are impaired require directed attention to the task, sequencing of cognitive processes, and often additional motor interaction. Other disturbances characteristic of Parkinson's disease are impaired perceptual motor or visuospatial function, especially the inability to perform sequential or predictive voluntary movements (Stern et al. 1984). This results in impaired internal spatial representation (from which may arise the initiation of independent thought and mental action); and articulatory difficulty without impaired language reception or production. In fact, Parkinson's disease is distinct from other neuropsychiatric disorders because of the paucity of language impairment, a significant boon to the psychiatrist trying to do psychotherapeutic work.

Memory is often slowed without being impaired. Trouble with word finding, which worsens with increased motoric symptoms in some parkinsonian patients, was considered a form of the "tip of the tongue" phenomenon similar to anomia in aphasics with frontal lesions. Mayeux (1984) summarized a review of the literature of Parkinson's disease and Huntington's disease by stating that "nearly every patient with a movement disorder has some type of behavioral dysfunction, whether it is personality change or intellectual impairment."

The psychiatrist may wish to observe the patient's mood, cognition, organization, and general well-being during physical therapy or occupational therapy. The close link of motor and mental action may be turned to advantage by using a number of behavioral techniques (Duvoisin 1984).

Patients should be encouraged to participate in regular moderate exercise, especially if their occupation is sedentary. Fitness does not stop the progression of Parkinson's disease, but helps patients cope with symptoms. Free-moving calisthenics and sports such as swimming are best, but safety, especially with patients who freeze motorically, must be considered.

Sensory, rhythmic, and other cues should be used to keep the bradykinetic patient moving. A patient can put tap-like nails in the shoes to provide an auditory cue to keep the rhythm of walking constant and to prevent festination. A small piece of raw carrot in the mouth may remind the patient to swallow and prevent drooling. Many techniques helpful to movement and mental state seem mechanical: wearing slippery rather than rubber soles to permit shuffling without falling, dispensing with canes and walkers when there is retropulsion, raising the back legs of chairs and toilet seats 2 inches to facilitate rising, and removing doorsills to prevent doorway freezing. Other measures are more cognitive, such as teaching patients how to initiate rising from a chair by placing their hands on the arms of the chair. Similarly, patients can be taught ways to initiate sexual intercourse when rolling over in bed is difficult. As a feedback device, I rigged an earphone radio with a mercury switch attached to the eyeglasses that kept a favorite station going only when the patient stood up straight.

Parkinson's disease is a disorder of knife-edge tolerances and balances. The response to L-dopa is so dramatic that the patient and family are exquisitely conscious of the central role of drug effects. Indeed, they become such "believers" in their medication that it is difficult to pry them beyond a mechanistic view of their movement disorder and beyond their demanding dependence on the neurologist to monitor their prescriptions. Because of

this fervent pharmacologism, the psychiatrist must deal with the symbiotic relationship between patient and drug that includes not only motor and mental improvement but also an array of side effects. Patient and family, building on this medication response, may try to convince the psychiatrist that a cumbersome apparatus is being dealt with, a thing rather than a person. The psychiatrist should avoid becoming so totally immersed in the intricacies of such compelling medicomotor phenomena as on-off reactions and sudden transient freezing that the emotional issues are neglected. Often, antiparkinsonian drugs lose their efficacy with time. This can result in severe disillusionment to parkinsonian patients and their families. Supportive care and treatment of reactive depressions by the psychiatrist are critical at this point. In addition, as the parkinsonian patient's symptoms become less responsive to antiparkinsonian medications, the doses of these medications are increased or several antiparkinsonian agents are used in combination. Psychiatric side effects of antiparkinsonian agents often become prominent at this point. For example, psychosis often emerges with the increase of L-dopa. At this point, a psychopharmacologic "see-saw" may result (Yudofsky and Rosecan 1979). Adding antipsychotic agents improves the psychosis but makes the motoric components of Parkinson's disease more prominent. Adding more antiparkinsonian agents, on the other hand, may improve the motoric components but aggravate the psychosis. Several investigators have reported that electroconvulsive therapy (ECT) has been shown to be effective in patients with advanced parkinsonian disease. Yudofsky and Rosecan (1979) recommended the use of ECT in patients with advanced parkinsonian disease and psychosis. They theorized that the reported improvement in both psychosis and motoric behavior is secondary to beneficial effects of ECT at the site of the dopamine receptor.

The early parkinsonian patient should be watched closely for symptoms of depression. The increased suicide risk should be seriously considered, especially in males who overvalue physical mobility and power and are extremely anxious about their continued performance in competitive and exacting sports. Activities less aggravating for the mild parkinsonian patient should be encouraged. The psychiatrist should also explore the patient's image of the disease process. Parkinson's disease is sufficiently common to be a vivid Charlie Chaplinesque caricature in the minds of some patients, who seem to exaggerate the motor tendencies of the aged that are assumed by stage actors and comics. Fear of humiliation because of such an image may be allayed by emphasizing the medical manageability of the condition. Later symptoms of emotional flattening, apathy, and impoverishment of the ability to relate to loved ones are especially painful for the spouse on whom the patient may greatly rely without much gratitude or recognition. These feelings often are not articulated by the spouse unless encouraged by the psychiatrist.

Huntington's Disease

In a large kindred of Huntington's disease families living along the shores of Lake Maracaibo in Venezuela, where in 1983 the G8 DNA marker was localized to chromosome 4, all descendants are said to "inherit" the disease; only those who are affected by it are said to "have" it. Wexler (1985) pointed out that while this distorts genetic truth, it expresses psychological truth about being at risk as a distinct state of mind. Because this state is stressful and conflict-ridden, the psychiatrist may be consulted on various issues.

Ambiguity about whether one will be affected, as with any late-onset autosomal dominant disease, may dominate the mental life of people at risk. Administration of the genetic test for persons at risk requires much sensitivity to the emotional dimensions of determining whether one possesses the gene. Testing should always be embedded in a personal physician-patient relationship.

Additionally, patients with the disease must face the ambiguity about when the disabling symptoms will begin. The peak onset is in the third and fourth decades; patients who do not know their genetic state can be comforted by a lower probability of inheriting the illness after they pass these decades symptom-free. Most individuals translate the 50/50 risk into a 100 percent certainty they will or will not develop the disease (Shoulson 1978). Instead, people should be told that they have a 50 percent chance of *not* doing so. Lack of control over one's destiny also may lead to feelings of helplessness or to the development of an overcontrolling personality. The psychiatrist should be aware of such responses and treat the patient appropriately. The overlap of initial symptoms of Huntington's with symptoms of normal clumsiness, irritability, or infrequent lapses of memory can lead

to hypochondriacal worries. Symptom seeking can lead to the loss of years of healthy productivity when a premature decision is made that the disease has begun. On the other hand, symptom denial may prevent acceptance of help when needed. The psychiatrist may help the patient by taking over the responsibility of the symptom search, distinguishing between those symptoms that overlap with normality and the disease, or by teaching the patient to delegate this function to the neurologist.

Stigmatization as part of a Huntington's disease family may affect employment and, even in the absence of evidence that the person is affected, lead to job discrimination. Most people feel some irrational guilt about a problem with their genetic inheritance and, unless specifically helped, may accept discrimination against them as rightful.

Patients at risk may have difficulty getting married unless testing has shown them not at risk. With prenatal prediction, even affected persons may bear children free of the Huntington's gene, but they may not be willing to do so because the disease may render their parenting abnormal and deficient. In most cases, persons at risk have seen one of their own parents deteriorate before reaching their own childbearing age. Survival guilt arises in the unaffected family member who consciously or unconsciously wished the disease on other family members in exchange for their own health. The psychiatrist should explore such feelings in patients and emphasize that genetic probabilities determine the outcome and not one's fantasies. Salutary effects in being at risk are not to be ignored. Many persons at risk, fearing their healthy life may be limited, may be superproductive, may develop an internal locus of control to a high degree as a compensation, and may have warm relations with their healthy parents and others.

Approach to Affected Patients. Knowing one has the disease and knowing which parent is affected often leads to blaming of the gene-donating parent. Psychotherapy can help patients deal with their longing for a healthy parental model and control primitive rage against unaffected siblings. Psychotherapy can also help the patient with fantasies that the disease is a punishment and that alternative behaviors could have prevented it.

Patients with Alzheimer's exhibit other symptoms in addition to a progressive dementia. Speech is frequently impaired. Huntington's patients remain oriented to their surroundings, are able to recognize family and caregivers, and are able to convey their likes and dislikes somewhat better than patients with Alzheimer's disease. In part, as a result, they also exhibit more depression and less psychosis. The presence of choreic movements may increase their caloric needs to 6,000 calories/day while impairing the coordination required to eat and swallow. The psychiatrist should help the patient and family to accept the expert assistance of psychiatrists and nutritionists with feeding. Family and staff ambivalence may arise around the sad irony of the daily struggle to keep the patient adequately nourished, in view of the disease's progressive downhill course and the possibility that the patient may one day die of choking. But there is a comfort for the family and staff in having treated the patient properly and in having managed the nutrition in an efficient way. Care of Huntington patients is a great burden, and those who do it need to monitor and pace themselves to avoid undue discouragement.

Multiple Sclerosis

Whitlock (1984) reviewed the variety of affective conditions in multiple sclerosis (MS) and concluded that it is difficult to separate the reactive from the organic (frontal and limbic) sources. The influential view of Cottrell and Wilson (1926) that 63 percent of the patients were unusually euphoric has been supplanted by numerous studies, beginning with that of Braceland and Giffin (1950), which showed more depression.

Certain specific interventions for dealing with psychosocial issues in MS patients are presented. They are adapted from Simons (1984) and the New York City Chapter of the National Multiple Sclerosis Society (personal communication 1985)

Psychiatrists should help the patient focus on the lack of certainty in prognosis in a positive sense rather than on the myriad of possible symptoms. Point out that the absence of sure knowledge by the doctor resembles life generally, including variability of the disease over time. The accurate diagnosis of MS is improving, and uncertain cases need not be labeled "possible" MS. Emphasize the presence of medical support and treatment rather than the lack of cure. The psychiatrist should be aware that the mysterious nature of the disease encourages magical theories of self-blame.

Psychiatrists should not reinforce the sick role in patients but emphasize that, although suffering

from a disease, the MS patient is not ill in the traditional sense, or disabled. However, the patient should be encouraged to omit those activities that are onerous or that reinforce the sick role. Psychiatrists should also be aware of differences in patients' expectations about self-reliance and involvement in their own care. Some patients may become quite dependent on their physicians and not display much independent activity.

An important task for the psychiatrist is to distinguish between organic and psychogenic sexual dysfunction in males by nocturnal penile tumescence monitoring. A crude way that is cheaper than a sleep lab is to have the patient paste a circle of postage stamps around his flaccid penis for three consecutive nights. If they are torn apart, the erection mechanism is intact. If indicated, instruct the patient about techniques of cooperative intromission, despite lack of erection, as discussed by Barrett (1984). Altered sexual response can precede severe disability and does not imply loss of libido or loss of love toward one's spouse. Approach this area cautiously and involve the spouse in sexual counseling. Remember that many people have erectile difficulties and anorgasmia unrelated to MS.

Because extensive frontal lobe involvement greatly impairs analytic ability, planning and organizing, flexibility, and emotional lability and limits the value of psychotherapy, do not reach beyond reasonable therapeutic goals or attempt sweeping revision of defenses when neuropsychiatric assessment suggests such involvement.

Psychiatrists should help patients to manage fatigue and other limitations by assisting them in selecting and planning participation in activities rather than withdrawing or regressing as a result of frustration at attempting too much. Focus on what the patient is able to do, not on disabilities. Advise the patient to avoid undue stress, which temporarily worsens symptoms; reassure the patient that these flare-ups do not permanently advance the disease.

Psychiatrists should know that the patients' greatest fears are of becoming wheelchair bound, blind, and incontinent. Keep newly diagnosed patients from attending support groups with very advanced patients. Apprise them of the likelihood of remission or successful management of their symptoms.

The following case is illustrative of many of the needs that are expressed directly and indirectly by patients with MS.

A 44-year-old married woman whose MS was associated with sensory symptoms and neurogenic bladder lay curled in a fetal position on her hospital bed trying to rest despite being very concerned about the noise of activities outside her door. During the interview she revealed in a plaintive voice a preoccupation with toxic and nutritional theories of MS and resentment toward her parents for having expected her to work long hours at a family business that exposed her to benzene fumes. Her physician was receptive to her complaint that the hospital was serving the improper diet but added that there was no evidence that fatigue or toxins caused MS to be worse. She was encouraged to find that she enjoyed nontiring activities on the ward. Psychotherapy focused on her guilt about having MS and disappointing her parents, which was implicit in her self-justifying listing of all the things she had done for her children and her complaints about her hospital care.

Brain Tumor

Because of the variety of sites and resulting deficits, the neuropsychiatric approach to neoplastic disease is difficult to generalize and arises from the needs of each particular case. Psychiatrists are consulted most for tumors of the temporal lobe producing epileptic behavior. Blumer and Benson (1975) noted the difficulties for psychotherapy that are caused by the viscous type of verbal expression in temporal lobe epilepsy patients, including a deepening of emotional response that is not reversed by anticonvulsant therapy, hyposexuality, and episodic aggressivity. Blumer and Benson argued in favor of nondrug psychiatric management of temporal lobe emotional features. Hochberg and Slotnick (1980) used neuropsychologic tests of higher cortical functions to examine 13 survivors of primary astrocytomas who failed to return to premorbid educational or vocational levels. In the absence of tumor regrowth, all had trouble solving problems or coping with novel situations, although previously acquired abilities, overlearned material, and psychometric intelligence appeared unchanged. The difficulties were diffuse and not related to tumor type or location and not explained by focal deficits, psychotic or depressive thought disorders, metabolic difficulties, or hydrocephalus. Blumer and Benson stated that the "pseudodepressed" change in personality caused by lesions of the convexity of the frontal lobes warrants early and ongoing rehabilitative efforts. Patients with the "pseudopsychopathic" alteration of personality, more attributed to lesions of the orbital surface,

have misbehavior that tries the patience of family members. They may benefit from psychiatric support. In patients with recurrent or inoperable central nervous system tumors, more diffuse signs of increased intracranial pressure sometimes supplant the specific personality changes already mentioned. Communication of underlying fear should always be expected, as when a patient with brain tumor denied all distress but lay with his arms crossed over his chest, as in a coffin (J. Jaffe, personal communication).

☐ RELATIONS WITH STAFF

Nurses are often privy to material from patients that would be helpful and time saving for the doctors, especially psychiatrists. Often the patient seems to feel that the physicians are too busy to be asked personal questions that are crucial to ensure compliance with treatment regimens. Patients may have simple questions about the necessity of taking medications precisely at 9, 1, and 5. Patients may not bring up bowel and sexual questions with the physicians who are perceived as authority figures, punitive and removed from patient concerns. An example is the patient who asked the nurse about whether his brain tumor could affect his sexual capabilities and was much relieved by the nurse's negative answer and explanation.

Consulting psychiatrists who take the time to listen to intimate emotional, interpersonal, and bodily data may be perceived by patients as occupying a position between medical authority figures (perceived as feared objects of higher status) and helping, nonmedical staff who are perceived as loved objects of lower status. A psychiatrist must balance the physician's status needs against the patient's real need for compassion. As a result, the psychiatrist may emerge as the practical doctor who understands the patient deeply. When doctors fail to consult nurses, it may be out of a need to play the doctor-nurse game of omniscient physician, rather than reevoke memories of our intern days when the nurses helped us survive. Understanding of illness and comprehension of regimens are more difficult for the patient in many neurologic syndromes, and the effect of diseases on the brain, which controls memory, thought, and emotion, may be more devastating for patient and family than diseases on other body systems. Patients need all the help that nurses can provide.

☐ SELF-HELP GROUPS AND SELF-HELP BOOKS

For a discussion and directory of patient support groups, almost half of which are for neurologic conditions, consult Manber (1984). Self-help groups for neuropsychiatric patients and their families disseminate information about new treatment approaches and combat feelings of being alone as a sufferer of an unusual disease. They may also increase the patient's anxiety, especially after diagnosis when the patient comes in contact with persons with the most advanced stages of the disorder and, worse, with those who have had poor treatment results. For example, a man with essential blepharospasm received useful negative feedback about medication and surgical approaches but was put in contact with very chronically disabled cases whose results terrified him. However, when the new treatment of periorbital injection with botulinus toxin was proposed, he had additional corroboration of its safety and limitations from self-help publications.

Self-help books can also cause problems. One of the best and most technically complete is Duvoisin's (1984) on Parkinson's disease, but the patient and the patient's spouse may focus on the chapters about advanced disease. Many patients who are newly diagnosed, especially those who overvalue physical mobility and power, are extremely anxious. Some even pose a suicide risk that requires immediate psychotherapeutic attention, even though the disease is treatable and slowly progressive. Too much cognitive knowledge, without emotional preparation or integration into the person's resources for coping, can be needlessly disturbing. The psychiatrist will find that psychotherapy at such a crisis time of new and threatening knowledge can be productive because of high motivation arising from unmet needs and openness of the defensive structure for revision and help.

☐ REFERENCES

Aronson MK: Alzheimers and other dementias. Carrier Letter # 102, November 1984, pp 1–5

Artiola A, Fortunay I, Briggs M, et al: Measuring duration of post-traumatic amnesia. J Neurol Neurosurg Psychiatry 43:377–379, 1980

Barrett M: Sexuality and MS, in Multiple Sclerosis: Psychological and Social Aspects. Edited by Simons AF. London, William Heinemann Medical Books, 1984, pp 54–71

Berry V: Partners/families and professionals together: a model of posttraumatic rehabilitation. Ranch Treatment Center Head Injury Articles, Austin, TX, 1984, pp 8–11

Blumer D, Benson DF: Personality changes with frontal and temporal lobe lesions, in Psychiatric Aspects of Neurologic Disease. Edited by Benson DF, Blumer D. New York, Grune & Stratton, 1975, pp 151–170

Bodenhamer E, Achterberg-Lawlis J, Kevorkian G, et al: Staff and patient perceptions of the psychosocial concerns of spinal cord injured persons. Am J Phys Med 62:182–193, 1983

Braceland FJ, Giffin ME: The mental changes associated with MS (an interim report). Res Publ Assoc Res Nerv Ment Dis 28:450–55, 1950

Bracken MB, Shepard MJ: Coping and adaptation following acute spinal cord injury: a theoretical analysis. Paraplegia 18:74–85, 1980

Bracken MB, Shepard MJ, Webb SB Jr: Psychological response to acute spinal cord injury: an epidemiological study. Paraplegia 19:271–283, 1981

Childs AH: Brain injury: "now what shall we do?" problems in treating brain injuries. Psychiatric Times, April 1985, pp 15–17

Cottrell SS, Wilson SAK: The affective symptomatology of disseminated sclerosis: a study of 100 cases. J Neurol Psychopathology 7:1–30, 1926

Critchley M: The Divine Banquet of the Brain and Other Essays. New York, Raven Press, 1979, pp 115–120.

Cummings JL: Clinical Neuropsychiatry. New York, Grune & Stratton, 1985a

Cummings JL: Organic delusions: phenomenology, anatomic correlates and review. Br J Psychiatry 146:184–197, 1985b

Davidson AW, Young C: Repatterning of stroke rehabilitation clients following return to life in the community. J Neurosurg Nurs 17:123–128, 1985

DeJong G, Branch LG, Corcoran PJ: Independent living outcomes in spinal cord injury: multivariates analyses. Arch Phys Med Rehabil 65:66–73, 1984

Ditunno PL, McCawley C, Marquette C: Sensation-seeking behavior and the incidence of spinal cord injury. Arch Phys Rehabil 66:152–155, 1985

Duvoisin RC: Parkinson's Disease: A Guide for Patient and Family (2nd ed). New York, Raven Press, 1984

Evans RL, Northwood LK: Social support needs in adjustment to stroke. Arch Phys Med Rehabil 64:61–64, 1983

Folstein MF, Folstein SE, McHugh PR: "Mini-Mental State:" a practical method of grading the cognitive state of patients for the clinician. J Psychiatr Res 12:189–198, 1975

Forrest DV: E.E. Cummings and the thoughts that lie too deep for tears: of defenses in poetry, Psychiatry 43:13–42, 1980

Forrest DV: Therapeutic adaptations to the cognitive features of schizophrenia [chapter 7] and Therapeutic adaptations to the affective features of schizophrenia [chapter 11], in Treating Schizophrenic Patients. Edited by Stone MH, Albert HD, Forrest DV, et al. New York, McGraw-Hill, 1983

Freud S: On Aphasia: A Critical Study. New York, International Universities Press, 1953

Freud S: Project for a scientific psychology (1895), in Complete Psychological Works. Standard Edition. Vol. 1. Translated and edited by Strachey J. London, Hogarth Press, 1966

Goldstein K: Aftereffects of Brain Injuries in War. New York, Grune & Stratton, 1942

Goodstein RK: Overview: cerebrovascular accident and the hospitalized elderly: a multidimensional clinical problem. Am J Psychiatry 140:141–147, 1983

Green BC, Pratt CC, Grigsby TE: Self-concept among persons with long term spinal cord injury. Arch Phys Med Rehabil 65:751–754, 1984

Hallet M: Physiology and pathophysiology of voluntary movement. Current Neurology 2:351–376, 1979

Hartmann H: The Nightmare. New York, Basic Books, 1984

Hochberg FH, Slotnick B: Neuropsychologic impairment in astrocytoma survivors. Neurology 30:172–177, 1980

Howell T, Fullerton DT, Harvey RF, et al: Depression in spinal cord injured patients. Paraplegia 19:284–288, 1981

Jain S: Operant conditioning for management of a noncompliant rehabilitation case after stroke. Arch Phys Med Rehabil 63:374–376, 1982

Jenicke MA: Alzheimer's disease: diagnosis, treatment and management, in Clinical Perspectives on Aging. Wyeth Labs, 1985, pp 8–10

Kotila M, Waltimo O, Niemi ML, et al: The profile of recovery from strokes and factors influencing outcome. Stroke 15:1039–1044, 1984

Labi MJ, Phillips TF, Greshman GE: Psychosocial disability in physically restored long-term stroke survivors. Arch Phys Med Rehabil 61:561–565, 1980

Luria AR: The Working Brain: An Introduction to Neuropsychology. New York, Basic Books, 1973

Malec J, Neimeyer R: Psychologic prediction of duration of spinal cord injury rehabilitation and performance of self care. Arch Phys Med Rehabil 64:359–363, 1983

Manber MM: Patient support groups: a natural resource for physicians. Medical World News, 13 December 1984, pp 24–38

Mayeux R: Behavior manifestations of movement disorders: Parkinson's and Huntington's disease. Neurol Clin 2:527–540, 1984

Mayeux R, Stern Y: Intellectual dysfunction and dementia in Parkinson disease, in The Dementias. Edited by Mayeux R, Rosen WG. New York, Raven Press, 1983

Newcombe F: The psychological consequences of closed head injury: assessment and rehabilitation. Injury 14:11–136, 1983

Oddy M, Humphrey M, Uttley D: Subjective impairment and social recovery after closed head injury. J Neurol Neurosurg Psychiatry 41:611–616, 1978

Oddy M, Coughlan T, Tyerman A, et al: Social adjustment after closed head injury: a further follow up seven years after injury. J Neurol Neurosurg Psychiatry 48:564–568, 1985

Palmer JB: Depression and adrenocortical function in spinal cord injury patients: a review. Arch Phys Med Rehabil 66:253–256, 1985

Rabins PV, Mace NL, Lucas MJ: The impact of dementia on the family. JAMA 248:333–335, 1982

Rao N, Jellinek HH, Woolston DC: Agitation in closed head injury: haloperidol effects on rehabilitation outcome. Arch Phys Med Rehabil 66:30–34, 1985

Rathbone-McCuan E, Goodstein RK: Elder abuse: clinical considerations. Psychiatric Annals 15:331–339, 1985

Reisberg B: Alzheimer's disease update. Psychiatric Annals 15:319–322, 1985

Rohrer K, Adelman B, Puckett J, et al: Rehabilitation in spinal cord injury: use of a patient-family group. Arch Phys Med Rehabil 61:225–229, 1980

Romano MD: Sexual counseling in groups. Journal of Sex Research 9:68–78, 1973

Romano MD: Preparing children for parental disability. Soc Work Health Care 1:309–315, 1976

Romano MD, Lassiter RE: Sexual counseling with the spinal-cord injured. Arch Phys Med Rehabil 53:568–573, 1972

Rosenstiel AK, Roth S: Relationship between cognitive activity and adjustment in four spinal-cord-injured individuals: a longitudinal investigation. J Human Stress 7:35–43, 1981

Sands H: Psychodynamic management of epilepsy, in Epilepsy: A Handbook for the Mental Health Professional. Edited by Sands H. New York, Brunner/Mazel, 1982, pp 135–157

Sarno MT: The nature of verbal impairment after closed head injury. J Nerv Ment Dis 168:685–692, 1980

Schiffer RB: Psychiatric aspects of clinical neurology. Am J Psychiatry 140:205–211, 1983

Schuler M: Sexual counseling for the spinal cord injured: a review of 5 programs. J Sex Marital Ther 8:241–252, 1982

Shoulson I: Clinical Care of the Patient and Family with Huntington's Disease. New York, Committee to Combat Huntington's Disease, 1978

Simons AF: Problems of providing support for people with M.S. and their families, in Multiple Sclerosis: Psychological and Social Aspects. Edited by Simons AF. London, William Heinemann Medical Books, 1984, pp 1–20

Smith-Brady R: Assessing adherence in stroke regimens. Nurs Clin North Am 17:499–512, 1982

Steinglass P, Temple S, Lisman SA, et al: Coping with spinal cord injury: the family perspective. Gen Hosp Psychiatry 4:259–264, 1982

Stern DN: The Interpersonal World of the Infant: A View from Psychoanalysis and Developmental Biology. New York, Basic Books, 1985

Stern Y., Mayeux R., Rosen J: Contribution of perceptual motor dysfunction to construction and tracing disturbances in Parkinson's disease. J Neurol Neurosurg Psychiatry 47:987–989, 1984

Stevens JH, Turner CW, Rhodewalt F, et al: The Type A behavior pattern and carotid artery atherosclerosis. Psychosom Med 46:105–113, 1984

Thomsen IV: Late outcome of very severe blunt head trauma: a 10–15 year second follow up. J Neurol Neurosurg Psychiatry 47:260–268, 1984

Tyerman A, Humphrey M: Changes in self concept following severe head injury. Int J Rehabil Res 7:11–23, 1984 van Zomeren AH, van den Burg W: Residual complaints of patients two years after severe head injury. J Neurol Neurosurg Psychiatry 48:21–28, 1985

Weinstein EA: Sexual disturbances after brain injury. Medical Aspects of Human Sexuality 8:10–31, 1974

Weinstein EA, Friedland RP: Behavioral disorder associated with hemiinattention, in Advances in Neurology, Vol. 18. Edited by Weinstein EA, Friedland RP. New York, Raven Press, 1977, pp 51–62

Wexler NS: Genetic jeopardy and the new clairvoyance. Prog Med Genet 6:277–304, 1985

Whitlock A: Emotional disorder in multiple sclerosis, in Multiple Sclerosis: Psychological and Social Aspects. Edited by Simons AF. London, William Heinemann Medical Books, 1984, pp 72–81

Wilson T, Smith T: Driving after stroke. Int Rehabil Med 5:170–177, 1983

Woods BT, Short MP: Neurological dimensions of psychiatry. Biol Psychiatry 20:192–198, 1985

Wool RN, Siegel D, Fine PR: Task performance in spinal cord injury: effect of helplessness training. Arch Phys Med Rehabil 61:321–325, 1980

Yudofsky SC, Rosecan JS: Parkinson's disease, depression, and ECT: a clinical and neurobiologic synthesis. Compr Psychiatry 20:579–581, 1979

Psychopharmacologic Treatment in Neuropsychiatry

Steven L. Dubovsky, M.D.

PSYCHOTROPIC MEDICATIONS ARE used extensively in patients with neurologic illnesses. This chapter addresses each of the major classes of physical intervention used in psychiatry, with special attention to general principles of use and modifications that are necessary in the neurologic setting. Discussions of structure, metabolism, dosage, and psychiatric uses are followed by sections on uses in the management of neurologic illness, major side effects, and important interactions. Each section is more or less self-contained to permit easy access by the clinician to information about each topic.

☐ HETEROCYCLIC ANTIDEPRESSANTS

First reported to be effective in depression in 1957 after imipramine was synthesized in a search for a structural analogue to chlorpromazine, heterocyclic antidepressants have become the first line of drug therapy for depression. All cyclic antidepressants are of approximately equal efficacy; their side-effect profiles, however, permit considerable flexibility in treating patients with neurologic illnesses. Nomifensine, a new cyclic antidepressant, was recently withdrawn from the market because of reports of fatal autoimmune hemolytic anemia associated with its use. Buproprion, another new antidepressant, may be about to be released. Antidepressants currently available in the United States are summarized in Table 1.

Antidepressants referred to as heterocyclics have a number of different structures, all of which include rings containing carbon, nitrogen, and/or oxygen atoms (Figure 1). The tricyclics are structurally related to the phenothiazines. The tertiary (i.e., 3-methyl-group) amines imipramine and amitriptyline differ from each other only in the presence of a nitrogen versus a carbon atom in position 5 of the middle ring. Desipramine and nortriptyline, the secondary amine congeners of these tri-

TABLE 1. CURRENTLY AVAILABLE HETEROCYCLIC ANTIDEPRESSANTS

Drug	Trade name	Structure	Usual daily dose (mg)	Upper daily limit (mg)	Usual daily dose in elderly (mg)
Amitriptyline	Elavil	Tertiary amine[a]	150–300	300	50–100
Nortriptyline	Pamelor Aventyl	Secondary amine[a]	75–125[b]	150[b]	25–50
Protriptyline	Vivactil	Secondary amine[a]	30–40	60	15–20
Imipramine	Tofranil	Tertiary amine[a]	150–200	300	25–100
Desipramine	Norpramin Pertofrane	Secondary amine[a]	150–250	300	25–100
Trimipramine	Surmontil	Tertiary amine[a]	150–200	300	50–100
Doxepin	Sinequan	Tertiary amine[a]	150–250	300	25–50
Amoxapine	Asendin	Dibenzoxazepine	150–300	600	75–300
Maprotiline	Ludiomil	Tetracyclic	150–200	300	50–75
Trazodone	Desyrel	Triazolopyridine	150–400	600	50–150

[a]Tricyclic.
[b]Dosage should be adjusted according to blood level.

cyclics, have one less methyl group. Newer antidepressants provide variations on the tricyclic structure or novel arrangements such as tetracyclic or bicyclic formulas.

Because cyclic antidepressants are extensively metabolized by the liver following oral administra-

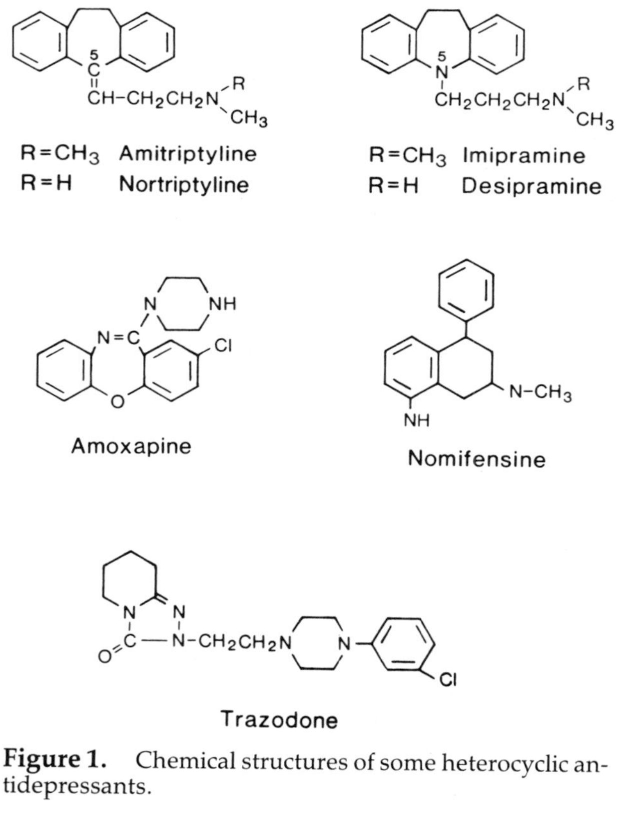

Figure 1. Chemical structures of some heterocyclic antidepressants.

tion, conditions that affect hepatic microsomal activity can significantly alter antidepressant levels. Alcohol, anticonvulsants, barbiturates, and antidepressants themselves may stimulate liver enzymes, decreasing blood levels of the antidepressant and leading to unexpected treatment failures or relapses in compliant patients. Some substances (e.g., phenothiazines and methylphenidate) compete with heterocyclics for metabolizing enzymes, slowing the rate of breakdown of both the antidepressant and the other drug. This may be one basis for the possible synergistic action of neuroleptics and stimulants with antidepressants (Baldessarini 1985). The long half-life of most heterocyclics—from 10 to 20 hours for imipramine to 80 hours for protriptyline (Baldessarini 1985; Lydiard 1985)—makes once-daily dosing possible for all preparations except trazodone and bupropion.

Inherited patterns of metabolism of heterocyclics probably account for two clinical phenomena. First, patients with a blood relative who has responded to a particular medication are more likely to respond to that drug themselves. Second, there is wide interindividual variation in blood levels produced by the same dose of a given drug. The clinical significance of the latter observation is complicated because response to antidepressants has been shown to be clearly correlated with blood levels only for nortriptyline, imipramine, and possibly desipramine (Lydiard 1985; Task Force on the Use of Laboratory Tests in Psychiatry 1985), and questions have even arisen about these correlations (Lydiard 1985).

Nortriptyline has a therapeutic window of 50 to 150 ng/ml. The likelihood of clinical response increases as blood levels of imipramine approach 200 to 250 ng/ml; higher levels may lead to more side effects without a better clinical effect. Desipramine is more predictably effective at concentrations greater than 125 ng/ml. Although the relationship between blood levels and effectiveness of other antidepressants remains to be clarified, preliminary observations suggest that a range of 125 to 300 ng/ml of parent compound plus demethylated metabolite may be satisfactory for most patients (Baldessarini 1985; Lydiard 1985).

Antidepressant blood levels are most appropriately used to adjust the dose of nortriptyline, to investigate the reason for failure to respond to an adequate dose of other antidepressants, and possibly to determine the correct dose of an antidepressant under urgent circumstances (Task Force 1985). Blood levels should be measured in adults about 1 week after each dose adjustment (90 percent of the steady-state concentration is achieved in 3.3 half-lives). Up to 2 weeks after a dosage change should elapse in the elderly and the medically ill before blood levels of antidepressants are measured (Baldessarini 1985; Lydiard 1985).

Mechanisms of Action

For many years the effectiveness of antidepressants was attributed to blockade of uptake into the presynaptic neuron of brain monoamine transmitters, especially norepinephrine, serotonin, and, to a lesser extent, dopamine (Richelson 1984). Although it is still thought that the beneficial effect of some antidepressants could, in part, be related to increased functional availability of serotonin (Charney et al. 1984), recent research suggests that some of the chronic actions of heterocyclics on receptor mechanisms actually may decrease net noradrenergic activity (Siever and Davis 1985; Sugrue 1983). Such changes might be a primary action, or they could be homeostatic responses to increased amounts of neurotransmitter resulting from reuptake blockade. As they have begun to look beyond single transmitter systems, investigators have speculated about a diversity of additional mechanisms, from interactions with opiate receptors (Goodman and Charney 1985) to modulation of erratic functioning of multiple transmitter systems (Siever and Davis 1985) to antagonism of the action of intracellular calcium (Dubovsky and Franks 1983). These and

other hypotheses remain more or less inferential, and any observed effect of antidepressants on a particular biologic system may be incidental to the action that actually produces therapeutic benefit.

Psychiatric Uses of Heterocyclics in the Presence of Neurologic Disease

Heterocyclic antidepressants have been found useful in the treatment of depression, panic anxiety, bulimia, posttraumatic stress disorder, and possibly obsessive compulsive disorder (Goodman and Charney 1985). Using antidepressants for psychiatric indications in neurologic patients requires great skill when the psychiatric disorder is caused, obscured, or complicated by disease of the brain, and when side effects of the medications can aggravate the neurologic illness.

Depression and Organic Brain Disease

A number of drugs (see Table 12) and illnesses can produce depression, which may or may not be accompanied by signs of delirium or dementia. Anticonvulsants, tranquilizers, and adrenal steroids are common causes of depression in neurologic patients. Of patients taking prednisone, 1 percent of those taking 40 mg/day, 5 percent of those taking 40 to 80 mg/day, and 18 percent of those taking 80 mg/day develop depression, mania, delirium, or psychosis, especially if the dose is increased or decreased rapidly (Rogers 1985). Psychiatric symptoms usually begin within 10 days of beginning steroids and remit shortly after the drug is discontinued, but the onset of symptoms may be delayed and they may continue after withdrawal of the medication (Rogers 1985).

The most appropriate approach to organically induced depression is to treat the underlying disorder or withdraw the offending drug. However, if the illness cannot be reversed immediately or if it would be unsafe to reduce the dose of medication, an antidepressant may ameliorate the depressive symptoms. Precautions discussed later for administering antidepressants to patients with compromised brain reserves should be observed.

Antidepressants may also be useful for patients in whom depression mimics or is accompanied by organic brain disease, even when an obvious irreversible cause of dementia is present. For example, depression may further slow thinking, increase confusion, or make the patient less inclined to marshal whatever intellectual resources remain, resulting in an apparent cognitive deficit that is out of proportion to the actual degree of organic impairment. A course of antidepressant therapy may therefore be reasonable for newly diagnosed demented patients without reversible causes, as well as for patients who may have depressive pseudodementia.

A different problem occurs when organic disturbances that affect the right hemisphere or the balance between the hemispheres impair the ability to express emotion normally. Instead of being obvious, depressive affect, thinking, and behavior in these instances may be expressed as such distorted derivatives as failure to recover from the neurologic illness, emotional lability, negativism, paranoia, hostility, confusion, mutism, catatonia, assaultiveness, noncompliance, and expression of a wish to die (Ross and Rush 1981). Only a course of antidepressants or electroconvulsive therapy (ECT) may resolve the behavioral disorder, which may persist after the underlying neurologic disorder has been successfully treated (Dubovsky 1986; Ross and Rush 1981).

Because they can further impair cortical function or depress the reticular activating system, strongly anticholinergic and sedating antidepressants can be problematic in patients with organic brain syndromes. Appropriate heterocyclics for demented patients include desipramine, maprotiline, trazodone, or amoxapine. The risk of tardive dyskinesia with the latter drug must be borne in mind, especially in elderly and brain-damaged patients.

When heterocyclics are ineffective or produce intolerable side effects in patients with organic brain disease, substitution of methylphenidate in a dose of 10 to 40 mg divided over the course of the day may ameliorate depression. Addiction and tolerance have not been problems in medically ill patients taking this drug, which can often be discontinued after a month or two without a return of depression (Kaufman et al. 1984). ECT, which is discussed in a later section, is an option in more severe cases, even if dementia is present.

Antidepressants in the Elderly

Because organic brain syndromes and other neurologic syndromes frequently occur in elderly patients, it is important to know about differences between patients in this age group and younger patients that influence dosage and choice of anti-

depressants (Salzman 1985). First, demethylation of tertiary amines, which tend to produce more anticholinergic, sedative, and hypotensive side effects, to the less toxic secondary amines is slower. The clearance of all antidepressants is slowed in the elderly, and this leads to higher blood levels and prolonged activity of all compounds. At the same time, the central nervous system (CNS) of the elderly is more sensitive to toxic as well as therapeutic effects of antidepressants. For these reasons, secondary compounds are often less troublesome than tertiary preparations, as are methylphenidate and newer antidepressants with less anticholinergic and sedating potential. In the elderly, the dose of all antidepressants should be increased slowly, and the final dose should be lower than for younger patients (Table 1).

Antidepressants in Patients with Seizure Disorders

Many antidepressants lower the seizure threshold in epileptics, and spontaneous seizures have occasionally been reported in patients without a history of epilepsy who were taking these drugs (Fiori 1977). Maprotiline appears to be the worst offender (Pinder et al. 1977), but the manufacturer of buproprion reports that this drug may cause an even higher incidence of spontaneous seizures when the recommended maximum dose (450 mg) is exceeded. Because amoxapine frequently causes seizures when taken in overdose, it should probably also be avoided in epileptics (Litovitz and Troutman 1983). Doxepin and monoamine oxidase inhibitors (MAOIs) may be relatively safe for epileptics, and secondary amines may be preferable to tertiary amines.

Antidepressants and Movement Disorders

The incidence of depression is high in Parkinson's disease, and L-dopa may increase or produce depression in susceptible patients. From a theoretical standpoint, at least, the more anticholinergic antidepressants such as amitriptyline, protriptyline, doxepin, trimipramine, and imipramine should benefit parkinsonian patients. However, because many of these patients are elderly, the same side effect can prove troublesome.

Because it can produce extrapyramidal syndromes, amoxapine is contraindicated in parkinsonian patients. This drug might be useful, however, for depressed patients with Huntington's disease and Gilles de la Tourette's syndrome. Its structural relationship to loxapine, a neuroleptic, may also make amoxapine useful in depression associated with bizarre or psychotic symptoms, which are sometimes expressed as atypical physical and neurologic complaints.

Antidepressants and Urologic Syndromes

Some urologic complications of neurologic disease require careful adjustment of antidepressant regimens. Because anticholinergic side effects can be particularly risky for uncatheterized patients with neurogenic bladder, drugs with low anticholinergic potency, such as amoxapine, trazodone, and desipramine, are preferable. Methylphenidate is even safer when urinary retention is a major concern. Desipramine, amoxapine, maprotiline, and methylphenidate seem less likely to aggravate erectile dysfunction, which can be a problem with other antidepressants, but trazodone has produced priapism leading to irreversible impotence in a few patients.

Antidepressant Withdrawal

Antidepressants are usually discontinued slowly (e.g., imipramine 25 mg/month) to monitor for return of depression. More rapid discontinuation (25 mg every 3 to 5 days) is possible but abrupt withdrawal of heterocyclics may result in abstinence symptoms that appear within a few days and last up to 2 weeks after stopping the drug (Lawrence 1985). Withdrawal phenomena, which have been estimated to occur in 3 to 100 percent of cases of abrupt discontinuation of heterocyclics, include anorexia, nausea, vomiting, abdominal pain, diarrhea, influenza-like symptoms, insomnia, nightmares, mania, panic attacks, akathesia, and delirium.

Neurologic Uses of Antidepressants

Antidepressants have a number of actions that can be beneficial in some neurologic syndromes even if depression is not present. For example, amitriptyline has been found to ameliorate pathologic laughing and crying (pseudobulbar affect) associated with organic brain disease (Schiffer et al. 1985), and protriptyline may be helpful to some patients with sleep apnea. Amitriptyline, imipramine, and

doxepin appear to have analgesic effects in chronic pain in doses lower than the usual antidepressant dose (e.g., amitriptyline 75 mg/day) (Rosenblatt et al. 1984). Amitriptyline, imipramine, and trazodone in relatively low (e.g., imipramine 100 mg/day) and usual antidepressant doses have reduced pain from diabetic neuropathy in a few patients (Hoogiverf 1985). Depression is common in patients with chronic pain, and chronically depressed patients frequently complain of pain. However, the antinociceptive action of antidepressants may be unrelated to their effect on depression because the doses for the two disorders are different and one condition may improve while the other remains unchanged.

In usual doses, amitriptyline has been widely used as a prophylactic agent for migraine headaches (Mathew 1981). Other antidepressants have not been studied systematically in this context, although there is no reason to believe that amitriptyline should be the only effective drug. However, propranolol and other standard antimigraine drugs produce the same or better migraine prophylaxis (Goodman and Charney 1985). Histamine-2 receptor blockade may explain the beneficial effects of trimipramine (25 to 50 mg/day) and doxepin (50 to 150 mg/day) in peptic ulcer disease (Richelson 1985b). These drugs are as effective as cimetidine, but cheaper, easier to monitor, and less toxic. Their anticholinergic effects, however, are additive with other anticholinergic drugs taken by ulcer patients.

Neurologic Side Effects of Heterocyclics

Heterocyclics have a number of side effects that require consideration in neurologic practice. Important syndromes and drugs that commonly cause these side effects are listed in Table 2 (Baldessarini 1985; Demuth et al. 1985; Fiori 1977).

Interactions of Heterocyclics with Neurologic Drugs

Cyclic antidepressants interact with many medications that are used in neurologic and psychiatric practice. Some prominent interactions reported (Baldessarini 1985; Bernstein 1983; Graham et al. 1974; Lydiard 1985; Salzman 1985) include:

1. Additive anticholinergic effects with antiparkinsonian drugs, antihistamines, and neuroleptics.

TABLE 2.   SIDE EFFECTS OF HETEROCYCLICS

Side effect	Manifestations	Drugs
Anticholinergic	Delirium with tachycardia, warm dry skin, mydriasis	Amitriptyline, trimipramine, protriptyline, doxepin (especially when combined with other anticholinergic drugs)
Postural hypotension (alpha-adrenergic blockade)	Dizziness, unsteadiness, light-headedness, stumbling on standing up	Tertiary amines, protriptyline, trazodone, maprotiline
Cardiovascular	Sinus tachycardia	Especially anticholinergic compounds
	Suppression of ventricular arrhythmias	
	Worsening of conduction defects	All but trazodone
	Cardiac depression	
	Sinus bradycardia	
	Worsening of ventricular arrhythmias	Trazodone
Sedation	Oversedation, impaired cognition, worsening of organic brain syndrome	Amitriptyline, trimipramine, trazodone, doxepin, maprotiline
Decreased seizure threshold	Spontaneous seizures or exacerbation of epilepsy	Amoxapine, maprotiline, tertiary amines
Priapism	Priapism and permanent impotence	Trazodone
Neuromuscular	Fine tremor, myoclonic jerks	Most tricyclics, maprotiline, trazodone
	Peripheral neuropathy	Amitriptyline
	Proximal myopathy	Imipramine
	Phospholipid accumulation in nerve tissue	Imipramine
Extrapyramidal	Parkinsonism, tardive dyskinesia	Amoxapine; imipramine and amitriptyline in high doses
Sleep changes	Increased REM latency, decreased total REM, increased stage 4, nightmares occasionally when entire dose taken at night	Most heterocyclics (except trimipramine)
EEG changes	Suppressed alpha	Amitriptyline
	Increased synchronization at low doses	Especially tertiary amines
	Arousal in high doses	
Hypersensitivity	Lupus-like syndrome	Nomifensine
	Drug fever	
	Hemolytic anemia	
	Photosensitivity, eosinophilia, skin rashes	Tricyclics and maprotiline
Abstinence syndromes	Anxiety, agitation, insomnia, influenza-like symptoms	Possible with all heterocyclics on abrupt discontinuation

2. Increase of antidepressant levels by neuroleptics, methylphenidate, amphetamine, and disulfiram.
3. Increase of neuroleptic and stimulant levels by antidepressants.
4. Decrease of antidepressant levels by alcohol, anticonvulsants such as phenytoin, barbiturates, oral contraceptives, cigarette smoking, and chloral hydrate. (Benzodiazepines do not have a significant effect on antidepressant metabolism.)
5. Increased antidepressant effect due to displacement of binding of antidepressants to albumin produced by phenytoin, aspirin, phenothiazines, phenylbutazone, aminopyrine, and scopolamine.
6. Potentiation by antidepressants of norepinephrine and amphetamine.
7. Blockade by antidepressants of substances that must actively be taken up into presynaptic nerve terminals, such as guanethidine, bethanidine, debrisoquin, and tyramine.
8. Blockade of central antihypertensive effect of clonidine.

☐ MONOAMINE OXIDASE INHIBITORS

Following the discovery that iproniazid, an MAOI antituberculous drug, could produce euphoria and hyperactivity, there was great enthusiasm for this class of drug as a potential antidepressant. Later, the risk of hepatotoxicity with iproniazid, the need for dietary restrictions, and studies (probably using inadequate doses) suggesting that MAOIs were not effective antidepressants led to an equally rapid decline in their use, at least in the United States. More recent research has solidified the place of MAOIs in the psychiatric armamentarium, especially for the treatment of "atypical" and "neurotic" depression, anxious depression, depression resistant to other therapies, phobic-anxiety states, panic anxiety, agoraphobia, bulimia, obsessive compulsive disorders, and posttraumatic stress disorder (Baldessarini 1985; Bernstein 1983; Klein et al. 1980; Pare 1985).

Four MAOIs are now in use in the United States: the two hydrazines, phenelzine and isocarboxazid, and the two nonhydrazines, tranylcypromine and pargyline (Table 3). Nonhydrazines are theoretically safer for patients with liver disease; the risk of hepatic damage is greatest with isocarboxazid. Tranylcypromine inhibits monoamine oxidase (MAO) faster than other MAOIs and may have amphetamine-like properties related to release and blockade of reuptake of norepinephrine.

MAOIs are usually given in divided doses. With the possible exception of pargyline, the last dose of an MAOI should not be taken too late in the day or activation produced by the drug may result in insomnia. One principal route of metabolism for MAOIs other than phenelzine appears to be by acetylation in the liver (Klein et al. 1980; Pare 1985). About half of the normal Caucasian population are "slow acetylators"; this makes them more sensitive to MAOIs because of higher levels with the same dose. "Rapid acetylators," on the other hand, may not achieve therapeutic concentrations easily.

Serum concentrations of MAOIs generally are not measured in clinical practice. Inhibition of platelet MAO may be a more valid measure of activity of drugs that affect this enzyme, 80 to 85 percent inhibition being necessary for the effect to become clinically apparent. Because there is often a good correlation between dose administered and response, this test is usually not only impractical but unnecessary in routine practice. Platelet MAO inhibition may be helpful in deciding whether to increase the dose beyond the usual range in compliant but unresponsive patients who may be rapid metabolizers. Brain MAO inhibition lags 2 to 3 weeks behind the rather immediate inhibition of platelet MAO by MAOIs (Klein et al. 1980).

Located on mitochondria, MAO is a ubiquitous enzyme whose function is to inactivate such biogenic amines as norepinephrine, serotonin, dopamine, and tyramine. The enzyme exists in two forms. MAO-A exhibits a preference for serotonin and is the principal form of MAO in the lungs, intestine, and placenta. MAO-B preferentially breaks down phenylethylamine and is the principal isoenzyme in platelets and kidney. The brain and liver contain both MAO-A and MAO-B (Baldessarini 1985), although the brain may contain more of the B form (Tabakoff et al. 1985).

The currently available MAOIs irreversibly destroy both forms of MAO, which take up to 2 weeks to regenerate themselves after the drug is stopped. For this reason, dietary restrictions should be ob-

TABLE 3. MAOIs AVAILABLE IN THE UNITED STATES

Class	Drug	Trade name	Structure	Usual daily dose (mg)	Acceptable limits of dosage (mg)
Hydrazine	Phenelzine (-NHNH-)	Nardil		45–60	45–90
	Isocarboxazid	Marplan		20–30	20–40
Nonhydrazine	Tranylcypromine	Parnate		20–40	20–60
	Pargyline	Eutonyl		10–25	10–100

served for 2 weeks after drug discontinuation. Because MAO-A metabolizes tyramine in the gut and limits the amount that is absorbed, inhibition of this enzyme allows increased amounts of tyramine to enter the bloodstream. The inherent pressor effects of tyramine are augmented because more is absorbed while its inactivation throughout the body is slowed.

Two strategies have been investigated to limit adverse reactions related to increased tyramine absorption produced by MAOIs. The first is to develop MAOIs that are selective for one or the other isoenzyme. For example, clorgyline inhibits only MAO-A, whereas deprenyl (selegiline) is selective for MAO-B. Because deprenyl does not affect the intestinal form of MAO (i.e., MAO-A), the rate of tyramine breakdown in the gut is not decreased, tyramine absorption is not increased, and hypertensive reactions to ingestion of tyramine-containing foods are supposed to be less likely to occur.

Still in its early stages of development, the second approach to reducing the adverse effects of alteration of tyramine metabolism has been to explore "reversible" MAOIs. Theoretically, tyramine could compete with such drugs everywhere in the body, which would then be temporarily inhibited but not destroyed by the MAOI. If too much tyramine were ingested, the increased amounts would displace the MAOI from the enzyme and would then be metabolized normally.

Mechanisms of Action

It would be tempting to attribute the clinical effectiveness of MAOIs to increased availability of monoamines secondary to reduced degradation; however, this is only one of the actions of MAOIs. In addition, there may be more than one action that is responsible for the clinical effect, or a combination of mechanisms may be important. For example, inhibition of MAO leads to accumulation not only of neurotransmitters but of substances (e.g., octopamine) that are normally present only in trace amounts. Octopamine, and possibly other compounds, may function as false noradrenergic transmitters that alter functional activity in systems that use those transmitters. Any acute effects on neurotransmitter availability may also be balanced by more enduring changes in receptor functioning. Further research into possible mechanisms of action of the MAOIs will undoubtedly be stimulated by the recent resurgence of clinical interest in this class of drugs.

Psychiatric Uses of MAOIs in the Presence of Neurologic Disease

MAOIs may be very useful in the treatment of depressed neurologic patients who are not taking medications (discussed below) that might interact with the antidepressant. Although they can exacerbate confusion and memory loss in more severely demented patients, they may be less troublesome than the more sedating and anticholinergic of the heterocyclics. The principal risk in cognitively impaired patients is that the patient will forget to adhere to the dietary restrictions.

Pargyline, an MAOI marketed as an antihypertensive, probably has antidepressant properties as well (Bernstein 1983). To a lesser extent, phenelzine can also ameliorate high blood pressure and, therefore, may be useful in hypertensive depressed patients. The potential hypotensive effects of MAOIs warrant slow and cautious increases in dosage in patients with marginal cerebrovascular reserve, who cannot tolerate a decrease in blood pressure.

Because MAOIs may have advantages in the treatment of depression with prominent anxiety as well as primary anxiety states (Klein et al. 1980; Sheehan et al. 1980), these drugs should probably be considered more frequently in neurologic patients whose symptoms are caused or exaggerated by anxiety, especially when mixed with depression. Patients with lightheadedness, dizziness, numbness, paresthesias, and other symptoms of hyperventilation, who may be misdiagnosed as having labyrinthitis, vestibular neuronitis, multiple sclerosis, or hypoglycemia, may be particularly good candidates, especially if heterocyclics have been ineffective or difficult to tolerate.

MAOIs in the Elderly

Lower doses and slower increments in dosage are necessary when MAOIs are used in the elderly. For example, treatment with phenelzine should be initiated at a dose of 7.5 mg, with increases of 7.5 to 15 mg every 3 to 6 days to a therapeutic range of 15 to 60 mg/day. The starting dose of tranylcypromine in the elderly should be 5 mg, with 2.5- to 5-mg increments daily to a total dose of 5 to 15 mg (Salzman 1985).

Elderly patients are particularly vulnerable to the effects of hypertensive reactions that can result from adverse MAOI interactions (described below). However, hypertensive crises do not occur more frequently in older individuals than in anyone else (Jenike 1984). Some older patients, and some younger ones, become paradoxically sedated from MAOIs, but tolerance tends to develop to this side effect.

MAOIs in Patients with Other Neurologic Syndromes

MAOIs are generally safe for use in patients with epilepsy; however, seizures have occurred in some nonepileptic patients following overdose. Interactions with antiparkinsonian drugs can complicate the use of the anticholinergic MAOIs such as phenelzine, although deprenyl has been used to treat Parkinson's disease. Patients with carcinoid and pheochromocytoma should not receive MAOIs.

Neurologic Uses of MAOIs

Deprenyl, a selective MAO-B inhibitor, has been used as an antiparkinsonian drug. Because they strongly suppress rapid eye movement (REM) sleep, currently available MAOIs have been used to treat narcolepsy. Furazolidone, an MAOI antibiotic, may prove useful as a treatment for peptic ulcer and gastritis (Huai-Yu et al. 1985).

Neurologic Side Effects of MAOIs

A serious but infrequent adverse effect of the hydrazine-type MAOIs is hepatocellular damage, which, in rare cases, can be fatal. Hydrazines can also cause reversible peripheral neuropathy, which may be a result of direct neural toxicity or of interference with pyridoxine metabolism. Other MAOI side effects that are important in a neurologic setting are summarized in Table 4 (Bernstein 1983; Lieberman et al. 1985; Meyler and Herxheimer 1968; Pare 1985).

Interactions of MAOIs with Neurologic Drugs

The most dangerous interaction of an MAOI is the hypertensive reaction that can occur when it is combined with certain foods and medications, some of which are listed in Table 5. Headache, fever, agitation, vomiting, and chest pain signal a hypertensive crisis; these may progress to intracerebral bleeding or heart failure. Some authorities recommend that patients have available one or two 50-mg chlorpromazine tablets to take for the alpha-blocking effect if they accidentally violate the di-

TABLE 4. ADVERSE EFFECTS OF MAOIs

System	Manifestation
Autonomic nervous system	Orthostatic hypotension, dry mouth, constipation, delay in micturation
CNS	Toxic psychosis, insomnia, irritability, headache, ataxia
Neuromuscular	Muscle twitching, myoclonus, motor tension, tremor, muscle and joint pain, peripheral neuropathy, carpal tunnel syndrome, hyperreflexia
Liver	Jaundice, hepatocellular damage, elevated liver enzymes
Genitourinary	Impotence, anorgasmia in men and women (may respond to cyproheptadine)
Miscellaneous	Edema, skin rash, blood dyscrasia (rare), aggravation of asthma, fever, constipation

etary restrictions and develop symptoms of a hypertensive crisis (Baldessarini 1985). Other authorities are concerned that hypotension from the chlorpromazine might be more dangerous than mild hypertension resulting from most "cheese reactions" (Bernstein 1983). In any event, the definitive treatment of severe hypertensive crises is 2 to 5 mg of intravenous phentolamine.

Although hypertension, rigidity, tremor, fever, convulsions, and coma can occur when MAOIs are combined with cyclic antidepressants, these two classes of drugs are frequently administered together without adverse consequences. In fact, by blocking uptake of tyramine into nerve terminals, heterocyclics may protect to some degree against hypertensive reactions related to ingestion of tyramine (Pare 1985). However, because hydrazine and nonhydrazine MAOIs may interact severely with each other, it is advisable to wait 2 weeks before switching from one class of MAOI to the other.

Because it takes 2 weeks for MAO to recover after it has been inhibited by MAOIs, most clini-

---

TABLE 5.   SUBSTANCES TO AVOID FOR PATIENTS TAKING MAOIs

Do not eat the following foods until at least 2 weeks after you have stopped taking the drug

- Pickled herring
- Liver
- Dry sausage (including Genoa salami, hard salami, pepperoni, and Lebanon bologna)
- Soy sauce
- Broad bean pods (fava bean)
- Aged cheese (cottage cheese and cream cheese are OK)
- Fermented beer
- Red wine
- Yeast extract
- Any spoiled, aged, pickled, fermented, or smoked meat, fish, or dairy product
- Yogurt
- Sour cream
- Avocados
- Overripe bananas
- Raisins

Go easy with

- Chocolate
- Caffeine

Do not take

- Cold preparations
- Any nasal decongestant
- Hay-fever medications
- Sinus medications
- Asthma inhalants
- Antiappetite drugs
- Amphetamines or cocaine
- Weight loss pills
- Pep pills
- Demerol
- Tricyclic antidepressants

If you get a cold or allergies, you can take:

- Aspirin
- Diphenhydramine (Benadryl)
- Acetaminophen (Tylenol)
- Cēpacol
- Chloraseptic
- Robitussin
- Ipsatol-DM

Call about any other medication you plan to take.

---

cians wait this length of time after completely discontinuing MAOIs before allowing the patient to take a food or medication that might lead to a hypertensive reaction if MAO were still inhibited. De-

cline in blood level of the drug and increase in MAO activity following abrupt discontinuation of MAOIs are gradual, but withdrawal reactions have occurred where MAOIs are withdrawn too rapidly. Withdrawal syndromes have included psychosis, insomnia, headache, tremors, nightmares, weakness, paresthesias, and delirium (Lawrence 1985). MAOIs should therefore be gradually discontinued by decreasing the dose by one pill every few days.

In addition to hypertensive reactions, the following potentially dangerous interactions have been reported with MAOI (Baldessarini 1985; Lieberman et al. 1985; Meyler and Herxheimer 1968; Pare 1985):

1. Ataxia, hyperreflexia, ankle clonus, myoclonus, nystagmus, dysarthria, and paresthesias when L-tryptophan is added.
2. Potentiation of general anesthetics, sedatives, antihistamines, and narcotic analgesics. There is still some concern that for these reasons anesthesia for surgery or ECT should be delayed until MAOIs can be discontinued; however, anesthesia has been administered safely to patients who are still taking MAOIs.
3. Potentiation of the pressor effects of amphetamine and tyramine but not norepinephrine and epinephine.
4. Additive anticholinergic effects with neuroleptics and antiparkinsonian drugs.
5. Potentiation of the sedative effects of alcohol.
6. Severe hyperpyrexia with meperidine.
7. Increased hypoglycemic effect of insulin.

☐ LITHIUM

Lithium was introduced in 1859 as a treatment for gout, and it could be found in patent medicines during the late 19th and early 20th centuries (Bernstein 1983). The modern use of this ion began in 1949 when Cade, an Australian psychiatrist who believed that urate might be an endotoxin in mania, injected lithium urate into guinea pigs and found that it tranquilized them. Theorizing that lithium was the active agent, he found that it did indeed calm a small group of manic patients.

At the same time that Cade reported on its effectiveness in mania, lithium chloride was in wide use as a salt substitute. Unfortunately, the combination of strict sodium restriction, which increased lithium resorption by the kidney, and liberal use of the substitute resulted in fatal lithium intoxication in a number of hypertensive patients. Fears of lithium that arose from these catastrophes delayed approval of this ion in the United States as a psychiatric drug until 1970.

Lithium carbonate, which is less irritating to the gastrointestinal tract than other lithium salts (Baldessarini 1985), is available in 300-mg capsules and tablets. Lithium citrate comes in liquid form. There is no parenteral preparation.

Lithium is metabolized primarily by direct excretion by the kidney. Equilibrium between ingestion and excretion takes about 5 to 6 days, and the half-life of lithium in chronic administration is about 24 hours. Even during long-term therapy, a peak in blood level that is 2 to 3 times the steady-state concentration is reached an hour or two after each oral dose. Because there is only a two- to threefold difference between therapeutic and toxic concentrations, lithium is usually but not always administered in divided doses to avoid peaks that might be high enough to be problematic. Lithobid, a sustained release preparation, is absorbed relatively slowly and is associated with less drastic increases in serum levels; this form, too, is generally administered in at least two daily doses (Baldessarini 1985).

The dose of lithium is always adjusted according to blood level, which is measured 10 to 12 hours after the last dose to ensure an accurate estimate of the steady-state concentration. Acutely manic patients usually require 0.8 to 1.5 mEq/l, which is generally achieved at a dose of 1,200 to 2,400 mg/day (Baldessarini 1985; Bernstein 1983; Klein et al. 1980). Levels above 1.2 mEq/l rarely are necessary; levels greater than 1.5 mEq/l almost always result in more side effects than therapeutic benefit. Maintenance blood levels are usually in the range of 0.5 to 1.0 mEq/l (900 to 1,500 mg/day), but even lower levels may be prophylactic.

Mechanisms of Action

Lithium inhibits the release of norepinephrine from brain synaptosomes and may also be serotonergic. The ion substitutes incompletely for sodium, calcium, and magnesium in many biologic systems, inhibiting their action (Singer and Rotenberg 1973). Recent interest has focused on antagonism by lithium of both membrane phospholipid second messengers (Berridge 1984) and intracellular actions of calcium ions (Dubovsky and Franks 1983). The exact relationship of the intracellular actions of lithium to its clinical actions remains to be clarified.

Psychiatric Uses of Lithium in the Presence of Neurologic Disease

Lithium is the drug of choice for prophylaxis of recurrent mania. It is also effective in the treatment of acute mania. Because the clinical effect is not completely manifest for 1 to several weeks after lithium is initiated, neuroleptics frequently are also required during acute treatment. There seems little doubt about lithium's ability to prevent or attenuate antidepressant-induced mania and recurrent bipolar depression. Whether or not lithium is a useful treatment or prophylaxis of acute or recurrent unipolar depression is controversial. Many clinicians have found that lithium can augment the antidepressant effect of heterocyclics, especially in bipolar patients (Roy and Pickar 1985).

Mood stabilization by lithium may have several other less well-documented benefits, including reduction of psychotic symptoms in schizoaffective patients and decrease in alcohol consumption in alcoholics with affective features. Lithium may also help to control impulsive, aggressive, and antisocial behavior in some emotionally labile patients with personality disorders and brain damage. It has recently been used to treat premenstrual syndromes.

Lithium and Organic Brain Disease

When a patient being treated with lithium becomes delirious, the first consideration is lithium intoxication. Lithium should therefore be withheld until the cause of an acute organic brain syndrome is determined, and the illness treated. Hypothyroidism, which may be induced by lithium treatment itself, can aggravate lithium toxicity.

Even at therapeutic levels, lithium may aggravate preexisting organic brain syndromes. Demented patients who require treatment for a bipolar disorder and who become more confused on lithium may benefit from one of the alternative treatments listed in Table 6. Of these experimental

TABLE 6. EXPERIMENTAL ALTERNATIVES TO LITHIUM

Bromocriptine	Naloxone
Carbamazepine	Physostigmine
Clonazepam	Propranolol
Clonidine	Reserpine
Diltiazem	Valproic acid
ECT	Verapamil
Lorazepam	

alternatives, carbamazepine and ECT have been studied most thoroughly. Verapamil has been given to a small number of manic patients with dementia without adverse effects (Dubovsky et al. 1986). Propranolol or clonazepam may at least theoretically be safe and effective in this context. None of these drugs has been studied systematically in brain-injured patients.

Lithium in Patients with Other Neurologic Disorders

Because it lowers the seizure threshold and occasionally induces seizures in nonepileptic patients (Massey and Folger 1984), increased doses of anticonvulsants may be necessary when patients with epilepsy take lithium. The antiepileptic drugs carbamazepine and clonazepam (Table 6) are logical alternatives to lithium when seizure control is difficult. Chronic lithium therapy occasionally produces extrapyramidal syndromes (Klein et al. 1980), which can be a problem for parkinsonian patients. Sodium depletion leads to increased renal conservation of lithium; hypokalemia increases the risk of neurologic and cardiovascular side effects, even at therapeutic lithium concentrations (Jefferson and Griest 1977).

Lithium in the Elderly

Even if renal clearance is normal, a generalized decrease in organ reserve makes the elderly more vulnerable to confusion and to other toxic effects of lithium (Table 7). The dose of lithium should therefore be increased more slowly in the elderly, and the final dose should be lower (e.g., maintenance serum concentration, 0.3 to 0.6 mEq/l) than in younger patients. Because lithium suppresses automaticity of the sinoatrial (SA) node and conduction through the atrioventricular (AV) node, patients with cardiovascular disease require very close monitoring. Alternate treatment should be considered if electrocardiogram (EKG) changes occur or if adverse effects on the heart develop.

Neurologic Uses of Lithium

In anecdotal reports and uncontrolled studies, lithium has been said to ameliorate cluster headaches, Huntington's disease, and spasmodic torticollis; it has also been subjected to preliminary trials in tardive dyskinesia (Baldessarini 1985). The leukocy-

tosis induced by lithium makes it a useful therapy for leukopenia induced by chemotherapeutic agents. Lithium-induced diabetes insipidus may counteract the syndrome of inappropriate secretion of antidiuretic hormone, which can be a primary disorder or a complication of some tumors of the brain and lung.

Neurologic Side Effects of Lithium

Lithium produces two types of psychological side effects: those at therapeutic levels and those that are due to toxicity (Table 7). Toxic reactions are common when blood levels are greater than 1.5 to 2 mEq/l, but they may occur at therapeutic levels in some patients. The onset of toxicity is heralded by a coarse tremor, ataxia, vertigo, dysarthria, disorientation, nausea, and vomiting. These signs and symptoms may progress to muscle fasciculation, gross confusion, delirium, hyperreflexia, arrhythmias, seizures, coma, irreversible brain damage, and death. Treatment of lithium intoxication involves stopping all drugs, hydration, diuresis, maintenance of electrolyte balance, and, if toxicity is extreme, dialysis. Lithium has been reported to cause increased intracranial pressure (Saul 1985).

Interactions of Lithium with Neurologic Drugs

Ever since a report of irreversible neurotoxicity in patients treated with lithium plus haloperidol (Cohen and Cohen 1974), there has been considerable debate about the risks of combining lithium with neuroleptics, particularly with haloperidol and thioridazine, and with carbamazepine. Even though some experts feel that these combinations present no increased risk of neurotoxicity (Baldessarini 1985; Bernstein 1983), reports of irreversible neurologic syndromes, often following lithium intoxication, still arise (Izzo and Brody 1985). All clinicians agree that careful monitoring is necessary when lithium and these drugs are administered together. The interaction of lithium and ECT is discussed in the next section.

Lithium levels are increased by sodium-wasting diuretics, and potassium-wasting diuretics can increase the risk of toxicity even at therapeutic levels (Bernstein 1983). A number of antibiotics, especially tetracyclines, spectinomycin, and metronidazole, may increase lithium levels, although this association has not been established definitively. Theophylline and possibly caffeine may oc-

TABLE 7. COMMON LITHIUM SIDE EFFECTS UNRELATED TO TOXICITY

Side effect	Manifestations	Comment
Tremor	Irregular, fine resting of fingers and hands most likely to appear after rapid increase in dose; myoclonic jerking may also occur	May respond to decreasing the dose, adding propranolol or amantadine, or switching to lithium carbonate in slow-release tablets (Lithobid).
Mental symptoms	Difficulty concentrating, dazed feeling, impaired memory, confusion, dizziness	Can appear in normal subjects as well as affective patients. May respond to decreasing the dose.
Polyuria and polydipsia	May be due to nephrogenic diabetes insipidus (metabolic effect) or tubular damage (structural effect)	Lithium-induced kidney disease is probably mild and clinically is insignificant. Nevertheless, renal function should be monitored regularly and the lowest possible dose prescribed. Patients should be advised to avoid dehydration. Thiazide diuretics may paradoxically decrease polyuria.
Thyroid dysfunction	Hypothyroidism or enlarged thyroid with normal T4 but increased thyroid-stimulating hormone; decreased thyroid function may initiate rapid cycling in some bipolar patients	Treatment with thyroxine or discontinuation of lithium usually restores normal thyroid function.
Cardiac changes	Decreased automaticity of SA node	Arrhythmias and conduction disturbances are much more common at toxic levels. A baseline EKG should be obtained if there is any suspicion of preexisting cardiac disease to compare suspected postlithium changes.
EEG changes	REM suppression, high-voltage slow waves, superimposed beta, epileptiform discharges, disorganization of background rhythm	Seizures may occur in nonepileptic patients at therapeutic levels.
Gastrointestinal, dermatologic, metabolic, and endocrine effects	Diarrhea, indigestion, skin rash, acne, hair loss, weight gain, hyperparathyroidism	Weight gain is probably due to fluid retention plus altered carbohydrate metabolism. Cataracts, depression, or renal disease on lithium should prompt serum calcium studies.

casionally lower serum lithium concentrations (Perry et al. 1984).

☐ ELECTROCONVULSIVE THERAPY

Convulsive therapies were initially developed as a treatment for schizophrenia because it was thought that schizophrenia and epilepsy rarely occurred together. The original convulsants were gases and liquids, but in 1938 an electrical stimulus was shown to be easier to administer and control. Epilepsy was eventually shown not to protect against schizophrenia, and ECT turned out seldom to be truly useful in schizophrenia. However, double-blind studies comparing real to sham ECT provide strong evidence that ECT is a highly effective treatment for depression (Brandon et al. 1984).

ECT is administered under barbiturate anesthesia with succinylcholine or similar muscle relaxants to spare the patient the peripheral manifestations of major motor seizures. An anticholinergic drug such as atropine or glycopyrrolate (which does not cross the blood-brain barrier) may be administered to dry secretions and prevent bradycardia caused by central stimulation of the vagus nerve. Many psychiatrists begin ECT with unilateral non-dominant electrode placement, which may minimize memory loss, and proceed to bilateral treatment if satisfactory seizures cannot be obtained or if the patient does not improve. The usual course is 6 to 12 treatments or 200 to 600 seizure seconds (Fink 1981).

Mechanisms of Action

ECT induces changes in a number of transmitter systems, particularly norepinephrine and serotonin (Fink 1974), down-regulates beta adrenergic receptors, and may decrease cerebrospinal fluid (CSF) calcium levels (Carman and Wyatt 1977). It is also conceivable that, analogous to cardioversion, an electrical stimulus to the brain could suppress reentrant or hyperactive circuits that have been provoked by recurrent stimulation (kindling) (Dubovsky 1986). There are as yet insufficient data even to generate a specific hypothesis about the mechanisms of ECT, but it is clear that the effect of the electrical current on the brain and not peripheral manifestations of the seizure, memory loss, adjunctive medications, or the psychological meaning of the treatment is the source of its beneficial action.

Psychiatric Uses of ECT in Patients with Neurologic Disease

ECT is usually reserved for severely depressed patients who have not responded to medication or who are too ill to wait for antidepressants to take effect. It may also be effective in mania and catatonia and in some cases of schizophrenia (Bernstein 1983). To prevent relapse, patients who respond to ECT should be maintained on antidepressants for at least 6 months (Bernstein 1983).

Contraindications to ECT are space-occupying lesion in the brain or any condition with increased intracranial pressure (Bernstein 1983; Fink 1974). However, ECT has been administered to a few patients with brain tumors and one patient with elevated intracranial pressure without ill effects (Dubovsky 1986). Obviously, the potential benefits would have to outweigh the considerable risks to justify the use of ECT in such patients. A few reports of irreversible brain damage suggested that ECT should not be used within several months of carbon monoxide poisoning (Dubovsky 1986).

A number of papers have reported that ECT has improved physical as well as psychiatric states in occasional patients with neurologic illnesses that have included epilepsy, Parkinson's disease, multiple sclerosis, pituitary insufficiency, anterior cerebral artery occlusion, hypertensive retinal hemorrhage, neurodermatitis, and diabetes mellitus (Dubovsky 1986). These anecdotal studies do not prove that ECT is helpful or even benign in most patients with neurologic disease, but they do suggest that ECT does not necessarily have to be withheld under these circumstances. There is no convincing evidence that ECT permanently worsens dementia or causes brain damage (Weiner 1984).

Neurologic Uses of ECT

According to the American Psychiatric Association Task Force Report on Electroconvulsive Therapy, most American psychiatrists "would find it strange" to use a treatment that can produce an acute organic brain syndrome in delirious patients (Dubovsky 1986). In Scandinavia, however, ECT is considered an appropriate therapy for delirium. Over the years, a number of studies of single and small groups of patients have reported that ECT induces rapid clearing of delirious states associated with intoxication and withdrawal from numerous drugs, delirium tremens, cerebritis, meningitis, encephalitis, uremia, pneumonia, and delirium superimposed on dementia (Dubovsky 1986). One to four treatments have usually been sufficient for these conditions, even when the underlying pathologic process has not yet been corrected. There are no controlled studies of this application of ECT, but it remains a potential therapy for life-threatening delirium.

Because repeated seizures raise the threshold for further convulsions, ECT has been used as a treatment for intractable epilepsy and as a means of clearing prolonged postictal clouding of consciousness (Dubovsky 1986). The beneficial effect of ECT in some parkinsonian patients noted above makes it at least worthy of consideration in cases of depression and intractable Parkinson's disease.

Neurologic Side Effects of ECT

Confusion and memory loss are the major neurologic side effects of ECT. A small number of patients continue to complain that their memories or personalities have been permanently damaged following ECT, but objective studies have not yet provided evidence of memory loss persisting more than 6 months after treatment (Weiner 1984). It is not clear whether such problems do not really occur or whether they just cannot be measured.

With modern anesthetic management, serious complications or death develop in fewer than 1 in 8,000 patients, making it one of the safest interventions that utilize general anesthesia (Fink 1974). Any morbidity or mortality that does occur is usually secondary to cardiovascular complications such as arrhythmia, myocardial infarction, or hypertension. The major risks are those associated with brief general anesthesia.

Interactions of ECT

Concerns that heterocyclics might predispose to cardiac complications and that MAOIs could potentiate pressor agents and anesthetics or could cause severe hypotension lead many clinicians to discontinue these drugs 2 weeks before beginning ECT. While this is the safest course, some recent research suggests that ECT can be safe even when antidepressants are still being taken (Azar and Lear 1984; El-Gazour et al. 1985). Lithium may increase the risk of post-ECT confusion and memory loss (Baldessarini 1985) and has also been reported to enhance the action of succinylcholine (Bernstein 1983; Packman et al. 1978). It is therefore a good idea to discontinue lithium a few days prior to ECT. Anticonvulsants and benzodiazepines may make it more difficult to initiate a seizure during ECT.

☐ ANTIPSYCHOTIC DRUGS (NEUROLEPTICS)

Chlorpromazine, the first of the modern antipsychotic drugs, was synthesized in France in 1950 in an attempt to find a new agent that would potentiate general anesthesia. Since it seemed to have marked sedative properties, it was given to manic and then to schizophrenic patients. This resulted in the discovery of its antipsychotic potential. Five classes of antipsychotic agents are now available in the United States: phenothiazines, thioxanthenes, butyrophenones, indolones, and dibenzoxazepines.

Antipsychotic drugs are characterized by their ability to control symptoms of psychosis (not limited to schizophrenia) and to produce neurologic side effects. Available preparations differ primarily in their anticholinergic properties and their ten-

dency to produce sedation and hypotension. The oral and intramuscular doses of these drugs are summarized in Table 8. Although high doses are sometimes necessary for severely psychotic patients, doses above 1,000 mg/day of chlorpromazine or its equivalent are probably no more effective in controlling psychotic symptoms than doses of 300 mg/day for most patients (Davis and Andriukaitis 1986). Fluphenazine decanoate, 12.5 mg (0.5 ml), is usually administered intramuscularly every 2 to 3 weeks for every 10 mg of fluphenazine hydrochloride given daily; 10 to 15 mg of haloperidol decanoate should probably be administered intramuscularly every 4 weeks for every 1 mg of oral haloperidol given daily (Kane 1986).

There are a number of different metabolic pathways in the intestine and the liver for antipsychotic drugs (Ko et al. 1985). Chlorpromazine and thioridazine have many active metabolites, whereas butyrophenones and thioxanthenes may be metabolized only to inactive compounds. Parenteral administration avoids hepatic first-pass metabolism that occurs after oral dosage, increasing availability of the neuroleptic 4 to 10 times (Baldessarini 1985). Some low potency neuroleptics such as chlorpromazine and thioridazine may induce their own metabolism, resulting in decreased drug levels after a few weeks of treatment (Baldessarini 1985).

Blood levels vary widely in different patients given the same dose of a neuroleptic. Because there is no clear correlation between serum concentration and clinical response, blood levels are used only to determine if levels are very low in nonresponders and not as a standard approach to adjusting the dose (Ko et al. 1985). The half-life of all antipsychotics is long (20 to 40 hours), and metabolites may be detected in the urine months after the drug is discontinued. This may explain why recurrence of psychosis may be delayed when medication is stopped.

Mechanisms of Action

The potency of neuroleptics appears to parallel their ability to block dopamine D2 receptors, suggesting that dopamine blockade may be important in their antipsychotic action (Creese et al. 1976). However, the usual cautions should apply before assuming that an observed action of a drug, and not some as yet unsuspected mechanism or combination of actions, explains why it is effective in a particular disorder. For example, neuroleptics also block muscarinic, histamine, alpha adrenergic, and serotonin

TABLE 8. ANTIPSYCHOTIC DRUGS AVAILABLE IN THE UNITED STATES

Class and drug	Trade name	Usual daily oral dose (mg)	Usual single im dose (mg)	Sedative properties	Anticholinergic properties	Hypotensive effects	Parkinsonian effects
Phenothiazines							
Chlorpromazine	Thorazine	300–800	25–50	Very high	High	Moderate–high	Moderate
Trifluopromazine	Vesprin	100–150	20–60	Moderate	Moderate	Moderate	High
Thioridazine	Mellaril	200–700	—	High	Very high	Moderate–high	Low
Mesoridazine	Serentil	75–300	25	High	Moderate–high	Moderate	Low
Acetophenazine	Tindal	60–120	—	Moderate	Moderate	Low	Moderate
Perphenazine	Trilafon	8–40	5–10	Moderate	Moderate–low	Low–moderate	Moderate–high
Trifluoperazine	Stelazine	6–20	1–2	Low	Low	Low	High
Fluphenazine	Prolixin	1–20	12.5–50[a]	Low	Low	Low	High
Thioxanthenes							
Chlorprothixene	Taractan	50–400	25–50	High		Moderate	Moderate
Thiothixene	Navane	6–30	2–4	Low–moderate	Low	Moderate	Moderate–high
Butyrophenones							
Haloperidol	Haldol	6–20	2–5	Low	Very low	Very low	Very high
Dibenzoxazepines							
Loxapine	Loxitane	60–100	12.5–50	Low–moderate	Moderate	Low	Moderate
Dihydroindolones							
Molindone	Moban	50–100	—	Low–moderate	Moderate	Very low	Low–moderate

[a]1.25–2.5 cc q 1–3 weeks.

receptors (Richelson 1985a). An action on the brainstem reticular formation may account for the attenuating effect of neuroleptics on schizophrenics' tendency to become overwhelmed by sensory input (Richelson 1985a).

Psychiatric Uses of Antipsychotic Drugs in the Presence of Neurologic Disease

Antipsychotic drugs are used to treat psychotic and agitated states. Their widest application has been in the treatment of schizophrenia, mania, and delusional depression. In acute treatment, neuroleptics ameliorate negative symptoms such as indifference, withdrawal, blunted affect, and anergia more rapidly than positive symptoms such as delusions, hallucinations, and agitation, but long-term control of positive symptoms with neuroleptics is better than long-term control of negative symptoms (Schooler 1986). Family therapy enhances the beneficial effects of neuroleptics in schizophrenia (Schooler 1986).

Combined data from formal studies of over 3,500 patients reveal an average relapse rate of 57 percent in schizophrenics taking placebo compared with 16 percent of patients on neuroleptics, a difference that has less than a 10^{-100} probability of having occurred by chance (Davis and Andriukaitis 1986). The relapse rate in treated schizophrenics is lower (10 to 15 percent) in more stable patients and higher (40 percent) in less stable schizophrenics (Schooler 1986). In chronic schizophrenics, psychotic symptoms return an average of 4.5 months after neuroleptics are discontinued. The risk of relapse appears to be the same no matter how long the patient has been taking the neuroleptic. Each month after a group of schizophrenics discontinues antipsychotic drugs, a relatively constant percentage of additional patients will relapse (Davis and Andriukaitis 1986).

Some impulsive borderline patients with transient psychotic symptoms benefit from the short-term use of low doses of nonsedating neuroleptics such as haloperidol. The use of neuroleptics in the treatment of organic brain syndromes is considered in the next section. The risk of tardive dyskinesia makes neuroleptics poor choices in nonpsychotic anxiety and most types of insomnia.

Because neuroleptics produce extrapyramidal syndromes, they are usually contraindicated for patients with Parkinson's disease. Theoretically, at least, if a parkinsonian patient requires an antipsychotic drug, compounds with strong anticholinergic potential such as thioridazine should be tried or an alternative treatment considered. Many antipsychotic drugs lower the seizure threshold, especially low potency preparations, such as chlorpromazine, thioridazine, and haloperidol. Fluphenazine and thiothixene are not as likely to aggravate epilepsy, and molindone seems safest in seizure-prone individuals (Baldessarini 1985). The dopamine blockade produced by neuroleptics increases prolactin secretion, which is a definite problem for patients with prolactin-secreting pituitary tumors and a possible concern for patients with breast cancer.

As with many drugs, lower doses of neuroleptics are required in the elderly; the initial dose should be about one-third of the usual adult starting dose (Raskin 1985). High potency drugs with lower anticholinergic and hypotensive potential, such as haloperidol, molindone, loxapine, fluphenazine, trifluoperazine, and perphenazine, are safer in older patients with heart disease (Baldessarini 1985). Thioridazine, which has been reported to cause cardiotoxicity, and chlorpromazine, which has quinidine-like myocardial depressant properties, should generally not be first-line treatments for cardiac patients.

Alternatives to Neuroleptics

When acutely psychotic patients are in urgent need of treatment but cannot tolerate neuroleptics, several alternative strategies may be considered. If the patient is manic, one of the experimental alternatives listed in Table 6 may be useful. ECT may be effective in extreme situations, especially if the psychosis is depressive, manic, schizophreniform, or schizoaffective, and it may reduce psychotic symptoms in some schizophrenic patients (Van Valkenberg and Clayton 1983). Clonidine and lorazepam may augment the action of neuroleptics in ameliorating acute psychotic symptoms, thereby reducing the amount of neuroleptic needed. Clonidine may not be effective by itself but lorazepam may at least tranquilize severely agitated psychotic patients (Salzman et al. 1986). Other benzodiazepines, reserpine, baclofen, droperidol, and L-tryptophan have also been used as antipsychotic agents (Richelson 1985a). Short-acting barbiturates such as amobarbital (see below) may be used for emergency tranquilization if a contraindication to their use does not exist (Salzman et al. 1986).

Neurologic Uses of Antipsychotic Drugs

Increasing experience has been gained in recent years with intravenous haloperidol as a treatment for agitation and psychosis caused by delirium. Single intravenous doses of haloperidol as high as 75 mg, and total 24-hour doses as large as 530 mg, have been administered without any ill effects (Tesar et al. 1985). Control of delirium is achieved within 20 to 90 minutes in many cases (Adams et al. 1986). According to Ayd (1984b), haloperidol is safe even for delirious cardiac patients because it "has virtually no effects on cardiac, pulmonary, renal, hepatic or hematopoietic functions and no absolute contraindications to its use" (p. 33). Extrapyramidal reactions are also rare with high intravenous doses of haloperidol.

Intravenous haloperidol therapy is begun with a 5-mg dose. Cassem's group recommends escalating the dose rapidly to 30- to 75-mg boluses administered as frequently as necessary to control agitation and psychosis in delirious patients (Tesar et al. 1985). Adams et al. (1986), who has studied this drug in patients with metastatic brain cancer, recommends adding to the haloperidol intravenous lorazepam in 1- to 10-mg increments for a total dose of 36 to 480 mg/day of lorazepam, when individual intravenous doses of haloperidol reach 3 to 10 mg, mixing the two drugs in the same syringe (Ayd 1984b). Either regimen may be considered for delirium of most etiologies and for severe agitation, the cause of which has not yet been determined; special caution is necessary if the patient has epilepsy. On the other hand, frequent intramuscular doses of high potency neuroleptics in large doses are no more effective in acute schizophrenia than standard approaches, and are more likely to cause extrapyramidal syndromes (Escobar et al. 1984; Modestin et al. 1983).

For many years, low doses of high potency neuroleptics (e.g., haloperidol 0.5 to 2 mg 1 to 4 times/day) have been used to control recurrent agitation in demented patients when nonpharmacologic measures such as keeping a light on at night have failed and when it is clear that intercurrent delirium is not present. Ideally, the drug should be administered intermittently to coincide with anticipated episodes of agitation. The risk of tardive dyskinesia is significant in this group of patients.

Propranolol is a safe and effective alternative to neuroleptics for controlling violent outbursts in brain-damaged patients. In an initial dose of 20 mg 3 times/day, gradually increased to a maximum of 640 mg/day and titrated according to heart rate, this drug has been found to ameliorate unpredictable attacks of rage and assaultiveness in adults and children with a variety of organic brain syndromes (Silver and Yudofsky 1985; Yudofsky et al. 1983). Some patients respond immediately; others take up to 1 month to improve. Carbamazepine may also be a useful treatment for intermittent agitation associated with organic brain disease (Silver and Yudofsky 1985).

Most neuroleptics (except for thioridazine) have antiemetic properties that make them useful treatments in low doses for nausea and vomiting induced by chemotherapy, vestibular stimulation, dysautonomia, and related physical factors (Baldessarini 1985; Richelson 1985a). For unknown reasons, chlorpromazine in low doses orally, intramuscularly, or as a suppository can ameliorate intractable hiccups. The phenothiazine trimeprazine (Temaril), which does not have antipsychotic properties, is an antipruritic agent in a dose of 10 mg/day. A well-known use of the potent neuroleptics, especially haloperidol, is for control of chorea and agitation in Huntington's disease and of involuntary movements and obscene vocalizations in Gilles de la Tourette's syndrome.

Neurologic Side Effects of Antipsychotic Drugs

Neuroleptics have many side effects that mimic or exacerbate neurologic disease. The most familiar of these are the various extrapyramidal syndromes.

Parkinsonism consists of a resting tremor, shuffling gait, bradykinesia, stooped posture, excess salivation, and a mask-like face. Some of these symptoms can be mistaken for schizophrenic mannerisms and withdrawal, leading the clinician to increase the dose of medication inappropriately. Akathesia, a feeling of intense inner restlessness and need to keep moving, may sometimes be confused with psychotic agitation; dystonia and oculogyric crises may be interpreted as psychotic posturing. Recognizing these syndromes is important because they usually call for a decrease rather than an increase in dosage.

Acute extrapyramidal syndromes usually appear shortly after neuroleptic therapy is instituted. They may resolve within 3 months, making it possible in some cases to discontinue medications used to treat the side effect. Some experts recommend routine prophylactic treatment with antiparkinsonian drugs during the initial stages of neuroleptic treatment to prevent this complication and enhance compliance (Bernstein 1983). Others prefer to wait to see if extrapyramidal side effects appear before prescribing an antiparkinsonian agent to avoid administering medications that may not be necessary and that have adverse effects (usually anticholinergic) of their own (Baldessarini 1985). Prophylactic antiparkinsonian therapy is definitely indicated for patients at risk of acute dystonic reactions, such as individuals with a past history of acute dystonia with neuroleptics and adolescent and young adult males receiving high potency neuroleptics (Ayd 1986). Because the duration of action of neuroleptics is much longer than that of agents used to treat extrapyramidal syndromes, these side effects may reemerge when antiparkinsonian and antipsychotic drugs are discontinued at the same time (Baldessarini 1985). Lithium can aggravate neuroleptic-induced extrapyramidal syndromes.

A great deal of concern exists about tardive dyskinesia, a syndrome of involuntary movements of the tongue, lips, extremities, and trunk described in Table 9 that usually but not always appears after long-term neuroleptic therapy. The risk of tardive dyskinesia may be proportional to the total amount of neuroleptic that has been taken (Ko et al. 1985). Other risk factors include being older, female, and brain damaged (Kane et al. 1985). In a study of 668 patients taking neuroleptics for an average of 8 years, it was found that 40 percent had tardive dyskinesia, which persisted for more than 6 months in 22 percent of the entire sample

TABLE 9.   NEUROLOGIC SIDE EFFECTS OF NEUROLEPTICS AND THEIR TREATMENT

Syndrome	*Manifestations*	*Treatment or Prevention*
Akathesia	Motor restlessness and feeling of inability to remain still	Propranolol; diphenhydramine po or iv (Benadryl); intramuscular antiparkinsonian drug (e.g., benztropine, trihexyphenidyl);
Acute dystonia	Spasm of muscles of neck, tongue, face, eyes, or trunk	Decrease dose of neuroleptic
Parkinsonism	Stiffness, tremor, bradykinesia, shuffling gait, salivation	Oral antiparkinsonian drug for 4 weeks–3 months; decrease dose of the antipsychotic drug
Perioral ("rabbit") tremor	Perioral tremor usually appearing after long-term therapy	Decrease dose or change to a medication in another class
Tardive dyskinesia	Dyskinesias of tongue and face, choreoathetoid movements of extremities, and abnormal movements of neck and trunk, usually but not always appearing after years of treatment following a reduction in dose; incidence higher in the elderly and brain damaged Symptoms are worsened by antiparkinsonian drugs and masked but not cured by higher dose of neuroleptic	No treatment known; may be prevented by prescribing the least amount of drug possible for as little time as is clinically feasible, and utilizing drug-free holidays for patients who need to continue taking the drug
Anticholinergic delirium (acute OBS)	Psychotic symptoms, dry skin, hyperpyrexia, midriasis, tachycardia	Discontinue drug, iv physostigmine for severe agitation or fever
Neuroleptic malignant syndrome	More commonly caused by high potency drugs; appears days to months after beginning treatment; elevated CPK, white blood count, and urinary myoglobin; hyperthermia, muscle rigidity, autonomic instability; parkinsonian symptoms, catatonia stupor, neurologic signs; 10–30 percent fatality	Obtain serum CPK if altered neurologic status, fever, and muscle rigidity appear; if CPK and urine myoglobin elevated, discontinue neuroleptic and give iv dantrolene plus po bromocriptine; ensure hydration and cooling
Alpha adrenergic blockade	Orthostatic hypotension, more common with low potency drugs; inhibition of ejaculation (may also be related to calcium channel blockade)	Advise patient to stant up slowly; treat acute hypotension with norepinephrine, not epinephrine; avoid beta adrenergic stimulation; change to another medication
Heat stroke	Decreased sweating; thirst and possible hypothalamic dysfunction cause fever, decreased sweating, and collapse	Discontinue drug; hydrate and cool
Leukopenia and agranulocytosis	Sudden appearance within the first 2 months of treatment	Advise patient to call immediately for sore throat, fever, etc., and obtain immediate blood count; discontinue drug; prophylactic blood counts are of no value
Pigmentary retinopathy	Reported with doses of thioridazine equal to or greater than 800 mg/day	Stay below 800 mg/day of thioridazine
Photosensitivity	Easy sunburning	Advise patient to avoid strong sunlight and to use sunscreens
Jaundice	Rare complications of low-potency phenothiazine use	Switch to a low dose of a low potency agent in a different class

(Kane et al. 1985). Patients with a history of severe acute extrapyramidal reactions may be more likely to develop tardive dyskinesia later, but it is not known whether aggressive treatment of these early side effects will decrease the risk of the later syndrome. Anticholinergic drugs may unmask covert tardive dyskinesia, which can be temporarily suppressed but not cured by an increase in the dose of neuroleptic. Discontinuing the neuroleptic improves tardive dyskinesia in some patients, but no specific treatment is known.

The most dreaded complication of neuroleptic treatment is the neuroleptic malignant syndrome (NMS). This potentially lethal condition (mortality, 20 to 30 percent) occurs in 0.5 to 1 percent of patients taking neuroleptics (Guze and Baxter 1985). NMS is more likely to occur with intramuscular administration of antipsychotic drugs and may be more common with high potency preparations, especially haloperidol, thiothixene, fluphenazine, and trifluoperazine (Mueller 1985), but it has also been reported in patients taking chlorpromazine, promethazine, thioridazine, carbidopa-levodopa, and a variety of other drugs and after withdrawal of amantadine and carbidopa-levodopa (Mueller 1985; Pelonero et al. 1985). Patients are more vulnerable to develop NMS if they are less than 40 years old, male, unresponsive to the usual doses of neuroleptics, and debilitated, and if they have nonschizophrenic disorders and neurologic illnesses associated with the psychiatric condition (Mueller 1985).

NMS may appear soon after the offending medication is begun, or its onset may be delayed for months. The major manifestations affect temperature regulation, muscle tone, autonomic regulation, the extrapyramidal system, and mental status. Severe hyperthermia can lead to heat stoke and brain damage. Muscular rigidity may progress to rhabdomyolysis with myoglobinuria and renal failure. Other disturbances include dyspnea, dysphagia, autonomic instability with hypertension, diaphoresis, tachycardia, parkinsonian symptoms, delirium, catatonia, and psychosis. NMS is associated with elevations of white blood count, serum creatine phosphokinase (CPK), and urinary myoglobin. This syndrome requires intensive medical treatment that usually involves cooling, hydration, bromocriptine 5 mg 3 times a day by mouth, and intravenous dantrolene in a dose of 1 mg/kg (Mueller 1985).

Patients who recover from NMS frequently still require treatment for the underlying psychiatric disorder. Although there are no proven guidelines for managing this situation, a number of suggestions have been offered by experienced clinicians (Guze and Baxter 1985; Mueller 1985; Pelonero et al. 1985). The most appealing option is to use one of the alternative treatments described earlier in this chapter. If a neuroleptic is necessary, it has been recommended that a low potency compound of a different class than the drug that caused the NMS be tried. Supplementation with benzodiazepines may make it easier to use the lowest possible dose. The patient's temperature, blood pressure, pulse, and mental status should be monitored closely, and the neuroleptic should be discontinued if early signs of NMS reappear.

Descriptions of parkinsonian syndromes, tardive dyskinesia and NMS, as well as other important neurologic side effects of neuroleptics, are provided in Table 9.

Interactions of Neuroleptics with Neurologic Drugs

Sedating neuroleptics potentiate other CNS depressants, while anticholinergic effects are additive with other anticholinergic drugs. Neuroleptics are sometimes used to increase the analgesic effect of narcotics, but respiratory depression may be potentiated as well. Like the heterocyclic antidepressants, chlorpromazine and some other neuroleptics can interfere with the action of antihypertensive agents like guanethidine. Anticonvulsants that induce microsomal enzyme systems (e.g, phenytoin) enhance metabolism of neuroleptics, sometimes decreasing blood levels substantially (Baldessarini 1985). Antiparkinsonian drugs also lower neuroleptic levels and decrease the therapeutic efficacy of the antipsychotic drug (Ayd 1986).

☐ ANTIANXIETY DRUGS

Bromides were the first sedatives to be introduced, in the mid-19th century, followed about 50 years later by barbiturates. Bromides proved to be toxic, and the risks of dependence and death with overdose when barbiturates were used to treat anxiety became evident by the early 1950s. Propranediol carbamates such as meprobamate were developed at about this time, but these drugs also proved to be addicting and dangerous in overdose. Since the introduction of chlordiazepoxide in 1961, the benzodiazepines have proved to be both more effective and safer than other drugs in the treatment of anxiety and insomnia. These medications, too, can produce tolerance and excessive sedation, problems that may be reduced with newer nonbenzodiazepine anxiolytics such as buspirone.

Technically, the term *benzodiazepine* refers to the fusion of a benzene ring and a 7-atom diazepine ring. Most benzodizepines in clinical use also have a 5-aryl substituent ring. Alprazolam and triazolam have, in addition, a triazolo ring fused to positions 3 and 4 (Figure 2). Properties and doses of some benzodiazepines and other safe antianxiety drugs are described in Table 10. Since barbiturates and related drugs are generally no longer recommended for anxiety and insomnia, they are not discussed at length in this chapter.

Benzodiazepines are well absorbed orally but, with the exception of lorazepam, they have unpredictable availability after intramuscular use. Most benzodiazepines are metabolized in the liver by a complex variety of enzyme systems. Unlike the barbiturates and many other psychoactive drugs, benzodiazepines do not induce their own metabolism or the breakdown of other medications. With a few exceptions (e.g., lorazepam), the inactivation of benzodiazepines is inhibited by cimetidine and oral contraceptives.

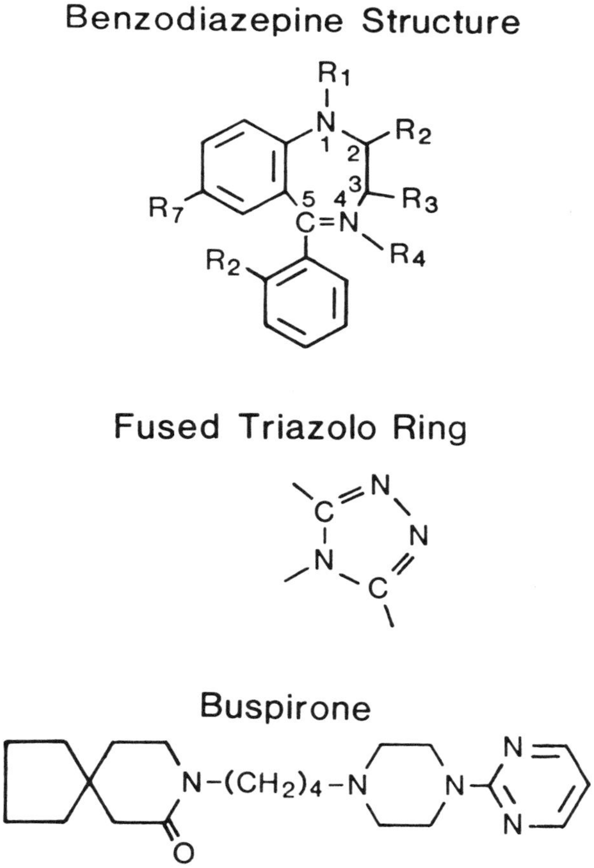

Variable patterns of metabolism of benzodiazepines to active or inactive metabolites result in a broad range of half-lives (Table 10). Because blood-level peaks can produce undue sedation, benzodiazepines are often given 2 to 4 times/day for daytime anxiety despite half-lives of 2 days or more (Baldessarini 1985).

Mechanisms of Action

Much has been learned about the potentiation by benzodiazepines of gamma-aminobutyric acid (GABA), the transmitter that inhibits activation of monoamine-containing neurons (e.g., in the locus ceruleus) that mediate arousal and anxiety-related behaviors (Harvey 1985). Receptors for benzodiazepines and GABA appear to be linked to each other as well as to chloride channels in these neurons. Interactions of benzodiazepines with their receptors heighten the affinity of the GABA receptor for its neurotransmitter, and the resulting increased activity at the GABA sites increases the permeability of the chloride channel so that more chloride ions flow into the cell. This increases the internal net negative charge, hyperpolarizing the neuron so that it is more difficult to stimulate it to discharge. Barbiturates may increase the affinity or numbers of GABA and benzodiazepine receptors. Buspirone, which reduces anxiety without producing muscle relaxation, elevated seizure threshold, or sedation, appears not to affect the GABA system directly, but it may indirectly affect this locus as well as serotonergic, noradrenergic, and cholinergic systems (Ayd 1984a). More complex interactions of diverse antianxiety drugs with intracellular mechanisms will undoubtedly be discovered as the necessary technology and conceptualization develops further.

Benzodiazepine Structure

Fused Triazolo Ring

Buspirone

Figure 2. Chemical structure of benzodiazepines.

Psychiatric Uses of Antianxiety Drugs in the Presence of Neurologic Disease

Antianxiety drugs are most appropriately used to treat time-limited anxiety or insomnia that repre-

TABLE 10. COMMONLY USED ANTIANXIETY DRUGS

Class and drug	Trade name	Usual daily dose (mg)	Onset of effect
Short-acting benzodiazepines[a]			
Lorazepam	Ativan	2–6	Intermediate
Oxazepam	Serax	45–100	Slow
Alprazolam	Xanax	1.5–6	Intermediate
Halazepam	Paxipam	20–120	Fast
Temazepam	Restoril	15–30	Intermediate
Triazolam	Halcion	0.125–0.5	Fast
Long-acting benzodiazepines[b]			
Diazepam	Valium	2–40	Fastest
Chlordiazepoxide	Librium	10–100	Intermediate
Clorazepate	Tranxene	7.5–60	Fast
Prazepam	Centrax	10–60	Slowest
Flurazepam	Dalmane	15–30	Slow
Nonbenzodiazepines			
Buspirone	Buspar	5–20	Slow
Antihistamines			
Hydroxyzine	Atavax	100–200	Slow
Diphenhydramine	Benadryl	100–200	Slow
Beta-blockers			
Propranolol	Inderal	40–120	Slow

[a]Half-life 5–20 hours.
[b]Half-life 20–200 hours.

sents a response to an identifiable stress or change in sleep phase. Because all anxiolytics, with the possible exceptions of alprazolam and buspirone, can aggravate depression, they should not be administered long-term to depressed patients with secondary anxiety.

Antidepressants are more effective than tranquilizers for panic attacks. Alprazolam and clonazepam are the only benzodiazepines that may ameliorate panic anxiety, but it can be extremely difficult to withdraw these agents from some patients. A single dose of propranolol has been helpful to patients with stage fright, and atenolol may decrease social phobia (Gorman et al. 1985). Because buspirone (Dommisse and DeVane 1985) produces dysphoria at higher doses, it may not be addicting. This drug also is not sedating, making it useful for patients who cannot tolerate decreased alertness.

Abstinence Syndromes

It is not uncommon in neurologic practice to encounter patients who have been taking a benzodiazepine, barbiturate, or other CNS depressant for many years. Some of these patients utilize a tranquilizer to cope with the stresses of daily living or to prove that they have a "real" illness requiring treatment with a medication. Others have become physically dependent and experience increased anxiety, rebound insomnia, or other withdrawal symptoms when they attempt to abstain, to which they respond by increasing the dose to suppress withdrawal. These patients frequently underestimate their drug intake and may obtain CNS depressants from different doctors and family members. It is very common for prescription CNS depressants to be combined with alcohol.

The risk of physical dependence (i.e., tolerance and/or withdrawal) is greatest in patients who take 40 to 60 mg/day of diazepam or its equivalent for more than 1 month or who take lower doses for more than 8 months (Dubovsky and Weissberg 1986). Even one dose of a benzodiazepine hypnotic can produce some rebound insomnia (Harvey 1985), and as many as 45 percent of benzodiazepine users experience some form of abstinence syndrome (Harvey 1985). Withdrawal from all CNS depressants (Table 11) is phenomenologically similar. Abstinence symptoms are more intense with shorter-

TABLE 11. SYMPTOMS OF WITHDRAWAL FROM CNS DEPRESSANTS

Dysphoria, irritability, depression
Anxiety,[a] anorexia, agitation, panic
Headache, sweating, faintness, dizziness
Myalgia, tremor, muscle twitching
Rebound insomnia, bad dreams
Delirium, paranoia, psychosis
Seizures

[a]Daytime anxiety may be a symptom of recurrent withdrawal when short-acting benzodiazepines are taken chronically at night for sleep.

acting preparations; withdrawal appears 1 or 2 weeks later and is more prolonged and attenuated with the longer-acting benzodiazepines.

The real cause may not be apparent when acute psychosis, agitation, delirium, or a generalized seizure are secondary to benzodiazepine withdrawal, especially when the patient conceals the extent of drug use. These symptoms may not appear for some time after the patient has been admitted to the hospital if a long-acting benzodiazepine is being abused or if the patient continues to take the medication after admission. Family members may provide important information about drug intake, but the patient's history is frequently unreliable.

Because CNS depressants cross-react with each other, withdrawal from any combination of them may be diagnosed by administering one known substance, usually phenobarbital or pentobarbital. Once signs and symptoms of withdrawal appear, 200 mg of pentobarbital or 60 to 100 mg of phenobarbital are administered orally after the patient has been npo for 12 hours. If pentobarbital is used, the amount necessary to suppress abstinence is estimated from the amount of intoxication that is observed 1 hour after administration of the test dose. Intoxication is judged by the degree of such signs as sedation, nystagmus, dysarthria, postural hypotension, and ataxia. It is important to record the level of these findings both before and after the test dose is given because all but nystagmus may be seen in both intoxication and withdrawal. Multiple significant signs of intoxication using this method indicate that there is no tolerance and that no further treatment is needed. Moderate intoxication suggests that 200 to 300 mg of pentobarbital every 6 hours are needed to suppress withdrawal. No intoxication after the test dose suggests that 400 to 500 mg of pentobarbital are needed every 6 hours to prevent the abstinence syndrome. These doses, or an equivalent amount of phenobarbital, are then

administered for 1 to 2 days, following which the barbiturate is withdrawn at a rate of 10 percent every day to every other day.

If phenobarbital is the initial medication, 60- to 100-mg doses are administered every 3 to 6 hours until the patient is intoxicated. The total amount is given the next day in divided doses every 6 hours and then withdrawn initially at the same rate as for pentobarbital. More rapid withdrawal may be necessary after 4 to 7 days because the long half-life (24 to 120 hours) may result in drug accumulation when a steady state is reached. Nevertheless, this drug is preferable to pentobarbital because seizures are less likely to occur if dosage reduction is too rapid and because phenobarbital is available in injectable form if the patient refuses treatment. Within the guidelines listed above, each dose of pentobarbital or phenobarbital should be adjusted according to the patient's clinical status. A flow sheet indicating signs of withdrawal or intoxication before and after each dose makes it easier to judge the patient's overall response and the amount of the next dose.

Organic Brain Syndromes and CNS Depressants

When anxiety is a symptom of organic brain disease, steps should be taken to compensate for the underlying disturbance of concentration, attention, and memory while the medical or neurologic disorder is being diagnosed and treated. This is accomplished by such measures as frequent orienting, keeping a light on at night, and avoiding unnecessary changes in the patient's surroundings. Benzodiazepines and barbiturates are often ineffective anxiolytics in delirious and demented patients because these medications further depress cortical- and reticular-activating-system function, which clouds the patient's sensorium even more. Low doses of benzodiazepines with shorter half-lives (e.g., oxazepam and lorazepam) may be less disruptive, but propranolol or haloperidol are probably more appropriate. Antihistamines (e.g., hydroxyzine 50 to 100 mg orally or intramuscularly) are sometimes used to sedate patients with organic brain disease who require an electroencephalogram (EEG) because these drugs have minimal effects on the EEG. Antihistamines have also been used as sleeping pills for elderly and demented patients, but their anticholinergic properties may be problematic and their antianxiety effect is unpredictable.

Even after special tests, it is occasionally not clear whether complex symptoms such as memory loss, confusion, agitation, or psychosis are due to a psychiatric or a neurologic disorder. If the patient does not have a space-occupying lesion, increased intracranial pressure, porphyria, or allergy to the drug, 100 to 400 mg of amobarbital (Amytal) very slowly administered intravenously can sometimes distinguish between the two. With a little sedation, the patient may become more cooperative with mental status testing. Dramatic transient improvement when the patient is tranquilized suggests a functional etiology. Worsening of symptoms during the amobarbital interview, which is usually due to intensification of the underlying disorder of consciousness by the CNS depressant, suggests an organic cause.

The amobarbital interview may also help to distinguish between organically based and functional paralysis, blindness, deafness, aphonia, and sensory loss. The latter disorders may disappear briefly under amobarbital, whereas the former only improve slightly or are unchanged. Failure of symptoms to remit does not exclude a psychogenic syndrome.

Antianxiety Drugs in the Elderly

As with other centrally acting drugs, lower doses and smaller increments in dosage are necessary for older patients. Shorter-acting benzodiazepines such as triazolam are preferable as sleeping pills to longer-acting ones such as flurazepam. Benzodiazepines with simpler metabolic pathways such as lorazepam or oxazepam are probably safer than medications with multiple active metabolites. Many elderly patients who complain of insomnia do not require a hypnotic because they are experiencing the normal decrease in total nightly sleep that is encountered with aging or because difficulty sleeping is a symptom of another major disorder such as dementia, depression, gastroesophageal reflux, sleep apnea, or restless legs syndrome.

Neurologic Uses of Benzodiazepines and Related Drugs

Phenobarbital is familiar to most clinicians as a first-line anticonvulsant. Clonazepam is a new benzodiazepine anticonvulsive drug with a half-life in the range of 20 to 40 hours that is used to treat generalized, myoclonic, and absence epilepsy (Chouinard and Penry 1985). This benzodiazepine

may be helpful in some cases of trigeminal neuralgia and pain syndromes elsewhere in the body that are associated with paroxysmal dysesthesias, pain on stimulation of normal tissue, burning sensations, and hyperesthesia (Bouckonis and Litman 1985). Clonazepam has utility in paroxysmal choreoathetosis that might predict effectiveness in the treatment of tardive dyskinesia (Chouinard and Penry 1985). A dose of 1.5 to 4 mg/day has been used for neuralgia, whereas in a dose of 4 to 16 mg/day, clonazepam may have antimanic properties (Chouinard and Penry 1985). Carbamazepine has been found useful in restless legs syndrome and pain syndromes associated with dysesthesias (Larsen et al. 1985).

Neurologic Side Effects of Antianxiety Drugs

The most important adverse effects of CNS depressant use are tolerance and abstinence syndromes (Table 11). Paradoxical reactions such as anxiety, irritability, aggression, agitation, and insomnia are common in children, the elderly, and brain-damaged patients. Because characteristically hypervigilant patients may become panic stricken, suspicious, or belligerent when their faculties are dulled by the sedating effects of tranquilizers, antianxiety drugs should either be avoided or used in very low doses when they are absolutely necessary. Benzodiazepines are rarely fatal when ingested in overdose unless they are accompanied by other CNS depressants (Baldessarini 1985).

Like the barbiturates, low doses of benzodiazepines decrease alpha activity on the EEG and increase low-voltage fast activity (Harvey 1985). In contrast with the barbiturates, EEG changes with benzodiazepines are more obvious in the frontal regions and are less likely to spread through the brain. Most benzodiazepines increase stage 2 non-REM sleep and decrease stage 4 sleep, making them useful in treating some nightmares (Harvey 1985). Low doses of flurazepam, temazepam, and possibly other benzodiazepines do not shorten the total time in REM sleep; even when time in each REM period is decreased, the number of REM cycles is increased. Patients with depression who have increased REM density may spend even more time in REM sleep when they take benzodiazepines.

Interactions of Antianxiety Drugs with Neurologic Drugs

Barbiturates induce hepatic microsomal systems that metabolize many other drugs, including a number of anticonvulsants. This is not true of benzodiaze-pines, but ethanol and phenytoin decrease ben-zodiazepine breakdown slightly (Harvey 1985). A more significant problem is the additive CNS depressant effect of most anxiolytics with other depressant drugs, including anticonvulsants. Benzo-diazepines can augment respiratory depression in-duced by opioids other than meperidine. Buspi-rone has not yet been found to have any clinically significant interactions (Ayd 1984a).

□ PSYCHIATRIC SIDE EFFECTS OF NEUROLOGIC DRUGS

Most drugs that affect the CNS can produce changes in thinking, emotion, and behavior that mimic pri-mary psychiatric syndromes. The psychiatric symptoms may appear in a clear sensorium, or they may be accompanied by signs and symptoms of delirium. Antiparkinsonian drugs (e.g, trihexyphen-idyl, benztropine) and some neuroleptics and an-

TABLE 12. PSYCHIATRIC SIDE EFFECTS OF NEUROLOGIC DRUGS

Symptom	Medications	Comments
Depression	Amantadine	Common at usual doses
	Anticonvulsants	Usually at higher blood levels
	Corticosteroids, ACTH	More common with high doses; may occur on withdrawal
	Benzodiazepines	Can occur at usual doses
	Barbiturates	
	Narcotics	
	L-Dopa	Greater risk with prolonged use
	Antihypertensives	Has been reported with many preparations
	Propranolol	Can occur at usual doses
	Vinblastine	Rare
	Asparaginase	Common side effect usually with higher doses
	Cimetidine	
	Oral contraceptives	In as many cases as 15 percent
	Ibuprofen	Rare
	Metoclopramide	Usual doses
Mania	Baclofen	Usually appears after sudden withdrawal
	Bromocriptine	Symptoms may continue after drug is
	Captopril	withdrawn
	Corticosteroids, ACTH	Usually at higher doses
	Dextromethorphan	
	L-Dopa	More frequent in elderly; risk increases with prolonged use
	Antidepressants	In bipolar patients with higher doses
	Digitalis	
	Cyclobenzaprine	Reported in one patient
Hallucinations	Amantadine	Rare; more common in elderly
	Anticonvulsants	Visual and auditory
	Antihistamines	Especially with higher doses
	Anticholinergics	Usually with delirium
	Corticosteroids, ACTH	See above
	Digitalis	Usually at higher blood levels
	Indomethacin	Especially in elderly
	Methysergide	Occasional
	Propranolol	At usual or increased doses
	Methylphenidate	More likely in children
	L-dopa	See above
	Ketamine	Common
	Cimetidine	Usually with higher doses and in elderly
Nightmares	Antidepressants	When entire dose taken hs
	Amantadine	Especially in elderly
	Baclofen	Usually after sudden withdrawal
	Ketamine	Also produces hallucinations, crying, changes in body image, and delirium

TABLE 12.   (Continued)

Symptom	Medications	Comments
	L-dopa	Often after dosage increase
	Pentazocine	During treatment
	Propranolol	See above
	Digitalis	See above
Paranoia	Asparaginase	May be common
	Bromocriptine	Not dose related
	Corticosteroids, ACTH	See above
	Amphetamines	Even at low doses
	Indomethacin	Especially in elderly
	Propranolol	At any dose
	Sulindac	Reported in a few patients
Aggression	Bromocriptine	Not dose related; may persist
	Tranquilizers and hypnotics	A rebase phenomenon
	L-dopa	See above
	Phenelzine	May be separate from mania
	Digitalis	See above

tidepressants can produce an anticholinergic delirium characterized by agitation, psychosis, hallucinations, tachycardia, mydriasis, fever, and warm dry skin. Common specific disturbances and their causes are summarized in Table 12 (Dubovsky and Weissberg 1986; Medical Letter 1985).

☐ REFERENCES

Adams F, Fernandez F, Andersson BE: Emergency pharmacotherapy of delirium in the critically ill cancer patient. Psychosomatics 27(Suppl):33–37, 1986

Ayd F: Buspirone: a review. International Drug Therapy Newsletter 19:37–42, 1984a

Ayd F: Intravenous haloperidol-lorazepam therapy of delirium. International Drug Therapy Newsletter 19:33–35, 1984b

Ayd F: Prophylactic antiparkinsonian drug therapy: pros and cons. International Drug Therapy Newsletter 21:5–6, 1986

Azar I, Lear E: Cardiovascular effects of electroconvulsive therapy in patients taking tricyclic antidepressants. Anesth Analg 63:1140, 1984

Baldessarini RJ: Drugs and the treatment of psychiatric disorders, in The Pharmacological Basis of Therapeutics. Edited by Gilman AG, Goodman LS, Rall TW, et al. New York, Macmillan, 1985, pp 387–445

Bernstein JG: Handbook of Drug Therapy in Psychiatry. Boston, John Wright-PSG, 1983

Berridge MJ: Inositol triphosphatate and diacylglycerol as second messengers. Biochem J 220:345–360, 1984

Bouckonis AJ, Litman RE: Clonazepam in the treatment of neuralgic pain syndromes. Psychosomatics 26:933–936, 1985

Brandon S, Crowley P, MacDold C, et al: Electroconvulsive therapy: results in depressive illness from the Leicestershire trial. Br Med J 288:22–25, 1984

Carman JS, Wyatt RJ: Alterations in cerebrospinal fluid and serum total calcium with changes in psychiatric state. In Neuroregulators and Psychiatric Disorders. Edited by Usdin E, Hamburg DA, Barchas JD. New York, Oxford University Press, 1977, pp 488–494

Charney DS, Heninger GR, Sternberg DE: Serotonin function and mechanisms of action of antidepressant treatment. Arch Gen Psychiatry 41:359–365, 1984

Chouinard G, Penry JK: Neurologic and psychiatric aspects of clonazepam: an update: proceedings of a symposium. Psychosomatics 26(Suppl):1–37, 1985

Cohen WJ, Cohen NH: Lithium carbonate, haloperidol and irreversible brain damage. JAMA 230:1283–1287, 1974

Creese I, Burt DR, Snyder SH: Dopamine receptor binding predicts clinical and pharmacologic potencies of antischizophrenic drugs. Science 192:481–483, 1976

Davis JM, Andriukaitis S: The natural course of schizophrenia and effective maintenance drug treatment. J Clin Psychopharmacol 6:25–105, 1986

Demuth GW, Breslov RE, Drescher J: The elicitation of a movement disorder by trazodone: case report. J Clin Psychiatry 46:535–536, 1985

Dommisse CS, DeVane CL: Buspirone: a new type of anxiolytic. Drug Intell Clin Pharm 19:624–628, 1985

Dubovsky SL: Using electroconvulsive therapy for patients with neurological disease. Hosp Community Psychiatry 37:819–825, 1986

Dubovsky SL, Franks RD: Intracellular calcium ions in affective disorders: a review and an hypothesis. Biol Psychiatry 18:781–797, 1983

Dubovsky SL, Weissberg MP: Clinical Psychiatry in Primary Care (3rd ed). Baltimore, Williams & Wilkins Co, 1986

Dubovsky SL, Franks RD, Allen S, et al: Calcium antagonists in mania. Psychiatry Research 18:309–320, 1986

El-Gazour AR, Ivankovich AD, Braverman B, et al: Monoamine oxidase inhibitors: should they be discontinued preoperatively? Anesth Analg 64:592–596, 1985

Escobar JI, Barron A, Kiriakos R: A controlled study of "neuroleptization" with fluphenazine hydrochloride injections. J Clin Psychopharmacol 3:359–363, 1983

Fink M: Induced seizures and human behavior, in Psychobiology of Convulsive Therapy. Edited by Fink M, Kety S, McGaugh J, et al. Washington, DC, VH Winston & Sons, 1974, pp 1–20

Fiori MG: Tricyclic antidepressants: a review of their toxicology. Curr Dev Psychopharmacol 4:72–94, 1977

Goodman WK, Charney DS: Therapeutic applications and mechanisms of action of monoamine oxidase and heterocyclic antidepressant drugs. J Clin Psychiatry 46:6–22, 1985

Gorman JM, Liebowitz MR, Fyer AJ, et al: Treatment of social phobia with atenolol. J Clin Psychopharmacol 5:298–301, 1985

Graham LF, Fredricson-Overo K, Kirk L: Influences of neuroleptics and benzodiazepines on metabolism of tricyclic antidepressants in man. Am J Psychiatry 131:863–866, 1974

Guze BH, Baxter LR: Neuroleptic malignant syndromes. N Engl J Med 313:163–166, 1985

Harvey SC: Hypnotics and sedatives, in The Pharmacological Basis of Therapeutics, 7th ed. Edited by Gilman AG, Goodman LS, Rall TW, et al. New York, Macmillan, 1985, pp 339–371

Hoogivrf B: Amitriptyline treatment of painful diabetic neuropathy: an inadvertent single-patient clinical trial. Diabetes Care 8:526–527, 1985

Huai-Yu, Guszhen L, Jundong G, et al: Furazalidone in peptic ulcer. Lancet 2:276–277, 1985

Izzo KL, Brody R: Rehabilitation in lithium toxicity. Arch Phys Med Rehabil 66:779–782, 1985

Jefferson JW, Griest JH: Primer of lithium therapy. Baltimore, Williams & Wilkins Co, 1977

Jenike MA: The use of monoamine oxidase inhibitors in the treatment of elderly patients. J Am Geriatr Soc 32:571–575, 1984

Kane JM: Dosage strategies with long-acting injectable neuroleptics, including haloperidol decanoate. J Clin Psychopharmacol 6:205–235, 1986

Kane JM, Woerner M, Borenstein M, et al: Integrating incidence and prevalence of tardive dyskinesia. Paper presented at the 4th World Congress of Biological Psychiatry, Philadelphia, 8–13 September 1985

Kaufman MW, Cassem N, Murray G, et al: The use of methylphenidate in depressed patients after cardiac surgery. J Clin Psychiatry 45:82–84, 1984

Klein DF, Gittelman R, Quitkin F, et al: Diagnosis and Drug Treatment of Psychiatric Disorders: Adults and Children (2nd ed). Baltimore, Williams & Wilkins Co, 1980

Ko GN, Korpi ER, Linnoila M: On the clinical relevance and methods of quantification of plasma concentrations of neuroleptics. Clin Psychopharmacol 5:253–262, 1985

Larsen S, Telstad W, Sorensen O, et al: Carbamazepine therapy in restless legs: discrimination between responders and nonresponders. Acta Med Scand 218:223–227, 1985

Lawrence JM: Reactions to withdrawal of antidepressants, antiparkinsonian drugs, and lithium. Psychosomatics 11:869–877, 1985

Lieberman JA, Kane JM, Reife R: Neuromuscular effects of monamine oxidase inhibitors. J Clin Psychopharmacol 5:217–220, 1985

Litovitz TL, Troutman WG: Amoxapine overdose: seizures and fatalities. JAMA 250:1069–1071, 1983

Lydiard RB: Tricyclic-resistant depression: treatment resistance or inadequate treatment. J Clin Psychiatry 46:412–417, 1985

Massey EW, Folger WN: Seizures activated by therapeutic levels of lithium carbonate. South Med J 77:1173–1175, 1984

Mathew NT: Prophylaxis of migraine and mixed headache: a randomized controlled study. Headache 21:105–109, 1981

Medical Letter: Drugs that cause psychiatric symptoms. Medical Letter 26:75–78, 1985

Meyler L, Herxheimer A: Side Effects of Drugs. Baltimore, Williams & Wilkins, 1968

Modestin J, Toffler G, Pia M: Haloperidol in acute schizophrenic inpatients: a double-blind comparison of two dosage regimens. Pharmacopsychiatry 16:121–126, 1983

Mueller PS: Neuroleptic malignant syndrome. Psychosomatics 26:654–662, 1985

Packman AM, Meyer DA, Verdun RM: Hazards of succinylcholine administration during electrotherapy. Arch Gen Psychiatry 35:1137–1141, 1978

Pare CMB: The present status of monoamine oxidase inhibitors. Br J Psychiatry 146:576–584, 1985

Pelonero AL, Levenson JL, Silverman JL: Neuroleptic therapy following neuroleptic malignant syndrome. Psychosomatics 26:946–947, 1985

Perry PJ, Calloway RA, Cook BL, et al: Theophyllus-precipitated alterations of lithium clearance. Acta Psychiatr Scand 69:528–539, 1984

Pinder RM, Brogden RN, Speight TM, et al: Maprotiline: a review of its pharmacological properties and therapeutic efficacy in mental states. Drugs 13:321–352, 1977

Quitkin F, Rifkin A, Klein DF: Monoamine oxidase inhibitors: review of effectiveness. Arch Gen Psychiatry 36:749–760, 1979

Raskin DE: Antipsychotic medication and the elderly. J Clin Psychiatry 46:36–40, 1985

Richelson E: The newer antidepressants: structures, pharmacokinetics, pharmacodynamics, and proposed mechanisms of action. Psychopharmacol Bull 20:213–223, 1984

Richelson E: Pharmacology of neuroleptics in use in the United States. J Clin Psychiatry 46:8–14, 1985a

Richelson E: Treatment of peptic ulcer disease with tricyclic antidepressants. International Drug Therapy Newsletter 20:21–23, 1985b

Robinson RG, Lipsey JR, Price TP: Diagnosis and clinical management of post-stroke depression. Psychosomatics 26:769–778, 1985

Rogers MP: Rheumatoid arthritis: psychiatric aspects and use of psychotropics. Psychosomatics 26:915–925, 1985

Rosenblatt RM, Reich J, Dehrung D: Tricyclic antidepressants in treatment of depression and chronic pain: analysis of the supporting evidence. Anesth Analg 63:1025–1032, 1984

Ross ED, Rush AJ: Diagnosis and neuroanatomical correlates of depression in brain damaged patients. Arch Gen Psychiatry 38:1344–1354, 1981

Roy A, Pickar D: Lithium potentiation of imipramine in treatment-resistant depression. Br J Psychiatry 148:582–

583, 1985

Rubin EH, Biggs JT, Preskorn SH: Nortriptyline pharmacokinetics and plasma levels: implications for clinical practice. J Clin Psychiatry 46:418–424, 1985

Salzman C: Clinical guidelines for the use of antidepressant drugs in geriatric patients. J Clin Psychiatry 46:38–44, 1985

Salzman C, Green AI, Rodriguez-Villa F, et al: Benzodiazepines combined with neuroleptics for management of severe disruptive behavior. Psychosomatics 27(Suppl):17–21, 1986

Saul RF: Pseudotremor cerebri secondary to lithium carbonate. JAMA 253:2869–2871, 1985

Schiffer RB, Herndon RM, Rudide RA: Treatment of pathological laughing and weeping with amitriptyline. N Engl J Med 312:1480–1482, 1985

Schooler NR: The efficacy of antipsychotic drugs and family therapy in the maintenance treatment of schizophrenia. J Clin Psychopharmacol 6:115–195, 1986

Sheehan DV, Ballenger J, Jacobson G: Treatment of endogenous anxiety with phobic, hysterical and hypochondriacal symptoms. Arch Gen Psychiatry 37:51–59, 1980

Siever LJ, Davis KL: Overview: toward a dysregulation hypothesis of depression. Am J Psychiatry 142:1017–1031, 1985

Silver JM, Yudofsky S: Propranolol for aggression: literature review and clinical guidelines. International Drug Therapy Newsletter 20:9–12, 1985

Singer I, Rotenberg D: Mechanisms of lithium action. N Engl J Med 289:254–260, 1973

Tabakoff B, Lee JM, De Leon-Jones L, et al: Ethanol inhibits the activity of the B form of monoamine oxidase in human platelet and brain tissue. Psychopharmacology 87:152–156, 1985

Task Force on the Use of Laboratory Tests in Psychiatry: Tricyclic antidepressants: blood level measurements and clinical outcome. Am J Psychiatry 142:155–162, 1985

Tesar GE, Murray GB, Cassem VH: Use of high-dose intravenous haloperidol in the treatment of agitated cardiac patients. J Clin Psychopharmacol 5:344–347, 1985

Van Valkenberg C, Clayton PJ: Electroconvulsive therapy and schizophrenia. Biol Psychiatry 20:699–700, 1983

Weiner RD: Does ECT cause brain damage? Behav Brain Res 7:1–53, 1984

Yudofsky S, Williams D, Gorman J: Propranolol in the treatment of rage and violent behavior in patients with chronic brain syndrome. Am J Psychiatry 138:218–220, 1983

Chapter 24

Cognitive Rehabilitation of Patients with Neuropsychiatric Disabilities

Michael D. Franzen, PH.D.

Carl Rollyn Sullivan, M.D.

FOR YEARS THE CONVENTIONAL WISDOM has been that there is very little that can be done for individuals who suffer physiologic brain impairment due to anatomic lesions. Brain-impaired people were discharged to their families if their care needs were not too great or were sent to nursing homes or other long-term care facilities if their families were unable to meet their care needs. However, today there is greater interest in treating the brain impaired. There are several reasons for this. For one, there has been a veritable explosion in the neurosciences in the past 15 years. What was previously thought to be impossible or unknowable is now regarded as possible.

The second reason for the increased interest in treating brain-impaired individuals includes social and political influences. Due to acute care innovations such as paramedic teams, procedures such as cardiopulmonary resuscitation (CPR) and equipment such as the "jaws of life," more people are surviving myocardial infarcts, cerebral vascular accidents, and high-speed motor vehicle accidents. Caveness (1977) estimated that each year as many as 900,000 individuals may experience some form of traumatic brain injury in the United States. These people may be alive, but many are in need of rehabilitation and treatment for their resulting conditions. The families of these people are lobbying for care facilities and for funds for research.

A third reason is the ever-increasing proportion of aged in our population. These older people are at higher risk for cerebral impairments of all types, and they too are lobbying for care facilities. The partial result of these political and social pressures has been the growth of coma and inpatient cognitive rehabilitation centers. In the private sector, rehabilitation hospitals such as Braintree and the chain of LEIR (Lake Erie Institute of Rehabilitation) hospitals have been started.

A consequence of this set of circumstances is that the demand for, and provision of, treatment services for the brain impaired may actually exceed the current technological capacity to provide such services. Few psychiatrists, just as few other professionals, receive sufficient training in the treatment of brain-impaired individuals. However, it is reasonable to expect that increasing numbers of psychiatrists will be called on to do just that. It is necessary, therefore, that psychiatrists acquaint themselves with the theories and operations of cognitive rehabilitation. This chapter will attempt to introduce psychiatrists to some of the concepts involved. Additionally, we will outline the points at which a psychiatrist's professional expertise is likely to be enlisted.

First, we will consider the ideas regarding the diminution of transient effects including the amelioration of temporary effects, diachisis, inhibition and deinhibition, and restoration. Then, we will examine the ideas regarding attempts of the brain to repair itself.

☐ TRAUMATIC BRAIN IMPAIRMENT

The treatment of traumatically brain-impaired individuals is variably called cognitive rehabilitation, cognitive retraining, or neurotraining. Although the focus of cognitive rehabilitation is on the optimal remediation of deficits subsequent to traumatic injury, treatment must also attend to the disruption in social, vocational, emotional, and family functioning to be successful. Cognitive rehabilitation is a multidisciplinary effort requiring the cooperation of various medical and nonmedical personnel. The psychiatrist can play an extremely important role in this process. This role begins in the early stages of rehabilitation and continues into the extended, long-term aspects of recovery and rehabilitation. There are many psychiatric complications and sequelae that will impinge on the successful treatment of a brain-impaired individual. To understand the role of a psychiatrist, it is important to understand the course of recovery and the effects of the patient's reaction at each stage.

☐ THEORIES OF RECOVERY

Brain impairment is a complex phenomenon that includes many different etiologies. A useful categorization system involves the dichotomy of congenital versus acquired brain impairment. To focus the scope of this chapter more directly, only acquired brain impairment will be considered. However, much of the discussion contained in this chapter will also be relevant to a consideration of the psychiatric needs of individuals with congenital brain impairment.

Despite the many recent advances in the neurosciences, it is safe to say that little regarding brain function is definitively known. However, we can learn much about behavioral and emotional recovery from brain injury by examining studies of more discrete, physiologic recovery. Miller (1984) proposed a useful distinction between the recovery of brain function as a means and the recovery of brain function as an end. This distinction closely parallels the difference between brain function as viewed by the basic scientists and brain function as viewed by the applied behavioral scientists. The recovery of function as a means involves the recovery or replacement of physiologic functions. Research in this area has involved mainly animal studies. The recovery of function as an end involves the recovery of behavioral and emotional processes that are observable. Research in this area involves both passive observations of brain-injured individuals over time and treatment studies with humans.

An understanding of the theories of recovery is also essential to an understanding of cognitive rehabilitation interventions. Because brain damage is a multifaceted phenomenon with many different etiologies, treatment of brain damage is multifaceted. Intervention methods will vary with the type of injury and with the time since injury. A detailed discussion of the many different possible treatment methods is beyond the scope of a single chapter. However, we will outline some of the possible treatments at each appropriate stage of recovery.

Recovery of Function as Means

There are two main ideas in theories of recovery as a means. According to the first idea, for which there is greater evidence regarding the processes involved, recovery occurs as the result of the diminution of transient, acute effects of the injury. According to the second idea, recovery occurs as the result of attempts of the brain to compensate for the injury physiologically or to repair itself.

Amelioration of Temporary Effects. There are several processes that accompany brain injury and that can account for the immediate severe observable effects. Especially following a traumatic brain injury, there may be edema and swelling of brain tissue. This will result in unconsciousness or, at a lesser level, disorientation and confusion (Garoutte and Aird 1984). Because the entire brain is affected by these processes, the observable effects tend to be widespread and severe. However, as the edema subsides, the widespread effects tend to dissipate, leaving deficits only in those areas that contain necrotic tissue. Lowering abnormally high levels of fluid in the brain will result in more normal neurochemical processes. Reduction of swelling will reduce pressure on areas in the brain that were not directly affected by the traumatic injury but that were affected by the resultant compression. The removal of waste products can also partly explain recovery. When a neuron is lysed secondary to structural damage, the leakage of its intracellular material will temporarily disrupt activity in adjacent cells (Kalat 1981). Over time, this material is washed away by brain fluid processes, and normal brain processes resume.

Early in the recovery process when behavioral deficits are still thought to be due to the presence of edema, treatment is conservative. Time is allowed for the subsidence of edema before rehabilitation begins. Usually a comprehensive assessment is not even begun until after it is determined that the edema has largely subsided.

Diachisis. Another proposed process involved in the production of temporary cognitive and behavioral deficits following brain injury is more complex. This process is known as diachisis, a concept proposed by von Monakow (1914.) Diachisis is a multileveled concept with far-reaching implications. Partly due to its complexity and partly due to its assumptions regarding brain physiology, there are few experimental or empirical evaluations of the accuracy of diachisis. At the risk of oversimplifying the theory of diachisis, its implications for the recovery of brain function can be outlined in a few sentences. Basically, diachisis requires a consideration of the brain as a system. The different components of this system operate in an interacting set of checks and balances. Successful operation of

the system requires not only the intact physiologic functioning of the areas most responsible for a given cognitive or behavioral function, but also the intact physiologic functioning of areas of the brain that provide the checks and balances on that original area of interest. Injury to a single area results in a disruption of function in those areas that are related to the original area either by spatial contiguity or by fibrous connections. Over time, the other areas regain their function as a new system of checks and balances develops. Although theoretically attractive, diachisis is an idea that is difficult to test empirically. Furthermore, experimental tests of this model have resulted in equivocal results (Finger and Stein 1982).

The implications of diachisis for treatment are similar to the implications of the presence of edema. Comprehensive assessment and treatment are held until the effects of these two processes are minimal.

Inhibition and Deinhibition. Luria et al. (1969) also addressed the issue of temporary widespread effects of traumatic brain injury followed by eventual recovery of function in areas untouched by the actual damaging event. They first stated that some temporary effects were secondary to edema, cerebral swelling, changes in blood flow, changes in the circulation of cerebral spinal fluid, and lowering of cortical tone due to disruption. But they also suggested the existence of inhibition as an explanation for temporary deficits. Inhibition was defined as the blocking of remaining uninjured nerve cells. This temporary blocking was viewed as protective and due to increases in the concentration of cholinesterase. Clinical case data in which neostigmine and galanthamine appear to reverse the effects of inhibition were presented, a process Luria et al. labeled deinhibition. However, more clinical and experimental work needs to be done before this idea can be rigorously evaluated.

Restoration. LeVere dismissed the role of repair of brain tissue in recovery from brain damage. In a series of experiments involving rats (LeVere 1975, 1980; LeVere and LeVere 1982), LeVere outlined a process by which he hypothesized behavioral recovery to occur. LeVere stated that the use of the word *recovery* can be misleading because it is not the ability that is recovered. Instead, there are three mechanisms by which behavior that is not seen immediately following brain damage can reappear at a later time. The first involves the notion of reaccessing. According to LeVere, what is lost is not the ability to perform a behavior but the ability to access the engram containing instructions to perform the behavior. Therefore, recovery occurs when the engram is reaccessed. Second, the system of inhibition and facilitation in the brain is damaged. This system is later restored, resulting in reemergence of the behavior. Third, organisms may shift from a damaged system to a nondamaged system in the production of the behavior in what LeVere called reactivation.

According to this theory, early treatment will involve simple practice of discrete skills, with feedback regarding the accuracy of the patient's behavior. Later treatment will involve training the patient in new behavioral strategies to produce the behavioral skill of interest.

Theories of Repair. The second main idea in the recovery of function as means involves both metabolic and structural changes following brain injury. The metabolic changes can be considered adaptations. These theories rely on the existence of preserved intact neurons in areas where damage has occurred. Following incomplete injury to tissue that utilizes catecholamine, the remaining intact tissue demonstrates increased synthesis and release of selected neurotransmitters (Agid et al. 1973; Hefti et al. 1980). Postsynaptic hypersensitivity is also sometimes seen (Marshall 1984). These processes generally take place over time in the early acute phases following brain injury. As such, they can be used to explain early (less than 72-hour) recovery but may have little impact on recovery in the later stages.

There is also limited evidence for structural changes at the cellular level, which may account for recovery of function. Although regenerative growth is a rare event in central nervous system structures, it appears that grafting embryonic tissue may facilitate this growth (Bjorklund et al. 1975). Similarly, collateral sprouting, although infrequent, may help account for some recovery (Bach y Rita 1981b; Kerr 1975).

The complete relation of these processes to recovery from brain injury in humans is largely unknown. Knowledge of their existence indicates that the treatment of brain-impaired individuals may not be a futile endeavor. However, most of the work done in the rehabilitation of brain-impaired individuals relies on theories that do not require the recovery of function as means, but rather concentrate on recovery of function as ends.

Recovery of Function as Ends

Proven treatments to facilitate the recovery of function as means are yet in the future. Partly because of our limited knowledge regarding the processes involved, research with human subjects has concentrated on theories of recovery of function as ends. The main thrust here is to recover the behavioral end product of brain functions. Although some theories state that this can be accomplished spontaneously, most theories require either manipulation of the subject's behavior or of the subject's environment.

Theories of spontaneous recovery involve alternate representation. The theory of alternate functional systems allows for spontaneous recovery as well as for the effects of treatment. Retraining and substitution both consider only the effects of treatment.

Theories of Alternate Representation. Some theories state that recovery of function as ends occurs because of redundant representation of cognitive functions in multiple areas of the brain (Rosner 1970). One example of this idea relies on Jackson's (1958) theories of the hierarchical organization of brain functions. Jackson posited that behaviors that may seem identical are subserved by different areas of the brain, depending on specific aspects of the context of the behavior. For example, the behavior of speaking the word *no* is mediated by different areas of the brain, depending on whether automatic speech, volitional speech, or speech under emotional arousal is required. The patient can produce speech when the areas subserving volitional speech are damaged if conditions fostering automaticity or emotional arousal are engendered. Another example of this is in the clinically observed capacity of some aphasic patients to sing verbal communication when declaratory speech is impaired.

Other theories state that recovery of function as ends occurs when homologous regions "learn" to produce the behavior of interest (Bach y Rita 1981a). While recognizing limitations in the actual occurrence of this process, Luria et al. (1969) stated that the possibility of it occurring helps explain recovery in certain cases. This process is more probable for those functions that are usually lateralized. Teuber (1974a) and Milner (1974a) relied on this mechanism to explain some aspects of recovery and stated that it is more probable in younger individuals who have yet to develop the more strict lateralization present in adult individuals. In particular, children with congenital left hemispherectomies will still develop speech capacity. Teuber (1974b) and Milner (1974b) pointed to relative decrements in spatial skills in these children as evidence that the speech functions were developed by the right hemisphere, "crowding" out the full representation of spatial skills in that hemisphere. This idea has been challenged by Woods and Carey (1979) and Dennis and her colleagues (Dennis and Whitaker 1976; Dennis et al. 1981), who argued that although speech does develop in these children, it has different linguistic characteristics than does speech in normal individuals. They presented convincing data to document their proposal but were unable to explain the relative deficits in spatial skills as well as Teuber and Milner.

Alternate Functional Systems. Yet another theory of recovery relies on the concept of the functional system, which is one of the cornerstones of Luria's (1981) theory of brain function. In this theory, observable behaviors are considered to be too complex to be represented in any one area of the brain. Only discrete molecular skills that are unobservable can be strictly localized. The successful production of molar, observable behavior relies on the cooperation of multiple areas of the brain. Luria likened the functional system to a chain. Damage to a given area of the brain (or a certain link of the chain in this metaphor) results in unsuccessful attempts to produce the desired behavior.

These functional systems are learned. However, an alternate functional system may be learned using a replacement link for the damaged one. Through psychological interventions based on learning procedures, the behavior may again be successfully produced. The behavior is first produced only with conscious effort as the individual purposefully uses the alternate link. However, the alternate functional system becomes second nature with practice. In this way, brain-impaired individuals can be rehabilitated by relying on preserved areas of strength. Often these alternate functional systems may be less efficient than the original functional systems in producing the behavior of interest. However, they are more successful and efficient at producing the behavior of interest than are the damaged original functional systems.

Retraining. A different approach relies on intensive retraining to rehabilitate the individual. This retraining is an integral part of the system proposed by Diller and Gordon (1981) and by Reitan (Franzen 1985). In this approach, a deficit is identified and retrained using the learning theory concepts of componential learning, approximation, and reinforcement for success. Diller and Gordon's method is better articulated. The method tries to increase performance by varying the characteristics of the stimulus as well as the complexity demands of the response. Both systems use a standardized battery (the Halstead-Reitan Neuropsychological Battery) to identify areas of deficits. However, while Reitan's approach relied strictly on retraining, Diller and Gordon also attempted to rehabilitate the individual back into a vocational and social setting.

Substitution Methods. Still another type of cognitive rehabilitation relies on the use of behavioral prosthetics or environmental manipulations to rehabilitate the brain-impaired individual. These approaches are sometimes referred to as substitution methods (Rothi and Horner 1983). With the behavioral prosthetic approach, the individual is trained to substitute an intact behavioral response to compensate for deficits. An example of a behavioral prosthetic would be teaching alternate visual scanning procedures to an individual with visual-field defects. With environmental manipulation, aspects of the environment are rearranged so as to reduce the demands on the individual. An example of environmental manipulation would be using color-coded carpeting to demarcate the path an individual needs to take to get to the dining area of a residence hall. There is evidence to suggest that these external strategies may have effects on the brain itself (Bakker 1984). For example, Zihl (1981) found that in training subjects with visual-field cuts to use alternate scanning strategies, their visual field was increased even when the effects of spontaneous recovery were accounted for.

Time Course of Treatment

It is likely that different approaches are necessary explanatory aids at different stages of the rehabilitation process. For example, theories of recovery of functions as means are likely to be important in the early stages of recovery. Even as part of its theory, diachisis is a time-limited operation. The changes in extracellular composition and receptor hypersensitivity can also be seen to have time-limited spheres of possible influence. Some theorists have proposed that therapy at this point should include stimulation with the hope that restitution will be facilitated. As mentioned above, Luria et al. (1969) even suggested a form of chemotherapy during the early stages following traumatic brain injury. This might be followed by a period where therapies that foster brain reorganization are used. Finally, when the patient is 12 to 18 months postinjury, therapy can focus on manipulation of the patient's behavior and environment (Rothi and Horner 1983). These suggestions are highly speculative and are far from universally accepted. However, they do point out the need to fit the rehabilitative therapy to the stage of recovery of the patient.

The early stages of recovery will occur in an inpatient setting, optimally either a coma center or later an inpatient cognitive rehabilitation center. The middle stage of recovery may begin in the inpatient setting, but will continue into the early parts of outpatient rehabilitation, or in a day hospital setting. The late stage of recovery, which not all patients will reach, occurs in an outpatient setting. Because of the changes in staff that accompany transition from one stage to another, it is recommended that there be continuity in the psychiatric care provided for the patient and the patient's family.

The Early Stage of Recovery. The early stage of recovery occurs while the patient is still disoriented. After coming out of the coma, the patient may be confused and disoriented even to person. Treatment here consists largely of providing the necessary nutritional and hygienic needs of the patient. As the patient progresses through the early stages of recovery, more directive interventions may be utilized. For example, the patient may be given the command to raise an arm. If the patient cannot respond accurately, the command may be repeated as the patient's arm is guided through the appropriate motion. The idea is to help the patient regain the connection between the information in the verbal request and the motor output required to satisfy the request. Treatment may also consist of retraining the patient in self-care behaviors such as dressing, bathing, and eating if necessary. Feedback regarding orientation to person and place are provided on a daily basis if necessary. The patient is given cues for the identification of the place in which the patient is being cared for (usually a hospital). Cues are also given for the identification of the

season. These cues are repeated daily until the patient demonstrates accuracy in orientation.

In the early stage of recovery, the patient is not able to benefit from psychotherapy. If conscious, the patient is disoriented and may display signs of restlessness or agitation. The patient will show signs of perplexity and confusion, and may exhibit amnesia. There will be an impaired attentional capacity. At this point, the psychiatrist may be consulted to help control the agitation. Conversely, there may be signs of depression. Although there is heterogeneity of psychiatric symptoms in brain-impaired individuals, it is clear that subjects with cerebral disorders are more likely to manifest psychiatric disturbances than are subjects with peripheral nervous system disorders (DePaulo and Folstein 1978). For example, Lewin et al. (1979) found, in a long-term follow-up study, that individuals who suffer closed head injuries are at risk for endogenous depression. Folstein et al. (1976) compared stroke victims with orthopedic injury victims equated for degree of impairment and found that while only 10 percent of the orthopedic subjects exhibited depression, 45 percent of the stroke victims exhibited depression.

Care must be taken in the pharmacologic treatment of brain-impaired individuals because of the greater risk of developing side effects from antidepressants or antipsychotics (Yudofsky and Silver 1985). Instead of the usual antipsychotics, propranolol has been recommended as a treatment for rage attacks and violent behavior in brain-impaired persons (Yudofsky et al. 1981).

The degree of psychiatric impairment is correlated with the length of posttraumatic amnesia (Lishman 1968). The type of injury may also play a role in the development of specific psychiatric impairment. In a series of penetrating head wounds, Lishman found that lesions of the temporal lobes were more often associated with schizophrenic-like symptoms than lesion of the frontal, occipital, or parietal lobes. For some areas this relationship holds conceptual validity. Memory disorders and disorders of auditory comprehension can easily be seen as conducive to the development of paranoia as the subject feels that people are talking behind his or her back or conspiring to perform a revisionist reconstruction of past conversations or activities involving the patient. The relationship between the injury and the behavioral manifestation may be less obvious in other cases, as in the case of rage attacks following frontal lobe injury (see Chapter 10).

These emotional-behavioral consequences of brain injury are frequent. Some of the consequences may be secondary to metabolic concomitants of the cerebral insult including electrolyte imbalance, anoxic episodes, blood loss, or infection. For these problems, treatment of the primary causative factor is likely to be sufficient for the amelioration of psychological symptoms that are temporary, leaving the more enduring consequences. The behavioral and psychological disability following traumatic brain injury may take several forms. There may be an exacerbation of premorbid personality characteristics, or the disappearance of former coping strategies. The individual may become impulsive or argumentative, and show poor judgment.

Some authors reported the production of schizophrenic-like symptoms following brain injury (Levin et al. 1982). More common is the production of symptoms resembling affective disorders. There is evidence to suggest that a disruption of catecholaminergic (Van Woerkman et al. 1977) or cholinergic (Grossman et al. 1975) processes may be responsible for the affective symptoms. There are other possible reasons for the development of affective symptoms following brain injury. Gainotti (1972) examined affective symptoms in a sample of individuals with lateralized brain damage. He found a fairly consistent catastrophic reaction with left hemisphere damaged subjects and an indifference reaction with right-hemisphere-damaged subjects. He hypothesized that the catastrophic reaction in the left-hemisphere-damaged subjects was an understandable reaction to awareness of the loss of skills consequent on the injury. He further hypothesized that the right-hemisphere-damaged subjects suffered from a form of agnosia in which they did not become aware of the scope of their injuries and therefore did not become depressed.

Alternate explanations also attempt to explain the differential reactions of the two groups of subjects. Heilman and Bowers (1982) related the indifference reaction to an impaired ability of the right-hemisphere-damaged subjects to perceive or express emotional material adequately. Heilman and Bowers noted that both reception and production of affective communication require the perception and manipulation of spatial, tone-oriented, and simultaneous material, all of which are skills that are known to be disrupted by right hemisphere injury (Tucker et al. 1977). Regardless of the etiology of the affective symptoms, pharmacologic treatment should be conservative because of instances of receptor hypersensitivity following traumatic brain injury.

Although the patient may not be receptive to psychotherapy in the early stages of recovery, family members can be targeted as individuals in need (Rosenthal 1984). Crisis intervention methods can also be useful. The first reaction of family members is likely to be shock and disbelief. Because of their very nature, traumatic injuries do not allow family members to prepare themselves emotionally. As a result, the impact of these injuries can be devastating. The family members may be in a state of shock and may need occasional counseling. In addition, family members are unlikely to have a realistic appraisal of the amount of damage. As part of their denial of the seriousness of the injury, they may engage in magical thinking. They may harbor unrealistic expectations that the patient will regain consciousness and resume premorbid functioning in a matter of days. This wishful thinking probably plays an adaptive role in the early states. However, it would not be beneficial to allow these expectations to continue. Gentle but firm reminders of the patient's actual condition and of the usual course of recovery in such cases can be helpful. Family members will also seek out and retain signs that the patient's condition is not that serious. Random movements and reflexive motor activity may be interpreted as purposeful movement. At these times, gentle reality-testing strategies can help the family accept the patient's condition.

Because of medical training, the psychiatrist is in a good position to assess the family's level of understanding of the patient's condition. Modern medical technology can be incomprehensible even to educated laypersons. The hospital and its electronic machinery may seem frightening to the family members, who would then need reassurance. Without an adequate understanding of the actual condition of the patient, family members are free to believe in their own wishes. The psychiatrist can ask the family to restate their conception of the medical procedures to assess the level of understanding.

As postinjury time increases and the patient shows less of the quick recovery that characterizes early stages, family members may become despondent over what they perceive as a lack of progress. Alternately, they may develop anger at the physicians for not "curing" their relative quickly enough. Either of these affective responses are likely to impede treatment of the patient. Therefore it is important that they be recognized early enough to be dealt with in an appropriate fashion instead of waiting until a decision regarding the next course of treatment presents itself. Although some of the most marked psychiatric symptoms occur in the early stages of recovery, a substantial proportion also occur in the middle and late stages (Goethe and Levin 1984).

The Middle Stage of Recovery.   In the middle stage of recovery, the patient is conscious and may be able to care, in part, for basic needs. The pervasive confusion of the early stage is usually not present. Instead, pockets of impairment remain. The area of impairment, as well as the degree of impairment, varies from individual to individual. These will include cognitive as well as psychiatric impairment.

In these stages of recovery, the patient is at least partly able to perform basic self-care behaviors. Treatment will turn to more complex self-care behaviors such as taking responsibility for personal possessions and for meeting needs. Earlier, the patient was only expected to be able to self-feed once food was provided. Now the patient is expected to be able to find the dining room. If there are spatial deficits, these will be treated through analog training methods and by practice of the required behavior in the environment or in a naturalistic setting. The behavior of the patient is given appropriate prompts, which are removed as the performance of the patient improves.

Earlier the patient was provided feedback regarding orientation to person and place. Now the patient is given feedback regarding orientation to time. The patient is taught cues to determine the time of day, such as looking out the window to see if it is light or dark. The patient is reminded to use a clock, or if visual-spatial impairment exists, to use a digital watch.

At this stage, it is possible to identify areas of impairment using a comprehensive assessment technique. Treatment is then directed toward the area of impairment. For example, if the patient demonstrates deficits in color recognition, color identification tasks may be given in occupational therapy (OT). Guided training in OT tasks may also be used to help regain eye-hand coordination. The identified behavioral deficit is broken down into its smallest components, and the patient is started at the level commensurate with current level of competence.

Speech therapy may also be indicated for those individuals who demonstrate deficits in any of the speech-related skills. Depending on the patient's specific problem, there may be training to relearn the symbolic referent nature of words or in articulation. Because speech is so important in our culture, brain-damaged individuals may be more motivated to regain speech skills than they are to regain other skills. Also, because of the importance of speech skills in our culture, successful treatment of speech deficits sometimes precedes attempts to treat other areas.

In the later portions of the middle stage, treatment may also include structured group experiences to provide the patient with learning experiences in social interactions. Supervised expression of feelings and personal wants to other people can help a patient regain social skills. Practice in understanding the communications of others is also an important part of this stage of treatment.

Lezak (1978) outlined some of the more common problems exhibited by individuals in this stage. These include impaired social perceptiveness, impaired capacity for self-control and self-regulation, an impaired capacity to learn from experience (especially social experience), impulsivity, impatience, and restlessness. The psychiatrist may be consulted to help provide a program to manage the patient. Additionally, patients may become distraught over their current condition, losing motivation to remain in the rehabilitative effort. Again, the psychiatrist can be helpful in treating these problems.

Secondarily, but no less importantly, individuals in the social environment may be in need of services from the psychiatrist. Family members may start to exhibit negative affect toward the patient. The patient may be blamed for the occurrence of the traumatic event or for the perceived slow rate of progress. This may be especially true in those cases where the patient demonstrates diminished motivation or an attitude of indifference. These family members can benefit from an opportunity to express these emotions in an appropriate manner or in a nonjudgmental environment.

Muir and Haffey (1984) discussed the reaction of family members in the context of a model of mourning. Certainly, the injury of the patient may represent a loss of the individual in the premorbid role. Acceptance of a realistic appraisal of the patient's extent of injury may result in depressed affect or, in some cases, a full depressive syndrome.

By following the family members, the psychiatrist can propose treatment at early stages of this reaction.

The Late Stage of Recovery. The late stage of cognitive rehabilitation involves the reentry of the individual into society at a level that can realistically be handled. Cognitive rehabilitation at this point is largely directed at behavioral and environmental manipulation, which requires the cooperation of the patient. As discussed earlier, there may not be much potential for brain reorganization by the late stages of recovery, necessitating the reliance on behavioral and environmental prosthetics.

When training of discrete skill areas is complete, the patient can be directed toward linking these discrete areas into molar collections of behaviors that are required for operation in the environment and in the workplace. Here the vocational aspects of rehabilitation become more important than they were in earlier stages. The patient may be guided through analogs of work-task requirements. Feedback regarding speed and accuracy are given, and the patient is encouraged to improve performance.

The patient is usually out of the inpatient setting by this time, either in a group home or some other form of sheltered care. Here there is ample opportunity to provide supervised experience in social interactions. Social skills are important for success in both the residential and the workplace setting. Treatment aimed at increasing the level of social skills can have an essential role in ensuring the success of the entire rehabilitation program.

The psychiatrist can provide consultation on increasing compliance of the patient to the treatment regimen at this stage. As the patient attempts to resume normal activity, there may be discouragement because of the extreme difficulty in performing what used to be simple tasks. The patient may also experience anxiety and exhibit apprehension when faced with the reentry process. Addressing these concerns can facilitate the rehabilitation process.

The family is also in need of intervention. The patient formerly occupied a position in the social arrangement of the family. Now the roles are likely to be drastically changed. A new level of stability needs to be reached. Families may be unable to adjust to the changes efficiently, especially as the patient returns home. Besides the financial and emotional burden occasioned on the family members, there are time burdens. Rehabilitation may now be conducted in an outpatient setting. Because patients may be unable to transport themselves to the clinic, family members are called on to provide that service. Also the cognitive rehabilitation is likely to contain a significant home practice component that is a further demand on the time of family members. A former wage earner is now a dependent, meaning that another member of the family has to assume the wage-earner role. All of this may contribute to feelings of resentment, which can subvert even the best-planned rehabilitation effort. Family counseling sessions may help to identify and treat these problems.

☐ CONCLUSION

The rehabilitation of brain-impaired individuals is a multidisciplinary endeavor. The psychiatrist can provide necessary services at each stage of the process. Behavioral and emotional disturbances are extremely common following brain injury. Left untreated, these disturbances can severely limit rehabilitation of the brain-impaired individual. Family members may also be seen as in need of psychiatric services. However, the psychiatrist who wishes to provide these services must first be acquainted with theories of recovery and with the different types of rehabilitation. This chapter can be used only as a starting point.

☐ REFERENCES

Agid Y, Javoy F, Glowinski J: Hyperactivity of remaining dopaminergic neurones after partial destruction of the nigro-striatal dopaminergic system in the rat. Nature 245:150–151, 1973

Bach y Rita P: Brain plasticity as a basis for development of rehabilitation procedures for hemiplegia. Scand J Rehabil Med 13:73–83, 1981a

Bach y Rita P: Central nervous system lesions: sprouting and unmasking in rehabilitation. Arch Phys Med Rehabil 62:413–417, 1981b

Bakker DJ: The brain as dependent measure. Clin Neuropsychol 6:1–16, 1984

Bjorklund A, Baumgarten HG, Lachemayer L, et al: Recovery of brain noradrenaline after 5, 7-dihydroxy-tryptamine-induced axonal lesions in the rat. Cell Tissue Res 161:145–155, 1975

Caveness W: Incidences of cranial-cerebral trauma in the United States. Transactions of the American Neurological Association 102:136–138, 1977

Dennis M, Whitaker HA: Language acquisition following

hemidecortication: linguistics of the left over the right hemisphere. Brain Lang 3:404–433, 1976

Dennis M, Lovett M, Weigl-Crump CA: Written language acquisition after left or right hemidecortication in infancy. Brain Lang 12:54–91, 1981

DePaulo JR, Folstein MF: Psychiatric disturbances in neurological patients: detection, recognition, and hospital course. Ann Neurol 4:225–228, 1978

Diller L, Gordon WA: Rehabilitation and clinical neuropsychology, in Handbook of Clinical Neuropsychology. Edited by Boll TJ, Filskov SA. New York, John Wiley & Sons, 1981

Finger S, Stein DG: Brain Damage and Recovery: Research and Clinical Perspectives. New York, Academic Press, 1982

Folstein MF, Maiberger R, McHugh PR: Mood disorder as a specific complication of stroke. J Neurol Neurosurg Psychiatry 40:1018–1020, 1976

Franzen MD: Reitan Evaluation of Hemispheric Abilities and Brain Improvement Training, in Test Critiques, Vol. 2. Edited by Keyser DJ, Sweetland RC, Kansas City, Test Corporation of America, 1985

Gainotti G: Emotional behavior and hemispheric side of lesion. Cortex 8:41–55, 1972

Garoutte B, Aird RB: Behavioral effects of head injury, Psychiatric Annals 14:507–514, 1984

Goethe KE, Levin HS: Behavioral manifestations during the early and longterm stages of recovery after closed head injury. Psychiatric Annals 14:540–546, 1984

Grossman R, Beyer C, Kelly P, et al: Acetylcholine and related enzymes in human ventricular and subarachnoidal fluids following brain injury. Proceedings of the Fifth Annual Meeting of the Society for Neurosciences 76:506, 1975

Hefti F, Melamed E, Wurtman RJ: Partial lesions of the dopaminergic nigro-striatal system in rat brain: biochemical characterization. Brain Res 195:123–137, 1980

Heilman K, Bowers D: Affective disorders induced by hemispheric dysfunction, in The Neurology of Aphasia. Edited by Kirshner HS, Freeman FR. Lisse, Swets & Zeitlinger BV, 1982

Jackson JH: Selected Writings. New York, Basic Books, 1958

Kalat JW: Biological Psychology. Belmont, Calif, Wadsworth, 1981

Kerr FWL: Structural and functional evidence of plasticity in the central nervous system. Exp Neurol 48:16–31, 1975

LeVere TE: Neural stability, sparing, and behavioral recovery following brain damage. Psychol Rev 82:344–358, 1975

LeVere TE: Recovery of function after brain damage: a theory of the behavioral deficit. Physiological Psychology 8:297–308, 1980

LeVere ND, LeVere TE: Recovery of function following brain damage: support for the compensation theory of behavioral deficits. Physiological Psychology 10:165–174, 1982

Levin HS, Benton AL, Grossman RG: Neurobehavioral consequences of closed head injury. New York, Oxford University Press, 1982

Lewin W, Marshall TF de C, Roberts AH: Long term outcome after severe head injury. Br Med J 2:1533–1538, 1979

Lezak MD: Subtle sequelae of brain damage: perplexity, distractibility, and fatigue, Am J Phys Med 57:9–15, 1978

Lishman WA: Brain damage in relation to psychiatric disability after head injury. Br J Psychiatry 114:373–418, 1968

Luria AR: Higher Cortical Functions in Man (2nd ed). New York, Basic Books, 1981

Luria AR, Nayden VL, Tsvetkova LS, et al: Restoration of higher cortical function following local brain damage, in Handbook of Clincial Neurology, Vol. 3. Edited by Vinken PJ, Bruyn GW. Amsterdam, North-Holland, 1969

Marshall JF: Brain function: neural adaptations and recovery from injury. Annu Rev Psychol 35:277–308, 1984

Miller E: Recovery and Management of Neuropsychological Impairments. New York, John Wiley & Sons, 1984

Milner B: Hemispheric specialization: scope and limits, in The Neurosciences Third Study Program. Edited by Schmitt FO, Worden FG. Cambridge Mass, MIT Press, 1974a

Milner B: Sparing of language function after unilateral brain damage. Neurosci Res Program Bull 12:213–217, 1974b

Muir CA, Haffey WJ: Psychological and neuropsychological interventions in the mobile mourning process, in Behavioral Assessment and Rehabilitation of the Traumatically Brain-Damaged. Edited by Edelstein BA, Couture ET. New York, Plenum, 1984

Rosenthal M: Strategies for intervention with families of brain injured patients, in Behavioral Assessment and Rehabilitation of the Traumatically Brain-Damaged. Edited by Edelstein BA, Couture ET. New York, Plenum, 1984

Rosner BS: Brain function. Annu Rev Psychol 21:555–594, 1970

Rothi LJ, Horner J: Two theories of recovery with applications to neurobehavioral treatment. J Clin Neuropsychol 5:73–81, 1983

Teuber HL: Recovery of function after lesions of the central nervous system: history and prospects. Neurosci Res Program Bull 12:197–209, 1974a

Teuber HL: Why two brains? in The Neurosciences Third Study Program. Edited by Schmitt FO, Worder FG, Cambridge, Mass, MIT Press, 1974b

Tucker D, Watson R, Heilman K: Affective discrimination and evocation in patients with right parietal disease. Neurology (NY) 27:947–950, 1977

Van Woerkman TCAM, Teeklan AW, Minderhoud JM: Differences in neurotransmitter metabolism in frontotemporal lobe contusion and diffuse cerebral contusion. Lancet 1:812–823, 1977

von Monakow C: Die Lokalisation im Grossheim und der Abbau der Funktion durch Kortikale Herde. Wiesbaden, JF Bergmann, 1914

Woods BT, Carey S: Language deficits after apparent recovery from childhood aphasia. Ann Neurol 6:405–409, 1979

Yudofsky SC, Silver JM: Psychiatric aspects of brain injury: trauma, stroke and tumor, in Psychiatry Update: The American Psychiatric Association Annual Review. Edited by Hales RE, Frances AJ. Washington, DC, American Psychiatric Press, 1985

Yudofsky SC, Williams D, Gorman J: Propanolol in the treatment of rage and violent behavior in patients with chronic brain syndromes. Am J Psychiatry 138:218–220, 1981

Zihl J: Recovery of visual function in patients with cerebral blindness. Exp Brain Res 44:159–169, 1981

Legal Aspects of Neuropsychiatry

Robert M. Wettstein, M.D.

NEUROPSYCHIATRY PRESENTS A VAST ARRAY of legal psychiatric issues to the clinician and researcher. Of necessity, then, this chapter can only selectively highlight certain clinical legal issues as they pertain to neuropsychiatry. A comprehensive discussion of legal psychiatry is beyond the scope of the present effort, and the interested reader is referred to the numerous texts in this area (Cavenar 1985; Gutheil and Appelbaum 1982; Halleck 1980; Stone 1975; Slovenko 1973, 1985).

This chapter will provide a brief overview of some conceptual and methodical issues in psychiatry and the law. It will subsequently describe certain legal principles in several areas of the criminal and civil law, which will than be applied to various areas in the diagnosis and treatment of neuropsychiatric disorders.

☐ OVERVIEW OF LAW AND PSYCHIATRY

The general field of psychiatry and the law may be divided loosely into two subareas. Law and psychiatry, or the legal regulation of psychiatry, deals with those aspects of constitutional, statutory, and regulatory law that define its practice. Once internally regulated or self-regulated, the practice of psychiatry has shifted toward a system of external and governmental control. Law in the practice of psychiatry thus raises issues of informed consent, voluntary and involuntary treatment, professional negligence (malpractice), liability for acts to third parties, confidentiality, evidentiary privilege, record keeping, billing practices, employment contracts, staff privileges, advertising, relationships with nonphysician health care providers, and insurance for health care.

In some cases, the law goes as far as to define mental illness in its mental health code, forbid certain mental disorders (e.g., alcohol abuse, substance abuse, mental retardation, dementia) from involuntary treatment, prohibit certain forms of psychiatric treatment entirely (e.g., electroconvulsive therapy or ECT, psychosurgery). In this area of psychiatry and the law, patients' rights are both delineated and limited; practitioners' privileges are defined yet constrained.

Distinguished from law and psychiatry, psychiatry in the practice of law, or forensic psychiatry, is the application of psychiatry to legal issues for legal purposes. In this case, psychiatric intervention is directed primarily to legal issues in which the patient is involved; psychiatric consultation relates primarily to the ends of the legal system, not with the therapeutic needs of the patient (Gross and Weinberger 1982). The forensic psychiatrist provides psychiatric data and consultation in such areas as competency to stand trial, criminal responsibility for an alleged offense, competency to be sentenced for criminal charges, competency to make a will (testamentary capacity), child custody, termination of parental rights, personal injury, and workers' compensation (posttraumatic stress disorder).

The principles of forensic psychiatry differ in significant respects from those of the practice of general psychiatry. The general psychiatrist serves the patient and secondarily society; the forensic psychiatrist primarily serves a third party (e.g., the patient's lawyer, the court, or other individuals involved in the legal system). The forensic psychiatrist, influenced by legal values, goals, and principles, responds to legal inquiries rather than clinical ones (Rappeport 1982). This application of the use of psychiatry for legal purposes converts the forensic psychiatrist to an agent of society; the psychiatrist must attempt to answer specific legal questions by translating psychiatric knowledge or data about the patient-litigant into the language of the legal profession. The forensic psychiatrist must be familiar with the specific legal standard, definition, or rule at litigation and must be knowledgeable about the legal meaning of all psychiatric terms (e.g., mental illness) in the case in question.

It is important to note, too, that psychiatry and the law (and by corollary psychiatric and judicial decision making) derive from and reflect different conceptual and ideological traditions. For years these differences have been noted to contribute to the conflict and antagonism of their respective adherents. For one, medicine and psychiatry rely on deductive reasoning (drawing conclusions from the general to the particular) whereas the law prefers inductive reasoning (from the specific case to the broader principle). Second, the adversarial nature and process of the judicial system in the United States finds no parallel in the collaborative relationships of mental health professionals. Third, mental health professionals are primarily con-

cerned with individual patients' needs and welfare whereas the judicial system focuses on their rights. Fourth, scientific reality, the result of empirical study and research, is fundamentally different from judicial reality, a product of legal precedent (stare decisis) and rules of evidence (Gutheil and Mills 1982). Lastly, the law is primarily concerned with correcting past wrongs (achieving justice) whereas medicine focuses on accessing and controlling biologic events in the present and the future (Rachlin 1985).

Medical and judicial decision making also differ with regard to concepts of causation. The law postulates that individuals retain free will, the ability to decide how to conduct themselves. Medicine and psychiatry, however, whether biologic or psychological, reflect a determinism that minimizes free choice. The law carefully delineates procedures through which decisions are rendered (procedural law); the clinical practice of medicine and psychiatry emphasizes the substantive factors.

The law also carefully defines the levels of conviction (standards of proof) for legal decision making. The law requires that an individual will be convicted of a crime when the evidence against the defendant has been presented "beyond a reasonable doubt" (with a certainty that exceeds 95 percent). Similarly, the patient may be involuntarily hospitalized in a psychiatric hospital when evidence of mental illness and dangerousness are presented to a "clear and convincing" standard (approximately 75 percent certainty). Lastly, a psychiatrist is found negligent in the patient's treatment when evidence of professional misconduct is presented to a "preponderance of the evidence" standard (beyond 50 percent certainty). The degree of certainty with which the physician makes a diagnosis of temporal epilepsy or prescribes treatment for delirium, for example, is no doubt rarely conceptualized in such a manner. The clinician rarely rejects statements of third parties whereas the court rarely permits them (hearsay).

CRIMINAL LAW

Criminal Competency

Legal Principles. According to the common law, several competency issues can be raised prior to trial when an individual is charged with a criminal offense. These may be generically referred to as criminal competencies and include competency to waive Miranda rights (competency to confess), to testify at trial, to stand trial, to be sentenced, and, particularly, to be executed. Competency to stand trial, the most frequently raised issue, has been said to be the most significant mental health inquiry in the criminal justice system (Stone 1975).

Questions about the defendant's competency to stand trial, or any of the component competencies (including competency to plead or plea bargain), develop whenever a defense attorney, prosecuting attorney, or judge believes that the defendant's mental condition may interfere with the defendant's capacity to participate in the trial process. The issue of competency to stand trial relates only to the defendant's mental condition at the time of the hearing; in contrast, criminal responsibility deals with the defendant's condition at the time of the alleged crime. A defendant's competency to stand trial, therefore, may fluctuate over time prior to trial.

The competency to stand trial doctrine has common law origins that related to the prohibition of trying a defendant in absentia. In contemporary times, a determination of the defendant's competency to stand trial serves several needs of the judicial system. First, the competent defendant, present in both body and mind, is able to provide an attorney with essential information, especially when known only to the defendant. Second, the defendant could not be said to have been fairly convicted unless able to understand the defenses, their consequences, and the nature of the proceedings. Third, retribution and individual deterrence, both aims of the criminal law, could not be well served if the defendant failed to understand the reason for the trial. Last, it has been argued that the judicial process is demeaned if the defendant is disruptive during hearings and trial (Stone 1975).

The United States Supreme Court has held that a trial judge has a duty to raise the competency issue when a bona fide doubt as to the defendant's competency is evident, even when the defendant fails to raise the issue (Pate v Robinson, 383 U.S. 375, 1966).

Prevailing legal criteria for competency of defendant are: "Whether he has sufficient present ability to consult with his lawyer with a reasonable degree of rational understanding, and whether he has a rational as well as factual understanding of the proceedings against him" (Dusky v U.S. 363 U.S. 402, 1960). Several components of this defi-

nition have been specified: the defendant's appraisal of available legal defenses, quality of the relationship with the attorney, planning of legal strategy, appraisal of the roles of courtroom participants, understanding of courtroom procedure, appreciation of charges, appreciation of the nature and severity of possible penalties, appraisal of likely outcomes, capacity to challenge prosecution witnesses, and capacity to testify relevantly and behave manageably (McGarry 1973).

A defendant whose competency to stand trial has been questioned may be detained, usually in correctional facilities without the privilege of being released on bail. Prolonged inpatient examinations may occur, depending on local statutory or procedural requirements, availability of local psychiatrists, or the custom of the court. Physical and psychiatric examinations, laboratory studies, psychological tests, family interviews, and observations of the defendant's behavior over a period of time may be used in formulating the psychiatric expert's opinion about the defendant's competency.

In most jurisdictions, the competency issue is decided by the court, although some jurisdictions allow a jury determination. While the psychiatric and psychological experts are permitted to testify about the defendant's mental and physical condition and, in their opinion, competency to stand trial, the ultimate decision of the defendant's competence is made by the trier of fact. Contested hearings, with multiple mental health professionals providing psychiatric input about the defendant's current mental status, diagnosis, and prognosis throughout the anticipated period of trial, sometimes occur.

If the court determines that the defendant is incompetent to stand trial, the defendant may be remanded for inpatient psychiatric treatment without a civil commitment hearing for treatment to render the defendant competent to stand trial. Treatment duration may be prolonged but is limited to a period defined by statute or that necessary to determine if restoration of competency is foreseeable. While some statutes and case law have limited the duration of incompetency commitments to the maximum sentence authorized for the offense charged, others may permit extended periods of incarceration for many years, particularly in the case of the most severe offenses.

Once a defendant has been restored to competency to stand trial and adjudicated at a subsequent due process hearing, the defendant is remanded to stand trial. Given the fluctuating nature of many psychiatric disorders, subsequent reexaminations for incompetency or recommitments as incompetent may occur should the patient relapse. Criminal charges are sometimes dismissed if minor, particularly if the patient has been confined and treated at a psychiatric hospital for a period of time and can be returned to the community. A continuing dilemma exists, however, for those defendants who can never be restored to fitness for trial. Many such individuals fail to meet civil commitment criteria, yet cannot be maintained indefinitely in a hospital as incompetent to stand trial.

Defendants determined to be incompetent to be sentenced or executed are managed similarly to those alleged or determined to be incompetent to stand trial. After conviction, those determined to be incompetent to be sentenced or executed may be remanded for psychiatric treatment to restore their competency for sentencing or execution. These competencies relate to the accused's ability at the present time to understand the nature and purposes of the proceedings, and his ability to collaborate effectively in them, in contrast to mental status at the time of the previous criminal offense.

Applications to Neuropsychiatry. Defendants with neuropsychiatric disorders present a complex array of problems to the criminal justice system with regard to criminal competency. It should be noted at the outset that the presence of a psychiatric disorder, even schizophrenia, does not per se render the defendant incapable of standing trial. Most empirical studies of criminal defendants referred to competency evaluations reveal that functional psychiatric disorders rather than neuropsychiatric ones predominate (Reich and Wells 1985). Yet individuals with irreversible dementia, seizure disorder, cerebral vascular disease, head trauma, substance-induced organic mental disorders, organic affective disorders, organic personality disorders, and functional or organic amnesias are commonly evaluated or adjudicated for incompetency to stand trial, incompetency to waive Miranda rights, and incompetency to be sentenced.

Any psychiatric disorder (whether functional or neuropsychiatric) that presents with significant impairment in cognitive or communicative capabilities is likely to affect the defendant's criminal competency. Impairments in sensorium, concen-

tration, language, speech, intellectual capacity, memory, behavioral control, affective stability, judgment, problem solving, abstracting ability, spatial recognition, or orientation may render a defendant unfit to stand trial. In such cases, it is critical to relate the neuropsychiatric impairment to the specific demands of the legal process for the defendant. In conjunction with a comprehensive neuropsychiatric examination and laboratory assessment of the defendant, an assessment must be made as to the defendant's current ability to cooperate with counsel and participate in the criminal proceedings, as well as the capacity to do so for the foreseeable time of the criminal proceedings. Defendants who are initially confined as incompetent on the basis of a significantly reversible disorder (e.g., substance-induced hallucinations) may, over a period of time, regain lost neuropsychiatric function to a degree that permits trial competency. Other defendants, with profound intellectual or speech deficits on the basis of significant head trauma, may safely be said never to be likely to be restored to sufficient competency to stand trial. Sometimes such prognostic statements, however, should not be offered until adequate longitudinal assessment of the defendant's functioning has been conducted while adjudicated incompetent. Similarly, treatable emotional or behavioral changes associated with traumatic brain injury, cerebral vascular disease, or tumor—such as affective lability, anxiety, psychosis, episodic dyscontrol, and impulsivity—may, after psychiatric hospitalization and intervention, permit restoration of competency. Assessment of prognosis in such cases requires review of the defendant's premorbid personality and psychological functioning, given that many defendants with new and treatable organic lesions have had preexisting impulsivity, aggressivity, behavior disorder, and previous arrests or convictions.

Comprehensive neuropsychiatric assessments and laboratory procedures, while frequently available outside of the criminal justice system, may not be easily obtained in the public sector criminal justice and forensic facilities where many such individuals are referred. The need for experienced and qualified personnel and facilities in such situations cannot be overstated. Special arrangements for appropriate referrals to qualified personnel outside the forensic facility must frequently be arranged, despite their significant cost.

Amnesia is perhaps one of the most frequent neuropsychiatric impairments seen in the pretrial forensic psychiatric arena. Defendants commonly claim to fail to remember the alleged criminal conduct, or a significant period of time during which it allegedly occurred. This may be consistent with the prevalent use of intoxicating substances during the course of many criminal offenses (Collins 1981). Although it may appear to the observer that the defendant's memory for the alleged criminal offense would be particularly critical to the ability to defend oneself, amnesia is not in practice given much support for an incompetency plea, whether the amnesia is organic or functional in nature (Annotation 1972; Koson and Robey 1973). Defendants adjudicated incompetent to stand trial on the basis of functional or reversible neuropsychiatric disorders with associated amnesia often find that psychiatric treatment in the form of psychotropic medication or psychotherapy facilitates the recovery of lost events. Malingered amnesia, often suspected, may also dissipate spontaneously over time.

The use of psychotropic medication may be critical to restoring the defendant's competency to stand trial. While courts are undoubtedly unconcerned by a diabetic defendant's need to take insulin during the trial, they have not uniformly accepted competency of patients restored by psychotropics. Some courts have referred to these patients as "synthetically sane" and have demanded that the accused come to trial free from psychotropic medication. Additionally, psychotropics (including anticonvulsant medications) may have side effects that interfere with a defendant's cognitive and communicative abilities prior to and during trial (Rivinus 1982). Use of such medications in such circumstances might be counterproductive. Occasionally, too, defense attorneys prefer that their clients be removed from medication to appear as bizarre as possible during their criminal trial for purposes of trial tactics. Consultation with the defendant's attorneys and the court is sometimes necessary around these issues (Winick 1977).

Criminal Responsibility

Legal Principles. Psychiatric participation in the adjudication of criminal responsibility of a defendant for an alleged offense has been accompanied by considerable controversy for many years. A brief review of several aspects of the criminal law is necessary to an understanding of the psychiatrist's role in this area.

Under our current system of law, criminal responsibility cannot occur in the absence of a blame-

worthy state of mind. Evidentiary proof of this state of mind must be legally established by the court or jury. Thus, with few exceptions, such as traffic offenses or regulatory offenses, there are two central components to a criminal offense: antisocial conduct (actus reus) and criminal intent (mens rea). Current social policy in criminal law is based on the belief that an individual cannot be held culpable for committing a crime if he lacks the mens rea or criminal intent for that act. For example, homicide may be committed by accident, in self-defense, under duress, under the influence of substance use, as a result of a mental disease or defect, by a 4-year-old child, or with premeditation and deliberation; the law individualizes responsibility for the offense accordingly. The mental or culpability elements of an offense may be purpose (or intention), knowledge, recklessness, negligence, or lack of culpability with regard to engaging in the conduct or being aware of its circumstances.

The law recognizes a great variety of identifiable conditions or circumstances that may preclude conviction for an offense. These may include alibi, amnesia, brainwashing, convulsion, defense of others or property, diplomatic immunity, duress, entrapment, executive immunity, extreme emotional disturbance, impaired consciousness, insanity, voluntary and involuntary intoxication, justification, mistake of law or fact, necessity, provocation, self-defense, somnambulism, subnormality, and unconsciousness (Robinson 1982). Traditional defenses using evidence of psychiatric conditions and disorders generally fall into three broad categories. First, evidence of psychiatric disorder at the time of an alleged offense may be used to negate the mens rea necessary for conviction to occur. Thus the defendant would lack the mens rea required for the crime, and acquittal on that charge would result. Intoxication or delirium at the time of an alleged offense, for example, may be used to rebut the premeditation required for a conviction of first-degree murder in some jurisdictions. The presence of intoxication or delirium might not, however, bar conviction for a lesser criminal charge (e.g., manslaughter). In this case, evidence of mental disorder is not a complete defense but merely a means of reducing the criminal charge. Thus mental disorder here may be used to negate some or all elements of a criminal offense. This has sometimes been referred to as the mens rea approach to diminished capacity (Morse 1979).

Second, the defendant's mental condition at the time of a criminal offense may relieve the defendant of criminal liability through the special verdict of insanity. In this case, the defendant's mental disease or defect fails to negate the mens rea elements of the offense, as in the case of a delusional individual who intentionally kills another in response to the delusional thought. Such a mental disorder exonerates the defendant from criminal responsibility when it impairs cognitive and volitional capacity to conform conduct to the law, according to the legal insanity standard of each jurisdiction. Under the M'Naghten standard, a defendent can establish a defense of insanity when it has been clearly proved that, at the time of the act, the defendant was laboring under such defective reasoning from disease of the mind as not to know the nature and quality of the act; or, if the defendant did know it, that the defendant did not know that what was being done was wrong. The American Law Institute standard incorporates a volitional test with the cognitive test of M'Naghten: A person is not responsible for criminal conduct if at the time of such conduct, as a result of mental disease or defect, the person lacks substantial capacity either to appreciate the criminality of the conduct or to conform conduct to the requirements of the law. The American Psychiatric Association (1983) recommended a compromise of these two standards: "A person charged with a criminal offense should be found not guilty by reason of insanity if it is shown that as a result of mental disease or mental retardation he was unable to appreciate the wrongfulness of his conduct at the time of his offense" (p. 685). With rare exceptions, the special verdict of insanity, in one form or another, is available to a criminal defendant in all state and federal jurisdictions.

Subsequent to an acquittal of the charges by reason of insanity, the acquittee may be subjected to involuntary hospitalization under the supervision of a civil or criminal court for prolonged periods of time. The defendant may be held in some secure psychiatric facility independently from other civilly committed psychiatric patients.

Third, psychiatric disorder at the time of a criminal offense may be used to find a defendant guilty but mentally ill (GBMI) of the charges in those jurisdictions that have such statutes. Here the defendant has been found to have a mental illness at the time of commitment of the alleged offense, but that mental illness is not sufficient to acquit the defendent by reason of insanity. A patient with a schizophrenic disorder may, for example, be found GBMI on charges of theft or burglary when the criminal conduct occurs independently of the psychiatric disorder, despite its presence at the time of the offense. Defendants found GBMI are customarily referred to correctional facilities where treatment may or may not be provided, depending on the needs of the patient and the resources of the system.

Applications to Neuropsychiatry. The role of the psychiatric expert in criminal responsibility evaluations is to provide medical fact or opinion when relevant to the ultimate legal determination. The forensic psychiatrist is initially required to identify the medical and psychiatric data applicable to psychiatric disorders, and then to relate these data to the legally defined mental disorder and ultimate legal standards of criminal responsibility. In practical terms, the psychiatrist must decide whether or not the defendant was mentally ill at the time of the alleged offense, was able to appreciate the wrongfulness of the behavior, and had the capacity to control the behavior at the time of the offense, and whether the psychiatric disorder relates to the legal tests at issue (Bursten 1982).

The few empirical studies that exist in the area indicate that a wide variety of psychiatric diagnoses are made of individuals acquitted by reason of insanity. While a diagnosis of some form of schizophrenic disorder is made in approximately two-thirds of insanity acquittees at the time of hospitalization following acquittal, neuropsychiatric disorders may represent 10 to 15 percent of all diagnoses (Pasewark et al. 1979). Substance abuse disorders, whether primary or secondary, are also highly represented among insanity acquittees. Neuropsychiatric disorders are even more prevalent among defendants referred for criminal responsibility evaluations regardless of outcome. Such research is often confounded by the significant time interval between criminal offense and psychiatric examination, such that the disorder may remit after a brief period of incarceration or hospitalization.

Certainly one of the major areas of controversy in determinations of criminal responsibility relates to the scope of the definition of mental disease or defect for purposes of exculpation. Defendants have been acquitted of criminal charges on the basis of nonpsychotic disorders in a substantial percentage of cases (Pasewark 1981) in certain jurisdictions. It has been argued that disorders such as posttraumatic stress disorder, pathologic gambling, multiple personality, pedophilia, antisocial personality disorder, or other disorders of volition or behavior should not be permitted to support the special defense of insanity (Rachlin et al. 1984). The traditional legal criteria for granting exculpation or diminished capacity has depended on the presence of major mental disorder of psychotic proportions, whether functional or organic. Thus severe disorders of intellectual or behavioral control, such as dementia, organic delusional syndrome, organic hallucinatory syndrome, or organic affective syndrome, may fall within the rubric of disorders eligible for exculpation.

The task of the forensic neuropsychiatrist and neuropsychologist in these cases is to complete a diagnostic assessment of the defendant, not at the present time, but at the time of the alleged criminal offense, some time previously. The criminal responsibility evaluation, noted by the Supreme Court as a constitutional right of each criminal defendant when mental status at the time of an offense is at issue (Ake v Oklahoma, 105 S. Ct. 1087, 1985), thus entails a retrospective reconstruction of the defendant's mental condition at a previous point in time rather than an assessment of current functioning. It is frequently necessary in such situations to supplement one's evaluation with corroborating evidence of the defendant's earlier mental state through reports or statements of witnesses and victims of the crime; friends and relatives of the defendant; or earlier medical, psychiatric, and neuropsychiatric evaluations. Current laboratory or neuropsychological evaluations may or may not provide helpful data about the defendant's earlier psychiatric condition, depending on the nature of the disorder. These data would be useful, where the neuropsychiatrist is asked to evaluate the defendant subsequent to acquittal by reason of insanity to ascertain the appropriate disposition. Reconstruction of the defendant's earlier mental status is frequently complicated by the spontaneous resolution of the neuropsychiatric disorder at the time of the offense, or as a result of treatment provided during incarceration pending trial.

Further complexities of the evaluation are often presented by the defendant's prevalent use of alcohol or illicit substances during the course of the criminal conduct. As noted earlier, simple intoxication at the time of a criminal offense may permit a partial but not complete defense against the criminal charges. When substance use eventuates in bona fide psychotic symptoms such as hallucinations, delusions, or thought disorder, however, the substance-induced mental disorder (even if voluntary) may sufficiently impair the defendant's cognitive and volitional capacities so as to permit a complete defense of insanity.

Fluctuating neuropsychiatric disorders also present special problems to the criminal responsibility evaluation. It must be recalled that this evaluation focuses exclusively on the defendant's mental condition at the time of the alleged offense; *insanity*, a legal term, is, in a manner of speaking, always temporary. Problems are also presented by the individual who displays a chronic behavior disorder with antisocial features, who may have clinically evident attentional deficit, learning disability, soft neurologic signs, or a variety of specific neuropsychiatric deficits in the absence of a formal DSM-III-R Axis I disorder (American Psychiatric Association 1987). Courts may essentially consider such individuals as having antisocial personality disorders, inappropriate for complete or partial psychiatric defenses.

Perhaps the most problematic of all criminal responsibility determinations in neuropsychiatry pertain to the epileptic. As noted earlier, the elements of a criminal offense include both objective and mens rea elements. A defendant is not guilty of a criminal offense unless the defendant's conduct includes a voluntary act, usually considered to be part of the objective element of the offense. Evidence of unconsciousness or automatism constitutes a defense to a crime in either of two ways: by negating the actus reus (i.e., the criminal act is not a voluntary one) or by the defense of insanity. Some courts or statutes have explicitly held that automatism or unconsciousness constitutes a distinct defense to a crime; others have held that this represents a type of insanity defense (Annotation 1984). In the former case, no evidence of mental disease, mental defect, or mental illness need be presented, as in the latter. The distinction is more than semantic. Automatism as a recognized defense may result in unconditional acquittal; as a form of insanity defense, however, it may result in acquittal with subsequent prolonged and possibly inappropriate psychiatric hospitalization (cf. Matter of Torsney, 394 N.E. 2d 262, NY 1979). The confused state of the law in this area, which pertains particularly to epilepsy (motorist liability), head trauma, and somnambulism (Oswald and Evans 1985), reflects the hesitancy on the part of the legislatures and judiciary to expand avenues of criminal exculpation.

Criminal behavior may occur ictally, postictally, or interictally; particular attention has been directed to ictal violence. Several epidemiologic studies in correctional populations have noted that the prevalence of epilepsy in jails and prisons exceeds that of age-matched nonprisoner controls. This may, however, be a reflection of socioeconomic factors, including head trauma in correctional populations, rather than evidence of any intrinsic relationship between epilepsy and aggression (Whitman et al. 1984). Gunn (1981) noted that several relationships between antisocial conduct and epilepsy may be inferred: (1) antisocial act caused by a seizure; (2) cerebral malfunction causing both epilepsy and antisocial behavior; (3) antisocial behavior with the consequence of low self-esteem and social rejection suffered by patients with epilepsy; (4) antisocial behavior symptomatic of a mental disorder as a result of epilepsy; (5) psychosocial environmental deprivations causing both epilepsy and antisocial behavior; and (6) antisocial behavior that produces accidental brain trauma.

Delineation of the precise relationship between epilepsy and antisocial behavior must be undertaken in the criminal responsibility evaluation. Interictal criminal behavior as a result of an epileptic's shame, humiliation, and social rejection would be unlikely to support a defense of insanity. On the other hand, criminal conduct as a result of a psychotic episode in an epileptic may support an insanity defense (Bacon and Benedek 1982).

Nevertheless, many defense attorneys have presented epilepsy as a defense to criminal charges for their clients; as of 1981, some 15 such cases had reached the appellate courts (Delgado-Escueta et al. 1981). Most reports tend to indicate that directed ictal violence occurs extremely rarely, if at all (Gunn and Fenton 1971). Stereotypic acts, particularly of a defensive nature, may occasionally occur during an ictal episode and may technically constitute criminal conduct. Postictal violence and aggression, however, may be a more prevalent if unappreciated concern (Devinsky and Bear 1984).

In an attempt to standardize practice in this area, Delgado-Escueta et al. (1981) presented five criteria to determine whether a seizure resulted in a specific violent crime: (1) the diagnosis of epilepsy should be established by a neurologist with special competence in seizure disorders; (2) the presence of an epileptic automatism should be documented by electroencephalogram (EEG) telemetry and closed circuit television; (3) ictal aggression should be verified in a videotape-recorded seizure with concomitant epileptiform patterns on EEG; (4) the patient's aggressive or violent acts should be characteristic of the patient's seizure disorder according to the history; and (5) a neurologist should provide a clinical judgment that the alleged crime is the result of a seizure episode.

Such a procedure is further complicated by the occasional claim that the defendant's criminal behavior and seizure episode were precipitated by the ingestion of alcohol or other nonprescription substances. EEGs conducted during the use of alcohol in laboratories are sometimes performed to assess this possibility; documentation of the validity of their use for this purpose remains unclear. Courts have generally held that impaired consciousness or automatic behavior due to the voluntary use of alcohol and/or drugs can only serve to rebut the specific intent or element of an offense, rather than result in acquittal of all charges (Annotation 1984).

☐ CIVIL LAW

Personal Injury and Workers' Compensation

Legal Principles. Under tort law, the law of civil wrongs, physical and emotional injuries sustained by a plaintiff may sometimes be compensated by the defendant—tort-feasor. Although particular acts may be both criminal and tortious, this discussion will focus on civil rather than criminal litigation.

A successful tort action (e.g., personal injury, professional negligence, or malpractice) must maintain four separate elements: (1) a legal duty was owed to the plaintiff by the defendant; (2) the defendant breached that duty; (3) the plaintiff was damaged; and (4) the injury occurred as a result of the defendant's breach of the duty.

An often-stated principle in the common law of torts (case law, not statutory law) states that any wrong suffered through the conduct of another is entitled to redress. This axiom has, however, to be more consistently applied over the years to bodily injuries than emotional ones, although the law allowing recovery for emotional distress continues to evolve.

Courts have generally allowed monetary recovery for negligently inflicted injuries as well as their psychological sequelae; the emotional injury is compensated as a "parasitic tort," or considered to be an element of additional damages for the physical injury claim. The plaintiff may receive damages for somatic symptoms as well as for the consequent emotional disturbance.

In recent years state courts have also considered cases of negligent infliction of emotional distress in the absence of physical injury. Case law has begun to expand and has sided with the plaintiff, thus recognizing the infliction of emotional distress as an independent tort. In some of these cases, the uninjured plaintiff may recover monetary damages for emotional distress when placed in some physical danger while witnessing a nearby injury to a third person that results from the defendant's negligent conduct (zone of physical danger rule). In still more liberal jurisdictions, the uninjured bystander may recover for emotional damages even if not in physical danger when observing a physical injury to a close relative from a distance (zone of emotional risk rule). Courts have only cautiously expanded the recovery for the negligent infliction of emotional distress in these cases because of fear that emotional distress claims could too easily be feigned or exaggerated, are unassessable, would multiply excessively, or do not by themselves constitute real damages (Langhenry 1981).

The law also requires that there be a causal relationship between the defendant's negligent act and the plaintiff's injury (i.e., proximate causation). The law recognizes that there may be multiple causes to a harm, and requires that the alleged negligence constitute a substantial or principal cause of the injury. The law is thus not concerned with the premorbid vulnerabilities of the victim, but only whether the accident precipitated or caused a new disorder or aggravated a preexisting one.

In contrast to tort litigation, occupational injuries are compensated through out-of-court workers' compensation programs, administered on a state-by-state basis. The injured worker need not prove that the employer was negligent, but only that the harm arose out of and in the course of the worker's employment. Courts have been increasingly willing here, too, to compensate injured workers for emotional injuries in the absence of physical trauma (Carter v General Motors 106 N.W. 2d 105, 1960). Workers thus receive certain, defined, and limited compensation for their industrial injuries.

Applications to Neuropsychiatry. The forensic neuropsychiatrist is called on to address several issues in personal injury or workers' compensation actions where neuropsychiatric damages are al-

leged. These include differential diagnosis, prognosis, treatment planning, and causation.

The nature, extent, and duration of neuropsychiatric disability must be elucidated by the examiner (Gilandas and Touyz 1983). This may require repeated examinations; assessment of nervous system structure and function, especially neuropsychological evaluation; review of records of prior medical, psychiatric, social, vocational, and family histories; and interviews with relevant family members and others (Golden 1984). Attention should be given to both the neurologic injuries and their psychiatric sequelae, both short- and long-term. The evaluator must be acquainted with the scientific literature on the outcome of head injuries to address prognosis and indications or type of recommended intervention. Malingering and conscious or unconscious secondary gain disorders must also be considered in the assessment process.

Proximate causation must be addressed by considering the victim's premorbid functioning in conjunction with the presenting trauma and any coexisting factors (e.g., other recent life events). The following questions need to be answered: would the disorder have occurred but for the traumatic event; to what extent did the traumatic event contribute to the appearance and development or aggravation of the current disorder; and to what extent would a preexisting disorder naturally result in the current impairment in absence of the present trauma (Robitscher 1966; Weissman 1984).

Preparation of forensic neuropsychiatric reports is frequently necessary in personal injury and workers' compensation cases. Deposition and trial may also occur in personal injury litigation. It may be helpful for the neuropsychiatrist inexperienced in such matters to consult with an experienced colleague before entering this unfamiliar territory (Gutheil and Appelbaum 1982).

Civil Competency

Legal Principles. A variety of civil competency issues are presented by the neuropsychiatric patient. These include problems relevant to the practice or regulation of psychiatry as well as to the use of psychiatry for legal ends. In the former case, questions may be raised about a patient's competency to consent to or refuse diagnostic procedures, treatment (hospitalization, medication, convulsive therapy), or research. In the latter, questions are raised about the competency of neuropsychiatric patients to marry, divorce, drive an automobile, enter into a contract, write a will (testamentary capacity), manage personal affairs or estate, testify in court, and assume parental responsibilities.

In either situation, the law indicates that competence and incompetence are always specific and time-dependent variables that refer to a patient's competence to perform a certain task, rather than global or general ones. An individual may, for instance, be competent for some purposes but not for others. Similarly, various competencies may fluctuate over time, along with changes in mental status.

Generally, competence involves the ability to understand the nature and consequences of one's actions in the particular situation at issue. Regarding questions of testamentary competence, for example, the relevant elements are an awareness that one was signing a will, ability to assess the quantity and quality of one's property, ability to understand who are one's heirs, and absence of undue influence of any party to the process (Spaulding 1985).

Court challenges to a patient's competencies are typically lengthy, cumbersome, and costly. It is also frequently difficult to obtain individuals willing to serve as guardians. Jurisdictions generally differ in some civil competency areas, particularly guardianship, where several varieties of guardianships are extant. Limited guardianships specify which functions are assumed by the guardian; temporary guardianships indicate the duration of such limitations. Guardianships of the estate are confined to financial matters; plenary guardianships involve the loss of almost all legal decision-making authority by the ward. Some guardianships are predicated on the existence of a mental disorder or disability, others a physical disability; some statutes fail to differentiate between these.

Applications to Neuropsychiatry. Competency is a legal concept; patients are presumed to be competent in all respects until determined otherwise according to due process requirements. Nevertheless, the neuropsychiatrist in clinical settings makes functional determinations of competence on a routine basis. A distinction, therefore, is sometimes made between legal competency and de facto competency (Meisel 1979). In the presence of significant questions about a patient's functional competency, the psychiatrist is called on to initiate such a legal determination. The presence of a neuro-

psychiatric disorder does not per se render the patient legally or functionally incompetent.

Despite the duty of the clinician to ensure that the patient is competent to consent to or refuse the procedure or treatment at issue, there is no clear legal or clinical consensus about the tests or standards to be used in such assessments. Several standards noted in the literature include: (1) evidencing a choice with regard to the procedure or treatment; (2) reasonableness of the patient's choice; (3) the patient's rationale for the choice; (4) the patient's ability to understand the risk, benefits, and alternatives to the diagnosis or treatment procedures; and (5) the patient's actual understanding of this information (Roth et al. 1977). The tests clearly differ with regard to their breadth and reliability. Clinicians also appear to select the competency test to be used according to the risk–benefit ratio of treatment under consideration, as well as to whether the patient consents to or refuses the intervention. Competency tests are sometimes selected to achieve a desired medical or social outcome, particularly in cases of ambiguous competency.

Neuropsychiatric evaluations of a patient or litigant's civil competencies must be comprehensive, functional, and sometimes interdisciplinary (Hafemeister and Sales 1984). Historical, interview, and laboratory data should be obtained and supplemented by third-party reports of the individual's specific functioning. The use of static (i.e., diagnosis) or structural data does not primarily determine the individual's competency in a functional or legal sense. Functionally based neuropsychological or occupational assessments, on the other hand, generally provide much greater contribution to this determination (Nolan 1984). Information should be sought about the individual's sensory and motor capacities, ability to manage activities of daily living, and adequacy as well as safety of the home environment.

In particular, the neuropsychiatrist may become involved either as the primary or consulting physician in petitioning for appointment of a guardian or conservator, in examining the prospective ward prior to the court hearing, in providing written reports for or testimony at the hearing, and in recommending placement for the ward. Neuropsychiatric input may also be sought in the process of determining whether the guardianship should be terminated.

The neuropsychiatrist may also become involved in providing treatment to the legally incompetent patient under guardianship. In this case, consent for treatment must be obtained from the legal guardian. For some interventions (e.g., civil commitment or sterilization), the guardian's authority may be limited, and application must be made directly to the court. Although not legally obligatory, the physician is also advised to maximize the participation of the incompetent patient in the treatment decision, particularly where the guardian may not be personally familiar with the attitudes and values of the ward.

The neuropsychiatrist will frequently encounter situations in which there are doubts about the functional capacity of a legally competent patient to consent to treatment. It is generally advisable to involve interested family members in the decision-making process in such cases. It should be kept in mind, however, that such proxy decision making is rarely authorized by law (Kapp and Bigot 1985). Effort should also be made to increase the patient's comprehension of the necessary treatment information by making consent forms more readable, individualizing the consent material to the abilities of the patient, allowing patients to be exposed to the information over an extended period of time prior to decision making, and developing an adequate rapport with the patient and family (Appelbaum and Roth 1981; Stanley 1985) (Table 1).

Psychopharmacology

A review of the many legal issues pertinent to psychopharmacologic treatment and research would itself occupy a sizable volume. Space limitations merely permit brief mention of several contemporary issues in this area.

As noted above, only legally competent patients or their surrogates are permitted to consent to or refuse medical-psychiatric diagnostic and therapeutic procedures. The decision of the patient or surrogate must be a voluntary one, and it must be informed. The physician is required to provide information to the decision maker about the nature and purpose of the proposed treatment, its anticipated benefits and risks, the alternatives to the proposed treatment, and, in some cases, the prognosis without treatment. The extent of the disclosure is, however, ambiguously articulated, depending on local case law or statute. Jurisdictions that have adopted a professional standard approach define the requisite disclosure by the customary practice of a practitioner in a similar situation. Jurisdic-

---

TABLE 1. ASSESSMENT OF COMPETENCY TO CONSENT TO TREATMENT

Procedures
- Evaluate patient on two or more occasions if non-emergency.
- Obtain corroborating data from third parties (family, friends, treatment staff) regarding patient's global and specific functioning.
- Request the attending physician to be present during the competency evaluation to describe the nature, risks, and benefits of the proposed treatment to the patient.
- Consider the effect of the setting and personnel on the informed consent process.
- Assess the psychodynamic basis for the patient's consent and refusal.
- Provide a differential diagnosis and therapeutic recommendations to the referring physician with regard to the patient's decision-making incapacities.

Hierarchy of Competency Criteria
- Does the patient verbally accept or reject the proposed treatment?
- Is the patient's decision a reasonable one?
- Is there a rational basis for the decision?
- Is the patient able to understand the risks, benefits, and alternatives to the proposed treatment, including the possibility of no treatment?
- Does the patient actually understand the risk, benefits, and alternatives to treatment after they have been explained?
- Does the patient have a critical and reflective appreciation of the illness and treatment based on personal and emotional considerations?

---

tions with a patient-centered standard require that the physician disclose information (usually the risks of treatment) that a hypothetical, reasonable patient would find material to the medical decision at issue. Even so, these somewhat general rules provide considerable room for uncertainty with regard to the necessary disclosures. Risks in the use of psychotropic medication that are common or serious, even though rare, for instance, should be disclosed. The physician may be able to postpone or avoid these disclosure requirements in an emergency, when the patient waives the right to the information, or when the physician believes that the information would be significantly detrimental to the patient (Meisel 1979).

The neuropsychiatrist risks professional liability when prescribing psychotropic medication if the patient's injuries result from the physician's negligence. Such situations include (1) failure to disclose relevant information to the patient or guardian; (2) failure to obtain an adequate history, physical examination, or laboratory examination prior to treatment; (3) prescription of a drug when not indicated, in the wrong dosage, or for the wrong treatment interval; (4) failure to recognize, monitor, and treat side effects and toxicity; and (5) failure to consult with the necessary experts (Wettstein 1983).

The development of tardive dyskinesia by patients receiving antipsychotic medication has presented particular cause for apprehension to the psychiatric community because of the widespread use of these medications and the relatively common prevalence of the disorder. Indeed, litigation in this area has occurred, although most cases have arisen because of improper monitoring for side effects (Wettstein 1985). Prescribing physicians should also be cognizant of the difficulties in educating patients who receive antipsychotic medications about the presence or development of tardive dyskinesia (Irwin et al. 1985; Munetz and Roth 1985).

It is therefore generally recommended that prescribing physicians regularly monitor for the presence and severity of tardive dyskinesia, repeatedly present to the patient and guardian information about the risks of treatment throughout the treatment course, provide written information sheets or inserts to patients, question the patient about his understanding of the illness and its treatment, and document evidence of the informed consent process in the medical record. Similar procedures might be employed by physicians when dealing with other serious risks of psychotropic medication, including teratogenicity, retinopathy, and renal failure. Informed consent discussions should also be thorough when medications approved by the Food and Drug Administration (FDA) are used for nonapproved purposes, a generally inconspicuous but relatively common practice in psychiatric referral centers (e.g., carbamazepine for the treatment of affective disorders; medroxyprogesterone acetate for the management of the paraphilias; lithium carbonate for the treatment of aggression).

Finally, the interested reader is referred to the considerable literature on other psychopharmacologic issues and the law: right to refuse psychoactive medication, product liability, and informed consent to research for adults and minors (Gutheil and Appelbam 1982; Halleck 1980).

□ REFERENCES

American Psychiatric Association: Diagnostic and Statistical Manual of Mental Disorders, 3rd ed Revised (DSM-III-R). Washington, DC, American Psychiatric Association, 1987

American Psychiatric Association: American Psychiatric Association's statement on the insanity defense. Am J Psychiatry 140:681–688, 1983

Annotation: Amnesia as affecting capacity to commit crime or stand trial. American Law Reports 3d 46:544–569, 1972

Annotation: Automatism or unconsciousness as defense to criminal charge. American Law Reports 4th 27:1067–1143, 1984

Appelbaum PS, Roth LH: Clinical issues in the assessment of competency. Am J Psychiatry 138:1462–1467, 1981

Bacon PD, Benedek EP: Epileptic psychosis and insanity: case study and review. Bull Am Acad Psychiatry Law 10:203–210, 1982

Bursten B: The psychiatrist-witness and legal guilt. Am J Psychiatry 139:784–788, 1982

Cavenar J: Legal psychiatry, in Psychiatry, Vol. 3. Philadelphia, Lippincott, 1985

Collins JJ: Drinking and crime. New York, Guilford Press, 1981

Delgado-Escueta AV, Mattson RH, King L, et al: Special report: the nature of aggression during epileptic seizures. N Engl J Med 305:711–716, 1981

Devinsky O, Bear D: Varieties of aggressive behavior in temporal lobe epilepsy. Am J Psychiatry 141:651–656, 1984

Gilandas AJ, Touyz SW: Forensic neuropsychology: a selective introduction. J Forensic Sci 28:713–723, 1983

Golden CJ: Luria-Nebraska neuropsychological battery and forensic assessment of head injury. Psychiatric Annals 14:532–538, 1984

Gross BH, Weinberger LE: The mental health professional and the legal system. San Francisco, Jossey-Bass, 1982

Gunn J: Medical-legal aspects of epilepsy, in Epilepsy and Psychiatry. Edited by Reynolds EH, Trimble MR. Edenburgh, Churchill Livingstone, 1981

Gunn J, Fenton G: Epilepsy, automatism and crime. Lancet 1:1173–1176, 1971

Gutheil TG, Appelbaum PS: Clinical handbook of psychiatry and the law. New York, McGraw-Hill, 1982

Gutheil TG, Mills MJ: Legal conceptualizations, legal fictions, and the manipulation of reality: conflict between models of decision making and psychiatry and law. Bull Am Acad Psychiatry Law 10:17–27, 1982

Hafemeister TL, Sales BD: Interdisciplinary evaluations for guardianship conservatorships. Law and Human Behavior 8:335–354, 1984

Halleck SL: Law and the practice of psychiatry. New York, Plenum, 1980

Irwin M, Lovitz A, Marder SR, et al: Psychotic patients' understanding of informed consent. Am J Psychiatry 142:1351–1354, 1985

Kapp MB, Bigot A: Geriatrics and the Law. New York, Springer, 1985

463

Koson D, Robey A: Amnesia and competency to stand trial. Am J Psychiatry 130:588–592, 1973

Langhenry JG: Personal injury law and emotional distress. Journal of Psychiatry and the Law 9:91–109, 1981

McGarry AL: Competency to Stand Trial and Mental Illness. Rockville Md, Department of Health, Education and Welfare, 1973

Meisel A: The exceptions to the informed consent doctrine: striking a balance between competing values in medical decisionmaking. Wisconsin Law Review 1979:413–488, 1979

Morse SJ: Diminished capacity: a moral and legal conundrum. Int J Law Psychiatry 2:271–298, 1979

Munetz MR, Roth LH: Informing patients about tardive dyskinesia. Arch Gen Psychiatry 42:866–871, 1985

Nolan BS: Functional evaluation of the elderly in guardianship proceedings. Law, Medicine & Health Care 12:210–218, 1984

Oswald I, Evans J: On serious violence during sleepwalking. Br J Psychiatry 147:688–691, 1985

Pasewark RA: Insanity plea: a review of the research literature. Journal of Psychiatry and the Law 9:357–401, 1981

Pasewark RA, Pantle ML, Stedman HJ: Characteristics and disposition of persons found not guilty by reason of insanity in New York State, 1971–1976. Am J Psychiatry 136:655–660, 1979

Rachlin S: Legal encroachment on psychiatric practice. San Francisco, Jossey-Bass, 1985

Rachlin S, Halpern AL, Portnow SL: The volitional rule, personality disorders and the insanity defense. Psychiatric Annals 14:139–147, 1984

Rappeport JR: Differences between forensic and general psychiatry. Am J Psychiatry 139:331–334, 1982

Reich J, Wells J: Psychiatric diagnosis and competency to stand trial. Compr Psychiatry 26:421–432, 1985

Rivinus PM: Psychiatric effects of the anticonvulsive regimens. J Clin Psychopharmacol 2:165–192, 1982

Robinson PH: Criminal law defenses: a system analysis. Columbia Law Review 82:199–291, 1982

Robitscher JB: Pursuit of agreement, psychiatry and the law. Philadelphia, JB Lippincott Co, 1966

Roth LH, Meisel A, Lidz CW: Tests of competency to consent to treatment. Am J Psychiatry 134:279–284, 1977

Slovenko R: Psychiatry and law. Boston, Little, Brown and Co, 1973

Slovenko R: Law and psychiatry, in Comprehensive Textbook of Psychiatry (4th ed). Edited by Kaplan HI, Sadock BJ. Baltimore, Williams & Wilkins, 1985

Spaulding WJ: Testamentary competency. Law and Human Behavior 9:113–139, 1985

Stanley B: Geriatric Psychiatry: Ethical and Legal Issues. Washington, DC, American Psychiatric Press, 1985

Stone AA: Mental Health and Law: A System in Transition. Rockville, Md, Department of Health, Education and Welfare, 1975

Weissman HN: Psychological assessment and psycholegal formulations in psychiatric traumatology. Psychiatric Annals 14:517–529, 1984

Wettstein RM: Tardive dyskinesia and malpractice. Behavioral Science and the Law 1: 85–107, 1983

Wettstein RM: Legal aspects of neuroleptic induced movement disorders, in Legal Medicine Annual, 1985. Edited by Wecht C. New York, Praeger, 1985

Whitman S, Coleman TE, Patmon C, et al: Epilepsy in prison: elevated prevalence and no relationship to violence. Neurology 34:775–782, 1984

Winick BJ: Psychotropic medication and competency to stand trial. American Bar Foundation Research Journal 1977:769–816, 1977

INDEX

465